CULTURE AND PERSONALITY

The Dorsey Series in Anthropology

Culture and Personality

Victor Barnouw

Emeritus Professor of Anthropology
University of Wisconsin-Milwaukee

Fourth Edition   1985

THE DORSEY PRESS
Chicago, Illinois   60604

ISBN 0-256-03237-8

Library of Congress Catalog Card No. 84–72284

Printed in the United States of America

4 5 6 7 8 9 0 MP 2 1 0 9 8

Preface

The present edition of *Culture and Personality* has three new chapters: Chapter 11 on Biological and Evolutionary Perspectives on Human Nature, Chapter 19 on Altered States of Consciousness, and Chapter 21 on Ethnic Minorities. Much new material has been inserted in Chapter 18, Culture and Mental Disorders, especially dealing with cross-cultural research on schizophrenia and depression. Melford Spiro's *Oedipus in the Trobriands* (1982) is discussed in Chapter 4, and Derek Freeman's recent criticism of Margaret Mead's research in Samoa is reviewed in Chapter 5. Former Chapters 6 and 7 have now been combined into one (Chapter 6), while former Chapter 19 has been broken up into three chapters. Chapter 15 has new material on projective testing of Yukon Delta Eskimos, Taiwanese, and Japanese, and Chapter 23 has a new section on Melanesian cargo cults. There is also new material in other chapters.

I would like to express my gratitude for helpful comments and suggestions to Robert B. Edgerton of the University of California, Los Angeles; George De Vos of the University of California at Berkeley, and John Hobgood of Chicago State University.

Victor Barnouw

Contents

Mead on Balinese Character: *Balinese Childhood. The Tjalonarang Drama.* Some
General Considerations.

CULTURE AND PERSONALITY

PART ONE

Basic Concepts
and Approaches

1

An Introduction to the Field

Culture-and-personality, or psychological anthropology, is an area of research where anthropology and psychology come together—more particularly where the fields of cultural and social anthropology relate to the psychology of personality. Ethnologists, or cultural anthropologists, are students of culture—of the different ways of living that have developed in human societies in different parts of the world, while psychiatrists and (at least some) psychologists are analysts of human personality whose work involves an effort to understand why and how individuals differ from one another as they do. Serving as a bridge between ethnology and psychology, the field of culture-and-personality is concerned with the ways in which the culture of a society influences the persons who grow up within it.

Sociology and social psychology are allied social sciences related to this field, although studies by sociologists and social psychologists have generally been made within the setting of modern Western culture. It is not always possible, or necessary, to draw boundary lines between these disciplines. The present work, however, focuses primarily on contributions made by anthropologists who have an interest in the psychology of personality. It is mainly concerned with cross-cultural studies; these have generally been pursued by anthropologists, although analyses of some of their data (e.g., Rorschach records) have often been made by specialists in other fields. The recently developed field of cross-cultural psychology, concerned mainly with cognitive processes, is another overlapping area.

Ethnologists get most of their information from observing behavior and from interviewing. The usual job of the ethnologist is to record and analyze ethnographic data and to study the customs and social organization of a particular society. In addition to this, researchers in the field of culture-and-personality are concerned with observing behavior expressive of personality to see how culture and personality patterns are related in the society. In contrast to psychologists, ethnologists seldom make use of controlled experiments, although they have sometimes used doll play under controlled conditions. They do not usually give paper and pencil tests, for very often they work in nonliterate societies. Anthropologists have, however, made use of projective tests, such as the Rorschach and modified Thematic Apperception Tests (TATs), which do not require literacy.

Much of our knowledge of human personality has come from the work of psychiatrists and psychoanalysts, such as Freud. Although this knowledge is of the greatest value, it has two limitations. First, it is necessarily derived from people who were unhappy enough to go to a psychiatrist for help. Although everyone has problems, this makes for a rather biased sample of human beings. The second limitation is that most psychiatric patients whose cases have been analyzed are Europeans or Americans. We need to study the lives of successful and relatively unneurotic persons as well as the emotionally disturbed, both in our own society and in others with contrasting cultures.

An ethnologist studies human beings in their natural sphere of action, not in a clinic or laboratory, and may spend several weeks or months with a particular family or group of families. These persons are not apt to pour out their troubles to the anthropologist as a patient does to a psychiatrist, so the anthropologist probably takes much longer to learn something about them. But he or she sees them in the course of their daily lives in a variety of activities and circumstances, and not in an artificial setting. This is not to say that the information thus acquired is more enlightening or of greater value than that provided by the psychologist or psychiatrist. It is open to the criticism of being less scientific than that of the psychologist, in that it is not based on controlled experimentation. However, culture-and-personality research provides a valuable alternative way of learning about human personality which can check and supplement the findings of psychology and psychiatry.

Unfortunately, the terms *culture* and *personality*, which give the field its name, are hard to define in clear-cut unambiguous fashion. Both are associated in popular usage with older colloquial meanings which differ from those given in social science literature. ("He has a lot of culture," we might say, "but she's the one with the personality.") We must first consider these two terms in some detail.

THE DEFINITION OF CULTURE

E. B. Tylor, in 1871, was the first to use the word *culture* in English in the sense now accepted by anthropologists and sociologists. Following the lead of some German writers who used *Kultur* in this sense, he named his pioneer work *Primitive Culture* and defined the term at the outset of his work as "that complex whole which includes knowledge, belief, art, morals, law, custom, and any other capabilities and habits acquired by man as a member of society" (Tylor 1877:1).

This may be called an omnibus or sum-total definition, in that it lumps together a number of different categories which serve to make up the term defined. One weakness of such a definition is that it omits the element of integration found in every culture, although that is hinted at in the phrase "complex whole." Another weakness is that the list of categories cannot be complete. However, Tylor's definition was an important achievement in its time, for it set forth the subject matter of the then new science of cultural anthropology. Under this view, culture could be studied as a sphere apart from psychology or biology, because cultural phenomena were believed to have their own laws.

Years later, Ralph Linton (1945:32) offered a definition of culture which stressed the factor of integration: "A culture is the configuration of learned behavior and results of behavior whose component elements are shared and transmitted by the members of a particular society." Here some have objected to the inclusion of "results of behavior" in the definition, for opinions are divided as to whether objects—"material culture," so called—are to be regarded as culture. Note that Linton has defined a culture and not culture in general. The broader term is useful in clarifying how human behavior differs from that of other animals, which do not have a language and which cannot, therefore, transmit culture in the human sense. But anthropologists more frequently speak of particular cultures—of "Blackfoot culture," for example, meaning the way of life characteristic of the Blackfoot Indians of Montana in the early 19th century.

If we do not include artifacts, tools, buildings, and the like in a definition of culture, we have a cognitive or mentalistic definition like that of Ward Goodenough (1957:167–68): "A society's culture consists of whatever it is one has to know or believe in order to operate in a manner acceptable to its members." This emphasis is similar to that of Geertz (1965:106–07): "Culture is best seen not as complexes of concrete behavior patterns—customs, usages, traditions, habit clusters . . .—but as a set of control mechanisms—plans, recipes, rules, instructions (what computer engineers call 'programs')—for the governing of behavior."

The definition of a culture that I propose to use for this text is as follows: *A culture is the way of life of a group of people, the complex of shared concepts and patterns of learned behavior that are handed down from one generation to the next through the means of language and imitation.* The nub of this definition is the first clause: "the way of life of a group of people." The phrase "complex of shared concepts and patterns of learned behavior" implies that there is some integration and cohesion in this way of life, which is transmitted through language and imitation—not through instinct or any direct action of the genes. These patterns are only relatively fixed. For example, in our culture it has long been the custom for men to wear pants and women to wear skirts. But this pattern is amenable to change; for women often wear slacks, and some Scotsmen wear kilts. Culture, then, is marked by plasticity and change, although some societies have gone through centuries, even millennia, with very little change.

The culture of a society provides a number of ready-made answers to the problems of life. The child learns these as he or she grows up and comes to see the world through the particular spectacles of the culture. The culture provides the means for coping with the world; mastery of these methods increases one's sense of confidence. The culture also has a body of doctrines about the world—religious traditions and folklore—which give some orientation and reassurance to the individual. But the culture may also provide threatening influences, such as beliefs in evil spirits, malevolent gods, sorcery, and so forth, which may structure a view of the world as dangerous.

From a logical point of view, it is surprising how seldom people question the tenets of the culture into which they are born. But usually they do not have the perspective to do so. In some ways cultural behavior is like that of persons under posthypnotic suggestion, who perform actions without realizing why they do so. Humans would be lost without culture—hardly different from the apes. But while gaining so much from culture, human beings are also brainwashed, to some extent, by the culture to which they are exposed from birth. Equipped with a collection of stereotypes with which to face the world, we are apt to lose sight of possible alternative modes of behavior and understanding.

THE DEFINITION OF PERSONALITY

The definition of *personality* is an even more vexed question than that of culture, and there are many types of definition to choose from.[1] For example, there are omnibus definitions, such as this one from Morton Prince (1929.532): "*Personality* is the sum total of all the biological innate dispositions, impulses, tendencies, appetites, and instincts of the individual, and the acquired dispositions and tendencies—*acquired* by experience."

Such definitions are open to the same objection as is Tylor's definition of culture—the omission of an element of integration. Another type of definition puts the emphasis on just this factor—the integrative nature of personality, which gives some consistency to the behavior of the individual. Allport's definition (1937:48) may be cited as

---

[1] For a brief history of this term, from its beginnings in the Greek word *persona*, meaning mask, see Allport (1937).

an example: "Personality is the dynamic organization within the individual of those psychophysical systems that determine his unique adjustments to his environment."

Not all psychologists would accept such a definition. Those influenced by positivistic and behaviorist traditions might regard it as an unwarranted reification or even as an effort to reintroduce soul or psyche into psychology. Avoiding such dangers, Watson (1930:274) refers to personality as "the sum of activities that can be discovered by actual observation over a long enough period of time to give reliable information," while, for McClelland (1951:69), personality is "the most adequate conceptualization of a person's behavior in all its detail that the scientist can give at a moment of time."

Parallel problems appear in defining *culture* and *personality*. As we have seen, each term has been given sum-total definitions and also definitions which emphasize configuration or integration. For both terms, some definitions include and some exclude behavior. McClelland's definition, which stresses that personality is an abstraction in the mind of the scientist, has its counterpart in Osgood's definition of culture (1951:208): "Culture consists of all ideas of the manufactures, behavior, and ideas of the aggregate of human beings which have been directly observed or communicated to one's mind and of which one is conscious."

One's definition of culture or personality, then, evidently reflects one's central assumptions. A behaviorist's definition of personality will differ from a psychoanalyst's. American academic psychology has been much influenced by the behaviorist viewpoint. However, the American anthropologists who have done the most research in culture-and-personality have, for better or worse, been influenced more by psychological and psychiatric schools of European origin, such as the Gestalt and psychoanalytic schools; and they have tended to accept a view of personality which stresses its integrative, configurational character and to think of personality as something which influences behavior, rather than equating it with behavior itself.

A statement about personality with which I agree, though with some reservations, is one given by the authors of *The Authoritarian Personality:*

> personality is a more or less enduring organization of forces within the individual. These persisting forces of personality help to determine response in various situations, and it is thus largely to them that consistency of behavior—whether verbal or physical—is attributable. But behavior, however consistent, is not the same thing as personality; personality lies *behind* behavior and *within* the individual. The forces of personality are not responses but *readiness for response* . . . (Adorno et al. 1950:5).

An objection that can be raised here is that consistency of behavior might be ascribed to culture or to the social role of the individual, rather than to personality. Consistency of verbal behavior, if we mean speaking English or Chinese, is certainly a matter of culture, not of personality. Consistency of physical behavior (sitting on chairs in our culture, or squatting in a primitive tribe) may also be more readily ascribed to culture. If a man is consistent in going to work every morning at a certain hour by subway and returning home at a predictable time in late afternoon, this consistency is the product of a particular sociocultural system and the man's role within it, although the performance of this dull routine may well require a particular kind of personality organization. But this is not what the authors of the statement in *The Authoritarian Personality* had in mind.

With the reservations noted, their view of personality is one which I share. Moreover, I believe that part of the consistency inherent in personality relates to the acquisition of values and attitudes by the individual. The analysis of a Thematic Apperception Test, for example, or of a life history document, brings to light the characteristic attitudes and values of the subject, and it is assumed that there is some degree of stability in these patterns. Personality is also characterized by certain patterns of perception and cognition, as may be manifest in a subject's Rorschach protocol. In modifying the statement in *The Authoritarian Personality*, let me conclude with this suggested definition: *Personality is a more or less enduring organization of forces within the individual associated with a complex of fairly consistent attitudes, values, and modes of perception which account, in part, for the individual's consistency of behavior.*

CONSISTENCY IN PERSONALITY

Those who hold a view of personality along some such lines as these are apt to see everything that a person does, or the way in which he does it, as expressive of his personality to some degree. Experiments have shown that individuals have characteristic and consistent patterns of walking, gesturing, and even of sleeping (Wolff 1943:88–100; Krout 1935; Johnson and Weigand 1927–28: 43–48; Hartmann 1973). We recognize that our friends have certain predictable styles of behavior and modes of expression—something well illustrated by the works of composers and painters. A music lover may correctly identify a piece of music as being by Mozart even if he hasn't heard that particular piece before, just as one can recognize a painting as the work of Rembrandt or van Gogh, or a passage of prose as being by Hemingway or Henry James on the basis of style. But is there a general consistency in such matters as posture, gait, vocal expression, and so forth? That is to say, did Mozart, for example, have a particular way of walking or writing? Did Hemingway put out a cigarette very differently from Henry James, and would that way of putting it out express something of the writer's inner nature?

Werner Wolff (1943:20–21) has approached this sort of problem through some ingenious matching experiments. He showed a group of 20 subjects three specimens of musical notations, one by Bach, one by Beethoven, and one by Mozart; and he asked them to guess which musician wrote which (see Figure 1). Sixteen of the subjects made

FIGURE 1
Musical Notations to Be Matched to the Names of Three Composers: *A.*, Bach; *B.*, Beethoven; *C.*, Mozart. Correct Matchings: I*B*, II*C*, III*A*.

Source: Werner Wolff, *The Expression of Personality. Experimental Depth Psychology.* New York: Harper & Brothers, 1943, pp. 20–21.

correct matchings, the four mistakes being made with the samples of Mozart and Bach. While this experiment turned out successfully, it raises some questions. One wonders if Beethoven in his earlier years, when his music was more like Mozart's, had a more Mozartian calligraphy and style of writing notations? And did Mozart, in his later years, when his music became more like Beethoven's, write in a more Beethovenish handwriting? Such second thoughts show how intricately culture and personality are interrelated. A particular literary or musical style may come to be imitated by people of very different personality characteristics. Yet, as one may see in the Impressionist school of painting (or any other), individual differences still persist. All the children in a particular class may have learned how to write from the same teacher; nevertheless, each soon develops idiosyncratic peculiarities of style and a characteristic handwriting which friends and relatives can recognize at once.

Wolff carried out various other matching experiments similar to the one just described. In one of these, 23 students were asked to write this sentence: "Good day, I wonder whether these experiments will yield any results." Each subject then spoke the same words into a sound recording device. At a later period the students received three specimens of handwriting and listened to three recordings of the sentence. Their task was to match the voice with the handwriting. The number of correct matchings in this case was from one and a half to two times the chance numbers. Similar experiments in matching voice with other manifestations of behavior have been made by W. Huntley, G. W. Allport, and H. Cantril, with results much better than chance.

Individuals show consistency in dealing with certain cognitive tasks, for example, in the speed with which they can find a hidden figure embedded in a picture. Herman A. Witkin and his associates (1954, 1967, 1971) termed those who are quick to discover the hidden figure "field-independent," while those who are slow to do so are "field-dependent." Field-independence, which represents a greater degree of psychological differentiation, increases with age. At the same time, the level of psychological differentiation is relatively stable during development, so that a child who is more field-dependent than his age-mates will tend to have a similar position as a young adult. On the basis of a wide range of psychological tests, it has been claimed that field-dependent persons have a less differentiated body image than field-independent persons, tend to repress their impulses, to lack insight, and to be passive, readily giving in to feelings of inferiority. Thus, in various ways, persons show consistency over time in certain cognitive and emotional patterns of behavior.

To affirm that personality is characterized by consistency is not to deny that a personality may have its internal conflicts and inconsistencies. A man given to swagger and boastfulness is not necessarily a person with a deep sense of confidence in himself; perhaps quite the contrary. A boy who feels himself to be physically inferior may develop overcompensating tendencies and "act tough"; but inconsistencies of this sort are not basic. Such a mechanism may be seen as part of the total personality. There are also apparent inconsistencies stemming from situational conditions of status and role. (A *status* is a person's position in relation to others, as son to father or husband to wife; while a *role* is the behavior associated with a status, through which it is maintained.) Thus a boy may behave differently with his parents than with friends at school. But the playing of different roles does not negate an underlying consistency of personality. We must grant that personality may change over time. Despite much carry-over, the adult is a different person from the child. Gordon Allport who has done so much to demonstrate the consistency of personality, has also emphasized the "functional autonomy" of adult life. According to Allport (1937:194), adult motives may grow out of antecedent childhood systems, but are functionally independent of them. Thus, there are both consistency and change in personality, just as there are both consistency and change in culture.

CONTRASTING VIEWS OF PERSONALITY

As the variety of definitions has implied, there are many different conceptions about the nature of personality. Different schools of thought present contrasting views. A useful way of grouping such schools is Salvatore R. Maddi's classification (1976). Maddi, a professor of psychology at the University of Chicago, points out that most writers on personality make two kinds of generalizations. One is about the inherent nature of human beings, concerning those features common to all people which do not change much in the course of life. Such statements concern the *core* of personality. The other kind of generalization has to do with behavior which is generally learned, more circumscribed, and which differentiates people from one another. Maddi calls this sphere the *periphery* of personality. Theorists may be grouped according to their differing conceptions of the core of personality.

The Conflict Model

Following Maddi's scheme, there are those who assume that a person is always caught in a clash between opposing forces, between which he must make compromises. Maddi calls this the conflict model. The outstanding representative of this approach is Sigmund Freud, the founder of psychoanalysis. For Freud the core tendency of human beings is to maximize instinctual gratification while minimizing punishment and guilt. Human selfish instincts inevitably come into conflict with the taboos of society. As Philip Rieff (1959:197) has phrased it, "human culture is established through a series of renunciations. The sacrifice of self is the beginning of personality." One way in which man protects himself against the inevitable frustrations of life and the attendant anxiety is to develop unconscious defenses, such as repression, projection, reaction formation, and sublimation, among others.

From the orthodox Freudian point of view, personality is subdivided into three main units: the id, ego, and superego. The id is a deep, inaccessible part of the personality, filled with instinctual energy which seeks discharge. The ego is a portion of the id in contact with the environment. The maturing ego learns to replace the pleasure principle of the id with the reality principle. Freud compared the relationship between ego and id to that between a rider and horse. The horse supplies the power of movement; the rider directs its course. The last unit of the personality to develop is the superego, which represents the internalized voice of the parents and their code of ethics (Freud, 1933).

Much criticism has been made of these hypothetical entities, which have no particular somatic localization; but Freud's model, for which he provided a diagram in the work cited, helped him to speculate creatively about psychological processes. That is why Gregory Bateson (1972:84) termed psychoanalysis "a monument to the importance and value of loose thinking."

The conflict model involves a form of childhood determinism, according to which personality is largely fixed by the age of five or six, as the result of experiences undergone during the early years of life. Methods of weaning, toilet training, and sexual disciplines are held to significantly affect the personality of a growing child, and the Oedipus complex, the "primal scene" (the child's witnessing of its parents' intercourse), and real or imagined castration threats may establish attitudes and reactions of lifelong importance. Later influences on the individual, such as status and occupation, are seen as playing only relatively minor roles in the shaping of personality. Character attitudes, according to Freud, represent compromises between instinctual impulses and the controlling forces of the ego. "The permanent character-traits are either unchanged prolongations of the original instincts, or sublimations of those instincts, or reaction-formations against them" (Freud, 1908:175). Anthropologists who have followed a Freudian conflict model include Weston La Barre, George Devereux, and Melford Spiro.

The Fulfillment Model

In contrast to the conflict model, the fulfillment model assumes only one great force, located in the individual. Conflict may exist, but it is not held to be inevitable or continuous. Life is seen as an unfolding or realization of possibilities. Carl R. Rogers, for example, sees an actualizing tendency in all living things; in the case of man there is an attempt to actualize the self, involving the realization of a need for the approval of others and approval of one's self.

Other exponents of a fulfillment model include Gordon W. Allport and Abraham Maslow. Maddi classifies Erich Fromm in this group (correctly, I believe), although Fromm has been much influenced by Freudian theory. Few attempts have been made to explicitly apply a fulfillment approach to the field of culture-and-personality, but one example may be cited: Joel Aronoff (1967) made use of Maslow's self-actualization theory in a culture-and-personality study of a community in the West Indies.

The Consistency Model

Third is the consistency model. Here there is little emphasis on forces, whether in conflict or not. Life is seen as an effort to maintain consistency. There is less emphasis on an inherent human nature than in the other two models. "For consistency theorists, the content of personality is largely learned, and represents the history of feedback resulting from interacting with the world" (Maddi 1976:141).

George A. Kelly, for example, believed that a person tries to predict and control events on the basis of personal constructs built up in the past. When his or her constructs fail to adequately predict or control events, the individual experiences anxiety, which may lead to a modification of constructs.

Looking at efforts toward consistency in another way, everyone has some general notion of what sort of person one is or would like to be. Since a person may feel anxiety when there is a discrepancy between self-evaluation and the ideal model, one tries to behave in a reasonably consistent fashion. The term *cognitive dissonance* has been applied to a discrepancy between a person's concepts or between expectation and actual outcome. Leon Festinger and other social psychologists who have used this term assume that whenever cognitive dissonance is experienced, the individual acts to reduce it.[2]

Donald W. Fiske and Salvatore R. Maddi believe that the core tendency in an individual is to maintain the level of neuropsychological activation to which he or she has been accustomed.

Few attempts have been made to explicitly apply a consistency model of personality in cross-cultural studies.[3] But it is likely that many anthropologists have sometimes assumed a consistency model of personality without formulating it as such. For example, in commenting on the displeasure occasioned by observing bad table manners, Franz Boas (1963:57) remarked: "bad manners are always accompanied by rather intense feelings of displeasure, the psychological reason for which can be found only in the fact that the actions in question are contrary to those which have become habitual."

It could be argued that anthropologists who have used the concept of "world view" or "mazeway," assume a consistency model and that the personal constructs delineated by George A. Kelly could be compared with the cultural constructs which make up the world view of a particular society. Ruth Benedict's cultural determinist approach, discussed in Chapter 3, could be similarly categorized. Attempts at cultural integration constitute a kind of consistency. Although Benedict did not use the term *cognitive dissonance*, she did discuss the difficul-

---

[2] For a review of literature on cognitive dissonance and allied theories, see Zajonc (1968). For a massive reader on the subject, see Abelson et al. (1968).

[3] For two attempts, see Triandis and Fishbein (1963) and Campbell and LeVine (1968).

ties experienced in discontinuities in the process of growing up, when expected adult patterns contrast with earlier learned childhood patterns of behavior, so that an individual must unlearn what he has previously learned. Little children, for example, do not have to be responsible, but adults do. Submissiveness and obedience may be expected of children, but when they become adults they may have to assume dominant attributes of behavior. There are also contrasts in sexual roles between the childhood and adult states. Some cultures allow for easier transitions in these areas than do others. There are often problems at puberty or adolescence when formerly consistent self-concepts are altered and new patterns of consistency assumed (Benedict 1938).

In a consistency model of personality, the important elements in the determination of consistency are cognitions, such as attitudes and opinions.

Conceptions of Culture in the Three Models

These different models of personality imply somewhat different conceptions of the nature of culture. In the conflict model, culture is seen as inhibiting or repressive, a view epitomized in the title of Jules Henry's book, *Culture against Man*. Associated with this idea may be the Rousseauistic conclusion that cultural development has involved an increase of human frustration and that simpler cultures (such as Samoa or Trobriand) are less conducive to neurosis than our complex one. This notion was expressed in Robert Redfield's (1941) folk-urban continuum, according to which folk societies are homogeneous and well integrated, while urban cultures are diverse, impersonal, and socially disorganized. Implicit in Karen Horney's title *The Neurotic Personality of Our Time* is the suggestion that maybe people were less neurotic in former times. We will return to this question in Chapter 18, "Culture and Mental Disorders."

The fulfillment model involves a more beneficent view of culture, which may be seen as providing various channels for self-realization. This conception would be in keeping with Bronislaw Malinowski's functional view of culture, which he saw as fulfilling human needs. "The functional view of culture insists upon the principle that every type of civilization, every custom, material object, idea, and belief fulfills some vital function, has some task to accomplish, represents an indispensable part within a working whole" (Malinowski 1926:132). Malinowski could hardly have used the phrase "Culture against Man." Rather, it is through culture that man's various needs are met and his goals attained.

This fulfillment approach of Malinowski's may have been part of the difficulty he experienced in trying to test the application of Freudian theory to Trobriand culture, a topic to be discussed in Chapter 4.

Malinowski did not see why, given their assumptions, psychoanalysts should consider the Oedipus complex to be so harmful. "After all, to a psychoanalyst, the Oedipus complex is . . . the beginning of religion, law, and morality" (Malinowski 1955:237).

The consistency model seems to be more neutral in its assessment of culture than the two preceding ones. Presumably, any cultural routine which has become familiar will allay anxiety if it is adhered to.

A weakness of the consistency model, as Maddi has pointed out, is that it does not account for boredom. People do not always like familiar routines; some dissonance may be pleasurable. At the same time, it is true that a culture, in providing pattern and meaning, is a source of security. This becomes evident in the sense of disorientation known as "culture shock," when persons are exposed to an unfamiliar way of life. In Chapter 18, we will consider the relationship between migration and mental disorder; the mental breakdowns which attend migrations to foreign countries may often be related to the experience of culture shock.

If they are consistent in their views of culture, adherents of a conflict model of personality should be more tempted to rebel against the system, while those who prefer a fulfillment model should be more conservative and aware of the advantages of tradition.

PHYSIOLOGICAL DETERMINANTS

Oddly enough, in his discussion of the three models of personality, Maddi devotes no space to genetic, biochemical, or constitutional determinants of personality; but these should surely be seen as influential factors that help to explain both individual differences and consistency in personality. For example, Roger J. Williams (1956) has drawn attention to the enormous range of variation among human beings in the functioning of different organs and organ systems. To give only one example, although the "standard" number of parathyroid glands in humans is 4, the number may range from 2 to 12. Kinsey and his associates (1948) have similarly pointed out the great variation in the strength of the sex drive in males.

It may be noted that some individuals suffer more readily than others from vitamin and other deficiencies. Niacin deficiency may produce profound psychoses, which disappear when the deficiency is remedied, and psychoneuroses may result from thiamin deficiency. Calcium deficiency may lead to the development of hysteria; pellagric psychosis may develop from vitamin deficiency. It is well known that marked effects on consciousness are produced by such substances as LSD, amphetamine, and alcohol.

Attempts have been made to relate some mental disorders to chromosomal or genetic factors. In some cases the relationships are clear enough; in others there is uncertainty about causal factors. Some pathological disturbances result from the presence of too many or too few chromosomes; mongolism and Klinefelter's and Turner's syndromes are examples. The latter two involve sexual aberrations related to an abnormal number of sex chromosomes.

Many studies have been made of the possible role of heredity in the genesis of schizophrenia. The most common research approach to this problem has been to study twins, sometimes twins who have been reared apart and thus exposed to different environmental conditions. Twin studies have been made with both monozygotic (identical) and dizygotic (fraternal) twins. The problem is to find the rate of *concordance* in pairs of twins; that is, whether, when one twin develops schizophrenia, the other does also, and whether the concordance rate for monozygotic twins is greater than that for dizygotic twins, which would presumably indicate the presence of a genetic factor. David Rosenthal has reviewed such twin studies and has made the following points: (1) the concordance rate for monozygotic twins is always less than 100 percent and sometimes much less, suggesting that nongenetic factors may also play a role in the development of schizophrenia. (2) The concordance rate is always greater for monozygotic than for dizygotic twins, sometimes with a ratio of as much as six to one. (3) There is a wide range in the rates reported both for monozygotic and dizygotic pairs (Rosenthal 1971:72–74).

In summarizing data from a number of studies, Bernard Rimland presents the following table to show that the likelihood that a person

TABLE 1
Incidence of Schizophrenia Related to Presence of Schizophrenia in Blood Relatives

	Percent
No schizophrenic relatives	1
Grandparents, cousins, nephews, and nieces	3–4
One schizophrenic parent	16
Both parents schizophrenic	39–68
Half-siblings	7
Sibling	5–14
Fraternal twin	3–17
Identical twin	67–86

Source: Arnold Buss, *Psychopathology* (New York: John Wiley & Sons, 1966), p. 319. © 1966 John Wiley & Sons. Reprinted by permission of John Wiley & Sons, Inc.

will be schizophrenic is a function of the presence of schizophrenia in his blood relatives (Rimland 1969:730, based on Buss 1966:319).

Another approach to the possible genetic factor in schizophrenia is through adoption studies involving cases in which parents and children have been separated early in life, and when the incidence of schizophrenia in the children and their families has been studied. In reviewing studies of this kind, Rosenthal asserts that ". . . the evidence has turned up so consistently and so strongly in favor of the genetic hypothesis that this issue must now be considered closed. Genetic factors do contribute appreciably beyond any reasonable doubts to the development of schizophrenic illness" (Rosenthal 1971:84). (See also Davis and Flaherty 1976:108–15.)

Another school of thought, represented by E. Kretschmer and W. H. Sheldon, places the emphasis on constitutional type. Kretschmer (1925) made physical measurements of 260 psychotic patients suffering from schizophrenia and manic-depression. On the basis of his findings, Kretschmer claimed that there is an association between schizophrenia and body builds tending to be lanky, or (sometimes) athletic, while manic-depression is found to be associated with more plump physical types. Kretschmer believed that there is continuity between normal and abnormal states and that the different constitutional types have characteristic differences in temperament; the lean asthenics tending to be more schizoid—sensitive, inhibited, and cold; while more plump individuals tend to be moody and changeable— but more sociable and realistic than the asthenics.

W. H. Sheldon (1940, 1942), who measured and tested Harvard students and other groups in the United States, followed Kretschmer's lead but developed different methods of measurement, classification, and terminology. According to Sheldon, thin individuals tend to be tense introverts, plagued by skin troubles, fatigue, and insomnia. Muscular athletic types tend to be energetic persons delighting in noise and adventure, exercise, and open air; while those who tend to be fat are apt to be comfortable extroverts, fond of food, company, and luxurious surroundings. Sheldon believed that there is a regular correlation of this sort between physique and temperament, although not in any one-to-one fashion. There has not been much research along these lines in recent years.

SITUATIONAL APPROACHES

Although they differ in their respective emphases, Maddi's three models and Sheldon's constitutional approach all agree that there is an internal consistency in personality. But there are some sociological and psychological schools of thought that tend to play down the continuity and integration of personality and to emphasize the constraining influence of particular roles, statuses, and situational factors. Included in this group are social behaviorists and interactionists. The latter argue that a person's conception of himself or herself is formed through consistent relations with others. If someone is treated by others as subordinate, he or she will be apt to develop feelings of inferiority. However, a person's status may change, and the nature of his or her interactions with others may undergo modifications as a result—perhaps ultimately leading to changes in the individual's self-concept. The playing of a new role may reverse earlier patterns.

George A. Kelly, who was himself an officer in the navy at one time, was struck by the effect on individuals of assuming an officer's rank. He noted that men often assumed officerlike qualities much more successfully than their past record would have led one to suspect. "Even men who are literally on the borderline of feeble-mindedness make fairly convincing officers. Perhaps it is because they *construe* themselves as officers" (Kelly 1955:367).

But one does not always assume a role so easily. There may be a sense of incongruence between the self and the role to be enacted, or there may be a conflict between two or more roles which the individual enacts.

The interactional school of psychology emphasizes the importance of current situational factors in a person's life (see Endler and Magnusson 1976). Such an emphasis also leads to different approaches in psychotherapy than in the more childhood determinist psychoanalytic approach. For example, behavior therapy places more stress on the here and now; it is not felt necessary to dredge up a patient's childhood memories and traumas (see Rimm and Masters 1974). Critics of the situational approach, on the other hand, insist that a person always responds to a particular role or situation in terms of his or her past experience.

LONGITUDINAL STUDIES

It would seem that the best way to find evidence for consistency in personality is through long-range longitudinal studies, following a subject or group of subjects from infancy to late maturity. That is easier said than done, of course; for if an investigator is a graduate student, let us say, when he or she is beginning to observe the behavior of a group of infants, the investigator may be planning for retirement by the time the infants have matured. And how many people would want to be life-time subjects for such an investigation?

There are various problems in longitudinal studies. One is that the methods of observation and measurement considered appropriate for working at one age level may not be suitable for a later one. However, some longitudinal studies have been successfully carried out—notably one by Lois B. Murphy, Alice E. Moriarty, and their colleagues, in which a group of about 30 children were studied from infancy to adolescence. One aspect of this research was the making of fairly successful predictions about the later preschool behavior of subjects on the basis of observations carried out during their infancy. Correlations between infant and later preschool behavior were also noted. It was found, for example, that infants who protested against disliked food and terminated feeding tended later, at the preschool stage, to show determination and clarity of self-concept (Murphy and Moriarty 1976:127–39).

PRIMATE TRAITS

In seeking to understand core aspects of personality, an anthropologist is tempted to examine general primate characteristics before turning to human beings. Let us briefly review some general characteristics of primates—the order of mammals to which we belong along with the apes, monkeys, lemurs, and tarsiers. Primates are creatures with prehensile (grasping) five-digited hands and feet. These grasping hands and feet are useful in getting about in the arboreal habitat shared by most primates and also in exploring and manipulating objects. They are important for monkeys in infancy, since monkeys are born with a clinging reflex, which enables them to hang onto the mother's fur, leaving her arms free when she climbs through the trees.

The mother-child relationship is closer and longer lasting among primates than in most other animal species. A general trait of mammals is that females suckle their young. This results in a continuing relationship, at least for a while, between mother and offspring in all mammals; but the relationship is longer lasting in primates than in the other orders of mammals, since the complex nervous system and brain development of the primates needs time to become coordinated. The young are born in a relatively helpless condition, which increases dependence on the mother. While a baby deer can walk about on the day of birth, a baby primate clings to its mother's body for the first weeks or months of life.

A primate is usually born into a social group that includes a male or males as well as a female or females. Some primate groups, such as those of the gibbon, are small, consisting of only a male, female, and offspring, while others, such as the baboons, have large bands with many males and females of different ages. Adult males in most primate groups are either tolerant or helpful toward the young.

Especially for terrestrial species, reports have been made of protective behavior by adult males, who may rescue a threatened infant or juvenile. But the main contact a young primate has during the first weeks or months of life is with the mother. Among rhesus monkeys, for example, an infant is in continuous close contact with the mother and is held by her at night. After the first week or two, it makes short trips away from the mother—within a two-foot radius, close enough for rescue by her.

Primate groups may have several infants of about the same age. Gradually, as the young primate gets older, it makes contact with these peers and spends more time with them. The mother may encourage this tendency by rebuffing the young, but this varies in different species. Baboon mothers engage in rebuffing behavior after the infant is 10 months old, but chimpanzee and gorilla mothers do not seem to do much rebuffing, and chimpanzee mothers carry their children about until they are around four years old.

Young primates spend a lot of time in rough-and-tumble play with one another as their dependence on the mother decreases. Thus a juvenile primate typically interacts with peers, older males, and older females.

Primate groups of the same species may behave quite differently in different ecological settings and situational contexts. Rhesus monkeys in Hindu temple compounds show more aggression than those who live in the forest. Most striking were the results of Harry Harlow's experiments with rhesus monkeys raised in isolation since infancy: After about a year and a half, when they were brought into contact with other members of their species, they did not know how to interact with them. The males could not perform the sexual act, and when the formerly isolated females were impregnated by normal males, they did not behave in a maternal manner toward their offspring but treated them cruelly. However, when deprived infant monkeys were allowed to play with other young members of their species for 20 minutes a day, they developed in a normal fashion. These experiments show that sexual and maternal behavior, which we might assume to be instinctive among monkeys, depends on the development of adequate patterns of social interaction with other members of the species (Harlow 1962).

While human beings share the general features of primates just reviewed, they have a still more developed brain and complex central nervous system than other primates, and consequently have an even longer period of dependency on the mother. Every human being starts out as a helpless, dependent, and nonresponsible creature but must learn to become relatively competent, independent, and responsible. This development toward maturity and competence, involving the actualization of inherent human potentialities, gives support to the fulfillment model for the core of personality. However, the same data also give some support to a conflict model, since the long period of dependence on the mother sets the stage for the Oedipus complex and other problems of incompatible dispositions, such as dependence-independence.

Various anthropologists who have observed primate groups in the field have used the term *personality* to apply to apes and monkeys. In a brief survey of such literature, John O. Ellefson (1968:137) suggests that: "The modal or normative personalities of species have adaptive significance; that is, norms of personality are the result of an adaptive process, an interplay between natural selection and the genetic variation intrinsic to sexual reproduction and mutation through time in populations."

"Personality" differences between primate species may represent adaptations to different environments. It has been suggested, for example, that the aggressive temperament of baboons is related to their adjustment to terrestrial life on the savannahs, where they are exposed to predators, while arboreal primates are under less pressure of that sort.

A contrast has often been noted between the calm, aloof behavior of the gorilla and the noisy sociable behavior of the chimpanzee. V. Reynolds (1965) has argued that these contrasts are related to differences in social organization and foraging patterns. The food supplies of the chimpanzees are more varied, located in different places at different times, and their social organization is looser, permitting groups to split up and later regroup. Their loud chorusing alerts chimpanzees to areas of plentiful food.

While there seem to be differences in personality or temperament between such species as gorillas and chimpanzees, individual differences are also found within a species. George B. Schaller (1963:80) has written: "Free-living gorillas exhibit great individual variation in their affective behavior, and the spectrum of emotions exhibited by the members of the same group to my presence varied from excitement to seeming disinterest; in other words, there were nervous individuals and calm ones, aggressive individuals and shy ones."

Can one say, then, that gorillas have personalities? That would, of course, depend on one's definition of personality. The definition given earlier refers to "a complex of fairly consistent attitudes, values, and modes of perception which account, in part, for the individual's consistency of behavior." If attitudes and values are derived from culture, involving the use of language, then nonhumans and human infants could not be said to have personalities, and personality could not antedate culture. But if some other definition of personality, such as Allport's, were used, there would be no logical inconsistency in saying that our earliest hominid forebears had personalities before speech or the use of tools were developed. Their personalities, indeed, may have tended more toward the chimpanzee model than a gorilla or other primate model, as Ellefson has suggested (1968:147–47). We will return to a consideration of primate and early human characteristics in Chapter 11.

HUMAN DEVELOPMENT

Having examined some general features of primate development and behavior, let's now focus on our own species, dealing first with some universal aspects of maturation during the first years of life.

A newborn child has some capabilities not present in other mammals at birth. In contrast to puppies, which are blind and deaf at birth, newborn humans can see and hear and they also have a sense of smell and are sensitive to pain and touch. However, human beings are quite helpless at birth, in comparison to such rapidly maturing mammals as deer and antelope, and they taken even longer to grow up than other primates because of their more developed brain and complex central nervous system. Hence, there is a longer period of dependency on the mother and other adults.

A crying infant can usually be soothed by being picked up, held, and rocked. Its crying disturbs the adult, and body contact comforts the infant. These reactions help to establish a strong mother-child relationship, further strengthened by the development of the smile.

Despite their helplessness, human infants start to imitate the actions of grownups at a surprisingly early age:

> children of two weeks can stick their tongues out or clench and un-
> clench their hands when they watch someone else do these things.
> . . . The baby in this sort of imitation has to watch another person
> sticking out a tongue; he then has to realize that his own tongue is
> equivalent to the other person's, in spite of the fact that he has never
> seen his own tongue (Macfarlane 1977:89).

In an experiment with two-week-old babies, Genevieve Carpenter showed that they spent more time looking at their mothers' faces than at a strange woman's face (Macfarlane 1977:78–79). When suckling, an infant looks at the mother's face, not at her breast. Some psychological experiments indicate that the eyes, in particular, are sought out (Freedman 1974:31).

Freud termed the first stage of psychosexual, or libido, development during the child's first year as the *oral* stage, when the child's main contact with the environment is through the mouth in the suckling process.[4] Pleasurable sensations are also centered around the mouth. Babbling is another oral activity of the first year. By around the 9th or 10th month a babbling child begins to imitate sounds he or she hears, which lays the groundwork for the acquisition of language.

By four months of age, the child can give a smiling response, usually to a human face, whether strange or familiar, but at seven or eight months the child may show fear of strangers and cry on seeing an unfamiliar face. The child may now be upset by the absence of the mother and be reassured when she returns. Some writers believe that all forms of anxiety are based on separation anxiety—the original fear of separation from the mother. If a child becomes willing to let the mother out of sight, that indicates a sense of trust and continuity of

---

[4] Although the general tenor of this account of child development is eclectic, Freudian formulations are presented in this section because of the childhood determinist approach of this conflict-model school and the consequent fact that the Freudians have made more specific distinctions about stages of development in childhood than appear in the fulfillment or consistency models of personality.

experience. For Erik Homburge Erikson (1963) the establishment of a basic sense of trust is the crucial accomplishment of the first year, failing which the child develops a basic sense of mistrust.

By around eight months of age a child can stand with help. Soon it can creep; it can walk with assistance at 11 months and alone at 15 months. This opens up new areas for exploration, which seems to have an exhilirating effect on the child. Although the toddler can now leave the mother, it often returns to her, just as the exploring rhesus infant does. This behavior has been interpreted by some writers as "emotional refueling," as if the child needed this reassurance and contact in order to return to its exploration of the world.

Language

Another aspect of the encounter with the world is the learning of language, the basis for human culture. In this respect human beings differ significantly from the other primates.

The first learning of language by a growing child marks an adaptation to a realm quite different from the visible environment; it is a new world of concepts. From this point on, the child is strongly influenced by the prevailing cultural conceptions of the society into which he or she is born. It is hard for us to imagine the direct contact with reality, without names for things, that children have before this point. Since it must be very different from our own structured picture of the world, it is probably nearly impossible to remember that earlier period.

The first words are spoken around the end of the first year. Children begin to combine words at 18 to 24 months ("Where Mommy?"), but by around four years of age they have somehow learned the rules of grammar of their language and an understanding of about 1500 words or so.

The use of language gives a child a new sense of control. Now he or she can ask for things. The child learns its own name and the pronoun "I" as well as "Mommy," "Daddy," and the names of siblings and others.

While upright locomotion opens up new worlds for the child, it also creates new hazards and physical dangers for the child, and sometimes for the property of the parents. "No! No!" becomes a warning that the child learns to internalize, thus creating the beginning of a superego, the Freudian term for the inner voice of conscience. Through language the parents can now instruct, scold, and reason with the child, who thus learns what values and attitudes they hold. Language also makes possible the new pleasures of storytelling and symbolic play.

Among the child's dealings with grown-ups the issue of toilet training may be stressed, although this varies greatly in different cultures. This may be the child's first encounter with outside interference in its instinctual impulses, and toilet training may become a source of conflict between parent and child. Retention of urine and feces involves a new demand for autonomy on the part of the child, who may be made to feel ashamed of lapses. Freud termed the second phase of libido development (after the oral stage) the *anal* stage, since pleasurable sensations are now focused on the anal zone. Erikson sees the second year as establishing either a successful sense of autonomy or else feelings of shame and doubt. Stubbornness and negativism are common reactions in the second and third years, expressing the child's defense of its new sense of identity and autonomy.

Maternal Deprivation

A controversial issue in relation to human development is the significance of maternal deprivation during the first two years of life. John Bowlby, René Spitz, Mary Ainsworth, and others have written about the trauma of early maternal separation and its effects on the later development of human personality. Bowlby (1969, 1973) studied children who were placed in a nursery because of the mother's hospitalization and were separated from the mother for more than 12 days to as much as 21 weeks. Not only did the long-separated children become depressed and apathetic, but on reunion with their mothers they did not cheer up right away but tended to remain apathetic and aloof.

Bowlby claims that, if such a child is between 15 and 20 months old and has had an adequate relationship with the mother before separation, it will exhibit successive, overlapping stages of protest, despair, and detachment. A briefer separation may be followed by ambivalent phases of alternate rejection and demands for attention. After longer separations, Bowlby thought that an attitude of detachment might persist indefinitely. He claimed that it is stressful to start nursery school before a child's third birthday. After the age of three, separations are better endured.

René Spitz (1945) contrasted the development of infants in a foundling home, where they had no close contacts with adults, with infants in a prison nursery, where there were daily sessions with mothers. The foundling home infants showed states of depression, physical deterioration, and sometimes even death. Spitz believed that the lack of mother love was the cause of these negative developments. However, Freedman claims that the foundling home was located in an area characterized by protein deficiency, even for home-reared babies, and that "no temperate zone worker has ever found such lethal results from lack of mothering" (1974:47).

William Goldfarb (1945) compared early institutionalized children with children reared in foster homes, giving Stanford-Binet and

Wechsler-Bellevue intelligence tests and collecting life history data. Goldfarb concluded that early maternal deprivation and institutionalization brings about defects in intellect and emotion, weakness of concept formation, difficulty in learning songs, rhymes, and stories, grasping number concepts, and learning concepts of time and space. The institution-reared children studied by Goldfarb were hyperactive, disorganized, and often threw temper tantrums. They seemed to have an insatiable need for love without being able to love others in return. However, institutionalization does not always have such adverse consequences.

John Bowlby (1946) compared a group of 44 juvenile thieves at a child guidance clinic with a control group of 44 children at the same clinic who were emotionally disturbed but did not steal. Bowlby found that the thieves included several with "affectionless" personalities who had often experienced separation from their mothers during the first five years of life, while only two members of the control group had suffered such experiences.

In another study, a test of these implications brought negative or inconclusive results. Siri Naess (1959) reviewed a group of 42 Norwegian delinquent boys aged 10–18, all of whom had nondelinquent brothers who provided a control group, thus keeping the home environment a constant factor. Oddly enough, there was found to be more separation from the mother in the nondelinquent group.

Some authors (for example, Morgan 1975; Clarke and Clarke 1976) have criticized the general argument about maternal deprivation presented by Bowlby, Spitz, and others. Since there are studies of children institutionalized from early infancy who show no ill effects (e.g., Lewis 1954; Douglas and Blomfield 1958), the bad results reported by Spitz and Goldfarb are not inevitable. Besides, such effects may be reversed in later years. In a book published in 1973, *Children of the Crèche*, Wayne Dennis described foundlings in Lebanon who made great progress in intelligence test performance after moving before age two from an institution to adopting homes. Similar improvements are noted in another work, *Adopting Older Children* (1970), by A. Kadushin, about children who were adopted at a much later age, between 5 and 12.

The Clarkes present some cases of children brought up under conditions of extreme isolation but who nevertheless turned out remarkably well in later years. One concerns two monozygotic twins born in Czechoslovakia in 1960, who were not only kept in isolation but were occasionally beaten and mistreated by their guardians. They lived in a small unheated closet and were often locked up in a cellar for long periods. The twins were discovered and removed from their family in 1967. At that time their speech development was very retarded, and they could barely walk; but after living for a while in a children's home and later in a foster home they made steady progress. The author of the report, Jarmila Koluchová (1972, 1976), described them in the 1970s as being agile, cheerful, and popular at school; they swam, skied, rode bicycles, and played the piano well. The twins did well at their studies, had IQs of 100 and 101, and showed no damaging personality defects.

In her book, Patricia Morgan makes the following criticism of Spitz's study of institutionalized children:

> if an institutionalized sample is compared with a family-reared sample, some of the differences which emerge may be due to constitutional differences present in the children since birth. If other evidence strongly suggests that mental retardation or psychosis are related to genetic and organic factors, then a preponderance of children with these defects in an institution does not demonstrate that they are caused by that institution's regime. Children abandoned to institutions may have been abandoned because their mothers were too mentally backward or psychotic or handicapped to look after them (Morgan 1975:114–15).

A selective process results in the removal of the healthier and more intelligent children, who are more apt to be adopted. Apart from possible genetic defects, Morgan also suggests that the deficiencies of the children in the foundling home studied by Spitz did not stem from lack of mother love but from the absence of the opportunity to practice such skills as walking and learning language. She writes: "In Foundling Home . . . the babies were kept in cubicles for fifteen to eighteen months. After they were weaned there was no human contact except when they were fed. Sheets were hung around the cots so that all they could see was a white ceiling. . . . They had no toys and played only with their hands and feet. They saw no other baby. They were kept entirely on their backs" (Morgan 1975:123).

The situation is similar to that in two institutions in Iran described by Wayne Dennis (1960a), where children suffered behavioral retardation because they were not sufficiently handled by their attendants. They were not placed in prone or sitting positions and consequently did not learn to creep, sit up, and move about. In a third institution in Iran, where such handling was better, children developed normally in those respects.

One way to examine the effects of maternal separation is to observe children who have had to be hospitalized, although here the health of the child is another confusing variable. However, in a study by R. S. Illingworth cited by Morgan (from *The Lancet*, December 17, 1955), it was found that 32.4 percent of 1-to-4-year olds, 56.8 percent of 5-to-6-year olds, and 72.4 percent of 7-to-14-year olds in the hospital seemed to be quite contented. The younger the children, the more the upset. Boys were more affected than girls.

Morgan (1975:177) notes that: "There is little indication in research that upset occurs if a separated child is left at home with father or grandparents." Even if the child leaves home, he or she may be less affected if accompanied by a sibling. One study of separated children (Douglas and Blomfield 1958) found that those who stayed at home during the separation experience showed no differences, when matched with controls, suggesting that the total environmental change is important, not just the presence or absence of the mother.

The criticisms by Patricia Morgan and the Clarkes indicate that such writers as Bowlby and Spitz may have overstated the dangers of maternal deprivation and the overriding importance of the first year or two of life. While these years are, of course, of great importance, so are later years. A criticism made of Bowlby, Spitz, and others of this group is that they have underestimated the resilience of growing children and the increasingly wider experience of later years that may offset earlier deprivation. For example, Martha Wolfenstein (1955a:114–15) has described French childhood as a period of restriction and preparation for adult life, full of hard work; yet the French grow up with a great capacity for enjoyment of life. "It remains one of the puzzles of French culture how this effect is achieved: that the restraints to which children are subjected have only a temporary influence and do not encumber the adult with lasting inhibitions."

Some psychologists, such as G. H. Frank, have explicitly denied the idea that early childhood experiences are major determinants in the development of psychopathology. "A review of the research of the past 40 years failed to support this assumption. No factors were found in the parent-child interaction of schizophrenics, neurotics, or those with behavior disorders which could be identified as unique to them or which could distinguish one group from the other, or any of the group from the families of the controls" (Frank 1965:191).

A different kind of discontinuity between childhood and adulthood has been noted by some anthropologists. Child upbringing in some societies (for example, the Hopi, Navaho, St. Thomas Negroes) may be ideal from a Freudian point of view, but the typical adult personality found in these groups may nevertheless be tense and anxious. (See Eggan 1943; Goldfrank 1945; Leighton and Kluckhohn 1947:68, 111; Campbell 1943:43, 89.)

Role of the Father

Another criticism of writers who have emphasized the dangers of maternal deprivation is that they have given too much attention to the mother at the expense of other members of the family who also interact with the child. In many societies, including our own, maternal roles may be filled by other persons—grandmother, aunt, older sister, foster mother, and others. The father, too, may play a maternal role. Watson and Lindgren (1973:188) write: "Fathers [in our culture] are performing many services for infants that were formerly provided only by mothers: feeding, diapering, bathing, burping, cuddling, and the like."

Studies have been made of father-deprivation as well as of maternal deprivation. One study was made of Norwegian boys whose fathers are away at sea from nine months to two years at a time. These boys were compared with boys whose fathers worked and lived at home. This study, and several other such studies, found that the father-absent boys are more immature and dependent and have poorer relations with their peers than the control group (Lynn and Sawrey 1959). Apparently sex identification is easier for a boy who has a father around to serve as a model. However, a father surrogate could also fill this role. Boys in father-absent homes often develop exaggerated protest masculinity, and their gang behavior has sometimes been interpreted as a way of demonstrating their masculinity.

The effects of father-absence on girls has not been studied as much as the effects on boys; but some studies suggest that such girls also tend to be more dependent as adults. The earlier the separation from a father figure, the greater the effects are judged to be. But negative effects are not invariable or universal, and much depends on the personality of the mother.

Besides mother and father, older siblings often play an important role in child-rearing. This is less true in the United States than in many non-Western societies, and for that reason American anthropologists may not have been sufficiently alert in studying the caretaking roles of older siblings in other societies. In a recent survey of this subject it was found that in less than 20 percent of the 186 societies studied is the mother the principal caretaker after infancy (Weisner and Gallimore 1977). Other siblings play this role in some of the societies discussed later in this book. Margaret Mead (1928), in her study of Samoa, was one of the first writers to draw attention to this topic.

Years Three to Five

The period from about the third through fifth years is termed by Freud the *phallic* stage of psychosexual or libido development, when pleasurable sensations begin to be found in the genital areas. It is a period of rapid physical development and locomotion when, according to Erikson, a sense of initiative is developed, but also feelings of guilt. The problems emphasized by psychoanalytic theory are now unfolding: incest taboos, the Oedipus complex, and castration fears.

Freudians consider the mother, through the suckling experience, to be the child's first love object; she remains such for the little boy, while the girl comes to transfer her attachment to the father. To quote Freud (1916–17:322–33): "Well, it is easy to see that the little man wants to have his mother all to himself, that he feels the presence of his father as a nuisance, that he is resentful if his father indulges in any signs of affection towards his mother and that he shows satisfaction when his father has gone on a journey or is absent. He will often express his feelings directly in words and promise his mother to marry her." Indeed, Freud adds, he may try to seduce her, "which puts beyond doubt the erotic nature of his tie with his mother."

That is why, according to Freud, modern civilized men, even today, are moved by Sophocles' *Oedipus Rex*, for this play represents the enactment of a forbidden wish—the desire to murder the father and marry the mother. This wish, although repressed, is seen to lurk in the subconscious of every man, but is particularly pressing and insistent among neurotics and psychotics who have failed to successfully "resolve" the Oedipus complex.

> For the son this task consists in detaching his libidinal wishes from his mother and employing them for the choice of a real outside love-object, and in reconciling himself with his father if he has remained in opposition to him, or in freeing himself from his pressure if, as a reaction to his infantile rebelliousness, he has become subservient to him. These tasks are set to everyone; and it is remarkable how seldom they are dealt with in an ideal manner—that is, one which is correct both psychologically and socially (Freud 1916–17:337).

In Chapter 4 we will consider Bronislaw Malinowski's criticism of some of these generalizations, based on his research in the Trobriand Islands, where the family system differs in some respects from that of Europe and the United States.

In Piaget's scheme of cognitive development, the period between two and seven years of age represents the stage of preoperational thought, in which symbolism, including symbolic play, becomes important. During this period the child's view of things is essentially egocentric, by which Piaget means that it is difficult for the child to comprehend another person's point of view.

In a study of children in the first three years of life, Jerome Kagan and his colleagues found little evidence of *intraindividual stability* for such factors as attentiveness, excitability, or fearfulness.

> Change, not stability seems to be the most prominent characteristic of the opening years of life. We suspect . . . that the late childhood and adolescent personality traits we are fond of—like self-confidence, intellectual ability, motivation, hostility—do not become firmly established until the child is six to ten years old, after attitudes toward self and others have become structured as a result of identification with parents, class, and ethnic groups, and following opportunities to arrive at conclusions regarding one's competences and liabilities relative to peers (Kagan, Kearsley, and Zelazo 1978:280–81).

On the other hand, a study by Neilon (1948) suggests considerable continuity from early childhood to late adolescence. She got in touch with adolescent subjects whom Shirley (1933) had studied during the first two years of their lives.

> General personality descriptions were made of these young men and women without knowledge of what they were like as infants. These descriptions were then given to a number of judges to see how well they could be matched to the descriptions reported at two years of age. Matching was well above chance so that at the global level of personality description it was possible to demonstrate continuity from 2 through about 18 years of age (Freedman 1974:112).

Latency

Latency is a period of sexual quiescence between 6 and 12 years of age, during which children are relatively well behaved, pliable, and educable (Sarnoff 1976). Malinowski claimed that the latency stage is not a universal aspect of human development, for Trobriand children maintain an interest in sex throughout this period, which suggests that the sexual quiescence may be due to suppression or repression. Sarnoff states that latency is characterized by an involvement in fantasy. In our culture, boys become inveterate collectors at this time and display a somewhat compulsive character, which Freudians see as a manifestation of defense and reaction formation characteristic of the anal stage. Conflicts are avoided through a combination of repression, sublimation, and escape into fantasy. This need for fantasy comes at a time when children are first learning their culture's myths, which help to establish guidelines for them.

The manageable quiescence of latency makes possible the transmission of much cultural material. Sarnoff (1976:169) refers to the development during latency of behavioral consistency, which is the capacity to retain consistent behavioral guidelines even without supervision. In our culture, school attendance demands both self-control and consistency of behavior. Despite their restlessness, children are able to absorb an amazing amount of knowledge during the first year or two of school: the letters of the alphabet, the numeral system, and the abstractions involved in reading, writing, and arithmetic. It is during this time that children in some cultural settings reach the stage of concrete operational thinking, in Piaget's terms: They can group objects according to different attributes, such as color and size and arrange items in a series, as from smaller to larger. Aspects of concrete operational cognition have been tested with children in different cultures, a topic to be dealt with in Chapter 9.

Puberty and Adolescence

With the glandular changes occurring at puberty, the sexual quiescence of latency comes to an end. Increases in weight and height and the development of secondary sex characteristics bring about a new self-consciousness about the body image, often with feelings of awkwardness and embarrassment. At the same time there is a requirement to assume adult roles. This is traditionally a difficult time, although we will see later (in Chapter 5) that Margaret Mead did not find it so among girls in Samoa.

In Freudian terms, puberty and adolescence bring about the psychosexual stage of *genital primacy*. Erich Fromm's scheme includes a *productive orientation* in the mature adolescent, in contrast to the earlier receptive, exploitative, and hoarding orientations of childhood. According to Freudian theory, if an individual meets with sufficient frustration at this point, he or she may regress to an earlier level of libido development, possibly becoming neurotic or psychotic.

The rate of sexual maturation seems to be influenced by cultural factors. The average age at menarche, or first menstruation, in the United States is now 12.9 years, although a generation ago it began a year or half a year later. Girls of lower socioeconomic class tend to mature later. Farm girls in rural Poland begin menstruation later (over 14) than nonfarm girls (before 14) (Laska-Mierzejewska 1970).

TABLE 2
Freudian and Modified Freudian Stages of Development

Ages	Freud	Erikson	Fromm
First year	Oral stage	Basic trust versus basic mistrust	Receptive orientation Exploitative orientation
Second year	Anal stage	Autonomy versus shame and doubt	Hoarding orientation
Third through fifth years	Phallic stage	Initiative versus guilt	
Sixth to about eleventh year	Latency period	Industry versus inferiority	
Puberty and adolescence	Stage of genital primacy	Identity versus role confusion	Productive orientation
Young adulthood		Intimacy versus isolation	
Adulthood		Generativity versus stagnation	
Maturity		Ego integrity versus despair	

CULTURAL DIFFERENCES IN CHILD DEVELOPMENT

The foregoing review of early human development gives some idea of common features in the process of growing up. However, the varied cultures of the world have many different ways of dealing with them, and children must adjust to different kinds of situations. Some children are born into monogamous families, as in the United States. Others are born into polygynous households, in which a man may have several wives, as in some African tribes. Still others are born into polyandrous households, in which a woman has two or more husbands, as in Tibet and adjacent regions. The family unit may be a small nuclear one, as among ourselves, or a large joint family household, as in parts of India. The number of persons with whom a child interacts may differ very much from one society to another.

Stages of development may vary in some respects due to cultural features. Balinese babies do not have a crawling phase, since their mothers or other caretakers always carry them about and disapprove of creeping on all fours. Children in Uganda are said to be precocious in development, when compared with European children of the same age, in such features as prehension, manipulation, sitting, crawling, standing, and walking. One explanation for the alleged precocity is in terms of the close mother-child relationship and intimate physical contact during the first year of life (Ainsworth 1967; but see also Warren 1972 and Super 1981b). In some other respects, cultural factors do not seem to alter patterns of maturation. Hopi children who were strapped on a cradleboard during the first year of life learned to walk as soon as Hopi children who were not put on cradleboards and who had more freedom of movement (Dennis and Dennis 1940).

Birth order and institutionalization seem to affect the maturation process in some respects. Later born children speak later than first-born, and institutionalized children speak later than children in families (Munroe and Munroe 1975:62).

Relations between mother and child show much cultural variation. The suckling period may be quite short, as it is in the United States, when compared with most nonliterate societies. In a cross-cultural study of child-training practices in 75 societies, the median age for beginning to wean was found to be two and a half years (Whiting and Child 1953:70). The situation is very different in our society. A survey of 379 mothers from New England in the 1950s showed that only about two fifths of the children were breast fed, the large majority for less than three months (Sears, Maccoby, and Levin 1957). According to the Whiting and Child (1953:74) cross-cultural survey, slightly over half of the primitive societies begin toilet training between the ages of one and a half and two and a half. American families tend to begin toilet training much sooner. From a survey of 582 mothers in Detroit in the 1950s, it was found that 57.6 percent of the mothers began toilet training between six and nine months (Miller and Swanson 1958:219). Sexual disciplines also vary considerably. Childhood erotic play is condoned or regarded with amusement in some societies and severely punished in others. In some societies the child is tightly swaddled soon after birth, while in others there is no such restriction. Play patterns differ in different societies; in some there is a great variety of children's games, while in others there are very few. In many peasant societies children are assigned tasks and chores from an early age, while in other societies they have a great deal of freedom until puberty. In some societies all young boys go through severe initiation ceremonies into adulthood, while others have no such rituals. In some societies there is formal education and schooling for many years, while in others there is none. Different societies hold up different ideals to the growing child. In past times, for example, the Cheyenne Indian boy was encouraged to be a brave self-assertive warrior and raider of horses, while a Hopi child was encouraged to be cooperative, submissive, and mild-mannered in behavior. Culture and personality, or psychological anthropology, deals with contrasting patterns such as these and their influences on personality formation.

SUGGESTIONS FOR FURTHER READING

For the reader who is unfamiliar with literature on the psychology of personality, Gordon W. Allport's book, *Personality, A Psychological Interpretation* (New York: Henry Holt, 1937), is suggested as a good place to begin. Three more recent texts are Salvatore R. Maddi, *Personality Theories: A Comparative Analysis*, 3d ed. (Homewood, Ill.: The Dorsey Press, © 1976); Walter Mischel, *Introduction to Personality* (New York: Holt, Rinehart & Winston, Inc., 1971); and Irving L. Janis, George F. Mahl, Jerome Kagan, and Robert R. Holt, *Personality: Dynamics, Development, and Assessment* (New York: Harcourt, Brace & World, 1969). The latter book has a psychoanalytic orientation; Mischel's has a more behaviorist approach. There are several readers in culture-and-personality, of which the best, it seems to me, is Douglas G. Haring, ed., *Personal Character and Cultural Milieu* (Syracuse, N.Y.: Syracuse University Press, 1956).

For reviews of cross-cultural studies of child development, see Robert L. Munroe and Ruth H. Munroe, *Cross-Cultural Human Development* (Monterey, Calif.: Brooks/Cole Publishing, 1975); Emmy Elizabeth Werner, *Cross-Cultural Child Development* (Monterey, Calif.: Brooks/Cole Publishing, 1979); and Ruth H. Munroe, Robert L. Munroe, and Beatrice B. Whiting, eds., *Handbook of Cross-Cultural Human Development* (New York: Garland STPM Press, 1981).

2

The Concept of Social Character

We turn now to the question of whether there may be similarities in personality among people who share the same culture. It is this notion which underlies such concepts as "basic personality type," "national character," and "social character." Explaining the latter term, Erich Fromm (1941:277) writes: "we are interested . . . not in the peculiarities by which these persons differ from each other, but in that part of their character structure that is common to most members of the group. We can call this character the *social character*."

Some critics do not believe that there is such a thing as social character. Instead of arguing about this question in abstract, theoretical terms, let us consider three separate areas where research has been done. These areas are (1) an Egyptian peasant village in Aswan Province, (2) the Aymara Indians of Bolivia and Peru, (3) present-day Japan. The descriptions that follow deal with progressively larger groups: first a village, then a tribal group, and finally a nation. (Naturally, more documentation is required as larger populations are considered.) In each case, as we proceed, we will see what evidence there may be for the existence of a social character.

THE EGYPTIANS OF SILWA

The source for our first example is a single work, *Growing Up in an Egyptian Village* by Hamed Ammar (1966). It would, of course, be better to have reports by other observers on the same people; but the Egyptian study has one signal, rather unusual advantage: its author was born and grew up in the village which he describes. Although Ammar left the community at the age of seven to go to school, he never lost contact with the village and spent his holidays there. For him there were none of the problems of learning an alien language and introducing himself to the villagers which face most ethnologists in their fieldwork. This point is important, since the author cannot be charged with having an outsider's bias. It might be argued, however, that the experience of encountering a freer way of life outside his native village led Ammar to become critical of it, so that he acquired a bias of a different sort, like that of Sinclair Lewis in writing about Babbitt and Main Street. Nevertheless, Ammar's account is written in a careful, objective manner.

Generalizing about the villagers of Silwa (and Ammar is writing only about them, not about "Egyptian national character"), the author remarks:

> Hearty laughter is rare, and it usually occurs amongst adults in their sarcastic allusions to others, and in belittling their esteem, while apparently seeming to praise them. Suspicion of the evil intentions of others is institutionalized in the evil eye, seeing potential danger in practically everybody. The small family guards its private affairs with great caution, especially its misfortunes, for fear that others may exult or gloat at their expense. . . . The villagers mutually describe each other as greedy, envious, and malicious, and, as they usually put it, "people would distribute your property while you are alive. . . ." (Ammar 1966:230)

Ammar makes the point that this character should not be seen as something neurotic but as an understandable result of adjustment to a particular set of realities, experienced by each Silwa villager as he grows up. What are some of these realities?

Silwa is a small, rather isolated town in Aswan, the southern border province in Upper Egypt, having a population of nearly 3,500. Almost all the men are farmers, and land is the most valued possession. To sell land is calamitous; to buy land is a sign of God's blessing. Descent is traced patrilineally, in the male line. There is no primogeniture; a dead man's property is divided among his children. During a man's lfietime, his children have no legal right to own any of his property.

There is a definite sexual division of labor. Women's place is in the home; men work in the fields. A man who does not mix with other men is called "man of the oven." A woman who often leaves her house is called a "strayer." When walking in the street, men walk down the middle; women keep to the wall. When meeting a man in the street, a woman turns her head away or pulls her head covering across her face, while the man lowers his gaze. Women do not go to the mosque to worship. During the first year of marriage, a wife does not eat with her husband. After they begin to eat together, she should eat later than he does.

Children are suckled for an average of between one year and a year and a half, sometimes for two or three years. They are never weaned before the end of the first year. According to the views of Freud and Erikson, we might expect this to establish feelings of basic trust and "oral optimism." But there is much finger sucking among children, which is encouraged by their mothers; and in later childhood years there is much concern about food, expressed in children's stories, conversations, reports of dreams, and responses to projective tests. There is a realistic basis for this concern, for Ammar gives evidence that in post-weaning years the children of Aswan province are very undernourished when compared with children elsewhere. Little meat is eaten in Silwa, and the diet is deficient in proteins and fats. Adults are described as being secretive and careful with food.

There is no special stress on toilet training in Silwa. When a child learns to walk, it is taught to indicate when it wants to defecate. After the age of 3 or 4, this is usually done outside the house; but after the age of 12, girls defecate in a special room indoors. There is no disgust about feces and urine, for these people are peasants who often handle animal dung for fertilizer or fuel.

Scaring techniques are used as a sanction to cultivate submissiveness in children. Bogeys are invoked, including a huge animal that eats its young after suckling them, and a hairy beast which attacks children while they sleep.

Children must show their respect for elders. Until the age of four or five, a child touches an older person's hand with his lips and forehead.

There is much sibling rivalry in Silwa, although brothers are taught that they must show strong solidarity. Sibling rivalry is deliberately encouraged, since it is believed to be healthy, especially for boys, and helps the child to stand up to rivals. A mother may encourage such rivalry by saying to a child, "Eat this before your brother takes it," or else she praises the other child. When a visitor meets a boy, he asks, "Who is better, you or your brother?" Siblings of different ages play in separate groups, especially after the age of six or seven.

Boys are circumcised between the ages of three and six. Girls go through a clitoridectomy at around seven or eight years of age. This is thought to reduce sensuality and prevents the girl's future husband from suspecting that she is not a virgin. Girls may be married by 12 or 13, but boys usually marry after 18, on completing their military service.

Children start to work early and work hard. Since hired labor is difficult to obtain, a father makes his sons help him in the fields. This may lead to father-son conflict, and some boys run away from the village, if they are overworked. But deference to the father is emphasized in the culture. Disobedience to parents is a major sin, according to the Koran, and is severely punished in the afterworld.

A boy walks behind his father, not abreast. A mature son does not sit beside his father in a gathering of men. If the father is sitting on a bench, the son sits on the ground or on another bench.

The oldest son is the father's representative and gives orders to the younger sons. When walking to the fields, brothers do not walk together but follow, one behind the other to avoid the evil eye.

In this society the evil eye is particularly feared from relatives. There are many popular sayings which express tension among relatives, such as "Relatives are like scorpions," and "Who brings disaster but relatives?"

Ammar describes the adolescents of Silwa as being timid, apprehensive, and withdrawn, with little drive or self-assertion. Sex is regarded with shame, embarrassment, and guilt. There seems, in general, to be a constricted personality. For those who accept a fulfillment model of personality, Silwa would seem to be a community which does not encourage much self-actualization but inhibits it.

The foregoing account, which attempts to summarize Ammar's work, could be criticized on the grounds that it overemphasizes negative features. After all, the villagers of Silwa must get enough satisfaction from life, and they have to be people of a particular kind in order to lead the kind of life they must lead. For Erich Fromm the social character functions to make men desire to act as they have to act.

This view suggests, though, that the Silwa villagers *want* to be submissive, hardworking toilers. Not all wish to do so, evidently, since some young men run away from the village. Such young men are in the minority, however; those who remain come to terms with the system for which they have been prepared throughout childhood. As Ammar (1966:231) puts it, "Adults continually wean their offspring from flights of imagination and spontaneity of action till they almost completely achieve their end by the time their offspring reach adolescence." The adult scaring techniques used in childhood, the segregation between the sexes and age levels, which emphasize prudery and respect for elders, all contribute to forming a personality in which submissiveness is combined with undercurrent feelings of fear, resentment, envy, and hostility, as suggested by the quotation from Ammar which introduced this discussion. The general picture may be overdrawn, but it does seem to give support to Fromm's concept of social character. Insofar as the personality traits in question are determined by common childhood experiences, support would also be given to the concept of "basic personality type" which will be discussed in Chapter 6.

THE AYMARA INDIANS

Let us now consider another group of people who have also been described in rather discouraging terms, the Aymara Indians of Bolivia and Peru, who live in the Andes Mountains around Lake Titicaca. Here we are dealing, not with a single village such as Silwa, but with a population of over 700,000; so our two examples are not exactly comparable.

In presenting data on the Aymara, my purpose is, first of all, to provide some evidence that a rather consistent Aymara "social character" has been reported by several observers over a considerable period of time, although it may be undergoing some changes at present. The second purpose is to use the Aymara data as a vehicle for discussing various possible determinants of personality and to show how one could go about testing their relative importance. In this case, unlike the data for Silwa, we have no report by a native Aymara inhabitant. The descriptions are by outsiders, which opens the door to possible enthnocentric bias.

Among the anthropologists who have worked among the Aymara are Harry Tschopik, Jr., Weston La Barre, William E. Carter, John M. Hickman, Dwight B. Heath, Hans C. Buechler, and Judith-Maria Buechler. Some of the earlier travelers to this region have described the Aymara in very consistent terms. From many of their accounts we get a general picture of these Indians as being submissive, gloomy, anxious and mistrustful, dirty and slovenly in personal habits, quarrelsome, and capable of cruelty and malice. The Aymara seem to have little in the way of aesthetic interests; and Tschopik has characterized them as "utilitarian," meaning by this that they stress the useful and practical, although the term does not imply any special resourcefulness or ingenuity on their part.[1] Tschopik tells us that the Aymara, brought up to be submissive to authority, are reluctant to assume leadership. Hostility is suppressed or repressed among them, but may break through in drunken acts of violence. Above all, in Tschopik's view the Aymara are an anxious people:

> among the Aymara anxiety is so general and intense, so ever-present and all-pervading, that it has left its particular mark on virtually every individual and has colored the entire fabric of the culture. . . . Anxiety is, in fact, the keystone of Aymara "modal" personality, the central principle in terms of which other personality characteristics become intelligible (Tschopik 1951:174).

Tschopik points to the inordinate use of alcohol and coca, the many omens which bode ill, and the frequent resort to divination as indications of the prevalent anxiety.

If only one writer had described the Aymara in these terms, one might suspect exaggeration in this picture—at least some degree of personal projection or subjectivity. But many published accounts, while differently expressed, reflect the same state of affairs—and one apparently persisting over a period of time.

---

[1] For quotations about the Aymara by early writers, see Tschopik (1951:172–73) and La Barre (1948:39).

Thinking about the Aymara in these terms, one can't help but wonder why they have come to be such anxious, unhappy people. A number of possible reasons—indeed, a whole battery of them—appear in the accounts of Tschopik and La Barre. There is first the matter of adjustment to high altitudes. *Sorroche* is a native term for high-altitude sickness, brought about by lack of oxygen. Among the symptoms are headache, nausea, a sense of oppression and fatigue, and sometimes even temporary psychosis. Commercial pilots who are often exposed to anoxemia are said to suffer from grouchiness, as an almost standard occupational disease (La Barre 1948:174). Perhaps, then, high altitude is one of the contributing factors to the Aymara personality picture.

We learn from La Barre (1948:48, 65) that intoxication at high altitudes has more drastic effects than at sea level, and that "The Aymara are a notoriously drunken group. . . . All travelers have remarked on the quantities of alcohol the Aymara can consume, and the states of intoxication to which they can attain, and I can only confirm that I have never anywhere seen American Indians more thoroughly intoxicated than at the usual Aymara fiesta." Alcohol, then, must be another contributory factor, as well as being an indicator of the degree of anxiety among the Aymara.

In addition to liquor, the Aymara are widely addicted to the chewing of coca, from which the narcotic cocaine is derived. Frequent coca chewing, as medical experiments have shown, may lead to pallor and muscular weakness. Gutierrez and Von Hagen state that ". . . coca chewers present emotional dullness or apathy, indifference, lack of will power, and low capacity for attention. They are mistrustful, shy, unsociable, and indecisive" (quoted in Tschopik 1951:187). Perhaps, then, this is the source, or one of the sources, of the observed Aymara traits.

Moreover, we learn from Tschopik that the houses of these highlanders give poor protection. They are crowded, unheated, dirty, and unhygienic. Their clothing is inadequate, too, and men often walk without sandals in subfreezing weather. The children are poorly clad. According to a medical survey in Ichu, the diet of at least some Aymara groups is inadequate—low in fats, vitamins A and C, iron, and calcium, and energy-producing foods (Tschopik 1951:157–58).

Little wonder that there is a good deal of sickness, especially respiratory and heart ailments, but also skin diseases, smallpox, scarlet fever, typhus, and venereal disease, among others. The Aymara, indeed, are said to have the highest infant mortality rate in the New World—one in seven during the first year (La Barre 1948:47, 126).

We learn from the Buechlers (1971:23–26) that Aymara infants are tightly swaddled from birth to the fourth month. If one took a childhood determinist approach, one might attempt to derive some Aymara characteristics from this experience. According to the Buechlers' brief account, children seem to be treated indulgently. Children are suckled for an average period of two years and fed on demand. They are played with by their parents and siblings and not allowed to cry for long. As in Silwa, children begin to work early, starting to herd pigs by the age of four or five, and later, sheep. They also take care of young siblings and carry water.

Childhood does not seem to be an especially difficult time, but the high rate of child mortality and sickness must be kept in mind.

High altitude, excessive drinking and coca chewing, combined with unsanitary homes, inadequate clothing, poor diet, and much sickness—is there any wonder that the Aymara are said to be unhappy?[2] Yet these are not the only factors that may be responsible for their alleged character traits. There is also the historical background of these people and their social relationships with the Mestizos toward whom they play a submissive role.

During the Spanish colonial period, the Aymara were made to work in the mines at forced labor. The Spaniards treated them brutally, and it has been estimated that 8 million natives, the majority of them Aymara, died during this time (La Barre 1948:31). The Aymara rebelled repeatedly, but with little success, and they have remained in a subordinate position for the past five centuries. Their present overlords, the Mestizos, now command all the important political offices, own the best farmlands and better houses, and are, in general, much better off than the Aymara, who tip their hats submissively to the Mestizos as they pass, and who kiss the hands or garments of the Mestizos in gratitude for favors conferred (Tschopik 1951:159).

Among the Aymara, to consider another aspect, there is a growing shortage of land. Ideally, members of an extended family are expected to cooperate with one another, but the land shortage leads to individualistic self-assertive behavior and to conflicts within the extended family. According to Tschopik (1951:62–63), this results in more uneasiness and anxiety. Moreover, there is a good deal of tension within the average family. Marriages are unstable, infidelity and divorce common. The children born to such families are given relatively little affection.

There are, then, a multitude of possible causes for the alleged character traits of the Aymara—climatic, toxicological, historical, and sociological. Granted that all the factors cited have played a role in the shaping of Aymara personality, have they all been equally important? Have not some exerted a more telling influence than others? How could we weigh their relative importance?

How significant, for example, is the factor of high altitude? If the Aymara lived at lower levels, would they be different? Are all moun-

---

[2] Another possible factor is hypoglycemia and its alleged relationship to aggression among the Aymara (Lewellen 1981) or Qolla (Bolton 1984).

taineers and highlanders anxious and grouchy? We have no intensive personality study of the Nepalese or Tibetans, but judging from the accounts of travelers, the high-dwelling Himalayan peoples seem to be quite different from the Aymara, often being pictured as cheerful, cooperative, and self-reliant. For example, C. J. Morris has written:

> The most striking element in the character of the Gurkhas [Nepalese] is their unfailing cheerfulness even in the most adverse circumstances; and this, more perhaps than any other single factor, distinguishes them so markedly from the peoples of India proper . . . ; they are happy and contented—on good terms with life—and the stranger who is prepared to accept them as they are cannot help but feel the same (Morris 1935:437).

Yet some Nepalese live at even higher levels than the Aymara. Moreover, both La Barre (1948:39, 40, 156) and Tschopik (1951:173) claim that the depressing personality picture of the Aymara which they present applies more specifically to the Aymara of towns and haciendas than to the more independent Indians who live in *ayllus,* the traditional social units of the highland region. This is not a difference in altitude, but in the texture of social life. Social and cultural factors may therefore be the more important determinants in this respect.

The Aymara Reexamined

The foregoing account of the Aymara, with some minor changes, appeared in the first edition of this book. Since then, this negative picture of the Aymara has been criticized by some anthropologists who have recently worked in Peru, although others have supported it in part.

John M. Hickman spent 10 months doing fieldwork among the Aymara of Chinchera. In addition to getting a series of depth interviews, Hickman trained 50 Indian interviewers to give an extensive survey schedule to 1,810 Indian adults in six communities—four Aymara and two Quechua—to get information about values and attitudes concerning culture change. In 1964, Hickman (1964:3498) wrote: "The quality of life is one of general 'amoral familism' that places the family as the only center of concern and effort. The degree of suspicion, insecurity, hostility, ambivalence, and alienation as a group is high, corresponding to reports of previous investigators." On the other hand, Hickman also noted that the Indians were optimistic about the future and that an increase in their level of education now made them less dependent on the ruling class. An eagerness to learn among the younger Aymara was also noted by A. Bouroncle Carreón (1964). Some Aymara have now entered advanced professions: the law, medicine, education, priesthood, and aviation. They have also taken an active role in politics, including Bolivia's recent revolution (Heath 1966).

In 1966 there appeared a paper by John F. Plummer in which he took issue with the traditional negative view. Plummer points out that most travelers in the Aymara region used Mestizo or white interpreters, who were hated by the Aymara. According to Tschopik, in Chucuito a person had to be either an Indian or a Mestizo, and the Tschopiks were perforce classed as Mestizos. Plummer also notes that most travelers in the region seldom stayed long in one place and had no opportunity to get to know the Indians well.[3] As for the accounts by Tschopik and La Barre, Plummer points out that both made various positive comments in their writings which serve to modify the dominantly negative impression. For example: "The Aymara does laugh and joke as do other human beings, and affection, love and friendship are far from non-existent in this society" (Tschopik 1951:148). Plummer also quotes passages from Tschopik's unpublished diaries and letters which stress the friendliness of individual Aymara.

According to William E. Carter (1977) the Aymara are not alcoholics since their drinking is mainly limited to ceremonial occasions.

On the other hand, supporting the traditional negative viewpoint, in 1966 Weston La Barre published an analysis of a series of Aymara folktales, which seem to depict a dog-eat-dog universe. Themes of aggression and duplicity are recurrent, and there is an obsessive emphasis on food. La Barre had evidently not changed his views about the Aymara by this time, for he concluded:

> If the Aymara, as evidenced in their folktales (and indeed throughout the rest of their culture), are apprehensive, crafty, suspicious, violent, treacherous, and hostile, one important reason for this may be that such a character structure is an understandable response to their having lived for perhaps as long as a millennium under rigidly hierarchic and absolutist economic, military, and religious controls (La Barre 1966:143).

Perhaps one could accept this as a valid statement of the traditional Aymara world view and at the same time acknowledge the changes now occurring as reported by Hickman, Carreón, Heath, and Plummer.

The reader may have noted that, although the characterizations of the Aymara are more extreme, there are some similarities between the Aymara and the people of Silwa, Egypt. The latter do not drink or use drugs (at least, Ammar gives no information about such practices), but otherwise, there are many similarities. In both areas, we have peasants living under conditions of poverty and malnutrition, brought up to be submissive and fatalistic, and feeling much anxiety

---

[3] This seems to have been true in Plummer's case as well. He writes: "Unfortunately, we were never able to stay in one place for more than a few days at a time. It is true that the Aymara avoided us when we first appeared, but the longer we stayed, the more friendly they became" (1966:70).

and suppressed resentment. These features seem to be characteristic of many peasant communities. Similar descriptions of Mexican peasants have been given by Erich Fromm and Michael Maccoby (see Chapter 22), of Rajput peasants in India (see Chapter 8), and of Italian peasants (see Banfield 1958). In his study of Tepoztlán, Mexico, Oscar Lewis (1951:Chap. 4) described the Tepoztecans as being mutually suspicious, envious, unsmiling, and constricted. The normal type of personality in Aritama, a peasant community in Colombia, is described by the Reichel-Dolmatoffs (1961:449) as extremely controlled and rigid. "There is mistrust of all motivations in others, little submission, and never rebellion, but rather avoidance of all close relationships. . . . Gloominess and cynical self-accusations are frequent."

Generalizing about peasant societies on a large scale, George M. Foster (1965) has offered the concept of "the image of limited good," by which he means that peasants tend to assume that all the good things in life and in the environment exist in finite quantity in scarce amounts. Since there is no way to increase the supply, an individual or family can only improve a position at the expense of others.

This picture can be supported by various field studies of peasant communities. For example, the Blums write of Greek villagers:[4]

> it was said that when good things happen to a villager, the other villagers express their envy in gossip, criticism, and calumny. The villagers described their life altogether as an uneasy one, with each family feeling competitive and jealous toward any other that might achieve success or happiness (Blum and Blum 1965:128).

The notion of "limited good" has some basis in the realities of peasant life; most peasants are poor, land is in limited supply, and so are other goods. This state of affairs could easily be projected onto the world at large. Thus, Foster considers sibling rivalry to be influenced by the conception of a mother's love as being finite and directed mainly to the youngest child; hence the jealousy of older siblings. Foster notes the expectation of sibling rivalry and jealousy in Mexican villages as well as in Ammar's Egyptian village.

Foster remarks that peasant families can be relatively self-sufficient and individualistic; so each family sees itself in a competitive struggle with others for the scarce values of life. They do not compete for outward symbols of success or display; instead, everyone tries to be inconspicuous and to look like everyone else, in order to avoid evoking jealousy, envy, and criticism.

Much of this cognitive approach may be true of nonpeasant societies as well as of peasant societies. Also, there are peasant societies which do not fit the scheme very well. For example, the villagers of Niiike, Japan, are described as having little anxiety or aggression but

---

[4] See also Friedman (1967).

with a high stress on achievement. There seems to be little tension compared to what has been described of Silwa or the Aymara (De Vos 1965a). The people of Niiike engage in much cooperative activity. Perhaps a crucial factor which distinguishes this Japanese village from the other peasant communities we have considered is that it is relatively prosperous (Beardsley, Hall, and Ward 1959).[5]

What interests the anthropologist is not only the similarities which may be found in some peasant communities, but also the differences. Why are the peasants of Taira, Okinawa (discussed in Chapter 8) apparently more trusting and cooperative than those of Silwa? Why is alcoholism attributed to Aymara but rare among poor Italian and Sicilian peasants, despite their similarly dull rounds of experience?

Comparisons in different contexts may also help to elicit the significant determinants of personality patterns. If high altitude, for example, is said to account for some personality traits of the Aymara, one can compare Aymara who live at high altitudes with Aymara who live in low-lying jungle areas, as some of them do, and see if there are any significant differences between these groups. Or one can compare the high-altitude Aymara with other peoples, like the Nepalese, who live at high altitudes. If the Aymara are said to have suffered mainly from the oppression of Mestizos, one can compare the Aymara of towns and haciendas with the more independent Indians who live apart from white or Mestizo control, or make comparisons of Aymara before and after the Bolivian revolutions, before and after the acquisition of education.

PRESENT-DAY JAPAN

Some of the best work in culture-and-personality research since World War II has been done in Japan. Much of this work has focused on child-rearing patterns, and the review that follows will thus emphasize childhood experiences.

One justification for attempting generalizations about Japan is that its people long shared a relatively homogeneous culture. As Richard K. Beardsley (1965:360) put it: "Few areas of comparable population anywhere in the world have had such culturally homogeneous people who were so long isolated from other peoples. . . . In isolation,

---

[5] Arthur J. Rubel (1977:233–34) has pointed to some similarities between Foster's "image of limited good" and reference group theory. The former has been a topic of discussion among anthropologists, while the latter has been a focus of research among sociologists and social psychologists. Rubel believes that Foster's model is more applicable to closed corporate, relatively homogeneous peasant societies. It requires some modification when dealing with more stratified societies, such as Foster's own Mexican village of Tzintzuntzan, in which it seems likely that "a resident will compare his own abilities and relative well-being to the condition of those whom he perceives to be most similar to him, and he will reject as reference individuals those whose social characteristics are least similar to his own."

the Japanese missed what most peoples have experienced, a constant rubbing of elbows with outsiders. . . ."

One of the best community studies in anthropological literature, which incidentally involves research in culture-personality relations, is the study of the village of Niiike in the southwestern part of the island of Honshu. In their Foreword the authors note that even in 1959 almost half the Japanese population was rural, living in small rice-growing communities like Niiike. Moreover, a large proportion of city dwellers are recent migrants from such villages, which to some extent represent "the traditional cultural foundation of all modern Japan" (Beardsley, Hall, and Ward 1959:viii).

The case for Japan's cultural homogeneity may be overstated here, but a consideration in its favor to which Nyozekan Hasegawa has drawn attention is that while other ancient Eurasian civilizations developed from walled cities, the civilization of Japan grew up in unwalled communities open to the outer world. To be sure, there was much fighting in the feudal Japanese period, and the *daimyo*, or feudal overlords, did have walled, fortified castles, but there were no walled cities such as those of Europe and China (Hasegawa 1966:37). In the survey that follows, data from both urban and rural communities (including Niiike) will be presented.

Sleeping Arrangements

One way in which Japanese families differ from American and European families is in their characteristic sleeping arrangements, the subject of a study by William Caudill and David W. Plath (1966). Caudill and Plath interviewed parents about the sleeping arrangements in their families. They have data on 323 households—198 in Tokyo, 99 in Kyoto, and 26 in Matsumoto. The sample had an average of 4.8 persons per household. There were no one-person or two-person households. The sample was close to the 1960 census which found an average of 4.8 persons per household for all urban areas. No important differences in sleeping arrangements were found for different social classes. (This seems surprising, for one would expect more crowding in the lower classes.) Almost all the rooms counted had *tatami* mat covering, with people sleeping on quilts (*futon*) which are spread out each evening and removed in the morning after the people get up. Only 10 percent of the people used beds of Western style.

It was found that children sleep with parents to a much older age than is usually done in the United States. "The sharpest break in sleeping arrangements comes between the children who are 11 to 15 years old and those who are 16 to 20 years old. The former have a 50 percent chance of co-sleeping in a two-generation group (with a parent or extended kin member), whereas the latter have only a 17 percent chance of so doing" (Caudill and Plath 1966:352–53). The authors believe that the onset of puberty for a boy and of menstruation for a girl set the stage for withdrawal from co-sleeping with older persons. On the basis of their tables the authors state that a child can expect to co-sleep with an adult until he is 10 years old. The period from 11 to 15 years is one of transition. "After the age of 16, a child is more likely to co-sleep with a sibling or to be alone, but there always remains a fair chance (at about the 20 percent level) that he will co-sleep with a parent" (Caudill and Plath 1966:353). After 16, daughters are more apt than sons to co-sleep with a parent. Sons are more likely to sleep alone. Caudill and Plath (1966:363) conclude that: "sleeping arrangements in Japanese families tend to blur the distinctions between generations and between the sexes, to emphasize the interdependence more than the separateness of individuals, and to underplay (or largely ignore) the potentiality for the growth of conjugal intimacy between husband and wife in sexual and other matters in favor of a more general familial cohesion."

The authors point out that age periods when people commonly sleep alone coincide with age periods when suicide rates are high, as in adolescence and old age. They do not suggest that sleeping alone causes suicide but indicate that it may add to the sense of isolation for a person who has been used to co-sleeping patterns for most of the rest of his life. Where causal factors are concerned, much of the stress during adolescence in Japan seems to be related to the competitiveness of academic life and the struggle to be admitted into good schools and colleges. (This will be discussed later.) The physical isolation of the lone sleeper may add to his or her anxiety and depression.

One consequence of the Japanese sleeping arrangements seems to be some inhibition of sexual activity. In a study of a rural agricultural community in northern Shikoku, Robert J. Smith (1962:188) reports that sexual relations are engaged in as quickly as possible after a married couple's children have gone to sleep; neither partner disrobes fully, and there is almost no foreplay. A similar picture is given of marital relations in the village of Niiike (Beardsley, Hall, and Ward 1959:333), and in Ezra F. Vogel's study of middle-class Tokyo suburban families (1963). Vogel claims that married couples in the suburban community called Mamachi have intercourse less frequently than American couples and have less foreplay. He gives comparative figures for frequency of intercourse per week for different age brackets in the United States and Japan, with the American figures coming from the Kinsey report on *Sexual Behavior in the Human Female* (1953) and the Japanese figures being drawn from a study by Nobuo Shinozaki, "Report on Sexual Life of Japanese" (1957), based on a sample of 635 persons in or near Tokyo. In the Japanese sample, 38.9 percent reported no foreplay before intercourse, while all of the American sample reported foreplay. The American frequencies for intercourse were higher for each age bracket than the Japanese (Vogel 1963:220).

Statistical assessments like these may be open to question, but the findings seem to be consistent. According to Vogel, sexual repression makes it difficult for young wives to enjoy sexual relations soon after marriage.

Japanese and American Infants: Some Contrasts

Some different patterns in the early infancy of Japanese and American babies from middle-class homes have been noted by William Caudill and Helen Weinstein (1969). The authors made observations in the homes of 30 Japanese and 30 American firstborn normal three- to four-months-old infants and their families. All the families were judged to be middle class on the basis of occupation and level of education. The Japanese mothers in the sample were a little older than the American mothers and more frequently breast-fed their babies. 18 of the Japanese, but only 5 of the American mothers, were breast-feeding at the time of the observations.

The authors used a time-sampling procedure for about four hours on each of two days. "In this method, one observation of approximately 2 seconds in duration is made every 15th second in terms of a set of predetermined variables concerning the behavior of the infant and of the caretaker" (Caudill and Weinstein 1969:19). Four observations were made each minute; 40 in a 10-minute period. 1800 observations were available for each case for two days. On the first day, observations were made from 9:30 A.M. until noon; on the second day from 1:30 P.M. until 4:00 P.M.

The two samples, of course, are very small; although it is questionable how representative they may be of Japanese and American middle-class mothers and infants, some of the findings suggest that there may be considerable differences in the behavior of Japanese and American babies as early as three or four months of age. The American infants, for example, were more active than the Japanese babies. The American children played more with objects and gave more "happy" vocalizations. The Japanese infants were quieter, more passive, with more "unhappy" vocalization. The American infants were left alone more.

Differences were also noted in the behavior of the respective caretakers. The American mothers talked more to their babies, while the Japanese mothers rocked and lulled them more. The American mother seems to be trying to stimulate her baby, whereas the Japanese mother seems to have a more soothing effect, trying to keep the baby quiet and contented.

Perhaps the behavior of the infants in the two national settings was differentially affected by the contrasting behavior of the two sets of mothers. On the other hand, an inborn genetic explanation is also possible. Daniel G. Freedman and Nina Freedman in a study of 24

Chinese and 24 Caucasian newborns, found that Caucasian babies cried more readily and were harder to console. "The Chinese-American newborns tended to be less changeable, less perturbable, tended to habituate more readily, and tended to calm themselves or to be consoled more readily when upset" (Freedman 1974:154). Freedman (1979b) has noted other studies which point to a possible Mongoloid-Caucasian difference in these respects, but there are also some studies which do not agree with such conclusions (see Super 1981a:196).

Patterns of Bathing and Carrying

The closeness of Japanese mother and child is reflected in bathing customs. Middle-class Japanese families have private wooden bathtubs, usually heated by gas. They are narrower and deeper than American bathtubs. The tub is filled to the top with very hot water, and the bather crouches in it with the knees drawn up. Soaping and washing are done beforehand, outside the bath. Pleasure is derived from sitting and soaking in the tub. The washing must be done beforehand, since the water must stay clean for all the family members. Father, the head of the household, usually goes first, followed by sons in order of age, and then by the female members. If the mother is cleaning the dishes, she may take her bath last. The mother takes her young baby into the bath with her, in contrast to the bathing situation in the middle-class American home, where the mother stands outside the bath and bathes her baby.

Poorer families and those who have no private bath go to public baths, where there are usually separate baths for men and women. Boys below two or three years of age are taken by the mother to the women's side, but boys older than that are taken by the father to the men's bath.

Close contact with the mother is also represented by carrying techniques. For the first year or two of life the baby is carried on the mother's back with a special strap. In wintertime, when she goes out, the mother may wear a coat which covers both herself and the child. Babies being carried this way generally look quite contented. If the baby cries, the mother may jiggle it. According to Ruth Benedict (1946:257), this form of carrying is conducive to passivity in the child and develops a capacity (which Benedict attributes to the Japanese) of being able to fall asleep anywhere, anyhow.

One reason why the child is so constantly carried during the first year of life is that there are some dangers during the crawling period, particularly in the open floor-level toilet, into which the child might fall. The places for cooking and heating are also dangerous for children. Moreover, parents do not want their children to poke fingers through the sliding paper doors (Smith 1962:192; Beardsley, Hall, and Ward 1959:293).

Early Oral, Anal, and Sexual Disciplines

In the responses to Betty B. Lanham's questionnaire on child care in the city of Kainan, the lowest ages for completing weaning were between nine months and one year and two months; the highest was six years, eight months. Weaning generally takes place after the first year (Lanham 1956:567; see also Vogel 1963:231). This would support Benedict's statement (1946:261) that children are usually weaned after they can understand what is said to them. A mother teases a child who wants to continue suckling, comparing him unfavorably with a younger child who has already been weaned.

In the mid-1940s, during World War II both Geoffrey Gorer (1943b) and Weston La Barre (1945) published articles claiming that the Japanese had compulsive personality tendencies stemming (as Freudian theory would have it) from early strict toilet training; but in the early postwar years, articles by Sikkema (1947), Lanham (1956), Haring (1956), and Norbeck and Norbeck (1956) cast doubt on the severity of Japanese toilet training. On the basis of her questionnaire survey in the city of Kainan (449 respondents), Lanham (1956:581) concluded that "Toilet training may not be too different from what occurs in the United States." Concerning a rural area, Robert J. Smith (1962:190) wrote that children are expected to have control over elimination processes by the age of two, "but because toilets in rural Japan are so dangerous, most parents do not permit the child actually to use the toilet alone until he is three or four years old."

The Japanese do not have a puritanical rejecting attitude toward sex. Both Ruth Benedict (1946:270) and Robert J. Smith (1962:193) write that Japanese do not condemn childish sexuality or regard masturbation as dangerous.   •

Methods of Achieving Compliance

Children, then, seem to be treated with much permissiveness and indulgence. With regard to the frequency of punishment, however, there are conflicting reports in the literature. Beardsley, Hall, and Ward (1959:296) write that "Loud-voiced commands, repetitions, and detailed instruction, scolding or tongue-lashing, and physical beating are relatively rare and disapproved in Niiike homes." The same point is made by Vogel (1963:244) in his description of Mamachi parent-child relations; mothers seldom yell at, scold, or spank their children. "Several Japanese mothers, visiting the United States, have expressed their shock at the cruelty and crudity of American mothers who spank and yell at their children in public places such as supermarkets."

However, Betty B. Lanham's questionnaires did elicit high percentages of reports of slapping and spanking used by parents to enforce compliance in children. Lanham (1956:578) estimated the frequency of slapping to be quite similar to what might be expected in the United States. These conflicting findings may reflect subcultural differences.

The literature also contains conflicting conclusions about "spoiled" behavior in children. Some writers, including John F. Embree, Ruth Benedict, and Geoffrey Gorer, claim that Japanese children are spoiled and that boys are rude and aggressive to their mothers. In his work on Suye Mura, the only important community study made in Japan before World War II, Embree (1964:184–85) wrote that Suye Mura children ". . . can and do strike their mothers in a rage and call them the favorite Japanese epithet of *baka* (fool). Anything a child asks for or cries for long enough he gets." Benedict (1946:264) echoed Embree's statement that the little boy may strike his mother with his fists. Such tantrums ". . . in both villages and upper-class homes . . . are looked upon as an ordinary part of child life between three and six. The baby pommels his mother, screams, and, as his final violence, tears down her precious hair-do. His mother is a woman and even at three years he is securely male. He can gratify even his aggressions." But on the basis of her questionnaires, Betty B. Lanham (1956:581) denies that mothers generally acquiesce to such abuse from their sons. Two of her tables show ". . . that in a majority of families the mother as well as (or instead of) the father, is used as a threat to enforce proper behavior on the part of her young son. In slightly under half the families reporting, the mother punishes by slapping the boy." In these areas, then, there is evidently much variation.

Besides slapping, other methods of achieving compliance are used. Threats and scaring techniques are employed, frightening the child by saying that he will be punished by god, or harmed by devils, the thunder god, goblins, the dead, and various animal spirits. Policemen, beggars, neighbors, or teachers may be invoked as threatening figures.

In Lanham's questionnaire, 17 percent of the parents reported the use of moxa cautery, which involves burning a cone of moxa powder on the child's skin, leaving a scar. This is done not only as a punishment but as a therapeutic technique, which may lessen its traumatic effect on the child. "He has at least some chance of perceiving moxa treatment as an act of love, however painful it may be" (Beardsley, Hall, and Ward 1959:294). Shaming, scolding, and ridicule are also used as sanctions for good behavior.

Vogel presents a very interesting account of how Mamachi middle-class mothers achieve obedience and compliance in their children. Part of the secret is that the mother teaches only when her child is in a cooperative mood. She wants to establish such a close relationship with him that he will automatically go along with her suggestions. The mother avoids situations where she must force the child to do something against his will. She tries to anticipate difficulties and to resolve them before they develop. On shopping trips she carries a supply of candies to dispense if the child starts to get restless. Flattery and praise are given for good behavior. In addition to these positive sanctions, which do not always work, Mamachi mothers also make use of threats, shaming, and ridicule (Vogel 1963:243–51).

Another technique used by Japanese mothers, according to George De Vos (1960) on the basis of an analysis of Thematic Apperception Tests[6] given in Niiike, is the assumption of quiet suffering. The mother reproaches herself if her children behave badly or fail to become successful. This somewhat masochistic response is encouraged by popular literature directed toward Japanese women. "Among the favorite themes of movies, television, drama, and magazine fiction is that of the quiet suffering of a girl, young wife, or elderly mother whose self-sacrifice makes her a lovable person and wins copious tears from the responsive female audience" (Beardsley 1965:375). A person who fails in life, and who has thereby hurt his mother, may feel guilt in consequence.

School Education

The pressure to achieve begins when children start going to school. Japanese children are required by law to complete nine years of schooling. Once admitted to school, no student is failed. While this may diminish the pressure somewhat, Japanese students work hard at their home assignments. Examinations are required for entrance to schools and colleges. According to Vogel (1963:46–51), there are special schools in Tokyo to prepare three-and-four-year olds for their kindergarten entrance examinations. Great anxiety attends all school examinations, not only on the part of the child but also on that of the mother, often resulting in sleeplessness on nights before examinations.

Mamachi middle-class mothers help their children with their homework. "In a sense, parents become assistant teachers, checking frequently with the regular teachers about the work the parents should be doing to help educate and train their children. Therefore, to a large extent the parent-child relationship is the relationship of teacher and student" (Vogel 1963:65).

The child's performance in school reflects on his family. If he does badly, he lets them down. According to both Ruth Benedict (1946: 273–74) and Geoffrey Gorer (1943b), when a teacher sends in a bad report about the child, the family turns against the child.

The Sense of Obligation

Ruth Benedict devotes four chapters of her book to discussing the Japanese emphasis on payment of obligations, for which the Japanese

---

[6] For a description of the Thematic Apperception Test, see p. 293ff.

have a special vocabulary. Two words in particular are emphasized in her account: *on* and *giri*. Benedict defines *on* as a load, an indebtedness, or burden which one must repay. One receives *on* from the emperor, from one's parents, and from one's teacher or superiors. Somehow one must make a return for the benefits received from these sources. *Giri* is another term for obligation, such as repayment for a kindness. Benedict speaks of *"giri* to one's name," which involves keeping the family reputation unsullied. This emphasis may lead to such features as stoicism, dignified comportment, and living up to one's commitments in life (Benedict 1946:chapters 5–8).

Notions of obligation were emphasized by both Buddhist and Confucian teachings, particularly among members of the warrior class of samurai during the Tokugawa period (1600–1867). While such notions are still part of the Japanese tradition, Benedict probably exaggerated their importance in relation to Japan of the 1940s. One of the criticisms made by Japanese scholars who read *The Chrysanthemum and the Sword* after the war was that it seemed too much like a description of Japan during the feudal period (Bennett and Nagai 1953).

Achievement Motivation

Several writers have drawn attention to the stress on achievement motivation in Japan. We find evidence of this stress not only in middle-class suburban Mamachi but also in rural Niiike, as manifest in Thematic Apperception Test stories told by the villagers. In analyzing Niiike TAT stories, George De Vos (1965a) identifies four types: (1) self-motivated achievement, (2) encouraged or inspired achievement, (3) achievement as repayment, and (4) achievement as expiation. In the first category, there is an emphasis on persistence and success at all costs, which De Vos believes to be characteristic of the Japanese in comparison with other cultures. In the second category, the father is usually the source of inspiration, an example to his son. The third category involves *on* relationships; since parents undergo hardships to raise and educate their children, the children must succeed as a way of repaying them. The same theme occurs in the fourth category; a person who has let down his parents and thus incurred guilt tries to make amends by hard work and dedication.

One source of guilt in many of the Niiike TAT stories is the choice of a love marriage in opposition to one's parents. Guilt is not expressed for sexual transgressions; rather, the main transgression is rebellion against the parents. The worst eventuality is seen to be excommunication from the family or community.

It is rather surprising to find such an emphasis on achievement motivation in a farming village. De Vos draws attention to a contrast with characteristic American middle-class achievement stories, in which a young man leaves home to strike out for himself. In the

Niiike stories the protagonist does not want to leave home, and if he does leave to study and work elsewhere, the story often ends with his return home.

Some Generalizations on Personality

Let us now review some aspects of child development as described in the foregoing pages and see what effects they may have in personality formation. Perhaps the most striking feature is the very close mother-child relationship manifest in sleeping arrangements, bathing, carrying, suckling, and education. One consequence of these patterns may be some sexual inhibition. Caudill (1962:206) writes that the close mother-child relationship results in a strong attachment to the mother and a sense of trust in others but also in ". . . a chronic mild depression and nostalgia in later life concerning the loss of childhood gratification," which he says is expressed in Japanese plays, movies, and songs.

L. Takeo Doi (1962) thinks it significant that the Japanese have a term *amaeru*, for which there is no English equivalent. It refers to an attempt, usually on the part of a child, to get into a state of close dependence on another person. Doi writes that the desire to *amaeru* affects people in adult life and becomes manifest in therapeutic sessions. He cites a number of other Japanese terms related to the concept of *amaeru* for which, again, there are no English equivalents, although the feelings and attitudes to which they refer are universally recognizable. Doi mentions that Japanese do not say that an infant does *amaeru* until he is about one year old. This suggests that by that time the child has come to realize that his wish to *amaeru* may be frustrated.

The closeness of early familial ties combined with some inevitable suppression and renunciation must lead to a certain constraint in personality. In a work on the psychology of the Japanese, Hiroshi Minami notes that the Japanese seldom express happiness, for which there are relatively few words in the Japanese language, although there are many Japanese words for unhappiness (Norbeck and De Vos 1961:24). In looking up words for happiness in Obunsha's *Essential English-Japanese Dictionary* (revised edition), to check on this generalization, I found that there are, after all, quite a few Japanese words for happiness, but these do not refer to the more extreme ranges suggested by such English terms as gaiety, exhiliration, exuberance, rapture, and ecstasy.

As for unhappiness, Hiroshi Minami et al. (1959) note that it is a common theme in postwar popular songs which often deal with loneliness, helplessness, parting and "giving up." However, this may mainly reflect the confusion of the postwar period. Despite such themes of sadness, there seems to be no overt expression of sadness in everyday life. The people of Niiike are described as living in an atmosphere of quiet tranquility, which comes ". . . in good part from the restraint put on all expression of emotion. Exuberance is repressed; so is every form of violence. The people smile readily and often; they laugh not infrequently, but gently, never in boisterous guffaws" (Beardsley, Hall, and Ward 1959:66). Also writing of Niiike, De Vos (1965a:55) refers to the muted quality of emotional expression; ". . . few opportunities exist for the expression of feelings with any vehemence or abandon. . . . Both happy and disturbed feelings generally remain muted and suppressed." In Ruth Benedict's terms, the Japanese seem to be more Apollonian than Dionysian (see Chapter 3). This is suggested by a passage in Nyozekan Hasegawa's *The Japanese Character* (1966:10). The emotional outlook of the Japanese, he tells us, ". . . is less subjective than objective, less romantic than realistic, less extreme than middle-of-the-way, less grandiloquent than concise, less pretentious than unassuming, less out-of-the-way than commonplace, less heroic than sensible."

With the strong sense of responsibility, obligation, and need for achievement discussed earlier, there must be a concomitant sense of tension. William Caudill (1970:42) believes that there is an underlying excitability among the Japanese which is held in check by compulsive orderliness.

Fortunately, Japanese culture has developed many institutions for relaxing tension and adding to the enjoyment of life: the family meal, the daily hot bath, *sake* parties, bars and geisha houses for the men, massage houses, and such refinements as the tea ceremony and the enjoyment of gardens. Ruth Benedict (1946:180) even includes sleeping as "one of the most accomplished arts of the Japanese. They sleep with complete relaxation, in any position. . . ." Tensions, in any case, are handled and reduced in various ways.

The foregoing composite sketch of "Japanese national character" which I have drawn from various sources—the writings of Benedict, Caudill, De Vos, Beardsley, Hall, Ward, Lanham, Smith, Vogel, and others—seems to present a consisent picture. It should be taken with a grain of salt, all the same, since subjective factors enter into any assessment of national character. This is evidenced by the fact that wartime American analyses of Japanese national character emphasized negative features—compulsiveness, anality, and fanaticism—while postwar American assessments have been much more positive and favorable—stressing collaterality, good maternal care, and the Japanese need for achievement. All the same, there does seem to be a good case for the existence of a widespread social character among the Japanese. Many writers have thought so, including both foreigners and Japanese themselves.

It would seem, then, that the three examples given in this chapter—the Egyptian village of Silwa, the Aymara of Bolivia and Peru, and the

Japanese—present sufficient evidence to justify further investigation of the influence of culture on personality in different sociocultural settings. The concept of social character may be more applicable to a small tribal or village group that to a large nation which has class stratification and an elaborate division of labor; yet even in Japan, which is so highly industrialized, there seem to be consistent patterns of culture and personality.

SUGGESTIONS FOR FURTHER READING

For a discussion of the concept of social character, see Erich Fromm and Michael Maccoby, *Social Character in a Mexican Village. A Sociopsychoanalytic Study* (Englewood Cliffs, N.J.: Prentice-Hall, 1970), especially Chapters 1 and 11. For a criticism of some of Fromm's views, see Reinhard Bendix, "Compliant Behavior and Individual Personality," *American Journal of Sociology* 58 (1952), pp. 292–303.

There has recently been a heated debate about whether the Aymara can be described as aggressive and, if so, whether their aggression is related to hypoglycemia. The negative view, on both counts, is presented by Ted C. Lewellen, "Aggression and Hypoglycemia in the Andes: Another Look at the Evidence," *Current Anthropology* 22 (1981), pp. 347–61. The affirmative position is held by Ralph Bolton, "The Hypoglycemia-Aggression Hypothesis: Debate versus Research," *Current Anthropology* 25 (1984), pp. 1–53. Despite the reasonable arguments by both protagonists and the well-informed commentators who give their own views, the issues seem to remain unresolved.

For a review of national character studies, see Alex Inkeles and Daniel J. Levinson, "National Character. The Study of Modal Personality and Sociocultural Systems," in Gardner Lindzey and Elliot Aronson, eds., *Handbook of Social Psychology*, 2d ed. (Reading, Mass.: Addison-Wesley, 1968), vol. 4, pp. 418–506.

See also Francis L. K. Hsu, *The Study of Literate Civilizations* (New York: Holt, Rinehart & Winston, 1969).

For surveys of work done in Japan related to culture-and-personality, see Takao Sofue, "Japanese Studies by American Anthropologists. Review and Evaluation," *American Anthropologist* 62 (1960), pp. 306–17; and Edward Norbeck and George De Vos, "Japan," in Francis L. K. Hsu, ed., *Psychological Anthropology. Approaches to Culture and Personality* (Homewood, Ill.: The Dorsey Press, 1961), pp. 19–47. See also William Caudill, "The Study of Japanese Personality and Behavior," in Edward Norbeck and Susan Parman, eds., *The Study of Japan in the Behavioral Sciences* (Houston, Tex.: Rice University Press, 1970), vol. 56, pp. 37–52.

For a reader on Japanese culture and personality, see Bernard S. Silberman, *Japanese Character and Culture. A Book of Selected Readings* (Tucson: University of Arizona Press, 1962). Articles on Japanese character by George De Vos, Hiroshi Wagatsuma, and others have been collected in George De Vos, *Socialization for Achievement. Essays on the Cultural Psychology of the Japanese* (Berkeley: University of California Press, 1973).

PART TWO

Pioneer Studies

3

Ruth Benedict's *Patterns of Culture*

Patterns of Culture has been described by Margaret Mead (1949b:460) as "one of the great books of the second quarter of the twentieth century." Geoffrey Gorer (1953:247) paid a still greater tribute in these words: "I should choose 1895, the year of the publication of Freud and Breuer's *Studien Über Hysterie,* as the year in which the scientific study of individual psychology was born, and 1934, the year of the publication of Ruth Benedict's *Patterns of Culture,* as the birth year of the scientific study of national character."

One reason for the book's success is that it was written with a sense of style, for Benedict was a poet as well as an anthropologist. She came to the study of anthropology when she was 32—"to have something really to do," as she put it—first taking courses at the New School of Social Research (1919–21), then at Columbia University, where ultimately she became an assistant and colleague of Franz Boas.

Boas was the leading anthropologist in the United States, the teacher of the first generation of professional American anthropologists. He was a resolute opponent of the genetic determinist views of racists and eugenicists who promoted the "nature" side in the nature-versus-nurture controversy. Boas, in opposition, stressed the "nurture" side in his book, *The Mind of Primitive Man,* first published in 1911. George Stocking (1968:303) has described Boas as tending toward the theoretical approach of cultural determinism, "the explanation of human behavior in purely cultural terms." While Boas was not a full-fledged cultural determinist in this sense, his teaching must have led Ruth Benedict to explore the implications of this approach. *Patterns of Culture* emphasized human plasticity and the greatly contrasting types of cultures into which people are born and to which they accommodate themselves.

Patterns of Culture was a compilation of some previously published articles, combined with the descriptions of three primitive societies: Pueblo, Dobu, and Kwakiutl. In the following pages I will not deal with her description of the Dobu, which was based entirely on the work of one anthropologist, Reo Fortune (1952), who spent only six months among these islanders.[1] Her fullest discussion dealt with the Pueblo Indians of the Southwest, to which we turn first.

PUEBLO CULTURE

The Pueblo Indians of the American Southwest consist of several tribes which share a similar culture, although they speak at least four distinct languages. The Hopi of Arizona and the Zuñi of New Mexico are the two best-known Pueblo tribes. They are agricultural people who added to their aboriginal corn, beans, and squash some fruits introduced by the Spaniards, such as peaches and apricots, and the use of sheep, burros, and horses which the Spaniards also brought to the Southwest.

The Hopi and Zuñi have matrilineal descent, tracing clan membership in the female line, so that one is a member of one's mother's clan. They also have matrilocal residence, the custom of a married couple taking up residence with the wife's female matrilineal kin. Marriages are monogamous.

In a semidesert environment, farmers must work hard, and it is not surprising that their religion centers around the need for rain and fertility. To that end masked men perform carefully rehearsed dances in a calendrical cycle. They represent the *kachinas* (or *katcinas*), ancestral spirits who bring rain. When uninitiated children see these masked beings, they believe them to be spirits, but they learn the truth when they are initiated into the tribalwide kachina cult, between the ages of 6 and 10 at which time they receive a whipping in an underground chamber known as a *kiva*.

Ruth Benedict spent the summers of 1924 and 1925 doing field research among the Zuñi. Later she did fieldwork among the Pima, the nearest neighbors of the Zuñi to the southwest, and wrote to her mentor, Franz Boas, that the contrast between the Zuñi and the Pima was "unbelievable" (Mead 1959:206).

Other writers before her had been struck by differences between the Pueblos and other American Indians. As early as 1916, H. K. Haeberlin had written an article which foreshadowed some of the themes in *Patterns of Culture*, called "The Idea of Fertilization in the Culture of the Pueblo Indians." Haeberlin pointed out that many religious ceremonies and other aspects of culture could be found common to both the Hopi and Navaho Indians, but that there were differences of emphasis in these societies. A ceremony designed to heal the sick among the Navaho was directed toward securing fertility

---

[1] This is not to deny the merits of Fortune's monograph, which was highly praised by Malinowski in an introduction to the book.

for the fields among the Pueblo Indians. The bull-roarer was used among the Hopi to produce rain, but among the Navaho it was applied to the body of a patient by the shaman as part of a cure. The myth of the Twin War Gods, while similar in the two groups, had different emphases and associations—with fertility among the Pueblos, with healing among the Navahos. A game associated with the buffalo among the Plains tribes was associated with crops among the Hopi. Haeberlin explained this local refashioning as due to a psychological orientation. In the case of the Pueblo Indians this orientation could be designated under the heuristic catchword of "the idea of fertilization."

Ruth Shonle (1925:58) discussed the distribution of the peyote cult, pointing out that it was never accepted by the southwestern tribes, "probably because it did not fit into their seasonal division of ceremonies," and noting that areas where the vision quest existed were receptive to the cult.

In 1928, the same year in which Ruth Benedict first set forth her views about the Pueblo area in "Psychological Types in the Cultures of the Southwest," Benedict's friend Edward Sapir published an article entitled "The Meaning of Religion" in the September issue of *The American Mercury*, in which he contrasted Pueblo and Plains religions. Sapir pointed to the emphasis on ritual among the Pueblos and their repudiation of anything orgiastic. Thus, Protestant revivalism might be taught to a Blackfoot Indian, but never to a Zuñi.

In 1930, Barbara Aitken published an article called "Temperament in Native American Religion," in which she showed, again, that there were different emphases between the religions of the Pueblos on the one hand and certain Woodland and Plains tribes on the other. Among the Winnebago and other tribes in the latter group there was an individual emphasis in the guardian spirit quest. Every man sought his own religious experience. The religion had a "Protestant" tone. Among the Hopi, however, everything was related to agriculture, and there was a stress on mutual confidence, cooperation, and "being happy." The guardian spirit search was absent.

A few writers, then, had been attracted to this theme of contrasting the Pueblo with other Indian groups. Ruth Benedict found a key to this contrast in the writings of Nietzsche.

Nietzsche discussed two opposing approaches to existence: the Dionysian and the Apollonian. The Dionysian seeks to escape from the humdrum round of daily life and to achieve excess, ecstasy, or unusual psychic states. The Apollonian distrusts such experiences and prefers to follow an orderly routine life. Benedict remarked:

> It is not possible to understand Pueblo attitudes toward life without some knowledge of the culture from which they have detached themselves: that of the rest of North America. It is by the force of the contrast

that we can calculate the strength of their opposite drive and the resistances that have kept out of the Pueblos the most characteristic traits of the American aborigines. For the American Indians as a whole, and including those of Mexico, were passionately Dionysian (Benedict 1934:80).

Benedict's strategy here is like that used by Oswald Spengler when he tried to demonstrate the existence of a prevalent world view in a particular society by showing its response to adjacent cultures and the selective borrowing of culture traits. Spengler showed that borrowed items of culture usually undergo some kind of transformation in the new setting and are tailored to fit the culture into which they have been introduced. Thus, when Buddhism diffused from India to China, it became a new, quite different religion (Spengler 1939, vol. 2:57). The ways in which such borrowed items are modified tell us something about the prevalent values or attitudes of the incorporating society. The rejection of uncongenial culture traits is diagnostic in the same way. Spengler pointed out that, although the ancient Greeks were in contact with the Egyptians, Babylonians, and Persians, they did not take over such culture patterns as the pyramid, pylon, or obelisk of Egypt, or either the hieroglyphic or cuneiform writing (Spengler 1939, vol. 2:58).

Benedict's method was similar. She first provided evidence for the widespread Dionysian tendency among American Indians, such as fasting and self-torture in the vision quest and in the ceremonial use of drugs, peyote, and alcohol to induce religious intoxication. Then she went on to show that these patterns were uniformly rejected by the Pueblo Indians because they ran counter to the Apollonian values cherished by these people. The Hopi and Zuñi had never brewed intoxicants or accepted drugs, although they were surrounded by Indian groups who did. Drinking was consequently no problem on Pueblo reservations. Self-torture was also incomprehensible to the Pueblos; and while whipping took place during the puberty ceremonies, this ordeal was merely a symbolic beating that drew no blood.

In a similar vein the author went on to delineate the rejection of the "Dionysian" Ghost Dance of the Great Plains, the shamanistic trance, the tradition of boasting, and other un-Apollonian patterns, such as competition for prestige, cruel punishment for adultery, frenzied lamentation at funerals, recourse to suicide, sense of sin, and dualism in cosmology.

This long list of items, so persuasively tied together, is cumulatively impressive. But there are some dubious assertions. It is hard to accept the statement that "the American Indians as a whole, and including those of Mexico, were passionately Dionysian." This would presumably link together such varied cultures as the hunting bands of Labrador, the fishing communities of the Northwest Coast, the caste societies of southeastern North America, and the complex civilization of the Aztecs. In labeling them all "Dionysian," Benedict seems to commit the error for which she castigates the armchair anthropologists of the 19th century, who made facile generalizations about "primitives" and who failed to recognize the tremendous diversity of nonliterate cultures.

A good case could be made for the "Apollonianness" of many American Indian cultures. Even if we take the Cheyennes, who provide some fine examples of Dionysian behavior—self-torture on the part of the young men, suicidal bravado in battle, and so forth—it will be seen that a firm set of Apollonian values was also present—as in the exemplary behavior expected of chiefs,[2] in the chastity required of unmarried girls (they wore chastity belts), in the police control exercised by the military societies, and in the low rate of ingroup aggression. Indian cultures were, of course, not uniform; and one could hardly assert that they were uniformly Dionysian.

At the same time, Benedict seems to have made Pueblo culture itself out to be more homogeneous than seems warranted. E. A. Hoebel has taken Benedict to task on this point:

> The Western Pueblos (Hopi and Zuñi) are uxorilocal, matrilineal, and have strong clans. But it is wrong to leave the impression that this is a universal Pueblo characteristic. Among the several Keres-speaking Pueblos of Central New Mexico . . . clans, although matrilineal, are weak. Moieties, which are lacking in the west, are strong. Fraternal associations also play a correspondingly greater role. Among the Eastern Pueblos north of Santa Fe . . . clans are patrilineal and relatively important. Patrilineal moieties dominate social life. Houses are owned by the men, and residence is consequently virilocal (Hoebel 1949:450).[3]

Although her chapter on the Pueblos is entitled "The Pueblos of New Mexico" and deals primarily with the Zuñi, Benedict included the Hopi under the general rubric of Pueblo, for she felt it necessary to argue that the Hopi snake dance is not really Dionysian.

Turning now to Benedict's items which illustrate the Apollonian nature of Pueblo culture, she claims that in contrast to the situation on Indian reservations elsewhere, the Pueblos have no drinking problem, since drunkenness is repulsive to them. After reading this, it comes as a surprise to learn, in Smith and Roberts' report on Zuñi law

---

[2] "In the Cheyenne view, the first duty of a chief . . . was that he should care for the widows and orphans; and the second that he should be a peace maker—should act as mediator between any in the camp who quarreled. The dignity of a chief did not permit him to take part in any quarrel; he might not take personal vengeance for an offense committed against himself; to do so would result in loss of influence. . . . A good chief gave his whole heart and his whole mind to the work of helping his people, and strove for their welfare with an earnestness and a devotion rarely equalled by other rulers of men" (Grinnell 1923, vol. 1:336–37).

[3] While Benedict says that her discussion of Northwest Coast culture is largely confined to the Kwakiutl, that section of her book is entitled "The Northwest Coast of America," which, again, would seem to slight cultural differences between such groups as the Haida, Tsimshian, and Coast Salish (see Codere 1950:62).

(1954:58) that by far the most common crimes at Zuñi are drunkenness and drunken driving. "In 1949 there were 57 arrests for drunkenness on the first night of the Shalako festival and 150 bottles of liquor were confiscated." The anthropologist E. A. Hoebel (1954:452) informs us that "Field work among the Central Pueblos in 1945 to 1947 revealed the Pueblo governments almost helpless in the face of uncontrollable drunkenness and violence." And Edmund Wilson (1956:23) describing a visit to Zuñi in 1947, tells how his car was searched for liquor by the police when he entered the pueblo at the time of the Shalako festival. He adds: "This, I was later told, failed almost completely in its purpose, since the Zuñis, by way of their grapevine, would send the word back to Gallup for their bootleggers to come in around the hills."

No doubt a strong disapproval of drinking exists, particularly among the older and more conservative members of many Pueblo communities. Nevertheless, people do drink, particularly the younger men, and especially since World War II. But these tendencies are not necessarily new. Ruth Bunzel (1933:44) wrote: "Long ago, before the drinking of whiskey was forbidden, the Zuñis suffered much from its effects. People sold all their goods to get liquor, got drunk, and fought with each other." Matilda Coxe Stevenson (1904:253) also described prevalent drinking, particularly around the time of the Shalako festival. It seems that there must be a crack in the Apollonian structure, as far as drinking is concerned. The repugnance felt for liquor can apparently be overcome among these people.

Turning to another point, Benedict (1934:69) describes the Pueblos as being invariably mild people, averse to any show of violence or aggression. "In Zuñi," she writes, "whipping is never used as a corrective of children. The fact that white parents use it in punishment is a matter for unending amazement." Here again Benedict has probably overstated the case. We know, at least, that whipping of children is familiar to the Hopi. Don Talayesva, the Hopi Indian whose autobiography is such a rich mine of information, tells us that he was whipped by his parents, grandfather, and father's brothers, but "The relatives that a boy needs to watch closest are his mother's brothers and clan brothers. They have a right to punish an unruly lad severely and almost kill him" (Simmons 1942:70).

Dorothy Eggan (1943:366n) quotes a 42-year-old Hopi man on the same subject: "I was 'licked' when I was a kid, by my father, mother, mother's and father's brothers, and even by an older sister sometimes." Clearly the whipping of children was not a matter of "unending amazement" to the Hopi.

Benedict admitted that whipping of children takes place at Pueblo puberty ceremonies. But she treated this lightly: "In the initiation children are supposed to be very frightened, and they are not shamed if they cry aloud. It makes the rite the more valuable" (1934:69). And again: "The Pueblo practice of beating with stripes is . . . without intent to torture. The lash does not draw blood. . . . The adults repudiate with distress the idea that the whips might raise welts. Whipping is 'to take off the bad happenings' . . ." (1934:91).

However, according to the observations of some other writers, these initiation whippings are not so mild. This is evident with regard to the Hopi, at any rate. H. R. Voth (1901:104) described the floggings at Oraibi as being "very severe," and added that "pandemonium reigns in the kiva during this exciting half-hour"—which doesn't sound Apollonian. In his autobiography, Sun Chief confessed that he suffered permanent scars as the result of his initiation. Describing the blows, he wrote:

> I stood them fairly well, without crying, and thought my suffering was past; but then the Ho Katcina struck me four more times and cut me to pieces. I struggled, yelled and urinated. . . . Blood was running down over my body. . . . I was led home and put to bed on a sheepskin. The next morning when I awoke, the pelt had stuck fast to my body, so that when I tried to get up it came with me (Simmons 1942:83).

There are Dionysian features in the behavior of members of the Néwekwe society at ceremonials who drink urine, eat filth, and aim "to outdo the others in everything disgusting" (Stevenson 1904:107n; see also Parsons 1939, vol. 1:131).

There would certainly seem to be Dionysian elements in the practices followed by some Zuñi medicine societies of walking on red-hot coals and swallowing swords. Benedict (1934:71–72) refers to these in passing, but without comment on their possible Apollonian or Dionysian significance. Elsie Clews Parsons (1939:879) has observed: "The curing society is the part of Zuñi ceremonialism least known to recent observers who therefore underestimate, I think, the orgiastic potentiality of Zuñi character, also the hold of witchcraft belief."

Turning to another point, Benedict says that the ideal man in Zuñi avoids office. However, in a criticism of Benedict's analysis, Li An-Che (1937:69), a Chinese anthropologist who did fieldwork in Zuñi, asserts that "not only do ordinary forms of struggle for individual supremacy exist, but violent forms also occur once in a while." He proceeds to give some examples.

In general, Benedict seems to underplay the tension and conflict in Pueblo society. Much has been written about the clash of factions in the Pueblos, but one gets no hint of factionalism in Benedict's description, since the stress is all on the unity of the society and its cooperative spirit.

Ruth Bunzel (1952:xv) has written that when she and Benedict first arrived at Zuñi the village was in one of its "periodic" states of upheaval in which anthropologists figured. "The 'progressive' faction, favorable to Americans and friendly to anthropologists, had been ousted after unsuccessful attempts by anthropologists to photograph the midwinter ceremonies, and its members were so discredited that any contact with them would have been disastrous."

One would never suspect such a state of affairs from reading *Patterns of Culture*. The Pueblo culture, as she describes it, seems somehow disembodied and unrelated to our historical world. This timeless quality may be related to Benedict's emphasis on the underlying ethos of the culture, which seems to be self-perpetuating and unchanging.[4]

A better sense of the current situation may be gained from reading Robin Fox's short but lively article "Pueblo Baseball: A New Use for Old Witchcraft," which shows how problems of factionalism and the surfacing of aggressive emotions have been stimulated by the appearance of competitive baseball teams. Rivalry is greatest among women related to the players, who bring accusations of witchcraft into the fray.

Benedict evidently saw Pueblo culture in a particular light. She was selective in what she responded to. To some extent, this is inevitable in fieldwork. John Bennett (1946) has shown that different ethnologists have responded very differently to Pueblo culture, and he has grouped them roughly into two divisions: (1) an "organic" school, which stresses the integration of the culture with its "sacred" values and its ideal type of the nonaggressive cooperative individual; (2) a "repressive" school, which stresses the covert tension, anxiety, and suspicion in everyday life. These two viewpoints are not, to be sure, incompatible, and Bennett observes that there are competent ethnographers in both groups, Ruth Benedict and Laura Thompson being classified under the first heading; Esther Goldfrank, Dorothy Eggan, and Mischa Titiev under the second. Evidently, one's values and attitudes partially determine what one will see in the field and how one will describe what is seen. It is fortunate, therefore, that a number of different investigators have worked among the Pueblos.

KWAKIUTL CULTURE

Ruth Benedict's prime example of a Dionysian culture was that of the Kwakiutl Indians of the Northwest Coast of North America, the last of the three cultures which she described in her book. Benedict did not do fieldwork among the Kwakiutl; her data came from Franz Boas, whose studies of Northwest Coast culture covered a period of

---

[4] There is probably a relationship between this timelessness and the emphasis of Boas on getting ethnographic accounts of American Indian cultures before their imminent collapse. This was a kind of salvage ethnography which tended to focus on the precontact elements of Indian culture and to discount concomitant modern features. Thus an ethnographer would be apt to ignore the gasoline station and the grocery store as irrelevant intrusions and to direct his attention to what remained of the Indian way of life.

over 40 years, and she had access to Boas's published and unpublished material, both voluminous.

The Kwakiutl and other Indian tribes living in the coastal regions of British Columbia in aboriginal times depended on hunting, gathering, and fishing. They were not farmers like the Hopi and Zuñi. Yet they had a sophisticated culture, living in villages with large plank-walled, gable-roofed houses. This sedentary life was made possible by the rich resources of the streams and sea, which included salmon, cod, candlefish, halibut, flounder, shellfish, seals, and porpoises. Many kinds of berries and roots were available. The elaborate culture of the Northwest Coast tribes was also made possible by trade with white fur traders, beginning in the late 18th century. Iron knives and other cutting tools facilitated housebuilding, wood carving, and the making of masks, totem poles, and cedar storage boxes, all carved in the strikingly distinctive style of Northwest Coast art.

The fur traders also introduced Hudson Bay blankets, which became a kind of currency and figured prominently in the distribution of goods at the feasts known as potlatches. Hammered copper sheets, worth hundreds of blankets, were also distributed on these occasions. A basic potlatching unit was the *numaym*, a named landholding group whose members were usually related to their chief through patrilineal descent. A chief would give a potlatch to establish his heir, or to announce some other change of status, such as a girl's first menstruation or a wedding. Goods were accumulated by members of the *numaym* and finally distributed at the feast. A potlatch could also be given by a tribe to other tribes. This set the stage for competitive displays, boastful speeches, and sometimes destruction of property to show off the wealth of the hosts.

The drama of Kwakiutl life was also expressed in their winter ceremonials, when elaborate performances were enacted with splendid masks and costumes, involving the use of magic tricks and other stage effects.

Six years before the publication of *Patterns of Culture*, Franz Boas sketched out a theme that Benedict was to elaborate on in her book:

> Wherever there is a strong, dominant trend of mind that pervades the whole cultural life it may persist over long periods and survive changes in mode of life. This is most easily observed in one-sided cultures characterized by a single controlling idea. . . . On the North Pacific Coast the importance of hereditary social rank, to be maintained by the display and lavish distribution of wealth, determines the behavior of the individual. It is the ambition of every person to obtain high social standing for himself, his family, or for the chief of his family (Boas 1928:151–52).

Boas saw the stress on status, associated with wealth and property, as the integrating principle in this culture. Benedict added to this the

Dionysian motif. After a very brief summary of the geographical environment and subsistence techniques on the Northwest Coast, Benedict plunged at once into an account of the dramatic religious ceremonials—an approach which places the emphasis on the Dionysian nature of the culture.

She described how—for the high point of his performance—the chief dancer at a Kwakiutl ceremony should try to lose his self-control, and should tremble and froth at the mouth. Before the ceremony a neophyte Cannibal Society dancer was isolated in the woods, where he fasted.

> That which distinguished the Cannibal from the members of all other religious societies was his passion for human flesh. He fell upon the onlookers with his teeth and bit a mouthful of flesh from their arms. His dance was that of a frenzed addict enamored of the "food" that was held before him, a prepared corpse carried on the outstretched arms of a woman (Benedict 1934:178).

This certainly sounds Dionysian! But, in a discussion of this ceremony, Philip Drucker (1955:151–52) writes that it is highly improbable that corpses were actually used. The Kwakiutl had a remarkably developed interest in sleight-of-hand and stage effects—dramatic mock murders, decapitations with false heads, disappearances through trapdoors, wounded men gushing blood from concealed seal's bladders, and so on.[5] Drucker suggests that the carcass of a small black bear, fitted with a carved head, could easily resemble a human corpse, especially by the dim firelight.

As for the biting of bystanders, this seems to have occurred, but it did not happen at random. People were contacted by the "cannibal" ahead of time. They would agree to the biting beforehand, and later the victim would be compensated by special gifts. This places the ceremony in a different light. It cannot have been so wild and Dionysian then. The "cannibal's" behavior was not so frenzied and uncontrolled, but rather carefully planned, at least to the extent that he did not dash about just biting anyone.

Charles Nowell, in the Kwakiutl autobiography, *Smoke from Their Fires*, explains that when he displayed aggressive ceremonial behavior in the bear's skin, going from house to house to smash dishes, he was accompanied by a man who kept track of everything he broke, so that the owner could be compensated later (Ford 1941:117). Dionysian? Yes, to some extent, but in a controlled setting. Benedict's picture ignores the elements of staging and planning, so important in these dramatic ceremonials. The enormous amount of time spent in food getting and in the production of standardized goods also shows that there must have been a strong "Apollonian" core in Kwakiutl soci-

---

[5] For some striking examples of such staged effects, see Ford (1941:118–22).

ety.[6] And when we examine the magnificent art products of the Northwest Coast, we are struck by the emphasis on form. This is not a wild expressionistic art; the elements of tension and the occasional strong colors are bound by strong forms and definite outlines.

Clellan S. Ford makes the interesting suggestion that the Kwakiutl ceremonies were violent, not because the Kwakiutl were habitually violent people, but quite the contrary—because the daily life of the Kwakiutl demanded so strict a control over aggression. And he asks (1941:27): "Can it be that they derived pleasure from thus participating in acts of violence which they badly wanted to do yet dared not?"[7] One thinks in this connection of the extraordinary amount of violence in American films—in westerns, gangster films, and animated cartoons. Some might interpret the popularity of these films as an indication of the bloodiness and violence of American life; but a more likely explanation, it seems to me, would be in terms of Ford's hypothesis of repressed aggression and the tensions of everyday life.

At any rate, there were Apollonian features in Kwakiutl life, just as there were Dionysian ones in the Pueblos. Indeed, it would seem inevitable that there would be some mixture of these human tendencies. Dionysian people cannot very well be always Dionysian. Could a society exist in which everybody was engaged in pursuing ecstatic experiences, cutting off fingers, taking dope or hashish, getting drunk, and going into trances? Of course not. Some Apollonian core of sobriety and responsibility must be found in any culture, or else it will fall apart. At the same time, Dionysian elements can usually be discovered in any culture, no matter how "middle of the road" it may be.

Meanwhile, how are we to characterize forms of integration which exist outside of the Apollonian-Dionysian polarity? Should we find a new catchword for each culture (Babbittian? Confucian? Nanookian?) with each label representing a different principle of integration? Obviously, this is an unsatisfactory stratagem, as Benedict (1934:228–29) admitted in an almost self-disparaging passage: "It would be absurd to cut every culture down to the Procrustean bed of some catchword characterization. The danger of lopping off important facts that do not illustrate the main proposition is grave enough even at best. . . . We do not need a plank of configuration written into the platform of an ethnological school."

Although I have expressed some criticisms of Benedict's descriptions of Pueblo and Kwakiutl culture, I do not want to give the impression that I reject them outright, for I think that much of the

---

[6] See Codere (1950:18–19). According to Codere, they were a peaceable people, who did not engage in much warfare (see p. 115).

[7] There are some passages in Ford's book which could, however, be cited as evidence for a Dionysian tendency in Kwakiutl culture. See the descriptions of children's games and Nowell's account of a rather bloody ceremony in which he participated (pp. 65 f., 115 f).

analysis, in both cases, must be valid. A difficulty in both cases is Ruth Benedict's tendency to overstatement. For instance, there is her extravagant assertion (1934:117) that suicide is "too violent an act, even in its most casual forms, for the Pueblos to contemplate. They have no idea what it could be." Here it is sufficient for Hoebel (1954:452) to cite three Pueblo suicides (all after 1939) to refute her. But the easy refutation that is possible in this case should not blind us to the reality of a difference between the Pueblo and Plains tribes in their attitudes toward suicide and aggression. Benedict's overstatements tempt one to throw out the baby with the bath water. If she had written "Suicide is rare," no one would have objected.

Overstatements seem to abound in Benedict's description of the Kwakiutl, who are characterized as "megalomanic," "paranoid," and so on. Helen Codere has written an article in which she seeks to modify this harsh picture. "The Kwakiutl are more real, more complex, more human than they have been represented to be," Codere tells us (1956:349–50). This is a necessary corrective and is in line with the less sensational emphasis in the accounts of Northwest Coast culture written by Ford and Drucker, which seem more plausible than Benedict's highly colored one. However, in accepting this milder view there is a danger that we may develop a blind spot to the significance of Boas's rich material. Boas, after all, was closer in time to the living culture than later workers in this area, and the amount of work he did was prodigious. Moreover, we should not let our notions of plausibility influence us too far in this connection. Those who have lived through the era of the Nazi regime have some vivid evidence of the extreme forms which cultures may assume. If we had simply read about the Nazis in an anthropologist's account of a remote people, we might well reject the whole report as exaggerated.

With regard to the Northwest Coast, there is abundant evidence that the culture was characterized by a set of values and attitudes which permeated the whole life of the people. Boas is not the only one who provided evidence for this. We find similar impressions in Aurel Krause's work on the Tlingit, first published in German in 1885. Krause (1956:115,169) writes of the Tlingit's highly developed sense of ownership, his vanity and selfishness, even in dealing with friends and near relatives. Krause's account seems to be in keeping with Boas's characterizations.

It seems to me that a revised picture of Northwest Coast culture, although incorporating modifications suggested by the work of Codere, Ford, and others, should retain some of the insights of this sort made by Krause, Boas, and Benedict. For Benedict and Boas may have been on the track of something valid. I feel, for example, that Benedict (1934:187–88) convincingly showed that the motifs of rivalry and self-glorification appear not only in the potlatch, but also in connection with marriage and shamanism. And surely the boastful speeches of Kwakiutl chiefs quoted by Benedict are striking evidence for the attitudes she describes.

SOME GENERAL CONSIDERATIONS

One important problem which Benedict did not pursue in *Patterns of Culture* concerns the means by which individuals are "Apollonianized." In other words, how do the Hopi manage to become such submissive, gentle people? And how were "Dionysian" attitudes cultivated among the Blackfoot in each new generation? In this book Benedict seemed to assume that the whole thing works by contagion. Thus, an individual born into an "Apollonian" culture and exposed to it long enough automatically becomes an "Apollonian" person, just as an Eskimo baby naturally learns to speak Eskimo rather than another language and eventually "takes over" Eskimo culture.

An implicit consistency model of personality is suggested here, although a fulfillment model is also possible. At any rate, Benedict (1934:251–54) explicitly rejects a conflict model, stating several times that there can be no inherent antagonism between society and the individual. There is no conflict because human nature is so malleable.

> Most people are shaped to the form of their culture because of the enormous malleability of their endowment. They are plastic to the moulding force of the society into which they are born. It does not matter whether, with the Northwest Coast, it requires delusions of self-reference, or with our own civilization the amassing of possessions. In any case the great mass of individuals take quite readily the form that is presented to them (Benedict 1934:254–55).

This was in the days before Ruth Benedict had become interested in problems of child-rearing—a matter to which she turned her attention in later works. There is a passing reference in *Patterns of Culture* to the probable absence of the Oedipus complex among Zuñi. Beyond this, there is not much evidence of psychoanalytic orientation in this work, although Clyde Kluckhohn (1944:597) has written concerning "Psychological Types in the Cultures of the Southwest" and "Configurations of Culture in North America" that "every page is colored by an attitude that can only be called 'psychiatric' and which must be traced eventually from the influence of psychiatry."

It may seem paradoxical in the light of Leslie White's polemics against the "Boas school," but Benedict was something of a culturologist, at least in *Patterns of Culture*. Her emphasis was always on the culture rather than on the individual. There is no study of individuals in Benedict's book and no life histories. What Benedict analyzes is Pueblo *culture*, especially its ideal form. The only determinism which Benedict stressed in this work was a cultural determinism, but with the saving implication that man may develop some culture consciousness and insight into the mold of his own culture and thereby change or transcend it in some way. In this respect, perhaps, her viewpoint was close to that of her teacher, Boas (1938:201–202), who once wrote: ". . . my whole outlook upon social life is determined by the question: how can we recognize the shackles that tradition has laid upon us? For when we recognize them, we are also able to break them."

While Benedict expressed a relativist position, she was, at the same time, a reformer, who evidently believed that some solutions to human problems are better than others. It was as a reformer that she wrote books and pamphlets combating racial prejudice.

Could we not say that in some societies people seem to be "happier" than in others, or that there are fewer mental and emotional disturbances in society A than in society B? From reading *Patterns of Culture*, one receives the very definite impression that the Pueblo tribes are "happier" than the Dobu. "Life in Dobu fosters the extreme forms of animosity and malignancy which most societies have minimized by their institutions," Benedict (1934:172), tells us while Pueblo culture is described as "a civilization whose forms are dictated by the typical choices of the Apollonian, all of whose delight is in formality and whose way of life is the way of measure and sobriety" (p. 129).

In which society would you rather live? Or does it make no difference? One would think that Ruth Benedict would rather be a Zuñi than a Dobu or a Kwakiutl. Yet, in the final paragraph of her book, she speaks of the "coexisting and equally valid patterns of life which mankind has created for itself from the raw materials of existence" (p. 278). At the same time, at other points in *Patterns of Culture* she seems to approach absolute criteria for the evaluation of social systems. "It is possible," she suggests, "to scrutinize different institutions and cast up their cost in terms of social capital, in terms of the less desirable behavior traits they stimulate, and in terms of human suffering and frustration" (p. 248).

Elgin Williams (1947:88) has discussed the internal contradictions and inconsistencies in Ruth Benedict's work. "Formally she sticks to relativism," he observes. "Her pragmatism is not so much at the tip of her tongue as bred in the bone. Try as she may to maintain the pose of relativism, the test of consequences intrudes." He is aware that Benedict's concern for tolerance was expressed in her cultural relativism, but he inquires whether this relativism, if carried to a logical conclusion, would not lead to an acceptance of Jim Crowism and other manifestations of intolerance.

THEMES AND POSTULATES

Reference was made earlier to Benedict's statement (1934:228–29): "We do not need a plank of configuration written into the platform of an ethnological school." In line with this self-criticism, Morris Opler (1945) argued that cultures are rarely dominated by a single integrative principle, and proposed, instead, the concept of *themes*, "dynamic affirmations" which are found, in limited number, in every culture and which structure the nature of reality for its members. An example of a theme would be the high valuation of long life and old age among the Chiricahua Apache. Opler points out evidence for the significance of such a theme in various Chiricahua culture patterns. But there is another theme, "validation by participation," which limits the first. An old man is admired and respected as long as he is active and fit, but when he can't keep pace with younger men, his years and knowledge do not prevent his retirement. Themes, then, are not necessarily pervasive in a culture but interact with and balance one another.

Opler (1968) applied a thematic analysis to the culture of North India, in which the 11 themes he singled out are sometimes in conflict with one another.

Similar to themes are basic propositions shared by members of a society which E. Adamson Hoebel (1954:13–14) has called *postulates*. Like themes, postulates may be at odds with one another. Hoebel suggests that the degree to which they are consistent and harmonious with one another in a particular society is a measure of the integration of its culture. In his book on law, Hoebel used the concept of postulates in a cross-cultural study of legal institutions in a series of societies: Eskimo, Ifugao, Comanche, Kiowa, Cheyenne, Trobriand, and Ashanti. Later, in a work on the Cheyenne, Hoebel (1960:98–99) singled out 16 postulates which underlay Cheyenne culture in general.

Francis L. K. Hsu (1969) has suggested the use of postulates as a way of comparing and contrasting the cultures of complex literate societies like China and the United States. The postulates would be underlying assumptions about the nature of things which carry with them various associated corollaries. The postulates and corollaries of a particular society may be inferred from a study of the society's literature, philosophies, ethical systems, laws, mores, and from studies on abnormality, crime, and other forms of breakdown.

To give an idea of Hsu's suggested approach, here is Hsu's Postulate I on China: "An individual's most important duty and responsibility are toward his parents, which take precedence over any other interest, including self-interest. The essential expression of this is filial piety. Filial piety is the individual's way of repaying parents for giving him life and raising him" (Hsu 1969:65). Associated with this postulate are 15 corollaries. There are 14 postulates in all.

A problem with concepts like these is that different analysts can draw up different lists of themes or postulates for a particular society. What specific operations should be followed in drawing up such lists, and how could agreement be achieved in conflicting cases?[8]

---

[8] Other concepts which have been proposed for cultural configurations are *world view* (Redfield 1957:30–34; 1960), and *mazeway* (Wallace 1970a:15; 1970b).

ETHOS AND SCHISMOGENESIS

Another concept showing Benedict's influence is that of *ethos*, as used by Gregory Bateson.

In 1933 Bateson was living among the Iatmul of the Sepik River region in New Guinea. In the preface to his book *Naven*, he mentions the good fortune of being joined there by Margaret Mead and Reo Fortune "at a time when I was hopelessly sick of field work." While the three were working together on the Sepik River, part of the manuscript of Ruth Benedict's *Patterns of Culture* arrived, which Bateson (1958:x, 258) says profoundly influenced his thinking and gave him a clearer idea of what he wished to do in anthropology. The Iatmul among whom Bateson was living were headhunters living in villages with large pile structures and men's houses. They engaged in the cultivation of sago and fishing.

To give an example of what he means by ethos, Bateson describes a group of young intellectual English men or women who are accustomed to having a witty and cynical kind of conversation which establishes, at least for the time being, a tone of appropriate behavior, that is, an ethos. With the suggestion that this state of affairs might apply to whole societies, particularly small isolated ones, Bateson proceeds to examine the Iatmul from this point of view. Here he finds not one ethos but two—one for the men and one for the women. Iatmul men are occupied with dramatic activities centered in their ceremonial house, where they swagger about self-consciously, engaging in angry debates, with violent gestures. Pride and exhibitionism characterize the men, whose dramatic shows are appreciatively watched by the more unobtrusive women.

Women have a humbler way of life centered in the home and concerned with the mundane business of food getting, cooking, and bringing up children. These are largely private rather than public activities. The women are described as being jolly and readily cooperative, in contrast to the touchy, self-assertive males who find it hard to cooperate. At times the women assume something of the male ethos, for on ceremonial occasions they elaborately dress up and display among their decorations some ornaments normally worn by the men. At these times the women march with a "fine proud bearing" quite different from their usual manner, and receive the admiration of both men and women in the audience (Bateson 1958:122–51). In contrast, when men don women's clothes in the ritual activities concerning their sisters' sons, they make themselves look ridiculous, thus indicating the superiority of the male ethos.

To help account for this ethological polarity and its persistence in Iatmul society, Bateson (1958:175) presents the concept of *schismogenesis*, which he defines as "a process of differentiation in the norms of individual behavior resulting from cumulative interaction between individuals." Among the Iatmul, for example, women provide an audience for the men's spectacular shows. Their presence no doubt spurs the men to further exhibitionistic behavior. This in turn promotes more passive, admiring behavior among the women. In this sort of complementary fashion, the characteristic ethos of each sex is reinforced.

Boys become impressed by the men's preoccupation with headhunting, the production of theatrical displays, initiations, and the like, while girls are influenced by the routines of food getting and child-rearing. Bateson (1958:189) saw schismogenesis as a process in which each party reacts to the reactions of the other, and he suggested that this process of differentiation must follow some mathematical law. We see here the origin of Bateson's later involvement in systems theory and cybernetics. He distinguished between two types of schismogenesis. One is the complementary type, just reviewed. The other is a symmetrical form in which reciprocal behavior of the same type occurs, so that boasting by one side leads to boasting by the other. An armaments race exemplifies this symmetrical sequence. In different cases, then, Bateson conceives of a system within which certain units such as individuals or groups interact and mutually influence one another. Although Bateson's use of *ethos* seems to have been influenced by his reading of *Patterns of Culture*, the concept of schismogenesis provides a dynamic interpretation which contrasts with the more static picture of culture that we find in Benedict's book.

SUGGESTIONS FOR FURTHER READING

A biography of Ruth Benedict is available in Judith Schachter Modell's *Ruth Benedict. Patterns of a Life* (Philadelphia: University of Pennsylvania Press, 1983). Concerning Ruth Benedict as a teacher, see Victor Barnouw, "Ruth Benedict" in *Masters. Portraits of Great Teachers*. Edited by Joseph Epstein (New York: Basic Books, 1981), pp. 165–77.

Among Benedict's numerous contributions to culture-and-personality, two can be singled out as of special interest: "Continuities and Discontinuities in Cultural Conditioning," *Psychiatry* 1 (1938), pp. 161–67; and *The Chrysanthemum and the Sword, Patterns of Japanese Culture* (Boston: Houghton Mifflin, 1946) which was briefly discussed in the preceding chapter.

An explicit attempt to see the Dionysian-Apollonian polarity in a cultural evolutionary context has been made by Alvin W. Gouldner and Richard A. Peterson, who, on the basis of a factor analysis of data drawn from 71 primitive societies described in the Yale cross-cultural files, assert that Apollonianness, or impulse control, has increased with the development of technology and civilization. See Alvin W. Gouldner and Richard A. Peterson, *Notes on Technology and the Moral Order* (Indianapolis: Bobbs-Merrill, 1962).

4

Malinowski's Criticism of Freudian Theory

In dealing with the writings of Benedict, we were not concerned with the effects of childhood experiences on personality, but this will be our theme in this and in many subsequent chapters. A pioneer work in the cross-cultural study of this subject was Bronislaw Malinowski's *Sex and Repression in Savage Society* (1953), the first part of which appeared as a pair of articles in *Psyche* in 1925. Some conclusions in these articles were challenged by Ernest Jones, the psychoanalyst who later became Freud's biographer. In the second half of *Sex and Repression*, Malinowski dealt with the criticisms of Jones and other Freudians. The present chapter will set forth Malinowski's argument, the data he presented, and an evaluation of this work.

Bronislaw Malinowski (1884–1942) was one of the leading figures in modern anthropology. He was born and educated in Poland and received a Ph.D. degree in physics and mathematics at Cracow in 1908. Later, however, after a period of illness, Malinowski became so interested in anthropology (through reading Frazer's *Golden Bough* in convalescence) that he went to study under C. G. Seligman and others in England. In 1914, he traveled to Melanesia and lived for two years in the Trobriand Islands, where he learned the native language and intimately observed the life of the people.

TROBRIAND CULTURE AND SOCIAL ORGANIZATION

The Trobriand Islanders are horticulturalists who raise yams, catch fish, and engage in trade with other Melanesian peoples. The kula trade ring was described in detail by Malinowski in his *Argonauts of the Western Pacific* (1922). Malinowski's lengthy stay in this region provided him with the material for a series of books which made both him and the Trobriand Islands famous (Malinowski, 1922, 1926, 1929, 1948, 1959).

Like Joseph Conrad, Malinowski was a Pole who preferred to write in English and did so with great skill. He made the Trobriand scene vivid and immediate to the reader. In this chapter we will be concerned with only one corner of his work: his criticism of Freudian theory. The reader should keep in mind that there is much more to be found in Malinowski's survey of Trobriand life—the study of economic institutions, law, magic and religion, all of which, as a true "functionalist," Malinowski saw as being intricately interrelated.

In *Sex and Repression in Savage Society*, Malinowski examined Freud's concept of the Oedipus complex. He asked the telling question: Is the Oedipus complex as described by Freud to be considered a universal human phenomenon found in all cultures, or is it the product of a particular type of family system? Freud clearly considered the Oedipus complex to be a universal, inevitable aspect of human life, since it is rooted in biology and in the processes of growing up.

Malinowski asked whether this was really so. He pointed out that the composition of the family varies in different societies. Would an Oedipus complex be apt to appear in a society having a matrilineal type of family? Malinowski was in a position to throw light on this question, for the Trobriand Islanders have matrilineal descent. Moreover, as he went on to show, the role of the father in Trobriand society is quite different from that in the Western world.

In the first half of *Sex and Repression*, Malinowski described the Trobriand family situation as follows: Descent is traced in the female line. At birth one becomes a member of one's mother's clan. From a woman's point of view, residence after marriage is virilocal; that is, the bride goes to live in her husband's community. But the term *avunculocal* residence is more appropriate, for at the time of marriage, or shortly thereafter, the husband leaves his father's village, where he was born, and goes to live in the village owned by his mother's subclan, where his mother's brother lives. Except for chiefs, who may have many wives, marriages are monogamous.

> Every man and woman in the Trobriands settles down eventually to matrimony, after a period of sexual play in childhood, followed by general license in adolescence, and later by a time when the lovers live together in a more permanent intrigue, sharing with two or three other couples a communal "bachelor's house" (Malinowski 1953:9). [As we shall see later, this is not all strictly true for "every man and woman."]

The Trobriand Islanders recognize no relationship between sexual intercourse and pregnancy. They believe that a child is inserted in the mother's womb by a dead female relative of hers. The male head of the household, therefore, is not considered to be a progenitor of the child, who is regarded as solely a product of the mother, related to her family, not his.[1] However, the "father" does take an active, indulgent interest in "his" children, and spends much more time playing with them than the usual European or American father does.

Since this is a matrilineal society, a Trobriand boy does not inherit property from his "father" but from his mother's brother, whom he looks up to as the principal family authority. The father's role in the Trobriands also differs in that he is not the traditional food provider or breadwinner for his family, as with us. Instead, every man turns over most of his garden produce to his sister, even though he usually lives in a different village, sometimes as much as six to eight miles away. The "father" is not a disciplinarian; he exerts no special authority over the children. It is the maternal uncle who disciplines the boy when he is old enough—at around seven—to go and work in his uncle's village and to learn from him the techniques of agriculture and the traditions of his clan.

Within the family circle, Trobriand children never see their mother brutalized or in abject dependence on her husband. "They never feel his heavy hand on themselves; he is not their kinsman, nor their owner, nor their benefactor. He has no rights or prerogatives" (1953:31). Here Malinowski exaggerates somewhat, forgetting for the moment that residence is virilocal. (He writes elsewhere: ". . . the man is considered to be the master, for he is in his own village and the house belongs to him . . .") (Malinowski 1929:18). However, the status of the Trobriand woman is high. She has her own possessions; her brother supplies the family with food, and next to him she is the legal head of the family.

Trobriand children grow up with much freedom to do as they like, freedom which includes the sphere of sex. Children play sexual games in imitation of adult copulation, which is regarded with amused tolerance by their elders. But there is one important taboo which governs sexual behavior: an incest taboo proscribing any intimacy between brother and sister. A kind of avoidance relationship is consequently established between them at the approach of puberty. To a lesser degree this taboo extends to clan "sisters" as well. According to Malinowski, there is no latency period among Trobriand children. They maintain an interest in sex throughout childhood during

---

[1] Various writers have expressed skepticism about the Trobrianders' nescience of the facts of life. The same lack of knowledge has been attributed to the Australian aborigines, whose "spiritual" conception of conception is somewhat similar to that of the Trobriand Islanders. However, Géza Roheim, William Lloyd Warner and others have reported that Australian groups whom they have studied really do understand the male role in procreation. This topic has been discussed at length in M. F. Ashley-Montagu's *Coming into Being among the Australian Aborigines* (1937). However, one cannot generalize from the Australian to the Melanesian scene. As far as I know, no one has disproved Malinowski's account of Trobriand beliefs concerning conception. Malinowski was challenged on this matter by Alex G. Rentoul (1931, 1932). Malinowski (1932) responded sharply. It seems to me that Malinowski got the better of the argument. (I am indebted to John B. Gatewood for these references.) The issue of Trobriand knowledge about the male role in procreation is discussed further on pp. 89–90.

the period which Freud described as marked by diminution of such interest.

During adolescence, boys live in bachelors' houses to which they bring their girl friends. After a few years of casual affairs with different partners, they finally get married, thus assuming full adult status. At puberty, ideally, the boy leaves his father's community to live in the village of his mother's brother.

This is the village associated with his clan, where he will inherit property, and which he will ultimately come to regard as his own village, rather than the village of his father, where his father's clan members may even regard him as a sort of outsider (Malinowski 1929:7). However, the move to the uncle's village may not be made until between 18 and 22 years of age (Malinowski 1935:205).

While living at the bachelors' house, the boy continues to have meals at his parents' home (Malinowski 1929:75). He brings his bride there, while his own dwelling is being built, and they spend a "protracted honeymoon" under his parents' roof (Malinowski 1929:91, 109; see also 86–88). In some cases, as with the sons of chiefs, no shift in residence takes place. Once a couple is married, fidelity is expected of both partners, and a rather stiff propriety replaces the earlier free and easy license. Husband and wife never hold hands or otherwise touch one another in public and do not exchange amorous glances or smiles while others are present. Nevertheless, most married couples are said to be on excellent terms with one another.

It was Malinowski's impression that the Trobrianders were a very well-adjusted people, lacking in neuroses or perversions. "In the Trobriands, though I knew scores of natives intimately and had a nodding acquaintance with many more, I could not name a single man or woman who was hysterical or even neurasthenic. Nervous tics, compulsory actions or obsessive ideas were not to be found" (Malinowski 1953:87). Nor was there any evidence of homosexuality, except among boys and girls who had been penned up in the Mission Station.

What of the Oedipus complex? Was there any evidence for repressed longings for the mother? Obviously, this is not an easy thing to find out. Malinowski tried to get accounts of dreams from his Trobriand friends but discovered they dream very little. Malinowski did learn that sex dreams occurred and asked his informants if they ever dreamed in this way about their mothers. Although there were denials to this, there were admissions of sexual dreams about sisters. No Oedipus legends occur in Trobriand folklore; on the other hand, brother-sister incest forms an important motif in their mythology. Malinowski could not unearth a single case of mother-son incest, but did find some involving brother and sister.

Were there reports of hostility felt toward the father? Here again, findings were negative. Sons seemed to entertain warm feelings toward their fathers, but sometimes expressed hostility for maternal uncles. No cases of parricide were reported. Malinowski's conclusion was as follows:

> In the Trobriands there is no friction between father and son. . . . The ambivalent attitude of veneration and dislike is felt between a man and his mother's brother, while the repressed sexual attitude of incestuous temptation can be formed only towards his sister. Applying to each society a terse, though somewhat crude formula, we might say that in the Oedipus complex there is the repressed desire to kill the father and marry the mother, while in the matrilineal society of the Trobriands the wish is to marry the sister and to kill the maternal uncle (Malinowski 1953:80).[2]

Malinowski (1953:134) thought that this Trobriand complex might apply to other matrilineal societies as well, for he claimed that myths of incest between brother and sister are often found among matrilineal peoples, especially in the Pacific, while stories of hostility between a man and his maternal uncle are also widespread.

The principal conclusion in the first part of Malinowski's *Sex and Repression* is that we are "not to assume the universal existence of the Oedipus complex, but in studying every type of civilization, to establish the special complex which pertains to it" (p. 82). This is a clearcut position, but in the second half of his book Malinowski surrenders much of it. During the first half of the book we are led to believe that Malinowski rejects the universality of the Oedipus complex.[3] In the second half, although continuing to criticize aspects of Freudian theory, such as the dubious myth of the primal parricide,[4] Malinowski retreats from his original stand and affirms agreement with his Freudian critic, Ernest Jones, on some crucial points.

Jones insists on the presence of the Oedipus complex in the Trobriands. The father is hated here, he says, as elsewhere; this hatred, in fact, is the "reason" for the Trobriander's denial of the male role in procreation. But hatred for the father in this society is deflected toward the maternal uncle. Thus we have a "decomposition of the primal father into a kind and lenient actual father on the one hand and a stern and moral uncle on the other" (Malinowski 1953:138). Malinowski observes: "For Dr. Jones, then, the Oedipus complex is fundamental; and the 'matrilineal system with its avunculate complex arose, . . . as a mode of defense against the primordial Oedipus tendencies.' " Malinowski's next sentence comes as a considerable

---

[2] Malinowski usually writes as though a boy had only one sister and one uncle. We do not know whether, if a boy had several uncles, he would hate all of them or only one or two—perhaps those with most authority.

[3] "this complex is assumed to exist in every savage or barbarous society. This certainly cannot be correct . . . they cannot reach correct results when they try to trace the Oedipus complex, essentially patriarchal in character, in a matrilineal society. . . ." (Malinowski 1953:5–6).

[4] On the primal parricide, see pp. 215–17.

surprise: "All these views will strike the readers of the first two parts of this book as not altogether unfamiliar, and sound in all the essentials" (1953:138). He expresses agreement with the idea that "hate is removed from the father and placed upon the maternal uncle" (p. 139).

But this means to concede the presence of an Oedipus complex among the Trobrianders, for why should there be any hatred for the father in the first place? In the early part of his book Malinowski gives the impression that where such hatred is found in Europe it is apt to stem more from resentment at the authoritarian role of the European father than from any sexual rivalry (1953:27–29). It would be consistent with this view that in the Trobriands no hostility is reported as being felt for the father (who is not a disciplinarian), while there is hostility expressed toward the maternal uncles, who are authority figures. Malinowski's point, comparable to one of Erich Fromm's (1941:178), would seem to be that sexual rivalry need not be involved to account for the hostility which sons may feel for their fathers. Indeed, Malinowski (1953:241–5) writes: "The statement that 'a young organism reacts sexually to close bodily contact with the mother' appears to me now absurd. I am glad that I may use this strong word, having written the absurd statement myself." Why, then, should there be any hatred for the Trobriand father, with whom children have such a good relationship? Such hatred must presumably exist if it is to be "removed from the father and placed upon the maternal uncle." While appearing to criticize Freud, Malinowski, in effect, concedes the basic Freudian premise.

Géza Roheim, an orthodox Freudian analyst who has done ethnological fieldwork in Melanesia and Australia, asserts, as does Jones, that the Oedipus complex is present among the Trobrianders. He points out that the composition of the Trobriand family is essentially like ours, consisting of husband, wife, and children. The mother's brother does not play an intimate part in the life of this family, for he generally lives in another village. In Freudian doctrine, the crucial events concerning the Oedipus complex are believed to occur before the age of seven, but it is not until then that the boy goes to work in his uncle's village. The uncle, therefore, does not become an important figure in the boy's life until after that time. Roheim (1950:167, 191) also claims that the Trobrianders have Oedipal legends in their mythology.[5]

Malinowski (1929:54) tells us that Trobriand children witness much of their parents' sexual behavior, and that no special precautions are taken to prevent their watching. Since it is Freud's view that such "primal scenes" (often interpreted by the child as the father's aggres-

---

[5] Oedipal motifs seem to be widespread in Oceania. William A. Lessa (1956) believes that this is largely due to diffusion and that such stories may be told in societies where there would seem to be little likelihood for an actual Oedipus complex to develop.

sive attack on the mother) implant resentment in the son, the conditions for an Oedipus complex would seem to be present in Trobriand society, if one accepts the Freudian premise. As we shall see later, Trobriand lovemaking is characterized by some sadomasochistic behavior, which would heighten the impression of an aggressive attack, although, as it happens, it is the male who is on the receiving end of most of the sadism.

To be sure, the free sexual behavior of children and adolescents would, at the same time, seem to obviate the building-up of tensions. But this raises another point. Judging from Malinowski's data, the free sex life he describes is not open to everyone, although in *Sex and Repression* we get the impression that it is. In *The Sexual Life of Savages,* however, we discover that patrilateral cross-cousin marriage is often practiced, that is, the marriage of a man to his father's sister's daughter. Such marriages are arranged by parents when their children are infants and are considered binding. "The betrothed are spoken of as husband and wife, and thus address one another" (1929:105). A girl so betrothed may not sleep with other men or go on girls' sexual expeditions to other villages. At the same time, the boy's father tries to control his son's behavior in these respects. Betrothed couples are not expected to have affairs (pp. 106–7).

Cross-cousin marriages are popular in the families of chiefs, village headmen, and men of rank, wealth, and power. Unfortunately, Malinowski (1929:98) does not tell us what percentage of marriages conforms to this pattern, although he writes: "Whenever there is a possibility of it, a cross-cousin marriage will be arranged. . . ."[6] Malinowski (1929:101) believes that cross-cousin marriage (which results in matrilocal or uxorilocal residence in this culture) represents a compromise between the conflicting principles of mother-right and father-love, but this is an unlikely idea, at least as a general principle, since cross-cousin marriage is found in so many different kinds of societies, including patrilineal ones.

There are other individuals beside those betrothed in infancy who do not experience the traditional Trobriand sexual freedom. Chiefs and other men of high rank may have plural wives. A chief takes a wife from each subclan in the villages of his territory, his wealth stemming from the fact that all of his brothers-in-law contribute to his store of yams. The chief of Kiriwina, for example, had 60 wives and received from 300 to 350 tons of yams a year (1929:132). At the death of such a wife, her community of origin provides a substitute. These are among the prettiest girls in the village, for "the chief simply indicates which of the girls pleases him best, and, irrespective of her previous attachments, she is given to him" (p. 137). These girls, then,

---

[6] In the context of this passage it is not certain whether the statement is meant to apply only to chiefs or to others as well.

are also removed from the life of the *bukumatula*, the bachelors' house, and from the girls' erotic expeditions to other villages. While intrigues occur among the younger wives of chiefs and their boyfriends, they may be punishable by death (p. 140). Not everyone, therefore, has an unrestricted sex life in childhood and adolescence in the Trobriand Islands. Those betrothed in infancy and the many wives of chiefs do not take part in the casual liaisons described by Malinowski. We do not know what percentage of the population was thus restricted. If a free sex life is given as a reason for the well-adjusted character of the Trobriands, what are we to say of those who do not experience it?

This brings us back to Malinowski's generalizations about the absence of neuroses and perversions among these people. These generalizations, it must be said, are based largely on impressions. Malinowski had no extensive psychiatric background, administered no psychological tests, employed no "depth interviews," and was not equipped to give the sort of medical or psychiatric examinations which might have revealed neurotic trends. Even though Malinowski lived a relatively long time among the Trobrianders, learned their language, and was a keenly perceptive person, he was probably not qualified to speak as a psychiatrist about the incidence of neurotic tendencies among them.

The Sexual Life of Savages contains various indications of sadomasochistic behavior. Malinowski tells us that girls in the Trobriand Islands generally inflict a good deal of pain in their lovers by scratching, beating, or stabbing them before engaging in lovemaking. Apparently the young men do not object to this treatment but welcome it as evidence of love and temperament in their girl friends. Malinowski once had to dress the wound of a Trobriand boy who had received a deep cut beneath his shoulder blades. The girl, who had struck harder than she realized, was very concerned about the wound, but the young man did not seem to mind, although he was obviously in pain. Malinowski was told that the boy received his reward that same evening (1929:257). Apparently, women inflict more lacerations on men than the men do on women. Malinowski saw larger telltale scratches and wounds on men than on women.

Malinowski describes an erotic festival which was said to have been formerly celebrated in the Trobriands but was suppressed in more recent years. It had not been held in about 20 years, at the time of the anthropologist's visit. However, Malinowski believes in the accuracy of the accounts given him. According to these reports, the women at this festival used to attack men and boys with shells, bamboo knives, pieces of obsidian, and small sharp axes. Again, the men do not seem to have objected to being cut up in this fashion; it was a sign of manliness and popularity to receive many gashes. A woman's aim, on this occasion, was to slash as many men as she could. A man's aim was to receive wounds from the more attractive women, from whom he would seek his reward. Malinowski (1929:257) tells us that sexual intercourse took place openly in public on this occasion.

Even if this alleged festival were only a fantasy of Malinowski's informants, the nature of the fantasy is instructive. There are also Trobriand traditions, or fantasies, about gangs of sexually ravenous women in distant villages who attack men, passing strangers, and subject them to violent sexual indignities (1929:274–29, 422–25). It is the women, incidentally, who are feared as witches in this society (pp. 45–46).

In Malinowski's description of Trobriand lovemaking, he refers to biting and scratching as part of the erotic techniques employed. As mentioned earlier, it is the woman who inflicts the greater wounds. The man, however, bites off the woman's eyelashes during intercourse. Malinowski (1929:475) says that this is done "tenderly"; so perhaps there is nothing sadistic about this practice. Malinowski does acknowledge that there may be some sadistic and masochistic elements in the erotic behavior of the Trobriand Islanders; but he says that flagellation as an erotic practice is unknown and that he does not consider the Trobriand lovemaking practices to be perversions. Here agreement or disagreement with Malinowski would depend on one's definition of *sadism* and *perversion.*[7]

It may be noted that a recurrent motif in the folktales presented by Malinowski is the cutting off of a woman's clitoris (1929:406–08). There are also stories of self-castration by men (pp. 412–15). Why should such motifs appear in a society of genitally adequate people who lack neurotic traits? If stories of this sort were generally found in all, or most, human cultures, their presence might not seem unusual. But according to Clyde Kluckhohn (1959), who made a survey of the mythology of 50 cultures with a widely scattered distribution, following Murdock's six major cultural regions, there were only four cases from all the material he surveyed where actual castration was mentioned. One of these was the Trobriand self-inflicted castration.

To my mind, *The Sexual Life of Savages* presents data which show that the picture of Trobriand life presented in *Sex and Repression* is oversimplified. I also feel that the handling of the central question concerning the Oedipus complex is unsatisfactory and leaves the problem still unsettled.

It must be admitted, however, that Malinowski did demonstrate the point that sex may be differently regarded and expressed in other

---

[7] It is interesting to note, incidentally, that the Normanby Islanders, a matrilineal people who live near the Trobrianders and who have a similar culture, are reported by Roheim to have strong sadomasochistic patterns. "Coitus itself is openly sadistic and masochistic. Both parties bite, scratch, and hit each other. This is done before and during the sexual act, but they will avoid it when somebody is in the house and they do not want to make a noise. We have here one of the most significant facts in understanding the psychology of these people, *they pretend to be so mild and they are so violent.* Cruelty is an outstanding character trait. Prisoners of war were made to walk up and down between two fires until they were gradually roasted" (Roheim 1950:175. Roheim's italics.).

cultures, and that there may be variations in the structuring of the family romance. Anthropologists have since provided further illustrations of these themes. For example, among the Hopi there is a sexually tinged joking relationship between a boy and his "father's sisters," the female members of his father's clan. The husbands of such women affect to feel (or perhaps do feel) resentment and jealousy of the boy and may threaten to castrate him. Some examples of such behavior are given in Don Talayesva's autobiography (Simmons 1942:33–40, 76, 108).

Curiously enough, there is also a sexual joking relationship between a boy and his father's sister among the Trobriand Islanders. Malinowski (1929:534–35) states that sexual intercourse would be permitted in this case, but it is not common because of the difference in age. (Nothing is said about the jealousy of the husband.) A paternal aunt's daughter, however, is a preferred sexual and marriage partner. Among the Trobrianders a man should not simultaneously be in the presence of both a sister and a paternal aunt, since the first is an inhibiting relationship and the second a relaxing one.[8]

In the writings of A. R. Radcliffe-Brown and Claude Lévi-Strauss, we find some suggested structural explanations for attitudes toward mother's brother and father's sister. In an essay on "The Mother's Brother in South Africa" (1952), Radcliffe-Brown pointed out that in different societies there may be two antithetical kinds of attitudes toward a mother's brother. In the one case, the mother's brother represents family authority and is feared and respected. In the second case, the nephew treats his maternal uncle with familiarity and may take liberties with him. The first type is associated with matrilineal descent, the second with patrilineal descent. "In groups where familiarity characterizes the relationship between father and son, the relationship between maternal uncle and nephew is one of respect; and where the father stands as the austere representative of family authority, it is the uncle who is treated with familiarity" (Lévi-Strauss 1967:39).

In patrilineal societies, the mother's brother may be considered a "male mother" and is sometimes called by such a term. A young man in such a society may expect more indulgence from his mother than from his father, and this feeling may be extended to other members of her family and lineage, including the mother's brother. Similarly, the father's sister may be regarded as a kind of "female father" and must accordingly be regarded with deference and respect in a patrilineal society (Radcliffe-Brown 1952:19–20). But in a matrilineal society, where the maternal uncle is head of the family, a more familiar, friendly attitude may be taken toward the father, and this attitude of

---

[8] Here, again, Malinowski writes as though a boy had only one father's sister, just as he seems to have only one sister and one mother's brother.

indulgence may in turn be extended to his sister. This might account for the parallel attitudes toward the father's sister among the matrilineal Hopi and Trobriand Islanders. However, the Hopi do not seem to have the same kinds of attitudes toward the mother's brother as the Trobriand Islanders do, and they have matrilocal rather than avunculocal residence.

Another difference between these two matrilineal societies is that the Hopi do not have brother-sister avoidance, which is such an important feature of Trobriand social life. In this respect the Hopi seem to be atypical of matrilineal societies. Of 15 matrilineal societies studied by David M. Schneider, Kathleen Gough, and their associates, 12 are known to have taboos affecting brother-sister relationships, apart from the incest taboo. The main exceptions are the Hopi and the Ashanti of West Africa. Gough (1961:598–99) offers as a possible partial explanation for this the fact that among the Hopi and Ashanti brothers-in-law seldom co-reside. Brother-sister taboos seem to be strictest among the Minangkabau of Indonesia and the Nayars of central Kerala, India, where brothers share a joint household with their sisters and often have contact with their sisters' husbands. In both cases, brothers are not allowed to enter their sisters' rooms.

There seem to be many variations as well as parallels among matrilineal societies. They do not all share the features which Malinowski described for the Trobriand Islanders. The role of the mother's brother varies in different matrilineal societies. It appears to be strong among the Ashanti, the Nayars, and to some extent among the Plateau Tonga. In the last chapter (p. 64) there was a quotation from Don Talayesva about the powerful role of the mother's brother among the Hopi. However, the maternal uncle does not seem to figure prominently in the everyday life of the Navaho Indians (Schneider and Gough 1961:84, 169–70, 291). Thus the "matrilineal complex" proposed by Malinowski cannot apply generally to matrilineal societies, although they often do have brother-sister avoidance and other parallel features.

Sex and Repression was the first important study to test Freudian propositions in a nonliterate non-Western society. Moreover, Malinowski pointed to some possible areas of culture-and-personality research for the future. He claimed that the Amphlett Islanders differed from the neighboring Trobrianders in some respects. "Though matrilineal," he remarked of the former group, "they have a much more developed patriarchal authority and this, combined with the sexual repressiveness, establishes a picture of childhood more similar to our own" (Malinowski 1953:86).

In yet another group, the patrilineal Mailu, there was a still greater strictness and the presence of people whom Malinowski classed as neurasthenic. Recognition of such variations led Malinowski to formulate an imaginative proposal of research:

The problem would . . . be: to study a number of matrilineal and patriarchal communities of the same level of culture, to register the variation of sexual repression and of the family constitution, and to note the correlation between the amount of sexual and family repression and the prevalence of hysteria and compulsion neurosis. The conditions in Melanesia, where side by side we find communities living under entirely different conditions, are like a naturally arranged experiment for this purpose (Malinowski 1953:89).

Malinowski had a remarkable knack for asking significant questions. Here he foreshadowed, to some extent, the Linton-Kardiner concept of "basic personality structure."[9]

SPIRO ON THE TROBRIAND OEDIPUS COMPLEX

Except for some additions to Footnote 1, the foregoing pages of this chapter remain as they appeared in the previous edition; but now it is necessary to take account of a work by Melford E. Spiro, *Oedipus in the Trobriands* (1982), which argues that the Oedipus complex is universal. Far from it being absent in the Trobriand Islands, Spiro finds that the Trobriand Islanders have a particularly strong Oedipus complex. Spiro has done no fieldwork in the Trobriands. His conclusions are based on an analysis of Malinowski's data.

Spiro begins by discrediting the alleged matrilineal complex. He points out that the Oedipus complex comes to an end before Malinowski's matrilineal complex even begins, and the latter does not have the triangular character of the Oedipus complex, in which hostility to the father is related to the boy's love for his mother. "In the matrilineal complex, the boy sustains a diadic and separate relationship with each of the other actors, his love for his sister having no bearing on his hostility to the mother's brother" (Spiro 1982:10). If the boy's libidinal attachment to his mother dissolves because of his sexual freedom, why would that not also be true of his feelings for his sister?

Malinowski implies that the uncle's jural role accounts for the boy's hostility toward him, but Spiro (1982:30) complains that there is no real evidence on this important issue. "Nowhere in any of his writings does Malinowski provide an on-the-ground description of the relationship between the boy and his uncle." (p. 30). At one point

---

[9] It is unfortunate that Malinowski's picture of Trobriand life has sometimes been assumed to be characteristic of matrilineal peoples in general, as if the Trobriand Islanders represented a stage in man's cultural evolution, before the development of a sexually repressive stage of patriliny. Misleading notions of this sort are expressed in the writings of Wilhelm Reich (1946:73 ff.; 1949:xxiv) and Erich Fromm (1951:chap. 7; 1955:44 ff.; 1959).

The dour Dobu are matrilineal. So were the Ashanti of West Africa, who insisted on virginity in their brides, severely punished adultery, and inflicted the death penalty for various sexual offenses. The Nuer of the Upper Nile River, on the other hand, are patrilineal, but allow a good deal of experimental lovemaking before marriage, and there are many patrilineal peoples in northeastern India which take an indulgent view of premarital relations between boys and girls. The Todas of South India, famous for their lax sexual mores, are also patrilineal.

Malinowski indicates that the matrilineal complex begins at puberty, for that is when the boy becomes subject to his uncle's discipline. But elsewhere he writes that at puberty a boy's relations with his mother's brother are at their best, and it is not until some later unspecified time that friction develops between them (Spiro 1982:32).

After reviewing other inconsistencies and stressing the lack of evidence, Spiro concludes that it is unlikely that the boy's early feelings for the mother would spontaneously disappear or that the sister should become the focus of his desires and the mother's brother the main target of his hostility.

Spiro next turns to what he calls "the absent-father pattern." As we have seen, the father is absent in the sphere of reproduction from the Trobriand point of view. This is also true of mythology, in which, according to Malinowski, the father is never mentioned. Dreams are a third domain in which the father is said to be absent. In each case, according to Spiro, the real reason for the father's absence is denial and repression. The ambivalence of the son's feelings leads to a blotting out of the father image.

The weakest of the three domains for Spiro's argument is that of dreams, for Malinowski did not make a collection of dreams and he did not state that the father rarely appears in them; but since the sister and mother are said to appear frequently in Trobriand dreams: "It seems safe to infer from his silence that father dreams are virtually absent" (Spiro 1982:46). Malinowski notes that the Trobrianders have little interest in dreams and seldom report on them, which Spiro (p. 49) interprets as repression, especially involving hostility toward the father. The evidence here is slight, and the explanation is "entirely speculative," as Spiro acknowledges.

The case for the mythology is somewhat better, for a small collection of myths is available for analysis. Spiro (p. 49) proposes to follow a structural principle that "if . . . there is a persistent pattern of the absence of a person (or object) whose presence is normally to be expected and if, instead, some other person (or object) has taken its place, the clue to his absence is often provided by his replacement." He recounts the myth of a Trobriand culture hero, Tudava, the son of a virgin who was abandoned by her brothers when a cannibalistic ogre attacked the village. The mother raises the boy and teaches him magic, of which Tudava makes use when he becomes old enough to fight and kill the ogre. Tudava cuts off the ogre's head and buries it in a taro pudding. Then he sails off in search of his mother's brother. When he finds him, Tudava gives him the pudding. The uncle reacts with horror, dismay, and guilt when he discovers the head, regretting the former abandonment of his sister and her son, whom he should have protected, according to Trobriand tradition.

Following the structural principle mentioned earlier, Spiro identifies the ogre as the boy's father who is unaccountably missing from the family unit in this story, and he considers this to be evidence for the Oedipal hostility felt by Trobriand boys. Since the father is a benevolent friend to his children, the hatred due to rivalry over the mother cannot be consciously directed at the father. So in the myth the father disappears altogether, and the ogre is not consciously connected with him. "This would indicate why the father as such is absent from the myth, patricidal and filicidal wishes being too threatening to acknowledge even when attributed to the characters in a myth" (p. 53). In this way, Spiro accounts for the absence of father figures in Trobriand mythology.

However, there is another, less psychological explanation for the absence of fathers. Malinowski emphasizes the fact that fathers are not mentioned in origin myths, which recount how different clan groups came from the earth through holes in the ground. In these myths a woman always appears as an ancestral figure, sometimes accompanied by a brother but never by a husband. This pattern is quite understandable in view of the matrilineal emphasis in this culture and the lack of knowledge about the male role in procreation. We will come back to this issue later.

Spiro recounts another Trobriand tale in which a father does, after all, play a prominent role. An old man with his son and grandson go on a kula expedition in which the man acquires a valuable necklace but conceals it from his son. Angry on discovering that, the son abandons his father on an island and sails away. His father throws a stone to sink the canoe, but he misses. Eventually the old man makes his way back to the village and turns into an evil spirit.

Spiro thinks that the presence of father-son hostility in this story strengthens the likelihood that such hostility is also expressed in the Tudava myth and other myths in which ogres figure. On the other hand, the story shows that Trobriand Islanders are quite capable of telling such tales and do not have to block hostile father figures from consciousness. Spiro strengthens his case, however, by stating that most deaths are attributed to sorcery, and that in the case of a male, "the principal suspicion of sorcery attaches always to the wife and children" (Malinowski 1929:161), although Malinowski does not specify that the children are male.

Spiro turns next to the third domain involving the absent father: reproduction beliefs. Here he echoes the view of Ernest Jones that hatred of the father is the reason for the Trobriand denial of male physiological paternity. This view assumes that somehow the Trobrianders really do know the facts of life. Spiro cites an article by Lorna McDougall (1975) which vaguely implies this. In the kula trade the white armbands are thought to be female, while the red necklaces are thought to be male. They travel in opposite directions through the island circle. The natives speak of the "marriage" of kula objects. But kula objects are also referred to as the "children" of the men, "the only infant that the Trobriand father will ever be able to procreate, according to native philosophy" (McDougall 1975:80–81). The names of the objects are important to the men," . . . a means of being recognized after a man is dead, or of carving out a place in time, paralleling the matrilineal system of inheritance of Trobriand society" (pp. 80–81). "Kula asserts, in a symbolic form, a fact necessary to the continuation of life in society itself: that men are indeed biological fathers" (p. 99).

When Malinowski tried to explain the male role in procreation to Trobrianders, he was surprised by their fierce opposition to his explanation. Spiro interprets this vehemence as due to their resistance to an unwelcome idea.

Spiro feels, then, that he has demonstrated the existence of Oedipal hostility to the father in the three domains of dreams, myths, and reproduction. "Since the father is absent from the three domains in which his presence would be most expected, and since, for all three, father absence is plausibly explained as an indication of the son's hostility toward him, the fact that his hostility is coped with by repression, denial, and father banishment suggests that the hostility to the father in the Trobriands is of more than ordinary intensity" (Spiro 1982:73).

While this demonstration is ingenious, I am not sure that myths and reproduction beliefs really constitute two separate domains; besides, the domain of dreams strikes me as too poorly represented to be worth considering. Myths and reproduction beliefs, which could be grouped together under the general heading of *world view*, are unified by the Trobriand conception of conception, to which the male makes no contribution. Given the Trobriand set of beliefs, there is no reason why the father should appear in origin myths, and a father does appear in one of the myths Spiro recounts which is not concerned with origins.

Spiro criticizes Malinowski for not being enough of a functionalist and for failing to point out relationships among such variables as ignorance of physiological paternity, the postpartum sex taboo, the infrequency of recalled dreams, the extrusion of males at puberty, and folktales about attacks on the clitoris. Malinowski is said to have dealt with these items separately "under such standard ethnographic rubrics as sex, myth, household composition, and the like" (Spiro 82:142). This is an astute observation, but in his use of the three domains, Spiro employs his own system of compartmentalization to show the extent of father-banishment in Trobriand culture. This part of Spiro's demonstration does not seem convincing to me.

I think that Spiro makes a better case for the likelihood of an Oedipus complex in the Trobriands in the information he gives about child-rearing. Malinowski tells us that the Trobriand Islanders observe a long post-partum sex taboo with exclusive mother-child sleeping arrangements. This combination, which has been noted for several societies, will be discussed in a later chapter (see pp. 139–40). Among the Trobrianders the child stays with its mother until weaned, at age two at the earliest, according to Spiro.[10] The father sleeps separately.

Cross-cultural surveys indicate that such a close mother-child relationship is likely to create a strong attachment to the mother, which may be sexually tinged, especially since the mother may feel sexually frustrated by the long separation from her husband. Spiro (1982:93) claims that, when the father returns to his wife's bed, at the end of the postpartum taboo period, the son is apt to resent the displacement. However, according to a recent ethnographic work, the Trobriand father does not replace the child in the mother's bed. Instead, Annette Weiner states that the child moves to the father's bed. "On the night that a woman leaves her nursing child, the baby begins to sleep with its father and continues to sleep in its father's bed until about the age of 10 or until a younger child is weaned. Husbands and wives have separate beds; a woman always sleeps with her nursing child or alone, and her husband always sleeps with a child who is a bit older" (Weiner 1976:124).

Under these conditions the newly weaned child may resent the mother's absence and the father's inability to suckle, but at least it still has close body contact with an older person during the night, and the father is very attentive to the child during the day.

> He will fondle and carry a baby, clean and wash it, and give it the mashed vegetable food which it receives in addition to the mother's milk almost from birth. In fact, nursing the baby in the arms or holding it on the knees . . . is the special role and duty of the father. . . . The father performs his duties with genuine natural fondness; he will carry an infant about for hours, looking at it with eyes full of such love and pride as are seldom seen in those of a European father (Malinowski 1929:20–21).

One wonders whether a young boy would continue to hate such a father. However, as noted earlier, the son is likely to witness the primal scene, and between 12 and 14 years of age boys are extruded from the family home. Malinowski (1929:62) says that this is done "so as not to hamper by their embarrassing presence the sexual life of their parents." Spiro's assumption is that this sequence of events fosters the boy's hostility toward his father. But if the boy's resentment concerns sex, one would think that the children's free sex life (which according to Malinowski starts well before this time and now becomes more serious) would soon dissipate it.

In a final chapter entitled "Is the Oedipus Complex Universal?,"

---

[10] Annette Weiner (1976:124) says that a child is weaned abruptly some time between a year and a year and a half. Malinowski (1929:233) put the age of weaning at "some two years after its birth."

Spiro (1982:62) answers his own question by saying, "How could it possibly not be?", thus clearly adhering to a Freudian conflict model of personality. This raises a new question: If hatred of the father is universally present, and if the mechanisms of denial and repression operate as Spiro describes, why is it that almost all human groups acknowledge the relationship between intercourse and pregnancy? If it is so painful to think of the father as genitor and mother's lover, how was this association ever made, and how could it have become so generally accepted? One would have expected the same father banishment to have taken place in all societies. The only way out of this dilemma is to assume that the Oedipus complex is much stronger in the Trobriand Islands than elsewhere, which would make Malinowski's contribution to this subject paradoxical indeed.

While Spiro has made a fair case for the Trobriand Oedipus complex, his demonstration is all based on circumstantial evidence. What would be required to clinch the case would be to get an adequate sample of Trobriand men to stretch out on the beach, if not on a psychiatrist's couch, and bring up some reminiscences and free associations. Then, perhaps, we'd know for sure—unless, of course, times have changed since Malinowski's day, and Trobriand young men have changed as well.

SUGGESTIONS FOR FURTHER READING

The Oedipus complex will be discussed further in Chapter 7. For the titles of Malinowski's other works on the Trobriands, see the *references cited*. A brief general description of Trobriand culture may be found in Elman R. Service, *A Profile of Primitive Culture* (New York: Harper & Brothers, 1958), pp. 222–42.

For more on the problem of the universality of the Oedipus complex and local variations thereof, see Anne Parsons, "Is the Oedipus Complex Universal? The Jones-Malinowski Debate Revisited," in Anne Parsons, *Belief, Magic, and Anomie. Essays in Psychosocial Anthropology* (New York: Free Press, 1969) pp. 3–66.

In 1967, 25 years after his death, a diary kept by Malinowski during his Trobriand fieldwork was published: Bronislaw Malinowski, *A Diary in the Strict Sense of the Term* (New York: Harcourt, Brace & World, 1967). It is of interest because it shows that Malinowski, surprisingly enough, had intolerant, prejudiced attitudes toward the natives. It might also be deduced that Malinowski had something of an Oedipus complex, judging from some of the entries: "At last I begin to feel a deep, strong longing for [Mother] in my innermost being" (p. 22). "Main interests in life: Kipling, occasionally strong yearning for Mother—really, if I could keep in communication with Mother I would not mind anything and my low spirits would have no deep foundation" (p. 41). "Mother is the only person I care for really and am truly worried about" (p. 52). But the biggest surprise in this diary, perhaps, is to learn that Malinowski hated doing fieldwork. "As for ethnology: I see the life of the natives as utterly devoid of interest or importance, something as remote from me as the life of a dog" (p. 167). "Ethnographical problems don't preoccupy me at all. At bottom I am living outside of Kiriwina, although strongly hating the *niggers*" (p. 264).

The reader of Malinowski's voluminous ethnographic works would never infer such attitudes on the author's part. It is a tribute to his determination and hard work that Malinowski was able to accomplish so much in spite of his depression and malaise. For an interesting review of this diary, see Clifford Geertz, "Under the Mosquito Net," *New York Review*, September 14, 1967, pp. 12–13. For some rejoinders to Geertz by loyal students of Malinowski who protest that the diary gives a misleading impression of the man, see letters to *New York Review* by Hortense Powdermaker and Ashley-Montagu, November 9, 1967, pp. 36–37.

Balanced reviews of this topic are provided by George W. Stocking, Jr., "Empathy and Antipathy in the Heart of Darkness: An Essay Review of Malinowski's Field Diaries," *Journal of the History of the Behavioral Sciences* 4 (1968), pp. 189–94; and Murray L. Wax, "Tenting with Malinowski," *American Sociological Review* 37 (1972), pp. 1–13.

5

Margaret Mead's *From the South Seas*

Margaret Mead was one of the most influential and widely read contributors to the field of culture-and-personality. Her three best known works, the subject of this chapter, were brought out together in one volume under the title *From the South Seas* (1939). This trilogy comprises *Coming of Age in Samoa* (1928), *Growing Up in New Guinea* (1930), and *Sex and Temperament in Three Primitive Societies* (1935). With these books Mead introduced a new pattern into American anthropology—fieldwork centered about a problem. The traditional fieldwork of the Boas school in which Mead received her training had been all encompassing, with the ethnographer noting down everything that he or she could about the culture under investigation. Franz Boas, realizing that primitive cultures in different parts of the world were giving way under the impact of modern Western civilization, wanted anthropologists to get out and record as much as possible about them while there was still time. While Mead has published some ethnographic reports in this tradition, her best known works have been directed to questions which have some relevance to our own life.

Coming of Age in Samoa

Boas himself deserves some credit for this deviation from his own approach, for he helped to suggest and to discuss Mead's research problems with her before she went to Samoa on her first field trip. In a letter of 1925, Boas wrote:

> One question that interests me very much is how the young girls react to the restraints of custom. We find very often among ourselves during the period of adolescence a young rebellious spirit that may be expressed in sullenness or in sudden outbursts. . . . I am not at all clear in my mind in how far similar conditions may occur in primitive society and in how far the desire for independence may be simply due to our modern conditions and to a more strongly developed individualism (Mead 1959:289).

Coming of Age in Samoa was concerned with this relationship between adolescence and culture. In it, Mead (1928:11) asked the question: "Are the disturbances which vex our adolescents due to the nature of adolescence itself or to the civilization?" We tend to think of adolescence as a time of emotional conflict and rebellion against authority. Is such a state of affairs due to the physiological changes occurring at puberty, or is it largely brought about by certain social and cultural conditions in our society? If the former alternative is true, adolescence should present similar characteristics in all cultures. If it does not do so, the social and cultural conditions would seem to be the more significant determinants.

To answer these questions, Mead lived for nine months in Samoa, studying 50 girls in three small neighboring villages. She found, in brief, that adolescence was not a difficult period for Samoan girls. This was partly because of the generally casual nature of the society. Among these people, according to Mead, there is a lack of deep feeling or involvement. Children grow up in family units where there are many adult figures, and their emotional relations to others become diffuse and relatively shallow. Premarital sexual relationships are accepted naturally, but with little emotional investment in the partner. The facts of life—birth, sex, and death—are learned at an early age and are not hedged about with secrecy. Samoan life, moreover, lacks the confusing alternatives found in the United States, where an adolescent must choose between a host of ideologies, political doctrines, religious tenets, standards of morality, and occupational choices. Thus adolescence in Samoa is not characterized by tension, emotional conflict, or rebellion. The source of such characteristics in American youth must, therefore, lie in the social institutions and traditions of the Western world.

Coming of Age in Samoa in some ways recalls Malinowski's work. There is the same sense of problem, together with a literary skill which makes an exotic culture more vivid to the reader. One wonders, however, whether it was necessary, in dealing with the problem of physiological versus sociocultural factors affecting adolescence, to go to Samoa for an answer. Couldn't one simply have studied some adolescents in the United States? There must be some young people in this country who are relatively well adjusted and for whom adolescence involves no great upheaval. Such a group could be contrasted with a more maladjusted one, and an attempt made to see what significant sociocultural factors were involved in differentiating the two groups. Difficulties of learning a new language and establishing rapport in a strange culture would be obviated by an investigation of this sort, and it would be easier to study boys as well as girls. (For Mead's conclusions can have reference only to girls.) However, this is a minor quibble. Margaret Mead was an anthropologist, and anthropologists are expected to go to primitive cultures.

A more crucial question may also be raised. In chapter XI Mead describes a few girls whom she calls "deviants" who did show evident conflicts. One wonders whether some of the other girls, although outwardly placid, might not have similarly harbored internal stresses and strains. Day-to-day interaction with these girls, even over a period of months, might not necessarily disclose emotional tensions. We have no Rorschach or Thematic Apperception Test records for them, for this study was made in the days before these tests became popular.

We do, however, have such projective tests for two rather similar cultures—Truk and Ifaluk in Micronesia. In Truk there is the same absence, as in Samoa, of Western socioeconomic complexity and division of labor. There is the same casualness and acceptance of sex, and there are also many similarities in the nature of family life and childhood experiences. Yet, according to Seymour B. Sarason, the Rorschach and Thematic Apperception Test records express a great deal of conflict over sex—more than one would find in a Western society (Gladwin and Sarason 1953:449). This seems surprising in a society with premarital sexual freedom. At any rate, it shows that such freedom does not obviate tension; nor does the simplicity of the socioeconomic order.

The same may be said of Ifaluk, as described by Melford E. Spiro. Here again, premarital sexual activity is sanctioned, and life is leisurely and placid; there is little economic specialization, the climate is quite pleasant, and there is little need for long or strenuous work.

> Ifaluk social structure seems to evoke as little conflict or anxiety as its physical setting. Absent from its economic system are important inequalities in, and social classes based on, wealth. . . . Absent, too is economic competition, either for subsistence or for prestige goals (Spiro 1959:144).

The Ifaluk ethos stresses kindliness, cooperation, generosity, and peaceful behavior. Nevertheless, according to Spiro, indications of tension and hostility are found in Ifaluk, manifest in the concepts about ghosts, in legends, in the content of dreams collected by Spiro, in Thematic Apperception Test protocols, and in various aspects of Ifaluk behavior. Spiro describes three cases of apparently psychogenic mental illness, in which the underlying tensions of Ifaluk culture are most clearly expressed.

The data from Truk and Ifaluk show that in an easygoing "simple" culture there may still be stresses and strains, not always readily discernible, but manifest in certain areas. The use of projective tests helps to indicate their presence in these two studies. The point made here is that a similar condition may have been true of Mead's community in Manu'a.

Incidentally, based on her observations of chimpanzee behavior,

Jane van Lawick-Goodall (1971:173) has written that "Adolescence is a difficult and frustrating time for some chimpanzees just as it is for some humans. Possibly it is worse for males, in both species." Older, more mature male chimpanzees are quick to punish signs of insubordination in adolescents. Van Lawick-Goodall writes that nearly all the adolescent males she had known spent long periods of hours or even days away from the rest of the group.

In an appendix to *Coming of Age in Samoa,* Dr. Mead listed all the cases she learned of in Manu'a of mentally defective and mentally ill people. From these figures, Ellen Winston has estimated the rate of mental disorder to be 100 per 100,000 population. Winston (1934) estimates the rate in rural areas in the United States to be about the same. In view of these estimates, one wonders whether the picture of a tension-free Samoa may not, to some extent, be a projection or wish-image.

Another kind of question is also suggested by *Coming of Age in Samoa.* In most of Mead's account we get the impression that she is describing a traditional and relatively unchanging "primitive" culture. Christianity has been taken over, to be sure, together with some other trappings of Western civilization, but these have been rather minor in their effects, mainly having the consequence of making the lives of the people more comfortable. Yet, in some passages, principally in an appendix, Mead presents evidence of far-reaching cultural changes in this area. We learn that, formerly, household heads had life and death powers over their family members and that girls could be punished for sexual lapses by being severely beaten or having their heads shaved. On the marriage of girls of high rank, a defloration ceremony was performed to test the bride's chastity. The authority of household heads has since been broken by the American legal system and missionary teachings; beatings and head shavings have been discouraged, and the defloration ceremony is now forbidden by law.

There have been sweeping changes in other areas of Samoan life as well. Formerly all young men were tattooed, an important *rite de passage,* before which a youth was not considered an adult and could not marry or go to war (Turner 1884:88). Warfare was an important activity for young men, a source of power and prestige—and status considerations were of great importance in Samoa. This warfare was characterized by some rather curious formal behavior—courtesy rituals between opposing armies before the affray—but the fighting was real and earnest enough (Brown 1910:164–76; Turner 1884:192 ff.). Ritual tattooing and warfare have by now been put down by the white authorities. This may make Samoan living conditions more "comfortable," but it does involve a profound change in the way of life of these people. Many former sources of prestige and excitement for young men have been disallowed. The former class of master craftsmen has vanished through the introduction of modern technology. Long sea voyages by canoe have been given up and large canoes are no longer made. Much of the old social and ritual life has disappeared. Keesing wrote, as of 1930:

> The *taupo* system, by which the ceremonial life of each community revolves around the person of a village virgin, is passing: chiefs who are entitled by tradition to the honor of having a *taupo* find the entertainments connected with the position too costly; again, due to the breakdown of the old order, the marriage of such maidens has lost its former value in securing political alliances and economic and ceremonial advantages; the missions have discouraged the custom as heathen. . . (Keesing 1934:142).

The social world of both men and women, then, has greatly changed from "aboriginal" Samoan conditions. The navy, the missions, and the schools have largely brought about these changes. In 1911 school attendance was made compulsory for all children between the ages of 6 and 13 (Holmes 1958:72). Robert W. Williamson (1939:157–86) suggested that immorality was not so general in Samoa as some writers have made it out to be and that some "retrogression" may have taken place in Samoan sexual mores. Keesing (1937:8) also speaks of "a general loosening up as regards the sexual conduct of young folk," and adds that "The old village system with its segregation of the young and unattached people (the *aualuma*, and the corresponding groups of youths and men, called *aumanga*) apparently put certain constraints upon the mingling of the sexes that are now gone." Mead herself suggested that young female sex delinquents had a harder time of it in aboriginal Samoa.

The point made here, then, is that the picture of adolescent behavior presented in *Coming of Age in Samoa* should be seen in a particular historical context. Mead was aware of this context, but felt that the historical changes in the recent past were irrelevant for her purposes. Hence a consideration of them was left to the appendix.

Freeman's Criticism of Mead's Work

In 1983 Derek Freeman published a polemical attack on Mead's pioneer Samoan study in which he took issue with most of her findings. Freeman is an anthropologist who studied the Samoan language between 1940 and 1943 and was given a chiefly title, which enabled him to attend chiefly assemblies. Life was not easy going during the 1920s, Freeman tells us. It was a time when strong protests were being made by Samoan leaders against the American naval government, which made it inappropriate or incorrect for Mead (1928:198) to write that in Samoa "no one suffers for his convictions." Nor was family life so casual and easy going. Mead wrote that children did not have strong emotional ties to their parents and easily moved to the homes of other relatives to escape punishments, which tended to be slight in any case. In a survey that he made in Sa'anapu village in 1967, Freeman (1983:202) found that 92 percent of those under 19 years of age lived with their parents, and they were often severely punished. A child was not allowed to change residence without parental permission, which was seldom given before the age of 12.

Virginity for girls was highly valued in Samoa, and Freeman is skeptical about the casual liaisons reported by Mead. Rape is not "completely foreign to the Samoan mind," as Mead claimed, for "the incidence of rape in Samoa . . . is among the highest to be found anywhere in the world (Freeman 1983:244).[1] Adolescence is a stormy period, not an easy one. Freeman (1983:260) presents charts showing ages at first conviction for offenses in Western Samoa and in England and points out that at age 16 there is a peak in offenses against authority, especially by males.

There is a good deal of aggression and competition in Samoa, according to Freeman, in contrast to Mead's picture of a relaxed and peaceful world. Bradd Shore, who lived in Samoa for five years, seems to share this view. In his *Sala'ilua. A Samoan Mystery* (which deals with a violent murder) Shore (1982:199–200) discusses competition in symmetrical sets (for example, between brothers), and he cites an unpublished Ph.D. thesis on Samoan temperament by R. Maxwell concerning the Samoan's "inclination to dominate others" (p. 152).

On the other hand, Shore seems to agree with Mead's picture of Samoan adolescent lovemaking, for he was quoted in *Time* (February 14, 1983:69) as saying "They are both sexually free and sexually restrained. Virginity is prized as an ideal and widely violated." Some young men, at least, value free-impulse expression, as quoted by Shore (1982:187): "If hunger comes, you eat. And if the desire for sex comes, then you leap and zap! it's done" (see also Holmes, Tallman, and Jantz 1978:459).

Freeman accounts for the alleged errors in *Coming of Age in Samoa* by describing Mead of that period as a relatively untrained 23-year-old girl who had a mental set imbued with the cultural determinist philosophy of her teachers Franz Boas and Ruth Benedict. Besides, instead of rooming in native quarters, as she did on later field trips, Mead lived in the household of American representatives of the naval government. Most of her time was spent with 25 girls aged 14 to 20, who visited her in the government medical dispensary.

Boas sent Mead to Samoa to assess the relative weighting of biology and culture as they affect the adolescence of Samoan girls. In downplaying the biological significance of adolescence in Samoa, Mead provided what was, according to Freeman, a crucial "negative

---

[1] Freeman's figures refer to Samoa as a whole for a later time, the 1960s, while Mead's observations referred to a small island, Ta'ū, in the 1920s.

instance" to support the cultural determinist viewpoint. In refuting Mead's findings, Freeman believes that he has canceled out this "negative instance," and he argues for the development of a new synthesis between the biological determinist thesis and the cultural determinist antithesis, involving a more biologically oriented approach than Margaret Mead's.

However, *Coming of Age in Samoa* is not as one-sided as Freeman asserts, nor was Mead altogether blind to biological factors. Her later work with Gregory Bateson[2] shows a strong Freudian influence, which may already have been present to some degree in the 1920s, for Harold Gould (1971:793) claims that on her way home from Samoa, Mead told a group of graduate students and faculty at Berkeley that "the purpose of her field trip had been to test psychoanalytic hypotheses *in situ*," and A. A. Brill was quoted on the 1964 book jacket of *Coming of Age in Samoa* as stating that this book "corroborates, through practical demonstration, the psychosexual theories promulgated by Freud and his pupils." Mead was not just a stooge for Franz Boas, nor was Boas himself the doctrinaire cultural determinist that Freeman makes him out to be. Freeman uses the phrase "the Boasian paradigm" for the cultural determinist approach or "the explanation of human behavior in purely cultural terms." He drew this phrase from the work of George Stocking (1968:303; 1974:219–20), but Stocking himself considered Boas not to be a full-fledged cultural determinist. "Boas was transitional, and his own thinking retained strong residual elements of older thought about the nature of culture" (p. 230).

Growing Up in New Guinea

Growing Up in New Guinea has the subtitle, *A Comparative Study of Primitive Education*. It deals with the upbringing of children among the Manus of the Admiralty Islands north of New Guinea. At the time of Mead's 1928 field trip, the Manus whom she studied were living in houses raised on stilts above the waters of a lagoon. They lived primarily by fishing and trading and had a kind of Protestant ethic— valuing property, hard work, and financial success.

Switching to the "ethnographic present," this is a society with a high infant mortality rate, but the children who survive are healthy, self-confident, and alert. They learn to swim at the age of three and soon thereafter are paddling about in little canoes. This freedom and mobility makes them relatively independent of adults. One rule is instilled at an early age: respect for property. Otherwise, children are left to their own devices. They eat, play, and sleep when they wish and do no work. Girls begin to perform some household chores after

---

[2] See pp. 120–26.

they are 11 or 12, but boys do hardly any work until after they are married. Little deference is shown to parents or other adults.

According to Mead, Manus husband-wife relations are usually difficult and strained. Marriages are arranged by parents and entered into with reluctance. Residence is virilocal, the bride being a stranger in her husband's home. When a child is born or adopted, the father at once takes a proprietary interest in it, and a closer bond develops between him and his child than between mother and child.

Manus children, however, live largely in a world of their agemates. They spend their time in energetic play.

> The adults give the children no story-telling pattern, no guessing games, riddles, puzzles. The idea that children would like to hear legends seems quite fantastic to a Manus adult. . . . Where we fill our children's minds with a rich folklore, songs which personalize the sun, the moon, and the stars, riddles and fairy tales and myths, the Manus do nothing of the sort (Mead 1930:125–26, 130).

Hence Manus children do not develop animistic concepts. A naturalistic view of the universe, says Mead, is as congenial to a child as a supernatural one. He accepts the view provided by his elders. Hence there is little imagination in Manus play. And since there are no children without playmates, there are no imaginary playmates. The children believe in spirits but ignore them.

Mead's conclusion (1930:257–58) is: "If the children's imaginations are to flourish, they must be given food. Although the exceptional child may create something of his own, the great majority of children will not even imagine bears under the bed unless the adult provides the bear."[3] Mead thus drew attention to the enriching qualities of cultural tradition. In Manus there is little interest in the arts, the emphasis of the culture being on practical success. Little contact exists, in any case, between adults and children. With marriage, the adult world finally begins to bear down on the individual, and the carefree life of childhood is over.

In *Growing up in New Guinea*, Margaret Mead's unusual gifts—imagination, acute observation, and literary flair—find their fullest expression.[4]

---

[3] Wayne Dennis (1943) has taken issue with Margaret Mead's conclusion about the absence of animistic thinking in Manus children, arguing that the various tests given to the children to gauge animistic responses were inadequate for the purpose and did not make use of the methods developed by Jean Piaget to elicit animistic concepts in children. Dennis, who has given tests for animistic thinking among children in a number of different cultural settings, believes that animistic notions among children are probably worldwide.

[4] In 1953 Mead revisited the Manus—25 years later. She found the culture extraordinarily changed. The Manus no longer live on the lagoon but have moved ashore. The people now wear clothing of European type. The old religion has entirely disappeared. This is described and discussed by Mead in *New Lives for Old. Cultural Transformations—Manus, 1928–1953.* The reader interested in the Manus is also advised to consult Reo F. Fortune's interesting work, *Manus Religion* (1935).

Sex and Temperament

Sex and Temperament in Three Primitive Societies, the third in Mead's trilogy, deals with the influence of culture on sex roles and attitudes. In the preface of a 1950 paperback reprint, Mead remarks that this is her most misunderstood book. Part of the misunderstanding seems to hinge on the central theme of the book. In the original 1935 Introduction Mead wrote:

> This study is not concerned with whether there are or are not actual and universal differences between the sexes either quantitative or qualitative (Mead 1935:viii).

To the average reader, however, this seems to be just what the book is about. At any rate, in a concluding section of the book entitled "The Implication of These Results," Mead states:

> The material suggests that we may say that many, if not all, of the personality traits which we have called masculine or feminine are as lightly linked to sex as are the clothing, the manners, and the form of head-dress that a society at a given period assigns to either sex (Mead 1935:280).

Our conceptions of what constitute masculine or feminine characteristics, therefore, are the product of particular historical, cultural traditions, rather than of any innate biological differences between the sexes.[5]

Mead's conclusions about sex and temperament were based on fieldwork done in three New Guinea tribes—the Arapesh, Mundugumor, and Tchambuli—all of whom live within a hundred mile area and yet show remarkable differences in culture and temperament. Among the Arapesh, Mead found that both men and women act in a mild, maternal, cooperative manner, behaving as we expect women to behave. Mundugumor men and women, on the other hand, are fierce and aggressive, behaving as we expect men to behave. Neither of these two cultures harbors assumptions about the existence of sex differences in temperament. But in the third tribe, the Tchambuli, there are clear-cut differences between men and women; only here we have a kind of parody in reverse of the situation in the United States. Tchambuli women, who are the food-providers, are described as being hearty, efficient, and comradely among themselves. "Solid, preoccupied, powerful, with shaven unadorned heads, they sit in groups and laugh together . . ." (1935:257). The men, however, are principally concerned with art, with their hairdos, and their relationships with women.

About half the book deals with the Arapesh. Of the three, this was the culture in which Mead and Reo F. Fortune worked the longest

---

[5] However, in a reply to a review of *Sex and Temperament* Mead (1937:559) wrote: ". . . nowhere do I suggest that I have found any material which disproves the existence of sex differences."

and got to know best. Fortune paid a return visit in 1936. A number of publications by Fortune and by Mead about the Arapesh are available, so we have more to go on here than with the other two tribes.

In one of Mead's publications (1940:326–38), there is an excellent account of the field methods used in their work. Although Mead has often been accused of subjective impressionism, it is evident that her standards of fieldwork are high; her dedication to the job, as revealed in this monograph, is certainly impressive. Nevertheless, as we shall see, there are weaknesses in her descriptions of the three tribes. Let us start with the Arapesh.

Mead tells us in *Sex and Temperament* that the Arapesh " see all life as an adventure in growing things," and that "the duty of every man and woman is to observe the rules, so that the children and the food upon which the children depend will grow. Men are as wholly committed to this cherishing adventure as are women. It may be said that the role of men, like the role of women, is maternal." As a chapter heading tells us, this is a cooperative society. Nine tenths of a man's time is spent in responding to other people's appeals for assistance (1935:14, 22).[6]

Mead (1935:23) writes that warfare is practically unknown among the Arapesh. Their feelings toward a murderer and toward a man who kills in battle are not essentially different. No cult of military bravery exists. There are occasional brawls between villages over women who have been abducted, but "abductions of women are really the result of marital disagreements and the formation of new personal attachments, and are not unfriendly acts on the part of the next community."

This seems contradictory, especially since the same passage also refers to abductions as "unfriendly acts" which must be avenged.

In a brief paper Reo F. Fortune observes that warfare has been kept down since before 1914 by the colonial (originally German) administration. Thus, the absence of fighting does not necessarily express a peaceful maternal nature on the part of the men, since peace has been externally imposed. "A census of the war records of individual grey-headed old men revealed the fact that approximately 50% of them claimed one or more war homicides each to his credit" (Fortune 1939:28).

An externally imposed peace has also affected Mundugumor and Tchambuli life. In her description of the Mundugumor, Mead preferred to describe the life as it had been lived up to three years before she came to that area. The contrast between Arapesh and Mundugumor

---

[6] In a later publication, Mead (1947,3:205) wrote that the Arapesh should be characterized as "helpful" rather than as "cooperative," cooperation being defined as the sharing of a common end, in which the end is the essential goal, while helpfulness involves the activity of two or more persons toward an end conceived as belonging to only part of the group whom the others help.

Mead has written elsewhere (1937a:36): "In only a very few instances is there genuine cooperation and these are mostly in the interest of the Tamberan cult."

is therefore heightened by the fact that the Arapesh are described as of the post-colonial peace period, while the Mundugumor are described as of the precolonial period.[7]

In his article, "Arapesh Warfare," Fortune (1939:36) expresses doubt that the Arapesh expect a similar temperament in men and women. He cites a proverb. "Men's hearts are different; women's hearts are different," and mentions the existence of a class of men called *aramagowem*—"women male," or effeminate men. "The class of *aramagowem* is a definitely assigned class, with definite functions, given inferior food at feasts and special subordinate place."

There is no socially organized class of masculine women, but there are stories about individual women who had taken part in warfare, one of whom was buried by the men's secret society with a warrior's honors.

Mead (1935:32) herself presents evidence that different expectations are held about the behavior of men and women. Boys are preferred to girls. If there are already a number of girls in a family, a newly born daughter may be killed. Note that it is the *father* who makes this decision. Girls learn to control their fits of rage much earlier than little boys, who may still have temper tantrums at 15 without a sense of shame. (One wonders, incidentally, why the children of such maternal parents would have temper tantrums. Temper tantrums among the children in Alor, as we shall see later, are attributed by Kardiner and Du Bois to maternal neglect.) "Furthermore," observes Mead "as it is considered appropriate for big men to simulate anger and defiance in their public speeches, to wield a spear, stamp their feet, and shout, the little boy has a model of violent expression before him that the little girl lacks . . ." (Mead 1935:51–52). The men are described as being more restless than the women and given to traveling about on visits to relatives—a source of jesting reproach by the women.

Girls are described as having less curiosity than boys.

> A habit of intellectual passivity falls upon them, a more pronounced lack of intellectual interest than that which characterizes their brothers' minds. All that is strange, that is uncharted and unnamed—unfamiliar sounds, unfamiliar shapes—these are forbidden to women, whose duty it is to guard their reproductivity closely and tenderly. This prohibition cuts them off from speculative thought and likewise from art . . . (Mead, 1935:70).

When Mead showed them a brown life-sized doll, the women shrank away from it in fright, thinking it a corpse, but the men recognized the doll as a mere representation.

---

[7] At the same time, the Pax Britannica must be credited with a large share in affecting the roles of men and women in Tchambuli life, since Tchambuli men have been deprived of some formerly traditional male pursuits. This should be kept in mind when considering Mead's description of the Tchambuli.

Mead writes (1935:81): "The whole organization of society is based upon the analogy between children and wives as representing a group who are younger, less responsible than the men, and therefore to be guided." This sounds like a very important assertion of different expectations concerning the sexes in this society.

Mead mentions several cases of men beating their wives, but only one of a woman beating a man. It is men who fight over women and capture women from other communities, not vice versa. Polygyny, not polyandry, is practiced.

In a critical review of *Sex and Temperament*, R. Thurnwald (1936) pointed to various inconsistencies in Mead's description of the Arapesh. Although the Arapesh are described as being gentle and peaceful, the account contains such violent episodes as quarrels over women, a man and wife attacking each other with axes, and a mother trying to strangle her baby.

Much of the behavior cited by Thurnwald is drawn from a chapter on those who "deviate" from the Arapesh ideal. But as Thurnwald points out, their percentage is not recorded. This is the same problem that comes up in *Coming of Age in Samoa*, where exceptions to Mead's generalizations are dealt with in a chapter on "deviants." Mead does not hide or skirt seemingly contradictory information. By tagging it with the label of "deviancy" she brings it under control. To what extent, however, are the tensions manifest by "deviants" shared by other members of the society?

Mead's answer (1937b:558) to Thurnwald on the question of percentages is that under conditions of cultural breakdown, "practically every individual of a given age and sex may become in his own mind, and in the opinion of the community, a deviant." Deviants are people who fail to exhibit the approved personality of the culture. If the majority fails to manifest it, then the majority is deviant (see Mead 1932:93). Questions of percentage are therefore irrelevant, since deviants do not have to be a minority group. Besides, Mead (1937b:559) asserts, "Researches which depend upon statistical validation cannot be carried out among primitive peoples under the existing conditions of work."

Apparently Mead's way of studying a culture involves finding out the rules of the game, then looking to see whether these rules are broken. Thus, she is able to write of some Arapesh as follows:

> These aberrants' own misunderstanding of their culture was further aggravated by the existence of very stupid people among themselves— such as Menala, who further complicated Wabe's life by accusing him of a willful act of violence that had actually been carried out in strict accord with the rules of the culture, in which he had co-operated with her brothers in breaking up a marriage of which they disapproved (Mead 1935:154).

Again:

> The quiet responsive non-initiatory nature of men and women is blurred by those who watch Amitoa take an ax to Baimal, or Wabe beat both his wives and declare that he wishes he was rid of the pair of them (Mead 1935:160–61).

Mead evidently has a Platonic ideal conception of the culture as it should be. Although some members of the society evidently do not understand their own culture and thus confuse matters. Mead is able to make out its true form through the distortions of actual life. This Platonism is paradoxical in an ethnographer who has such a keen eye for immediate realities.

The Mundugumor, the next tribe discussed by Mead, are described as being violent, aggressive, and mistrustful cannibals. Unlike the situation in many parts of New Guinea, there is no village with a central plaza and men's clubhouse; there is no real community. Family groups, some polygynous, live in palisaded compounds, whose location the members try to keep secret. These isolated family units are rife with tension, since there is traditional hatred between brothers and between fathers and sons. "Between brothers," Mead (1935:177) tells us, "there is only one possible form of close contact; they can fight each other and abuse each other publicly".

A man is supposed to get a wife through brother-sister exchange—by giving his sister to someone in exchange for the other's sister. But a man may also trade off his daughter for an additional wife for himself. Anxious mothers keep warning their sons that the father may thus deprive the boy of a future wife. According to Mead (1935:180) the pattern of hostility between brothers and between father and son is repeated in every family group in varying degrees.

However, Mead (1935:191, 225) cites a Mundugumor saying, "He was not strong, he had no brothers," and tells us that the phrase "a man who has brothers" often occurs in their remarks, "and this means a man who, by a stroke of luck, has some weak-willed docile brothers who will follow his lead, and instead of disputing his progress will form a more or less permanent constellation about him in his middle age." So apparently there is sometimes cooperation between brothers, although Mead labels such cooperative individuals as deviants. At any rate, perhaps there should be some modification in the statement that "between brothers there is only one possible form of close contact; they can fight each other and abuse each other publicly."

Mead (1935:191) says that a wife who has become pregnant hurts a man at his most vulnerable spot: "she has taken the first step toward his downfall by possibly conceiving a son. And for herself, she has shifted her husband's active sexual interest into angry frustrated resentment—for what? Possibly to bear a daughter, who will be her husband's, not hers."

But Mead (1935:193) tells us that a man desires a daughter, the woman a son. And we learn that adoption is a very common practice, with girls being adopted more often than boys. In such cases "the wife is compensated for this by the better relationship to her husband."

The practice of adoption indicates at least some interest in children. "Even women who have never borne children are able in a few weeks, by placing the child constantly at the breast and by drinking plenty of coconut milk, to produce enough or nearly enough milk to rear the child, which is suckled by other women for the first few weeks after adoption" (p. 193).

Could one say, then, that these people show strong maternal tendencies? Apparently not, for Mead goes on, in the next few pages, to describe a frustrated, loveless childhood, and makes some contrasts with the Arapesh: "if an Arapesh child that has been weaned for several years is screaming with pain or fright, the mother will offer her slack, dry breast to comfort it; the Mundugumor mother will not even offer a still suckling child her full one" (p. 196). The weaning process is accompanied by cross words and blows.

However, the picture is not all black, for we learn that there are some adults who are fond of children. "Within every child's circle of kin there are likely to be one or two of these persons, a mild unassuming paternal uncle, or some remarried widow who lives a quiet, unaggressive life, not competing with her co-wives or thinking it worthwhile to be disagreeable to their children" (p. 200). If relationships between the parents and such kind persons are strained, the child may not be allowed to visit them. But perhaps these kind persons have children? At any rate, if every child knows one or two such people, there must be a fair number of well-disposed deviants in this society, although not enough, evidently, to modify Mead's grim picture.

Because of Margaret Mead's way with words, her books are much more readable than the standard ethnographic monograph. But her literary approach carries certain dangers. Like an official guided tour, it leads the reader to view the culture in a particular way. This is most evident in Mead's description of the Tchambuli.

Here Mead does not give us the news straight; she editorializes throughout, with her conclusions being constantly imbedded in the ethnographic description. For example:

> All that remains to the individual Tchambuli man, with his delicately arranged curls, his handsome pubic covering . . . his mincing step and self-conscious mien, is the sense of himself as an actor, playing a series of charming parts—this and his relationships to the women.

. . . each man sits daintily in his own place and observes his companions narrowly.

. . . the men moving self-consciously, abashed to eat, among the crowds of smiling, unadorned, efficient women.

. . . in a group of men there is always strain, watchfulness, a catty remark here, a *double entendre* there (Mead 1935:248, 239, 241, 253).

Of course, it is hard to be objective in the description of behavior. What one observer characterizes as "mincing" might be differently interpreted or phrased by another.

Jessie Bernard raised some pertinent questions about this account of the Tchambuli:

> Would everyone who saw what Miss Mead saw agree with the observations upon which she based these conclusions? . . . I would not consider Tchambuli men effeminate on the basis of the data she presents, nor do the women she describes seem masculine. . . . Miss Mead concludes that temperament is not sex-linked . . . but that it is overwhelmingly cultural. A skeptic, accepting her data, might argue to the contrary: that the reversion of cultural roles among the Tchambuli violated the natural masculine temperament to such a degree that the men were prone to neuroticism (Bernard 1945:285, 289).

It is probably because of such criticisms by Bernard and by Thurnwald that Mead referred to *Sex and Temperament* as her most misunderstood book. To some critics, the three cultures seemed to provide ready-made demonstrations for a point of view which Mead must have held in the first place. In her 1950 preface, Mead rejected such suspicions and claimed that "the seemingly 'too good to be true' pattern is actually a reflection of the form which lay in these cultures themselves." More fieldwork in these tribes by other anthropologists—if it is not too late—would seem to be the only way to settle this problem.[8]

Sex and Temperament, one can see in retrospect, reflected and also contributed to the environmentalist ideology characteristic of the 1930s. This was the period in which Marxism attracted many intellectuals and in which neo-Freudians like Horney and Fromm were emphasizing the importance of social and cultural factors affecting personality. This stress on the cultural environment was part of the liberal tradition, influenced, among other currents, by the philosophy of John Dewey. Related to this tradition was the repudiation of racism, as manifest in the South's Jim Crowism and in Hitler's Nazi movement. This was a period, too, in which women were attaining more freedom and recognition in many fields; indeed, a feminist

---

[8] Theodore Schwartz (1983:927–28), who accompanied Margaret Mead to Manus at the time of her restudy, gives some examples of Mead's having a preconceived mental set in relation to her fieldwork.

stance is not hard to detect in the writings of Benedict and Mead (see Chase 1959).

In Mead's case, her relativism was later modified by a greater influence of Freudian theory. Her influence on the feminist movement has been mixed. Martin and Voorhies (1975) enthusiastically endorse her contributions in this respect, but Betty Friedan (1975:126–41) is more ambivalent and critical.

The three works which make up *From the South Seas* were beginnings in a new kind of undertaking. They were vigorous, imaginative, and influential books. If there were shortcomings in them, Mead was herself aware of the fact, for in the preface to the combined volume she wrote:

> They are pioneer studies made by a method which I myself shall not use again; my future work, like my past three years' work in Bali and among the Iatmul of New Guinea . . . will be cooperative, in which at least two, and sometimes as many as six observers, armed with modern methods of recording, typewriters, or stenotypes, miniature cameras and motion-picture cameras, will bring a battery of observation to bear upon the behavior of native children or native mothers (Mead 1939:vii).

In later parts of this book we will deal with some of Mead's more recent work. For example, Mead's work with Gregory Bateson in Bali is discussed in the following chapter.

SUGGESTIONS FOR FURTHER READING

Mead's bibliography is enormous and runs on for pages. Only a few books will be mentioned here: *The Changing Culture of an Indian Tribe* (New York: Columbia University Press, 1932); *And Keep Your Powder Dry* (New York: William Morrow, 1942); *Male and Female* (New York: William Morrow, 1949); *New Lives for Old. Cultural Transformation—Manus, 1928–1953* (1956).

Mead has provided an autobiographical account in *Blackberry Winter. My Earlier Years* (New York: William Morrow, 1972). Letters written home have been collected in Margaret Mead, *Letters from the Field: 1925–1975* (New York: Harper & Row, 1977).

For the reactions of several anthropologists (Ivan Brady, Annette B. Weiner, Theodore Schwartz, Lowell Holmes, Bradd Shore, and Martin C. Silverman) to Derek Freeman's criticism of *Coming of Age in Samoa*, see Ivan Brady, ed., "Speaking in the Name of the Real: Freeman and Mead on Samoa," *American Anthropologist* 85 (1983) pp. 908–47. For my own comments on this controversy, see Victor Barnouw, "Coming to Print on Samoa: Mead and Freeman" *The Journal of Psychoanalytic Anthropology* 6 (1983), pp. 425–33.

6

Childhood Determinist Approaches

By the late 1930s, an increased interest in Freudian and Gestalt viewpoints could be noted in the United States. This was furthered by the influx of refugees from Nazi Germany. Neo-Freudians such as Karen Horney, Erich Fromm, Franz Alexander, and Erik Homburger Erikson, and Gestaltists such as Wertheimer, Koffka, Köhler, and others took up residence in this country. Their writings, perhaps especially those of Horney and Fromm, received wide circulation. In this new intellectual atmosphere, the time was ready for revised theoretical approaches and improvements in methodology in the field of culture-and-personality.

THE SCHOOL OF LINTON, KARDINER, AND DU BOIS

Some new approaches along these lines began to be threshed out in a seminar on culture-and-personality conducted by the psychiatrist Abram Kardiner in conjunction with a group of anthropologists. In 1936 and 1937, Kardiner and Cora Du Bois held a seminar at the New York Psychoanalytic Institute, at which Edward Sapir, Ruth Benedict, and Ruth Bunzel were guest lecturers.

After Ralph Linton came to Columbia University in 1937, he joined forces with Kardiner and the two held a joint seminar at the university, which continued for several years. At these seminars it was the practice for some anthropologist to describe a culture in which he had done fieldwork, after which Kardiner would present an analytic interpretation, which would then be discussed by the group. The first product of this seminar was an exploratory work, *The Individual and His Society* (1939), followed in 1945 by *The Psychological Frontiers of Society*, in which Linton, Du Bois, and James West collaborated with Kardiner. Meanwhile Cora Du Bois published *The People of Alor* in 1944.

Basic Personality Structure

A concept central to the whole investigation is that of *basic personality structure*, which Kardiner (1939:237) defines as "the effective adaptive tools of the individual which are common to every individual in the society." The concept applies only to particular societies, such as the Trobriand Islanders; its nature differs from one society to another.

Since Kardiner is a Freudian, albeit a modified one, he believes that the earliest years of life are crucial in forming the personality of an individual. Techniques of child-rearing, suckling, toilet training, and sexual and other disciplines all profoundly influence the growing child in one direction or another. Now these techniques of raising children tend to be fairly standardized within a particular society. While there may be individual differences in various respects, by and large the women tend to suckle their children for about the same length of time as their neighbors do, feed them the same foods, and apply the same kinds of discipline. Therefore, the children who grow up within a particular society pass through the same general gamut of childhood experiences. They are apt to react to such experiences in much the same ways and therefore develop many personality traits in common. As Linton has put it, "The *basic personality type* for any society is that personality configuration which is shared by the bulk of the society's members as a result of the early experiences which they have in common" (Kardiner et al. 1945:viii).

One possible weakness in this formula is that, even if all the children of a society have the same kinds of early experiences, all would not necessarily react in the same ways. There are constitutional differences among children, present at birth, and children also differ in their positions in the birth order of the family. These differentiating factors would have to be seen as subordinate by supporters of the basic personality approach.

This approach is essentially a form of childhood determinism. Economic factors are taken into consideration, but primarily as they affect the family and childhood upbringing. Attention is directed to such matters as weaning, toilet training, and sexual disciplines. "If the character of the human mind is integrative, then it follows that the earliest constellations are basic, and if they prove expedient they will form the groundwork of all subsequent integrations, because they become a part of the individual's appreciation of reality" (Kardiner (1939:484).

"Primary" and "Secondary" Institutions

Another term used by Kardiner is *institution*. He does not use this term as Malinowski has sometimes used it, or as some other social scientists have done. Kardiner (1939:7) defines an institution as "any fixed mode of thought or behavior held by a group of individuals (that is, a society) which can be communicated, which enjoys common acceptance, and infringement of or deviation from which creates some disturbance in the individual or in the group."

In *The Individual and His Society*, Kardiner (p. 471) distinguishes between "primary" and "secondary" institutions. The first group includes such features as "family organization, in-group formation, basic disciplines, feeding, weaning, institutionalized care or neglect of children, anal training, and sexual taboos including aim, object, or both, subsistence techniques, etc". This somewhat heterogeneous assemblage is held to be older and more stable than the "secondary institutions" and is less apt to be affected by changes in climate or economy. These primary institutions are accepted as natural and self-evident by the members of a society. Childhood disciplines may, however, be harsh in their effects, and the individual must accommodate himself or herself to them in some way. These primary institutions are instrumental in shaping the basic personality structure of a society. The personality thus formed may, in turn, exert an influence on the culture by creating certain "secondary institutions." The latter refer primarily to folklore and religious beliefs, concepts about deities, attitudes toward them, and techniques used in dealing with them. These are fashioned through projection—conceptions about the gods being modeled after the child's relationships with its parents.

Freud dealt with this theme in *The Future of an Illusion*, in which he wrote:

> When the growing individual finds that he is destined to remain a child for ever, that he can never do without protection against strange superior powers, he lends those powers the features belonging to the figure of his father; he creates for himself the gods whom he dreads, whom he seeks to propitiate and whom he nevertheless entrusts with his own protection (Freud 1927:24).

Kardiner carried these observations further by examining the characteristic features of the religions in the societies he studied and by noting their relationships to the form of the family and parent-child relations. An example of this will·later be given in the discussion of Alor.

The principal tenets set forth in *The Individual and His Society* are the concept of basic personality structure, the notion that the basic personality structure of a given society is shaped by its primary institutions, and the idea that the basic personality structure, through "projective systems," fashions its secondary institutions.

While the same general approach is continued in *The Psychological Frontiers of Society*, the terminology is a bit different, and we hear less about primary and secondary institutions. This is partly because the study of Alor showed that some practices (for example, maternal neglect of children) are not institutionalized but may have important consequences for personality formation. More important, however, it proved to be difficult to classify many institutions as either primary or secondary (Kardiner et al. 1945:25, 97).

Although they were close collaborators, Linton did not agree with Kardiner about primary and secondary institutions and pointed out that all societies have a long history, with most of the cultural content being borrowed from outside (Hsu 1954:270–71).

In his books Kardiner occasionally writes in a general theoretical vein, sometimes taking issue with other analysts. He criticizes Freud, Reik, and Roheim for assuming that repressions always fall in the same place in all cultures. He is also critical of the libido theory. Some internal contradictions, however, have been noted by Inkeles and Levinson in their discussion of Kardiner's work:

> . . . although he rejects the Freudian theory of psychosexual development, he speaks of "oral" and "anal" adult character types and seeks their origins in corresponding periods of childhood development. The conceptual status of these presumably de-instinctivized terms remains unclear. (Inkeles and Levinson 1954:986).

Kardiner is generally categorized as a neo-Freudian, but he has been critical of others who are so classified, and has written:

> The so-called culturalist schools of psychodynamics represented by such writers as Harry Stack Sullivan, Karen Horney, and Erich Fromm, have not produced any enduring contributions to the social sciences (Kardiner and Preble 1961:243).

Applications

The value of such concepts as those set forth by Kardiner must be tested by their application to ethnological data. In this respect some weaknesses appear in these books, particularly in *The Individual and His Society*. It should be kept in mind, however, that Kardiner warns in the preface (1939:xxii) that the emphasis of the book must fall on the method; the conclusions must remain provisional.

The Individual and His Society contains a brief discussion of five cultures: Trobriand, Kwakiutl, Zuñi, Chukchee, and Eskimo, and a longer treatment of two cultures described by Ralph Linton—the Marquesas and the Tanala of Madagascar. In *The Psychological Frontiers of Society* three more cultures are discussed—Comanche (Linton), Alor (Du Bois), and Plainville, U.S.A. (James West).

Linton's account of the Tanala has been severely criticized by Aidan Southall (1975), who worked in the region in 1966–67 and again in 1973. There are also some drawbacks in Linton's accounts of the Marquesans and Comanche. He was originally sent to Marquesas to study the local archaeology and material culture. Linton (1939:xvii) was not at that time interested in personality studies and had no knowledge of psychoanalysis. It is true that he made friends with various natives and came to know them closely during a year's stay. But Linton tells us that at the time of his visit Marquesan culture was already a broken one, although it was possible to reconstruct a picture of the old days from the reminiscences of old men still living in the islands (Kardiner 1939:137).

Linton's picture, therefore, is largely a reconstruction. The same is true of the Comanche study. While the psychological inferences made about these people may be correct, they would certainly be hard to check or verify. Projective tests could not very well be used, and Linton presented no life histories. If one wishes to make generalizations about the personality characteristics of a group, there should be adequate documentation for them, and in this respect the descriptions of Marquesas, Tanala, and Comanche are insufficient. James West's study of Plainville is fuller, but it does not provide a sufficient basis for the sweeping generalizations which Kardiner makes about the personality characteristics of Western man. We learn, for example, that the basic personality structure of our society is essentially the same for all economic classes, and that this basic personality structure has been common to all of the Western world since the time of Job (Kardiner et al. 1945:337–38, 365, 432–34).

When we come to the study of Alor, however, we find much better groundwork. Here is the account of a living culture presented by a competent anthropologist with some psychiatric training, who collected life histories and gave projective tests in the field.

The People of Alor

The People of Alor is the outstanding research study to come from the Kardiner–Linton–Du Bois group. Let us, therefore, consider this work in more detail. The first thing to note is a difference in terminology. Instead of *basic personality structure,* Du Bois uses the term *modal personality,* which involves a more statistical concept. Du Bois (1944:4–5) notes that in Alor both the test material and her own impressions indicate a wide range of variation. "Ranges, however, are measured on a common base line. On such a base line, data will show central tendencies that constitute the modal personality for any particular culture."

The People of Alor is a study of the village complex of Atimelang on the island of Alor in Indonesia, where Cora Du Bois worked for about 18 months between 1938 and 1939. In order to work with the Alorese, Du Bois learned Dutch, Malay, and also the native tongue, which had not been studied before, and which she named Abui. Autobiographical material was not recorded until after Du Bois had been at Atimelang for a year, by which time she could translate directly into English as informants gave their life histories. In addition to writing a general ethnography and getting eight rather lengthy biographies, Du Bois administered the Rorschach test to 37 subjects, a word association test to 36 subjects, and the Porteus maze test to 55 subjects; she also collected children's drawings from 33 boys and 22 girls. She set up a daily clinic, treating wounds, infections, and fevers, thereby establishing communication and rapport with the villagers.

Du Bois states that the autobiographies do not represent the ideal or "type" person of Atimelang. The more successful Alorese were too busy with their affairs to take time off to tell their life histories and were not sufficiently attracted by either the money or prestige involved in working with the anthropologist. Autobiographical interviews were limited to one hour each morning before the informant began his day's work. The informant was encouraged to tell his dreams and to discuss them. The autobiographical material makes up about half the book. Each life history is analyzed by Abram Kardiner, who also presents some general conclusions to the autobiographical data.

The Rorschach tests were submitted to Dr. Emil Oberholzer, a Rorschach expert, for a "blind" analysis. He knew nothing of Kardiner's conclusions, drawn from the life history material, nor did Kardiner know of his. Each worked independently. Oberholzer's analysis (pp. 588–650 in Du Bois, *The People of Alor*) is brilliant and presents many striking correspondences to Kardiner's.

The same procedure was used with the children's drawings, submitted for "blind" analysis to Dr. Trude Schmidl-Waehner. Here, again, the agreement with the findings of Kardiner and Oberholzer is noteworthy. These correspondences strengthen the likelihood that each analyst has been on the right track and has correctly identified some general tendencies in Alorese personality. Through this technique the possibility of bias and subjective impressionism in the ethnographer are minimized. This innovation in methodology, together with the outstanding fieldwork, makes *The People of Alor* a milestone in culture-and-personality research.

Let us now turn to some of the data presented by Du Bois. As among the Iatmul and Tchambuli, the women in Alor are the principal food producers, concerned with the cultivation and collection of vegetable foods. The men are occupied with financial transactions involving the exchange of pigs, gongs, and kettledrums. This sexual division of labor has an important consequence for Alorese personality development in infancy, for the mother usually returns to regular agricultural work from 10 days to two weeks after the birth of her child. She does not take the baby with her to the fields, but leaves it in the care of its father, brother, sister, or grandparent. The child may be nursed by other women than the mother, but these substitutes are not consistently available. Consequently, children suffer from oral deprivation, although the mother nurses and fondles the child on her return from the field in late afternoon and whenever she is at home and not too busy. One substitute for offering the breast is to massage the child's genitals. There is no stress on toilet training during the prewalking period, and no efforts are made to teach the child either to talk or to walk during infancy. But walking begins at about the same time as in the Western world—from the 12th to the 18th month. Weaning rarely occurs before this time.

The period from the age of first walking to about five or six is considered by Du Bois to be probably the time of greatest stress for the child. The oral frustration continues, and by now the child is no longer carried about much in the carrying shawl, and thus loses the constant skin contacts and support of the previous period. When the mother goes off to work, the child is left from about eight in the morning to about five in the afternoon. It is fed irregularly by older siblings and others, but often, presumably, goes hungry. If a younger sibling is born during this time, the weaning process is hastened. Children are generally weaned and toilet trained by the age of three.

Teasing of the child is sometimes resorted to, similar to that described by Bateson and Mead (1942) for Bali. That is, the mother may deliberately stimulate jealousy in her baby by showing preference for some other child. Oddly enough, there is not much finger sucking among Alorese children. Sexual disciplines are lenient. Children may masturbate freely in public, and knowledge about sexual matters is common by age five. If a child is the last born, it may continue to sleep with its mother until the age of seven or eight; if displaced by a younger sibling, it sleeps with an older one or with some adult.

Children are often frightened by their elders. "Constant threats, accompanied by the brandishing of a knife, are made to cut off children's ears or hands. The adult is playful in his intentions, but some children are seriously frightened by this form of teasing" (Du Bois 1944:48). Shame sanctions are used in dealing with children, to ensure conformity. But children may also be consoled with gifts, usually of food.

A striking aspect of Alorese childhood is the temper tantrums. "Rages are so consistent, so widespread, and of such long duration among young children that they were one of my first and most striking observations" (Du Bois 1944:81). A common precipitating cause of this behavior is the mother's morning departure for the fields. Du Bois describes a particular child whose paroxysms sometimes lasted as long as 20 minutes. "He would begin by pursuing his mother; then as she outstripped him he would throw himself on the ground, roll back and forth, and often beat his head on the earth" (p. 51).

Temper tantrums begin to cease at about age five or six, when the child starts to wear the loincloth, a first step toward adult status.

During the day, children—more particularly boys—roam about in groups, foraging for food. (They can expect meals at home at around 7 A.M. and 7 P.M.) Adults don't object to minor raiding, but may punish children if they catch them stealing food. During this period the lives of boys and girls become differentiated. Boys have more mobility and may attach themselves to young men whom they serve as fags, or they may take part in work groups in the fields, pulling out weeds. Girls, however, stay closer to their mothers, have less time to play, and learn to weave, sew, make bark cloth, and engage in agricultural work. Both boys and girls may be saddled with the care of younger siblings.

Girls are tattooed between 10 to 14 years of age—a sort of indication of adult status. Boys are sometimes tattooed as well, but their symbolic mark of adulthood is letting their hair grow long. At this time they strut about carrying shields, quiver, and other male accouterments.

During adolescence boys and girls go through a process of having their teeth blackened, an occasion that provides a kind of picnic, during which some sexual license takes place. Women often take the initiative in courtship.

A man seems to look for a mother in the woman he marries. This was expressed in a statement by Du Bois's interpreter, Fantan:

> Wives are like our mothers. When we were small, our mothers fed us. When we are grown, our wives cook for us. If there is something good, they keep it in the pot until we come home. When we were small, we slept with our mothers; when we are grown, we sleep with our wives. Sometimes when we are grown we wake in the night and call our wives "mother" (Du Bois 1944:96).

Marriage involves many financial transactions, but, although the masculine-controlled finance acts to stabilize marriage, Atimelangers average about two divorces apiece. There seems to be much tension between men and women. This tension is interpreted by Kardiner and Du Bois as being due to the ambivalent attitudes developed toward the mother in childhood and to the continuing search in the man for a nurturing mother. The average Atimelang woman cannot meet these needs and thus continues to be a frustrating figure for the man. Much jealousy is in evidence, largely on the part of the men. Feeling unsure of themselves, men find an avenue to self-importance through the elaborate financial exchanges in which they engage.

According to Kardiner, Alorese childhood experiences are such that parental figures are not idealized, and superego formation is weak. Spirit effigies are made in a careless manner, and are soon discarded. There is also an absence of artistic creation and of interest in the outer world—a lack which must also, ultimately, be traced to the maternal frustrations of childhood.

Much of this analysis seems convincing, and there is much supporting evidence in the autobiographical data and in Oberholzer's Rorschach analysis. For instance, in discussing the Alorese black-color responses, which generally manifest "black-color shock," Oberholzer writes:

> From this we assume that the Alorese are suspicious and distrustful; they are so not only toward everything that is unknown and new to them, such as foreigners, for instance, but also among themselves. No one will trust another. Moreover, they are fearful and timid in their heart of hearts, feeling uneasy and insecure (Du Bois 1944:596).

Oberholzer states that the Alorese organization of conscience is undeveloped and that they are indifferent and let things slide. They have little capacity for sublimation, creativity, or close friendships, and they are probably given to angry emotional outbursts.

The interested reader should examine Oberholzer's impressive analysis in full, for this summary does not do it justice. Although it may contain a few discrepancies with the views of Kardiner and Du Bois, the most striking thing is the close correspondence. The same may be said of Dr. Trude Schmidl-Waehner's drawing analysis, in which she speaks of the children's "feeling of aloneness," their poverty-stricken relationships, and absence of creativity (Du Bois 1944:584–85).

Perhaps the main question raised by Du Bois's study is whether the personality traits singled out by Kardiner, Oberholzer, Du Bois, and Schmidl-Waehner are primarily due to the maternal neglect in infancy. There are other possible etiologies; Du Bois (1944:81) touches on at least one in referring to the prevalence of dysentery, respiratory infections, malaria, and yaws. "The possible effect on personality of these debilitating diseases, often suffered in acute form during childhood, is worth bearing in mind." Might not lack of ambition, for example, be traced to such a cause? How could one decide which factors were the crucial ones?

In a review of this book, Hortense Powdermaker (1945:160) observed: "We are not sure that this absence of the mother, which is common among all horticultural people in Melanesia, would necessarily lead to the mother being an object of frustration. My fieldwork in New Ireland, where the pattern of childhood feeding was identical to that of Alor, did not give me the impression that it led to feelings of frustration." Powdermaker suggests that too much emphasis may have been placed on prohibitory factors in Kardiner's analysis and not enough on the permissive, restitutive ones mentioned in the ethnography.[1]

---

[1] For an example of the latter: "Everyone seems entranced by small babies and many people will ask to hold and fondle them" (Du Bois 1944:33–34).

Roheim comments on the Alor study as follows:

> The mothers could take the children along with them into the fields,
> but they don't do it. Other primitive mothers carry their children all
> day; if these mothers don't, it is evident that they resent either the
> children or the fact that they have to do all the field work (or nearly all)
> and also take care of the children. . . . We are driven to the conclusion
> that the mothers leave the infants at home simply because they have a
> lot of hostility toward them (Roheim 1950:261).

Such hostility, if it exists, might be more significant than the temporary absences of the mother, although in either case the mother
would come to be seen as frustrating by the child.

What is the more significant factor affecting personality in Alorese
children; food deprivation or maternal rejection? In a paper on the
Gurage of Ethiopia, D. N. Shack (1969) claims that nutritional deprivation is cross-culturally associated with such personality characteristics as selfishness, unrelatedness, emotional detachment, passivity,
dependency, and feelings of worthlessness. Ronald P. Rohner (1970),
on the other hand, asserts that parental neglect is a more significant
determinant of personality. He argues that parental rejection causes
feelings of anxiety, frustration, aggression, and a lowered sense of
self-esteem. The child comes to feel that he is not worthy of love; he is
also apt to become more dependent than an accepted child. As a
result of the frustrating experiences in childhood, the individual
tends to generalize his feelings so as to see the world as hostile and
unfriendly. Rohner expects that as adults such persons would find it
hard to form close emotional relationships and would, in turn, be
likely to reject their own children. They would also find it hard to
tolerate stress and would be less emotionally stable than persons who
had been accepted in childhood. In a crosscultural statistical study,
Rohner tested the foregoing hypotheses about the effects of parental
rejection as against Shack's hypotheses about the effects of food deprivation and found lack of confirmation for the latter but support for
the former.

Parental rejection is probably a more crucial determinant of personality in Alor than food deprivation per se. Rohner's findings seem to
fit in well with the conclusions of the Alor study.

Although these conclusions are consistent, and although the general picture carries conviction, there are still points where questions
and criticisms of the Alor study may be raised. One point which may
be noted is that Kardiner's analysis of Alorese infancy and its sequelae seems to be based on the wet season births. If birth takes place
during the dry season, when there is less agricultural work, the
mother spends more time with her child. The seasons seem to be
about equally long. Oberholzer was struck by the great variability
manifest in the Alorese Rorschachs, and this was attributed to the

variations in maternal and paternal care. But if there are such great variations, is it safe to make generalizations about the personality tendencies of this society? Eight biographies and 37 Rorschachs are the principal sources from which generalizations are made about modal personality characteristics in a population of about 600, although the latter number represents only a small part of the total Alorese population. Moreover, Du Bois tells us that the life histories are drawn from some of the less successful members of the society.

Even within the small group of biographies there seems to be a great range of variation in personality patterns. Anthony F. C. Wallace has drawn attention to Kardiner's difficulties in finding a basis for making generalizations. Kardiner wrote at first: "It is difficult to decide how typical Mangma is. I would venture to say that if he were typical the society could not continue to exist" (Du Bois 1944:227). But later Kardiner wrote, "Mangma is the most typical, and his character corresponds to the basic personality structure" (Du Bois 1944:549). Kardiner also wrote that Malelaka was difficult to evaluate but that, nevertheless, his life history was in every way typical. Wallace comments: "This is remarkable, because Malelaka was a notorious prophet who attempted to launch a religious revival. On the other hand he is said to be similar to Rilpada, another seer, who in turn was described as 'atypical.' And to complicate things still further, the analyst says that 'characters such as Mangma, Rilpada and Fantan can be found in any society' " (Wallace 1970a:125).

While it is right to question the adequacy of the sampling in this study, historical perspective must remind us that no one had previously collected so much psychological data of this sort in culture-and-personality research. Moreover, Cora Du Bois (1960:xxiv) has herself been conscious of these problems; for in answer to the question "If you were doing Alor again, how would you go about it?" she replied, in part, that she would be far more precise in sampling and interviewing, probably using sentence completion and multiple choice schedules.

BATESON AND MEAD ON BALINESE CHARACTER

The earlier works of Margaret Mead and Gregory Bateson were not clearly in a childhood determinist vein, but there is a strong Freudian influence in their work on Bali and an emphasis on the formative nature of the early years. After Bateson and Mead were married in 1936, they immediately began to do fieldwork in Bali, from March 1936 to March 1938 and for a six-week period in 1939. They had several co-workers, including Jane Belo, Colin McPhee, Katharane Mershon, and others. About 25,000 Leica stills and 22,000 feet of 16-mm. film were taken in Bali. Extensive use of the still photographs was made in two books: *Balinese Character* (Bateson and Mead 1942) and *Growth and Culture* (Mead and MacGregor 1951). The Bateson and Mead films, including *A Balinese Family, Karba's First Years,* and *Trance and Dance in Bali,* among others, have since become classics. Reference will be made later to these films.

Bali is an island in Indonesia, located south of the equator, with a present population of about 2.5 million but having less than a million in 1936–39. Most people are farmers. Bali is very well irrigated with extensive rice fields. Cooperative organizations of farmers see that there is a fair distribution of water resources. Every married man is a member of a village council. People live in joint family households with patrilocal residence. There is a wall around each house complex.

Bali was formerly divided into small kingdoms, each ruled by a rajah, but these lost their authority after Dutch rule was established. Bali has a caste system diffused from India, along with many aspects of the Hindu religion. There are temples everywhere in Bali. The names of the castes, Brahmana, Satria, Wesia, Sudra, correspond to those of the Hindu varna (Brahman, Kshatriya, Vaishya, Sudra).

In Bali a person uses different terms of address depending on whether he or she is speaking to a person of higher or lower caste. A person of lower caste should always sit at a lower level than a person of higher caste. Balinese seem to be very conscious of their relations in space—to one another and in relation to the mountains and the sea. The mountain represents holiness, while the sea is a zone of danger and evil spirits. Height is associated with purity. One should sleep with one's head toward the mountains and one's feet toward the sea. Family shrines are located on the inland part of house compounds, toward the mountains, while kitchens and latrines are in the coastward side, toward the sea. Village cemeteries are on the coastward side (Belo 1935; Bateson and Mead 1942:6).

Bali is unusual, especially for a peasant society, in its emphasis on the arts. Carving in wood and stone, painting, drama, and music are all very advanced and occupy much of the people's time. Some of this art elaboration was connected with the calendrical round associated with the temples. States of trance were cultivated in some aspects of Balinese ritual and also in the drama *Tjalonarang,* concerning the conflict between Rangda, Queen of the Witches, and Barong, a Chinese-dragon-like diety.

In their everyday life the Balinese seem to be very controlled and poised. They are described as being very unaggressive, even in childhood. Margaret Mead (1955:44) has written: "in over two years of living in Balinese villages, I never saw two children or adolescents fight. When conflict arises, the elder child is continually told to give in to the younger."

Although everyday life has this calm tenor, the dramas that the people enact and the puppet shadow plays that they watch are full of conflicts, fights, and battles. Battle scenes are a prominent theme for artists. Covarrubias (1937:191) writes that "Battle scenes are crowded, bloody, and desperate, a tangle of arms, legs, and blood-spattered bodies, with all the space around filled with flying arrows and strange weapons." When Jane Belo (1955:65) provided paper and drawing materials and asked Balinese children to draw pictures, she found that battle scenes were the most popular subject. An average of 66 percent of the drawings represented a flight or some form of attack. Cockfighting, in which the birds are equipped with steel spurs, is a popular sport for the men and may, like the dramas, provide vicarious satisfaction of aggressive impulses. The Balinese preoccupation with witchcraft and demons suggests a fear of aggression from without.

In some societies where aggression is normally inhibited, perhaps due to fear of sorcery, hostility becomes expressed during intoxication, and men fight when they get drunk. But the Balinese do not drink. Covarrubias (1937:109) writes that during his entire stay in Bali, he never saw a man really drunk "perhaps because the Balinese dread the sensation of dizziness and confusion, of losing control over themselves."

This concern does not seem to affect behavior during trance, perhaps because a person is not then really himself. Normally the Balinese are afraid of falling, but during the kris dance[2] in the *Tjalonarang* drama men fall and thrash about violently on the ground. Children are not supposed to crawl on all fours, since that is animallike behavior. But in some trance performances, men play the roles of pigs and monkeys and behave so violently that they have to be subdued and held down by several men until they have calmed down. Another occasion when violent emotion is expressed is during funeral ceremonies, when men engage in wild, riotous behavior, some plunging their hands into the rotting corpse (Bateson and Mead 1942:46). Apart from such outbursts, life in Bali seems to follow a calm, even course.

What contributions do Bateson and Mead make to understanding Balinese character? As noted earlier, the emphasis in their research in Bajoeng Gede, a mountain village in Bali, seems to have been more Freudian than in their earlier work. They paid special attention to the early years of childhood.

Balinese Childhood

According to their account, a child has continuous close contact with the mother during the first year or more of life. Since crawling on the ground is disapproved of as animallike, a baby is generally carried about in a sling supported on the mother's hip. The child

---

[2] The kris is a Malay or Indonesian dagger with a serpentine blade. The kris dance is described further on page 125.

adjusts passively to the carrier's movements. This passive adaptation is capitalized on by adults who teach the child such skills as walking, gesturing, dancing, and playing musical instruments by manipulating the child lightly from behind, with only a minimum of verbal instruction.

When a baby is suckled, its mouth is placed down on the nipple, so that it draws milk up into the mouth rather than down. But solid food prechewed by the mother is stuffed into the baby's mouth from above, which leads to choking and resistance. Bateson and Mead (1942:23) relate this early pattern to adult behavior in eating at festivals and other public occasions, when people turn their backs on one another and eat hastily. On the other hand, liquids and snacks at a vendor's stall are consumed cheerfully without embarrassment. Such occasions "must be compared, not with the baby's forced eating of prechewed food, but with the casual and gay suckling."

Parallel differences can also be seen in the attitudes toward defecation, which is secret and private, and urination, which children do publicly and casually.

Balinese children are said to have no crawling stage, for reasons already noted. A child learns to walk by going around a walking rail and hanging on, when necessary. When the toddler is able to explore further afield, the mother may call the child back to her with alarming cries of "Tiger!" "Snake!" which bring the child running to her arms.

Throughout childhood a Balinese mother is said to engage in teasing behavior. She provokes or stimulates the child and then abruptly turns away without allowing it to reach an emotional climax. She may borrow a neighbor's baby and offer it the breast to arouse jealousy or else hold a younger child over the head of her older one, which is considered to be insulting. This kind of treatment ultimately leads to the child's withdrawal and lack of responsiveness some time between the ages of three and six. "He skirts any group in which he thinks there will be someone to reach out a hand toward him. And once established, his unresponsiveness will last through life" (Bateson and Mead 1942:33).

For this reason the authors (1942:xvi) describe the ordinary adjustment of the individual as comparable to what we called schizoid. This tendency may have been expected by Mead and Bateson in the first place, since before they went to Bali they had been fascinated by Jane Belo's preliminary reports on Balinese art and trance: "it seemed the ideal culture within which to plan a project on the cultural aspects of schizophrenia" (Mead in Belo 1960:v). Their research in Bali was funded, in part, by the Committee for Research in Dementia Praecox (Bateson and Mead 1942:v).

Let us consider the evidence provided by Bateson and Mead for their generalizations about mother-child interactions. The evidence comes, first of all, in the form of their still photographs with accompanying field notes. Plate 47, for example, shows a series of nine photographs of a mother with her child in a sequence illustrating stimulation and frustration, while Plate 49 deals with borrowing babies to provoke jealousy. Other plates deal with children's sulks, tantrums, and sibling rivalry.

Documentation is also provided in the Bateson and Mead films, *A Balinese Family* and *Karba's First Years*. The family in *A Balinese Family* is said to be larger than most; so perhaps there is more sibling rivalry, and perhaps the mother is more overworked than most Balinese mothers and more predisposed to reject her children's demands for attention. Toward the end of the film, we learn that she has been ill for some time and unable to look after her daughter, whose sulky attitude may be due to that rather than to the teasing. The film does show teasing behavior by a few mothers. This teasing does not seem to be particularly cruel or frustrating, but perhaps it is from the child's point of view, for some of the children do give way to temper tantrums. There is, at any rate, a good deal of documentation in both still and motion photography to support the generalizations made by Mead and Bateson about Balinese mother-child interaction, although the sample is unavoidably small in relation to the total Balinese population. What we see, of course, is overt behavior. We cannot be sure what is going on in the minds of the participants.

Bateson and Mead also made a film called *Childhood Rivalry in Bali and New Guinea*, in which comparisons were made of the behavior of Iatmul and Balinese children. Mead presented a doll to a child in Bali and also to some children in a Iatmul community; their reactions in both cases were filmed. The Balinese child did not want to accept the doll; the mother used the doll to tease her son and pretended to suckle it, thus eliciting the child's jealousy, while the Iatmul children played quietly with the doll beside their mother, who did not engage in any teasing. An ear-piercing ceremony performed on children of similar age was filmed in both Bali and among the Iatmul. The older sibling (a girl) watching the ceremony in Bali showed no concern about the younger child's pain, while the Iatmul older sibling (a boy) registered much anxiety, evidently identifying with, and feeling sorry for, the younger child. Contrasting film shots showed the fostering of sibling rivalry in Bali and its deemphasis among the Iatmul. Although the sample of children shown in the films was small in relation to the total populations, their behavior seemed to follow characteristic patterns in the two cultures.

The Tjalonarang Drama

Bateson and Mead relate Balinese mother-child relations to the drama of Tjalonarang. Trance activity is prominent in this classic Balinese drama, which deals with Rangda, Queen of the Witches, who has long canine tusks and fingernails, staring pop eyes, and pendulous hairy breasts. In the play she is opposed by Barong, whose followers, young men armed with krises, rush upon Rangda and try to stab her. She is limp and offers no resistance, but merely waves her cloth, a baby-carrying sling. At this, the men fall to the ground. When they get up again in a trance state, they subsequently turn their krises on themselves, while leaning backward in an intense, straining manner. They finally fall down, exhausted, in convulsions, and are subsequently brought out of trance. Normally, they do not cut or hurt themselves, despite the violence of their behavior.

Following a theory of projection, such as that of Abram Kardiner[3] Bateson and Mead (1942:35) identify Rangda as a maternal figure and Barong as a father image. Of the young men's inward-turning aggression, they remark: "Thus symbolically they complete the cycle of the childhood trauma—the approach to the mother, the rejection, and the turn-in upon the self."

The identification of Rangda as a frustrating mother is debatable, but some supporting evidence lies in the fact that Rangda carries a baby cloth. It seems odd that she does so, since the name "Rangda" means "widow," and she is depicted as old, with long, hairy, pendulous breasts, and she has a daughter of marriageable age. Another clue, which might be taken as evidence for a connection with childhood experience, is the fact that male trance dancers report having strong feelings of hatred toward Rangda. What might be the roots of this hatred? Perhaps the maternal frustration described by Bateson and Mead. Since many of the men taking part in the trance dance are married, it also is possible that hatred is felt toward the wife. (Marriages are patrilocal, so mother and wife share the same compound.) Bateson and Mead (1942:36) write: "The dance sums up the besetting fear, the final knowledge of each Balinese male that he will, after all, no matter how hard he seeks to find the lovely and unknown beyond the confines of his familiar village, marry the Witch, marry a woman whose attitude toward human relations will be exactly that of his own mother." The fact that the young men cannot stab the Witch might be another clue to the tie with childhood. The mother is too important to the child; she is too powerful to be harmed by him. Also, the fact that the kris is turned against the man's chest may be significant, especially since one man described his feeling afterwards as being one of great satisfaction, as if he had eaten a big meal of rice. This suggests a fantasied gratification of oral needs after frustration. Blocked from suckling, attention is narcissistically directed to the person's own chest, which some men describe as having burning and itching sensations. This experience may have phallic sexual connotations, for there is a Balinese joke in which impotence is symbolized by a bent kris

---

[3] See page 112.

(Mead 1949a:211). Perhaps there is something to be said, then, for the hypothesis that mother-child relations are reenacted in the Tja- lonarang drama. Bateson and Mead (1942:34) also make the point that children often watch the enactment of this play, which "shapes their reading of the experiences to which they are subjected daily."

One final question is whether the trance behavior should be seen as indicative of schizoid tendencies. Although Jane Belo (1960:10) was an associate, friend, and admirer of Bateson and Mead, she took issue with this interpretation, seeing no indication of abnormality among the trance dancers, who seem to be no different from their fellows who do not go into trance. Nor were any differences revealed when psychological tests were given to a group of "strong trancers" and to a control group of nontrancers.

SOME GENERAL CONSIDERATIONS

A problem in all the studies discussed in this chapter is how far the generalizations may be extended. Is it safe to conclude that the modal personality described by Cora Du Bois for the people of Atimelang apply to the people of Alor as a whole, who number about 70,000? Similarly, is the village of Bajoeng Gede, where Bateson and Mead did their fieldwork, representative of the much larger island of Bali?

The kind of research done in studies like these depends on an intensive investigation by the fieldworker, who must not only be able to describe the general culture but must also discover prevalent per- sonality patterns through such means as the observation of behavior, collection of life histories, and administration of projective tests. This is a time-consuming process and cannot be done with very large numbers of people. Hence research is apt to be confined to a particu- lar community.

Even within such a community, a biased sample of informants may be involved. For example, the more successful Alorese were not rep- resented in Du Bois' life histories. People who are willing to spend a lot of time telling an anthropologist their autobiographies are often maladjusted persons.[4]

Some fieldworkers have tried to avoid a bias of this kind by select- ing informants from different status groups and different age levels. In a study of high caste Hindus in Rajasthan, Carstairs (1958) inter- viewed a roughly equal number of informants from each of the three castes he was studying (Rajput, Brahman, and Bania), members of different age brackets, and a roughly equal number of oldest sons and younger sons.

Particular attention to sampling was given by Thomas Gladwin in his study of Truk in Micronesia. At the beginning of his work,

---

[4] See page 250.

Gladwin devised a sort of popularity poll to guide him in this selection. Five men and five women were drawn by lot from all the adolescents and adults on the island. They were asked to rate all other persons on the island on a four-point scale of like and dislike. It was felt that if a person was consistently said to be liked or disliked, there was something distinctive about him in one way or another.

> With the ratings completed, the men and women of the island were ranked separately from highest to lowest. The six most "liked" and the six most "disliked" of each sex were set apart, and three were selected by chance out of each such group for intensive study; there were thus six persons of each sex in our sample who were putatively "unusual." Of those remaining in the middle range five of each sex were again selected by chance for inclusion in the sample, making a total of eleven men and eleven women (Gladwin and Sarason 1953:211).[5]

To this number a Trukese assistant of Gladwin's was added, giving a total of 12 men.

Each of the 23 subjects was given the Rorschach and Thematic Apperception Test by Gladwin and was asked to tell his or her life history.[6]

SUGGESTIONS FOR FURTHER READING

The concept of *basic personality structure* is discussed by Abram Kardiner in "The Concept of Basic Personality Structure as an Operational Tool in the Social Sciences," in *Personal Character and Cultural Milieu: A Collection of Readings,* ed. Douglas G. Haring (Syracuse, N.Y.: Syracuse University Press, 1949), pp. 469–83. Also in the Haring volume (pp. 241–53) is a brief account of Alor, "Attitudes toward Food and Hunger in Alor," by Cora Du Bois, pp. 241–53. For an analysis of American Negro personality, see Abram Kardiner and Lionel Ovesey, *The Mark of Oppression: A Psychological Study of the American Negro* (New York: W. W. Norton, 1951). For a general discussion, see Ralph Linton, *The Cultural Background of Personality* (New York: D. Appleton-Century, 1945). There is a biographical sketch of Linton in Adelin Linton and Charles Wagley, *Ralph Linton* (New York: Columbia University Press, 1971). Kardiner has written some interesting biographical reminiscences in Abram Kardiner, *My Analysis with Freud: Reminiscences* (New York: W. W. Norton, 1977).

---

[5] Gladwin has written that the method of sampling was intended only to establish putatively "normal" and "deviant" samples. No validity was assumed for the poll as a measure of actual popularity (personal communication to author).

[6] For some of the findings, see pp. 301–4.

PART THREE

More Recent
Studies

7

Cross-Cultural Surveys

While the basic personality approach was being advanced at Columbia University, a rather different approach was under way at Yale, where George P. Murdock and John W. M. Whiting were leading figures in the launching and development of Yale's Cross-Cultural Survey, which later became known as the Human Relations Area Files (HRAF). In contrast to the intensive investigation of a single culture, such as Du Bois's study of Alor, researchers making use of HRAF sources try to make generalizations from a large number of societies, usually selected from different culture areas of the world. These studies usually set forth some specific hypotheses which are made to either stand or fall on the basis of statistical evaluations.

The HRAF is an extensive filing system containing ethnological data about several hundred societies from different culture areas. The material is so classified and sorted that it is easy for anyone familiar with the coding system to rapidly find whatever one is looking for. If a student, let us say, wants information about fishing techniques among the Yurok, Tikopia, and Ainu, he or she simply finds the files for these three groups and draws out the cards dealing with fishing. This is much simpler than going through a lot of library references. Moreover, the files facilitate the discovery of recurring correlations, associated features between institutions, or what E. B. Tylor (1889), in an early cross-cultural survey, called *adhesions.*

Those who are attracted to cross-cultural surveys making use of the files tend to believe that human behavior is characterized by a good deal of regularity, which makes it possible to make predictions about what sorts of institutions are apt to go together. Thus hypotheses can be stated and tested. One proponent of cross-cultural studies, Yehudi A. Cohen (1968:405), suggests that two main principles form a basis for such research. The first is the principle of limited possibilities: "that there are a finite number of forms which any institution, belief, or custom can take." In other words, there is a limited number of solutions to particular problems. The second principle is "the psychic unity of mankind," or the notion that despite racial and cultural differences all men have essentially the same basic thought processes and feelings.

A cultural relativist such as Ruth Benedict would not be apt to find research with the HRAF files congenial. What facilitates such research, as Cohen (1968:403) puts it, is a "clearly defined point of view about the ways in which sociocultural systems operate." The views of Murdock, Whiting, and others at Yale were congenial to this approach, since they had some rather definite notions about the nature of personality and of cultural institutions. Although they shared with the Linton-Kardiner school the influence of psychoanalytic theory, they differed in also having a behaviorist orientation.

With their stress on the importance of culture, which involves learned behavior, many anthropologists have been attracted to behaviorism, since this school of psychology deemphasizes the role of instincts or inborn qualities. Behaviorist psychology also places emphasis on the observation of behavior, which is in line with the traditions of anthropological fieldwork. Clark L. Hull taught learning theory at Yale, where he influenced psychologists such as O. H. Mowrer, John Dollard, and Neal Miller, but also such anthropologists as Murdock and Whiting. Both Murdock and Whiting have tried to apply learning theory to cross-cultural data. They have also tried to express psychoanalytic concepts in the terminology of learning theory.

In this chapter we will deal with cross-cultural studies which concern the field of culture-and-personality. The HRAF files have been used for other kinds of studies as well, for example in relation to cultural evolution. As will be seen later, there are some disadvantages as well as advantages in cross-cultural surveys. But before attempting an evaluation of the method, let us first consider a series of examples of such research.

SORCERY AND SOCIAL CONTROL

Let us start with *Paiute Sorcery* by Beatrice B. Whiting, an interesting monograph which combines the investigation of a particular society with the cross-cultural survey approach. Beatrice Whiting did field research among the Harney Valley Paiute in Burns, Oregon, in the summers of 1936, 1937, and 1938. Most of her work concerns the Paiute, and it is only in a concluding chapter that the cross-cultural approach is used.

Paiute bands were small in number, fluctuating in size with the seasons, and the individual families that constituted the essential economic units often lived alone. Few economic activities involved the cooperation of more than one extended family. There were no true chiefs, no council of elders, and no police force. How, then, was social control achieved? Whiting (1950:13) suggests, as Hallowell has done for the Saulteaux or Canadian Chippewa, that fear of sorcery was a crucial factor. "Within the band, the most important mechanisms of social control were retaliation and the fear of sorcery and accusations of sorcery."

Control of aggression within the individual family was very strict, for the solidarity of the family unit was essential. Children were promptly punished for aggressive behavior.

Moreover, children saw that their parents inhibited their own aggression due to fear of sorcery. Parents warned their children never to make fun of anyone and to always be polite. Despite this control, intrafamily aggression sometimes did break loose, particularly in the case of men attacking their wives. Aggression was also turned inward, and Whiting tells us that the suicide rate was high. Within the memory of her informants, there had been as many as 23 suicides in a population of between 200 and 300.

It occurred to Whiting that some of the functional relationships which she found among the Paiute might appear in other societies as well. Much of her picture accords closely with that of the Chippewa, although these groups did not belong to the same culture area, geographic environment, or linguistic stock. Whiting's cross-cultural study shows that similar patterns appear in still other "atomistic" societies. Whiting does not, however, use this term. She speaks of societies as having either *coordinate* or *superordinate* systems of social control.

In societies with superordinate control, persons are delegated authority to settle disputes and exact punishment. These persons have high status, either ascribed or acquired. Societies with coordinate control lack such individuals or groups, and offenses are dealt with by retaliation on the part of the kin or local group. The Paiute are an example of the latter type; in their case, fear of sorcery is functionally related to coordinate control.

Whiting classified societies described in the Cross-Cultural Survey as having either coordinate or superordinate control on the basis of how murders were dealt with in the society. She also rated these societies with regard to the importance of sorcery as an explanation for sickness, establishing two groups: sorcery important and sorcery unimportant. Four tables with tetrachoric correlations are presented in her monograph, together with statistical evaluations. These tend to support the hypothesis of a functional association between sorcery and coordinate control.

THE FUNCTIONS OF ALCOHOL

Another cross-cultural study is Donald Horton's investigation into the functions of alcohol in primitive societies. Part of this study is related to the work of Beatrice Whiting just cited. Horton asserts that the primary function of liquor consumption is reduction of anxiety, although counteranxiety may also develop as a result of drinking—through punishment for acts committed under intoxication, hangovers, and so forth. Horton suggests some "theorems" which he proposes to test:

   1.   The drinking of alcohol tends to be accompanied by the release of sexual and aggressive impulses.
   2.   The strength of the drinking response in any society tends to vary directly with the level of anxiety in that society.
   3.   The strength of the drinking response tends to vary inversely with the strength of the counteranxiety elicited by painful experiences during and after drinking (Horton 1943:230).

Horton considers various sources of anxiety, including subsistence insecurity and acculturation. Societies described in the Yale files, for whom there were descriptions of drinking behavior, were classified into those having "high," "moderate," or "low subsistence insecurity." They were also grouped under the headings "strong insobriety" and "moderate or slight insobriety." Subsistence insecurity was found to be positively and significantly associated with male insobriety. This association was held to substantiate the posited relationship between the level of anxiety and strength of the drinking habit (Horton 1943:268).[1]

The same applies to acculturation, which also tended to be associated with strong insobriety. Less clear-cut relationships were found between warfare and insobriety and between sorcery and insobriety. Nor was the type of beverage directly related to the strength of the drinking response. "Where anxiety is low, people will remain relatively sober with distilled liquor; where anxiety is high, they will try to become intoxicated with beer or wine" (Horton 1943:279).

Horton notes that for many societies a similar sequence of behavior occurs during drinking. In early stages there is laughter and friendly conversation, but in the later stages of intoxication quarrelling and fighting often break out among the men. Women do not seem to engage in drunken aggression, as the men do, and in many societies women hide the men's weapons or otherwise try to forestall their outbursts. Drunken aggression was reported for 36 of 37 societies in the files whose drinking behavior was described. It is evident that normally inhibited aggression is released under intoxication.

Horton (1943:286) suggests that sorcery may be used as a measure of the level of inhibited aggression. "It was predicted that strong aggression and an active belief in sorcery would tend to occur together, and medium or slight aggression would tend to occur where

---

[1] Horton says that the "nuclear data" of this study concern 56 societies, each with a culture significantly different from the others (p. 236).

the belief in sorcery is not important." This prediction is supported statistically in a series of tables.

Horton cites Whiting's association between sorcery and coordinate control and points out that in societies having coordinate control there is no central authority or police force to restrain drunken aggression. Such outbreaks would therefore probably be dealt with less effectively than in a superordinate society.

Another cross-cultural study of drinking behavior is that of Peter B. Field (1962), who takes issue with some of Horton's findings. He points out that an anxiety theory of excessive drinking is inadequate, because it does not explain why other anxiety-reducing mechanisms are not resorted to, instead of drinking. Moreover, while acculturation may sometimes increase anxiety, it may in some cases decrease it by diminishing supernatural fears or by providing new rational solutions to old problems. Field's own cross-cultural examination leads him to conclude that excessive drinking is related to an informal type of social organization in which there is a good deal of personal autonomy and an absence of institutional constraints. This would generally apply to nomadic hunting-gathering societies, which are rated high on drunkenness. Where stability and permanence are characteristic of a society, and where there are corporate kin groups having collective ownership of property, there is less evidence of excessive drinking. Such institutions as patrilocal residence and the bride price are also associated with relative sobriety. Sociological factors such as these, rather than the level of anxiety, are for Field the significant factors accounting for the extent of drinking behavior.

The most comprehensive cross-cultural study of drinking is that of Bacon, Barry, and Child (1965), in which data are drawn from 139 societies, mostly nonliterate, incorporating the 57 societies used by Horton. The authors' correlations support the conclusions of Horton but not those of Field, finding little relationship between drinking behavior and egalitarian or informal social order. A prediction tested in this study is that drinking and drunkenness should tend to be frequent in societies that produce much conflict about dependence and independence. In a correlational analysis, the authors find that drinking is associated with low indulgence in infancy and childhood, with pressure for responsibility in childhood, and a low degree of indulgence of dependence or nurturance in adult life. These findings would support, or at least do not contradict, the hypothesis that drinking is partially motivated by a need to relieve frustrated or conflicted needs for dependency.

"Apollonianism": Some Correlations

Although Field's interpretation was not supported by the work of Barry, Bacon, and Child, his type of explanation might help to account for the relative "Apollonianism" of the Pueblos, when compared with formerly hunting-gathering tribes like the Chippewa. Two other cross-cultural studies are of interest in this connection. Barry, Child, and Bacon (1959) have argued that in pastoral and agricultural societies a future food supply is best assured by faithful adherence to routine. There is a fear of innovation, and child training emphasizes conformity and obedience. In hunting and fishing societies, on the other hand, individual initiative is at a premium. There is less fear of innovation; child training emphasizes initiative and self-reliance. The authors find evidence for these patterns in a cross-cultural survey of child-training patterns.

D'Andrade (1961) has followed up these findings with a cross-cultural survey on dreams. His hypothesis is that hunting and fishing societies will be more apt to use dreams to acquire supernatural power than will agricultural ones. D'Andrade reasons that anxiety about being isolated and under pressure to be self-reliant might lead to the development of fantasies and dreams about magical helpers. He has found statistical support for the postulated relationship between type of economy and use of dreams. Approximately 80 percent of the hunting and fishing societies in his sample used dreams to acquire supernatural power, in contrast to 20 percent of the societies having agriculture and animal husbandry. It might be argued that it was the shift to agriculture and the development of a corporate society that led to the appearance of those Apollonian features in Pueblo life which Benedict described, such as strong disapproval of drinking, emphasis on conformity, and absence of the guardian spirit quest. At least these cross-cultural studies seem to suggest such a conclusion, which would also be supported by the findings of the cross-cultural survey by Gouldner and Peterson (1962), in which the authors conclude that Apollonian impulse-control has increased with the development of technology.

CHILD TRAINING AND PERSONALITY

The first major culture-and-personality work to make use of the Human Relations Area Files is *Child Training and Personality: A Cross-Cultural Study* by John W. M. Whiting and Irvin L. Child (1953). This work is concerned with the mutual interplay of culture and personality and with the integration of culture through the mediation of personality. It focuses on one particular aspect of culture—customs relating to illness. One reason for this choice is that in primitive societies such practices are apt to be fashioned by projection and to be retained because of their compatability with personality tendencies. Whiting and Child are interested in seeing how early childhood experiences in a particular society predispose to the development of certain medical practices.

The authors make use of the concept of *fixation*, but without endorsing the whole psychoanalytic canon surrounding this term. They point out that psychoanalysts have derived fixation from two quite different experiences—on the one hand from excessive gratification, and on the other hand from excessive frustrations at a given level. Whiting and Child suggest that fixation which results from a high degree of gratification be called *positive fixation*, while fixation which results from severe socialization be called *negative fixation*.

The authors wish to determine how severity or lenience in particular childhood disciplines are related to curing practices and explanations of sickness. For example, does early oral gratification lead to "oral" forms of curing?

Whiting and Child (1953:149) propound a hypothesis of negative fixation as follows: "In any society, the greater the custom potential of socialization anxiety for a system of behavior, the greater will be the custom potential of explanations of illness which attribute illness to events associated with that system."

The systems of behavior to which the authors refer are oral, anal, sexual, dependence, and aggression. Their hypotheses of negative fixation and the other hypotheses which follow are tested with reference to data from 65 societies described in the cross-cultural files, plus 10 more societies for which relevant information was available. Three judges were selected to make ratings on various aspects of child experience. In relation to *socialization anxiety*, for example, they had to evaluate for each society "the brevity of the transition from freedom of indulgence of the initial habit to the requirement of complete acceptance of childhood or adult inhibitions" (Whiting and Child 1953:53). They also had to evaluate the severity of punishment, frequency of punishment, and signs of emotional disturbance in the children. The judges were required, moreover, to indicate how confident they felt about their judgments by labeling them either *confident* or *doubtful*. The judges did not always agree in their evaluations; hence their pooled judgments were used. Whiting and Child were satisfied with the degree of consistency or reliability characterizing the confident judgments of their judges.

Two of the judges were also given the task of deciding whether "oral," "anal," or other explanations for illness were present in the various cultures under review. This was done for each of the systems of behavior specified above—oral, anal, sexual, dependence, and aggression. The authors set forth their criteria for determining such judgments. Some of these criteria are open to question and will be discussed in the concluding section of this chapter.

It is to be noted that Whiting and Child did not make the various judgments themselves, lest their bias influence the results. An evident advantage in having judges who are unfamiliar with the hypotheses to be tested is that contamination and bias are avoided.

From their investigation the authors conclude that for every system of behavior there is evidence to support the hypothesis of negative fixation, but especially in the case of oral, dependent, and aggressive behavior; less so for anal and sexual behavior.

The authors also propound a hypothesis of positive fixation: "In any society, the greater the custom potential of initial satisfaction in any system of behavior, the greater will be the custom potential of therapeutic practices which involve the performance of responses in that system" (Whiting and Child 1953:192).

This hypothesis did not receive much confirmation. Other hypotheses were also tested with the cross-cultural data, but with inconclusive results. If this procedure constitutes verification, therefore, the main hypothesis verified in this work is the one concerning negative fixation.

In a final chapter, the authors present some conclusions to the effect that child-training practices are influenced by the "maintenance system," that is, the economic, political, and social organizations of the society. They give the following diagram, which is reminiscent of Kardiner: maintenance systems → child training practices → personality variables → projective systems (Whiting and Child 1953:310).

This brief summary of *Child Training and Personality* may seem rather arid and abstract, but in the course of the book much interesting information is revealed about ranges in lenience and severity in the child socialization practices of different societies. What adds to the interest is that modern American child-training practices are compared with those of the primitive societies. The American sample was drawn from two works by W. A. Davis and R. J. Havighurst: "Social Class and Color Differences in Child Rearing" (1946) and *Father of the Man* (1947). The representativeness of this sample may be questioned. However, Whiting and Child say that this was the best source that they could find for their purposes. The scores used in comparisons with primitive societies are relevant only to the white middle-class group in the Davis and Havighurst studies.

Some of the conclusions based on these comparisons are as follows:

1.   Oral indulgence is much more restricted in white middle-class American society than in the other societies studied. The nursing period is short and there are rigid schedules of feeding, limited in time and amount. The authors state that such an interference with free indulgence of oral satisfaction is unknown among the other societies in their sample.

2.   Anal training is much more severe in white middle-class American society than in the other societies studied, with the exception of the Tanala and the Chagga. Slightly over half of the primitive societies begin toilet training somewhere between the ages of one and a

half and two and a half. The American middle-class group is judged to start toilet training when the child is a little over six months old.

3. Concerning indulgence of the child's sexual self-stimulation, the American middle-class group was given a rating which fell just below the least indulgent of the primitive societies, "but still not extremely low on the basis of the absolute estimate of the judges" (Whiting and Child 1953:79). The American group was judged to be rather extreme in the severity with which children were punished for masturbation and was given the same rating as the most extreme of the primitive societies. However, in overall severity of sexual socialization, it fell halfway between the median and the upper extreme of the primitive societies.

This information is of value in giving Americans some perspective on their child training practices. Of course, there have been some changes in these practices in recent years, and there is evidence that the present-day American middle class tends to be more lenient in the various disciplines than was the middle class of the early 1940s.

Later in this chapter we will return to some further considerations of the Whiting and Child book. Despite the criticisms that may be made of it, it was clearly an imaginative pioneering work, which stimulated various other cross-cultural surveys along similar lines.

THE FUNCTIONS OF INITIATION RITES

Whiting, in collaboration with others, has made further investigations that make use of the cross-cultural files. One paper, written in collaboration with Richard Kluckhohn and Albert Anthony concerns the function of male initiation ceremonies. The authors set forth this hypothesis:

> Societies which have sleeping arrangements in which the mother and baby share the same bed for at least a year to the exclusion of the father and societies which have a taboo restricting the mother's sexual behavior for at least a year after childbirth will be more likely to have a ceremony of transition from boyhood to manhood than those societies where these conditions do not occur (or occur for briefer periods) (Whiting, Kluckhohn, and Anthony 1958:304).

The reasoning behind this proposition is that the mother-son sleeping arrangements must establish strong dependent relations on the part of a boy toward his mother. This may also involve attitudes of hostility toward the father, especially after the latter resumes sexual relations with his wife and displaces the son. It is necessary, with the advance of puberty, to sever the boy's emotional dependency, to remove the dangers of incest and father-son rivalry. Hence the features which are so widespread in initiation ceremonies among primitive societies—seemingly sadistic hazing of the boys, their separation from the women, and exposure to tests of endurance and genital operations.[2]

The hypothesis linking mother-son sleeping arrangements and post-partum sex taboos with the presence of initiation ceremonies was tested for 56 societies representing 45 of the 60 culture areas designated by George P. Murdock in his "World Ethnographic Sample" (1957). Of 20 societies where both the antecedent variables were found, 14 had initiation ceremonies and only 6 did not. Where both of the antecedent variables were absent, only 2 of the 25 societies had the ceremonies. There were, of course, some mixed cases, but over 80 percent of the cases corresponded with the prediction. Moreover, the authors were able to present some plausible explanations for the cases which did not jibe with their expectations.[3]

Later, Whiting (1961) made some modifications, no longer giving importance to the Oedipal rivalry posited earlier. He noted that exclusive mother-son sleeping arrangements have a high correlation with polygyny. The father usually has access to another wife or wives and thus is not apt to regard his son as much of a rival. Moreover, he does not replace his son in his wife's bed, for in more than half of the societies of this sort investigated by Whiting, the man never *sleeps* with his wife. A new formula was offered by Burton and Whiting (1961). An important result of exclusive mother-child sleeping arrangements is a boy's cross-sex identification with his mother. Such an identification cannot be allowed to persist in a society with patrilocal residence, in which males are dominant. Hence, it was predicted that in such societies there will be male initiation ceremonies at puberty to resolve this conflict and to firmly establish a masculine identification. A statistical analysis of cross-cultural data involving these variables supported the new interpretation by Burton and Whiting.

This topic has been further pursued by William N. Stephens in his book *The Oedipus Complex: Cross-Cultural Evidence* (1962). Again making use of the cross-cultural files, Stephens reports a series of correlations between certain institutions, leading to the conclusion that an Oedipus complex is intensified by a long postpartum sex taboo. This results in lasting sexual fears, castration anxiety (manifest in the extensiveness of menstrual taboos, according to Stephens), and severity of avoidance rules. In agreement with the Whiting, Kluckhohn, and Anthony study, Stephens believes that the occurrence of initiations for boys is partly determined by the intensity of father-son rivalry.

---

[2] A similar argument appears in Reik (1958) and in Badcock (1980, chap. 1.). A paper by Graber (1981) builds on Reik's argument and combines it with a cultural evolutionary approach, making the point that cultures which have both patrilocality and the state should be likely to have the custom of male genital mutilation. A statistical analysis of 250 cultures supports Graber's prediction.

[3] For a criticism of this paper and an alternative hypothesis more along the lines of the classic views of Arnold van Gennep, see Norbeck, Walker, and Cohen (1962).

Frank W. Young has proposed an alternative explanation for the occurrence of male initiation ceremonies, making use of the same cross-cultural methodology and data used by Whiting, Kluckhohn, and Anthony. His assumptions are more sociological and less psychoanalytic. Young (1962:380) claims that initiation ceremonies serve primarily to dramatize and reinforce the social solidarity of adult males. Male solidarity is particularly emphasized in what he calls "middle-level" societies, "where the variety of food exploitation patterns is limited and where the resources may be exploited by cooperative groups. Moreover, it is among such societies that intergroup hostilities conducive to male solidarity are possible."

But what about the reported association of mother-child sleeping arrangements and postpartum sex taboos with male initiation rites? Young (1962, 1965) interprets these as being common traits in polygynous societies characterized by male solidarity. Young also claims that when male social solidarity is controlled in his cross-tabulations, "no relation remains between the typology of child-care items and the presence of initiation ceremonies" (Young 1962:383).

Still another cross-cultural analysis (although not making use of the HRAF) is one by Yehudi A. Cohen, presented in two publications (1964a, 1964b). Cohen argues that while Whiting and his students have claimed that initiation ceremonies function to resolve conflict in sex identity, they have not been able to show that such a conflict actually exists.

Cohen believes that there are two stages of puberty. The first, from about 8 to 10 years of age, the "latency" period, does not have observable changes in sex characteristics as does the succeeding second stage, although biochemical hormonal changes are already occurring in the earlier stage. During the first period, it is common for people in different societies to weaken the child's ties with its family by instituting two practices. One is *extrusion*, the dislodgment of the boy from his home, so that he sleeps elsewhere, as in a men's house, dormitory, or the home of another relative. The second custom is brother-sister avoidance.

According to Cohen, initiation ceremonies usually take place during the second stage of puberty and are less drastic in their effects than the comparable experiences of the first stage. They are found in fewer societies than the customs of extrusion and brother-sister avoidance, which are also longer lasting. Cohen agrees with Young about the social functions of initiation rites in dramatizing male solidarity, and he suggests that initiation ceremonies tend to occur in societies which emphasize the importance of the wider kin group.

More complexities are presented in considering the significance of the genital operations which sometimes take place in male initiations. There are three types: circumcision, supercision, and subincision. Writers who have speculated about the underlying motives for these operations usually consider them to be equivalent. Despite their different views, both Whiting and Young see the operations as accentuating the sexual differences between males and females. Bruno Bettelheim (1954), on the other hand, sees them as making for sexual nondifferentiation, for through these operations the males want to make themselves like women, to have vulvas and to menstruate.

Charles Harrington (1968) has pointed out that Bettelheim's theory was based primarily on cases of supercision and subincision and that he then extended his interpretation to apply to circumcision as well. Harrington argues that since the effects of supercision and circumcision are quite different, they should be considered separately. Harrington's cross-cultural sample consisted of 21 societies having circumcision, 6 with supercision, and 81 with neither operation. His hypothesis is that in societies practicing circumcision at adolescence there will be a high degree of sexual differentiation in socialization practices, boys and girls being treated differently. But sexual differentiation should not be emphasized in societies which practice supercision. These predictions were supported by the statistical analysis.

From a cross-cultural survey of 111 societies, Michio Kitahara (1976) concludes that circumcision is likely to be found in societies where the son sleeps with the mother during the nursing period, while the father sleeps elsewhere. Hence his findings support a Freudian interpretation; they do not support Bettelheim's theory.

Whiting (1964) has pointed out that circumcision is more common in tropical than in temperate regions, and he has launched into wide-ranging speculations about the relationships between such factors as warm weather, people sleeping apart to stay cool, mother-child sleeping arrangements, and a long suckling period related to protein deficiency in rainy tropical areas. This chain of reasoning serves to explain why male initiation rites involving circumcision are often found in tropical regions. Here, again, Yehudi A. Cohen (1966) has offered an alternative explanation. From his point of view, the customs of extrusion, brother-sister avoidance, and initiation ceremonies at puberty are all related to kin-group solidarity, which tends to be found, although not exclusively, in horticultural and agricultural societies. Since warm climate is a precondition for such socioeconomic systems, initiation ceremonies tend to be found in warm (Cohen does not say tropical) climates.

Some cross-cultural studies by Munroe and Munroe (1971, 1973) tend to support the Burton and Whiting (1961) thesis about the functions of male initiation ceremonies, or at least they are consistent with it. Their studies concern the institution of the couvade and the incidence of male pregnancy symptoms. The *couvade* is a pattern of variable content in some societies, in which a man observes certain taboos and restrictions in relation to his wife's child-bearing cycle. He may rest before or after the birth, observe food taboos, and refrain from such actions as handling knives or sharp implements. Munroe, Munroe, and Whiting (1973) predicted that this custom would be found in association with two institutions: mother-infant sleeping arrangements and matri-residence. In such cases there should be low male salience throughout childhood, but male initiation ceremonies would not take place at puberty, as in the patrilocal societies considered by Burton and Whiting. Hence a boy's feminine identification should tend to persist. One way in which this identification could be expressed is in the custom of the couvade, in which a man acts like a pregnant woman and observes the same taboos that she does. Munroe and Munroe (1975:127) point out that couvade observances and male initiation ceremonies are seldom found in the same society. The prediction of an association between mother-infant sleeping arrangements, matri-residence, and couvade practices was supported in a survey of 74 societies (Munroe, Munroe, and Whiting 1973).

The same study included an investigation of Black Carib males, who have a large percentage of father-absent homes as well as the practice of the couvade. Also common are male "pregnancy symptoms" during the time of the wife's pregnancy, including such manifestations as vomiting, dizziness, headache, fever, and food cravings. These symptoms are especially found among men who are more highly involved in couvade practices. Although these men showed other indications of feminine identification (as in the choice of "women's words" and a preference for female roles), they adhered to a "tough male" stereotype and were rated as being brave, heavy drinkers, and gamblers, which Munroe, Munroe, and Whiting (1973:65) interpret as defensive masculinity.

While the literature of male initiation ceremonies has contained conflicting opinions, there has also been controversy about female initiation ceremonies and allied features. In his book, *Initiation Ceremonies*, Frank W. Young (1965:105–121) applies the solidarity hypothesis to girls' initiations and parenthood ceremonies, while in another crosscultural study, Judith K. Brown (1963) concludes that female initiation rites occur in societies in which the girl does not leave her parents' home after marriage. Since the girl remains in the same social setting, such a ceremony serves to give notice of her changed status to adulthood. No such ceremony is performed in societies where girls leave home upon marriage, since the mere act of leaving home marks this change. Brown also notes that female initiation rites are found in societies in which women make a notable contribution to subsistence.

Societies differ greatly in the attention given to first menstruation and subsequent menstrual periods, sometimes having such practices as secluding girls in separate huts and having them observe various taboos. William N. Stephens (1961) finds the origin of such customs in male castration anxiety, evidenced in a roundabout way in certain cultural institutions. Frank W. Young and Albert Bacdayan (1965), on the other hand, find menstrual taboos to be associated with male dominance and social rigidity, thus offering a sociogenic as opposed to Stephens' psychogenic explanation.

OTHER CORRELATIONAL STUDIES

Landauer and Whiting (1964, 1981) conclude from a cross-cultural survey that in societies where infants are exposed to such practices as piercing of nose, lips, or ears, stretching of arms or legs, exposure to extreme heat or cold, abrasions, massage, or painful swaddling, there is an increase in adult male stature, when compared with societies that do not have such practices. The stress should occur before the age of two to have an effect on growth. Early vaccination and mother-infant separation are held to have the same consequences. The authors point to experiments in the stimulation of infant rats and mice, which show a more rapid rate of development than do nonstimulated unstressed rats and mice, suggesting that early exposure to stress has stimulating effects on the endocrine system and growth.

Yehudi A. Cohen (1966) suggests an alternative explanation for the correlations found by Landauer and Whiting, hypothesizing that infants and children subjected to stress will eat more as a way of coping with anxiety, thus gaining in stature. Landauer and Whiting (1981:359) state that this possibility cannot be rejected entirely. "In one sense, such a hypothesis is not a denial that stress causes an increase in growth but simply a guess as to its mechanism."

On the subject of food, or food sharing, Cohen (1961b) has produced another cross-cultural study, arguing that societies in which young children are generously fed on demand will also have practices of food sharing among adults. This article is paired with a cross-cultural study of friendship, both making use of the same sample of 65 societies. In the second study, Cohen (1961c) finds different forms of friendship to predominate in differently structured types of societies.

Dorrian Apple Sweetser (1966:304) has examined the kinds of social situations in which avoidance relationships occur and argues that

> men will avoid their parents-in-law when unilineal affiliation is an important basis on which social relationships are organized, and yet residential family groups are fragmented and impermanent. Their wives will avoid their parents-in-law under the same conditions and when also the mother's brother has no special role to play; they tend not to avoid when such a special role exists.

In his avoidance behavior the person is saying, in effect, "I am affiliated with these people by marriage, not by blood. . . ." He also shows by such behavior that he is not disposed to sexual relations and thus respects the principle of family authority.

The foregoing survey of cross-cultural studies by no means exhausts the list. There are many more correlational studies which relate to culture-and-personality problems, but enough examples have now been given to illustrate the possibilities of the method.

ADVANTAGES AND DRAWBACKS

We may now discuss some of the advantages and drawbacks of the cross-cultural survey method. It must be said that the proponents of this method are quite aware of the criticisms that have been made of it; indeed, some of the best discussions of its difficulties appear in their works (Whiting 1954; Campbell 1961).

First among the advantages of the cross-cultural correlational study is that this method encourages the formulation of hypotheses and the attempt to test them. Another advantage of the cross-cultural correlational method is that it permits a cumulative building on previous studies. The only question is how successfully hypotheses are tested in this way. We have seen that different solutions to a problem were presented by Whiting et al. and by Frank W. Young on the basis of the same data. Correlations do not speak for themselves. When one tries to present a causal explanation, various alternatives are possible. The mere appearance of a correlation, moreover, does not necessarily prove anything, even when it is in the predicted direction. If two items are associated in a number of different cultures, this may be due to a number of different causes. We need not assume that the same complex of factors led to the association in each case.

Morris Cohen (1942:16) once wrote:

> correlations are often mere coincidences that do not indicate any significant connection, or any reason for expecting such correlation to continue. I have on several occasions referred to the high correlation of 87 percent for 13 years between the death-rate in the State of Hyderabad and the membership in the International (American) Machinists Union. If there are not many instances of this sort, it is because we do not, as a rule, look for them. . . . verification involves not only confirmation but the exclusion or disproof of alternative hypotheses.

This is one aspect of the problem. But there are other difficulties inherent in the cross-cultural survey method. One of its disadvantages is that there are so many steps in the procedure at which error can enter: (1) on the part of the ethnographer reporting a piece of behavior, (2) on the part of the judge who has to classify or evaluate this behavior, and (3) on the part of the writer who makes an interpretation based on the judge's rating.

At step number 2, in the classification or rating of behavior, errors are easily possible. Norbeck, Walker, and Cohen (1962:481) point out that in a discussion of the length of postpartum sex taboos in *Patterns of Sexual Behavior,* Clellan S. Ford and Frank A. Beach classify as short (from six weeks to ten months) four societies that Whiting classifies as long (over one year).

A more confused case is Arnold R. Pilling's criticism of Beatrice Whiting's analysis of Paiute sorcery. While noting that an anthropologist may misclassify his data before applying statistical methods and thus make the statistical operation meaningless, Pilling charged that Beatrice Whiting made some errors in classifying societies as having coordinate or superordinate control. The Paiute, Aranda, Trobrianders, and Zuñi were, according to him, wrongly classified. But in this case Whiting has been supported by M. M. Bax and A. J. F. Köbben. In a check on Whiting's classifications, Bax concluded that her judgments were, after all, correct (Köbben 1967:6). Such disagreements, however, make one doubtful about the procedures involved. And this is only one stage at which mistakes in judgment may be made.

Another difficulty is that the authors of cross-cultural studies sometimes have to find an indirect index for something they want to measure. The amount of inhibited aggression in a society cannot be measured directly. Horton therefore takes sorcery as an index of it; societies are rated as having either strong or weak belief in sorcery, and this is supposed to indicate which societies have much or little inhibited aggression. Murdock and Horton have both used premarital sexual freedom as an indirect measure of sexual anxiety. That is to say, they assume that societies which permit premarital sexual behavior have less sexual anxiety than those which restrict or taboo such behavior (Horton 1943:275–76). But while this seems reasonable enough, the case of Truk shows that premarital sexual freedom may be associated with considerable sexual anxiety.

In an interesting and almost convincing cross-cultural survey on the genesis of narcissistic personality, Slater and Slater (1965:241) frankly state the tenuous basis for their study: "(a) it treats cross-cultural correlations as essentially identical with cross-individual correlations; (b) it allows a structural pattern to serve operationally for an interpersonal process; and (c) it argues for causation, albeit of a circular kind, on the grounds of correlation alone." The authors add that these limitations are typical of cross-cultural studies having to do with socialization or personality.

To get indexes of negative fixation as expressed in beliefs about illness, Whiting and Child had judges determine whether "oral," "anal," or other explanations for illness were present in the cultures under review. Criteria were established to determine the necessary judgments, but the adequacy of some of these criteria may be questioned. For example, under "Oral Explanations" we find: "Verbal spells and incantations performed by other people are the material responsible for illness. This was selected as the one item which indicated concern about specifically oral activity in other people." But under "Anal Explanations" we find: "The use of charms, curses, spells or incantations in ritual is responsible for illness" (Whiting and Child 1953·150–51).

How is a conscientious judge to decide whether to label a spell oral or anal under these conditions? For both items the authors have psychoanalytic explanations. A verbal spell is related to the mouth-hence oral. A spell is related to compulsiveness, to ritual, and this "is a common outgrowth of severe toilet training" (Whiting and Child 1953:151); so it is anal. Here, incidentally, the authors use psychoanalytic criteria in the process of testing some psychoanalytic hypotheses. Whether this is justifiable or not, it is certainly an involved procedure. Indeed, the complexity of the Whiting and Child demonstration sometimes takes on the dimensions of a Rube Goldberg machine.

Many of the cross-cultural studies have to do with the influence of early childhood experiences. The earlier studies suffered from the fact that there were not many careful descriptions of child training and children's behavior in the ethnographic literature. When Whiting and Child report that their study is based on data from 75 societies, that sounds impressive, but for many of these societies little information is available on the relevant topics. The authors tell us that the material given to a judge for rating varied from about one printed page to several hundred (Whiting and Child 1953:49).

In the appendix the authors give the "confident" ratings for their 75 societies, omitting those classed as "doubtful." A review of these columns gives some idea of what the data are like. The following societies have either a high or full complement of confident ratings: Alor, Arapesh, Balinese, Chagga, Chiricahua, Dahomey, Hopi, Lepcha, Lesu, Manus, Marquesans, Navaho, Ontong-Javanese, Papago, Samoans, Siriono, Tanala, Tenino, Teton, Western Apache, and Wogeo. For these societies, then, good information about childhood seems to be available. But the following societies have fewer than 6 confident ratings out of 17: Abipone, Chewa, Jivaro, Kazak, Kiwai, Lapp, Omaha, Palaung, Riffians, Taos, Tiv, Wapisiana, Warrau, Yukaghir, Yungar, Zuñi. Of these societies the Kazak received no confident ratings at all, the Riffians only one, and the Zuñi two. If the conclusions of the Whiting and Child book are based mainly on the confident ratings, these conclusions are drawn from a relatively small number of societies.

As more ethnographic work of good quality is done, and as the files improve, these problems will become less serious. Meanwhile there is the question of the reliability or completeness of data in the HRAF sources.

A common criticism of cross-cultural surveys is that the method involves pulling items of behavior out of context and forcing them into pigeonholes for purposes of quantification. One may sometimes question the degree of identity of institutions and patterns of behavior in different cultures which are classified together.

Another point often made about cross-cultural studies is that the influence of diffusion tends to be ignored. Each society is counted as a separate entity. Both the Hopi and Zuñi are listed by Whiting and Child, although they share the same general cultural tradition. In statistical assessments these societies should probably count as one, not two. But what about the Papago and the Navaho, who are also listed? These societies have been influenced by Pueblo culture and are not sealed off cultural islands.

The problem of diffusion was raised by Francis Galton at the meeting of the Royal Anthropological Institute in 1889, when Edward B. Tylor presented the first cross-cultural survey, suggesting relationships between particular descent systems and kin avoidance practices. Avoidance relationships may have developed independently at many times and places, but they may also diffuse from one society to another. Harold E. Driver has, in fact, shown that this must have been the case in aboriginal North America. On the basis of a detailed survey, Driver (1966:148) remarked, "one can predict whether an unspecified society will have kin avoidance from knowledge of its culture area and language family membership with greater accuracy than from knowledge of its residence, descent, or kinship terminology. Geographical-historical factors are more powerful than these functional ones." The problem is how to control for diffusion in correlational cross-cultural studies. Various attempts have been made to cope with this difficulty.

Beatrice Whiting retested her hypothesis of the relationship between sorcery and coordinate control with a smaller number of societies (26) which she held to be distinct. This second test revealed significant correlations, as did the first. Whiting and Child retested their hypothesis of negative fixation separately for each of five major culture areas of the world: (1) Africa, including Madagascar, (2) Asia, including Japan, the Andaman Islands, and Lapland, (3) North America, (4) South America, (5) Oceania, including Australia, Indonesia, the Philippines, and Pacific islands. They found their hypothesis confirmed in these separate tests. The authors argue that this indicates "that the association between child training practices and explanations of illness is not simply spread by joint diffusion but is dependent upon some more or less universal functional relationship between them which creates the association anew within sets of societies living in any single region of the world" (Whiting and Child 1953:187).

Raoul Naroll has been active in suggesting various techniques for solving "Galton's problem," to control for diffusion (Naroll 1961,

1964; Naroll and D'Andrade 1963). He has also been concerned with the related problem of defining the cultural units to be used in cross-cultural comparisons. What are we to compare—communities, tribes, nations, linguistic groups? Naroll (1964:286) coined a new term for his proposed unit: the *cultunit*, which he defined as "a group of territorially contiguous people who not only are domestic speakers of mutually intelligible dialects but also belong to the same state or contact group." Naroll objected to the use of the local community as a unit in cross-cultural research. Whiting, Young, and Murdock however, all consider the local community to be the most appropriate unit for such investigations (Whiting 1968:968).

George P. Murdock and Douglas White (1969) have proposed a standard sample of well-described cultures to be used in cross-cultural studies. Each society is pinpointed to a specific date and locality. This becomes a necessary precaution when communities change in the course of time and are described by ethnographers at different periods. Formerly, each scholar who made cross-cultural studies chose his own particular sample of societies, and there was usually little overlap between samples. Murdock and White believe that there is need for a large world sample which could henceforth be used in many different studies, so that the results of each study may be intercorrelated with others. Hence the proposed standard sample, which includes 186 societies, divided as follows: 28 from Sub-Saharan Africa; 28 from the Circum-Mediterranean area; 34 from Eastern Eurasia; 31 from the Insular Pacific; 33 from North America; and 32 from South and Central America. In addition some past civilizations are included: Babylonia at the end of Hammurabi's reign; the Hebrews at the time of the Code of Deuteronomy; and the Romans of the early imperial period. Not all of these cultures are now represented in the HRAF files, which included 120 of the societies, or 64 percent, at the time of Murdock and White's publication. It seems likely that many future studies will make use of the proposed standard sample.

CONCLUDING COMMENTS

The kind of research described in this chapter is very different from most of the studies dealt with in preceding chapters. Malinowski, for example, made an intensive investigation of a single culture, trying to see it in all its complexity and to learn how its interrelated institutions impinge on the members of the society. Malinowski's effort to "get inside the native's skin" and to see the world as a Trobriander sees it has been called an "emic" approach to the study of culture, in contrast to an "etic" approach, which Marvin Harris (1968:575) has defined as follows; "Etic statements depend upon phenomenal distinctions judged appropriate by the community of scientific observers."

Like Malinowski, Franz Boas and many of his students had an emic approach. Marian W. Smith (1959:58) wrote that "Boas conceived of his main task as the adoption of an informant's mode of thought while retaining full use of his own critical faculties."

From Boas's point of view broad cross-cultural comparisons of institutions run into the difficulty that culture elements classified under the same rubric by an anthropologist might not be the same from the viewpoints of the peoples concerned. "If we choose to apply our classification to alien cultures we may combine forms that do not belong together. The very rigidity of definition may lead to a misunderstanding of the essential problems involved . . ." (Boas 1943:314).

The term *idiographic* is applied to the detailed study and understanding of a particular, unique entity, such as the personality of a particular individual, in contrast to the term *nomothetic*, which refers to the search for general laws or principles, such as generalizations that would apply to all personalities. Boas's approach to culture was idiographic and relativistic, in contrast to the nomothetic and etic approach of Whiting, Murdock, and others who make studies using the Human Relations Area Files.

While Boas's reservations should be kept in mind, it seems to me that there need be no essential conflict between emic and etic approaches; we can learn from both approaches, and they may supplement one another. Moreover, what is learned from the intensive study of a single culture may be further investigated in cross-cultural surveys. For example, Cora Du Bois described child-rearing in Alor and ascribed to typical Alorese childhood experiences the characteristics of Alorese personality discussed in Chapter 6. As we have seen, D. N. Shack suggested that food deprivation could account for some of these traits, often found in societies with poor nutrition, while Ronald P. Rohner argued that parental neglect was the more significant determinant. In a cross-cultural survey Rohner found that his own hypothesis received support, while Shack's did not. In the chapter that follows we will see that a generalization about concern with "toughness" among lower middle-class males in our own society has been considered in the light of cross-cultural survey data. There are bound to be more extensions of this sort, checking on generalizations arrived at in one society through cross-cultural survey studies of others. The first example of a cross-cultural survey in this chapter, Beatrice B. Whiting's study of Paiute sorcery, followed this pattern.

Despite the criticisms that have been made here and elsewhere, cross-cultural surveys do seem to have been a stimulating addition to the field of culture-and-personality. They serve as a useful supplement to the intensive study of particular cultures. Moreover, the hypotheses put forward in these studies will give fieldworkers a host of issues to check on in future field researches.

SUGGESTIONS FOR FURTHER READING

There is a comprehensive bibliography on cross-cultural research in Timothy J. O'Leary, "A Preliminary Bibliography of Cross-Cultural Studies," *Behavior Science Notes* 4 (1969), pp. 95–115. See also the massive compilation in Robert B. Textor, *A Cross-cultural Summary* (New Haven, Conn.: HRAF, 1967). A review of what has been learned from cross-cultural studies is provided by Raoul Naroll. "What Have We Learned from Cross-Cultural Surveys?" *American Anthropologist* 72 (1970), pp. 1227–88. See also John W. M. Whiting, "Methods and Problems in Cross-cultural Research," in *Handbook of Social Psychology*, 2d ed., ed. Gardner Lindzey and Elliot Aronson. (Reading, Mass.: Addison-Wesley, 1968), vol. 2, pp. 693–728.

For a review of some work in this field, emphasizing socialization, see Charles Harrington and John W. M. Whiting, "Socialization Process and Personality," in *Psychological Anthropology*, ed. Francis L. K. Hsu (Cambridge, Mass.: Schenkman, 1972), pp. 469–507.

A few outstanding works which make use of this method deserve mention here, although they do not deal mainly with culture-and-personality problems.

George Peter Murdock's *Social Structure* (New York: Macmillan, 1949) bears the influence of Albert G. Keller's sociology, the anthropological approach of Franz Boas, behavioristic psychology, and psychoanalysis. It applies statistical analyses to data on social organization in 250 societies. Chapter 10, which presents an analysis of incest taboos and their extensions, is the section of the book most nearly related to culture-and-personality research. Otherwise the book is not primarily concerned with culture-and-personality but, as the title suggests, with social structure; hence it has not been dealt with here. Another study making use of the HRAF files is Guy E. Swanson's *The Birth of the Gods. The Origin of Primitive Beliefs* (Ann Arbor, Mich.: University of Michigan Press, 1960). Again, this work touches only peripherally on the field of culture-and-personality. It is a cross-cultural study of religious beliefs in 50 societies. Such beliefs as monotheism, polytheism, reincarnation, and witchcraft are explored by seeing how they are correlated with certain institutions in these societies. To give two examples: (1) there is a correlation between monotheistic beliefs and societies having the most stable sources of food, namely grain agriculture with settled residence; (2) societies with social classes are significantly more likely than others to possess a belief in superior gods.

Another work peripherally related to culture-and-personality is George C. Homans and David M. Schneider, *Marriage, Authority, and Final Causes: A Study of Cross-Cousin Marriage* (Glencoe, Ill.: Free Press, 1955).

There have been some cross-cultural studies of suicide and homicide, including: Herbert H. Krauss and Beatrice J. Krauss, "Cross-Cultural Study of the Thwarting-disorientation Theory of Suicide," *Journal of Abnormal Psychology* 73 (1968), pp. 353–57; and Herbert H. Krauss, "Social Development and Suicide," *Journal of Cross-Cultural Psychology* 1 (1970), pp. 159–67; and David Lester, "Suicide, Homicide, and the Effects of Socialization," *Journal of Personality and Social Psychology* 5 (1967), pp. 466–68. See also Raoul Naroll, "Cultural Determinants and the Concept of the Sick Society," in *Changing*

Perspectives in Mental Illness, ed. Robert B. Edgerton and Stanley C. Plog (New York: Holt, Rinehart & Winston, 1969), pp. 128–55; and Stuart Palmer, "Murder and Suicide in Forty Nonliterate Societies," *Journal of Criminal Law, Criminology and Police Science* 56 (1965), pp. 320–24.

For a cross-cultural study of crime, see Margaret K. Bacon, Irvin L. Child, and Herbert Barry III, "A Cross-cultural Study of Correlates of Crime," *Journal of Abnormal and Social Psychology* 66 (1963), pp. 241–300.

On the subject of romantic love, see Paul C. Rosenblatt, "A Cross-cultural Study of Child Rearing and Romantic Love," *Journal of Personality and Social Psychology* 4 (1966), pp. 336–38; and "Marital Residence and the Functions of Romantic Love," *Ethnology* 6 (1967), pp. 471–79. See also Robert M. Coppinger and Paul C. Rosenblatt, "Romantic Love and Subsistence Dependence of Spouses," *Southwestern Journal of Anthropology* 24 (1968), pp. 310–19.

There are various studies which seek to relate patterns of early child training to concepts of the supernatural, attempting to find some cross-cultural statistical validation for the idea that religions are projective systems. One is "A Cross-Cultural Study of Some Supernatural Beliefs," by Melford E. Spiro and Roy G. D'Andrade, *American Anthropologist* 60 (1958), pp. 456–66. A second is W. W. Lambert, Leigh Triandis, and Margery Wolf, "Some Correlates of Beliefs in the Malevolence and Benevolence of Supernatural Beings: A Cross-Societal Study," *Journal of Abnormal and Social Psychology* 58 (1959), pp. 162–68. A third is another study by John W. M. Whiting entitled "Sorcery, Sin, and the Superego: A Cross-Cultural Study of Some Mechanisms of Social Control," in *Nebraska Symposium on Motivation,* ed. Marshall R. Jones, (Lincoln: University of Nebraska Press, 1959). Each of these studies in one way or another, tends to find confirmation for the projection hypothesis.

8

The Six Cultures Project

An important outgrowth of the work of John W. M. Whiting and his associates was the Six Cultures Project. Whiting recognized that there were deficiencies in the Whiting and Child volume, *Child Training and Personality*, discussed in the previous chapter. The ethnographic data available in the Yale files in 1953 had often been collected by anthropologists who were not particularly interested in child-rearing and reported on such matters only incidentally. The coverage of many aspects of childhood experience was not sufficient.

Several conferences were held among scholars from Cornell, Harvard, and Yale in 1953 and 1954 to plan a more extensive and intensive study of child-rearing in a few different societies. One product of these efforts was a handbook for fieldworkers written by Whiting and his associates, entitled *Field Guide for a Study of Socialization* (1966).

In 1954 and 1955, six field research teams made use of the field guide. Each team chose a community of between 50 and 100 families which became their unit of study. Special attention was given to 24 mothers in each society who had children between the ages of 3 and 10. These mothers were interviewed on a standard schedule, and their interaction with their children was systematically observed. It had been decided to rely on behavioral observation and interviews rather than use projective tests, although some Child Thematic Apperception Tests were given. In observation and interviewing, particular attention was given to nine behavioral systems: succorance, nurturance, self-reliance, achievement, responsibility, obedience, dominance, sociability, and aggression. Each research team spent between 6 and 14 months in the field. Efforts were made toward comparability of data, and the reports were drawn up along similar lines. Part 1 of each report, called The Ethnographic Background, starts off with a description of the local environment, village plan, house types, basic economy, social organization, family type, religion, recreation, and other aspects of the adult world into which the child is born and to which it must adjust. Part 2, called Child Training, deals with pregnancy and childbirth, infancy, weaning, and early and late childhood.

These reports were published together first in one volume, *Six Cultures. Studies of Child Rearing*, edited by Beatrice B. Whiting (1963), and later, along with Whiting's *Field Guide*, in a series of seven separate volumes. A later study, applying factorial analyses to the interviews with mothers in these reports, was *Mothers of Six Cultures. Antecedents of Child Rearing* by Leigh Minturn and William Lambert (1964). The last volume in the Six Cultures series is *Children of Six Cultures: A Psychocultural Analysis* by Beatrice B. Whiting and John W. M. Whiting (1975). This work presents some general findings based on observation of children's behavior. Before considering their conclusions, let us review some of the data in these studies.

THE GUSII

The Gusii of Nyansongo, East Africa, differ from the other societies in having polygynous marriage as an important institution. Mother-child households and mother-child sleeping arrangements occur, since the husband rotates in visiting the houses of his different wives. This should lead to what William N. Stephens has called "diluted marriage," in which husband and wife are not emotionally close to one another. There may also be coolness between husband and wife due to the fact that a Gusii man was apt to take a wife from a clan with which his own clan has been at war. They have a proverb, "Those whom we marry are those whom we fight." Considerable hostility is shown to a Gusii bride at her wedding by the groom's relatives, who shout insults at her. We are told that Gusii girls feel very ambivalent about the prospect of marriage. (Residence is patrilocal.) The stage would thus seem to be set for emotional distance between husband and wife, which would be accentuated by quarrels between co-wives. There is a special Gusii word which means "hatred between co-wives."

The Gusii are unusual in having a kind of avoidance relationship between father and son. Father and son should not bathe together, see each other naked, or discuss sexual matters in one another's presence. A father must never enter the house of a married son. A son is expected to be obedient and deferential toward his father, who tends to be feared in childhood.

In addition to avoidance behavior between father and son, there is also some avoidance between a mother and her adult son, who may not go behind the partition in her house but is served food in the foyer or outside. Feelings of sexual shame are strongest of all between father and daughter. Avoidance rules are extended to classificatory fathers but are less stringent.

Although no formal postpartum sex taboo is reported, most of the other elements cited by Stephens as fostering an Oedipus complex seem to be present among the Gusii. On the basis of cross-cultural studies, Stephens (1962:13) claims that peoples with a "diluted marriage complex" are unusually phobic and taboo-ridden, particularly about matters involving sex. Severity of avoidance relations would be related to this syndrome, which fits the Gusii case well. It is also in keeping with the theories of Whiting and Stephens that male (and also female) initiation ceremonies involving genital operations take place at puberty. However, one point does not jibe with Stephens' generalizations. There is no fear of menstrual blood among the Gusii, which would be expected by Stephens as an outcome of presumed male castration anxiety.

Despite the "diluted marriage complex," Gusii mothers do not seem to pour out their emotional feelings on their sons, as one might expect. The LeVines report that it is rare to see a mother kissing, cuddling, or hugging a child, although this may be done by grandmothers, child nurses, or other caretakers. Nevertheless, it is to the mother rather than someone else that a frightened child runs for comfort. The LeVines describe the Nyansongo child emerging from infancy as being fearful and dependent.

Weaning, which often occurs at around the 19th month, is described as being very upsetting to the child, and this may be aggravated by the birth of a younger sibling, leading to temper tantrums. Fear is an important sanction in controlling children's behavior, including threats and warnings of bogeymen. Caning and other physical punishments are used. There seems to be no severity in toilet training, but attitudes toward sex are strict. Masturbation is strongly disapproved of, and children are beaten for it.

Among adults, sex seems to be associated with tension. A bride is expected to put up a fierce resistance to her husband's first sexual advances, while it is a matter for boasting on his part as to how many times he has been able to have intercourse the first night. An explicit purpose in this is to hurt the bride, so that the man can make her cry or have difficulty in walking the next day. These attitudes are not limited to the first night but continue to be important in later marital relations.

It is striking that the Gusii have a remarkably high rate of rape and also a fairly high rate of homicide. Drinking beer, a leading form of recreation for the men, often leads to quarreling and aggression. The Gusii are also outstanding for their litigiousness and readiness to accuse others of offenses (LeVine and LeVine 1966).

More information about the Gusii is available in *Mothers and Wives. Gusii Women of East Africa* by Sarah LeVine (1979), which contains biographical and interview material on seven Gusii mothers. Some recurrent themes in these life histories are complaints about absent, often shiftless husbands who do not support their wives, bad relations with in-laws, including the mother-in-law, and (often related to the latter) fears of witchcraft and sorcery.

THE RAJPUTS OF KHALAPUR

Khalapur, about 90 miles north of Delhi, seems to be a typical north Indian village, in which the Rajputs are the dominant landowning caste. Although they are very different in culture and historical traditions, the following similarities may be noted between the Rajputs and the Gusii: both are agriculturists with military traditions; both have patrilineal descent, patrilocal residence, and live in joint family households; both have mother-child sleeping arrangements, with the Rajputs also having a postpartum sex taboo. Both have long suckling periods. If the Rajput sacred thread ceremony may be so considered, both have initiation ceremonies for boys. Both have some respect-avoidance relationships, especially affecting father-in-law and daughter-in-law. Both have ancestor cults.

As for differences, the Rajputs do not have polygyny or genital operations at puberty. Their marriages are arranged, whereas Gusii can choose their own mates. Gusii mothers, more than Rajput mothers, punish their children for aggression against themselves. In *Mothers of Six Cultures*, they were rated as highest of the six cultures on this item. Rajput children were not reported to be upset by weaning as were the Gusii children. They have fewer chores to perform than Gusii children and were rated lowest of the six cultures in this respect. Girls in particular are given little work to do, for they are regarded as "guests" in their homes, which they must leave after marriage.

The Rajput and Mixtecan mothers were rated the least warm among the six samples.

Two important institutions in Khalapur are the caste system and the custom of purdah, or segregation of women. Both institutions serve to maintain social distance. Purdah, in particular, keeps women confined to their courtyards. A woman pulls her sari across her face in the presence of her husband or older men. She must always show respect to her mother-in-law, father-in-law, and other members of her husband's family. A man and his wife should not talk to one another in the presence of older members of his family. Minturn and Hitchcock say that since the mother-in-law is always around, and since the young wife cannot leave the courtyard, the only time they can whisper together is at night. But husband and wife do not sleep together. Men sleep in a separate men's house, sometimes visiting their wives briefly for sexual relations.

Men and women also eat separately. A woman takes her food to her own room or a corner of the courtyard. There is no family meal. Children are fed when they ask for food.

The confined life of the courtyard leads to occasional flaring up of temper among the women, quarrels, and sometimes divisions of the joint family. The Rajputs of Khalapur are described as being suspicious and mistrustful of the motives of other persons.[1]

A concern on the part of male Rajputs is to preserve their semen, which is thought to lead to vitality and spiritual strength. Sexual intercourse is therefore seen as weakening.[2]

A surprising aspect of Rajput childhood in Khalapur is the reported rarity of sibling rivalry. Minturn and Hitchcock explain this partly by noting that adults are not very affectionate with children, and infants are not given special attention, cuddled, or played with. Older children do not feel excluded or displaced. There are also many other older persons in a joint family household who can replace the mother in looking after a child. Temper tantrums seldom occur.

The explanations offered for the absence of sibling rivalry do not seem adequate. If the mother does not give much love, one might expect the child to be demanding for the little love available and to compete for it. Some writers about childhood believe sibling rivalry to be an inevitable development. If so, its apparent absence must be due to suppression or repression, which in turn might lead to psychosomatic complaints like skin rashes and asthma, or to nightmares, bedwetting, and feelings of anxiety, but we cannot say whether or not these are present in Khalapur.

In many ways the culture of Khalapur is similar to that of Silwa, Egypt, discussed in Chapter 2. In both of these peasant communities there is sexual segregation, purdahlike behavior among the women, and an emphasis on deference toward older persons. One difference is the encouragement of sibling rivalry in Silwa and its apparently successful discouragement in Khalapur.

In Khalapur, we seem to have another case of "diluted marriage." Marriages are arranged. Men and women eat and sleep separately. But development of an Oedipus complex may be inhibited by the fact that the Rajput mother, like the Gusii mother, does not demonstrate much affection and does not cuddle or play with her children much. The child-training process would seem to foster passive, dependent tendencies, which would be in keeping with joint family household life, arranged marriages, and the fact that occupation and clientele are largely determined by birth in a particular caste (Minturn and Hitchcock 1966).

---

[1] This is also reported by G. Morris Carstairs in *The Twice-Born. A Study of a Community of High-Caste Hindus* (1958:39–62). The community he describes is a Rajput-dominated town in Rajasthan, North India.

[2] This topic, briefly mentioned by Minturn and Hitchcock, is discussed at greater length in Carstairs, *The Twice-Born*.

TAIRA, OKINAWA

It was noted in Chapter 2 that in peasant communities, such as Silwa, Khalapur, and Tepoztlán, there is often a good deal of mutual suspicion and mistrust. Although Taira is a peasant community, it seems to be more cooperative and characterized by friendlier interpersonal relations than the communities just mentioned. People seem to be quite willing to work for other families in a rotation system, which appears to function effectively. Formal cooperatives have been successfully introduced. There are also mutual finance groups formed to extend credit for building construction, buying livestock, or other purposes. Taira seems to be relatively egalitarian. There is no caste system like that of Khalapur, nor any marked separation of the sexes as in both Khalapur and Silwa. Taira seems to be more progressive and modern in spirit than these other peasant communities. There is much more emphasis on education, much better schooling, and the involvement of parents in a PTA. Women have relatively high status. Some women are priestesses in the local religious cult. Although there are a few cases of polygyny, most marriages are monogamous. Courtship occurs, but there are more arranged marriages. One rather surprising item is that in a high percentage of marriages the wife is older than her husband. Few women marry before the age of 20. There is no postpartum sex taboo, and sexual intercourse is resumed after birth. Husband, wife, and child sleep together; so there is no evidence of diluted marriage, and there is no exclusive mother-child sleeping arrangement.

The Taira mothers were rated highest of the six cultures on "warmth." They were also rated less hostile than any other group. Children are indulged in Taira and are considered to be not responsible until six years of age. Since a child is carried about most of the time during its first two years or so, there is no crawling stage for children. There is a belief that the habit of crying is formed in the first four months of life; therefore, a child is comforted, cuddled, and nursed until he stops crying. The early period of indulgence is gradually withdrawn by the mother as she returns to the work of gathering firewood in the mountains, which keeps her away from home most of the day. The period after weaning is very frustrating for the child. It is then looked after by child caretakers who are less indulgent than the mother. Although mothers are indulgent, they have some severe punishments, particularly the application of moxa, burning powder on the skin. A child's hands and feet may also be tied as a punishment. Striking, slapping, and pinching are also used. However, these are all relatively rare, and praise and other positive sanctions are often used. Mothers are the main socializers. Fathers do not spend much time with their children, being gone most of the day, at work in the fields or hills.

A child is held to become responsible and teachable at seven. Children who die before this age are given unceremonious burials, but they have adult funerals after seven. This is the time of entrance into first grade at school, and also the time of assuming various chores, such as caring for younger children, cooking, cleaning, and bringing water. According to the Maretzkis (1966), Taira children are often eager to assume such new responsibilities. Four- and five-year-olds ask if they may carry younger siblings. Such nurturant behavior is encouraged by the custom of children carrying dolls on their backs.

In contrast to the Gusii and Rajputs, there are no avoidance relationships, and there is nothing like purdah. There is no initiation ceremony, as among the Gusii, unless admission to the first grade be so considered. There are no genital operations. There seem to be no avoidance customs relating to menstruation. In these respects Stephens' generalizations seem to be supported, since the people of Taira have no postpartum sex taboo or mother-child sleeping arrangements, and they do not seem to have "diluted" marriages.

Despite the period of frustration after weaning and birth of a younger sibling, children are not aggressive toward younger siblings but are quite nurturant. There does not seem to be much sibling rivalry. Grandmothers may make up for some of the frustration the children suffer from their mothers' frequent absence from the home when they are at work. There seems to be some general tension between boys and girls during the latency period while they are attending school. Boys tease and bully girls, and there is sexual segregation, which often occurs at this age in societies in different parts of the world.

Children have a lot of independent play, with much freedom to roam about the village. They usually play in groups of more than two; solitary play is discouraged. The people of Taira seem to be sociable and hard working but able to enjoy themselves in their free time. Although the community is relatively isolated, they are quite progressive in their adoption of new patterns and involvement in self-government and community responsibilities (Maretzki and Maretzki 1966).

THE MIXTECAN INDIANS OF JUXTLAHUACA, MEXICO

The Mixtecan community is a subgroup within a larger community. While the Rajputs are a dominant caste in Khalapur, the Mixtecans of Santo Domingo barrio form a sort of lower caste group looked down on by the people of the main part of town. Between the Mixtecan Indians and the townspeople there are differences in speech and dress and in food habits. They are divided by a geographical barrier, a *barranca* (ravine), between the barrio and el Centro, the center of town. Hostility is shown to the Mixtecans by townsfolk. Indian children go to school there, but the town children may throw stones at them and insult them. The Mixtecan children have been trained not to fight back. The authors say that this cleavage serves to emphasize barrio solidarity. Indeed, there is much cooperative behavior within the barrio. There is very little ingroup aggression even under intoxication, in contrast to the Gusii; and there is no fear of sorcery *within* the barrio.

Like the Rajputs, people live in compounds in extended family groups, such as two brothers and their families. Residence is patrilocal. But there are some differences from the Rajputs in the direction of more independence for the nuclear family. Each nuclear family has separate sleeping quarters and cooking facilities and eats apart from the others. The food used by a particular woman is kept separate from that of all other women in the compound. Unlike Khalapur, the community is endogamous. Unlike the situation in India, there is no head of the extended family. Adult males still in the prime of life have more or less equal status, and an older brother does not have authority over the younger. Cousins are equated with siblings, the same kinship terms being used for both. Cousins may act as caretakers as often as siblings. The same sort of behavior is shown toward cousins as toward siblings; no special distinctions are made. But a child gets food from its parents and sleeps in their house; and a child's father and mother are closer than its uncles and aunts. However, a father does not usually interact much with his children except for boys aged 12 and over who work with him in the fields. The mother spends most of her time with her youngest child and oldest daughter. She attends the nursing child and gives instruction to the oldest daughter. The authors say that neither men nor women play much with children. Between infancy and young adulthood the children spend their days apart from adults. A child sleeps with its mother in infancy. Weaning, initiated abruptly at age one or two, marks the end of the time when a child is carried in a shawl. It is now turned over to caretakers. From this point on the child has considerable separation from the mother. Before about two years of age children are considered to be "senseless," but after that become "children who know." (There is a much longer period in Okinawa for the time when a child is held to be without understanding.) At six or seven children are held to be teachable. Before that they are given few chores; they work more thereafter.

In *Mothers of Six Cultures,* the Mixtecan mothers were rated among the least warm, along with the Rajput mothers, who were rated still lower on the scale. The mothers rank fifth in the amount of time they spend with children. The Mixtecan mothers demand a good deal of work from their children, but they seldom praise them for work well done.

In *Mothers of Six Cultures*, Minturn and Lambert suggest a reason for the low ratings of Mixtecan mothers on maternal warmth. As in Khalapur, a woman lives in a compound shared with her husband's brothers' wives. Adult ties are more intimate than in Khalapur, however, for Juxtlahuaca is an endogamous community, and most mothers are related to their sisters-in-law by blood as well as by marriage. Those who favor their own children over their cousins would risk disrupting family ties. It would, therefore, be bad for a mother to take sides with her own children in disputes. "Treating all children with some emotional distance and strongly discouraging fights among the children are highly functional socialization practices in this type of community" (Minturn and Lambert 1964:207). The Mixtecan mothers were rated highest on punishment for aggression against peers. Since the adults themselves are unaggressive, the children have peaceful models with whom to identify. They are seldom beaten by their parents. The Romneys (1966) did not once see a parent strike a child.

Play groups in both early and late childhood are usually composed exclusively of closely related children. Unlike the situation in Okinawa, where mothers want their children to play with others, the Mixtecan mothers want their children to play alone—mainly to avoid getting into fights. This training against aggression seems to work. Although men drink a great deal at fiestas, they seldom fight. Children even avoided giving aggressive themes in Thematic Apperception Test stories. The Mixtecans think that anger and aggression may cause sickness or even death.

After the age of 12, boys work in the fields and assume adult tasks. School education is a recent development; not much emphasis is placed on it by parents. Many children do not go to school, or skip attendance. Discipline at school is described as being almost chaotic. There is little stress on achievement motivation, which might conflict with the barrio solidarity which the people value so highly (Romney and Romney 1966).

ILOCOS BARRIO, TARONG, PHILIPPINES

In *Mothers of Six Cultures*, the Tarong mothers were rated second in maternal warmth after the mothers of Okinawa and last in emotional instability. Like the Mixtecan mothers, the mothers of Tarong rate high in the proportion of time in which a nonparental adult takes care of the children. The Philippine mothers do not live in extended family compounds as the Mixtecans do; they have nuclear family households. But the homes that compose a *sitio* are crowded close together. Siblings, cousins, and other close relatives may live close by. Women seem very willing to look after other women's children. Minturn and Lambert (1964:212) write: "More than most mothers they tend to rear their children as a group. . . . Women sometimes nurse each other's children, a custom seldom found in other groups." Another woman is asked to suckle a child before its mother's milk comes.

The Tarong mother does not have to leave her home for work or marketing, as the Okinawan or Mixtecan mother must do. For the first month or so after childbirth, the mother and child are confined to the house, resting on a special, inclined bed, where the mother is supposed to undergo therapeutic "roasting" for two or three weeks, together with massage. The closeness between mother and child continues after the first month. The child sleeps between the parents until the next child is born, perhaps when he is two or three years old. The general picture is one of great indulgence and nurturance. There is some teasing of children, however. Grownups pretend that they are going to take away something the child values. When the child cries, the onlookers laugh. This kidding seems to be in line with the shaming techniques which help to bring about obedient, submissive personalities in this culture.

There is a long suckling period, although supplementary foods are given from four months on. Weaning takes place between one and four years of age. Two or two and a half is considered to be the ideal age. There is no preparation for this event, and weaning is abrupt and apparently quite traumatic for the child, who may throw temper tantrums. These are dealt with leniently by the parents, since they recognize that this is a difficult period, but later displays of anger or aggression are punished. If a child has been displaced by a younger one, it is said that its hostility is not directed toward the younger sibling but toward the mother. Lightening the blow of weaning is the fact that there are usually several substitute caretakers available who will show an interest in the child and look after it. Also the child has a new autonomy to replace the former relative lack of freedom. He becomes part of a children's group; play seems seldom to be solitary.

A mother need not worry about her child's straying from home; for all grownups in the community have a sense of responsibility for the children. While this gives a child security, it also means that it may be disciplined by any adult, not only the parents.

Training in responsibility begins early. Children of three are given chores to perform. By five, boys and girls carry water, feed stove fires, and help look after the baby. Older children run errands and learn to cook—boys as well as girls. Assignment of tasks by sex is not as rigid as in some other cultures. Children are praised if they undertake work associated with a higher age level.

One sanction in inducing good behavior is scaring techniques. Children are frightened by being told about evil spirits and other dangerous creatures. One bogeyman is a witchlike creature impersonated once or twice a year by a woman dressed up in a black cloak.

As seen by the people of Tarong, the world is divided into what is close, familiar, and trustworthy and what is foreign, uncertain, and dangerous. Quarrels within the *sitio* are kept under control, and efforts are made to smooth them over and forget about them. Interbarrio quarrels are more long-lasting. Outsiders and strangers may be feared and suspected of sorcery.

Children grow up playing mainly with siblings, cousins, and close relatives. By the age of eight or nine, they usually have a best friend of the same sex from whom they are inseparable.

School education is fairly recent, having begun only about 40 years ago, but education is valued. Almost all children attend the Tarong school for the first four years. Those who can afford it try to have their children graduate from sixth grade, and some go even further in education. Friendships at school seem to remain within *sitio* lines. The close friendships of the *sitio* group make possible the continued functioning of the men's cooperative work-exchange groups, an important aspect of the local community (Nydegger and Nydegger 1966).

ORCHARD TOWN, NEW ENGLAND

Orchard Town is a New England town with a population of about 5,000, in which the families are predominantly members of a Baptist church group. The men are salaried or self-employed wage earners. In *Mothers of Six Cultures* the mothers of Orchard Town were rated intermediate in maternal "warmth," ranking fourth in a group of high-ranking societies including the Okinawa, Philippine, and Gusii samples. They rank last with regard to physical punishment of children. The New England mothers have very little help in caring for their children. "They are significantly higher than any other group on the proportion of time they are in charge of babies . . . and, with the African mothers, higher than other groups on the proportion of time they care for older children . . ." (Minturn and Lambert 1964:191–92).

Orchard Town families are nuclear, usually with neolocal residence apart from the parents or relatives of either mate. Older children are all in school. This takes them away from home, leaving the mother alone with the preschool children. The husband is usually away at work during the day, but he often helps to look after children; 79 percent sometimes look after babies; 96 percent sometimes care for older children, a much higher proportion than in any other sample.

Persons other than the parents seldom look after children. Paid babysitters are a unique institution in this society, with no real equivalent in the other five societies. Older siblings do not look after young infants very much. Almost all the responsibility is thus in the hands of the mother. A "lack of clarity of norms, distrust of other people's judgment, and great concern that children be raised well, leads some mothers to avoid other caretakers even when they are available" (Minturn and Lambert 1964:193).

Most of the Orchard Town mothers seem to take their children's upbringing very seriously and want to do a good job at it, although some mothers feel their children to be burdens that prevent their self-fulfillment along other lines.

Although the mothers are attentive to their children's needs, they do not want to spoil them and may let a child cry if he or she seems to be crying only for attention. "Crying it out" is also thought to be good exercise for the lungs and may help to build character.

Sleeping arrangements involve more separation from the mother than in the other societies. An infant sleeps in a crib of its own for a year or more. If space is available, it may be placed in a separate room. Most preschool children sleep in a room having two beds.

Infants may be fed by bottle or breast. Ten out of the 24 Orchard Town sample children were nursed for a time by their mothers, for a period ranging from a few days to five months. The suckling period is thus shorter than in most societies.

Orchard Town infants are not swaddled or put on cradleboards and so their mobility is not restricted as in some other societies; but they are dressed more than children in the other five cultures, most of which are in tropical countries. Separate kinds of clothing, pyjamas and nightgowns, are worn at night.

Children learn few chores in this community, although they have to pick up their toys, which are more numerous than in the other societies. In some of the other societies children are taught to gather wood or carry water, none of which is required in Orchard Town, which has inside plumbing and central heating. They do not have to care for farm animals or help in the fields. Older children are seldom required to look after younger siblings, since they are not considered sufficiently responsible for that until they are around 12 years of age, but by that time they are busy with school attendance, club or scout meetings, and other activities (Fischer and Fischer 1966).

Obedience training is not strict. In *Mothers of Six Cultures* the Orchard Town mothers were ranked fifth in consistency obedience training and expectation of prompt obedience. They ranked lower than any other sample on consistency of rules about peer-directed aggression and higher than any other for reward for retaliation. In other words, children are not strongly dissuaded from fighting and may be praised for defending themselves against attack. Minturn and Lambert explain this in terms of the isolated family households in Orchard Town, in contrast to the compound dwellings in the Rajput and Mixtecan families, where related families live together and strongly punish peer-directed aggression.

SOME INTERPRETATIONS

Some interesting speculations about the six cultures data have been presented by Beatrice B. Whiting. She makes use of the data to explore a hypothesis of Walter D. Miller's about lower-class American males' concern with "toughness," especially among street gangs. Miller (1958:270) points out that "a significant proportion of lower-class males are reared in a predominantly female household and lack a consistently present male figure with whom to identify and from whom to learn essential components of a 'male' role. Since women serve as a primary object of identification during preadolescent years, the almost obsessive lower-class concern with 'masculinity' probably resembles a type of compulsive reaction-formation."

Whiting points to a cross-cultural survey of correlates of crime made by Margaret K. Bacon, Irvin L. Child, and Herbert Barry, III (1963), in which it was shown that both thefts and personal crimes, such as assault, rape, suicide, sorcery, and murder, are more common in societies having polygynous families and mother-child households than in societies with monogamous nuclear households. Whiting does not mention Stephens' concept of "diluted marriage," but she has the same assumptions about the relatively weak role of the father in polygynous societies with mother-child households. She refers to the papers by John W. M. Whiting and his associates on the relationship of this complex to male initiations at puberty, designed to break the mother-son bond and counteract the boy's cross-sex identity. As was noted in the previous chapter, some such ritual or its equivalent was held to be needed in a society in which the father plays a weak role in relation to the child during early childhood but in which males are more dominant and important than women in adult life. Feminine identification for a boy need not be a problem in a society in which men and women have roughly equal status. In such a case, there should be no need for masculine protest.

Turning to the Six Cultures data, Whiting (1965) notes that there is much more assault, homicide, and litigation reported for the Gusii and the Rajputs of Khalapur than for the other four societies. These are the two societies with the most diluted marriage, in which the husbands neither regularly sleep with nor eat with their wives. Nor do they work together with them. In Taira, Tarong, Juxtlahuaca, and Orchard Town, on the other hand, there are family meals, the father is home more often, and there is more shared activity, both in work and recreation, between men and women. Of the six cultures, then, it is in Nyansongo and Khalapur that we would expect to find "protest masculinity" and physical violence, in keeping with Miller's hypothesis and the cross-cultural findings of Bacon, Child, and Barry.[3]

This is a stimulating paper, but, as usual, other interpretations of the same data are possible. In contrast to the other four societies, the Gusii and Rajputs share traditions of cattle raiding and fighting, traditions which have their own momentum, with no necessary relationship to diluted marriage. One might expect to find violence and homicide in a society which emphasizes military virtues and masculine pride.

We are also brought back to the problem of which units are to be compared in cross-cultural comparisons. Following the recommendations of John W. M. Whiting, Murdock, and Young, the practice in Beatrice B. Whiting's paper has been to compare and contrast local communities. But Orchard Town is not an isolated social unit. It is part of a larger society in which there is a great deal of violence and homicide.

In *Children of Six Cultures* (1975) the Whitings' analysis is based on the observation of children's behavior made by the ethnographic teams in the six cultures. The methods employed in these behavioral observations are described in Chapter 12. The behavior that was observed and recorded involved social interaction, not solitary behavior, and generally covered a five-minute period for each sample of observation. The behavioral data were mailed to Cambridge, where they were coded according to 12 categories: *acts sociably, symbolic aggression, offers help, reprimands, offers support, seeks dominance, seeks help, seeks attention, suggests responsibly, assaults sociably, touches, assaults.*

When the material was quantified, the Whitings found that the children of Nyansongo, Juxtlahuaca, and Tarong were on the average more nurturant and responsible than dependent and dominant, while the reverse was true of the children from Taira, Khalapur, and Orchard Town. Children of the first three communities *offer support* significantly more and *seek help* and *seek dominance* significantly less than the children in the second group of three. It was decided that a significant factor in differentiating these two clusters of societies is degree of cultural complexity. Nyansongo, Tarong, and Juxtlahuaca are all characterized by subsistence farming, with little economic specialization and settlements composed mainly of dwellings, while Taira, Khalapur, and Orchard Town have more division of labor, some class or caste stratification, a centralized political and legal system, and communities containing specialized buildings of various sorts. Orchard Town and Khalapur also have an organized priesthood.

It seems reasonable to conclude that in the simpler cultures, children's contributions to the family work load are valued, and children

---

[3] Some support for the views of Miller and Whiting is provided in Charles C. Harrington's *Errors in Sex-Role Behavior in Teen-Age Boys* (1970).

are trained to be helpful and responsible. Chores such as bringing firewood and water, housecleaning, taking care of animals, farm work, running errands, carrying things, and looking after younger siblings are more often required of children in the simpler cultures than in the more complex cultures, and these chores are assumed at an earlier age than chores are assumed in the more complex cultures. The daily performance of such tasks, which represent real contributions, must give the child feelings of worth, responsibility, competence, and concern with the family welfare.

The tasks assigned to children in the more complex cultures may seem more arbitrary to the child, less self-evidently contributory to the welfare of the family or of the child himself. At the same time, school education plays a more prominent role in the more complex cultures and emphasizes individual achievement and egoism rather than concern for others. In the more complex cultures, children have to be trained for specialized roles for which they may have to compete. In this context, a stress on *seeking attention* and *seeking dominance* is understandable.

Punishment for disobedience or nonfulfillment of tasks was judged to be much more severe in the simpler than in the more complex cultures. Robert A. LeVine (1970) has suggested that the severe aggression training found in folk and peasant societies may be part of a general tendency to make children orderly, obedient, and pacific. The contrasts between the simpler and more complex cultures are also in keeping with the findings of John W. M. Whiting et al. in the Rimrock study discussed in Chapter 10 concerning the greater emphasis on individualism and need for achievement among the Texans than among the Zuñi. There seems to be an evolutionary progression from simpler to more complex cultures, reminiscent of the change described by David Riesman from tradition-direction to inner-direction discussed in Chapter 20.

The foregoing contrast between the simpler and more complex cultures was based on what the Whitings term *Dimension A:* nurturant-responsible versus dependent-dominant behavior. They also scored children's behavior for *Dimension B:* sociable-intimate versus authoritarian-aggressive behavior, based on such actions as *acts sociably, assaults sociably,* and *touches* on the one hand, and *reprimands* and *assaults* on the other. "Grouped by Dimension B, the children of Juxtlahuaca, Tarong, and Orchard Town were on the average more sociable-intimate and less authoritarian-aggressive than those of Taira, Khalapur, and Nyansongo" (Whiting and Whiting 1975:175). Here we have a different grouping. In this case the factors favoring a sociable-intimate tendency were nuclear household composition and flexible residence rules, with husband and wife usually eating and sleeping together. Such a household requires a less authoritarian disposition by the household head than does a patrilocal extended family, in which the head man must exercise authority over adult sons and their families. Children identify with and model their behavior after the adults in both types of families.

Despite the differences noted in the six cultures, the Whitings also found some uniformities according to age and sex. Generally, in the three-to-five age period, boys engage in more horseplay and rough-and-tumble play than girls, while girls seek help and touch others more often. At later age levels, nurturant behavior increases among girls but not among boys. Between 7 and 11, children tend to be bossy and self-righteous in all the cultures.

Despite the virtues of this careful study, the conclusions in the Whiting and Whiting volume do not seem to tell us much that was not already known about children. Perhaps more might have been extracted from the six studies if projective tests had been used. In their desire to be rigorously scientific, the researchers rejected such tests. As will be seen later in Chapter 15, various objections have been made by both psychologists and anthropologists to the use of the Rorschach Test and Thematic Apperception Test in non-Western cultures; these criticisms were apparently decisive in the Six Cultures project. The use of doll play was also rejected on the grounds that children do not play with dolls in all cultures. Besides, conclusions based on such sources are highly inferential. Hence, apart from the interviews with mothers, the observation of children's behavior became the main source of information. Moreover, solitary behavior was not observed, since it is hard to interpret, and better agreement has been obtained in the observations of different recorders when a child is interacting with others. The researchers do not seem to have considered drawings as a possible source of information, and yet, as will be seen later in Chapter 16, drawings often provide rich insights into children's values and attitudes. To depend so heavily on behavioral observation and questionnaires in the analysis of the six cultures seems unduly self-limiting. No use of films was made in this study. In view of the expense, that can hardly be raised as a criticism, but it does highlight the value of the earlier use of films by Bateson and Mead in their work in Bali.[4]

Despite the foregoing criticisms, the Six Cultures project remains an impressive accomplishment. The individual ethnographic reports of the six cultures are among the best studies in the field of culture-and-personality, and since Whiting's *Field Guide* has been used by other ethnologists in organizing their fieldwork,[5] more comparable accounts have now been added to the original six.

---

[4] John Hitchcock made a film of Khalapur, *North Indian Village* (International Film Bureau, color, 32 minutes); but this is a general "ethnographic" film about the community in general, the caste system, joint family household, purdah, and so on, and does not focus on mother-child relationships in particular, as the Bateson-Mead films do.

[5] Some titles are mentioned in the "Suggestions for Further Reading."

SUGGESTIONS FOR FURTHER READING

A work which made use of Whiting's *Field Guide* and is thus comparable to the reports described in this chapter is Thomas Rhys Williams, *A Borneo Childhood: Enculturation in Dusun Society* (New York: Holt, Rinehart & Winston, 1969).

Robert A. LeVine has published several articles on the Gusii. One which deserves mention is "Gusii Sex Offenses. A Study in Social Control," *American Anthropologist* 61 (1959), pp. 965–90.

The work by Carstairs cited in this chapter makes good supplementary reading to the Minturn and Hitchcock report on the Rajputs. It contains some interesting life history material and Rorschach data.

A suggested reading in connection with the report on the Mixtecans is John Gillin, *The Culture of Security in San Carlos*, Middle American Research Institute, Tulane University of Louisiana, Publication no. 16, 1951. Gillin distinguishes between the ethos of the dominant and aggressive Ladino "caste" and the submissive Indian "caste" in a Guatemalan community. The nonaggressive Indians he describes are reminiscent of the Mixtecans in Juxtlahuaca.

A picture of Philippine life somewhat similar to that of the Nydeggers is Ethel Nurge's *Life in a Leyte Village* (Seattle: University of Washington Press, 1965). Nurge made use of the same *Field Guide* that was used by the investigators in the Six Cultures project. Another description of Philippine childhood is available in F. Landa Jocano, *Growing Up in a Philippine Barrio* (New York: Holt, Rinehart & Winston, 1969). There is a review of Philippine culture-and-personality studies by Robert Lawless, "The Foundation of Culture-and-Personality Research in the Philippines," *Asian Studies* 5 (1967), pp. 101–36. The author gives a bibliography of 128 items. In general, he takes a dim view of Philippine culture-and-personality studies, which he says have been characterized by "inadequate methodology, unreliable operations, and unjustifiable conclusions" (p. 128). Lawless cites the Nydegger and Nurge studies and says that "this is probably some of the best writing on Philippine culture-and-personality, and certainly the best on child rearing" (p. 112). But he doubts that their findings can be generalized for the Philippine rural population, or that generalizations can be made about the "lowland Filipino," since there are so many regional differences in the Philippines. For a different view, see George M. Guthrie and Pepita Jimenez Jacobs, *Child Rearing and Personality Development in the Philippines* (University Park, Pa.: Pennsylvania State University Press, 1966).

9

Cross-Cultural Studies of Cognition

The study of cognition involves the investigation of processes of thinking, learning, remembering, and organizing information. Anthropologists have traditionally tended to support the notion of the "psychic unity of mankind" and to assume that ways of thinking are basically the same for both "primitive" and "civilized" human beings in different cultures. That, at least, was Franz Boas's view. In *The Mind of Primitive Man* (1911), Boas attacked racist views that stigmatized "primitive" mentality as inferior. He argued that one cannot draw conclusions about thought processes from the traditional beliefs held by the people; process and content should be distinguished. At the same time, anthropologists believe that biological and cultural evolution have taken place. Our distant ancestors are thought to have been small-brained australopithecines who probably did not have a language. The minds of those early beings were surely different from those of modern humans. Some authorities (Lieberman, Crelin, and Klatt 1972) have even argued that the large-brained Neanderthals of late Pleistocene times had a deficient use of language. Somewhere along the way human beings became more rational than they had formerly been. Lévy-Bruhl (1926) contrasted the prelogical reasoning of primitive peoples with the logicality of modern Europeans, and more recently Lévi-Strauss (1966:269) has contrasted the more concrete, magical and mythical thought of neolithic times with the more abstract and scientific thought of modern times (Goody 1977:7).

Apart from this long-range evolutionary perspective, recent testing programs have shown that performance on various cognitive tasks has been marked by a great deal of variability from one culture to another. The problem is to account for such variations.

The cross-cultural study of cognition has seen considerable expansion in the past 20 years or so. The *Journal of Cross-Cultural Psychology* was first published in 1970. Another journal dealing with the same general field is *International Journal of Psychology*. As the titles of these journals suggest, this is a field in which most of the contributions have been made by psychologists, although anthropologists have also been involved.

Before turning to the work of the psychologists, let us first consider the early Sapir-Whorf hypothesis about the relationship between language and thought. After that we will deal with more recent issues, such as the facilitation of recall by semantic organization, the question of the universality of Piagetian stages in cognitive development, the possible effects of environment on perception, and the contrasting cognitive styles of field dependence and field independence in relation to culture and ecology.

THE SAPIR-WHORF HYPOTHESIS

A leading figure in the early days of culture-and-personality research was Edward Sapir (1884–1939), a linguist and ethnologist to whom, according to Clyde Kluckhohn (1944:601) "more than to any other single person must be traced the growth of psychiatric thinking in anthropology." Sapir was in some respects a configurationist interested in the ways in which peoples' thought and behavior are patterned by language and culture. (He once wrote to Ruth Benedict that Spengler's *Decline of the West* struck him as "needlessly long and muddle-headed in places but fundamentally sound") (Mead 1959:185).

Sapir argued that every language structures the world in a particular way for its speakers. Thus, to learn an unfamiliar language is to enter a new realm of thought. "No two languages are ever sufficiently similar to be considered as representing the same social reality. The worlds in which different societies live are distinct worlds, not merely the same world with different labels attached" (Mandelbaum 1949:162). We have here a relativistic view that is similar to Benedict's view of culture. David Aberle (1960) has suggested that Sapir and Benedict followed a linguistic model in their writings about culture, and saw cultures as having some of the same characteristics as languages—being selective (choosing "a small number of actualizations from a large number of possibilities"); exemplifying patterning, some of which is unconscious; representing unique configurations; undergoing changes through "drift"; being functionally equivalent, neither "superior" nor "inferior" to others; and being shared by the members of a given community. A language, like the larger culture of a society, shapes its perception of the world.

Benjamin Lee Whorf, who has done more than anyone else to develop Sapir's line of thought along these lines, gave further examples of such patterning. Perhaps because of his training in the physical sciences and his broad interests in philosophy, Whorf particularly focused on conceptions of space and time implicit in different linguistic systems. From this point of view he contrasted Hopi and what he called SAE—"Standard Average European"—languages, Whorf claimed, for example, that the Hopi language contains "no words, grammatical forms, constructions, or expressions that refer directly to what we call 'time,' or to past, present, or future, or to enduring or lasting, or to motion as kinematic rather than dynamic . . ." (Carroll 1956:57).

The study of Hopi and other languages illuminated for Whorf some of the assumptions implicit in SAE languages.

> In our language, that is SAE, plurality and cardinal numbers are applied in two ways: to real plurals and imaginary plurals. . . . We say "ten men" and also "ten days." Ten men either are or could be objectively perceived. . . . But "ten days" cannot be objectively experienced. . . . Concepts of time lose contact with the subjective experience of "becoming later" and are objectified as counted QUANTITIES, especially as lengths, made up of units as a length can be visibly marked off into inches. A "length of time" is envisioned as a row of similar units like a row of bottles (Carroll 1956:139–40; Whorf's capitalization).

This facet of European languages is seen to have all sorts of far-reaching consequences. Here Whorf's writing takes on a Spenglerian tone. Our way of thinking about time, he tells us, has been influenced by our system of writing. Through the give-and-take between language and the total culture we get such developments as record-keeping, diaries, accounting, mathematics, a concern with exact sequences, dating, calendars, clocks, and an interest in archaeology and history (Carroll 1956:153).

It may be noted that many of the above features have appeared in complex civilizations speaking non-SAE languages, such as that of China. The significance of language in their etiology is thus not clear. However, just as Whorf traces some of the consequences of SAE languages for European cultural development, so he points to a relationship between Hopi linguistic and cultural behavior, for instance in "preparing" activities among the Hopi, for whom repetition represents the storing up of "an invisible charge that holds over to later events" (Carroll 1956:151). It is in these terms that Whorf considers such features of Hopi behavior as willing or praying and the repetitive steps of ceremonial dances.[1]

Whorf's essays are difficult and technical, and because of their specialized nature are hard to evaluate. Indeed, when one has read them, one wonders whether, after all, Hopi and Western conceptions of space and time can really be so different. Just because we call a ship "she" does not mean that we actually think of the ship as being feminine. Languages are not always so tyrannical, nor is grammar

---

[1] A somewhat similar approach to the study of Navajo language and culture appears in Gary Witherspoon's *Language and Art in the Navajo Universe* (1977).

necessarily an "invisible 'thought control' in our philosophical prison," as La Barre (1954:200) has put it. Evidence of this lies in the fact that communication is, after all, possible, though often difficult, across language barriers. While the diffusion of culture patterns may be slowed up by difficulties in communication, it need not be blocked thereby—as witness the worldwide spread of modern technology since the industrial revolution.

Moreover, as Hoijer (1954:102–104) has pointed out, peoples very similar in the rest of their culture sometimes speak languages that are wholly unrelated, while closely related languages are often spoken by peoples whose cultures are otherwise very different. For example, the Hopi and the Hopi-Tewa (pueblo of Hano) have lived together on First Mesa since about 1700 and share the same general Puebloan culture, but they belong to different language stocks. The Hupa and Navaho speak closely related Athapaskan languages, but otherwise their cultures are quite different. The same applies to the Hopi and the Southern Paiute, who are both Shoshonean speaking. This does not, of course, invalidate the Sapir-Whorf hypothesis. The latter may eventually prove to be very useful in the field of culture-and-person-ality, but at present this is only a potentiality. We still need to know more about how different languages structure the nature of interpersonal relationships and the general world view of their speakers. On the other hand, John B. Carroll and Joseph B. Casagrande (1958) have devised some experimental methods for exploring this field, which indicate that languages help to structure perception somewhat differently in different linguistic groups.

The term *forced observation* has been used for some characteristics of language that direct attention to particular aspects of reality. The fact that English has separate words for orange and yellow may facilitate our perception of differences in these colors. The Zuñi language does not distinguish between these colors but has one word which includes both. Roger Brown and Eric H. Lenneberg (1954) report on an experiment in which color tests involving discrimination between orange and yellow were given to monolingual Zuñi-speaking subjects, monolingual English-speaking subjects, and bilingual Zuñi who spoke both Zuñi and English. The monolingual Zuñi frequently confused orange and yellow in the stimulus set; the English-speaking subjects never did, while the bilingual Zuñi fell in between the two monolingual groups in the frequency of errors.

This implies a relativistic view of color perception. In contrast, Brent Berlin and Paul Kay have made a study which offers a challenge to a relativistic view. In a study of color naming in 98 languages from a number of unrelated language families, Berlin and Kay conclude:

> although different languages encode in their vocabularies different *numbers* of basic color categories, a total universal inventory of exactly eleven basic color categories exists from which the eleven or fewer basic

color terms of any given language are always drawn. The eleven basic color categories are *white, black, red, green, yellow, blue, brown, purple, pink, orange, and grey* (Berlin and Kay 1969:2).

The analysis of language can be a useful key to some features of the world view of a particular people, as suggested by Ruth Benedict's discussion of Japanese terms for the sense of obligation (see above, p. 52). But some authors have questioned the value of cognitive studies which involve formal semantic analysis. Robbins Burling (1964:27) asks: "when an anthropologist undertakes a semantic analysis, is he discovering some 'psychological reality' which speakers are presumed to have or is he simply working out a set of rules which somehow take account of the observed phenomena?" Is the anthropologist really getting at the cognitive system of the speakers of that language? Burling is skeptical about that.

As Oswald Werner (1970:157) has pointed out, a single language such as English or Chinese is capable of expressing a great variety of world views. Moreover, some aspects of a world view may be found in many societies without any necessary relationship to language. If, for example, patterns reoccur in peasant societies which conduce to the formation of a particular set of values and attitudes, this may have no necessary relationship to the languages spoken in those societies. The world views associated with Buddhism, Christianity, Islam, and modern science have influenced societies with different languages in many parts of the world, even though these views may have been locally modified in the process of absorption. These considerations would seem to limit the directive influence which language may have on cognition.

COGNITIVE TESTING AMONG THE KPELLE AND THE INFLUENCE OF LITERACY

As a graduate student in psychology, Michael Cole went to Liberia on a project to improve the mathematics education of tribal children. He worked among the Kpelle, who are mainly rice farmers. Liberian tribal children have difficulty learning Western-style mathematics. Moreover, both children and adults find it almost impossible to perform a sorting operation which is quite easy for American 12-year-olds. In this test a subject is given eight cards on which are pictured red or green triangles or squares, two or five on a card. The subject must sort them into groups, first one way, then another way, and then a third. This can be done according to shape, color, and number (Gay and Cole 1967:1, 38–39). Although Kpelle subjects found this very difficult, the adults did much better than a control group of

American Peace Corps trainees in estimating quantities of rice, a meaningful task related to Kpelle experience.

In Liberia, Cole and his colleagues set up an experiment in the recall of items. A list of objects was read to a subject who was then required to repeat as many of the items as possible. Kpelle children tended to do poorly on this memory test, when compared with American school children. Success in this task has been shown to involve an ability to organize items into clusters; "apple," "pear," and "orange" can be remembered better if classified together as fruit. When this test was given to American students, the latter used more semantic clustering of this sort than did the Kpelle subjects. But clustering became general among Kpelle students who had had more than four to six years of schooling. Clustering and rapid learning distinguished the high school students from nonliterates. Evidently, school education, at least in some cases, has something to do with the development of this kind of mental organization.

Cole and his colleagues found that they could encourage clustering by associating items to be remembered with particular external objects. An item was held over a chair with which the object was said to "belong." Thus, file, knife, hammer, and cutlass were associated with one chair; tie, trousers, shirt, and cap with another. This system considerably improved the rate of recall. The main conclusion of Cole et al. (1971:233) is that "cultural differences in cognition reside more in the situations to which particular cognitive processes are applied than in the existence of a process in one cultural group and its absence in another."

This study raises the question of the influence of literacy, printing, and formal education on cognition, a topic pursued by Goody (1977), who argues that writing makes it possible to put statements in a more or less permanent form and to compare contrasting statements, which facilitates criticism, skepticism, logic, and rationality. "the formalization of propositions, abstracted from the flow of speech and given letters (or numbers), leads to the syllogism. Symbolic logic and algebra, let alone the calculus, are inconceivable without the prior existence of writing" (p. 44).

Among the products of writing are tables, lists, and formulas, which facilitate the making of abstractions and generalizations. Much of the early Mesopotamian writing consisted of lists of goods and personnel made for the practical bureaucratic purposes of taxation and redistribution. But there are also Sumerian and Egyptian lists of classes of objects, such as animals and trees, which seem to have had no immediate practical purpose, although they may have figured in school exercises. In making such lists, problems of classification arise. (Is a tomato a fruit or a vegetable?) This, argues Goody (1977:105) "may be essential to the advance of systematic knowledge about the classification and evolution of natural species. And it is the kind of question generated by written lists." In the same way, the clustering used in the recall of items by school students would be encouraged by their literacy.

A number of studies in different areas have shown that schoolchildren, in classification tests, were "more likely to categorize by form or function as opposed to color. . . . were able to reclassify and array in a new way. . . . and were more adept at verbalizing the principles behind their categories . . ." (Nerlove and Snipper 1981:445).

An interesting question arises as to whether the reported differences in peformance between schoolchildren and nonschooled children could have been due to selective sampling. Perhaps those children were sent to school who showed more promise of academic success, or perhaps they came from more ambitious families or families who cared more about their children. In these cases the later observed differences between the schooled and nonschooled children might be due more to the differences in family background or to the preschool differences between the two groups of children than to the influence of schooling itself. This question was studied in an investigation of nearly 300 rural children in Guatemala *before they entered school*, with the following results: "Level of performance on nearly all the tasks in the Preschool Battery was higher for children who later attended school; nearly half the differences were statistically significant. Moreover, the children who attended school also lived in homes of better quality and received more frequent parental teaching before they entered school than did children whose parents kept them at home" (Stevenson 1982:210–11). However, in a study of nearly 1100 children in Peru, Stevenson and his colleagues found that there was an advantage in the schooling experience itself: "we conclude that the effects found in earlier studies indicating the influence of schooling on cognitive development cannot be solely accounted for by selective sampling. Children who go to school do not attain their higher scores on cognitive tasks simply because important environmental variables differentiate these children from those who are kept at home" (p. 224).

Another point to be considered is that, apart from the formal matter learned at school, there is the *hidden curriculum* which may also aid in children's performance in testing situations: "namely, the repeated practice in dealing with unfamiliar adults, in being presented with a variety of puzzles and problems, and being expected to persevere in solving them" (Nerlove and Snipper 1981:446).

On the other hand, tests carried out on cognitive abilities concerning conservation (see the following section) found no differences between schooled and nonschooled Tanzanian children, and some other reviews of Piagetian testing similarly found little association between schooling and performance on cognition (Price-Williams 1981:414).

PIAGETIAN STAGES OF DEVELOPMENT: CONCRETE OPERATIONS

One of the issues in cross-cultural psychological research has been whether the stages of cognitive development distinguished by Jean Piaget are universal. Piaget specified certain accomplishments which are made in the sensorimotor stage during the first two years of life. For example, *object permanency* concerns the child's ability to find a hidden object, showing a conviction of its continuing existence, although it is out of sight. Several researchers studying African babies have found that the structural properties and sequences within the sensorimotor stage are identical in both African and European babies (Dasen 1977:156–65).

A good deal of work has been done cross-culturally at the later stage of concrete operations.[2] One test of concrete operations involves the sorting of objects according to different properties, such as color and shape. We just saw, in the preceding section, that such a task is usually easy for American 12-year-olds but often difficult for Kpelle adults, although Kpelle adults did better than American adults at estimating quantities of rice.

One aspect of concrete operations is the concept of *conservation:* when water is poured from a tall, thin glass jar or beaker into a low, wide one, the amount of water remains the same, although its level is lower. Preschool children assume that there is more water in the tall, thin beaker. Conservation may also be shown with clay; when a compact wad of clay is rolled out into a long, thin strip, the amount of clay remains the same despite the differences in shape. European and American children generally acquire an understanding of conservation during the latency period. But testing in other cultural settings has shown great variability. Only about half of unschooled rural Wolof children tested in Senegal had achieved conservation by 11 to 13 years of age, although virtually all the schoolchildren had achieved it (Greenfield 1966), and only a small percentage of Australian aborigines had mastered conservation tasks by ages 14 to 15 (Dasen 1972). Western-type schooling and urban life have been suggested as factors which facilitate conservation and other aspects of concrete operations.

However, as we have seen, there are conflicting reports about the influence of school education in this respect (Price-Williams 1981:414). Thomas Weisner (1976:230) has reviewed studies dealing with the influence of urban life on cognition in different parts of Africa, Mexico, and elsewhere:

> Urban children in these studies were less influenced by the experimental "set" and were more flexible than rural children in the use of multi-

[2] See page 30 in the discussion of latency.

ple responses to expectations presumed in the test situation. . . . City residence seems to make children and adults less compliant, more "savvy," and perhaps more talkative in test situations, and hence more likely to display multiple classification criteria, to alter initial perceptual cues into more "abstract" ones, and generally to act in ways likely to be successful in many experimental settings.

Price-Williams, Gordon, and Ramirez (1969) tested for conservation among two groups of Mexican children, one of children from pottery-making families and one of children of similar age, social class, and education who did not make pottery. The authors predicted that the pottery-making children, through their experience with clay, would do better on tests of conservation than the control group, and their expectation was confirmed. This experiment suggests that we need to know, for a particular group being tested, what kinds of experience are common in everyday life. Such information may explain why the subjects score well on some cognitive tests and poorly on others.

ENVIRONMENT AND PERCEPTION

Do people who live in flat, treeless plains develop different habits of perception than inhabitants of dense tropical jungles? Do city dwellers, accustomed to rectangular rooms, see things somewhat differently than do African natives who live in round houses? The possibility that such differences do occur has been shown by experiments with geometric designs such as the Müller-Lyer figure (see Figure 2).

FIGURE 2
The Müller-Lyer Illusion

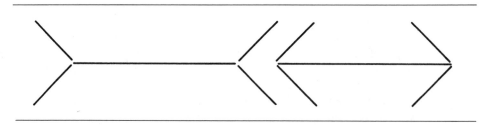

The Müller-Lyer illusion is that the horizontal line to the left in the figure looks longer than the one on the right but is actually shorter.

Around the turn of the century, the British anthropologist W. H. R. Rivers showed the Müller-Lyer figure and also a horizontal-vertical figure to Papuan natives of Murray Island and later to Todas of the Nilgiri Hills in South India. He found that both groups were less susceptible to the Müller-Lyer illusion than were his English subjects, but they proved to be more susceptible to the horizontal-vertical illusion. Rivers' findings are thus said to be bidirectional; the two non-

Western groups were more subject to one illusion, less subject to the other.

Rivers' experiments were done with rather small samples of subjects. A more recent large-scale cross-cultural investigation of the same problem involved showing a series of geometrical figures, including those used by Rivers, to 1,878 persons in 14 non-European areas and in the United States. This work was done over a six-year period by a team of anthropologists and psychologists. The bulk of the non-Europeans tested were natives from different parts of Africa. Some of these, as in Dahomey and Fang, live in rather dense, compressed environments which do not provide extended vistas; while others (for example, Senegal, Zulu) inhabit open savannahs. Two groups (Zulu and Bushmen) generally live in circular homes.

The findings of this ambitious and well-executed project were in agreement with Rivers' conclusions, with similar bidirectional results. The authors offer as explanations for their findings a set of hypotheses: that people who live in a "carpentered world" and who have an "experience with two-dimensional representation of reality" (as Western peoples do) are more susceptible to the Müller-Lyer illusion and the Sander parallelogram illusion than are non-Western peoples who have different kinds of visual environments and experiences. They also suggest that people who inhabit areas with broad horizontal vistas are likely to be more subject to the horizontal-vertical illusion than those living in restricted environments such as forests. The data provide a good fit for their hypotheses (Segall, Campbell, and Herskovits 1966).

But, according to Douglass R. Price-Williams (1975:11–14), some studies fail to confirm the ecological hypothesis, while others partially confirm it and partially do not. One of these studies was made by G. Jahoda (1966) with two groups of natives in Ghana, one of which was familiar with a more "carpentered" environment than the other. Despite the cultural contrasts between the two groups, they showed no significant difference in illusion susceptibility. Both groups, however, were less susceptible to the Müller-Lyer illusion than a European comparison group.

A quite different explanation for the illusion susceptibility than the "carpentered world" hypothesis is in terms of eye pigmentation. R. H. Pollack has argued that macular pigmentation of the eye is correlated with the ability to see contours and makes a person more visually analytic and less susceptible to the Müller-Lyer illusion (Pollack 1963; Pollack and Silvar 1967). This finding would be in keeping with the lack of significant difference between Jahoda's two native groups, while both were less susceptible to the Müller-Lyer illusion than the European group.

Marc H. Bornstein (1973a, 1973b) has not only offered a similar explanation for susceptibility to the Müller-Lyer illusion but has also suggested a psychophysiological explanation for different patterns in color naming in different cultures in terms of degree of eye pigmentation. However, Bolton et al. (1975) have reviewed Bornstein's hypotheses and present the results of tests of their own which suggest that they are inadequate.

COGNITIVE STYLE, CULTURE, AND ECOLOGY

In Chapter 1 reference was made (page 10) to Herman A. Witkin's distinction between field dependence and field independence as contrasting cognitive styles. The distinction is based on the speed with which a subject can discover a hidden figure embedded in a stimulus picture. Those who are quick to do so are termed *field independent*, while slower subjects are dubbed *field dependent*. Witkin's Embedded Figures Test has been used to test these differences in perceptual response.

Witkin and his colleagues (1962, 1967) have shown that there are positive correlations between subjects' performances on the Embedded Figures Test and on two other tests: the Body Adjustment Test and the Rod and Frame Test. In the Body Adjustment Test the subject sits in a small room on a moveable chair. The room and chair are adjustable and can be tilted in either the same or opposite directions. The subject must handle some controls so as to bring his body into the upright position. In the Rod and Frame Test the subject sits in a dark room in which he or she sees only a tilted luminous frame and a luminous rod within it. The rod can be moved, and the subject must bring it to the upright position, disregarding the tile of the frame. In the two latter tests the subject should overlook the visual cues and depend more on his or her own kinesthetic sensations to achieve the upright position. Witkin claims that field-independent subjects who do well in these tests have a greater sense of self-identity, are more active in dealing with the environment, and are more aware of their inner experiences. Field-dependent persons, on the other hand, are more passive and dependent, lack a clearly defined sense of personal identity, and are more inclined to accept the opinions of others.

Early writings on this subject suggest that since field-independence involves greater psychological differentiation, it is a more desirable condition, associated with maturity. In a review of factors affecting psychological differentiation during the socialization process, Witkin (1969) referred to strict training or excessive concern by the mother as tending to inhibit a child's sense of autonomy. More recently, however, Witkin has expressed a more relativistic view, finding positive qualities in field dependence. Field-dependent persons, according to Witkin (1977:88) are "high in social sensitivity and social skills," features in which field-independent persons are low.

Field-dependent persons are said to be better at remembering faces (Witkin et al. 1971:13).

In a cross-cultural study, John W. Berry (1966) reported on testing done on two very different groups, Eskimo and Temne.[3] The Temne of Sierra Leone are farmers, while the Eskimos are, or used to be, hunting-gathering people. Temne child-rearing is strict; that of the Eskimos is indulgent and permissive. The Temne are field-dependent, while the Eskimos score high on field independence. This is consistent with Witkin's findings, but there are some other variables which might have had a bearing on the differences in perceptual response. Sierra Leone has much vegetation; the Eskimo environment is bleak and treeless. The Temne produce almost no graphics, sculpture, or decoration, while the Eskimos are famous for their arts and crafts. Finally, according to John L. M. B. Dawson (1977:103) the Temne suffer from protein deficiency, while the Eskimos have a high protein intake. No doubt there is some integration and consistency in these sets of contrasts. Eskimo hunters must have sharp perceptual discrimination to kill game, game which provides their high protein intake; and child rearing must encourage potential hunters to be self-reliant.

In a more recent work, Berry (1976) generalizes on a broader scale and argues that nomadic hunting-gathering people are more field independent, while sedentary agriculturists are more field dependent. Testing has now been carried out in a sample of 21 groups. Besides the Temne and the Eskimos of Baffin Island, there are now data on the Cree of James Bay, the Tsimshian of the Northwest Coast, the Carrier of the Rocky Mountain Plateau, and the Ontario Ojibwa. These groups are all Canadian Indians, but two groups of Australian aborigines (Arunta and Koonganji) and two communities of New Guinea natives (Telefomin, Hanuabada) have been added. Since the hunting-gathering sample is mostly Canadian, it does not seem to provide an adequate basis for generalization about hunter-gatherers in general, especially since the Arunta proved not to be as field independent as had been expected (Berry 1976:223). The New Guinea groups are horticulturists. Berry's contrasts, therefore, seem to be mainly between Canadian hunter-gatherers and West African farmers. However, work is now being carried out with two groups in Central Africa: the Biaka pygmies, who are forest hunter-gatherers, and the Bangandu, agriculturists who live on the forest borders. Here environment is held relatively constant, while the subsistence bases are different (van de Koppel 1977).

The cultural evolutionary sequence posited by Berry, proceeding from more to less psychological differentiation, is at odds with the

---

[3] The tests used included Witkin's Embedded Figures Test, the Kohs Blocks Test, Morrisby Shapes, and Raven's Matrices.

ontogenetic development described by Witkin, moving from less to more differentiation. It seems reasonable, however, to argue that hunters must be able to disembed and make successful visual discriminations to detect and kill game. Moreover, Berry's findings are in keeping with the conclusions of Barry, Child, and Bacon (1959) that hunting-gathering people encourage initiative among their children, while agriculturists place more emphasis on conformity and obedience.

In a recent review Berry has suggested a way of looking at the cultural evolutionary sequence with regard to psychological differentiation:

> Over the middle range of subsistence patterns (hunting or agricultural ecological adaptations), cultural complexity increases while levels of psychological differentiation decrease. In the change to intensive agriculture and urban-industrial activity, the observed levels of complexity (particularly familial complexity) decline, while levels of psychological differentiation increase (Berry 1981:485).

THE QUESTION OF ESP

If different cognitive patterns appear in different cultures, the question may be raised whether there is more extrasensory perception (ESP) in some societies than in others. An initial problem with this issue is that not everyone believes that there are such faculties as telepathy (mind-to-mind ESP) or clairvoyance (direct extrasensory perception of objects or events not mediated through telepathy). There now seems to be a greater disposition among scientists to accept the existence of such faculties than there formerly was, for in 1969 the American Association for the Advancement of Science recognized the study of paranormal phenomena, including ESP, to be a valid subject for scientific investigation.

There are two main ways in which believers in the existence of ESP have argued their case. One is by citing anecdotal evidence of spontaneous cases; the other is through quantitative experimental work, such as the card-guessing experiments of J. B. Rhine. To give an example of anecdotal evidence, consider a report made on June 30, 1960, by Mrs. Mary O'Brien (pseudonym) of Manchester, England. She states that her husband is the manager of an ice-cream factory located about two and a half miles from their home. Since he often comes home between 11:00 P.M. and 6:00 A.M., she never worries if he is late. But one Saturday evening in December 1959, she suddenly felt uneasy about him. "After phoning unsuccessfully three times, I decided at 2:00 A.M. to walk to the depot. This I did; there was no reply and the door was locked, but feeling even more uneasy for no apparent reason, I took it upon myself to break a window and climb in. I found my husband locked in the cold store [walk-in refrigerator] and, on comparing notes, discovered it had happened only minutes before I felt I had to phone the first time." (Mr. O'Brien countersigned this account as correct.) Mrs. O'Brien added that she had never felt worried about her husband either before or since that episode. On the night that she walked to the depot, she had left her two-month-old daughter alone, something which she normally would never do (Stevenson 1970:55–56).

Against the argument that this was merely a coincidence, one may point to such unusual features as Mrs. O'Brien's unaccustomed uneasiness about her husband's welfare, leaving her infant alone at home, walking for two and a half miles to the factory at 2:00 A.M., and breaking a window to enter the ice-cream plant.

Here is another such anecdote. In a statement dated October 11, 1968, a Mrs. Hurth of Cedarburg, Wisconsin, describes how she suddenly had a sense of fear about her daughter, who had just left home to go to the movies. Mrs. Hurth was washing dishes at the time. "Quite suddenly while I held a plate in my hand an awesome feeling came over me. I dropped the plate, turned my eyes towards heaven and prayed aloud, 'Oh, God, don't let her get killed!'

"For some unexplainable reason I knew Joicey had been hit by a car or was going to be." Mrs. Hurth immediately dialed the phone number of the movie theater; she was told that her daughter had just been hit by an automobile but appeared to be all right. Corroboratory statements by the daughter, her father, and the theater manager confirm this account (Stevenson 1970:61–62).

We do not know whether Mrs. Hurth often had anxious feelings that her daughter had been hit by a car. If so, that would weaken the significance of this case somewhat. As it stands, however, it does suggest the likelihood of telepathic communication.

The second main kind of evidence for ESP besides anecdotal reports consists of experiments which produce quantitative scoring results. J. B. Rhine of Duke University developed a 25-card pack with five cards, each having standard symbols: circle, wave, square, star, and cross. In card-guessing experiments with a shuffled deck there should be one chance in five of getting a given call right. But some subjects have scored much better than chance. As Rhine (1947:35) reported:

> The best individual performer went through the deck of ESP cards well over 700 times during the first three years of work covered by my first report. . . . This man averaged about 8 hits per run of 25 trials. . . . To express the odds against averaging a score of 8 or better by chance alone for more than 700 runs would require a paragraph of figures. . . .

While many have been convinced by such experimental findings, by the spontaneous cases, or both, there are also many skeptics who fail to be impressed by either sort of evidence. It is interesting that parapsychologists have found that believers and nonbelievers score somewhat differently in ESP tests. Gertrude Schmeidler (1945; Schmeidler and McConnell 1958) gave the label of *sheep* to those who were willing to accept the possibility of extrasensory faculties, while skeptics were called *goats*. In Schmeidler's ESP tests, sheep tended to score better, on the average, than goats. These findings may have wider implications. As I wrote in 1946 (p. 9): "if paranormal faculties such as clairvoyance and telepathy do exist, one would expect them to appear more frequently in a culture which believes in their reality and rewards those who manifest them, than in one which is skeptical of their existence and ignores or suppresses their manifestations."

Almost all non-Western societies have been "sheep" societies. In societies with shamans or medicine men, who are believed to have paranormal abilities, such specialists tend to have high status. It has usually been the view of Western travelers, including anthropologists, that shamans are either deliberate frauds or self-deceived dupes; and yet some anthropologists, in the course of their fieldwork, have been given information by shamans that proved to be true. When Adrian Boshier (1974) first went to consult a female diviner in South Africa, she correctly gave him information about himself and later told him that he had had a dangerous encounter with a leopard, which was also true. A. I. Hallowell (1942a:46–47) asked a Chippewa shaman for news about his father, which proved to be correct. A Mexican curandero in a remote Mexican village gave Gordon Wasson information about his son, telling him that he was not in Boston, as the Wassons believed, but in New York and that he would soon be in military service, which was later shown to be true (Wasson and Wasson 1957, 2:264–65).[4]

Shamans usually have techniques which, rightly or wrongly, are believed to enhance their telepathic or clairvoyant abilities, such as fasting, concentration, crystal gazing, the use of drugs, singing or dancing to the point of exhaustion. In India, yoga techniques are sometimes held to develop paranormal abilities, and in our own culture some advanced technology has been devised for this purpose. According to Beal (1977:116): "Teaching machines and biofeedback equipment are now being used with some success as ESP teaching aids. . . . As an example, the Model 100A ESP teaching machine can be used either as a test instrument to measure ESP ability or as a feedback system for enhancing ESP ability."

Looking back at the two spontaneous cases recounted earlier concerning Mrs. O'Brien and Mrs. Hurth, it may be noted that the presumed telepathic communication in both cases was with a closely related person, a woman's husband and a daughter. It may seem

---

[4] More accounts of this kind are mentioned in Long (1977b:377).

obvious that such communication should be with a person with whom emotional ties exist, but the point is that such ties may be differently structured in societies which have contrasting forms of family organization. An early classic work of psychical research in England, *Phantasms of the Living*, dealt with apparitions coinciding with the death of a relative or friend. In Volume 2 of this work (Gurney, Myers, and Podmore 1886:723), the authors found that of 882 cases, 44.3 percent involved members of a nuclear family (husband, wife, mother, father, son, daughter, brother, and sister), while 9 percent were concerned with more remote relationships: grandparents, grandchildren, uncle, aunt, nephew, niece, and cousins. Friends accounted for 31.7 percent, acquaintances 10.7 percent, and strangers 4.3 percent. As far as I know, no similar large-scale study has been carried out in a non-Western society. If that were done, one might learn how telepathic links are structured in other social settings.

The two most ambitious attempts to study the operation of ESP in other societies have been those by Ronald Rose and Robert L. van de Castle. Ronald Rose and his wife gave the Rhine ESP test to Australian aborigines. The Roses recorded 16,625 guesses; chance would have given 3,325 "hits," but they recorded 3,870 correct hits (Rose 1956:227), which the Roses thought was evidence that Australian aborigines had ESP abilities. In a questionnaire which he submitted to the natives, most of Rose's subjects answered "Yes" to the question, "Would you know if a relative some distance away died, had an accident, or was seriously ill?" Rose cites some spontaneous cases along the lines of those described in *Phantasms of the Living*.

Robert L. van de Castle (1974) gave a modified form of ESP test to Cuna Indians of the San Blas islands of Panama. Instead of using the five standard Rhine symbols, van de Castle designed cards with five objects having some relevance to the Cunas: a jaguar, a shark, a conch shell, a canoe, and an airplane. Testing was done on a group basis among junior high school students in 1968, 1969, 1970, 1971, and 1972. Besides taking the ESP test, the students were also asked to write an account of their most recent dream. A total of 1,620 ESP runs was completed by 451 subjects (96 girls, 365 boys) with an overall negative deviation of six hits below chance; but the girls obtained 67 hits above chance expectation, while the boys scored 73 hits below chance. It was van de Castle's impression that the girls were a more obedient, cooperative group than the boys, which might account for the difference, but ratings on cooperativeness by teachers did not correlate well with ESP test performance.

The dreams of the subjects were scored for the amount of aggression involved, and it was found that dreams containing aggression were associated with higher ESP scores, especially among the girls. The presence of animals in dreams was also linked with above-chance scores, as were dreams which had some overt sexual activity. Long dreams were associated with above-chance scores and short dreams with those below chance, especially for boys.

While the overall group scores are not impressive, van de Castle's analysis of the scoring results and the dreams indicates that there seem to be some meaningful, consistent patterns in operation. In the discussion which followed presentation of this paper, it was suggested that the sex differences in the scoring results might have been influenced by the fact that van de Castle, a male, administered all the tests. It was suggested that a female experimenter might have been used to test this variable. Van de Castle offered the following suggestions about his findings:

> My speculation would be that the person who was more comfortable with his (their) impulse life, who can tolerate primary process thinking, who doesn't engage in as much censorship, who is open to an inner awareness in a sense, is the person who is going to do better at the ESP test. It's the person with the heavy denial and repressive mechanisms . . . who will not do well (van de Castle 1974:98).

Two anthropologists at the session, Ioan Lewis and George Devereux, opposed this interpretation, since they see the dream, in Freudian terms, as an expression of frustration or repression.

SUGGESTIONS FOR FURTHER READING

For two surveys, see Richard W. Brislin, Walter J. Lonner, and Robert M. Thorndike, *Cross-Cultural Research Methods* (New York: John Wiley & Sons, 1973); and Douglass R. Price-Williams, *Explorations in Cross-Cultural Psychology* (San Francisco: Chandler & Sharp, 1975).

General problems facing cross-cultural and other kinds of comparative studies are discussed in Michael Cole and Barbara Means, *Comparative Studies of How People Think* (Cambridge, Mass.: Harvard University Press, 1981).

For two critical evaluations of work in cross-cultural psychology, see Carol R. Ember, "Cross-Cultural Cognitive Studies," in *Annual Review of Anthropology*, ed. Bernard J. Siegel, Alan R. Beals, and Stephen A. Tyler. (Palo Alto, Cal.: Annual Reviews, 1977), vol. 6. pp. 33–56; and Lee Sechrest, "On the Dearth of Theory in Cross-Cultural Psychology: There is Madness in our Method," in *Basic Problems in Cross-Cultural Psychology*, ed. Ype H. Poortinga (Amsterdam: Swets and Zeitlinger, 1977), pp. 73–82.

A review of anthropological studies related to perception and cognition is available in David French, "The Relationship of Anthropology to Studies in Perception and Cognition," in *Psychology: A Study of a Science*, vol. 6. *Investigations of Man as Socius: Their Place in Psychology and the Social Sciences*, ed. Sigmund Koch (New York: McGraw-Hill, 1963), pp. 388–428. For another survey, see Harry C. Triandis, "Cultural Influences upon Cognitive Processes," in *Advances in Experimental Social Psychology*, vol. I, ed. Leonard Berkowitz (New York: Academic Press, 1964), pp. 1–48.

For some cross-cultural studies of cognition in children along Piagetian lines, see Jerome S. Bruner et al., *Studies in Cognitive Growth* (New York: John Wiley & Sons, 1966), chaps. 11–14. See also Robert A. LeVine, "Cross-Cultural Study in Child Psychology," in *Carmichael's Manual of Child Psychology*, 3d ed., ed. Paul H. Mussen (New York: John Wiley & Sons, 1970), pp. 559–612.

For ESP and related issues, see Benjamin B. Wolman, ed. *Handbook of Parapsychology* (New York: Van Nostrand Reinhold, 1977).

10

Cross-Cultural Studies of Values and Attitudes

A definition of personality offered in Chapter 1 was: Personality is a more or less enduring organization of forces within the individual associated with a complex of fairly consistent attitudes, values, and modes of perception which account, in part, for the individual's consistency of behavior. This definition draws attention to the importance of values and attitudes, which are discussed in this chapter.

Difficulties are evident in making cross-cultural studies of the dominant values held by people in different societies. The first question is how to go about it, whether to make use of a questionnaire or some other technique. A problem with questionnaires is that a person's answers may not necessarily express his or her actual values. Despite the various difficulties involved, a number of efforts have been made to deal with this subject.

Charles Morris of the University of Chicago has drawn up a document called "Ways to Live," in which 13 styles of life are described. Morris has affixed labels to these various ways, such as Apollonian, Dionysian, Promethean, Christian, Buddhist, Mohammedan, and Maitreyan. The subject is asked to read the descriptions of the 13 ways and to rate each of the ways on a seven-point scale as to how much he or she likes or dislikes it. This questionnaire formed the basis of Morris' cross-cultural investigation of the values of college students in the 1940s, although it was supplemented by interviews. The largest samples came from the United States (2,015 men, 831 women), China (523 men, 220 women), and India (724 men, 410 women). Smaller samples came from Japan, Norway, Canada, and some other countries. The responses were subjected to factor analysis, according to such factors as social restraint and self-control, enjoyment and progress in action, withdrawal and self-sufficiency, receptivity and sympathetic concern, and self-indulgence or sensuous enjoyment.

Morris (1956) found much similarity in the Indian, American, and Chinese ratings, although American students emphasized the values of flexibility and many-sidedness, Indian students stressed social restraint and self-control, and Chinese students were more actively and socially oriented.

James M. Gillespie and Gordon W. Allport (1955) made use of a questionnaire involving 50 items, designed to tap values. They also asked the subject to write an autobiography of the future, "From Now to 2000 A.D." The authors hoped to secure about 100 male and 100 female college students' sets of responses in 10 countries, but their final samples were sometimes smaller. The 10 countries were the United States, New Zealand, South Africa, Egypt, Mexico, France, Italy, Germany, Japan, and Israel. The materials were collected between 1949 and 1951.

Like Morris, the authors found much similarity among the different groups of students, which could be attributed to the fact that they are all liberal arts students exposed to a common international culture. Students in all nations, for example, favor permissive and affectionate parent-child relationships and express hope for more racial equality. There were also differences: more nationalism, for example, expressed by Afrikaners, Bantus, Egyptians, and Mexicans. American students in 1949 showed relatively little interest in social problems (no doubt changed by now). In agreement with Morris' findings, American students expressed a desire for a rich many-sided life. Associated with this was an attitude of "privatism," in contrast to more involvement in corporate loyalties among Egyptians, Bantus, Mexicans, and Japanese.

In the 1950s, Mary Ellen Goodman asked children in four Japanese and eight American schools to write compositions on the topic "What I want to be when I grow up, and why." About 1,250 Japanese and 3,750 American children from grades one through eight responded.

One contrast between the national groups was in connection with military service; no interest was shown by Japanese boys, while 7 or 8 out of 100 American boys looked forward to a military career. Japanese children showed much more interest in politics and holding public office than did the American children and also more interest in business pursuits. American children expressed more self-oriented individualism than did the Japanese (Goodman 1957).

VALUES IN FIVE SOUTHWESTERN COMMUNITIES

Probably the best cross-cultural study of values undertaken so far is Kluckhohn and Strodtbeck's *Variations in Value Orientations*. Value orientations are defined by Kluckhohn as "complex but definitely patterned (rank-ordered) principles, resulting from the transactional interplay of three analytically distinguishable elements of the evaluative process—the cognitive, the affective, and the directive elements—which give order and direction to the ever-flowing stream of human acts and thoughts as these relate to the solution of 'common human' problems" (Kluckhohn and Strodtbeck 1961:4).

The authors make the assumptions that: (1) All societies face a limited number of common human problems which must be solved; (2) The range of possible solutions is limited, neither random nor limitless; and (3) Although all alternative solutions are always present in all societies, some solutions to problems are differentially preferred. There is almost always a rank ordering of preferences.

Five basic problems are singled out:

1. What is the innate nature of man?
2. What is the relation of man to nature?
3. What is the nature of time orientation?
4. What is the modality of human activity?
5. What is the modality of man's relationships to others?

To each question a threefold set of possible answers or solutions is suggested. Human nature may be seen as (1) evil, (2) neutral or a mixture of good and evil, or (3) good. Man's relation to nature may be seen as (1) subjugated to nature, (2) in harmony with nature, or (3) dominating nature. The significant time orientation may be seen as directed to (1) past, (2) present, or (3) future. The significant activity orientation may be (1) being, (2) being-in-becoming, and (3) doing. The modality of human relationships may be (1) lineal, (2) collateral, or (3) individualistic.

Most of these alternatives are self-explanatory or readily understood. There is some difficulty, though, with the distinction between lineality and collaterality. Both refer to group relationships. Lineality has to do with the continuity of a group through time, as in the case of a Chinese family line. Collaterality concerns ties with laterally extended groups; but since these may include the family, the distinction between lineality and collaterality is not always clear.

Kluckhohn considers the dominant U.S. orientations to be individualism, future time orientation, mastery over nature, and doing. (An evil-but-perfectable conception of human nature is a heritage from our Puritan forebears but is now changing.) In contrast, Spanish-Americans of the Southwest are seen to have emphases on lineality (now changing), present time orientation, subjugation to nature, and being.

Every person is said to have a rank order of value orientations as part of his or her personality. According to this theory, the nature of the rank order is considerably influenced by the culture into which one is born.

Kluckhohn's theories were tested by the administration of a questionnaire schedule of 22 items in five communities within the same area of the American Southwest: Spanish-Americans, Texans, Mormons, Navaho, and Zuñi. Members of the research team made predictions in advance about the ranking of the value orientations in these five groups. They predicted that the Spanish-Americans would give priority to individualism (Ind) but with some stress on lineality (Lin) and preferences for present time orientation (Pres), subjugation to nature (Subj), and being. The Texans were predicted to give the following rankings: In relations: Ind > Coll > Lin. In time orientation: Fut > Pres > Past. In man-nature orientation: Over > Subj > With. In activity orientation, doing was given slightly more stress than being. The authors were more unsure about the Mormons but expected them to give about equal stress to collaterality and individualism. In time orientation: Fut > Pres > Past. In man-nature orientation: With > Over > Subj. The Mormons were expected to give priority to doing rather than being. The predictions for the Navaho were: In relations: Col > Lin > Ind. In time orientation: Pres > Past > Fut. In man-nature orientation it was predicted that priority would go to Harmony-with-Nature. These predictions were not made for the Zuñi. No predictions were made concerning the innate nature of man, since the questionnaire schedule did not cover that area. Nor was the being-in-becoming variant considered.

To give an idea of how value preferences were elicited, one of the 22 schedule items goes as follows:

> A man had a crop failure, or, let us say, had lost most of his sheep or cattle. He and his family had to have help from someone if they were going to get through the winter. There are different ways of getting help. Which of these three ways would be best?
>
> B (Coll) Would it be best if he depended mostly on his brothers and sisters or other relatives, all to help him out as much as each one could?
>
> C (Ind) Would it be best for him to try to raise the money *on his own* outside the community (his own people) from people who are neither relatives nor employers?
>
> A (Lin) Would it be best for him to go to a boss or to an older important relative who is used to managing things in his group, and ask him to help out until things get better? (Kluckhohn and Strodtbeck 1961:83–84).

Each question had three alternative choices. The subject was asked to give his first choice and then his preference for the remaining alternatives. He could give equal weight to two or all three alternatives if he wished.

The questionnaire was given to between 20 and 25 adult subjects in each of the five communities, roughly divided between males and females. The sample size was partly determined by the size of the Spanish-American community, which had no more adults than that. Random samples were drawn from persons over 20 in the Texan, Mormon, and Navaho groups. Random samples were not drawn for the Zuñi because of problems concerning rapport, and persons who had been working with the ethnographer were chosen as subjects.

This interesting experiment produced results in consonance with Kluckhohn's theories. Statistical analyses of the responses showed that there were both significant within-culture regularities and between-culture differences. The Spanish-American data accorded remarkably with the predictions which had been made. There was also much correspondence between predictions and data for the Texans, except that there was more stress on present time orientation than had been expected. The Mormon predictions were generally borne out, but the Mormons gave priority to over-nature rather than to with-nature in contrast to the prediction. The Navaho findings also accorded well with the predictions, especially in regard to activity orientation. No predictions were made for the Zuñi, whose responses were also those which gave the least conclusive results. This seems to provide very good support for Kluckhohn's theories about value orientations.[1]

A further study of values in the southwestern groups has been made by John W. M. Whiting and associates. This study was directed to a comparison of child-rearing practices in three of the five groups and the ways in which the characteristic values of each group are fostered. When the mothers of the three groups, Zuñi, Mormon, and Texan, were rated on a scale measuring intolerance of aggression by children against peers, 77 percent of the Zuñi and 69 percent of the Mormon mothers scored above the median for the three groups, while only 6 percent of the Texan mothers scored as high. Since the main contrast here was between the nuclear Texan families and the extended Zuñi families, the researchers considered whether this represented a characteristic difference between nuclear and extended families. Perhaps crowded living conditions require an emphasis on harmony and control of aggression. A cross-cultural correlational survey supported this hypothesis. "Twenty-five of thirty cases, approximately 80 percent, confirm our expectation. . . . 92 percent of the extended families are above the median in the severity with which children's aggression is punished, whereas but 22 percent of the societies with nuclear family households are equally severe" (Whiting, Chasdi et al. 1966:113).

Commenting on this study, Robert A. LeVine (1970:594) has suggested that in certain child-rearing practices the Texans may be roughly representative of northern Europe and the United States, while the Zuñi may be representative of folk and peasant populations

---

[1] A study making use of the same methods has been done in Japan with 619 subjects by William Caudill and Harry A. Scarr (1962). On the basis of his knowledge of the Japanese, Caudill successfully made predictions about their rankings of value orientations. Particularly striking was the Japanese emphasis on collaterality, which remained strong in different generations, being emphasized even more by the young than by the old.

of the New World, Asia, and Africa. The severe aggression training in such groups "may be part of a larger tendency to make children orderly, obedient, and pacific, producing an inhibitedness that manifests itself in performance on cognitive tasks." LeVine (p. 593) also makes the suggestion that this restraint of aggression in traditional societies is apt to give way in the process of Westernization. "Western child-rearing values seem to entail tolerance of children's fighting and other aggressive encounters, and it looks as if Westernization among nonindustrial agricultural peoples involves relaxation of traditional constraints on childhood aggression."

Another contrast in the three southwestern groups studied by Whiting and his colleagues was in the relative stress on need for achievement. This was tested by giving the Magic Man test to Zuñi, Mormon and Texan children.

> Once upon a time a magic man met a child and said, "I'm going to change you into something else. You can be any kind of person you like." If you were this child, what kind of person would you want to be? (Whiting, Chasdi et al. 1966:106).

Each child was also asked: If he could be changed into a father, mother, sister, or brother, which would he want to be? If he could be any age, how old would he want to be?

Whiting and his colleagues found that achievement was expressed by 57 percent of the Texan children, 38 percent of the Mormon children, and 20 percent of the Zuñi children. No cross-sex choices were made by the Texans, but 10 percent of the Zuñi boys chose to be females, and 23 percent of the Mormon girls chose to be males. No Mormon boys or Zuñi girls made cross-sex choices. Valued ages were higher for Texans and Mormons than for Zuñi. These answers seem to reflect the high status of Mormon men and Zuñi women in their respective cultures, the relative equality of sexes among the Texans, and the value of growing up and need for achievement among the Texans (Whiting, Chasdi et al. 1966:106–8).

Whiting and his colleagues present some speculations about the historical backgrounds of the value systems in the three groups and the reasons for their having adopted certain child-rearing practices. In the case of the Texans, they trace the emphasis on the nuclear family to frontier conditions in the New World. After 1750 the kinds of advice given to parents on child-rearing practices in counseling literature in North America stressed measures of encouraging independence in children. "The child rearing practices of modern Texans conform strikingly to this advice; they wean early, value individualism and early independence, and are permissive with respect to aggression" (Whiting, Chasdi et al. 1966:116).

There is a good deal of consistency in the findings of the southwestern values studies, those of Whiting and his associates and the earlier study by Kluckhohn and Strodtbeck. Also, there is correspondence with the analysis made by Whiting and Whiting of the differences between the simpler and more complex cultures in the Six Cultures project discussed in Chapter 8.

PASTORALISTS AND FARMERS

Pastoralists and farmers lead somewhat different ways of life, with pastoralists being more nomadic and often engaged in fighting and cattle raiding, while farmers are more sedentary, tied to the land. We might expect that, related to their different ways of life, contrasting sets of attitudes and values would characterize pastoralists and farmers. An investigation of this subject has been made by Robert B. Edgerton of the University of California at Los Angeles as part of a larger research project known as the Culture and Ecology in East Africa Project, organized by Walter Goldschmidt. The project involves a study of four East African tribes: the Hehe, Kamba, Pokot, and Sebei. These tribes engage in both pastoralism and farming. An effort was made to find groups in each tribe which were more limited to pastoralism or to farming. Eight communities were thus selected for investigation, with a pastoral and a farming group for each tribe.

With the help of native interpreters, Edgerton (1971a:39) gave a series of questionnaires and tests to samples from each group: 85 questions, the Rorschach Ink Blot Test, 9 "values pictures" showing scenes of native life to which the subjects were asked to respond, and 22 color slides. Edgerton interviewed about 30 men and 30 women in each of the eight communities.

One of Edgerton's conclusions from an analysis of the subjects' responses is that there is a good deal of uniformity within a tribal group, so that a Pokot pastoralist is more like a Pokot farmer than like a pastoralist from another tribe. At the same time, there were clear differences between pastoralists and farmers in each tribe, too numerous to be expected by chance (Edgerton 1971a:272). The farmers showed more anxiety, hostility, emotional restraint, indirection, and disrespect for authority, while the pastoralists were more open in their expression of feelings, and showed more independence, overt aggression, direct action, social cohesion, and respect for authority. These findings were in line with Edgerton's and Goldschmidt's expectations and with Edgerton's behavioral observations made in the course of fieldwork.

A plausible conclusion about the findings is that the farmer must repress or suppress his hostility, because he and his neighbors are tied to the land; they cannot move away. Pastoralists have more mobility and can separate if a quarrel breaks out. There is, therefore, less inhibition in pastoralists' expression of feelings. Resort to witchcraft would be more likely in a farming community, where hatred cannot be expressed as openly as in a pastoral society, a hypothesis for which Edgerton found partial confirmation (Edgerton 1971a:288–92).

In an epilogue to Edgerton's work, Walter Goldschmidt notes that a pastoralist's way of life reinforces patterns of direct action and decision making. The pastoralist cares for large mammals which have wills of their own; he has to direct them, impose his own will, and at the same time meet their needs. The farmer's daily routine is more passive and involves more drudgery. The pastoralist is always on the move, leading his animals to pasture and water, and keeping alert for enemies, raiders, and wild animals (Edgerton 1971a:296). The pastoral way of life involves a more striking division of labor between the sexes, emphasizing "masculinity" in the animal-tending, frequently warring males. Pastoralists would seem to have less reason than farmers to acquire an image of limited good, for an increase in one man's herd does not necessarily result in the decrease of another's (Edgerton 1971a:17–18).

The consistent findings about farmers' hostility, anxiety, and emotional constraint in Edgerton's research are in keeping with the generalizations about peasant societies cited earlier. Edgerton's and Goldschmidt's speculations help one to understand why such a complex of traits has been reported so often for peasant communities.

Goldschmidt (1976) has since published an excellent ethnographic account of the Sebei that provides further documentation for the contrasts between the more agricultural and the more pastoral segments of that tribe.

RIGHTISTS AND LEFTISTS

Lewis Austin (1977) suggests that being a rightist or leftist is more than just a political preference; it is a personality orientation embracing a particular set of values. Thus, the right is associated with order, self-control, tradition, and classicism; while the left is associated with freedom, self-expression, dynamism, and romanticism. Austin performed an experiment with 95 American and 376 Japanese subjects (mostly graduate students) who were shown a series of pairs of visual symbols. In each pair there was a choice between polar symbolic opposites, such as order and disorder or conflict and harmony. Each subject was asked to indicate his or her political viewpoint by making a checkmark on a line seven centimeters long. In this way subjects were divided into "left" or "right" groups. Responses to 14 of the 31 pairs of symbols showed distinctions at a statistically significant level. As expected (Austin 1977:312), conservatives showed a preference for order rather than disorder; for passive rather than active; for uniform rather than variant; for big rather than little; for push-down rather than push-up; for even rather than uneven; and for balanced rather than unbalanced. The "left" preferences were correspondingly opposite.

"Twelve of the thirty-one pairs of symbols distinguish between Japanese and American subjects at a statistically significant level. Of these, seven also distinguish between left and right. In six of the seven cases the Japanese preference is for the more conservative choice" (Austin 1977:319). This leads Austin to suggest that cultures may be distinguished according to degrees of "leftness" and "rightness," and that Japanese culture seems to be more conservative than American. Austin's imaginative test for preference of paired visual symbols should be given to more subjects in different cultures.

MALES AND FEMALES

In every society, men hold more or less stereotyped ideas and attitudes about women and vice versa. These notions may reflect the differences in status and role of males and females in the society. On the other hand, the stereotypes may be at odds with the sex roles, a situation which may ultimately lead to a change in the stereotypes. Melford E. Spiro has described a situation in Burma in which there is an inconsistency of this kind, but where there seems to have been little or no change in stereotypes for several generations.

In general, women in Burma have high status. There is no purdah like that of North India, nor is there foot-binding as in traditional China. Most retail trade is in the hands of women, who are active in large business enterprises and in the professions. In the villages, women do much the same sort of agricultural work that men do, for which they receive the same wages, despite the males' greater strength. Marriages are entered through free choice, in contrast to the pattern of arranged marriages which prevails in India, Malaya, Java, and Sri Lanka. "Legally, women are the equals of men. The family estate is divided equally between sons and daughters, women own property in their own name, and after marriage husband and wife own all property jointly" (Spiro 1977:257). In contrast to the patrilocal joint family system found in India, marriage in Burma is generally neolocal. Moreover, it is the woman of the household who manages the budget; the husband turns his earnings over to her. Divorce, which is easy to obtain, may be initiated by a wife as well as by a husband.

Despite all these indications of equality between the sexes, there is a prevalent Burmese view (shared by women, too) that men are superior to women. Spiro cites several proverbs to that effect, such as "A woman is not as noble as a male dog." Women are held to be more lustful, treacherous, and animallike than men.

These attitudes are projected into house arrangements. The eastern side of the house, where the men sit and where the Buddhist shrine is kept, is the noble side; while the western side, where the women sit and where childbirth takes place, is ignoble. In Buddhist ceremonies and school assemblies, the males sit in front and the females behind them.

According to Spiro, there is much quarreling between spouses and a good deal of extramarital affairs. Family tension may stem partly from the inconsistency between the traditional stereotypes and actual sex roles. Spiro remarks that men want to be dependent on women but also fear their domination.

Spiro (1977:277) collected self-judgments from 22 randomly selected married couples, in the village where he worked, about which partner was the dominant one. Twenty out of 22 named the husband.

> But when these same respondents were asked to identify the dominant spouse in other marriages, they most frequently—sixteen of the twenty-two—named the wife. It is probably fair to conclude that their self-judgments reflect the cultural ideology of male superiority and the cultural norm of husband dominance, while the judgments of others more accurately reflect the actual relationship.

Spiro also asked a panel of four men (the headman, two village elders, and the local native doctor) to similarly examine 39 marriages in the community. They judged that the husband was dominant in 17 marriages, the wife in 16, while six were ambiguous. The elders in two other villages stated that the wife is dominant in a majority of marriages. Despite possible flaws in these methods of assessment, acknowledged by Spiro, there seems to be consistency in these findings and support for Spiro's interpretation.

Buddhist monasteries provide an avenue of escape for men who find married life stressful. Buddhist traditions also uphold the doctrine of male superiority. Spiro conducted interviews with about 50 monks, especially a group of 21 to whom he administered a Thematic Apperception Test and Rorschach Test. According to Spiro (1970:343–48), the monks tend to be narcissistic persons. This is suggested by their attitudes to the wife and children left behind. A man must get his wife's consent to enter a monastery, but he often makes no provision for their support. Spiro (p. 345) quotes the statements of some monks about this: "I want to enter nirvana, and that's all that counts." "They will have to look after themselves. This is not my responsibility; I must think of my own nirvana. If they have good karma, they will be able to get along." "My wife and child will have to take care of themselves. That is no longer my worry." Moreover, most of these men enter the monastic order without first granting their wives a divorce, which would make it possible for the women to marry again. Such men are not censured but are admired for having cut off their ties to the world.

The incongruities between stereotypes and sex roles noted by

Spiro are not unusual. The Mundurucú, a horticultural tribe in Brazil, provide a somewhat similar example. In this society, descent is patrilineal, but residence is usually matrilocal. Hunting and fishing take the men outside the village, within which women form a compact group, processing manioc and carrying out other collective tasks related to horticulture. Despite the women's prominent position in Mundurucú society and their control of most food production and distribution, they are considered inferior to the men. A myth tells that women were formerly dominant and played sacred trumpets (now tabooed to them) which men took away from the women and stored in the men's house, where they are now kept. Yolanda Murphy and Robert F. Murphy (1974) suggest that the myth expresses the men's insecurity about their current dominance. The men formerly engaged in tribal warfare, which may have contributed to their former dominance in the past. While Spiro states that Burmese women—even highly educated ones—share the negative image of their sex, that is not true of Mundurucú women; according to the Murphys, they do not accept the male creed.

PREJUDICES

Prejudiced attitudes toward particular groups, involving stereotyped prejudgments, may be considered as forms of cognition. Value judgments are involved. Allport suggests as a definition of prejudice, "being down on something you're not up on." Ethnocentrism in some form may well be a universal feature of human life. But there is probably more prejudice in some societies than in others. Despite our traditions of democracy and Christianity, prejudice has a long history in the United States. "Racial segregation and an ideology of racial superiority have been part of the American culture for generations and in some sense every white American is implicated in this aspect of American life" (Campbell and Schuman 1968:62).

White racial prejudice antedated the slave trade; perhaps, without such prejudice, the slave trade would never have been allowed to expand (Jordan 1968:6–8, 30). We thus have a long heritage of prejudice behind us from which it may be difficult to extricate ourselves, especially since much of it is on a more or less unconscious level.

Within the past 30 years, a great deal of research has been done in the effort to understand prejudice and the personality of the prejudiced person. Prejudice may be seen either in terms of a consistency model of personality or in terms of a conflict model.

Prejudice is not a matter of personality alone, and there may be people who passively accept the prejudiced views of the culture in which they have grown up without experiencing any marked psychological sequelae as a result. But there is much evidence to indicate that, for many people, prejudice is a vital aspect of the personality, part of a defense system developed by an ego which is shaky and insecure.

The classic work on this subject is *The Authoritarian Personality* by T. W. Adorno et al. This massive study, based on the use of questionnaires, interviews, and projective tests, employed a psychoanalytic approach to delineate a complex of personality characteristics shared by persons holding right-wing authoritarian views. The authors suggest that such individuals come from relatively affectionless families in which the parents demand strict obedience to conventional modes of conduct. There is little opportunity for spontaneous development of the self. The expression of sex and aggression are tabooed. Children in such families develop compliant, submissive behavior and repress the hostility which cannot be directed toward the parents. Thus they develop a cleavage between the conscious and unconscious segments of the personality. Such individuals come to see the world as dangerous and threatening; safety lies in conforming to the conventional patterns of behavior required of them.

Persons of this sort are prone to projection and the displacement of hostility. For such a personality structure, prejudices play a functional role in supporting the self-image and in providing targets for the hostility which seeks an outlet. The individual who, at bottom, feels weak and insecure, places a high value on power and toughness, despises weak out-groups and admires strong leaders. This, in brief, is the "authoritarian personality" (Adorno et al. 1950). A discouraging implication of this picture is that as long as family conditions like those described continue to persist, prejudices will be hard to eliminate. Exhortation and propaganda for tolerance are not likely to have much influence on persons who desperately need to maintain their prejudices.

The Authoritarian Personality and succeeding volumes in the series edited by Max Horkheimer and Samuel J. Flowerman have been very influential and have stimulated much research along similar lines. A book of essays has been published which deals with *The Authoritarian Personality* and attempts to assess its contributions (Christie and Jahoda 1954). Herbert H. Hyman and Paul B. Sheatsley (1954) point to various methodological weaknesses in *The Authoritarian Personality*, such as inadequate sampling, overgeneralization from this sample, failure to validate questionnaire data, and absence of control over the variable of formal education. Edward A. Shils (1954) notes that the authors of *The Authoritarian Personality* never investigated the actual behavior and roles of their subjects in everyday life. Shils's principal criticism, however, is that the authors follow an outmoded assumption in placing right and left authoritarianism at opposite poles. They have ignored left-wing authoritarianism and dealt only with the right-wing authoritarian personality, not with the authoritarian personality per se.

While these and other criticisms in the same volume suggest that Adorno and his colleagues may not have proven their case, I feel that there must be a core of truth in their picture of the nature and etiology of the right-wing authoritarian personality. This conviction is strengthened by the fact that many other studies have presented corroborative data.

Else Frenkel-Brunswik (1949) has shown that children raised in restrictive authoritarian households develop what she calls "intolerance of ambiguity." They become accustomed to disciplines demanding the quick learning of rigid externally imposed rules which they do not understand but dare not violate. Patterns of this sort influence the children's performance in test situations involving perception and the solution of problems. Frenkel-Brunswik has reported on some tests given to children who scored either extremely high or extremely low on scales designed to measure degree of prejudice. In one test, children were shown pictures of a dog which, through a number of transitional stages, finally became the picture of a cat. At each stage the subjects were asked to identify the object depicted. The more prejudiced children tended to hang on longer to the original object and responded more slowly to the changes than did the unprejudiced children.

In another test, persons in a dark room were shown a point of light which, although stationary, appears to move in such conditions. Persons who scored high on the Berkeley Ethnocentrism Scale tended to soon establish a norm for themselves and reported the light as moving in a constant direction for a constant number of inches, while those scoring lower on ethnocentrism took longer to establish such norms (Block and Block 1951).

Milton Rokeach (1943, 1960) has devised a number of experiments in which a mental set is established by having the subject solve a problem in a particular way. Rokeach then poses a problem which may be solved either by the former method or else by switching to a different, more direct technique. In these tests, subjects rated as high on ethnocentrism tended to show difficulty in restructuring the field and persisted longer than did less-prejudiced individuals in maintaining the original set.

An important source of this kind of behavior is fear. People who cling to stereotypes are under pressure and seem to have a deep-lying fear of the environment which restricts their range of perception. A person who acquires such fears in early childhood develops a rigidity which is apt to persist into adult life.

The role of fear in relation to prejudice in the United States has also been touched on by Francis L. K. Hsu, although without reference to childhood. Hsu believes that a stress on independence and self-reliance is a core value for Americans. In a constantly changing world, the isolated individual in a competitive system is bound to feel anxiety. While he looks upward for loopholes to advancement, he is also afraid of the groups beneath him. Fearing contamination from less successful inferior groups, he tries to maintain social distance from them, including manifestations of racial and religious prejudice.

Hsu (1961b:222–25) claims that support for this thesis comes from the fact that there is less racial or religious prejudice in such traditional stratified Eastern societies as India, China, and Japan, where there is less need for competition and status seeking. Racial and religious prejudices, he argues, are most intense and widespread in the Protestant-dominated societies of the Western world.

A weakness in this argument is that there is much prejudice in India on the part of higher castes toward lower castes, particularly toward the 65 million or so Untouchables or Ex-Untouchables, as they have been called (Isaacs 1964). The writings of Isaacs, Berreman, De Vos, Wagatsuma, and others have shown not only how many parallels there are in prejudiced attitudes (and in the responses of discriminated-against minorities) in India and the United States, but also that similar patterns appear in Japan, where the Eta, formerly a leatherworking "caste," are still discriminated against today, although they are racially indistinguishable from the rest of the population, and although many of the Eta no longer have any connection with leatherwork or other traditionally defiling occupations (De Vos and Wagatsuma 1966).

A caste system may tend naturally toward the maintenance of prejudiced attitudes. The high-ranking castes adopt paternalistic attitudes of *noblesse oblige* toward the lower castes, approximating adult-child relations (Berreman 1966:309). Fear of contamination from contact with lower caste members can be cited for India, Japan, and the United States (Davis, Gardner, and Gardner 1941:16; Dollard 1957; Myrdal 1944).

In India, Japan, and the United States there have been similar self-improvement and protest movements and demands for integration on the part of the discriminated-against minorities. De Vos and Wagatsuma point out that Buraku (Eta) children score more poorly in IQ tests than do non-Buraku children, as do culturally underprivileged groups in the United States. In both cases they attribute this to early damage in social self-identity and self-respect. There is much truancy and delinquency among Buraku children. Thus there seem to be some cross-cultural regularities, not only in attitudes of prejudice but in responses to prejudice in India, Japan, and the United States. Of course, there are also differences in these respects.

The right-wing "authoritarian personality" is a product of Western culture. We cannot say to what extent prejudices in non-Western societies are associated with family backgrounds like those described by Adorno and his colleagues.

Bettelheim and Janowitz (1950:163) have suggested a relativistic view in relation to the etiology of anti-Semitism. "Although anti-Semitism has been present in slave societies, feudal societies, capitalist societies, and recently too in communist society, it appears in each case to have been a different social phenomenon."

But this is a matter which requires some investigation. The studies by Isaacs, Berreman, De Vos, and Wagatsuma cited earlier suggest that there are some universally operative mechanisms associated with prejudice.

SUGGESTIONS FOR FURTHER READING

On values: see Ethel M. Albert, "The Classification of Values," *American Anthropologist* 58 (1956), pp. 221–48; and Victor F. Ayoub, "The Study of Values," in *Introduction to Cultural Anthropology,* ed. James A. Clifton (Boston: Houghton, Mifflin, 1968) pp. 244–72.

For a comparative research study on values, stereotypes, and other aspects of "subjective culture," see Harry C. Triandis et al., *The Analysis of Subjective Culture* (New York: John Wiley & Sons, 1972).

On prejudice, for a balanced review and evaluation of different theories about prejudice, see Arnold M. Rose, "The Causes of Prejudice." in *Social Problems,* ed. Francis E. Merrill, (New York: Alfred A. Knopf, 1950), pp. 402–24. See also George Eaton Simpson and J. Milton Yinger, *Racial and Cultural Minorities, An Analysis of Prejudice and Discrimination* (New York: Harper & Brothers, 1958), especially chap. 3. See also S. Reichard, "Rorschach Study of Prejudiced Personality," *American Journal of Orthopsychiatry* 18 (1948), pp. 280–86; Nathan W. Ackerman and Marie Jahoda, *Anti-Semitism and Emotional Disorder. A Psychoanalytic Interpretation* (New York: Harper & Brothers, 1950); D. B. Harris, H. G. Gough, W. E. Martin, "Children's Ethnic Attitudes: Relationship to Parental Beliefs Concerning Child Training," *Child Development* 21 (1950), pp. 169–81; Gordon W. Allport, *The Nature of Prejudice* (Boston: Beacon Press, 1954).

On prejudice in India: see Gardner Murphy, *In the Minds of Men. The Study of Human Behavior and Social Tensions in India. Based on the UNESCO Studies by Social Scientists Conducted at the Request of the Government of India* (New York: Basic Books, 1953). For a fuller bibliography, which gives some references to studies of prejudice in non-Western countries, see Donald T. Campbell and Robert A. LeVine, "A Proposal for Cooperative Cross-Cultural Research on Ethnocentrism," *Journal of Conflict Resolution* 5 (1961), pp. 107–08.

11

Biological and Evolutionary Perspectives on Human Nature

The foregoing chapters of this book have dealt with many contrasts between human societies, with how the members of Society A differ from those of Society B. We have, for example, considered Apollonian-Dionysian contrasts, the differences between a Trobriand upbringing and a European one, between Samoan and American adolescence, and between the attitudes of pastoralists and farmers, to mention a few. But a quite different, although related issue should also be raised: How do human beings resemble or differ from other animals? Is there a special kind of human nature that is the product of our biological makeup and evolutionary history? Those who raise this question would concede that *Homo sapiens* is a culture-carrier but would insist that man is a culture-carrier of a particular sort, with a special kind of nervous system, endocrine glands, blood circulation, and so forth. Although this fact is generally acknowledged by most people, there was a tendency to downplay its significance in the early work of Ruth Benedict and Margaret Mead with their emphasis on human plasticity and cultural relativism. Human beings, it was argued, can adjust to almost any sort of culture.

There was an implicit criticism of this view in George P. Murdock's list of universal aspects of culture, published in 1945. A founder of the Human Relations Area Files, Murdock was in a good position to learn which aspects of culture appear in all societies for which there are adequate ethnographic descriptions, ranging from the simplest cultures to the most complex. Omitting a few items, here is Murdock's list following the alphabetical order in which he presented them:

> age grading, athletic sports, bodily adornment, calendar, community organization, cooking, cooperative labor, cosmology, courtship, dancing, decorative art, divination, division of labor, dream interpretation, education, ethics, ethnobotany, etiquette, . . . family, feasting, fire

making, folklore, food taboos, funeral rites, games, gestures, gift giving, government, greetings, hair styles, hospitality, housing, hygiene,
incest taboos, inheritance rules, joking, kin groups, kinship nomencla-
ture, language, law, . . . magic, marriage, mealtimes, medicine, . . .
mourning, music, mythology, numerals, obstetrics, penal sanctions,
personal names, postnatal care, pregnancy usages, property rights,
propitiation of supernatural beings, puberty customs, religious ritual,
residence rules, sexual restrictions, soul concepts, status differentiation, surgery, tool making, trade, visiting, weaning (Murdock
1945:124).

Some of these categories are ambiguous, and in some cases their
universality may be questioned; nevertheless we have here quite a
long catalog of allegedly universal aspects of culture. This suggests
that human beings are creatures of a particular kind who somehow
require an array of institutions along these lines. The presence of
some of the items is immediately understandable, since they are
closely related to human biology, such as feasting, obstetrics, postnatal care, pregnancy usages, and weaning; but many are aspects of
religion, including cosmology, divination, funeral rites, magic,
mourning, propitiation of supernatural beings, religious ritual, and
soul concepts. In these cases the reasons for their universality are less
obvious; we may need to resort to psychoanalytic, functional, or
other kinds of interpretation to account for them. Incidentally, in
view of the discussion that follows, it is worth noting that warfare
does not appear on Murdock's list.

Although relativistic views about human cognition were expressed
by the Sapir-Whorf and other schools of thought, there have been, at
the same time, an emphasis on universality in Noam Chomsky's
conception of the innate language-learning capacity of human beings,
in Berlin and Kay's study of color naming, and in Lévi-Strauss's ideas
about the ways in which the human brain structures experience according to binary contrasts. Thus human beings in different parts of
the world, with different histories behind them, have often arrived at
similar cultural solutions to the same experiences and problems.

Human beings everywhere not only share some general ways of
thinking, but they have the same sorts of emotions, including fear,
anger, hostility, envy, sexual impulses, and pride. We find many of
these emotional reactions in chimpanzees and other primates. The
biological and evolutionary basis for human emotions and behavior
was emphasized in a series of controversial books that appeared in
the 1960s, including *African Genesis* (1961) and *The Territorial Imperative*
(1966) by Robert Ardrey, *On Aggression* by Konrad Lorenz (1966), and
The Naked Ape by Desmond Morris (1967). Many such works by zoolo-
gists, ethologists, anthropologists, and sociobiologists have appeared
since. Ardrey, Lorenz, Morris, and others made comparisons and
contrasts between the behavior of human beings and other animals

and drew attention to the role of human evolution in establishing some abiding aspects of human nature, particularly with regard to aggression. Criticisms of such works also appeared in due course. Let us consider the issues involved in these controversies.

AGGRESSION

Lorenz, a naturalist observer of animal behavior, defines aggression as "the fighting instinct in beast and man which is directed *against* members of the same species." (1966:ix, Lorenz's emphasis). Thus his view is in keeping with that of Freud (1930:102) who referred to aggression as "an innate, independent, instinctual disposition in man." Like Freud, Lorenz believes that the aggressive drive may be redirected or sublimated in relatively harmless channels. He also sees aggression as being capable of spontaneous expression in the absence of an external challenge. This is because of the implicit assumption of a "hydraulic" model, that the impulse builds up like dammed-up water seeking release. "If the stimuli normally releasing it fail to appear for an appreciable period, the organism as a whole is thrown into a state of general unrest and begins to search actively for the missing stimulus" (1966:50).

Fredric Wertham (1966:25), a psychiatrist, takes issue with such views: "In contrast to hunger and sex, destructive aggression is not an instinct or even a drive, in the usual sense of these terms. It is not reduced by being expressed or acted out. It is greatly influenced by learning." John Paul Scott (1975:20), a psychologist, defines aggression as fighting, especially the initiation of an attack. He emphasizes that aggressive behavior is learned. From this point of view, the notion of spontaneous aggression seeking discharge is doubtful. "Defensive fighting can be stimulated by the pain of an attack, but aggression, in the strict sense of an unprovoked attack, can only be produced by training." Scott (p. 62) concludes that there is no such thing as a simple "instinct for fighting."

Some psychologists support the view of Dollard et al. (1939) that aggression results from frustration. This compromise between the Freudian view and learning theory is criticized by Scott (1975:35), who argues that "frustration leads to aggression only in a situation where the individual has a habit of being aggressive." While frustration may result in aggression, it may lead to other kinds of responses as well (pp. 33–34). Similarly, Ralph Holloway, an anthropologist (1968:39) writes: "There seems to be little doubt that frustration is a major stimulus for provoking aggressive responses, but it is debatable whether the original formulation that all aggression stems from frustration, or that aggression always follows frustration is accurate."

Very early frustration in human infants resulting from neglect or maltreatment is seen by Anthony Storr (1972:37–39) to produce a lifelong susceptibility to hostile feelings which, combined with a diminished sense of conscience, may give rise to a psychopathic personality. From a 22-year longitudinal study of 875 subjects, Leonard Aron of the University of Illinois at Chicago has concluded that the level of aggression remains very stable in individuals and may be well established before the age of eight (Milwaukee Journal, April 30, 1984).

Another approach to understanding aggression is in terms of the processes of identification and social learning which lead a child to behave as others do. It is for this reason that some psychologists warn about the bad effects of TV violence in children's programs. One experiment showed that children who saw adults beating a doll were more likely to later beat the doll, while a control group of children who saw the adults behave neutrally toward the doll were not as likely to beat it (Bandura and Walters 1959). In this case learned behavior is involved.

We find, then, a wide range of opinion, between *innate aggressionists* on the one hand (to use Ashley Montagu's term for writers such as Lorenz, Ardrey, and Morris) and psychologists such as Scott and psychiatrists such as Wertham who account for aggression mainly in environmental and situational terms.

Both Ardrey, a popularizer of biological and anthropological findings, and Morris, a zoologist, discuss early human ecological adaptations, especially the switch from a vegetarian gathering way of life to reliance on a carnivorous diet which turned our ancestors into weapon-wielding "killer apes." Aggression was directed against animals of other species and also, for territorial reasons, against members of the same species. "Man is a predator whose natural instinct is to kill with a weapon," says Ardrey (1961:316). In a similar vein, Morris (1967:34) writes: "The fundamental patterns of behavior laid down in our early days as hunting apes still shine through all our affairs, no matter how lofty they may be." The sociobiologist E. O. Wilson (1978:100) similarly believes that "human beings have a marked hereditary predisposition to aggressive behavior" and that human nature is "a hodgepodge of special genetic adaptations to an environment largely vanished, the world of the Ice-Age hunter-gatherer" (p. 196).

Are predation and aggression the same, or similar in nature? Lorenz (1966:22) claims that they are quite different: "a dog about to catch a hunted rabbit has the same kind of excitedly happy expression as he has when he greets his master or awaits some longed-for treat . . . the lion, in the dramatic moment before he springs, is in no way angry." Scott (1975:165) points out that herbivorous animals which never kill game may violently fight one another; and the hunting patterns used by carnivores differ greatly from their behavior in social fighting.

Where human hunters are concerned, many different kinds of attitudes are expressed, depending on the circumstances, the kind of prey, and local cultural traditions. For example, the Desana of South America regard hunting as a form of courtship. Their verb for "to hunt" has the meaning of "to make love to animals." In order to sexually excite the game and cause it to draw near, the hunter bathes and perfumes himself and applies face paint, using the same sort of love magic that is used in courting women (Reichel-Dolmatoff 1971:220–22). This example may be extreme, but it serves to show the differences that may appear between predation and aggression. However, it must be admitted that the Desana's wooing of game ends in the animal's death. Perhaps if the prey is elusive and the hunt drags on all day, the hunter may become aggressive in feelings as well as in the deed.

Lorenz (1966:142, 208–9) sees aggression as a benevolent instinctual reaction in some respects, for he remarks: "We do not know of a single animal which is capable of personal friendship and which lacks aggression. . . . A personal bond, an individual friendship, is found only in animals with highly developed intra-specific aggression; in fact, this bond is the firmer, the more aggressive the particular animal and species is." Washburn and Avis (1958:434) make a similar point in relation to hunting (aggression against other species) after humans adopted a carnivorous diet: "The very actions which caused man to be feared by other animals led to more cooperation, food sharing, and economic interdependence within the group." Eibl-Eibesfeldt (1972:123–24) finds the explanation for these associations not in aggression per se but in parent-child relations: "Love is not primarily a child of aggression, but has arisen with the evolution of parental care. . . . Among animals that do not look after their young, we know of no group defense and no fighting partnerships."

TERRITORIALITY

Both Ardrey and Morris deal with the relation between territoriality and aggression. Animals exhibit territoriality when they defend an area against incursions by other members of the same species. This sort of behavior occurs in all classes of vertebrates but is not universal and does not necessarily lead to fighting. As the ecologist Tinbergen (1968:1413) explains: "Animals of territorial species, once they have settled on a territory, attack intruders, but an animal that is still searching for a suitable territory or finds itself outside its home range withdraws when it meets with an already established owner." Threat displays are more common than fighting.

Although gibbons and howler monkeys, among others, exhibit territoriality, it is not strongly represented in the order of primates, to which we belong (Simonds 1974:75). This consideration weakens the strength of Robert Ardrey's contention (1966:15) that humans have an innate predisposition to defend their local turf: "If we defend the title to our land or the sovereignty of our country, we do it for reasons no different, no less innate, no less ineradicable, than do lower animals." According to Morris (1967) the ancestral carnivorous killer apes developed territoriality because packs of hunting males needed a home base where their females and young remained. Similar speculations about the development of territoriality by early human hunters of big game have been put forward by George B. Schaller and Gordon P. Lowther (1969) and also by Glenn E. King (1975), who points to parallel developments among hyenas, lions, and wolves.

Territoriality is found among some human hunting groups of recent times but not among all (Dyson-Hudson and Smith 1978). Concerning the Kung San of Botswana, one of the best-studied hunting-gathering societies, Richard B. Lee (1979:457) points to the practice of reciprocal land use by neighboring groups, which would tend to limit the emphasis on territoriality. "An individual's primary kin and close affines are always distributed at several different water holes, and through the far-reaching ties of the name relation he may establish close ties at a number of others . . . it is clear that the maintenance of *flexibility* to adapt to changing ecological circumstances is far more important in hunter-gatherer group structure than is the maintenance of exclusive rights to land." Julian Steward expressed his doubts about the territoriality of primitive bands as follows:

> First, the primary groups that comprise the larger maximum bands intermarry, amalgamate if they are too small or split off if too large. Second, . . . there is no more than a tendency for primary groups to utilize special areas. Third, most so-called "warfare" among such societies is no more than revenge for alleged witchcraft or continued interfamily feuds. Fourth, collecting is the main resource in most areas, but I know of no reported defense of seed areas (1968:334).

Since Morris, like Ardrey, considers the "territorial imperative" to be innate, he is pessimistic about efforts to control warfare. Early human aggression was relatively harmless, he explains, for its aim was only to subdue a rival, not kill him. A defeated primate displays submissive, appeasing gestures to the dominant animal, such as adopting a juvenile food-begging position, displaying a female sexual posture, or engaging in grooming behavior. But with the invention of long-range weapons, such measures ceased to work: "the result is wholesale slaughter on a scale unheard of in any other species" (Morris 1967:143).

With his "hydraulic" approach, Konrad Lorenz (1966:272) is more optimistic, since he believes that human aggression can be redirected along more harmless lines, such as participation in sports, and he noted that "The Olympic Games are virtually the only occasion when the anthem of one nation can be played without arousing any hostility against another." International sports events not only serve as a safety valve, but they also bring the people of different nations together in a common cause. Other such channels, Lorenz urges, should be utilized for the sake of world peace.

In opposition to the "innate aggressionists" are those who do not consider either aggression or territoriality to be at all instinctual. As we have seen, John Paul Scott belongs to this school of thought. He concedes that fighting occurs in all classes of vertebrates, although not in all species. But even within a species where fighting occurs, its appearance depends on circumstances.

> If male mice are brought together only once a day, they will begin to fight at about the age of thirty-two days. However, if a group of males are raised together in the same pen from birth, they do not automatically start to fight at thirty-two days. In fact, they may live peacefully together for many months with no fighting at all. The mice appear to have formed a habit of not-fighting while young, and this carries over into later life (Scott 1975:17).

Scott refers to this as the principle of passive inhibition, one form of learning: "the primary stimulation to fight must come from the outside. Heredity can enter the picture only in such a way as lowering or raising the threshold of stimulation, or modifying the physical equipment for fighting" (pp. 80–81). Young animals that grow up together are at first physically unable to fight. Just by not fighting, they learn not to fight, according to the principle of passive inhibition. The first agonistic behavior appears in playful form (p. 193).

NONAGGRESSIVE SOCIETIES

Ashley Montagu (1978:x), a physical anthropologist who holds that the notion of instincts in man "has no scientific validity whatever" has assembled descriptions by seven anthropologists of seven nonaggressive nonliterate peoples, including the Kung (Bushman) of South Africa and the Semai of Malaysia, to show that a peaceful way of life is quite possible in at least some human societies. However, some critics have pointed to examples of hostility, including murder, in these same groups (Wilson 1978:100; Paul 1978:76–77).[1]

American undergraduates, who have read about the Yąnomamö, "the fierce people," and who may have seen some of the fine films about those villagers of southern Venezuela, may well have come to think of the Yąnomamö as a most aggressive bunch of savages. This view, like the contrasting view of the Kung and Semai, should also be

---

[1] Richard B. Lee (1979:371) found 22 cases of homicide among the central Kung between 1920 and 1969. In a chapter entitled "Conflict and Violence," he describes various conflict cases in some detail.

modified, as their leading ethnographer, Napoleon Chagnon makes clear:

> First of all, the Yąnomamö do not spend all or even a major fraction of their waking hours making war on neighbors or abusing their wives. Second, warfare among the Yąnomamö varies from region to region and from time to time; it is extremely intense in some areas at particular times, and almost nonexistent in other areas. Even the most "warlike" villages have long periods of relative peace during which time daily life is tranquil and happy . . . (1976:162).

When we characterize a group of people as being aggressive or nonaggressive, we pay selective attention to certain features. (I do not mean to imply, though, that there are not great differences among such groups.) A group of people may be peaceful and cooperative in some respects but hostile in others.

Outward amiability may mask strong internal hostility, as A. I. Hallowell noted of the Saulteaux or Ojibwa Indians of the Lake Winnipeg region in Canada:

> These people have never engaged in war with the whites or with other Indian tribes. There are no official records of murder; suicide is unknown; and theft is extremely rare. Open expressions of anger or quarrels ending in physical assault seldom occur. A spirit of mutual helpfulness is manifest in the sharing of economic goods and there is every evidence of cooperation in all sorts of economically productive tasks. No one, in fact, is much better off than his neighbor (1955:278).

However, Hallowell believes that what Father Le Jeune, a Jesuit missionary, wrote about the Montagnais-Naskapi of Labrador in the 17th century applies to the Saulteaux as well: "It is strange to see how these people agree so well outwardly, and how they hate each other within. They do not often get angry and fight with one another, but in the depths of their hearts they intend a great deal of harm" (Hallowell 1955:277). Hallowell illustrated this point for the Saulteaux by referring to their malicious gossip and pervasive fears of sorcery, and he concludes: "while there are no *official* records of murder among the Saulteaux, this does not correspond with the psychological realities of this society. Within their behavioral world, murder has occurred again and again but always as the result of sorcery, not of overt physical aggression" (p. 282).

One wonders how well such observations might apply to other nonaggressive societies that have been described. Hallowell's analysis seems to imply acceptance of the Freudian-Lorenzian hydraulic model of aggression: If outlets are blocked in one area, other channels for its release will be found. But we do not find sorcery in all nonfighting societies. Colin Turnbull, who has done fieldwork among forest pygmies, remarks in a discussion on "Primate Behavior and the Evolution of Aggression," apropos of hunting societies: "In the two groups known to me, there is an almost total lack of aggression, emotional or physical, and this is borne out by the lack of warfare, feuding, witchcraft, and sorcery . . . the act of hunting is not carried out in an aggressive spirit at all" (Lee and DeVore 1968:341).

A crucial problem in discussions about aggression is how to define it. John Paul Scott defines aggression as fighting, while Hallowell has in mind a more pervasive undercurrent tension which may result in fighting or else in some other form of behavior. If aggression is defined in Hallowell's terms, it may be universal; if defined in Scott's terms, it may not be.

At any rate, an outburst of aggression is not the same thing as war, which is the result of deliberate decisions by the political leaders of a nation. Indeed, Theodore Abel (1941:855), in a review of world warfare, writes that "The evidence shows that the decision to wage war precedes by one to five years the outbreak of hostilities." It would be possible nowadays for a well-adjusted unemotional person to blow up a city. Although hostile feelings toward the enemy are apt to develop during a military campaign, a more important motive in modern warfare is obedience. Stanley Milgram's experiments have shown how strong this motive is in an experimental setting. Milgram's volunteer subjects were asked to give progressively stronger electric shocks to other volunteers when the latter made mistakes. The shocked victims, who howled in protest, were actually the psychologist's confederates, and they received no shocks at all; but the experimental subjects did not know that, and most of them continued to give the shocks at the psychologist's direction. 26 of 40 subjects carried out these instructions to the end, which involved giving a shock of 450 volts. This behavior does not seem to have been motivated by any sadistic or aggressive tendencies but, rather, by an earnest desire to carry out the orders of an authority figure (Milgram 1974).

Richard Sipes (1973) made a cross-cultural research study of the correlation between war and sports and also a diachronic study of the United States between 1920 and 1970 in order to test two rival doctrines which he calls Drive Discharge and Culture Pattern. According to the "hydraulic" Drive Discharge model, individual and group fighting result from innate aggressive drives. "Warlike sports serve to discharge accumulated aggressive tension and therefore act as alternative channels to war, making it less likely" (p. 64). The Culture Pattern model holds that aggressive behavior is mainly learned and culturally patterned. Because of cultural integration and the strain of consistency, "behavior patterns and value systems relative to war and to warlike sports tend to overlap and support each other's presence" (p. 65). Sipes's study showed that war and combative sports are positively correlated, in keeping with the Culture Pattern model, which tends to discredit the Drive Discharge Theory, with its innate, hydraulic assumptions. It may be noted that, seemingly at odds with the latter view, the amount and scale of warfare has greatly increased in the course of cultural evolution. In a cross-cultural study of 655 societies, Quincy Wright (1965:66) observes: "the collectors, lower hunters, and lower agriculturalists are the least warlike. The higher hunters and higher agriculturalists are more warlike, while the highest agriculturalists and the pastorals are the most warlike of all."

MALE DOMINANCE

Another aspect of human behavior that is traceable to our biological and evolutionary background, according to Lionel Tiger (1969), Robert Ardrey (1976), and others, is male dominance. Among the reasons for this view are the following considerations:

1. Terrestrial primates often show sexual dimorphism, differences in size and strength between males and females, with males being larger, stronger, and more dominant, and some males dominant over others.
2. Males are mainly involved in territorial defense and show more aggression than females.
3. In most human societies males carry out political roles and activities that are held to be more important than those of females. There seem to be no societies in which women actually control the political system.
4. Both among humans and nonhuman primates there is more rough-and-tumble play among juvenile males than among young females.
5. The male sex hormone testosterone is related to aggression.

In some animal species, when low-ranking animals were injected with male hormones, they rose to the highest positions in the dominance hierarchy. When testosterone was given to pregnant female rhesus monkeys, their "masculinized" female offspring showed more aggressive behavior than did an untreated control group of females (Young, Goy, and Phoenix 1964).

Both Ardrey and Tiger, and also Tiger and Fox (1971), trace the development of male dominance in the long hunting period of the early hominids, when group hunting and territorial defense led to what Tiger and Fox call *male bonding.* Females meanwhile tended their young in the home base, did some gathering, and prepared the meals.

The views of these male writers have been challenged by some female anthropologists. M. Kay Martin and Barbara Voorhies (1975) claim that women are really dominant in hunting-gathering societies, since gathering by women generally provides most of the diet. Ernestine Friedl (1975) claims that equality of the sexes is greatest in societies where men and women share the same subsistence tasks, as among the Washo of the Great Basin. The greatest male dominance occurs where hunting is almost the only source of subsistence, as among the Eskimos.

Divale and Harris (1976) explain the widespread existence of what they call the *male supremacist complex* in terms of the prestate warfare that was required to regulate population growth. They do not consider genetically determined sex differences sufficient to explain all aspects of the complex. Once again, the question of innate versus learned behavior appears. In a cross-cultural survey of 101 societies, Ronald P. Rohner (1976) found, as others have done, that boys are always more aggressive than girls; but Rohner also discovered that there is much more overt aggression in some societies than in others and that the level of aggression in the one sex tends to approximate that of the other within a particular society. The level of aggression is evidently influenced by general sociocultural conditions.

SEX

In nonhuman primates there are restricted periods of sexual activity, when the female is receptive, in contrast to the practically year-round receptivity of human females. Among our closest relatives, the chimpanzees, females are receptive for only 10 days per month, "provided they are neither pregnant nor lactating, which in older females means that they may be denied sexual activity for up to five years" (Van Lawick-Goodall 1971:191). The sex act itself is brief, lasting from only 10 to 15 seconds in chimpanzees (p. 83) and even less time in baboons. Nonhuman female primates do not normally seem to experience orgasm. For reasons such as these, Desmond Morris (1967:53) calls *Homo sapiens* "the sexiest primate alive."

There is much more precopulatory behavior among humans than among nonhuman primates, who do not go in for such activities as kissing and breast stimulation (Ford and Beach 1951:76). In most primates the male mounts from behind the female, but human copulation generally assumes the ventro-ventral position, although other positions may be used as well. The frontal position may be favored because human beings have upright posture and the genitalia of both sexes are directed forward (Harrison and Mantagna 1969:207). Morris (1967:62–64) points out that face-to-face sex is "personalized sex" in which the visual signals of lips and breasts are visible.

What was the function of this heightened sexuality among early hominids? Morris claims that it was to establish male-female pair bonds, something that is usually absent among nonhuman primates. Increased sexual activity between the male and female served to keep the hunting male together with the female who stayed in the home base with her offspring. Morris suggests that this was generally a monogamous relationship, a view regarded with skepticism by Robin Fox (1973:56–62), who believes that human males were then (and are today) essentially promiscuous, preferring polygyny if possible.

In any case, heightened sexuality would have some other consequences besides pair-bonding, including sexual rivalry, problems of incest, and the sexual molestation of children. In recent years Americans have become more educated than they formerly were about the existence of the latter problem. In April 1984, for example, there were revelations about the widespread rape, sodomy, and other sexual abuse of children in a school at Manhattan Beach, California. Is this a manifestation of latter-day decadence in American culture? Or have such abuses always existed but seldom been reported in the past? The latter alternative seems to be the more likely possibility. Although historical records on this topic are understandably scanty, Lloyd deMause has assembled evidence of much sexual exploitation of children in the classical past.

> Growing up in Greece and Rome often included being used sexually by older men. . . . Boy brothels flourished in every city, and one could even contract for the use of a rent-a-boy service in Athens. . . . Children were sometimes sold into concubinage. . . . Quintilian, after many years of teaching in Rome, warned parents against the frequency of sexual abuse by teachers. . . . Aristotle said homosexuality often became habitual in "those who are abused from childhood". . . . The favorite sexual use of children was . . . anal intercourse. . . . Intercourse with castrated children was often spoken of as especially arousing. . . (1975b:43–46).

From this sort of evidence one suspects that the potentiality for such behavior has always existed in human groups. Dorothy Willner (1983:141) relates sexual abuse of children to the question of the origin of incest taboos. She points out that the effects of abuse by a nonrelated male known to the child may not be very different from the effects of incest, and she suggests that this "might be an element underlying the extension of kinship categories and incest taboos to most or all adults of small local communities in tribal societies." Willner's explanation for the wide spread of incest taboos is: "incest is prohibited to reduce the trauma and psychic disruption that sexual activity can inflict on children when it is imposed by a more adult aggressor" (p. 139).

Sexual relations within a nuclear family have not always been tabooed. Brother-sister marriages were common in Egypt during the first three centuries B.C. From an analysis of household returns, Keith Hopkins (1980:304) has suggested that "one third, and perhaps more, of all brothers with marriageable sisters married inside the family." This shows that human groups have not always regulated sexual relations within the family in the same way, but generally they have tried to prevent incest.

One of the leading explanations for the existence of incest taboos is Sigmund Freud's concept of the Oedipus complex. The horror usually expressed at the idea of incest is seen as an unconscious defense against temptation: young boys, says Freud, wish to have sexual relations with their mothers. In practice, however, this seems to occur very rarely. Few cases of mother-son incest have been reported, in contrast to father-daughter incest, of which nearly 3,000 cases have been documented. Recorded cases of sibling incest range from less than one third to more than one half of father-daughter cases, although the actual incidence may be much higher (Willner 1983:139–40).

THE PRIMAL PARRICIDE

In Chapter 4 we considered the question of whether the Oedipus complex, as described by Freud, is universal. One aspect of Freud's argument, the so-called *primal parricide*, was mentioned but not discussed in that chapter. We deal with it now because the biological blacklash of recent years that produced the books by Ardrey, Morris, and others has led some writers to favorably reassess the Freudian myth set forth in *Totem and Taboo* (Freud 1913).

Freud drew from Darwin's writings the assumption that the earliest form of human social organization, the "primal horde," was headed by a dominant male who maintained a monopoly of sexual access to the females of the group, while his growing sons were driven off. At the dawn of the human era, according to Freud, a band of brothers jointly slew their father and ate him. But having done so, they felt a sense of guilt; so they tabooed to themselves the women for whose sake they had killed the father. This was the origin of the incest taboo and clan exogamy. The father then became symbolized by an animal, the clan totem, and the primal crime became symbolized by a jointly shared totemic feast in which the clan animal was eaten. Thus the primal parricide led to the beginning of social organization and religion. Memory of this ancient crime lives on in the unconscious minds of men today.

Freud's myth was subjected to severe criticism by A. L. Kroeber (1920) and by B. Malinowski (1953:123–52). Freud was familiar with their criticisms, but he continued to believe in the primal crime until the end of his life. In the posthumously published *Moses and Monotheism* (1955), Freud rejected the complaint that his hypothesis violated the biological principle that acquired characteristics are not inherited, for he found parallels in the instinctive behavior of animals, and he concluded: "After these considerations I have no qualms in saying that men have always known—in this particular way—that once upon a time they had a primeval father and killed him" (p. 129).

Since notions about inherited programming or "wiring" have

found renewed support (for example, Tiger and Fox 1971), it is perhaps not surprising that some writers have recently expressed belief in Freud's myth. In an article entitled "Did the Primal Crime Take Place?" Robert A. Paul (1976:341), an anthropologist, answers the question in the affirmative, claiming that the ancestral murder marked the transition from nature to culture, which must have been "a decisive and earth-shattering time; and this scenario is replicated in each of us, perhaps in our phylogenetic memory." Paul (1982) has written an interpretation of Tibetan religious symbolism in terms of the primal parricide and the Oedipus complex. Another recent convert to the primal parricide hypothesis is Robin Fox (1980:61) who states that "something like it must have taken place."

But the most detailed retelling of the Freudian myth is by C. R. Badcock (1980). From writings about primates by Clifford Jolly and J. H. Crook, Badcock concludes that Darwin and Freud were right about the composition of early human groups. He adds that a crucial shift took place when hunting replaced foraging. The sexually frustrated juvenile males were ideally preadapted for big-game hunting. Unlike the dominant father, they did not have to stay with the females and young, who would only be an encumbrance during the hunt. The young males were on relatively equal terms with one another and could learn cooperative techniques, forming a social group like those of carnivorous animals, such as the lion, hyena, and wolf. Hunting gave the young men an outlet for their aggressive feelings, but it also provided nutritious food, which gave them a cooperative edge over groups that remained foragers. Their collective action also increased their chances of survival.

The joint attack on the dominant male would have been carried out like a hunt, an act of cooperative aggression. But if the murder had been followed by a competitive scramble for possession of the females, the unity of the hunting group would have disappeared, and so, "the acquisition of females would have demanded notable increases in altruism and the suppression of internal conflicts within the hunting bands" (Badcock 1980:13). The use of a home base where the females and young could stay would help to maintain the structure of the male hunting group. All these developments would be aided by natural selection, which would also encourage the development of ambivalent emotions. "The reason is that the most successful hunters would have been those capable of the greatest resentment against their fathers, but also capable of the greatest love and respect for them" (p. 14). Aggression and altruism went hand in hand.

Then Badcock asks a new question: "Why should the sons of the original parricides not have committed incest with *their* mothers or sisters?" (p. 15). Part of the answer, following Reik (1958), lies in the men's creation of initiation ceremonies, which originally developed from a ritual of mourning over the slain father that involved masochistic self-chastisement, including genital mutilations. "Thus having initiated *themselves* . . . it was but a small step to initiating the sons . . . the original parricides who had maintained altruistic cooperation among themselves by forgoing incest and sexual and social hegemony, were bound to direct their aggression against temptations to violate those very same inhibitions" (Badcock 1980:25).[2]

Since Badcock closely follows and elaborates on Freud's original story, his ingenious version is open to the same objections that Malinowski and Kroeber raised in the 1920s. We still cannot be sure what sort of social organization characterized early human groups. Even if there was a dominant father figure, he might not have been able to keep all the females to himself. Hinde (1974:298) cites some reports about baboons which state that the highest ranking males, being occupied with controlling the group, copulate less than do inferior males. Jane van Lawick-Goodall describes a receptive female chimpanzee mating with several males in turn. Although adolescent males have less opportunity than the older ones, they sometimes approach the female. "The older males, although they may glance at the mating pair, seldom object to these expressions of youthful passion" (1971:85). Concerning mountain gorillas, Schaller (1963:255) writes: "I never observed the slightest indication that the dominant male chased others to the periphery, kept them from coming into the group, or prevented their having social intercourse with members of the group." We may ask, then: Did the sons of the primal horde have sufficient motivation to kill the father, and if they did, did they have to also eat him, too? If they killed and ate him, would they necessarily feel guilty? And would their guilt be so extreme as to make them repress their sexual impulses? These are among the questions raised by Kroeber (1920:49–50), who also remarked: "it is at best problematical whether blood sacrifice goes back to a totemic observance", and: "the fact that a child sometimes displaces its father-hatred upon an animal—we are not told in what percentage of cases—is no proof that the sons did so."

In short, belief in the primal parricide depends on too many unverifiable assumptions.

ALTRUISM

Some sociobiologists have attributed human altruism and cooperation to genetic factors, at least in part.[3] E. O. Wilson

---

[2] Although they do not invoke the primal parricide, a paper by Walsh and Scandalis (1975) has some similarities to Badcock's analysis. They point to parallels between warfare and male initiation ceremonies. In both cases young men are placed in a dangerous situation and threatened by older men, who both seek to instill group solidarity and also, at the same time, direct hostility toward them in a socially acceptable manner. Walsh and Scandalis derive this intergenerational hostility from the Oedipus complex.

[3] Wilson (1975:4) defines *sociobiology* as "the systematic study of the biological basis of all social behavior." He then explains that he attempts to "codify sociobiology into a branch of evolutionary biology and particularly of modern population biology."

(1975:382) states that the typical vertebrate society "favors individual and in-group survival at the expense of social integrity," while human societies, alone among the vertebrates, have something like the cooperative order of insect societies. Among vertebrates, including the mammals, "Selfishness rules the relationships between members . . . acts of altruism are infrequent and ordinarily directed only toward offspring" (p. 380). Thus the human accomplishment is quite surprising. "They have reversed the downward trend in social evolution that prevailed over one billion years of the previous history of life" (p. 380), which Wilson considers to be "the culminating mystery of all biology" (p. 382).

Reciprocal altruism is a common feature of human life which has been manifest in food exchanges, barter, and also, as Lévi-Strauss (1969) argued, in the exchange of women. Sociobiologists claim that reciprocal altruistic behavior is fostered through natural selection. There is no doubt, Wilson asserts, that such is the case among social insects.

> Natural selection has been broadened to include kin selection. The self-sacrificing termite soldier protects the rest of its colony, including the queen and king, its parents. As a result, the soldier's more fertile brothers and sisters flourish, and through them the altruistic genes are multiplied by a greater production of nephews and nieces (Wilson 1978:153).

Some sociobiologists argue that the same sort of explanation is applicable to human behavior, including self-sacrificial acts that would seem on the surface (as in the case of the termite soldier mentioned earlier), to be nonadaptive or self-destructive. Sociobiologists have coined the term *inclusive fitness* to cover such cases. As Daniel Freedman (1979a:2) explains: "Siblings share at least 50 percent of their genes. . . . If I give up my life to save three siblings who would otherwise die, I have, in effect, saved 150 percent of my gene component."

Rather than invoke a genetic explanation for altruism in human beings, it seems less strained to emphasize the influence of social ties and the process of identification. Mary Midgley (1978:131) points out that some nonhuman animals such as dolphins and elephants help to rescue adults of their species in distress, and some feed sick and injured adults. "When we consider what is involved in the relation of parent and child in a slow-developing species, and remember that this bond shapes the early experience of every member of that species, further gradual progress to mutual help among adults does not seem too hard to imagine. And in that context, rescue is intelligible enough" (p. 138).

In some comments in *American Psychologist* (1976:370), Wilson remarks, "to say that human altruism is genetically based at the species level is not to say that the variation *within* our species has any genetic foundation" (Wilson's emphasis).

According to Badcock (1980:35), however, there was genetic variation within the early human species: "natural selection must have favored those with the greatest ambivalence towards their fathers, for it was these individuals who had the greatest chance of solving the problems of altruistic behavior within the group and who would have thus handed on their psychological peculiarities most successfully to their offspring."

GENERAL CONSIDERATIONS

Many of the studies discussed in this chapter express opposition to environmentalist and relativistic views and emphasize the common underlying features of human nature that result from our biological and evolutionary background.

In an autobiographical sketch Melford Spiro (1978) described the gradual progress of his disillusionment with the cultural determinist philosophy that he had formerly held. Spiro's present viewpoint is set forth in his criticisms of Malinowski's work on the Oedipus complex[4] and also in his conclusions about current tendencies in Israeli kibbutzim.[5] Derek Freeman's criticism of Margaret Mead's picture of Samoan adolescence involves a similar opposition to a cultural determinist position.[6] In their different ways, orthodox psychoanalysis and sociobiology share the aim of understanding a human nature that is in large part biologically determined and far from infinitely malleable.

A cultural determinist approach that attributes great plasticity to the human child is usually congenial to liberals and radicals who hope to change human social conditions for the better. Nicholas Pastore (1949) made a good case for this point in an analysis of the views of 24 leading scientists who took sides in the nature-nurture controversy. Pastore classified 12 of these men as hereditarians and 12 as environmentalists. With regard to their political views, 11 of the 12 hereditarians were classified as conservatives, while 11 of the 12 environmentalists were classified as liberals or radicals. Although the sample is small, the findings are significant and seem to be consistent with what one might expect. It also seems likely that there would be less optimism among theorists who believe in innate human tendencies such as aggression, territoriality, and male dominance.

Perhaps, it is instructive to look at the periods when these two opposing ideologies became prominent. The early work of Ruth Benedict and Margaret Mead was done at a time when the new school

---

[4] See pages 87–92.
[5] See pages 452–54.
[6] See pages 98–100.

of behaviorism appealed to many anthropologists as well as psychologists, and when many liberals had a feeling of optimism about the novel experiment then under way in the Soviet Union. "Indeed, the years before and including 1928 were, in J. B. Watson's judgment, a period of 'social Renaissance, a preparation for a change in mores,' that was likely to become much more of an epoch in history than the scientific Renaissance which began with Bacon" (Freeman 1983:96).

One can see the basis for Watson's optimism (1930:82) in his assumptions about human plasticity: "Give me a dozen healthy infants, well-formed, and my own specified world to bring them up in, and I'll guarantee to take any one at random and train him to become any type of specialist I might select—doctor, lawyer, artist, merchant-chief, and, yes, even beggar-man and thief, regardless of his talents, penchants, tendencies, vocations, and race of his ancestors."

Sociobiology became popular in a more anxious time, when the fear of nuclear warfare and annihilation had become widespread. It is easy nowadays to believe that human beings are essentially killer apes who have an innate urge to defend their territories. Of course, our views about the nature of things should not be unduly influenced by our personal tendencies to be either optimistic or pessimistic, liberal or conservative (see Dobzhansky 1962:54–55). We must acknowledge that we are primates and mammals having much in common with chimpanzees and gorillas. At the same time, we do have some unique attributes. Human beings have used tools for nearly 3 million years. *Homo erectus,* dating between 1.5 million and 100,000 years ago, probably had a language. For a long time, then, our ancestors had a form of symbolic communication and ways of adjusting to the environment that differed significantly from those of other primates. The expansion of the human cortex and the undifferentiated nature of *Homo sapiens* allow for a good deal of plasticity, making the genetic determination of behavior less marked than in other species.

This brings us back to the question of the relative significance of instinct and culture. Mary Midgley (1978:286) argues that we should not see these as conflicting or alternative explanations for human behavior. "Man is innately programmed in such a way that he needs a culture to complete him. Culture is not an alternative or replacement for instinct, but its outgrowth and supplement." She notes that the stereotyping of behavior that culture entails is not so unusual among animals, which tend to be creatures of habit (pp. 307–10). Midgley suggests that the hominids who developed speech and culture must have had a particular kind of temperament that was "exceptionally cooperative, persistent and thorough."

> As Desmond Morris has pointed out, this kind of disposition is less common in primates, who do not usually work hard for their living, than it is in carnivores. The special development of people has led human life to converge in many structural properties with those of the

big dogs and cats. They have become (everywhere, not just in certain cultures) much more persistent, cooperative, strenuous, territorial, pugnacious, constant, acquisitive, and given to pair-bonding than most other primates—not just more intelligent (1978:250–51).

Apart from the inclusion of territoriality here, this view seems reasonable to me, as does Midgley's distinction between closed and open instincts or programs. Closed instincts are behavior patterns that are fixed in every detail, while open instincts are looser with strong general tendencies such as to get home or to seek water. More advanced animals are programmed in this more general fashion (pp. 52–53). Thus, hunting is both innate (in the open sense) and learned among carnivores. "The creature is born with certain powers and a strong wish to use them, but it will need time, practice, and (often) some example before it can develop them properly" (p. 54).

If we see human beings as creatures with open genetic programs, we can see why all human cultures should have the common outline, set forth by Murdock, which still allows for a great deal of variation and elaboration.

SUGGESTIONS FOR FURTHER READING

For a challenging approach to the topic of human nature that combines philosophy and ecology, see Mary Midgley, *Beast and Man. The Roots of Human Nature* (Ithaca, N.Y.: Cornell University Press, 1978). See also Melvin Konner, *The Tangled Wing. Biological Constraints on the Human Spirit* (New York: Holt, Rinehart & Winston, 1982).

There is an abundant literature on aggression. Apart from those discussed in the text, the following deserve mention: Arnold H. Buss, *The Psychology of Aggression* (New York: John Wiley & Sons, 1961); J. D. Carthy and F. J. Ebling, eds., *The Natural History of Aggression* (London: Academic Press, 1964); Morton Fried, Marvin Harris, and Robert Murphy, eds., *War: The Anthropology of Armed Conflict and Aggression* (New York: Natural History Press, 1968); Russell G. Green and Edgar C. O'Neal, eds., *Perspectives on Aggression* (New York: Academic Press, 1976); Irenäus Eibl-Eibesfeldt, *The Biology of Peace and War. Men, Animals, and Aggression* (New York: Viking Press, 1979); David A. Hamburg and Michelle B. Trudeau, eds., *Biobehavioral Aspects of Aggression* (New York: Alan R. Liss, 1981).

A textbook on ethology by a disciple of Konrad Lorenz is available in Irenäus Eibl-Eibesfeldt, *Ethology. The Biology of Behavior*, 2d ed., Erich Klinghammer, trans. (New York: Holt, Rinehart, & Winston, 1975). A good criticism of Konrad Lorenz's work is Daniel S. Lehrman's "A Critique of Konrad Lorenz's Theory of Instinctive Behavior," *Quarterly Review of Biology* 28 (1953), pp. 337–63. For a neo-Freudian view of aggression and of Lorenz's ideas, see Erich Fromm, *The Anatomy of Human Destructiveness* (New York: Holt, Rinehart, & Winston, 1973).

Two books that deal with the question of the relationship between human aggression and warfare are Martin A. Nettleship and R. Dale Givens, eds., *War, its Causes and Correlates,* (The Hague: Mouton, 1975) and, R. Dale

Givens, and Martin A. Nettleship, eds. *Discussions on War and Human Aggression*, (The Hague: Mouton, 1976).

On sex, see Clellan S. Ford and Frank A. Beach, *Patterns of Sexual Behavior* (New York: Ace Books, 1951).

For sociobiology, see E. O. Wilson, *Sociobiology: The New Synthesis* (Cambridge, Mass.: Harvard University Press, 1975) and *On Human Nature* (Cambridge, Mass.: Harvard University Press, 1978). See also Napoleon A. Chagnon and William Irons, eds., *Evolutionary Biology and Human Social Behavior. An Anthropological Perspective* (North Scituate, Mass.: Duxbury Press, 1979).

PART FOUR

Methods in Culture-and-Personality Research

12

Observation of Behavior and Interviews

Cultural anthropologists get most of their information by watching what people do, and from conversations and interviews. The traditional purpose of their observation is to develop a picture of the culture under review. In this chapter, however, we will consider the observation of behavior more from the standpoint of the assessment of personality. The fieldworker in culture-and-personality is concerned both with distinguishing culture patterns and with noting manifestations of personality, which places an undue burden on him as observer and recorder. For this reason, I think it is preferable for culture-and-personality studies to be carried out in societies where the ethnography has already been done, particularly if projective tests and life histories are to be collected. If the anthropologist is part of a team, that simplifies matters, although group research has its own complications, too (see Adams and Preiss 1960:chaps. 1–3).

A distinction may be made between two types of observation. In one case, a person simply observes what is going on, without limiting his observations to any particular categorized items of behavior. In the second case, or in what has been called *directed observation*, a previously prepared schedule focuses the observer's attention on certain selected acts. Other matters, irrelevant to these categories, are ignored (see Symonds 1931:30–31). Psychologists have done a good deal of work in the field of directed observation, which involves the rating or categorizing of items to be observed.[1] Some applied anthropologists and industrial sociologists have also made use of this approach (Guest 1960), and Elliot Chapple, an anthropologist, has developed techniques for recording rates of social interaction. Elements of this method can sometimes be noted in the field procedures of ethnologists. For example, there is something akin to directed obser-

---

[1] For a review of this literature, see Heyns and Lippitt (1954:372 f).

vation in Clyde Kluckhohn's (1938) quantitative study of Navaho ceremonialism—recording the number of days on which singers participated in ceremonies over a six-month period, and various other indexes to the extent of ceremonial behavior. But for the most part, anthropologists have not used this directed approach in their fieldwork; instead, their observations have been of the more general wide-ranging order.

What can one learn about people, simply from watching them? A good deal, sometimes. Martha Wolfenstein, for example, observed French children at play in various parks in France. She noted that they generally stay with the mother (or other adult) rather than mix indiscriminately with other children, so that the park seems to be populated by small family enclaves, with the adults keeping careful watch over their possessions (toys, buckets, and so forth) which are apparently felt to belong to the parent rather than to the child. Wolfenstein also noted that French children show a great readiness to play with children younger than themselves, in contrast to the American child's consciousness of age grades. (She suggests that this willingness may stem from the requirement of remaining within the family circle, or in the circle of children whose parents know one another.) She noted, too, that French children are not taught to fight their own battles, or to stick up for their rights, as Americans would put it. Instead, grownups intervene and scold the aggressor in a conflict. Physical aggression is inhibited, with verbal disputes developing in substitution. Wolfenstein was amazed at how long French children can sit still.

> A typical position of a child in the park is squatting at his mother's feet, playing in the sand. His hands are busy, but his total body position remains constant. . . . The squatting child keeps his bottom poised within an inch of the ground but never touching, only his hands getting dirty; activity and getting dirty are both restricted to the hands. . . . The requirement of keeping clean and the inhibition on physical aggression contribute to the restriction of motor activity, and so does the distrustful feeling about alien space, outside the family circle (Wolfenstein 1955:106–7).

In these few selections one can see that a variety of observations have been made in this study: observations on the composition of groups involved, on the nature of social interaction, on attitudes toward possessions, and on bodily postures. Of course, a number of questions can be raised about Wolfenstein's observations—how representative they may be and how widely one may generalize from them. But they serve here as an example of observation—rather sharp-eyed observation at that—of the sort that may be made in the field.

PSYCHOLOGICAL ECOLOGY

The observation of behavior is an approach that has been particularly emphasized by some social psychologists. For example, Roger G. Barker and Herbert F. Wright, veritable arch-observers, have presented a detailed account of one day in the life of a seven-year-old boy in a midwestern American town. We find entries such as these:

> 7:03: He pulled on his right sock.
> He picked up his left tennis shoe and put it on.
> He laced his left shoe with slow deliberation, looking intently
>   at the shoe as he worked steadily until he had it all laced.
> 7:04: He put on his right shoe (Barker and Wright 1951:17).

Eight observers (all but one of whom were adults familiar to the boy) took turns during the day in watching Raymond, carefully noting all his actions and remarks. Thus 14 consecutive hours of observation were recorded, each observer in turn dictating into a sound recorder as he trailed the boy, and indicating the passage of time at one-minute intervals (Barker and Wright 1951:6–8).

The authors have extended this approach (although not always so intensively) to a general study of children in Raymond's town (Barker and Wright 1955), and Roger G. Barker and Louise Shedd Barker (1961) have made a comparative study in which they contrast the "psychological ecology" of children in Midwest, Kansas, with that of children in Yoredale, Yorkshire, England. Observations in both areas were made in relation to what the authors call *behavior settings*—restaurants, stores, school classes, and so forth. They point to some features which behavior settings have in common: that is, each involves a characteristic pattern of behavior which is relatively independent of the presence of any particular person, and each has a particular spatial framework and boundary, so that a person knows when he is inside or outside the setting (Barker and Barker 1961:465–69).

Some of the conclusions based on this comparative study are rather surprising and of much interest. The authors find that "More of Midwest's than of Yoredale's settings are unsegregated; they are inhabited by persons of all ages, both sexes, and all social classes. The lesser segregation on the basis of age is especially marked in Midwest" (Barker and Barker 1961:470). (Here we may note a possible conflict with Martha Wolfenstein's comments on the rigid age grade play groups in the United States.) The Barkers assert that the average person in Midwest is more than three times as frequently in responsible settings as is his counterpart in the Yorkshire town.

> The average citizen of Midwest is busier in essential jobs in community behavior settings (as secretary, president, teacher, soloist, clerk, trustee, etc.) and does a larger share of the town's public work than is

true of Yoredale citizens. People, including children and adolescents, are in greater demand and in shorter supply. Midwest has fewer replacements; the average person is functionally more important.

Children are not exceptions. Sixty-four (11%) of Midwest's settings would have to shut up shop for lack of *operating* personnel if children and adolescents were removed from the town . . . (Barker and Barker 1961:470).

In the case of Yoredale, only 3 percent of the "settings" would have to close.

The authors give further evidence for the importance of children and adolescents in various spheres of activity in Midwest—the local newspaper, sports settings, concerts, programs, and so forth—and they point to the relative lack of participation in corresponding areas by the children and adolescents of Yoredale. The greater involvement of young people in community life in Midwest results in a greater sense of their importance than in the case of Yoredale young people. There are more areas for self-expression and achievement (and also more possibilities of failure). There is a more familiar, often first-name relationship between children and adults in contrast to the situation in the Yorkshire town, where a greater social distance prevails between the young and the mature (Barker and Barker 1961:472–74).

Comparative studies like these bring into sharper focus the significance of observed behavior.

METHODS IN THE SIX CULTURES PROJECT

Since comparability of data was emphasized in the Six Cultures project, a standard approach to the recording of behavior was recommended to the six teams of fieldworkers by Whiting, Child, Lambert et al. in *Field Guide for a Study of Socialization* (1966). The authors use the term *setting*, although in a different sense from the Barkers' usage. By settings they mean activities specified as to time and place in which the child spends a typical day, such as breakfast at home or playing in the schoolyard after school. By *situations* they mean conditions which instigate behavior, and by *responses* they refer to the child's reactions.

The authors recommend that three steps be taken in the observation of children's behavior. The first is to find out what the typical settings are in a child's day. "If possible, the child's waking day should be divided into hours and the record should be written in the form of a timetable, indicating where the child is, who is present, and what he is doing" (Whiting, Child, Lambert et al. 1966:93). The second step is to find out the frequency with which certain situations are met with in typical settings. For this purpose it is recommended that the fieldworker make 12 five-minute observations on each child. The third step is to draw up a protocol of P's behavior. (P stands for the particular child who is being observed, while O stands for a person with whom he interacts.) Finally, a record chart is kept for each child, with protocol numbers and dates recorded in the appropriate cells.

Difficulties were experienced when the fieldworkers tried to comply with some of these suggestions, and modifications were made, particularly in step three. The authors recommend that in future studies of child-rearing a variety of behavior observations be used. Besides recording a child's daily routine, efforts should be made to systematically sample and record the interaction of important dyads such as mother-child, father-child, and sibling-sibling.

FAMILY STUDIES

A pioneer in the field of family studies is Oscar Lewis (1951:63–72) who presents a nine-page chart detailing the activities of each member of a particular peasant family in Tepoztlán, Mexico, from 6:00 A.M., March 28, to 9:30 P.M., March 31, 1944.

In this case, the purpose was primarily to illustrate work patterns and the family division of labor; but Lewis's detailed family studies are also relevant to culture-and-personality research. In *Five Families,* Lewis (1959) gives extensive accounts of one day in the lives of five Mexican families. He tells us that in four of the five days the family conversations were recorded stenographically by an assistant. In two cases the assistant was a relative of the family; in a third, a close friend (p. 6).

Lewis has taken some liberties with his material, which may cause some raised eyebrows, but which probably contribute to the literary effectiveness of his accounts. For instance, the presence of the observer is never alluded to. Each family's day is described as if the observer were not there at all. Moreover, Lewis does not hesitate to present the thoughts and feelings of his subjects, along with their words and actions. Much material is presented in the form of flashbacks, to give something of the broader setting of the family life.

From these family accounts one gets a general picture of the greater importance of the mother in the lower-class Mexican home than of the father. The mothers tend to be devoted to their children. The fathers are more distant and authoritarian and spend a good deal of time away from home. Still, in most of the families, the children feel respect and affection for their fathers. Lewis believes that the younger generation in these five families has known more family stability than the parent generation experienced, an observation which somewhat lessens the prevailingly grim picture of the "culture of poverty" presented in this book.

STRUCTURED SITUATIONS

Two further categories may be distinguished in connection with the observation of behavior. In one category are studies, like those just cited, in which individuals are observed in the course of everyday life. A second category involves the observation of people in situations structured by the investigator. This approach may be more revealing for purposes of personality assessment, but fieldwork conditions do not usually lend themselves to it.

To give an example of the second category: during World War II members of the OSS assessment staff would assign a candidate two helpers whom he had to direct in the building of a frame structure within a 10-minute period. The "helpers" were really trained stooges, one of whom acted in a sluggish passive way, while the other behaved in an aggressive and critical manner toward the candidate. While they did not disobey direct orders, these men did whatever they could to slow things up. The assessment officers meanwhile watched how the candidate handled this problem (OSS Assessment Staff 1948:101–12).

Such stress situations can be most revealing, but, as has been indicated, anthropologists are not usually in a position to try this sort of thing. Perhaps a particularly well-endowed fieldworker could use the techniques popularized by Allen Funt in "Candid Camera"—training concealed cameras and microphones on unsuspecting subjects who are inveigled into an exchange with the investigator. (In one example Funt posed as a watchmaker and "fixed" a customer's clock by smashing it to pieces.) Funt does this for purposes of entertainment rather than science, but it would seem to be a possible technique for the investigation of personality—not the smashing of watches, necessarily, but some use of the general approach. This would not be very different from some attempts by psychologists to study such matters as the nature of children's fears—for instance, by exposing them to a strange room or awesome-looking objects, and noting their reactions (Arsenian 1943; Jersild and Holmes 1935).

DOLL PLAY

Perhaps the nearest approach made by anthropologists to the use of structured situations has been in studies of doll play. By watching how children play with dolls representing family members, anthropologists have found evidence for such patterns as sibling rivalry in cultures other than our own (Levy 1939; Henry and Henry 1944). From the play of Normanby Island children, Géza Roheim (1941) deduced the presence in that group of such Freudian items as the Oedipus complex, the phallic significance of the snake, and enactments of the primal scene.

The most extensive investigation of doll play made in a non-Western culture so far is the Henry Pilagá study. The principal play material used were a mother doll, a father doll, and several "child" dolls. The father doll was an "amputation doll," of a type used in David M. Levy's sibling rivalry experiments, with jointed and detachable arms and legs. The Pilagá children were also given scissors, a ball of plastilene, and a mechanical turtle. When a child was handed the dolls, each one was named after a member of the child's immediate family. Pilagá children often made breasts or genitalia of plastilene and stuck them on the dolls to differentiate the sexes. If a child did not make breasts and place them on the mother doll, the examiner suggested that he do so (Henry and Henry 1944:30–31).

It was hard to segregate individual children for observation in this study, since the Henrys' hut was invaded by swarms of children during the day and privacy was hardly possible. The observers, therefore, took notes on the activities of groups of children playing simultaneously.

The study of Pilagá doll play shows that sibling rivalry is present among these people as among ourselves. However, in contrast to David M. Levy's sibling rivalry experiments, Jules and Zunia Henry found that self-punishment on this account does not occur. A sense of guilt is not emphasized in Pilagá culture, as evidenced by the absence of confessionals, penitent speeches, self-flagellation, and traditions of suicide. There are no special rewards for love of a sibling and little punishment for injury to one. Hence Pilagá children openly detest their younger brothers and sisters and feel no guilt for doing so.

The problem of interpreting doll play is raised by David Landy, who expresses dissatisfaction with this approach to the study of children's personality patterns. Landy (1960) selected 18 families in a Puerto Rican village as representative of the largely lower class caneworkers there. A study was made of four sessions of doll play for one child from each family (10 boys and 8 girls between four and seven years of age). The dolls, representing mother, father, boy, girl, and baby, were made of pipe cleaners, cotton, and cloth. Play materials also included a roofless "house," furnishings, and outhouse.

Landy's approach involved directed observation. He had a scoring system for certain categories of acts: aggression, dependency, identification, nurturance, and noninteraction. Each child was brought alone to the doll play situation, with a Puerto Rican assistant being present. Landy scored and recorded each act performed by the child. He notes that much of the resultant doll play was routine and repetitive. These children were not encouraged in everyday life to act freely in the presence of adults and were not used to the sort of permissive behavior which Landy displayed. Landy (pp. 162–63) found it difficult to interpret the doll play of his Puerto Rican subjects and found it hard to determine when the technique elicited projective responses and when it reflected real-life situations. Partly because of uncertainty over the extent to which children's play is projection, and also because the observation and recording of doll play is very time consuming, Landy (pp. 166–67) concludes that he would not use doll play in another field situation and adds that he has obtained more data from child interviews in a later study among the Tuscarora.

Jane Ritchie (1957) made use of doll play in a study of Maori children in Rakau, New Zealand. Her study is hard to compare or contrast with those of Landy and the Henrys, since the three investigations made use of different kinds of dolls and followed different procedures. In this case 12 dolls, dressed to represent a large family group, were presented to the child subjects. There was no pattern here, as in the Henry study, of adding bits of plastilene; bodily parts do not seem to have been removable.

Landy's question of what the doll play represents poses no problem to Ritchie:

> Provided no extraneous stimulus material is introduced it seems that doll play directly echoes real life for the children and that they freely engage in projective activity without the mysteries, inhibitions, repressions and other subtleties which shroud such processes in adults. When a Rakau child said a doll was Mother he was speaking of his own mother (Ritchie 1957:107–8).

The author limits this generalization to the doll play of her Maori child subjects and does not mean to extend it beyond that area. Even here, however, one may note some exceptions to the notion that doll play reflects real life. In doll play, for example, the baby doll is rejected by the girls, but this does not take place overtly in real life. As Ritchie (p. 148) puts it, "The doll behavior is a fulfillment of a wish which cannot be granted in real life . . ."

Among these Maori children there was no boisterous sexual behavior like that of the Pilagá children, but only oblique sexual references, which were slightly more prominent among the boys than among the girls. The boys showed over twice as much aggression as the girls, while the girls showed a much greater need for love. In their doll play, moreover, there was much more concern with the arrangement of dolls and the maintenance of order. The girls' rejecting behavior was assessed as four times that of the boys. It is Ritchie's interpretation that the boys typically have affectionate relationships with more family members than do the girls, and they are not tied by obligations to the home. Hence the boys' needs for love are less intense.

The principal doll rejected by the girls (and boys as well) was the baby, indicating jealousy of the younger sibling. Ritchie observes:

> It is significant that the children do not often allocate themselves to other children or to parents, nor do they often allocate other family

members to themselves. . . . The Rakau child in the present material does not see himself in any natural relationship with the mother or the home. Instead, he sees the home as including bonds of relationship between other members of the family, but not between himself and other members (Ritchie 1957:113).

The baby doll accounts for 70 percent of the allocations and is thus seen by the children to be the most important figure in the home. A boy may openly express hostility for the baby, but the girls show more ambivalence, for they may attempt to "buy" parental love by caring for the baby."In order to get love she must continue in association with the cause of her rejection" (Ritchie 1957:114). (One wonders, in this connection, whether the doll play of youngest children differs from that of older siblings.)

Since the studies described earlier, little has been done in the psychological analysis of doll play in different cultures. Bushnell and Bushnell (1975) claim that this approach has been unfortunately neglected. The Bushnells made use of group doll play sessions in the highland village of San Juan Atzingo in Mexico and found that the results correlated well with findings from both the Rorschach and the Thematic Apperception Test.

It might facilitate research in this field if some generally agreed-on procedures could be adopted by those who make cross-cultural studies in doll play—that is, in the number and types of dolls to be used, methods of recording data, and so forth. Productive material does seem to have come from doll play studies, and while it is true enough that there are difficulties in the interpretation of such material, the same applies to all techniques used in the field—to the Rorschach, TAT, and interview materials as well. Moreover, they all take up much of the fieldworker's time.

POSTURE AND GESTURE

In connection with the Wolfenstein article on French children's play, it was noted that the author made different kinds of observations. Let us characterize these as observations on rates of social interaction, verbal exchanges, posture, gesture, and facial expression. It is important to note not only what people say but how they say it. Consider John Dollard's remarks on his methods of research in a southern town:

An important aspect of the method is to watch the feeling tone of the statements people make and the acts they do. This is often more definitive than the words uttered or the external character of the act. People can say *no*, for example, in such a way that it means *yes*, or vice versa. The feeling tone indicated in giving a permission may indicate that if it is acted on, the recipient can count on terminating his effective contact with the grantor (Dollard 1957:19–20).

Dollard's comments indicate the importance of noting facial expression, posture, and gesture as clues to underlying attitudes and personality patterns. There is a good deal of literature on the question of how successfully one may gauge emotions or personality traits from facial expression or bodily stance.[2] Most of the work done in this field has involved subjects making interpretations of drawings, photographs, or films. The anthropological fieldworker, however, has a much greater range of clues to work with. He or she lives with a group of people over a period of time, sees them in a variety of circumstances, and knows something of the context in which observed events take place. Hence the fieldworker has a great advantage over someone who is asked to interpret a collection of frozen split-second facial expressions in photographs of strangers. Gregory Bateson (1958:124, 151), for example, gave a vivid portrait of the swaggering posture of Iatmul men in the men's house and the"fine proud bearing" of Iatmul women when they dress up in men's regalia. These are psychologically significant observations. The ways in which people carry themselves, walk, and sit may tell us a good deal about them. As the studies of Werner Wolff, Allport and Vernon, M. H. Krout and others, cited in Chapter 1, have shown, individuals seem to have characteristic ways of walking and gesturing which remain as stable patterns over time.

Posture, of course, is much influenced by cultural tradition, as may be seen in Gordon W. Hewes's (1955) mapping of world distributions of postural habits. Cultural traditions may even modify sleeping postures.[3] Gesture and facial expressions are also considerably channeled by cultural tradition. La Barre (1947) has persuasively argued that there is no "natural" language of emotional gesture.

These considerations, of course, complicate the psychological interpretation of posture, gesture, and facial expression. A distinction may be made, however, between culturally standardized gestures, like the handshake and the military salute, and more personal gestural behavior, such as nose picking or ear pulling, which Krout (1935) calls "autistic gesture." The latter may be more significant psychologically than the former type of gesture. Even so, it may be of relevance to personality whether a particular individual, let us say, goes in for a good deal of handshaking.

Not much attention has been paid to the cross-cultural study of posture and gesture, and the work that has been done so far has been largely descriptive, with little attempt to relate characteristic postural

---

[2] For a review of such literature, see Bruner and Tagiuri (1954).

[3] To cite a rather extreme example, Prince Peter of Greece and Denmark (1953:145) has noted that, in order to keep warm, Tibetan caravaners sometimes sleep by kneeling together side by side, with shoulders and hips touching and their faces resting on the upturned palms of their hands placed on the ground before them. He also describes a seated posture in which Tibetans sometimes sleep.

or gestural features to personality patterns. These descriptions remain as valuable data, however, in which someone may yet find significant patterns.

Flora L. Bailey (1942), in an article on Navaho motor habits, tells us that a striking difference between Navaho and white American movements is the greater smoothness and flowing quality of Navaho motor behavior, while white American movements are seen as being more angular and staccato. Eating is performed daintily and slowly by the Navaho; walking is done with long strides, legs swinging freely from the hips, arms hanging loosely. The Navaho handshake is a limp clasp release, with no grip or up and down motion. The author does not speculate on any possible connection between these motor habits and Navaho personality characteristics.

W. D. Brewer (1951:237) has discussed the gesture language of the Levantine Arabs, who, like other Mediterranean peoples, are said to have a more "obvious" or "rotund and fluid" type of gesture than Americans. Brewer gives a list of symbolic and pictorial gestures and makes one observation of psychological relevance: "It is at least interesting that so many of the common Arab gestures described above imply injured innocence, unwillingness to assume responsibility or a mere desire not to be included with the group as a whole."

The most large-scale and methodologically rigorous cross-cultural investigation of gesture is David Efron's *Gesture and Environment,* the product of a two-year study of the gestural behavior of Eastern European Jews and southern Italians in New York City. These subjects never knew that they were under scrutiny. On-the-spot observations were made; 5,000 feet of film were taken, shot from hidden points of vantage (sometimes from adjacent buildings with a telephoto lens), and the artist Stuyvessant van Veen made sketches drawn from life. A great deal of data was thus amassed: 1,500 subjects were studied by direct observation, 600 in sketches, and about 750 in film.

Ingenious methods were developed to record and represent gestural motions:

> the film, taken at speeds varying from sixteen to sixty-four frames per second, was projected frame by frame upon coordinate paper. The position of motile bodily parts, such as wrist, elbow, and head, was marked in successive frame projections. When joined, these sequential positions give a precise representation of the fluent gestural movement (Efron 1941:41).

Efron (p. 43) found that the gestures of the "traditional," or unassimilated, Eastern European Jews, were more confined in radius than those of "traditional" southern Italians, much of their gestural motion taking place close to the chest and face, in contrast to the Italians, who might make gestures of full arms' length.

In the ghetto Jew the upper-arm participates seldom in the movement, and often is more or less rigid and attached to the side of the body. . . . The axis of gestural motion is often centered at the elbow.

There was a good deal of head movement among the traditional Jews, little among the Italians. Jewish gestures were made sequentially, not simultaneously with both hands or arms as among the Italians. Efron noted an irregularity of tempo and abruptness in Jewish gestures, while there was a more even flow in the Italian. The traditional Jew often touched the body of his conversational partner, and conversational groups were often closely massed. These features were not noted among the Italians. There was also a difference in the body planes at which gesturing characteristically took place.

The Eastern ghetto Jew exhibits a tendency to gesticulate chiefly in the vertical and frontal planes of his body. . . . In contrast to the "traditional" Italian, who is more likely to execute his gestural motions in a latero-transversal space-segment, i.e., at either side of his body, the Jew appears to direct most of his movements either in an up-and-down direction or in a direction toward the interlocutor . . . (Efron 1941:54).

Efron (pp. 56–136) found, finally, that assimilated southern Italians and assimilated Eastern Jews in New York City differed from their respective traditional groups and appeared to resemble each other in gestural behavior.

Efron does not attempt in this work to relate the type of gesturing to different personality tendencies in these two groups. His purpose seems to have been just to show that there are differences in gestural patterns in the two groups and that these patterns are culturally derived. Jurgen Ruesch and Weldon Kees (1956:23) have made some attempts at interpretation in this area and have discussed differences in posture and gesture in European national groups. For instance, concerning the Italians, they state: "The basic philosophy of this Mediterranean country is epitomized by a desire to express bodily and emotional needs in elaborate and somewhat outspoken terms while at the same time maintaining warm interpersonal contact." Unfortunately, the observations of these writers are loose and impressionistic and offered with little supporting evidence.

INTERPRETATIONS OF BALINESE POSTURAL HABITS

The culture where most has been done to relate posture and gesture to personality patterns, and, further, to account for the genesis of the ascribed personality traits, has been that of Bali. Since these efforts are almost unique in the literature of culture-and-personality, they will be dealt with here in some detail. Observations on Balinese posture and gesture have been made by Jane Belo, Margaret Mead, and Gregory Bateson in a number of publications. Jane Belo (1935) has drawn attention to the "absolute poise and balance" of the Balinese in their movements and gestures, which, however, is combined with a sort of carefulness of bearing, as if they were afraid to disturb a delicate equilibrium. Belo discusses, as Bateson and Mead also do, the sense of spatial and social orientation which is always part of the Balinese consciousness: the sense of one's relationship to the points of the compass, to up and down, and to the social standing of people of higher or lower caste. She also touches on the tempo of activity, pointing out that Balinese move slowly and deliberately.

This slowness of movement may be associated with the low tonus of Balinese children noted by Mead and Macgregor (1951:38–39).

There is a passivity in Balinese children which Mead traces to certain childhood experiences. Balinese children are carried about during most of their waking hours until they are from 15 to 18 months old. As was noted in Chapter 6, they have no crawling stage comparable to that of Western children because of the Balinese disapproval of crawling, and so do not show as much activity as American children of the same age. Children learn to adjust passively to the movements of the mother's body as they are carried about. The child's limbs are manipulated to teach it gestures and hand-dancing before he or she learns to walk. Both walking and dancing may be taught by holding the child from behind, so that it learns kinesthetically as well as from watching and a small amount of verbal instruction.

Another aspect of Balinese posture noted by Bateson and Mead is an economy of movement, which they see as involving a kind of dissociation.

> Where an American or a New Guinea native will involve almost every muscle in his body to pick up a pin, the Balinese merely use the muscles immediately relevant to the act, leaving the rest of the body undisturbed (Bateson and Mead 1942:17).

This dissociation is seen to be particularly evident in the hands, in which the fingers at rest rarely lie in seriated flexion, but may stick out at different angles. When a Balinese watches two cocks fighting, there may sometimes be noted a twitching of the different hands, symbolically identified with the two birds. Interestingly enough, Belo describes the case of a man whose hand was put into trance, while the rest of the man remained quite conscious (1960:203–4).

Bateson and Mead have also drawn attention to Balinese postures of withdrawal, illustrated in three photographs on pp. 132–33 of their work—a bent-over sitting position with the head held down over the knees. The implication of these postural details, from their viewpoint, is that there is a tendency toward narcissistic, schizoid withdrawal in the Balinese character. Bateson and Mead think that this tendency derives from maternal teasing and early childhood frustrations, as the result of which children learn, between the ages of three and six, to become aloof from the mother and other adults and turn in on themselves.

In contrast to the general mildness and passivity of everyday life in Bali, some very active and aggressive manifestations take place during trance, which in some villages is often induced on ritual occasions. At these times young men, and sometimes women as well drive the points of their krises against their chests, while leaning backward in an intense, straining manner.

Some men, it may be noted, are more violent than others in these attacks upon the self. Jane Belo (1960:128) describes one such case in which she employs a wealth of observations on facial expression, posture, and gesture. Rawa, the man in question, was particularly aggressive and exhibitionistic in trance. Reporting on his own sensations at such times, he said that demons want to attack his body. His chest itches as if it were being burned, and he feels a powerful desire to stab himself in the chest. "As for me, it is as if there were someone ordering me to stab. When it's like that, if I don't get hold of a kris, I should die, so strong is my anger." But after the self-stabbing, Rawa says that he feels extremely content, like a hungry man who has had a good meal of rice. Asked if desire for the kris were like desire for a woman, Rawa said that the former is stronger; he has had plenty of women.

Rawa's behavior in normal life showed some contrasting features. Belo says that Rawa had a soft, "almost wooing" manner with Westerners and was given to repeatedly shaking hands with them. "I have seen him seat himself beside a Westerner whom he hardly knew, lay his hand upon the man's knee and lean and fawn upon him for an extended period of time, without receiving any encouragement from the object of his attentions" (p. 129). Belo noted, however, that although Balinese often go around in pairs, with arms around each other's necks, she never saw Rawa with another Balinese in this fashion, and she guessed that perhaps he clung to Westerners because he was not on good terms with his own people.

Further fieldwork supported this inference. Rawa was not a native of the village in which he lived and was regarded by the local people as a sort of stranger. He was not liked, and Belo (p. 131 f.) gives an extensive account of one occasion when another man in trance violently expressed this generally antagonistic feeling toward Rawa. Such situational pressures may help to explain the particularly aggressive and exhibitionistic behavior which Rawa showed in trance, although its ultimate origin may also lie in the kind of childhood frustrations described by Bateson and Mead.

THE RECORDING OF BEHAVIOR

Since there is so much more going on in even the most lethargic society and so much to observe, there is a problem of how to record behavioral observations. The most usual method is the notebook. Margaret Mead (1940:326 f.), a particularly keen-eyed observer, followed the custom of recording bits of discrete data on slips of paper on the spot, with some reference category on each slip. Verbal behavior can be jotted down or recorded on tape. Without a camera it is hard to record details of facial expression, posture, and gesture, although systems of annotation are given in Efron's *Gesture and Environment* (1941) and in Ray Birdwhistell's *Introduction to Kinesics* (1952). If a group is doing fieldwork together, different kinds of observations may be assigned to different members, and Mead (1940:328) has suggested this parceling-out process for certain occasions, with one worker covering ceremonial behavior, another recording verbatim conversations, and so on. If possible, notes should be written up in full form while still in the field, for one is apt to forget many things.

Mechanical methods for recording data have sometimes been used, such as Chapple's interaction chronograph, the stenotype, and tape recorders (see Heyns and Lippitt 1954). Particularly valuable in the recording and presentation of field data are motion-picture film and still photography. Certainly, no technique can match sound film in conveying the quality of another culture, but unfortunately, it is too expensive for the average fieldworker.

Bateson and Mead apparently met with little objection to their constant photographing of the Balinese, and they assert that it is almost impossible for subjects to retain camera consciousness after the first dozen shots. They recommend that at least two workers collaborate, for a photographic sequence is of no value without a running account of what is going on, and one can't both take notes and handle a camera at the same time. Since they had to economize on film, Bateson and Mead (1942:49–50) saved the motion-picture camera for more active and interesting moments and stills for slower and less significant ones.

Videotape costs somewhat less than film, and artificial light is not required. It is less obtrusive than cameras focused by operators, since a TV camera with wide-angled lens can be set up and remotely operated while the investigator checks events on a monitor screen (Hutt and Hutt 1970:98). This provides a continuous record of behavior.

Marvin Harris (1964), who has made many suggestions regarding observation of behavior by ethnographers, has worked with graduate student associates in videotaping scenes of family interaction in lower class homes in New York City. In one study reported by Sharff (1975), two households were videotaped for two 24-hour days. The purpose was to test measures of relative authority in the household. Ethical problems of Big Brother prying are raised here, but some solutions have been found. In the study of some families in New York (where the head of the household was paid for the time the camera was in the house) members of the family had the right to see any of the tapes and could have them destroyed if they so requested (Schaeffer 1975:254–59). Videotape or film can be replayed at leisure for analytic purposes, and it is possible to check new hypotheses not developed in the field (Mead 1956b).

Schaeffer (1975:267) has described the advantages of portable videotape equipment in the field, it being light enough to be carried and handheld for fairly long periods of time when necessary. Future fieldwork will no doubt see an increase in the use of film and videotape.

PITFALLS IN OBSERVATION

There are some difficulties inherent in the process of assessing personality from observation of behavior. These difficulties are apt to be particularly pronounced in ethnological fieldwork. The anthropologist, of course, is not invisible. His or her presence affects, to some extent, the scene which is being observed. This is true of any observational study, unless one uses a one-way screen. But not only is the anthropologist visible, he or she is apt to stick out like a sore thumb. The people are usually very conscious of the stranger's presence, especially at first, before they have become used to having him or her around.

People have to find some explanation for an anthropologist's appearance in their community. The interpretation at which they arrive will, of course, influence their behavior in his or her presence. When Benjamin Paul and his wife first arrived in a Guatemalan Indian village, the villagers crowded their doors, peered through the windows, fingered their clothes, and inquired the price of each item. What later clarified this behavior for the Pauls was the explanation that the Indians thought that they were merchants, about to set up shop.

> We were not wholly wrong in judging the Indians to be curious about prices . . . but the avidity with which they crowded around to feel and look at everything made better sense in retrospect when we learned that our private residence was assumed to be a public shop. We had to revise our initial exaggerated estimate of their bold inquisitiveness (Paul 1953:433).

What an anthropologist sees, then, may be colored by the anthropologist's own presence and by the attitudes of the people toward him or her.

Another kind of difficulty which may affect the process of observation concerns the nature of the observer. An observer may project; he or she may have blind spots to certain aspects of behavior and be unduly attentive or sensitive to others. What he or she sees may be influenced by the individual's moods, attitudes, and values. This difficulty, again, may affect any observational study but applies particularly to ethnological fieldwork. The ethnologist finds himself or herself in an unfamiliar setting. One's mood, while working, may be influenced by any number of things—the nature of one's living quarters, the response one has met with in the community. He or she may feel somewhat homesick and ambivalent about fieldwork or may fall ill. Any of these factors, or others, may bring about distortions in what he or she observes and records. As some have put it, a culture may be seen as a sort of huge Rorschach blot, in which different ethnologists with different personality tendencies, may detect different patterns. While this is an overstatement, there is some truth in it, and that is why it is good to have descriptions of a particular culture made by a number of anthropologists, not just one or two. I don't mean to suggest that one must be skeptical of what anthropologists report. But we are dealing here with the assessment of personality from observation—a tricky undertaking, in which opportunities for projection abound.

INTERVIEWS AND QUESTIONNAIRES

Interviews, in ethnological fieldwork, supplement what one learns by observation. They may provide clarification of what one has seen. At the same time, an interview involves observation, too, for the ethnologist not only writes down what the informant says (or makes a mental note of what to write down later); but the ethnologist also watches how the informant behaves, talks, and gestures— blocks, pauses, and hesitations.

Interviews may be structured, loose, or "open ended," directive or nondirective, but most interviewing in the field is of the open-ended type. An ethnologist may have many brief exchanges with people which are not exactly interviews. He or she may engage in "participant observation"—take part in community affairs and to some extent identify with the people. In that case the ethnologist will have many contacts with individuals which are not interviews but which may be informative.

When the purpose is to get some insight into personality characteristics, the ethnologist must gain the acquaintance of some members of the community and somehow get them to serve as informants. Moreover, he or she must retain the goodwill of these people, so they will go on working and not back out. The problem facing the culture-and-personality ethnologist is that he or she wants to get the sort of information that a psychiatrist acquires from patients, while the ethnologist does not have the psychiatrist's role. A patient turns to a psychiatrist for help, even pays him large sums to listen to a variety of troubles. Since the patient wants to get well, there is a strong motivation to unburden. The ethnologist, on the other hand, has to seek out informants and may have to pay them to talk. They may be slow to open up, for there is no special reason, after all, why they should talk about their hidden secrets, their difficulties with marital partners, or their feelings about their parents. The ethnologist has to work warily, lest he or she lose the interest and friendship of the informants.

On the other hand, if it is true that people may talk more freely to a stranger than to a friend or acquaintance, the ethnologist has a certain advantage (Maccoby and Maccoby 1954:463). Oscar Lewis (1951:xvii), for example, found that the people of Tepoztlán were distant to one another but willing to open up to him and his co-workers. In the chapter dealing with life histories, some examples will be given of individuals who turned with gratitude to the ethnologist and were glad to confide.

Standardized questionnaires have sometimes been given in culture-and-pesonality studies, one example being in the Six Cultures project, in which the *Field Guide for a Study of Socialization* provided the English version of an interview to be used with the 24 mothers in each society. For example, the mother was asked what she did when her child cried, with follow-up questions such as:

a) How quickly would you try to tend to him?
b) How about when you were busy?
c) How about at night?
d) How did other members of the household feel about his crying? (Minturn and Lambert 1964:306).

A wide range of questions was asked covering various areas of discipline and interaction between the mother and child. These questions had to be translated into the local speech with the help of bilingual assistants, and they were sometimes altered to suit local conditions. The completed interviews were later read by coders who rated the mothers according to such factors as maternal warmth, maternal instability, mother's responsibility for baby and for child care, responsibility training, and aggression training (for both mother-directed and peer-directed aggression). Some of the findings of these ratings were cited in Chapter 8. For example, it was mentioned that the Mixtecan and Khalapur mothers were rated the least warm of the six groups.

One can get some idea of why coders might rate the Rajput mothers low on this dimension, if the following example, taken from the appendix of *Mothers of Six Cultures*, is representative of the questionnaire responses:

Q. What do you do when Mahender does not obey you immediately?
A. I beat him. I have no patience, I beat him with a stick. . . . . Mahender is a shameless boy. I have to tell him a thing four times and

then he does it. Other children do it when you ask them once and you feel so happy.

Q. What do you do when he tries to get his own way with you?

A. I beat him.

Q. How about when he tries to get his own way with other children?

A. Then I have to beat and scold (Minturn and Lambert 1964:312–13).

The interview continues along these lines. These responses may be compared or contrasted with the questionnaire answers of some of the mothers of the other cultures who were rated higher on maternal warmth, such as the mothers of Okinawa or the Philippines.

The use of a standard questionnaire makes cross-cultural comparisons possible.[4]

In the East African study discussed in Chapter 10, Robert B. Edgerton (1971a:310) used a questionnaire to elicit values and attitudes in each of the pastoral and farming groups of the four tribes he studied. To give a few examples of the questions asked: "Would the (Hehe, etc.) prefer to have sons or daughters? Why? What is the most important thing for parents to teach a toddler? . . . What is the most important thing for a young man to know before he gets married? . . . What is the best thing that can happen to a man?" The answers were coded and subjected to statistical analyses, providing basic data for the contrasts made by Edgerton between the farmers and pastoralists.

An "interpretative questionnaire" provided the main basis for the analysis of social character in a Mexican peasant community studied by Erich Fromm and Michael Maccoby. This was a series of open-ended questions that differed from most other questionnaires in that the answers were analyzed for their unintended unconscious meaning. The questionnaire was given to 406 adult villagers (200 men and 206 women), or 95 percent of the adult population.

After such routine questions as for the subject's name, age, place of birth, extent of education, whether parents were living, and so forth, questions such as the following were asked: "How frequently do you see your mother now?" "For what reasons, if any, have you consulted her during the last year?" "Would you act against her wishes?" "On what occasions have you done so?"

The subject was asked to give a brief description of his mother and of his father and to describe his idea of a good mother. He was asked if he beats his children and if children should fear their parents. The subject was asked what work he did, what he likes most and least about his work, what he does for recreation, and what he most enjoys in life. How often does he get drunk? How does liquor affect him? What does he think of *machismo*? What persons does he most admire?

---

[4] Interviews with children were also attempted in the Six Cultures project but worked out less successfully, partly because the number of interviews was insufficient and partly because of the lack of comparability of the situations. (Whiting et al., *Field Guide for a Study of Socialization*, pp. 118–23.)

What should a man do when his wife is unfaithful? Should women have the same rights as men? What is his concept of love?

There is a special set of questions for parents only, about their ways of dealing with children. Finally, there is a set of six story questions, of which the first may serve as an example: "A mother is ill and sends her son out to buy the food for the whole family. Because he stops to play, the boy loses the money and cannot buy the food. What do you think the mother did?" (Fromm and Maccoby 1970: 239–43).

The authors are aware of problems concerning questionnaires, such as the fact that answers to many questions may be stereotyped answers which do not really express the views of the subject, but they express faith in their method. Certainly, the questionnaire elicits a rich mine of information.

The villagers' questionnaires were scored according to the dominant character orientation evidenced by the subject's responses—receptive, exploitative, hoarding, or productive. They were also scored on such *modes of relatedness* as sadism, masochism, narcissism, love, indulgence, and conditional love, and *sociopolitical relatedness:* authoritarian orientation, orientation of traditional authority, democratic orientation, revolutionary orientation, submissiveness, active rebelliousness, and passive rebelliousness. They were scored on fixation to the mother and to the father and on the traits of enterprise-energy and depression.

In analyzing the tabulations of scores, it was concluded that the unproductive-receptive and (moderately) productive-hoarding types were the most frequent among the men. More men than women were narcissistic, while women were more masochistic. Most villagers of both sexes were fixated on the mother; only 4 percent were not, and 47 percent were scored as being "intensely fixated" on the mother.

As the result of a factor analysis, it was found that the most authoritarian and exploitative individuals were also the most narcissistic, and that the women tended to have more hoarding orientation than the men. A minority group of productive-exploitative villagers are the modern entrepreneurs who have been able to take advantage of new capitalistic opportunities, while the majority retain a helpless receptive orientation. Fromm and Maccoby (1970:83–133) found the latter type of orientation to be particularly associated with landowners who raised sugarcane. Cane brings much lower profits than rice or garden crops, but it requires much less work, and the refinery offers inducements to farmers who raise it, such as free medical care, life insurance, and scholarships for children, which appeal to those with a passive, receptive outlook on life. Cane growing was also found to be significantly correlated with exclusive attachment to the mother.

The authors found a significant agreement between their findings on the questionnaire and those from the Rorschach Test and Thematic Apperception Test. The detailed and convincing picture which Fromm and Maccoby have been able to draw of the social character of these Mexican villagers, based largely on the analysis of questionnaire data, shows, again, that questionnaires can be a useful instrument in culture-and-personality research.

A similar kind of standardized test potentially useful in cross-cultural studies is a Sentence Completion Test (SCT). Its use is advocated by Herbert P. Phillips (1965). Combined with behavioral observation, Phillips's SCT was the main source of data from which he drew conclusions about Thai peasant personality. The SCT was designed to elicit attitudes toward authority through such incompleted sentences as "When the [big man] told him to do it, he . . ." "When he is in the presence of a [big man] he feels . . ." "When his superior gave him an order which he knew was wrong, he . . ." "When placed in a position of power, he . . ." "The best way to treat a subordinate, is . . ."

Other kinds of attitudes were elicited by incompleted sentences, such as the following: "When he thinks of his mother, he thinks of . . ." "A real close friend is one who . . ." "When he found that his best friend spoke against him, he . . ." "People who never show their feelings are . . ." "His greatest problem was . . ." "The most important thing in life is . . ."

Phillips's SCT was given to 111 individuals representing an 11 percent stratified sample of the adult population of Bang Chan. Percentages of different types of responses are given for each SCT completion, but it is difficult to assess the significance of these percentages, since Phillips cites no comparable study using the same incomplete sentences.

If the same test is used in other cultures, the special characteristics of the Thai completions, if there are any, will emerge.

A large-scale cross-cultural application of a standardized Sentence Completion Test was undertaken by Takao Sofue (1979) making use of a 30-sentence test given to junior high school students in Japan (629 subjects), the United States (155 subjects), and Italy (284 subjects).[5] Some of the results are worth noting. To the sentence "When I am with my mother, I feel . . ." the Italians gave the strongest responses. Sofue remarks, "They have a very strong tone of sentimental dependency which does not exist in any of the American responses, nor in most of the Japanese responses" (p. 16). The Italians also gave the most positive completions to "When I am with my father, I feel . . .", although the emphasis was not as strong as for the mother. Attitudes toward strangers are expressed in completions to "When I am introduced to people. . . ." Here the Americans gave the highest number of positive responses and the Japanese the low-

---

[5] A small sample (9) of Eskimos from northern Alaska was also reported on by Sofue.

est, although female Japanese showed more flexibility than the males. The shyness of Japanese males is also shown in sentence completions concerning attitudes toward the opposite sex. In this respect there was no difference between the Italians and Americans. The phrase "People with authority . . ." drew negative responses from Americans and very positive ones from both the Japanese and Italians. The desire to become rich was expressed exclusively by a high percentage of American white males. Here are some of Sofue's conclusions (1979:25):

> The Japanese have a strong dependency need toward the mother and emphasize familistic ties with the parents. . . . They become easily depressed when ignored by others. Another characteristic trait is that they are strongly intrapunitive when faced with failure. Finally, Japanese are manifestly concerned with the improvement of both society and their own character.
>
> Americans are not dependent on their mothers, a tendency which is particularly evident among white females. They are positive and sociable toward strangers, and show a very strong hostility to authority. Blacks are especially hostile when rejected by others.

Sofue notes, however, that the SCT is a relatively superficial projective test and should be used in comparison with other sources of information.

Standardized questionnaires were not usually used very much by anthropologists formerly, but if efforts are made toward comparability between groups, as in the case of the Six Cultures project, questionnaires become a useful device, especially in view of the decreasing use of projective tests. However, Robert A. LeVine (1970:590) has complained about "noncomparability" when the "same" questionnaires have been used, as in the Six Cultures study, in Puerto Rico by Landy, in Lebanon by Prothro, and in the Philippines by Guthrie and Jacobs. ". . .[E]ach investigator had so altered the interview schedule or manner of reporting results that there were no comparable findings across the full range of published studies."

As Phillips's Thai study shows, there is not much point in giving standardized tests or questionnaires unless they are used in more than one cultural setting. But as LeVine's comment indicates, the administration of the same questionnaire in different cultural settings presents many problems. The same difficulty occurs with respect to structured situations such as doll play, although here the lack of comparability is greater, since in the studies done so far, different kinds of tools have been used and different instructions given.

In this respect, use of the Rorschach Test has some advantages, despite the other problems that attend it. Since every person taking the Rorschach Test sees the same set of inkblots presented in the same order, here, at least, is one situation that has been fairly well standardized.

Perhaps one should not expect too much of efforts toward standardization of questionnaires and test procedures and comparability of data from different groups, for not only is every field situation different from every other, but every fieldworker is different from every other fieldworker. Anthropologists vary in their interests, values, abilities in different spheres, and alertness to different aspects of the world around them. Even when administering the same tests or questionnaires, some will do so somewhat differently from others. Besides, in different cultures the questions will be asked in different languages, which may sometimes result in slight differences of meaning. For example, how could one replicate in another culture Fromm and Maccoby's questions about *machismo?* Equivalent terms in other languages, such as *manliness* or *masculinity* may not have quite the same connotations.

These questions are not raised to discredit the use of standardized interview schedules or questionnaires. This chapter has reviewed cases where their usefulness is well attested. But all research methods have their limitations, and it is best to be aware of them.

SUGGESTIONS FOR FURTHER READING

Karl E. Weick, "Systematic Observational Methods," in *Handbook of Social Psychology*, 2d ed. ed. Gardner Lindzey and Elliot Aronson, (Reading, Mass.: Addison-Wesley, 1969), vol. 2 pp. 357–451; and Charles F. Cannell and Robert L. Kahn, "Interviewing," in Lindzey and Aronson, pp. 526–95.

Traditional fieldwork methods in anthropology are well described in the Introduction of Bronislaw Malinowski's *Argonauts of the Western Pacific* (New York: E. P. Dutton, 1961), pp. 4–25; first published in 1922.

On the uses of photography in culture-and-personality studies, see Margaret Mead, "Some Uses of Still Photography in Culture and Personality Studies," in *Personal Character and Cultural Milieu*, 3d ed., ed. Douglas G. Haring (Syracuse, N.Y.: Syracuse University Press, 1956), pp. 79–105.

See also E. Richard Sorenson, "A Research Film Program in the Study of Changing Man: Research Filmed Material as a Foundation for Continued Study of Nonrecurring Human Events," *Current Anthropology* 8 (1967); pp. 443–69; and Paul Ekman and Wallace V. Friesen, "A Tool for the Analysis of Motion Picture Film or Video Tape," *American Psychologist* 24 (1969), pp. 240–43.

Films: The following black and white films made by Margaret Mead and Gregory Bateson are available at New York University Film Library (all have relevance to the field of culture-and-personality): *Childhood Rivalry in Bali and New Guinea* (17 minutes); *A Balinese Family* (17 minutes); *Trance and Dance in Bali* (20 minutes). Margaret Mead is commentator in a film about family life in four societies: *Four Families*, McGraw-Hill (60 minutes).

13

The Analysis of Life History Material

For the authors of that sociological classic, *The Polish Peasant*, personal life records, as complete as possible, constituted, "the *perfect* type of sociological material" (Thomas and Znaniecki 1958, vol. 2:1832). Franz Boas (1943), on the other hand, was skeptical of the value of life histories, which he regarded as little more than essays in retrospective falsification. However, Boas also believed that anthropologists should study individuals, in addition to compiling broader ethnographic accounts; and some students of Boas were pioneers in the collection of biographies from members of nonliterate societies. In the 1930s and 1940s, a growing interest in life histories was fostered by the influence of psychoanalytic doctrine, with its focus on the individual. Within a five-year period, three books were published which are still the fullest autobiographies we have by American Indians: *Son of Old Man Hat. A Navaho Autobiography*, recorded by Walter Dyk (1938); *Smoke from Their Fires. The Life of a Kwakiutl Chief*, edited by Clellan S. Ford (1941); and *Sun Chief. The Autobiography of a Hopi Indian*, edited by Leo W. Simmons (1942). Meanwhile, particularly after the appearance of a critique of *The Polish Peasant* by H. Blumer, efforts were made by some investigators in the social sciences to set up criteria by which life history documents could be judged and analyzed.

Life histories have figured prominently in culture-and-personality studies, such as those of Alor and Truk, Carstairs's study of high-caste Hindus in a Rajasthan community, and many others. In the United States, black American life histories have been analyzed for recurrent sociopsychological patterns in *Children of Bondage* by Allison Davis and John Dollard (1940), and in *The Mark of Oppression* by Abram Kardiner and Lionel Ovesey (1951).

An innovation that deserves notice is the *family autobiography*. In *The Children of Sánchez* (1961) Oscar Lewis presented the story of a lower-class family in Mexico City, as told by each of its members. Independent versions of the same episodes by the different individuals involved provide a check on the reliability and validity of some of the data. Moreover, one sees the same occurrence through different eyes, noting how it affects each individual differently. A dramatic incident, for example, is the early, unexpected death of Jesús Sánchez's wife, Lenore. Jesús tells this story; so do each of the children who remember the event vividly. Other episodes are similarly repeated, like recurrent motifs, in the individual autobiographies. In the process the reader gets to learn how the various members of the family feel about, and react toward, one another. This material was recorded by tape recorder, translated and edited by Lewis.

In *La Vida* Lewis (1968:xxvi) gave an extensive account of a poor Puerto Rican family consisting of five households. He described the Rios family members as having "an almost complete absence of internal conflict and of a sense of guilt. . . . The leading characters in *The Children of Sánchez* seem mild, repressed, and almost middle-class by comparison." The last in Lewis's series of autobiographical narratives is the posthumously published series, *Living the Revolution: An Oral History of Contemporary Cuba*, in three volumes: *Four Men, Four Women*, and *Neighbors* (Lewis, Lewis and Rigdon 1977). Lewis has made more use of biographical material than any other anthropologist, but he has presented the material as raw data, without much analysis of particular personalities.

Edward H. Winter (1959) collected life history material from an Amba man, his two wives, and another Amba male informant in Uganda. As in Lewis's studies, we get a vivid picture of the dynamics of family living from these autobiographies. In addition, the husband of the two wives was persuaded to keep a diary. He gives frank day-by-day accounts of his wives' quarrels and other matters. No projective tests were given to these subjects, but they are hardly necessary since the life histories are so revealing.

Norman B. Schwartz (1977) has published the autobiography of a Guatemalan *milpero*, together with an analysis which makes use of David Mandelbaum's concept of "turnings," periods when a person takes on a new set of roles or starts relations with a new set of people which brings about a new self-concept (Mandelbaum 1973:181). The subject's TAT responses are given in an appendix.

At their best, life histories are fascinating documents. The main difficulty lies in knowing what to do with them. How are they to be interpreted? Some collectors of such data have simply presented their narratives as raw material, leaving them to speak for themselves. In culture-and-personality studies, however, it seems preferable to make some effort at interpretation—not always an easy matter. There are other problems as well: questions of sampling, methods of procedure in recording data, and methods of presentation.

Most published life histories are either accounts of famous men or case histories by psychiatrists of their maladjusted patients.[1] The "average man" is not apt to be represented, being neither successful enough nor sick enough to attract attention. In cross-cultural studies it often happens that informants are drawn from the ranks of the less successful. In the discussion of Alor, for example, it was mentioned that Du Bois's biographies were given by some of the less-successful members of the society.

Clyde Kluckhohn (1945:99, 118) has suggested that American Indians who give autobiographies are apt to be drawn from the more maladjusted individuals in the group. There must, after all, be a fairly strong motive to talk, when an informant works with an ethnographer for many sessions. Well-adjusted subjects may be motivated only by financial rewards and may thus not give so sincerely personal an account. Don Talayesva, the narrator of *Sun Chief,* seems to have been a tormented person, ill at ease in his own society, who turned with gratitude to the white anthropologists who showed a friendly interest in him. John Chavafambira, the Manyika medicine man whose autobiography is presented by Wulf Sachs in *Black Anger* (1947), was also an unhappy man, and Sachs, a psychoanalyst, got his story through a number of analytic sessions. Lewis's Sánchez family members are painfully tormented people. Charles Nowell, the subject of *Smoke from Their Fires* (Ford 1941), on the other hand, seems to have been a rather successful nonneurotic man; his autobiography is also relatively colorless and nonpersonal when compared with those of Don Talayesva, John Chavafambira, and the Sánchez family.

For a balanced picture of the society being studied, of course, one should try to get material from the more successful and well-adjusted members of the group as well as from those less well adjusted. Gladwin handled the sampling problem ingeniously, as described in Chapter 6. Ideally one should have biographical data from young subjects as well as old, and of both sexes and of different status levels. Carstairs, who collected life history data from high-caste Hindus in a Rajasthan village, describes his own research design as follows:

> In drawing up plans for this research, my intention was to try to obtain prolonged interviews with twenty-seven informants, nine from each caste [i.e., Rajput, Brahman, and Bania]. In each case, three were to be relatively eminent and highly-regarded members of their community, three average, and three unquestionably low in their caste-fellows' esteem. Further, my ambition was to try to find one elderly, one middle-aged and one young man in each group of three (Carstairs 1958:37).

This design was not exactly achieved in practice, although the number of informants was increased from 27 to 37. A few of the pigeonholes were not filled. Carstairs also tried to keep a balance

---

[1] For the biographical work of psychohistorians, see pp. 407–10 and 417.

between the number of informants who were eldest sons and those who were younger sons. The sampling procedures of Gladwin and Carstairs show a great advance over earlier work in culture-and-personality in which there was often little or no concern with this problem.

Robert W. White has made a pioneer effort to record and analyze biographical material of normal persons in the United States. Three case histories are described in his book, *Lives in Progress* (1952). The procedures followed could be used in cross-cultural studies where communities are revisited after an interval of time. Each subject was interviewed on two occasions several years apart. In addition to giving an autobiography, each subject was given the Rorschach Test, Thematic Apperception Test, Wechsler-Bellevue Adult Intelligence Test, some self-rating scales, and other tests. The analysis of the personalities of the three subjects seem to be more successful and convincing than in most such efforts. They show that life history material can have much value for the understanding of individual personalities and their development over time.[2]

Some of the best life history documents are those which show the least prodding on the part of the ethnographer. During his Rajasthan fieldwork, Carstairs was fortunate in acquiring the already written autobiography, or journal, of a young man of a Bania family. The value of this document lies in its utter frankness and naiveté. Here is a man searching his heart, weighing his own assets and liabilities, complaining about his wife, father, and other members of the joint family, and expressing his longings and ambitions. This document is only about 40 printed pages in length, but it gives a remarkably full picture of a human personality.

Autobiographies recorded by ethnographers are not apt to be so spontaneous or so honest. The informant often lapses into silence or finds refuge in giving cultural data which have no personal significance. My Chippewa informant, Jim Mink, for example, used to launch into tedious explanations of how traps are made and other details of material culture. In such a case the ethnographer may direct the interview and ask quesions or specify the kind of information he wants. Where prodding of this sort occurs, it should be indicated in the published version. This is one deficiency in the otherwise splendid document, *Sun Chief.* We never know when a particular piece of information was spontaneously volunteered by Dan Talayesva and when it was elicited through cross-examination by Simmons. This criticism applies as well to Ford's *Smoke from Their Fires* and to *The Children of Sánchez* by Lewis.

The general question of editing is involved here. Kluckhohn

---

[2] For another good analysis among similar lines, see the case study of Morris Brown in Janis, Mahl, Kagan, and Holt (1969, chaps. 36, 38, 39, and 40). Analysis of life history material is combined with interpretation of the Rorschach, TAT, and various other tests.

(1945:97) believed that *Sun Chief* suffered from too much editing and condensation. (Only one fifth of the original data was published.) The material is presented in orderly chronological sequence and not as Don Talayesva told it. A different method was followed by Cora Du Bois, who presented the Alorese autobiographies as they were taken down, with no attempt at rearrangement. This method has the advantage of preserving chains of association. On the other hand, the Alorese life histories are hard to read or comprehend when compared with *Sun Chief* and some other edited biographies. The ethnographer must decide which method of presentation does most justice to his material.

Do not life history informants sometimes falsify and improvise? Of course they do, but this need not destroy their value as psychological documents. It was obvious to me that my Chippewa informant, Julia Badger, made up much of her information. She tended, for example, toward a dubious overspecificity; the numbers 56 and 57 kept coming up in her accounts. There were 56 people at a Winnebago peyote meeting she attended; her dormitory room at school had 57 beds. There were 357 boys and girls at one school she went to, which had 156 cows and where 856 loaves of bread were baked every day. But at another school that Julia attended there were 357 students, and 456 loaves of bread were baked every day. Many of Julia's anecdotes were evidently fantasies; all the same, they do provide psychologically revealing information, as will be shown in the next chapter.

The strange narrative by a Moroccan informant, Tuhami, seems to be largely made up of fantasy and fabrication. Vincent Crapanzano has described his relationship with his informant:

> At first Tuhami and I spoke mutually unintelligible languages. I was primarily interested in information, Tuhami in evocation. We did listen to each other, though, and soon our discourses began to vacillate between the informative and the evocative. We both tried to determine the direction: I with my prosaic questions, Tuhami, sometimes more extravagantly, with pronouncements (1980:14).

Crapanzano's text is of value in stressing the importance of the ethnographer's role in accounting for the character of the resulting life history document, something often ignored in earlier publications of this sort. He describes his own aims and his increasingly warm relationship with Tuhami. Moreover, Crapanzano realizes that his interpreter's role was also important, and he discusses that as well. Similarly, James M. Freeman (1978; 1979) has described his relationship with the Indian untouchable whose life history he collected, his own aims and purposes, and those of his interpreter.

Life histories are not always informative. Thomas Gladwin felt that the 23 Trukese biographies he collected told less about his subjects than the psychological tests which he used, the Rorschach and Thematic Apperception Test given to each subject. Gladwin's informants were not able to remember much about their early years, and since Trukese men are not given to introspection, their accounts "tend to consist in a series of flat statements about happenings and perfunctory and conventional expressions of their reactions to them . . ." (Gladwin and Sarason 1953:215). In a review of *The People of Alor*, Jules Henry (1945) expressed a similar disappointment in the Alorese life histories. He suggests that autobiography is a phase of the historical perspective associated with Western culture. One need not expect to find this interest in self-revelation in all cultures.

However, as *Sun Chief* testifies, rich life histories have been obtained from non-Western informants. To be sure, Don Talayesva is an acculturated individual, and Carstairs's introspective Bania diarist may also have been influenced by Western European traditions. Nevertheless, these men both belong to cultures which are still significantly different from that of the Western world. The same certainly applies to Winter's Amba subjects and to John Chavafambira.

For the purposes of culture-and-personality research, it is not necessary for life histories to be literarily satisfying. We hope to find clues in such material to the values and attitudes of the individual and to get some idea, if possible, as to why he has become the sort of person he is. For these purposes a fairly brief document may sometimes be sufficient. It is not always necessary to meet the demanding criteria which Dollard proposed for the life history. A life history can never be complete in any case. Even the fullest autobiography can be no more than a pale reflection of an individual's life in all its complexity. In analyzing a life history document, one looks for what the informant chooses to tell about himself and what values and attitudes he expresses, rather than attempt to reconstruct the whole sequence of his life.

SUGGESTIONS FOR FURTHER READING

Efforts to establish criteria by which life history materials can be judged and analyzed include the following:

H. Blumer, "An Appraisal of Thomas and Znaniecki's The Polish Peasant in Europe and America," Critique of Research in Social Sciences, no. 1, Social Science Research Council (1939).

John Dollard, *Criteria for the Life History, With an Analysis of Six Notable Documents* (New York: P. Smith, 1935).

Gordon W. Allport, *The Use of Personal Documents in Psychological Science*, Social Science Research Council Bulletin no. 49 (1942).

Lewis Gottschalk, Clyde Kluckhohn, and Robert Angell, *The Use of Personal Documents in History, Anthropology, and Sociology*, Social Science Research Council Bulletin no. 53 (1945).

Two attempts to interpret individual life histories may be noted: Alexander H. Leighton and Dorothea C. Leighton, *Gregorio, the Hand Trembler. A*

Psychobiological Personality Study of a Navaho Indian, Papers of the Peabody Museum of American Archaeology and Ethnology 40, no. 1 (1949).

David F. Aberle, *The Psychosocial Analysis of a Hopi Life History,* Comparative Psychology Monographs, Serial No. 107, vol. 21, no. 1 (1951).

For a review of life history documents, see L. L. Langness, *The Life History in Anthropological Science* (New York: Holt, Rinehart & Winston, 1965).

For psychoanalytic analyses of two famous charismatic men, see Erik H. Erikson, *Young Man Luther. A Study in Psychoanalysis and History* (New York: W. W. Norton, 1958); and Erik H. Erikson, *Gandhi's Truth. On the Origins of Militant Nonviolence* (New York: W W. Norton, 1969). The analyses of life history material, combined with the analyses of personality tests such as the Rorschach and Thematic Apperception Test are well carried out in Robert W. White's *Lives in Progress* and in Irving L. Janis et al., *Personality. Dynamics, Development, and Assessment* (New York: Harcourt, Brace & World).

For another review of life-history methods, see Gelya Frank, "Finding the Common Denominator: A Phenomenological Critique of Life History Method," *Ethos* 7 (1979), pp. 68–94.

14

The Interpretation of Dreams and Visions

G. P. Murdock (1945:124) lists "dream interpretation" as a universal aspect of culture. Not only does dreaming seem to be a universal human characteristic, but, if Murdock is right, an interest in dreams and an effort to understand them are found in all cultures. However, societies do vary considerably in the interest given to dreams. Among many American Indian tribes, where dreams were regarded as an avenue to supernatural power, this interest was intense, while among the Trobriand Islanders, according to Malinowski (1953:92), there is little concern with dreams; people seldom tell their dreams spontaneously, and have no system of symbolic explanation.

Dreams are very personal productions of the individual. The person who creates a dream is on his own; the setting, the cast, and the events of a dream are somehow of his own making. Due to their personal and intimate nature, the interpretation of dreams provides valuable clues to the personality of the individual. Because of the universality of dreaming, the study of dreams may be carried on cross-culturally.

It is evident that dreams reflect the culture in which one lives. Freud (1900:241) has discussed some "typical" dreams, "dreams which almost everyone has dreamt alike," and to which Freud says he has usually failed to obtain clarifying associations from the dreamer. One of these dreams is "the embarrassment-dream of nakedness." Such a dream, familiar enough in the Western world, can have no exact parallel among unacculturated Australian aborigines or other people who wear no clothing. Another "typical" dream cited by Freud is the examination-dream, which is also obviously the product of a particular type of culture characterized by formal schooling with competitive examinations.[1]

Griffith, Miyagi, and Tago (1958:1174) discuss the typical dream of

---

[1] Seligman (1924:40) reports this dream for ancient China, where competitive examinations were an avenue to political power.

finding money, which is said to be usually in the form of coins rather than bills. Whatever the denomination or form of currency, however, dreams of this sort can only appear in a society having some such medium of exchange. The dream of being chased by cows appears to be a typical dream in western Ghana, perhaps especially among disturbed individuals.[2] Culture, then, intimately influences the dreaming process.

Let us consider two general ways of studying dreams. First, one may collect dreams from a large number of individuals in a particular society and then look for characteristic features in this sample. Because of its group basis, such an investigation must be mainly concerned with the manifest content of dreams. Let us call this the *collective* approach. A second approach involves recording dreams in conjunction with life history material and other data concerning the individual, such as projective tests. In this case, especially if one can obtain free associations to the dream material, one may perhaps determine the latent content. Let us call this the *individual* approach. If one's sample of life history informants is large enough, these approaches could be combined.

THE COLLECTIVE APPROACH

Between 1933 and 1935 Lauriston Sharp collected 149 dreams from the Yir Yoront of Cape York Peninsula, Australia, in the course of fieldwork. The Yir Yoront are a hunting-gathering people whose culture is said to be much like that of the Murngin described by W. L. Warner in *A Black Civilization* (1958). The dreams collected by Sharp have been analyzed by David M. Schneider (1969). They seem to be often rather stereotyped, so they have been classified into a few categories: (1) dreams of sexual intercourse, (2) dreams of aggression, (3) dreams of death, (4) dreams of whites and white culture. Many dreams deal with hunting, spearing animals, and digging yams.

The 19 sex dreams—all from males—concern a young adult female who is not the dreamer's wife but who is of the appropriate kinship category in about half the cases—of the opposite moiety and a different clan. Although intercourse is usually completed, there are often inhibitory interruptions, the strength of which is related to the tabooed nature of the kinship tie. The Yir Yoront practice mother's brother's daughter marriage. It is interesting that the mother's brothers often figure as aggressors in dreams of aggression—eight times as often as sister's sons aggress against mother's brothers. Fights between these relatives are strongly tabooed in everyday life.

It seems rather unusual that in 18 cases the dreamer dies in the

---

[2] M. J. Field, *Search for Security* (1960), pp. 155, 157, 163, 164, 172–73, 176, 180, 195, 250, 285, 298, 310, 311, 368, 414, 427, 434.

dream. However, he does not usually stay dead but is resurrected, even though his body may have been dismembered. It is curious, too, that belief in resurrection is not part of Yir Yoront culture.

There is a good deal of evisceration and cutting up of bodies in Yir Yoront dreams, which may be related to the fact that hunters must often cut up and dismember game. It would be helpful to have collections of dreams from other hunting-gathering groups to see if the same pattern appears.[3]

Dorothy Eggan (1961) collected dreams from over 20 Hopi Indians over a fairly extended period of time. One of her informants was Don Talayesva, the narrator of *Sun Chief*, for whom she has over 230 dreams, 15 of which are discussed in a stimulating article (Eggan 1949). Her approach has therefore been both collective and individual. One of Eggan's conclusions, on a collective basis, is that:

> among the Hopi, the strength of tribal attitudes toward cooperative obligations to the tribe, frequently masked by surface changes, is well illustrated in dreams, as is also the superficiality of Hopi conversion to Christianity. A survey may show that 30% of a village is Christian in that they attend a missionary church; but their dreams indicate that the majority of the old Hopi who list themselves as Christian have as much respect for Masau'u, and many other Hopi deities, as they ever had (Eggan 1953:479).

A particularly interesting collective study of dreams is a detailed investigation of Zulu dreams by S. G. Lee (1958), which contains assessments of the latent content of the dreams. Lee asked 600 Zulu subjects, "How much do you dream?" and "What do you dream about?" In addition to recording their answers, Lee asked some 120 women the same questions, in each case following this up with further inquiries. These subjects were asked to describe two recent dreams in detail. Lee found that stereotyped typical dreams were very common—a circumstance which allowed quantitative comparisons to be made between groups, that is, between men and women, and between women of different ages and marital status. Because of their frequently stereotyped nature, all the dreams collected could be classified under less than 50 main content headings.

Women reported more dream activity than men, and more women dreamed of frightening objects, such as monsters, than did men. The men reported enjoying their dreams more than did the women. Men dreamed much more about cattle than did the women. Lee's explanation for this contrast is ingenious. Work with cattle used to be an exclusively male prerogative in the 19th century; and there was then a taboo on women handling cattle. Nowadays, however, women must take care of the cattle, since the men are often away from home under present work conditions. The cattle dreams reflect the sexual division

---

[3] Compare Laindjura's murders discussed on pp. 355–56 and in footnote 4 on p. 357.

of labor that existed 50 to 100 years ago but not the present situation. Lee argues that superego patterns are early instilled, and that dream content also tends to be derived from this early period. Hence the "conservatism" of the dream content. If Lee is right, this might explain the similarly conservative pattern of Hopi dreaming just noted.

When women do dream of cattle, their dreams have a different character from those of men. Women may dream of being pursued and gored by an ox or bull,[4] while the men have pleasant wish-fulfillment dreams of owning large herds.

More frequently than men, women dreamed of flooded rivers, water, snakes, and a priapic creature called Tokoloshe, who lives in rivers and assaults women sexually. While 32 percent of the women reported water dreams, only 5 percent of the men did so; 17 percent of the women dreamed of snakes as against 3 percent of the men; 16 percent of the women reported dreams of flooded rivers; while only 6 percent of the men did so. Tokoloshe dreams were reported by 7 percent of the women and 2 percent of the men.

The local interpretation of Zulu diviners is that "To dream of flooded rivers means that you will give birth to a baby." Lee points to the interesting parallel with orthodox Freudian symbolic interpretation here.

Lee goes on to examine the different age and marital status groups in which dreams are reported.

> Snakes, *tokoloshe,* and flooded river dreams were practically limited to women under the age of fifty—while dreams of "a baby" and children were reported by women of ages when childbearing might be considered very probable, between 18 and 35. Dreams of "a wedding" were found in an even younger group, mostly unmarried. "Fighting," a comparatively common dream in men, was a dream of a few unmarried women under 22. Overt aggression, after marriage, is forbidden the Zulu woman by her culture (Lee 1958:278–79).

Those who dreamed of a baby had the worst record of married infertility. Their dreams, evidently, represent simple wish-fulfillment. Those who dreamed of still water were more apt to be women who had borne no children and also married and widowed women who had borne relatively few. Flooded river dreams were mostly reported by married women with a very low rate of complete married infertility, but who were older than the "baby" dreamers. Such women have borne many more children than either of the other two "birth dream" groups and have a fear of further childbirth—a disinclination which is in conflict with social pressures to keep on bearing children.

If we are to make cross-cultural comparisons of the patterning of dreams, it would be useful to have data on the prevailing characteris-

---

[4] Compare the "typical" Ghana dream of being chased by cows, referred to in footnote 2.

tics of dreams in the United States. Fortunately, abundant information on this has been made possible by Calvin S. Hall's collection of 10,000 dreams and by his generalizations about them. Hall's generalizations (1959:19, 29–31, 37, 41) must be taken to apply to American dreams of the 1950s, not to dreams universally. Let us consider some of his findings. Hall claims that dreams generally concern the personal life of the dreamer and seldom have to do with current events, presidential elections, wars and other happenings reported in the newspapers. Nor does a person normally dream about his or her work or business activities. In 10 out of every 100 dreams, the dreamer is walking along a road; in about 15 out of 100, he or she is in some kind of conveyance. One out of three dreams occurs in a dwelling which is usually not the dreamer's own house. Family members and friends are commonly dreamed of, but about 4 of every 10 characters in our dreams are strangers. Strenuous activity is not generally characteristic of dreams; eating and drinking occur very infrequently, but swimming, dancing, and playing games are common. Unpleasant dreams are more numerous than pleasant ones; this ratio increases as one gets older. About one dream in three has color in it.[5] Domesticated animals appear more frequently than wild animals, with the three most common being horses, dogs, and cats—in that order. Horses appear about twice as often in the dreams of women as in those of men (pp. 62–63).

Another essay in the collective approach to the study of dreams is that by Griffith, Miyagi, and Tago (1958), who made a comparison of American and Japanese college students' dreams. In this case, instead of recording dreams, a dream questionnaire was used. Through the questionnaire Griffith collected figures on the occurrence of typical dreams and common dream contents from 250 American college students in Kentucky (134 males, 116 females), while his Japanese colleagues, using the same questionnaire, got similar data from 223 Tokyo college students (132 males, 91 females). The authors found that American and Japanese college students tended to have very similar types of dreams. Some differences, however, were noted in connection with aggressive dreams, and here the authors also seem to contradict one of the points made by Hall, who observes that aggressive dreams are common but outright murder rare. According to one report dealing with Hall's work, only 2 percent of the hostile dreams involved actual homicide (Robinson 1959:57). On this point one gets a different impression from the findings of Griffith, Miyagi, and Tago, whose analysis also brings out an interesting point of sex difference in the two national groups studied.

---

[5] This seems a surprisingly high percentage. Schachtel (1943) refers to a Japanese study by Tatibana, in which it is stated that of 100 subjects questioned, only 25 reported having seen color in their dreams; 60 percent of these 25 recalled only a single instance of having seen a color in their dreams.

To the question "Have you ever killed someone in your dreams?" 26 percent of the Americans responded "yes," versus 28 percent of the Japanese; of all the males combined, 29 percent reported the dream, versus 24 percent of the combined females. However, within the American culture, the males had the dream in proportion three to one over the females; the situation was completely reversed in the Japanese culture, where twice as many females as males reported the dream (Griffith, Miyagi, and Tago 1958:1176).

Two other differences noted in this study were (1) the rarity of nudity dreams in Japan and (2) the greater frequency of dreams of fire in that country.

Robert A. LeVine (1966) has carried out a complicated but well-conceived and well-executed study of dreams of English-speaking Nigerian boys attending secondary schools. His purpose was to find evidence of differences in the strength of the need for achievement (n-Achievement) in three ethnic groups: Hausa, Yoruba, and Ibo. A number of writers have commented impressionistically on the drive and enterprise of the Ibo, contrasting them with the more conservative Hausa. LeVine believes that the high achievement motivation of the Ibo is related to a greater degree of status mobility among them than in the other two ethnic groups.

In measuring achievement motivation the most usual method followed by David C. McClelland and his colleagues has been to use the Thematic Apperception Test (TAT). But LeVine did not think that this method would work well with his three Nigerian groups, which differ greatly in styles of clothing and other aspects of culture. Accordingly, LeVine obtained dream reports instead. Each student in a classroom was asked to write in English an account of a dream he had had more than once. Some of the reported dreams were probably daydreams, but LeVine and his colleagues made no distinction between such types, considering all the reports to be fantasies produced in response to an ambiguous stimulus.

LeVine's hypothesis was that the Ibo dream reports would show the most evidence of n-Achievement and the Hausa the least, with the Yoruba falling in between. The testing sample consisted of 342 male secondary students: 65 Hausa, 139 Yoruba, and 138 Ibo.

The students' dream reports were typed, disguised to obviate clues to ethnic identity, and scored for n-Achievement along the lines followed by McClelland. The scorers had no knowledge of LeVine's hypothesis or the ethnic groups. The results turned out to be in keeping with LeVine's hypotheses. The frequency of achievement themes was greatest for the Ibo, followed by the Yoruba and Hausa in that order.

The Nigerian students were also asked to write essays on "What is a successful man?" and "How does a boy become a successful man?"

Here the *n*-Achievement scores were not in the expected direction of Ibo–Yoruba–Hausa but, instead: Yoruba–Hausa–Ibo. However, differences between the groups were too small to be considered statistically significant. Another set of scores did accord with expectations. This time the essays were scored for the frequency of obedience and social compliance value themes, which proved to be highest for the conservative Hausa and lowest for the Ibo. LeVine cites similar findings in a nationwide public survey of Nigerian adults.

THE INDIVIDUAL APPROACH

The individual approach to the study of dreams is possible when one has life history material to which the dream can be related. Ideally, one should have the dreamer's associations to his dream. The Alorese study provides an example of this approach. Cora Du Bois (1944:191–92) began each day's work with her informants by asking for dreams of the previous night. She admits, however, that attempts to get associations to significant words in the dream were not very successful. Wulf Sachs (1947:179, 291) persuaded John Chavafambira and his wife to associate to their dreams, apparently with more success.

Once a dream or dream series has been recorded, either with or without associations, the problem of interpretation arises. A given dream may, of course, be interpreted in a number of different ways. Books on dreams, such as those of Wolff, Hadfield, and Boss, draw attention to contrasting systems of interpretation based upon different assumptions about dreams. Hadfield (1954:85–87) presents a dream and its analysis as it might be interpreted by (1) a Freudian, (2) an Adlerian, and (3) a Jungian. He also interprets some of Freud's dreams in a manner at variance with Freud's own analysis. Boss (1958:41) offers an interpretation of a recurrent dream which plagued the poet Rosegger—an interpretation which also contrasts with Freud's analysis of the same dream (1900:473–75). Wolff (1952:131–55), too, analyzes some dreams of Freud's that Freud had interpreted quite differently. Dream interpretations are, therefore, not self-evident. Each depends on a particular set of assumptions.

In the case of conflicting views, how can one decide which is the most justified? Calvin S. Hall (1947) has suggested some criteria in this connection. Somewhat condensed, these involve: (1) *agreement between individuals;* for example, two or more persons formulate explanations independently of one another and compare them; (2) *internal consistency;* that is, "The more facts that can be explained by a theory, the stronger is the presumption that the theory is correct"; (3) *external consistency;* for example, comparison with other data, such as Rorschach or TAT interpretation; (4) *prediction;* (5) *postdiction,* the reconstruction of past events. Since these may be verified, this method has an advantage over prediction, for which one must await the outcome.

Comments may be made on two of these criteria. In the case of *agreement between individuals,* it would not be surprising if two or more Freudians arrive at the same interpretation of a dream, but we can't say that this agreement would necessarily constitute corroboration. In connection with *external consistency,* a word of caution may be suggested. Hiram L. Gordon has made a comparison of the dreams and TAT stories of a group of 29 psychiatric patients (24 men and 5 women). He found that his subjects' dreams, as compared with their TAT stories, expressed more aggression, tension, and fear, and less depression and self-blame. The central character in dreams was more passive and inadequate than in the subject's TAT stories. Gordon's conclusion (1953:252–53) is that in dreams the subject "is less concerned with maintaining his idealized self-concept of adequacy and maturity and more concerned with escaping threats to his safety," while in the TAT stories he is more concerned with defending and enhancing an idealized concept of the self.

SYMBOLISM

The problem of symbolism is, of course, involved in the interpretation of dreams. Freud believed that most dreams of adults give expression to erotic wishes. To evade the "dream censor," these wishes may have to be disguised in symbolic form; hence, the familiar equations of the male genital organ with snakes, swords, sticks, and so forth, and of the vagina with containers, vases, boxes, and bags.

Though much influenced by Freudian theory, Calvin S. Hall doubts this concept of *symbolic disguise.* His reasons for skepticism on this point seem cogent:

> Having read hundreds of dream series in the past few years, I noticed that within the same series outspoken dreams occurred along with "symbolized" dreams. It is fairly common for one to dream of sexual activities in the frankest terms one night and in disguised terms the next. Open incest dreams alternate with camouflaged incest dreams. Patricide and fraticide are sometimes overt, sometimes concealed. I wondered what was the sense of preparing an elaborate deception in one dream when it was discarded in a subsequent dream (Hall 1953:172–73).

Hall also notes that many dream symbols for penis, vagina, and coitus are identical with slang terms given in Partridge's *A Dictionary of Slang and Unconventional English,* many of which terms are centuries old. They would, therefore, not be very effective disguises.

Freud gave another reason for symbolism in dreams—regard for representability. Thoughts, feelings, attitudes, and impulses are more vividly conveyed in pictorial form in dreams. The dream speaks in parables—not to confuse but to convey information. Hall prefers this view of symbolism to the disguise theory, which he thinks is diametrically opposed to the former. Whichever view of symbolism one accepts, however, the problem of interpreting symbols remains. Are we safe in translating sword or snake as penis, or handbag as vagina? May not such symbols have different overtones and associations in other cultures? The snake is certainly a symbol for penis in various cultures beside our own, but in some areas it symbolizes a variety of other things as well, for example, healing, immortality, wisdom, the rainy season, the rainbow, and the afterworld. In such cases one should investigate both the local cultural concepts about the symbolic referent and the dreamer's own associations as well.

The attitude of culture-and-personality anthropologists toward the question of symbolism has been ambivalent, for they have been influenced both by Freudian theory and by the cultural relativism of Franz Boas. A word must be said about these conflicting attitudes. According to the more orthodox Freudian and Jungian analysts, some symbols have a universal significance. They are "stable translations" (Freud 1915–16:151) and may be found in all societies because (for Freud) they are rooted in man's physiological functioning, common experiences, and associations,[6] or (for Jung) because they exist in the collective unconscious. Most anthropologists, as far as I can judge, take a more culturalist and relativist view of symbolism. A relativist approach stresses the differing cultural contexts in which a symbol may appear and which may alter the meaning of the symbol. This can be illustrated in Boas's treatment of design symbols.

Boas asserted that symbols, like all other aspects of culture, have a historical background. The form of a symbol, he argued, may diffuse from one society to another; but its associated meaning may or may not diffuse with it. As an example, Boas (1955:120) cited the design motif consisting of an isosceles triangle with short straight lines coming down from the base. This design is found in the decorative art of many North American Indian tribes, among whom it must have diffused from one group to another. Symbolic meanings are generally given to the design, but these vary from tribe to tribe. For one group it represents a bear's paw with long claws, for another a tent with tent poles, doorway, and pegs. Among the Pueblo Indians, concerned with rain and fertility, the design is interpreted as a cloud with falling rain, while another tribe sees it as a mountain with springs at its foot. The design, therefore, does not have a fixed symbolic significance for all tribes but assumes, rather, the character of a semistructured ink-blot into which varying interpretations may be projected.

---

[6] Freud (1915–16:199) also considered the possibility of transmission through a sort of collective unconscious. "It seems to me, for instance, that symbolic connections, which the individual has never acquired by learning, may justly claim to be regarded as a phylogenetic heritage."

Ruth Bunzel (1938:584) has similarly pointed out that many American Indian tribes use the cross in their decorative art. "To the Zuñi," she writes "it symbolizes the four quarters of the world; to the Arapaho, the morning star; to the Huichol it represents corn or peyote or a spark." Thus, certain meanings for a symbol may become standardized within a given tribe. Yet, within the group itself there may be differences of interpretation; the same individual, even, may give different explanations for a particular symbol at different times.

It must be noted, however, that the universal and relativist points of view need not be mutually exclusive. Perhaps the associations to design forms recorded by anthropologists represent only superficial, rational responses. It might be argued that on a deeper, more unconscious level some symbols may prove to have universal significance.[7]

But to demonstrate the existence of true universal symbols, one must rule out the influence of cultural diffusion. Most of Freud's evidence for symbolic meanings is drawn from the folklore, mythology, and proverbs of Western Europe. Even if we range further afield to India and China, we are still dealing with cultures in which the diffusion of folklore and beliefs has operated over long periods of time. To show true universality in symbolic associations one should examine the evidence from widely separated, historically unrelated cultures areas.

Let us consider these problems with regard to snake symbolism. Ernest Jones (1948:101, 123) considers the snake to be a good example of universal symbolism.

> The idea of a snake, which is never consciously associated with that of the phallus, is regularly so in dreams, being one of the most constant and invariable symbols; in primitive religions the two ideas are obviously interchangeable, so that it is often hard to distinguish phallic from ophitic worship.

This association is attributed by Jones to the objective attributes common to both snake and penis: "shape, erectibility, habits—of emitting poison and of creeping into holes," as well as to certain attitudes of horror and disgust which may sometimes be present, as in the case of prudish virgins.

Now, can we say that phallic associations and attributes of fear and disgust concerning the snake are universal? If we mean by this all peoples of the world, the answer would seem to be negative, for there

---

[7] Erich Fromm (1951:15, 18), who has so often mediated between psychoanalytic and sociological traditions, has suggested a distinction between *accidental* (entirely personal), *conventional* (restricted to a group sharing the same tradition), and *universal* symbols. "The universal symbol," he writes, "is one in which there is an intrinsic relationship between the symbol and that which it represents. . . . The universal symbol is rooted in the properties of our body, our senses, and our mind, which are common to all men and, therefore, not restricted to individuals or to specific groups." Unfortunately, Fromm's discussion of universal symbolism is rather weak. He gives two examples—fire and water—but offers so many "intrinsic" meanings of these properties that their symbolic significance remains unclear.

are some regions, in parts of northern Europe and Asia, the Arctic, and some oceanic islands, where snakes are not found. It is interesting to note, however, that in some of these areas traditions about serpents may persist in folklore and legend. Some Eskimo groups, at least—perhaps the most southern ones—have folktales about snakes (Rink 1875:186–88), and the Chukchee of eastern Siberia, where there are no snakes, have traditions about snakelike creatures which may be survivals of a period before the northward migration of the ancestors of the present Chukchee (Bogoras 1909:13). The tenacity of such traditions is remarkable. Even so, there are probably societies in snakeless regions where no such traditions exist. Moreover, it must be conceded that there are differences in attitudes toward snakes in different cultural areas. For example, among many African tribes, according to Hambly, the python is revered as "a god of wisdom, earthly bliss and benefaction." Here there seems to be no attitude of horror; however, Hambly (1931:11, 23, 75) also says that there are phallic associations to the snake among these tribes, also suggested, if not demonstrated, by Lee's material on Zulu dreams (1958:277).

Evidence for phallic associations to the snake is sometimes provided by linguistic clues. In Semitic languages, according to Howey (1949:127), the same root signifies serpent and phallus. In India "nāgalatā or climbing serpent, serpent-creeper, is one of the Hindoo names of the phallos" (de Gubernatis 1872, vol. 2:399). A Chippewa term for penis, kinébigustigwàn, translated literally, means "snake head" (A. I. Hallowell, personal communication).

Popular customs also may indicate such symbolic linkages. Rivet-Carnac has discussed some phallic implications of the Nāgpanchamī festival, as observed in Nāgpur, India, in the 1870s. At this time, he says:

> more than the usual license is indulged in. . . . Rough pictures of snakes, in all sorts of shapes and positions, are sold and distributed, something after the manner of Valentines. . . . In the ones I have seen, in days gone by, the positions of the women with the snakes were of the most indecent description and left no doubt that, so far as the idea represented in these sketches was concerned, the cobra was regarded as the phallus (Rivet:Carnac 1879:26).

According to Ronald M. Berndt (1951:21), the natives of northeast Arnhem Land frankly and consciously associate the penis with the snake.

An almost universal theme in folklore is the snake-lover motif; that is, stories in which a girl is penetrated by or has sexual relations with a snake. In going through the literature, I have found this motif reported for Italy, France, Portugal, Germany, South and Central India, Melanesia, Australia, and also in such American Indian tribes as the Hopi, Zuñi, Chippewa, Assineboine, Seneca, Sauk, Creek, and others. This motif would tend to strengthen the likelihood of a phallic association with the snake among these peoples. The evidence just presented does not, of course, demonstrate the universality of a phallic significance for the snake, but it does indicate the likelihood that such symbolism is not limited to Europe and the United States but obtains in many cultures in different parts of the world.

The same possibility may apply to other Freudian linkages: for example, the equation of feces and wealth. As suggested earlier, a dream involving coins or other currency can only appear in a society having some sort of monetary system. An equivalent may appear, of course, in societies such as the Yurok, where cowrie shells serve as a kind of currency (Posinsky 1956).

J. S. Lincoln (1935:107–108) has presented some of the evidence for a symbolic equation of feces and wealth in cultures other than our own—such as Seligman's example of a psychotic Melanesian who "when remonstrated with for defaecating on the verandah, replied, 'It is not faeces, but money.' "; the Ashanti explanation that a dream of falling into a latrine means that you are going to get money; the Siamese interpretation that to dream of excrement promises riches; the belief in Tangier that if you dream your clothes are full of excrement it means wealth; and a number of other such examples. Alan Dundes (1962:1041) has given some further examples, notably that the Nahuatl term for gold literally means "excrement of the gods."

One consideration that should be kept in mind in assessing the significance of such symbolism is that in some peasant societies, like those of India and China, manure has a real economic significance, either for fuel, as in northern India, or for fertilizer, as in rural China. Hence, when a human figure modeled of cow dung is constructed at the Gobardhan festival in northern India, and a man exclaims "Long live Grandfather Cowdung Wealth!" (Marriott 1955:200), this need not be invested with any special Freudian overtones, for cow dung *is* a form of wealth to the Indian villagers.

JULIA BADGER'S FANTASIES

To illustrate some of the issues that have been discussed, as applied to a particular case, I will present some fantasy material from my Chippewa informant, Julia Badger. These fantasies are not dreams (although part of their origin may be in dreams), but the basic problems involved are the same.[8]

When I collected this material in the summer of 1944 at Lac du Flambeau, Julia Badger was a 34-year-old woman married to Tom Badger, a conservative Mide priest in his 70s. Julia was a very bulky woman, "wall-eyed," and somewhat schizoid. During her childhood

---

[8] The following pages draw on Barnouw (1949).

she had had periods of temporary blindness and paralysis, and had worn a brace on her leg for several years. These ailments enforced absence from school for long periods and resulted in Julia's exposure to the gamut of conservative Chippewa curing practices: conjuring lodge, sucking doctor, bleeding, cedar bough medications, War Dance, Medicine Dance, and so forth. Eleven years of schooling could not erase this early impress of traditional Chippewa culture. Julia's parents seem to have rejected her in childhood, and she was brought up by grandparents, later going to school away from the reservation. After her return Julia had a brief marriage to a much older man, a Winnebago peyotist, by whom she became pregnant. This marriage was broken up by her relatives, who arranged a marriage with a Chippewa of whom they approved, but this man died not long after the birth of her child. Subsequently Julia married Tom Badger, who left his wife to live with her. When I worked with this couple in 1944, Tom and Julia had been husband and wife for 15 years, but there seemed to be a good deal of friction between them, partly because of Julia's refusal to perform the traditional chores of the Chippewa housewife. She preferred to lounge about and daydream. Tom, who was normally a mild and patient person, used to beat her when he was drunk.

On the first day of my work with Tom Badger (with Julia as interpreter) Tom told me about his encounter with a little man called Bebukowe, with whom he went sliding on the ice just before he (Tom) was born. Tom said that before he was born he was walking toward the sun, when he looked down and saw something shining. As he approached it, this turned out to be a river, frozen over. Behind him was the little man, Bebukowe. "When I was right next to that river, the man behind me spoke to me. We had reached a bend in that river, and this man said. 'Let's slide across to the bend there.' We slid along the ice. When I reached the bend, I was born."

When Tom had finished this story, Julia said that she, too, had seen Bebukowe. This happened when she was two months old. Julia had fallen very ill because a woman in mourning had stepped on her bonnet. This brought on paralysis and temporary blindness. A medicine man built a shaking tent to consult the spirits and took Julia into the tent with him, but meanwhile her spirit had already set out on the road to the other world. In the distance she could see the otter that stands beside the road. Julia heard a noise like jingling tin behind her. This was Bebukowe, who had come to take her back to her people. "He said, 'It isn't time for you yet.' Then he grabbed me by the waist and twisted and turned me around."

When she got back to the shaking tent, her parents were crying loudly. Bebukowe started to perform a dance. Julia said:

> Bebukowe looks a lot like a man—except that his face is different. His face is a little like a grasshopper's face around the nose. [Tom

Badger nodded in agreement to this description.] Bebukowe's face is handsome, though. And when he hollers, he's got a voice on him like any man's. He's dressed up in fine clothes, covered with bells. He likes to dance when he enters. He grabbed me around the waist like this. [Demonstrated.] Then he said, "You're going to play around with a lot of men like this. You can't go now."

Bebukowe took Julia's bonnet and whirled it around, causing a wind which made the bells ring and the wigwam tip over. During this account Mrs. Badger also described some other spirits who were present in the lodge—an old woman and two whitehaired old men.

In examining these fantasies, the first thing which struck my attention was the modification of the traditional picture of Bebukowe that appears in these accounts. Considering the respect and affection which Tom and Julia both felt for Bebukowe, it is curious to discover that Bebukowe does not at all play a kindly or beneficent role in Chippewa folklore. On the contrary, he is depicted as a villainous old fellow, an ugly hunchback with evil powers of sorcery. "He looks awful," said one informant, "He's humped way over. And he's everlastingly got the dirtiest nose. His snot hangs way down." In one story Bebukowe kills a handsome young hunter by shoving a heated stick down his throat. Then he changes bodies with the dead man, becoming a handsome fellow himself, and visits the dead man's girl in this guise; finally nemesis catches up with him, and Bebukowe is transformed back into his former ugly shape.

It might be suggested that Julia Badger's reinterpretation of this mythical character betrays a lack of contact with Chippewa tradition; but this does not seem to be an adequate explanation, because she is really very conversant with Chippewa folklore. Some characters in Chippewa folklore appear to be vague and flexible enough to admit of varying interpretations, for even *windigòg* (cannibal giants) can be friendly creatures in some anecdotes. Tom Badger also modifies the prevailing conception of Bebukowe, though in a much less dramatic fashion. Nevertheless, their conceptions of this figure do deviate markedly from the traditional patterns.

Such individual reinterpretations of local folklore provide a suggestive index of personality. In Julia's case we might say that her transformation of Bebukowe is typical of her approach to reality. She represses the painful aspects of her unhappy childhood, and in their place constructs a fantasy of happiness, gaiety, and affection. Bebukowe is an appropriate symbol for such a transformation. He is an ugly old fellow, crippled like herself, who temporarily takes on a handsome figure and masquerades under false pretenses.

Julia has seen fit to accept the temporary, handsome incarnation of Bebukowe, his false front, behind which the ugly reality lies hidden. Julia refuses to acknowledge the ugly reality; and so her picture of Bebukowe departs from that of others, just as her own version of reality is a private fantasy-tinged conception which others cannot share.

But Julia's Bebukowe has retained at least one characteristic of the original (in addition to the peculiarity of his nose); this is his libidinal quality. The traditional Bebukowe, although a villain, is at least aggressive in fulfilling his desires. While Julia's Bebukowe is lacking in villainy, he retains some of this erotic flavor. Perhaps one may say that in Julia's version Bebukowe has become a general incarnation of the life-affirming qualities, of the Eros principle, so to speak.

Bebukowe rescues Julia from death and restores her to her parents, whose lamentations demonstrate that they really loved her after all. Perhaps the circumstances surrounding Julia's narration of this story account for the compelling and emotional quality of her recital. For earlier that same day Julia had believed that Tom had deserted her, and the world looked black indeed for a while. But Tom had returned. He cared for her after all.

It may be said that the only positive figures in the foregoing story are the spirits of the supernatural world. Human beings are depicted as being rather helpless and incapable of solving their own problems without outside assistance. Julia's father calls on his parents for help when his daughter falls sick, and exclaims, "They say I'm going to lose my first baby, if I don't get busy and do something for her." Then the medicine man decides to summon the spirits, weeping as he does so, with the remark, "I'll try to do all I can. A lot of people never believe me."

Here, I think, is a general Chippewa attitude rather than a purely individual one. Hallowell describes a similar emphasis in Chippewa mythology:

> Among them *anicinábek* (men) are always the "receivers"; the *pawaganak* or *manitok* are always the ones who give help and "bless" human beings. They pity men and take cognizance of their needs, especially in misfortune. Human beings are conceived as being in constant need of help from birth to death. So essential is such help that no performance of any kind is due to an individual's own abilities or efforts (Hallowell 1947:554).

Julia Badger's Vision

On a later occasion Julia told me about a vision which she had had. It struck me that there were some thematic similarities in the visionary experience and in the Bebukowe fantasy. Julia said that the third time she went through the Midewiwin (Medicine Dance) it was because of a vision. One day when she was alone and feeling unhappy, she asked aloud, "What is there that I didn't do right?" Then she had a vision of walking along a narrow trail on a bright sunny day. She could hear a tinkling sound in the distance. "As I came nearer to the sound, I saw four men sitting around something that was round. [A drum. The four men represent the four directions, as she later made clear.] Above their heads was something across the sky like a rainbow. One of these men called me his grandchild."

These grandfather figures, the four directions, gave Julia advice and promised that she would live to old age if she heeded them and offered them tobacco now and then. When Julia returned along the trail, she met a large snake, who raised his head about four feet from the ground. He told her not to be afraid but to tell Tom what she had seen. The snake said, "I want to come into that place. [He meant her home, Julia later explained.] I like that place. It makes no difference how it looks. I'm coming there just the same."

After this, Julia made preparations for going through the Midewiwin, because a snake hide is given to a candidate who joins the Midewiwin for the third time. One afternoon, when Julia was alone at home, an unexpected visitor came in, saying, "I have come at last." He told Julia to look after him carefully and to wear her prettiest dress. Then he became a snake and went out.

Symbolism of the Snake

In this vision-fantasy sequence, the snake plays a role similar to that of Bebukowe in the earlier account, and Julia's private interpretation of the serpent is similarly at variance with the common conception. Snakes are generally feared by the Chippewa, since they are associated with the practices of medicine men and sorcery. Some medicine men were believed to obtain supernatural power by cutting off some of the flesh of giant serpents who inhabit swampy regions. According to Jenness (1935:35), serpents were not only held to be guardian spirits and agents of sorcerers, but were feared as the chief enemies of both man and the thunderbirds. They could travel underground unseen and steal away men's souls. Children were warned never to accept the serpent as a guardian spirit in a fasting dream, for their lives might be ruined by the association. According to Hallowell (1938:28), the animals feared most by the Saulteaux are snakes, toads, and frogs, although these are actually among the most harmless animals in their environment. A small variety of garter is the only snake present.

As she did with Bebukowe, Julia Badger seems to have effected a Nietzschean "transvaluation of values" in regard to her attitude toward the snake. However, the extent of Julia's personal reinterpretation need not be exaggerated. There are various instances in Chippewa folklore where the snake plays a beneficent role. In many Chippewa tales a serpent safely transports innocent people across a stream away from danger, and is respectfully addressed by those persons as "grandfather." The same serpent drowns malevolent people who ask him for a ferry ride across the river. As we learn from Julia's account, those who join the Medicine Dance for the third time receive a snakeskin hide and obtain some sort of supernatural bond with the serpent *manido*.

The snake is, therefore, not altogether evil in Chippewa conception; he has some beneficent associations as well. This element of ambiguity somewhat reduces the deviant character of Julia's conception of the serpent. But even when these qualifications have been made, it must be admitted that Julia's personal evaluation of the snake is most unusual in the general setting of Chippewa belief. Once again, we note Julia's tendency to construct a world of private meanings and to transform the ugly aspects of "reality."

Like Julia's Bebukowe, the snake-man seems to symbolize life, health, and love. There is certainly an erotic element in her references to this "visitor," with his expressed desire to enter into her home and be near to her. Julia, of course, associated the snake with the Medicine Dance and with the third degree of initiation; but the serpent very likely possesses a deeper symbolic significance at the same time. In this case the Freudian conception of the snake as phallic symbol seems to be appropriate, particularly in view of the Chippewa term, *kinébigustigwàn* ("snake-head") for penis.

Phallic Hunchbacks

Since publishing the article from which I have quoted, I have been struck by the phallic properties attributed to hunchback dwarf figures in aboriginal American folklore, which leads me to think that the parallel between Bebukowe and the snake may be stronger than I realized. In the Southwest of the United States, there were stories about a humpbacked flute player with a long penis called Kokopelli, who seduced young girls (Hawley 1937; Parsons 1938; Titiev 1939). (Bebukowe, incidentally, is also a flute player.) A curious similarity between Kokopelli and Bebukowe is that Kokopelli is considered by Elsie Clews Parsons (1938) to have been an insect, perhaps a locust, while Julia Badger described Bebukowe as looking like a grasshopper around the nose and referred to him as "the grasshopper man."

Ernest Jones (1948:93) has pointed out that the conception of the male organ as a "little man" is extremely widespread. He refers to stories of dwarfs, gnomes, and goblins—deformed, ugly, and wicked men, yet sometimes friendly and able to perform magical feats and "winning their way in spite of their obvious disadvantages." The character of Punch, with his long hooked nose, projecting hump, and pointed cap, is cited as an example of such a phallic figure.

Notice the similarity between Punch and Bebukowe, not only in the hump but in the prominent nose, which Freudian literature has often designated as a phallic symbol. It is the only other protrusion,

beside the penis, in the midline of the body. The snot-dripping quality of Bebukowe's nose seems to emphasize its phallic character. At
any rate, the parallels between Punch, Bebukowe, and Kokopelli are
rather remarkable and strengthen Jones's case. One might also point
to the *tokoloshe* figures discussed by Lee in his paper on Zulu dreams,
the priapic hairy creatures who come from rivers to attack women
sexually. Laubscher (1937:8) has pictured *tokoloshe* as follows: "He is
described as a dwarflike little man with short limbs and a powerful
thick-set body. He wears a sheepskin wrapped round his shoulders.
One of his outstanding physical characteristics is his huge penis."

Julia Badger's two fantasies, then, both appear to have an erotic
character. However, this does not seem to be their only significance.
As has been noted, Julia was very sickly, and her marital relationship
with Tom was not a happy one. Julia had her moments of deep
depression. Perhaps her "vision," therefore, represented a compensatory wish-fulfillment, which assumed the function of reviving the
thwarted life-affirming qualities in Julia's psyche, enabling her to face
life once more—just as Bebukowe rescued Julia from death in childhood and restored her to her parents.

The Four Directions serve somewhat the same function and give
"direction" to her life. These grandfather figures repeat the moral
instructions which Julia's own grandfather used to give her in childhood. They explain why she has gone wrong in the past, they encourage Julia to be more faithful about ritual observances in the future,
and they promise long life and health thereafter. Once again, Julia
played a purely passive role in relation to them and promised to obey,
although she did not always live up to such obligations afterwards.

In her dependent and introversive tendencies Julia Badger exhibited to a heightened degree some general Chippewa characteristics.
Remember that this was a society in which, not so long ago, great
emphasis was placed on dreams. At an early age children were regularly sent out to fast for a dream or vision of a guardian spirit. A
fasting child was supposed to be addressed by such a spirit with the
words, "My grandchild, I come to pity (cherish) you." It would not be
surprising if a young child, denied food and sent out into the woods,
might actually dream of such a nurturing figure. The stereotyped
expected dream would be compatible with the needs of a child who
has met with parental rejection and hunger.

The emphasis on the inner world of dreams in Chippewa culture is
in keeping with the Rorschach characteristics to be discussed in the
following chapter—the greater stress on human movement responses (of a passive quality) than on color, which is generally
avoided.

To be sure, Julia cannot be considered to be a "typical" Chippewa
woman. Dr. Bruno Klopfer was properly cautious in his Rorschach
evaluation of Julia when he observed, "*In our culture* she would be

called schizoid." But it should be noted that Julia was generally regarded as "queer" in her own community as well.

MOROCCAN FANTASY MATERIAL

In the life history of Tuhami, Vincent Crapanzano (1980:5) traces recurrent themes in a document that seems to be largely made up of fantasy. Tuhami was an illiterate, unmarried black tilemaker in his middle 40s. He believed himself to be married to 'A'isha Qandisha, a demanding female spirit. Apparently Tuhami was not unique in harboring such fantasies, which seem to have been culturally patterned. "Other Moroccan men were said to be 'A'isha's husbands; they were all peculiar in their way—loners, sexual inadequates, physical misfits, eccentrics, or men who for one social reason or another were unable to marry." Many of Tuhami's stories have the theme of enslavement by, or seduction by, women, either real women or ghouls such as 'A'isha Qandisha. Such tales are also common in Moroccan folklore, —"the inverse of the articulated standards of male-female relations, of sex and marriage" (p. 102).

In an article on Moroccan dreams, Crapanzano describes what he calls "visitational dreams," in which saints and *jnun* (plural of *jinn*) appear. Crapanzano (1975:145–46) comments as follows: "Elements, or figures believed to be external to the individual, such as demons, angels, and saints, can serve to symbolize certain 'psychological dispositions,' and the relationship that obtains between these elements may be symbolic of certain 'psychic structures' or 'psychological processes'." The saints or *jnun* that appear in Moroccan dreams may resolve conflicts or indicate what path the dreamer should take.

SUGGESTIONS FOR FURTHER READING

Articles on dreams by George Devereux, Weston La Barre, Dorothy Eggan, and A. Irving Hallowell may be found in G. E. von Grunebaum and Roger Callois, eds., *The Dream and Human Societies* (Berkeley: University of California Press, 1966). See also Carl W. O'Nell, *Dreams, Culture, and the Individual* (San Francisco: Chandler & Sharp, 1976); Calvin S. Hall, *The Meaning of Dreams* (New York: Dell, 1959); and Calvin S. Hall and Vernon J. Nordby, *The Individual and his Dreams* (New York: Signet Books, 1972).

Dorothy Eggan has contributed to the study of dreams in three interesting articles: "The Significance of Dreams for Anthropological Research," *American Anthropologist*, 51 (1949), pp. 177–98; "The Manifest Content of Dreams: A Challenge to Social Research," *American Anthropologist*, 54 (1952), pp. 469–85; and "The Personal Use of Myth in Dreams," *Journal of American Folklore* 68 (1955), pp. 67–75.

A special issue of *Ethos*, 9, No. 4 (1981) is devoted to dreams.

15

Projective Tests

The Rorschach (inkblot) and the Thematic Apperception Test (TAT), among others, are known as projective tests. The term *projection* has been given some different meanings. Freud first defined projection as a defensive process whereby the ego ascribes its own drives and feelings to other persons or objects and is thus able to remain consciously unaware of them.

In *Totem and Taboo*, however, Freud suggested another meaning for this term:

> But projection was not created for the purpose of defence; it also occurs when there is no conflict. The projection outwards of internal perceptions is a primitive mechanism, to which, for instance, our sense perceptions are subject, and which therefore normally plays a very large part in determining the form taken by our external world. Under conditions whose nature has not yet been sufficiently established, internal perceptions of emotional and thought processes can be projected outwards in the same way as sense perceptions; they are thus employed for building up the external world, though they should by rights remain part of the *internal* world (Freud 1913:64).

Leopold Bellak (1959:10), who distinguishes between various types of apperceptive distortion, believes that a person's past perceptions of his father influences his perception of father figures in the Thematic Apperception Test, and that "this constitutes a valid and reliable sample of his usual perceptions of father figures." Bellak goes on to argue that all perception is influenced by past perception and that every person distorts apperceptively to some extent. This is also true of what one remembers of the past (Bartlett 1932).

Such assumptions underlie the use of the Rorschach Test, Thematic Apperception Test, drawing analysis, and other projective techniques.[1]

---

[1] My survey of methods is not intended to be exhaustive. A number of projective tests which have been used cross-culturally are not discussed here, for instance, word association tests, the Picture-Frustration Test, the Szondi Test, the Bender Gestalt Test, the Lowenfeld Mosaic Test, and others. The Rorschach and Thematic Apperception Test seem to be the two most widely and successfully employed in cross-cultural studies; hence, they receive the fullest treatment here.

THE RORSCHACH TEST

The Rorschach Test was devised by Hermann Rorschach, a Swiss psychiatrist who died at the age of 37 in 1922, a few months after the publication of his book, *Psychodiagnostik*, in which the test was first described and discussed. The 10 Rorschach cards were originally published as part of this work. They represent a series of bilaterally symmetrical inkblots, half achromatic and half with some color. Rorschach experimented with thousands of different inkblots before finally choosing the 10 cards which are still used today.

The same 10 cards are shown, always in the same order, to every person who takes the test. The subject must tell what he sees in the blots, and the tester records his responses, also noting how long it takes him to respond. After the subject has completed all 10 cards, the tester usually goes through his responses with him, to make sure that he knows which parts of the blots have been used by the subject and, as far as possible, how the responses have been perceived, that is, whether a bat reported by the subject was seen to be flying or not, or whether the dark color of the blot contributed to the conception of the bat.

What the Rorschach analyst does is to examine the subject's responses for clues to his personality structure. His conclusions are based not so much on the content of the responses, but more on the manner of perception, accuracy of form discrimination, the nature of the determinants of responses given (such as movement, color, and texture); whether responses are given to the blot as a whole, to large details or small details, and so forth.

Human Movement and Color Responses

In this chapter frequent references will be made to human movement and to color responses. Since these are perhaps the most important "determinants" in the Rorschach Test, some preliminary discussion of them seems necessary.

Let us first consider movement responses. These are scored differently by different authorities. Rorschach scored as *M*, responses in which human movement was perceived; he excluded animal movement. His method of scoring has been followed by Samuel J. Beck (1952), but Klopfer and Kelley (1942) have added two new categories: *FM* (animal movement) and *m* (inanimate movement). I shall follow the Klopfer and Kelley scoring system in this book, since that is the one I learned and used myself.

Human movement responses (*M*) generally tend to be interpreted as indications of inner control, ego strength, intellectual capacity, imagination, introversiveness, and capacity for empathy. *M* responses are rarely found in young children, subjects with organic brain damage, or with rigid constriction. The presence of such responses suggests some capacity for the enjoyment of inner life and may be an index of how much at home a person is with herself or himself (Klopfer and Kelley 1942:254–64).

The way in which a subject handles color in the Rorschach Test is supposed to tell something about his or her characteristic response to outside emotional stimuli. Compulsion neurotics and people who are very depressed are said to give few or no color responses, while persons characterized by affective lability give many. According to Rorschach, the more stable the emotions, the better the form visualization. Thus, people who lack control over their emotions may give the "explosive" or formless color responses designated as C. If some form is vaguely associated with color response, but not very clearly, the response is designated as CF. When there is better control, expressed by a conjunction of definite form and color, the response is labeled FC.

Unfortunately, we do not know why color means what it is supposed to mean in the Rorschach Test, or why it is related to emotionality. Beck (1952:775) has remarked that "we know next to nothing about color as a psychologic stimulus." An association between color and emotion is implied by many phrases in our language, such as "seeing red," "rose-colored glasses," "feeling blue," and so forth, but why such associations have been made is not very clear.

Ernest G. Schachtel (1943) has made an attempt to explain this linkage. Color and emotional experiences have, he tells us, two things in common: "the *passivity* of the subject and the *immediacy* of the relation object-subject." One is visually assailed by a bright red color, so to speak, just as one is "seized" by a strong emotion. The subject in both cases plays a passive role. Views similar to Schachtel's appear in David C. McClelland's work, *The Achieving Society* (1961:309), in which the hypothesis is put forth that the person with a high need for achievement "might prefer colors like blue and green which he can 'act on,' as background, so to speak, as contrasted with reds and yellows that act on him."

The inner-directed "achiever" would presumably tend to avoid bright color, in contrast to the more other-directed extrovert, who, as Schachtel puts it, takes on the color of his environment.

Despite such insights, the relationship between emotion and color still seems rather mysterious. However, this relationship has some experimental support, and there is further evidence of a linkage between color and emotionality in the field of drawing analysis also.[2]

A full discussion of the Rorschach should examine the other determinants in the test, but the purpose here has been only to set forth some of the key concepts used in Rorschach interpretation. There is

---

[2] See Ruesch and Finesinger (1941), Alschuler and Hattwick (1947:15–50), and the discussion of Chippewa children's drawings in Chapter 16.

much more to Rorschach analysis than the interpretation of movement and color responses, but these are of special importance and, hence, they have been briefly dealt with here.

FIGURE 3
Rorschach Card I,
Reproduced at One Sixth
of the Original Size

Courtesy of Hans Huber
Publishers, Switzerland

To give some illustrations, let us consider some responses to the first card of the Rorschach Test given by three persons. Each was asked to tell what the blot might represent, what he could see in it. This is an achromatic card. All three subjects (two Chippewa Indians and one white man) looked at the same card, and yet they saw quite different things in it.

John Thunderbird (a pseudonym), a 54-year-old Chippewa Indian to whom I gave the test,[3] gave a single response. "Some kind of hawk, some kind of large bird. Indians years back would draw pictures of them. You see them on those poles there." The bird is sitting on a tree. This response made use of the blot as a whole. John Thunderbird pointed out the bird's eye, beak, feet, tail, and wings. The central portion was seen as the tree. "Must be a limb here, sticking out, that he's sitting on. An old tree top. The tree broke off up here. Probably the wind blew it off in a storm. It's an old stump."

To see this blot, or part of it, as a bird is quite a common response. John Thunderbird also projected into the blot the idea of an old stump, part of which has been broken off, blown away in a storm.

Another Chippewa subject, Julia Badger (aged 34), whose fantasies were discussed in Chapter 14, did not make use of the blot as a whole. Indeed, a characteristic feature of her Rorschach record was the extremely small percentage of Whole responses and the preference for small details. Mrs. Badger's first response was "Two snakes," which she later added were just heads sticking out, with their mouths open. (These are two small projections near the center

---

[3] John Thunderbird's autobiography, as told to me, is in the Appendix of my *Acculturation and Personality among the Wisconsin Chippewa* (1950:89–112).

of the top part of the blot.) It is interesting that snakes make an appearance here, as in her fantasies discussed earlier. Their mouths are open, suggesting Fromm's receptive orientation or oral character.

Julia Badger next saw a big hill on the left side of the blot with a valley and two large white rocks (the white space areas). This was an airplane view. In parts of the interior of the right-hand side of the blot, Mrs. Badger saw a man's face.

Our third subject is Amos Hale (a pseudonym), a 45-year-old white male bachelor schoolteacher. He gave 24 responses to Card I. The first four responses were Whole responses : "(1) *Os inominatum.* The ass. (2) Nose bone of nose. (3) Halloween false face. (4) A bat."

He next gave some responses to the central area of the blot: "(5) A toad. (6) A woman's thing. What do you call it?" (V.B.: "The vagina?") "Yes, that's what I mean." The line running down the center of the blot was next seen as (7) a road, a highway; and the small light area in the center was seen as (8) a diamond.

Two Whole responses followed: (9) "Clouds. (10) Entrance to caves." Then a small detail: (11) "A face." Then five Whole responses: (12) "Scattering of spots—ink. (13) Shell. (14) Butterfly. (15) Kindergarten cut paper. (16) Map, physiological map." Then a very small detail: (17) "Blemish on a face."

The last seven responses, most of which made use of irregular details, were: (18) "Broken glass. (19) Bottom of a bowl. (20) A cross. (21) Piles—coming out of the ass. (22) A coastline. (23) A child's paintbox. The whole thing. Just looks messy the way a child's paintbox looks when it's opened. (24) A long bug."

Notable in this series of responses to Card I is the depressing, negative content. Amos Hale sees things that are scattered, broken, or messy. (In the second card he saw "smashed umbrellas.") He sees, in sequence, a bat, a toad, and a "woman's thing" (which, in the context, does not seem to be positively regarded). Later, he sees a blemish on a face and a long bug. The anal responses (1, 21) suggest a hoarding orientation or anal personality. The subject gave similar anal responses to other cards, which were also characterized by depressing content.

The responses given by our three subjects show how much variation there is in the way different people perceive the same inkblot. They differed in the number of responses given (1 for John Thunderbird, 3 for Julia Badger, and 24 for Amos Hale). They differed in their use of the whole or part of the card. (A Whole response for John Thunderbird; none for Julia Badger, who used small details; while both Wholes and small detail responses were given by Amos Hale.) They also differed in the content of what they saw. It may be noted that in their responses to Card I none of our three subjects gave a human movement response.

The Cross-Cultural Application of the Rorschach Test

The main issue that concerns us with regard to the Rorschach Test is its cross-cultural application. Why has the Rorschach Test been used so often by anthropologists? One reason is that the Rorschach does not require literacy as do some other personality tests. Moreover, it is not culture-bound, for the blots do not represent anything in particular. Another advantage of the Rorschach Test is that it can be given to people of different age levels.

There are, however, some difficulties facing the use of the Rorschach in a non-Western culture. One is the language problem; another is the question of rapport between tester and subject.

If an ethnologist can become fluent in the language of the society he is studying, the Rorschach Test can be recorded in the native tongue, as was done by Jules Henry (1941) in the Pilagá records he obtained. Ethnologists are not always such good linguists, however. Reliance on partial knowledge of a language is less satisfactory than use of a good interpreter. Hallowell (1941) had recourse to an interpreter for some of his Berens River subjects and found no particular differences between the other protocols and those in which the interpreter was used. All the same, the possibility of distortion of a subject's responses through translation would seem to be present when an interpreter is used. Horace Miner found an ingenious solution to this problem, however. In his study of Algerians, Miner wire recorded the Rorschach inquiry, so that the informants' responses in Arabic and the French translations could later be played back for another interpreter. Differences in translation could then be noted and followed up.

Actually, Miner found few such differences. This method, however, would provide a check (Miner and De Vos 1960:13).

In giving the Rorschach Test in Lebanon, Herbert H. Williams and Judith R. Williams (1965) found some positive advantages in working with an interpreter. It gave them more time to record motor and verbal behavior, and their subjects often made revealing side remarks to the interpreter which might not have been made to them.

In order to get satisfactorily rich material from a Rorschach subject, the individual being tested should feel relaxed and at ease. In the nature of things, this desideratum is often hard to arrange in ethnological fieldwork. The anthropologist is a stranger in the community he is studying; his Rorschach blots are queer things, and his explanation of why he wants responses to them may not make much sense to the informant. Honigmann (1949:240) found that administration of the Rorschach Test was irksome for his Kaska subjects. "The situation often grew so painful that it was necessary to beg the subjects to remain for a few more minutes." Some of Spindler's (1955:61)

Menomini subjects were very reluctant to take the test, suspecting him, in some cases, of being a Communist, a federal investigator, or an agent of the superintendent. Or else they feared that the Rorschach Test might be some new technique for working sorcery. Kaplan's Zuñi informants showed much fear of the test. They were afraid that Kaplan (1954:5) was prying into their religion or testing them for possible war service: "the writer saw menace and hostility in every Zuñi who looked his way."

These are hardly ideal conditions for Rorschach administration. Of course, many excellent Rorschach protocols have been collected by anthropologists, but the situational factors affecting the test may result in an impoverishment of many Rorschach records. Compared with Western protocols, those from other cultures often seem rather barren. The total number of responses may be low, and there may be few movement or color responses. Two examples of this state of affairs may be given, in both of which the authors discuss the situational context and its possible effect on the subjects' responses. The first is a study of Northwest Coast Alaskan Eskimos by Caroline E. Preston (1964). Preston's Eskimo Rorschachs had relatively few responses, with few movement, color, or texture responses. The Eskimo TATs were characterized by prevailingly "unhappy" situations or feelings. Preston remarks that more than two thirds of her Eskimo subjects seemed anxious, angry, or inhibited in taking the tests, which she suggests as one explanation for the impoverishment of the records. The other example is the Lebanese study by the Williamses (1965) which was mentioned earlier. The number of Lebanese villagers' responses was very low, with a group mean of 12.4, and the records were very unproductive, lacking in movement, color, and texture responses, as in the case of the Alaskan Eskimos. The Williamses point out that tests of any kind are unknown to the villagers; being shown the inkblots and asked to give responses was a frightening experience for them. Erich Fromm and Michael Maccoby (1970:275) consider this to be a general peasant reaction to such testing, while Frank Riessman and S. M. Miller (1958) hold it to be typical of lower-class American subjects. The test, as Ernest G. Schachtel has indicated, is for many people something strange and fantastic. Their response to the test may be characteristic of their response to unfamiliar aspects of life in general. There are no rules for prescribing how one must respond in such a novel situation. In that sense, the impoverished Rorschach record of a frightened or constricted subject may express an important aspect of his personality. But one should try to minimize the dysphoric aspects of the test situation.[4]

Ideally, a Rorschach session should involve the isolation of the subject with the tester. Again, these conditions are often hard to

---

[4] On the effects of the Rorschach testing situation, see Klatskin (1952) and Schachtel (1966).

arrange in the field. Jules Henry (1941:231) has observed that in most primitive cultures people are never alone but are apt to be surrounded by relatives. Privacy may be suspect. Moreover, curiosity about the ethnologist's work will attract crowds.

In the case of the Lebanese villagers, the Williamses did succeed in getting each subject to take the test alone, but this only added to the frightening and unfamiliar nature of the experience. To be sure, matters are not always so difficult, and often the subject may be very relaxed. But ideal test conditions are not to be expected in the field.

The crucial question is sometimes raised of whether a test developed in our own culture, with Western-based norms, can be meaningfully applied in another culture. In a study by A. I. Rabin and Josefina Limuaco (1967), the point was made that the connotative meanings of the Rorschach blots may differ from culture to culture. More specifically, the authors point to differences in this respect in the Rorschach responses of American and Filipino college students. This led them to question the justifiability of the application of the test cross-culturally.

Some of the difficulties involved here can be illustrated in a Rorschach study of Samoan young men made by P. H. Cook (1942). Cook gave the test to a group of 50 high school "boys" (aged 16–27), 30 of whom came from families of chiefs. These students were all training to become pastors. They are thus not representative of the population as a whole.

One feature of these Samoan Rorschach records is a high percentage of white space (S) responses, which make use of white space areas within the blots. These are rather rare in Western records; when they occur they are usually interpreted as signs of oppositional tendencies. But almost three fourths of Cook's subjects gave S responses. Should this be interpreted in the traditional way? Perhaps not, for Cook mentions that 31 of the 50 young men reported white (regarded as symbolic of purity) as their favorite color.

The Samoans gave few texture responses. The interpretation of texture responses varies with the general configuration of the response, but they are usually seen to indicate sensitivity, sensuality, or a desire for contact. Such responses are often associated with animal skins or rugs, particularly seen in cards IV and VI. But furs and rugs are not generally known in Samoa; this response was not given once in Cook's sample. How, then, are we to interpret the low percentage of texture responses?

Cook's subjects gave many pure color (C) responses, in which no form was involved. As indicated in a preceding section, this would usually be held to express emotional impulsiveness. Cook tells us that the Samoans have not developed abstract names for colors. Their color words all have an object reference. For example, their word for red (*mumu*) means literally "like fire, flame." The idea of blood is also associated with this. The Samoan word for blue or green may mean either sky-colored or deep-sea-colored. Their color vocabulary is thus a limited one. Cook says that there is practically no artwork in this area except for crude designs in black and brown pigments stenciled on bark cloth. The culture offers little to foster any sensitivity to color nuances. Can Samoan color responses then be interpreted in the same way as Western European or American color responses?

Some Rorschach responses can only be made in cultures which have been exposed to Western influence. This applies at least to *k* responses, in which a blot, or part of it, is seen as an X-ray, although there could be an equivalent in which objects are seen through water. At any rate, considerations such as these, and the questions raised by Cook's Samoan protocols, have led some anthropologists and psychologists to deny the applicability of Western-based Rorschach norms to protocols from other cultures. Since interpretation becomes so difficult under these circumstances, the cross-cultural use of the Rorschach Test has been called into question.

The main argument on the positive side, however, is that use of the Rorschach Test has often proven to be very revealing and to yield information in close agreement with that drawn from other sources. Doubts about the cross-cultural applicability of the Rorschach Test assailed Emil Oberholzer, when he was asked to interpret the Alorese protocols.

> Not only was I confronted for the first time with the tests of individuals other than Europeans and Americans, but I did not know the norms of these people and had no way of working them out. I did not know the average of the numerical values for the various experimental factors. . . . Among the Alorese, I do not know, for example, what is an original and what is a popular answer; I do not know the border line between a normal and a small detail, since I do not know with certainty what constitutes with them normal and small details (Du Bois 1944:588).

As it happened, Oberholzer went on to interpret the Alorese protocols, despite his misgivings, and the results were most impressive. In Chapter 6 we noted the marked agreement between his conclusions, based on the Rorschach data, with other analyses drawn from the interpretation of life histories, children's drawings, and so forth. The Rorschach Test often seems to work; at least in a number of studies it has presented similar corroborative evidence. This is the best answer that can be given to objections about the cross-cultural use of the Rorschach Test. The Truk study can be cited, along with that of Alor, in this regard.

Another example of "blind" analysis presenting similar agreement with the ethnologist's observations is the study of Algerians made by Miner and De Vos. Miner's Algerian Rorschachs were submitted to Professor Max Hutt for blind analysis.

An attempt was made to test the validity of Hutt's psychological ratings by comparing them with evaluations based on personal acquaintance with the individuals concerned. Taking the seven Arabs best known to the field worker and the five psychological traits [*Fn:* Maturity, cathexis, anality, anxiety, and overt hostility] which he felt he could evaluate, fifteen ratings were made. They represented, therefore, the judgments about which he was the most sure. Of the fifteen ratings, thirteen were in conformity with those of Hutt, which is comfortably within the limits of statistical significance (Miner and De Vos 1960:108).

Still another procedure for validating Rorschach data has been used in the Rakau Maori study. On the basis of observation, James E. Ritchie (1956) drew up a series of generalizations about Maori personality development. From this picture he next drew up a series of predictions as to what the Rorschach records of the Maori would be like. A similar set of predictions was made by a psychologist who was familiar with Ritchie's generalizations about Maori personality development. The Rorschach Test, given to 41 male and 37 female Maori subjects, was then interpreted independently by Ritchie and by another analyst. The final step was to see how much agreement appeared between the two predictions and the two analyses. These proved to be very closely correlated.

The success of these various experiments lends considerable support to the cross-cultural applicability of the Rorschach Test. However, not everyone has been impressed by the successes of blind analysis. Ivan N. Mensh and Jules Henry suggested that the similarity of the Rorschach Test results with the anthropologist's impressions may be due to "contamination."

That is to say that the anthropologist biased the test results in favor of his own findings. This danger is obvious when the anthropologist does his own interpretation of the tests, but it is equally present when someone else interprets the results for the anthropologist. This is because the anthropologist consulted with his interpreting psychologist, and there are very few cases in which the anthropologist did not tell the psychologist much about the culture before, during, and after the process of interpretation of the test results (Mensh and Henry 1953:469).

This objection may apply to some culture-and-personality studies, but in many it would not hold. This circumstance may, in part, be due to publication of the Mensh and Henry criticisms and a subsequent concern to avoid contamination in more recent studies. Special pains were taken to rule out contamination in Gladwin and Sarason's work on Truk. Other cases where leakage from anthropologist to the psychologist seems improbable would include the Miner and De Vos Algerian study, a study by Kluckhohn and Rosenzweig (1949) and one by Clifton and Levine (1961).

If one wishes to be skeptical, another question could be raised concerning the correspondence of Rorschach results with other data. Might not the correspondences be largely due to chance? In cases where the anthropologist and the Rorschach interpreter found themselves in agreement, they would be eager to publish the results of their study, but less so in cases where there was little similarity in their findings. In the latter case they might feel that the experiment had not been a success, and they might therefore fail to press for publication. If this is so, studies in which correspondences were found between Rorschach and other data would tend to be published and to become better known than those where little agreement had appeared.

While this is a logical possibility, I don't think that skepticism should carry us so far. There are, after all, orderly processes governing the interpretation of Rorschach records. In some of the fuller publications the original records are given, and it is possible to check the data and to see how the analyst arrived at the results. In their analyses of the records from Alor and Truk, Oberholzer and Sarason make quite clear to the reader how they developed their interpretations from the test materials.

Criticisms of the Rorschach Test

Interest in projective tests, including the Rorschach, began to slacken in the 1950s. Joseph Zubin (1954) raised a series of criticisms of the Rorschach Test, claiming that it failed to provide an objective scoring system, lacked reliability, failed to provide sufficient evidence for clinical validity, and had little predictive power.

In the following year, 1955, there was a symposium on projective testing in anthropology, in which Jules Henry, one of the first anthropologists to apply the test in a non-Western culture, stated that he would not use the Rorschach if he were going into the field again.

In 1968, Walter Mischel, a psychologist from Stanford University, wrote:

> Clinicians have often suggested that the combination and integration of clinical techniques, rather than the use of single instruments in isolation, is important for effective assessment. A recent study (Golden 1964) investigated the incremental effects of combining the Rorschach, TAT, and MMPI [Minnesota Multiphasic Personality Inventory] tests as opposed to using them singly. Neither the reliability nor the validity of clinical inferences increased as a function of the number of tests, nor were there any differences among tests or pairs of tests. Again the clinicians were experienced, having interpreted a median number of 200 MMPIs, 250 Rorschachs, and 200 TATs (Mischel 1968:120).

Mischel cites a similar study by Soskin (1959), in which none of the test information improved predictions beyond what might be obtained just from the biographical data.

But if projective tests are rejected for use in cross-cultural studies, some other devices for gauging personality will have to be found, unless we must depend on behavioral observation and interviewing alone. The latter alternative would mean that the anthropologist would have no cross-checking devices; his or her description of the people being studied would be open to the criticism of subjectivity. In giving Rorschachs to Alorese subjects and submitting the protocols to a blind analysis, Cora Du Bois was able to diminish that difficulty.

An argument on behalf of use of the Rorschach Test in culture-and-personality studies is that different societies have different Rorschach patterns. The Pilagá Indian children tested by the Henrys give neither color nor movement responses (either animal or human). As we shall see, the Chippewa give movement responses but very little color. The Alorese give color, but little human movement. The Samoans, Algerians, and the Tuscarora give many Whole responses, while Zuñi children give very few, but emphasize small details. These group variations must mean something, although it is not always evident just what they do mean. But they would seem to strengthen the hypothesis that different societies are characterized by different modal personality types.

If the varied cultures of the world did not selectively influence perception and response to the Rorschach blots, we would expect that in different parts of the world people would all give pretty much the same kinds of Rorschach responses; but they do not. A. Irving Hallowell made an early study of the distribution of so-called popular responses—responses very commonly given to the blots in our culture. In examining Rorschach protocols from six American Indian cultures, Hallowell (1945) found that three categories of popular responses could be distinguished: one which did seem to be universal in the six American Indian cultures, a second group of populars which were found in some but not all of the six cultures, and a third group of "unique" populars found only within a single culture.

Bert Kaplan and Richard Lawless (1965) have examined the Rorschach records of adults from 11 cultures drawn from four main geographical world areas: American Indian, West Indies, Western Pacific, and South Asia (India, Pakistan). Kaplan and Lawless did find that there were differences in the characteristic responses of these groups, sometimes of quite a puzzling nature. "For example, both men and women in the Palau group give the response Bat to Card I, 40% of the time, but no Ifaluk or New Ireland individuals do at all; or on Card II, almost 50% of Menomini men give the response Bear to the whole card, a response which is found with substantial frequency in only one other group, the Hindus" (p. 310). This shows that there are problems in understanding the multifarious ways in which peoples of different cultures respond to a series of 10 inkblots. Let us now consider in more detail the Rorschach characteristics of some particular groups.

THE ANALYSIS OF GROUPS

Although studies of a single Rorschach Test (Mead 1949c) or of two subjects (Kluckhohn and Rosenzweig 1949; Boyer, Boyer, and De Vos 1982), have been made, Rorschach studies in the field of culture-and-personality more often involve the analysis of a fairly large sample of protocols drawn from a particular society. Sometimes comparisons are made between the Rorschach characteristics of two or more societies. In order to arrive at group generalizations and to make cross-cultural comparisons, some workers in this field have subjected their data to statistical treatment. What, for example, is the percentage of color responses in the group of subjects from Society X and how does this compare with the C percent in Society Y? Similar comparisons may be made with regard to other Rorschach categories.

Hallowell's Three Chippewa Groups

Before presenting Hallowell's Rorschach findings, it will be useful to have a brief ethnographic account of the Chippewa or Ojibwa, about whom data will also be presented later in connection with the Thematic Apperception Test, drawing analysis, and folklore motifs.

The Chippewa, an Algonkian-speaking Woodland people who lived in the region of the Great Lakes, were primarily dependent on hunting, fishing, and gathering as a basis of subsistence, although they raised small crops of corn and squash in summer, harvested wild rice in the fall, and tapped maple trees for sugar in the spring. Chippewa groups were first encountered by Europeans near Sault Ste. Marie (hence the name Saulteaux or Saulteurs), but largely through the influence of the fur trade and the pressure of tribes like the Iroquois, these Indians have since moved westward, so that Chippewa are now to be found in Michigan, Wisconsin, Minnesota, North Dakota, Montana, and the Canadian provinces of Ontario, Manitoba, and Saskatchewan.

They are one of the largest American Indian groups in population. The Chippewa cannot, however, be said to constitute a tribe, or even a collection of tribes. Their social order has been described as "atomistic." An atomistic society is one in which it is not difficult for the component units to break away and exist apart from the larger society of which they are a part; political authority is weak, and there are not many mechanisms for reinforcing larger-group social solidarity.

The Chippewa, especially before 1870, lived in small scattered bands. The time of greatest social interaction was in summer, when small villages, consisting of about a dozen families, were able to take advantage of relatively favorable food supplies—fish and agricultural crops, in addition to game. These village units, however, broke up in the fall, with families moving to shallow lakes where wild rice was harvested. After that, separate family groups occupied different hunting areas, to take maximum advantage of the sparse winter food resources. This dispersal appears to have been a deliberate policy, "a precaution which seems necessary to their very existence," as Peter Grant wrote in 1804 (Grant 1890:326–27).

In the spring, families moved to maple groves to tap trees and make sugar. Then the village life of summer was resumed. People generally returned to the same village, but there was much fluctuation. Landes (1937:3) says that such a village was not stable in numbers or location over any considerable period of time: "Almost any circumstance may cause people to drift to a given village or to leave it." Landes cites various reasons for such shifts of residence—visits to in-laws, hostilities, the abandonment of a site for sanitary or supernatural reasons, and so on.

In the Chippewa social order, one notes a marked contrast with the more integrated social organization of Plains tribes, such as the Cheyenne. In the latter a strong sense of social solidarity was manifest in the orderly camp circle, the communal buffalo hunt, the highly developed political organization with its council of chiefs and the soldier societies which served as police force. The Chippewa lacked such institutions; they had no organized council of chiefs, no policing system, no regularly constituted military societies, and no symbols of group unity like the "Medicine Arrows" or Sacred Hat" of the Cheyenne. There was no communal hunting comparable to that of the Cheyenne, and there was little economic cooperation outside the family unit. Even the major religious ceremonies were not conducted for the benefit of the group as a whole, as they generally were among the Cheyenne.[5]

The Midewiwin, the Chippewa Medicine Dance, was limited to members and required initiation payments. Perhaps the outstanding feature of their religion was the individual guardian spirit quest, which began at the age of four or five in this society. The powers of medicine men were supposedly derived from contact with guardian spirits who appeared in a dream or vision. There were no societies of medicine men.

The Chippewa had patrilineal clans, but almost their sole function was the regulation of marriage. They had little or no religious or political significance, as did the clans of some Central Algonkian tribes. This was particularly true of the more northerly Chippewa; for the southern groups there are indications of a formerly more devel-

---

[5] For some controversy on these points, see Hickerson (1960; 1962; 1967) and Barnouw (1961; 1967; 1977; 1978).

oped clan system. Dunning (1959:82) believes that the hunting economy prohibited the development of larger groupings and the social elaboration of the clan system in the north.

The Chippewa practiced bilateral cross-cousin marriage, which is reflected in their kinship terminology. The levirate and sororate were observed but often flouted (Landes 1938b:81).

The foregoing description has been phrased in the past tense, for much of it no longer applies to many groups, such as the Wisconsin Chippewa. Landes, who worked in 1932, 1933, and 1935 among Ontario Ojibwa, described a contemporary culture which retained much of the old way of life. The same is true of the Saulteaux studied by Hallowell in the 1930s. Even the Wisconsin Chippewa, however, are not far removed in time from the ethnographic picture just presented. My older Chippewa informants in 1944 and 1946 remembered and described this way of life. Some of them had lived in wigwams, traveled in birchbark canoes, and had worn breechclouts, leggings, and other traditional Indian clothing. They had fasted for guardian spirits in childhood, and they generally still believed in the thunderbirds, in Wenebojo, the culture-hero trickster, in the dangers of sorcery, in the efficacy of the Midewiwin and in the sucking doctor's cure.

Acculturation among these Indians can be adjudged to be either very old or very recent, depending on the aspects of culture selected for emphasis. Dunning writes that, from the 17th century on, it would not be true to consider the Chippewa an aboriginal population.

> Perhaps because of their strategic location at the Sault rapids on the main western trade route and their early contact with Europeans they became thoroughly identified with the development of European interests. Suffice it to say that they alone of the western lakes peoples cooperated with the explorers and fur traders. The Sioux, Cree, and Assineboine withdrew under the pressure of increasing economic development (Dunning 1959:4).

However, the nature of the Chippewas' contact with the fur traders was such as to perpetuate an aboriginal way of life based on hunting. New aspects of material culture were introduced—guns, traps, cloth, flour, tea, liquor, and so forth—but many groups do not seem to have had significant concomitant changes in other spheres, such as religion and kinship organization, until quite recent times. The precontact social order seems to have been atomistic, as defined above; the fur trade perpetuated and probably further emphasized this atomistic tendency. Many Chippewa bands lived in remote areas, having little contact with the outer world. As Hallowell (1955:119) has written, "not only was their subsistence economy retained, but the seasonal movements, institutions, attitudes, and beliefs that were closely integrated with it."

In his Rorschach study of these Indians, Hallowell made use of mean frequencies in a comparison of three Chippewa groups representing different levels of acculturation. Two are Berens River groups in Canada, the more conservative and unacculturated being termed Inland (with 44 Rorschach subjects) and the more acculturated group named Lakeside (58 Rorschach subjects). The third Chippewa population, at Lac du Flambeau, Wisconsin (represented by 115 Rorschach subjects), has experienced a still greater degree of acculturation. Hallowell (1955:350) presents a table giving the means of responses for various Rorschach determinants, locations, types of content, and certain percentage scores for each of the three groups.

This approach provides a composite group profile, comparable to the superimposition of a number of photographs of faces, one on top of the other, leaving a final picture which represents no one individual face but which does show something of the general features of the group in question. This group portrait can then be compared with those of other groups. Perhaps the comparison would be more apt if the procedure were described as one of finding the mean nose breadth, the mean distance between the eyes, and so on, of the members of the group, as a way of building up the composite picture.

Hallowell finds both similarities and differences in his three Chippewa groups. In all three there is a very low percentage of color responses and a low percentage of answers to the last three cards (which are all chromatic). In each of Hallowell's three groups, the mean for the sum of the color responses is very low: 0.5 for Inland, 1.7 for Lakeside, and 1 for Flambeau. By contrast, a sample American group (157 Rorschach subjects) cited by Hallowell has a mean of 3.11 (Hallowell 1956:527).

The low incidence of color responses would suggest that the Chippewa individual expects very little from others and is not apt to develop close emotional ties with them. The same rarity of color responses may be noted in Rorschachs collected by other investigators in the Chippewa area—Robert Ritzenthaler, Ernestine Friedl, Blanche Watrous, myself, and others. It seems to be a characteristic feature of Chippewa protocols.

The latter are also rather high in M. The mean for Hallowell's two Berens River groups is 4 for Inland and 3 for Lakeside (Hallowell 1955:350). The implication of this M percentage, combined with the low color percentage, is that traditional Chippewa personality is characterized by introversiveness, with fantasy playing an important role. The character of Chippewa M responses is also of interest. Most of them are passive in nature—people seen as sitting, standing, lying down, or watching. Hallowell says that 82.3 percent of the Ms of his adult subjects in the Inland group were of this type. At Lac du Flambeau the mean for M drops to 1—an indication of the disruptive effect of acculturation.

All three of Hallowell's groups have a mean of 3 for *FM*, or animal movement. Animal movement responses are believed by Klopfer and Kelley (1942:278) to represent the most instinctive layers in the personality. In a normal record the number of *M* should generally exceed that of *FM;* the reverse is believed to indicate emotional immaturity, as would an excess of *CF* or *C* over *FC*. In the Chippewa records, *M* and *FM* are generally on a par, except at Flambeau, where *FM* is higher. The relative increase in *FM* and the decline of *M* in the most acculturated group, together with some other Rorschach features, are seen by Hallowell (1955:351–52) to indicate a weakening of the rigid control characteristic of the traditional Chippewa personality, but without any new compensating factors in evidence. An apathetic type of personality has apparently developed at Lac du Flambeau, functioning with "a great paucity of inner resources."

Chippewa Children's Rorschachs

Hallowell's Rorschach studies of the Chippewa have been supplemented by Blanche G. Watrous, who has analyzed 102 records of children from Lac du Flambeau and compared them with 49 Berens River children's protocols. The children were grouped into two age groups; there were 54 children from Flambeau and 25 from Berens River aged 6 years to 10 years, 11 months; 48 from Flambeau and 24 from Berens River aged 11 years to 15 years, 11 months. No distinction was made in this study between the Inland and Lakeside groups. As in the Hallowell study, mean scores were computed and compared.

In general, the Flambeau children's records conformed to the traditional Chippewa picture. Both the Flambeau and Berens River children gave *M* responses at an early age—mostly passive *M*s, often seen in unusual tiny detail areas. Both groups produced fewer *FC* responses than has been reported for white children in the literature; *CF* responses exceeded the more controlled *FC*. Both Chippewa groups gave relatively few Whole responses, with more attention being paid to details, indicating a more practical than theoretical orientation. There was a high percentage of tiny details at Flambeau. Both groups show the introversive pattern characteristic of the traditional Chippewa; but it is interesting to note that the older children at Flambeau seem to be more "Indian" than the younger children. This is evidenced by a reduction in the total number of responses and a decrease in color responses.

More cards were rejected by the older children. At Flambeau there was an overemphasis on human and animal details in relation to whole human and animal responses. The Flambeau children, moreover, gave more *FM* responses and saw more active animal movement in the blots than did the Berens River children, which is interpreted to indicate a greater degree of emotional aggression. There is also a possible indication of greater anxiety in the larger number of texture responses at Flambeau. Blanche Watrous (1949:205) describes these children as having "oversensitive, hypercritical, fearful attitudes toward people, emotional aggression, underlying psychic conflicts, and an unsatisfactory rapport with their surroundings."

It will be seen in a later section of this chapter that a similar picture emerges from an analysis of Chippewa children's Thematic Apperception Test records.

The Menomini

A very detailed Rorschach study has been made by George and Louise Spindler of the Menomini, neighbors of the Wisconsin Chippewa, who shared with them the same general kind of Woodland Indian culture of former times, and who, like the Chippewa, speak an Algonkian language. Here again, a statistical approach was used, except that Spindler (1955) used the median, rather than the mean, as an expression of central tendency. Menomini males were studied first. Spindler divided his 68 male subjects into five segments representing different levels of adaptation to Western culture: (1) a *native-oriented* group, followers of the Medicine Dance, Dream Dance, and other traditional Indian patterns, (2) *Peyote cult members,* (3) a *transitional* group which is not clearly identified with either the native or Western-oriented groups, (4) a *lower status acculturated* group, and (5) an *elite acculturated* middle-class higher status group.

The native-oriented group is very similar, in its Rorschach patterns, to the traditional Chippewa (Spindler 1955:131, 137–38, 207). There is the same paucity of color responses. The Menomini, however, show more *FM* (animal movement) in relation to *M* than do Hallowell's Inland group. The "elite" group closely resembles a control group of local white subjects in their Rorschach patterns, showing a more controlled extroversion than the other Indian groups. The native-oriented group and the "elite" seem to represent polar points in a continuum, in which the intermediate groups show more emotional responsiveness to others than do the native-oriented subjects, but have less emotional control than the "elite." Nothing comparable to the latter's psychological shift has been found in the Chippewa groups studied so far, a circumstance which may perhaps be attributed to the relatively favorable economic situation on the Menomini reservation, where the Indians own and operate their own sawmill (Hallowell 1956:531–32). It may be, however, that Chippewa who have left the reservaion to live in cities such as Milwaukee and Chicago, and who were not available for testing on the reservation, approximate more closely to the Menomini elite acculturated group.

Louise and George Spindler (1961) have also made a Rorschach study of Menomini women, in which they found that they appeared to be more homogeneous psychologically than the men, despite the fact that they were differentiated socioculturally in the same ways as the men. Menomini men must adapt psychologically to the conditions of acculturation, while the women are able to retain more of the native-oriented personality structure at each level of acculturation. The women are more conservative than the men in personality tendencies and less tense and anxious. Similar observations have been made before for other American Indian groups including the Chippewa (Hallowell 1942a; Caudill 1949:425; Barnouw 1950:20–21 n).

The Yukon Delta Eskimos

L. Bryce Boyer and his colleagues worked among the Yukon Delta Eskimos in 1973, when 118 Rorschach protocols were obtained in an Eskimo village of about 500 people. Here we have another traditionally hunting-gathering society, although the Eskimos generally have a reputation for displaying more extroversion and sociability than do the northern Algonkians. This is partly borne out by the Rorschach records in which the Eskimos "tend toward the extratensive direction." While the Chippewa give more human movement than color responses, the reverse is true among the Eskimos, who give few M responses (Boyer et al. 1978:28).

However, the Rorschach records and Boyer's observations suggest that the Yukon Delta Eskimos are less sociable than they have usually seemed to other observers. Many of the records exhibit what Bruno Klopfer has called the "burnt child reaction," in which the subject gives more than twice as many achromatic responses as chromatic responses: "the individual's need for affectional response from others is so great that he has muted and inhibited his overt reactions to others lest he be hurt or rejected" (p. 30).

A reaction of this sort is believed to result when a gratifying early childhood is followed by traumatic experiences, including rejection. Boyer and his colleagues believe that this happens among the Yukon Delta Eskimos, where the mother-infant relationship is very close. The naked child is carried on the mother's back, close to her skin, sleeps with her at night, and suckles on demand. But teasing behavior starts early in life, some of it quite sadistic in nature. The child may be deliberately ignored, as if he or she weren't there, and may be subject to shaming and ridicule by the adults. It is this switch from early gratification to frustration that is held to bring about the "burnt child" syndrome, which leads to guarded, stereotyped behavior toward others.

In the Boyer et al. study, contrasts are made between the popular responses of the Yukon Delta Eskimos and the popular responses of Samuel Beck's sample of midwestern Americans. One difference is the much smaller number of Eskimo human movement (*M*) responses. One popular Eskimo *M* response which does occur is a frightening one, a threatening monster, giant, or man on Card IV, which the authors assume reflects anxiety concerning parental figures. Apart from popular responses, the number of *M* responses is low in general—held to reflect a lack of empathy with others. The number of animal movement responses (*FM*) is quite a bit higher than the *M* responses, which is interpreted to indicate an impulsive need for immediate gratification, a feature found in 78 percent of the records, while 60 percent of the Eskimo protocols exhibit Klopfer's "burnt child" syndrome (pp. 27, 32).

An encouraging aspect of the Rorschach Test is that Rorschach analysts continue to find new clues to interpretation. George De Vos, who analyzed the Yukon Delta Eskimo records just described, has examined the Rorschach protocols of both Arabs and Japanese living in traditional and acculturated settings, and he has found that while Arabs and Japanese differ in many ways in their "overall Rorschach configurations," there seem to be some cross-cultural regularities operating in the acculturated groups. That is to say, both among the Arabs and among the Japanese there is an increase in body-content material in Rorschach responses among the more acculturated groups and an increase in specific forms of hostile symbolism. De Vos (1961) finds evidence of this tendency among still other groups undergoing the pressures of acculturation.

A new development which may perhaps reanimate the cross-cultural use of projective techniques is the development of the Holtzman Inkblot Technique (HIT), devised by Wayne H. Holtzman and his associates (1961). Instead of the 10 standard Rorschach blots, the Holtzman test has two parallel forms: A and B, each consisting of 45 inkblots, with 2 practice blots, making up a total of 92 blots. These blots are more varied in color, form, and shading than the Rorschach blots; they are not all bilaterally symmetrical. The subject gives only one response per card instead of as many as he wishes in the Rorschach Test. This test was designed to meet some psychologists' objections to the Rorschach Test, such as lack of test-retest reliability for many scores, and the widely varying number of responses given to individual Rorschach cards. Holtzman (1968:160–62) believes that his test provides a more reliable scoring system. The test has been used cross-culturally, principally in Mexico. Reportedly universal "popular" responses to the HIT have been recorded for five areas: Denmark, Germany, Hong Kong, Mexico, and the United States.

THE THEMATIC APPERCEPTION TEST

The Thematic Apperception Test (TAT) involves showing the subject a series of pictures, for each of which, in turn, he or she is required to make up a story. The subject is asked to tell what led up to the scene depicted, describing the thoughts and feelings of the individuals involved, and to tell what the outcome of the episode will be. The test, designed by C. D. Morgan and Henry A. Murray (1935), contains some pictures which are shown only to male subjects, some only to females, some used only with children, while some are shown to all subjects. There is a standard order of presentation, although this has been varied in some studies. A few of the pictures are reproductions of paintings; some look like magazine illustrations; one is a blank white card. The traditional practice is to show 20 pictures to a subject and have him or her tell a story for each; many testers, however, do not give the full range of TAT pictures but select a few which they feel to be particularly productive.

The cards are designed to tap different areas in human life and interpersonal relationships: there are pictures eliciting stories about a man's relationship with a mother figure, with a father figure, with a girl friend, pictures which may elicit stories of ambition, tragedy, and so forth. These narratives are analyzed for recurrent or unusual themes and for what they reveal of the individual's underlying assumptions and attitudes. Attention is paid to figures and objects not depicted in the picture but introduced in the story, and also to items which may be prominent or significant in the picture but omitted in the story. It is noted whether the outcomes of the narratives tend to be successful or unsuccessful. Does everything end in failure? Are realistic methods employed to resolve a conflict, or is a *deus ex machina* solution improvised? Many points of this sort enter into the process of interpretation. Saul Rosenzweig and Edith E. Fleming (1948–49:502) have pointed to some interesting minor variations in TAT protocols. For instance in Card I, which represents a young boy contemplating a violin, some subjects may see the violin string as broken or else perceive the violin as otherwise damaged. This occurred only 8 times in a sample of 100 normal individuals whose TATs they investigated. But in a sample of 100 mental patients there were 23 such instances.

Nancy Scheper-Hughes (1979:55) gave the TAT to villagers and psychiatric patients in a disorganized community in western Ireland.[6] Concerning responses to this card, she writes: "Half the village boys and a quarter of the male mental patients told stories of despondency over a violin or fiddle that was broken or sadly out of tune." More than half the village girls told stories that ignored or misidentified the violin, referring to it as a gun or other object.

A number of different scoring systems have been devised for the TAT, but these will not concern us here. Our interest lies in the cross-cultural application of the Thematic Apperception Test. An inspec-

---

[6] See page 383.

tion of the Murray pictures will soon make it clear that this series would not lend itself well to administration in a culture which differs considerably from that of the Western world. In some of the pictures middle-class American interiors are depicted which would have little meaning to members of "primitive" societies. Facial features are "Caucasian," clothing of American type.

There are two solutions to this problem. One is to select a limited number of standard TAT cards which do not reflect Western cultural patterns so markedly. This approach can be followed when the society in question has undergone a good deal of acculturation and where the physical features are not particularly different from those of Europeans. This was the method William Caudill (1949) used in his study of Lac du Flambeau Chippewa children. In a study of adolescents in an acculturated Maori community in New Zealand, D. G. Mulligan (1957) made use of the full TAT series. The standard cards seem to have done the job successfully both at Lac du Flambeau and in the Maori group. The traditional Murray cards, then, may be shown, in whole or in part, when the group is sufficiently acculturated.

Modified TATs

With less acculturated groups a second alternative may be followed. This is to draw up a parallel series of cards in which the geographical setting, house types, clothing, and physical features correspond to the culture in question. In other words, an artist is commissioned to make a "modified" TAT series which will be meaningful to members of that society. This method has been used in Henry's study of Hopi and Navaho children (1947), in Gladwin and Sarason's work on Truk (1953), in Lessa and Spiegelman's investigation of Ulithian personality (1954), and in studies of various African groups (Lee 1953). A modified TAT, designed to elicit attitudes toward authority, the emperor, military service, and certain areas of interpersonal relations, has been given to Japanese subjects (see Appendix 2 in Stoetzel 1955). For use in Japanese rural areas, De Vos and Wagatsuma (1961) have employed a modified TAT which closely resembles the original Murray series.

One drawback in such tests is that a modified TAT is not the same test as the original series, although efforts have usually been made to parallel the Murray cards in a general way. William E. Henry (1951:263–64) has set forth some criteria for what a modified test should include. There should be mother-child and father-child scenes; a person alone; a heterosexual scene, a group scene, an authority scene; a typical environmental setting; and scenes of some characteristic economic activity. There should be one or two pictures of an "illogical arrangement of reality events," and one or two representing unreal or bizarre events. Henry suggests that there should also be some scenes characteristic of the culture in question, designed to touch on problems of local concern (for instance, caste groups in India). Such a modified series will, of course, differ in many respects from the Murray sequence and from modified tests in other areas. This is unintentionally illustrated in three plates reproduced in the Henry article just cited. In each of these, two young men are being addressed by an older, authoritative male. The first plate represents an American Indian group, the second a Mexican, and the third a South-West African group. Inspection of these drawings shows that they are not exactly equivalent. The ages of the younger males seem to differ, particularly in the Mexican and African plates. The Mexican adult is taller than the younger males, but the older adult is not equally so in the American Indian and African drawings. Facial expressions also differ slightly. Differences in responses to these drawings in the three groups might be due to differences in the plates rather than to differences in group personality tendencies.

Most modified TATs, like the ones used in Truk and Ulithi, do not try to imitate the style of the original Murray reproductions, but consist of line drawings which lack the shading and chiaroscuro of the original plates. This stylistic factor might make a difference. Caudill (1949:414) has noted that the Ojibwa children whom he tested told much longer stories than did the Hopi and Navaho children. Might not this disparity be a function of the nature of the plates in use, rather than a reflection of different group personality tendencies? For Caudill used the standard Murray pictures, while the modified TAT was used with the other groups. Perhaps experiments should be made to determine whether line drawings provide as productive results in TATs as do pictures with chiaroscuro.

Edward T. Sherwood (1957) who like Lee has devised a modified TAT for African subjects, has a series which bears somewhat more resemblance in style to the original TAT than do the Hopi, Navaho, and Micronesian TATs. Sherwood believes that the pictures should offer a good deal of variety to maintain the interest of the subject. Some should be close-up views, some seen at a distance; some should be dark in tone, some light. Some pictures should be in shade and highlight, others relatively monotone; and different graphic techniques should be employed in different cards.

In any event, it is clear that modified TATs do not lend themselves to the same sort of cross-cultural comparisons that the Rorschach Test allows. In the Rorschach Test every subject sees the same 10 blots in the same order, whether he or she be an Eskimo, a Bushman, or a Yale undergraduate. With modified TATs, however, we have a number of different tests providing different series of stimuli. This does not mean that modified TATs are not useful and productive. As we shall see, such tests have proven to be very informative. If the purpose is simply to produce fantasy material, a modified TAT will do what is required of it. But it cannot be used so successfully in global cross-cultural comparisons.

Some other drawbacks may be noted. With relatively "primitive" groups there may be a lack of familiarity with pictures and some consequent difficulty in seeing perspective depicted in the plates. This may affect the test results and produce some seemingly bizarre responses. One Ulithian, for example, interpreted large ocean waves illustrated in one card as being pigs (Lessa and Spiegelman 1954:280). Some Micronesian subjects who were shown the same modified TATs by Melford Spiro were unable to interpret some of the objects represented in the pictures and could not identify certain depictions of fire, smoke, and tree trunks. Perspective was not always understood. "Objects drawn above one another were seen as being above one another and not in spatially receding planes. A canoe, represented by the artist as being *in* a native canoe house, was seen as being *carried* by men standing in the foreground *outside* the house" (Hallowell 1955:45).

S. Biesheuvel found a similar lack of comprehension of perspective in some African subjects taking a modified TAT.

> A group of industrial operatives, presented with a picture of cattle grazing in a field, correctly identified those in the foreground, whilst those in the background, drawn smaller to simulate distance, were sometimes seen as hyenas or similar animals. A workman, standing on a box obscured by fellow-workers whom he was haranguing, against a background of factory buildings and chimney stacks, was seen by some as a giant catching the smoke that emanated from the stacks (Biesheuvel 1958:176).

However, such misunderstandings are not likely to be common. Recent cross-cultural testing by Jahoda and McGurk (1982:102) has shown that "the development of pictorial depth perception follows a similar pattern among children from a wide diversity of cultural backgrounds. . . ."

Group Studies

In the analysis of group protocols, different procedures have been followed by analysts, sometimes making use of statistical techniques along different lines. In their study of Ulithian personality, Lessa and Spiegelman (1954:268) make use of a quantitative approach involving certain categories set forth by Reuben Fine. The Ulithian records were scored according to these categories, and the interpretation (made blind) was based on the resultant quantitative findings rather than drawn from analyses of the TAT stories themselves. D. G. Mulligan's (1957:50) analysis of Maori TATs follows a similar quantitative approach based on Reuben Fine's method and makes use of the mean frequencies of certain types of responses. The blind analysis of the

Ulithian material yielded results with which the ethnographer agreed. There is also close agreement between Mulligan's TAT findings, observational data, and Rorschach conclusions in the Rakau study.

Most TAT analyses have followed a more informal procedure—of simply looking for recurrent patterns in the protocols. This seems, for instance, to have been the method followed by Sarason in his blind analysis of the Trukese TATs, which also proved to be in close agreement with the ethnographer's impressions of the people.

Let us now consider in more detail some of the TAT analyses which have been mentioned.

Hopi and Navaho Children

One of the first cross-cultural applications of the TAT was in connection with the study of Hopi and Navaho children, aged 6–18, equally divided as to sex. There were 102 Hopi and 104 Navaho subjects who took a modified TAT consisting of 12 line drawings drawn by an Indian artist. On the basis of their TATs, Henry found that, among the Hopi, the mother is the principal authority.

> There is considerable unconscious hostility to her although it is seldom expressed in direct form. . . . The dominance of the adult female in the fantasies of the children is so marked as to support the suggestion that their authority extends through the culture to all adult females rather than just to the mother-child relation. . . . The position of the father is one of far less importance than that of the mother. . . . In no case does there appear the hostility to him so characteristic of descriptions of the mother (Henry 1947:91).

In the large extended family setting, diffuse emotional attachments prevail. It would seem that a child can more easily move from one family unit to another than could a child in the white American middle class. Control of emotions is stressed and personal desires deemphasized. Individuality is suppressed in the interests of the group, but this is accompanied by a sense of anxiety in the individual. A frequent Hopi motif is "I want to rebel, but I know I can't." Henry (1947:93) makes the suggestion that "this is a society whose restrained, nonaggressive front, and rigorous system of social controls represent a system of defense against two kinds of events: the real or imagined threat to the psychological integrity and maintenance of the culture and the presence of intra-group hostilities."

The TAT evidence further suggests to Henry that the following channels of release may be resorted to: malicious gossip, indirectly expressed sibling jealousy, petty delinquencies such as stealing and acts of destruction, running away from home or school, and committing acts of cruelty to animals. Reference to the section on the Pueblos in Chapter 3 on Ruth Benedict will show that many observational studies are in agreement with this general picture, such as those of Dorothy Eggan, Esther Goldfrank, and others. Hostility toward the mother might not have been expected, however, at least not to the extent suggested by Henry's analysis.

As for the Navaho, life seems easier than for the Hopi. There is less weight of personal responsibility, and the environment is less threatening. At least, there is no anxiety about food. There is greater freedom and spontaneity in emotional life. More respect is shown for individuality within the family. Family relations are easier and less characterized by ambivalence. Sibling rivalry does not have the force of such rivalry among the Hopi, and there is greater impartiality in the treatment of children. In contrast to the Hopi, there is an absence of guilt feelings concerning infractions of rules. The mental approach is practical and matter of fact, but individuality and imagination are expressed in the arts and crafts, in clothes and jewelry.

This interpretation, again, coincides with impressions of those who have worked with these Indians. Henry quotes a statement made by Clyde Kluckhohn, one of the foremost authorities on the Navaho:

> I hope you will emphasize . . . the independence of the convergent views [of the two reports]. Last winter in Chicago, which was the first time I heard [your report on the Navaho], I was astonished and pleased at how in many details your results seemed to parallel almost identically things which already stood in this manuscript [*The People and Their Children*]—the psychological parts of which have not been substantially altered since then (Henry 1947:114 fn.).

A quantitative assessment of the test's validity was also attempted. Among 16 Navaho cases studied, 451 interpretations were made. "When these 451 points were compared with all other sources of data, 375, or 83.1 percent of them, were found to be substantiated and only 10, or 2.2 percent, were found to be incorrect statements" (Henry 1947:260). This is a careful, well-executed study.

Chippewa Children

William Caudill's analysis of Ojibwa children's records from Lac du Flambeau provides more psychological insights into this community and should be considered in relation to the Rorschach evidence and the life history materials that have been presented in previous sections. Caudill notes, as an outstanding feature of these TAT records, the tendency to catalog the contents of a picture, picking out small details.

> Both details of the natural environment and human details are treated equally as if all were inanimate objects. There is little more, if

any, warmth or involvement with a human detail than with an inanimate detail. . . . Another quality of this detailed approach is that the stories fail to relate one detail to another. More importantly, the human details are also seen with very little relationship to each other (Caudill 1949:414).

The stories display little emotional feeling of any kind. This is true even when stories deal with physical aggression and drunkenness—perhaps, as Caudill suggests, because these are accepted as part of everyday life.

Most endings of stories have a neutral quality. If a story ends unhappily, the unhappiness is stated without emotion. Caudill notes three types of deficiency in these records:

> (1) There is little indication of any emotional interpersonal relationships, and what there is involves hostility rather than warmth; (2) there is a total lack of any indication of ambition—no desire for education, for a better job, to be a good farmer or hunter; and (3) there are almost no remarks concerning moral or value judgments. Thus, going to jail simply happens, it is an ordinary part of life which is morally neither good nor bad (Caudill 1949:420–21).

From a total of 88 children's records, 41 show definite psychological maladjustment. A number show drastic personality damage in the direction of schizophrenia. There are constant references to hunger and eating. Caudill believes that the impact of Western culture cannot be the sole source of these psychological patterns, but that they must in part be traced back to aboriginal conditions. There is much correspondence with the work done by Hallowell, Watrous, and others who have worked among the Chippewa.

Japanese-Americans

Caudill also made a study of 70 Japanese-Americans in Chicago, utilizing the standard Murray series. This study shows the usefulness of certain key cards in eliciting material—for instance, 6BM and 7BM in tapping attitudes toward parental figures. 6BM shows an elderly woman looking somewhat vacantly out of a window, while a tall young man in the foreground looks down with a perplexed expression on his face. 7BM shows the faces of an older and a younger man. The features in these pictures are "Caucasian," but the Japanese-Americans do not seem to have had any difficulty in identifying with these figures.

A common response to 6BM concerns a son, a weakling who now realizes his mistakes and begs his mother's forgiveness.

In all the stories the mother is a very strong person. She may be very punitive toward the son; he is submissive. When rejected by her, the son feels a sense of failure and guilt. The mother may interfere with his own personal desires, especially in connection with marriage; and her voice seems to be decisive in such cases. The mother may support the attitude of the community or the law, if the young man has broken a rule. In general, the son is compliant, suppresses his feelings, and continues to feel a sense of obligation toward his mother.

> The most common adaptive mechanism utilized by Issei and Nisei is always to ask for parental advice and approval on any problem in order to avoid anxiety and guilt. This adaptive mechanism is extended by Japanese-Americans beyond the familial area and becomes one of constantly seeking advice on any important decision from older, and hence wiser, people. There is no defense against parental rejection, which usually results in feelings of masochistic guilt and personal failure (Caudill 1952:65).

The stories told about Card 7BM, which reflect father-son relationships, are also revealing. Other cards tap themes of ambition and illustrate the high aspiration levels of Japanese-Americans. In sum, this is an interesting study which throws light on the similarities and differences between Japanese-Americans and white Americans of lower and middle class.

Taiwanese and Japanese

In another TAT study, De Vos, Hauswald, and Borders (1979) compared Taiwanese and Japanese subjects. The Taiwanese sample consisted of 50 husband-wife pairs (with high school education) who were parents of elementary-age children. The Japanese sample was made up of 20 husband-wife pairs from Tokyo of upper-lower class origin. Like the Japanese-Americans, the Tokyo sample had an emphasis on achievement motivation and long-term future concerns, but this was not the case among the Taiwanese. The roles of mothers differed in the two samples:

> The Japanese mother evaluates success in her own life through the success of her children. . . . Through internalizing the mother's concerns, the child is allowed to become independent. . . . Chinese mothers are not so concerned with the independence of their children. Rather, simple nurturance and maternal control are the focus of mother-child interaction (1979:249).

Instead of autonomy being stressed in Taiwanese stories, there is an emphasis on the family as a whole.

Micronesian studies

Two studies of Micronesian TATs have been published. Both make use of the same modified series of cards. One study forms part of the

Gladwin-Sarason monograph on Truk; the other is the Lessa-Spiegelman work on Ulithi, to which reference has been made. In both cases TAT analyses were made blind and the results compared with the ethnographer's observations, although with some differences in method, as has been noted. Of the two studies, the analysis of Truk is more detailed and gives a more specific and complex picture of personality patterns, perhaps because Sarason worked more closely with the TAT stories themselves, while the psychologist in the Ulithian study based his analysis primarily on statistical breakdowns of categorized items. Sarason, moreover, had an additional source of information, for he had completed the group Rorschach interpretation before beginning his analysis of the TAT stories. Both psychologists had an added possible source of data on the culture—the pictures themselves, which might give some clues, as Lessa and Spiegelman (1954:300) imply.

Some of Sarason's generalizations, based on the Truk TAT stories, are as follows: Trukese parents treat their children inconsistently, sometimes kindly, at other times punishing and rejecting. This generalization would seem to be applicable to almost any parents, but Sarason goes on to underline the negative side of the picture. Parents, particularly the mother, are seen as fearsome, rejecting, and punishing figures against whom retaliation is best not attempted. Trukese children, moreover, experience severe oral frustrations. Indeed, anxiety over food is a common motif in the TAT stories. Sarason suggests that one would expect the Trukese to have little difficulty in "receiving" from others but much difficulty in giving of themselves. Many of the stories indicate the presence of a separation anxiety which seems to persist throughout life. Hostility and other strong feelings are suppressed and cloaked by overt conformity. Sarason sees little evidence of interests aside from food and sex, but a rather passive, lazy way of life. Sarason believes that men seek sexual conquests to prove their masculinity and to reduce feelings of inadequacy. But women are subtly dominating and undependable. Both sexes approach sexual relations in a narcissistic way (Gladwin and Sarason 1953:232–46).

The Trukese man is very jealous, but directs his hostility more to the woman in question than toward his rivals. Sarason hypothesizes that Trukese women are somewhat exhibitionistic—more so than the men. In general, social relations are superficial and unstable, one possible exception being the somewhat mutually supporting relationship between young "brothers." Women, on the other hand, do not seem to have such close relations with one another.

Gladwin, the ethnographer, expresses agreement on almost all of these points, and his description of the culture provides abundant documentation for them. But he does make some emendations. For example, Sarason stresses the men's concern with their genital adequacy, but Gladwin says that the women have the same kind of concern. There is a Trukese notion that a woman's vagina should be full of "little things"—prominent clitoris, labia minora, and so forth—which are believed to assure many lovers. Quarrels between women may lead to insults about each other's having inadequate vaginas, and this, in turn, may lead to mutual self-exposure of the genitals, whose relative merits are then assessed by bystanders. A woman who is proved inferior is greatly shamed (Gladwin and Sarason 1953:110, 244). In general, however, Gladwin is in close agreement with Sarason's interpretations based on the TAT stories.

The analysis of the Ulithian TATs, as noted earlier, is less detailed than Sarason's. Moreover, many of the psychologist's generalizations are of a cultural rather than psychological order. For example:

> Although cooperation is higher among males than females, the latter exceed the males a little on the category of Group Activity. One hypothesis to explain this difference is that the men are the main ones to gather food and that they do this in a cooperative way with other men, whereas the women may prepare and cook the food alone. The females' concern with group activity may be largely in connection with the goal of Amusement (*e.g.*, dancing) (Lessa and Spiegelman 1954:286).

Here are some of the more psychological TAT deductions concerning the Ulithians: These people are cooperative, basically optimistic people. Suicide and insanity are seldom mentioned in the stories and are probably rare. There is much concern with food and with work to attain it. Sexuality and menstruation do not seem to pose particular problems. Amusements are highly valued. Despite the basic optimism, there are many expressions of dysphoria in the stories. Feelings of anger and sadness are expressed, especially among adult males.

> They [the Ulithians] experience a full variety of emotions, but their general concreteness is evidenced here, as well, for their dysphoric emotions are confined to specific situations, are not extremely intense, and have no traumatic consequences. . . . Their concreteness and overwhelmingly group-oriented approach make for a lack of friction, but at the expense of abstract thought and individual differences (Lessa and Spiegelman 1954:298).

The ethnographer is in general agreement with these points. Incidentally, Sarason also speaks of "concreteness" in discussing the mental approach of the Trukese, but derives this from the Rorschach protocols rather than from the TAT stories (Gladwin and Sarason 1953:225–26).

The foregoing examples seem to me to show that the TAT is a useful projective technique in cross-cultural studies. But there are those who disagree. In a book on projective techniques which emphasizes the TAT, Bernard I. Murstein (1963:346–50) concludes that pro-

jective tests, including the TAT, have not demonstrated their usefulness in cross-cultural studies. However, he reports on only a few
such studies and seems to draw his negative conclusion largely from
a summary by Gardner Lindzey on the generally poor quality of this
research.

The anthropologists who have used the TAT generally seem to feel
that it is a good technique; some believe it to be preferable to the
Rorschach. This is Gladwin's view:

> Interpretation of the Rorschach in any setting necessarily requires
> more inference than the TAT because the Rorschach presents a less
> structured stimulus, and its interpretation rests on a larger series of
> assumptions about unconscious psychological processes derived from
> our own culture than does the TAT (Langness and Gladwin 1972:179).

Bert Kaplan has expressed a similar preference for the TAT over
the Rorschach. Sarason has discussed the different contributions
made by the two tests in the Truk study. The rigid "concrete" mental
approach of the Trukese was more evident in the Rorschach than in
the TAT, but the Rorschach gave no evidence about food anxiety
(Gladwin and Sarason 1953:220).

> From the Rorschach we were able to detect a sexual concern but
> from the TAT we were able to elaborate on the context of such concern.
> The Rorschach enabled us to see how the Trukese were likely to handle
> aggressive conflicts by avoidance and suppressive mechanisms, but the
> TAT tells us more about the situational contexts in which these conflicts
> arise (Gladwin and Sarason 1953:454).

This suggests (as Sarason recommends) that both tests should be
used in the field.

It may be pointed out that various special picture tests with limited
objectives have been used by anthropologists in ways similar to the
TAT, although for somewhat different purposes. Walter Goldschmidt
and Robert B. Edgerton (1961) have used a picture technique in
studying the value systems of Menomini Indians. Edgerton (1971)
made use of a series of drawings in his study of farming and pastoral
tribes in East Africa. William Caudill (1962a) showed a series of drawings to Japanese subjects as a way of eliciting prevalent emotional
themes and values. Seymour Parker (1964) used pictures as a stimulus to reveal attitudes toward ethnic identity among Eskimo villagers,
and George and Louise Spindler (1965) have used a set of drawings to
find out attitudes toward various activities and occupations among
the Blood Indians of Alberta, Canada. Richard H. Solomon (1971) has
shown a series of modified TAT-like pictures to Chinese subjects in
order to elicit attitudes toward authority. In each of these cases, drawings were made appropriate to a special cultural setting and designed
to elicit particular kinds of responses.

SUGGESTIONS FOR FURTHER READING

For a review of projective techniques see A. I. Rabin, ed., *Projective Techniques in Personality Assessment. A Modern Introduction* (New York: Springer Publishing, 1968). See also Bernard I. Murstein, *Handbook of Projective Techniques* (New York: Basic Books, 1965). For the cross-cultural application of projective techniques, see Gardner Lindzey, *Projective Techniques and Cross-Cultural Research* (New York: Appleton-Century-Crofts, 1961).

An interesting application of the Thematic Apperception Test to the study of bilingualism is available in Susan M. Ervin, "Language and TAT Content in Bilinguals," *Journal of Abnormal Psychology* 68 (1964), pp. 500–7.

Hallowell's essays on the Chippewa, including his Rorschach studies, are available in his *Culture and Experience* (Philadelphia: University of Pennsylvania Press, 1955).

This chapter dealt with projective tests; so no reference was made here to such tests as Witkin's Embedded Figures Test, Rod and Frame Test, Body Adjustment Test, Piaget's tests of conservation, and the Müller-Lyer illusion, discussed in Chapter 9, where each of these tests was briefly described. For a review of these instruments and the problems involved in their cross-cultural administration, see Richard W. Brislin, Walter J. Lonner, and Robert M. Thorndike, *Cross-Cultural Research Methods* (New York: John Wiley & Sons 1973).

16

Drawing Analysis

Much less use has been made of drawing analysis than of the Rorschach Test or TAT in culture-and-personality studies. Many anthropologists have collected drawings in the course of fieldwork, but few have done anything with them. This has been largely due to a general feeling that while there might be something in drawing analysis, it appears to be too intuitive and impressionistic a technique to have much validity, a feeling reinforced by the strong criticisms which some psychologists have made of interpretations of the Machover Draw-a-Person Test (Blum 1954; Swenson 1957). However, drawing analysis has been widely used in clinical practice in conjunction with the Rorschach and TAT. The approach would seem to have advantages for culture-and-personality studies. Drawings are relatively easy to collect in the field, are not time consuming, and do not require much equipment—mainly paper, pencils and crayons. Problems of verbal communication and translation are at a minimum. The technique is particularly useful with children, with shy subjects, and with people who, for one reason or another, find it difficult to communicate verbally. Drawings provide a permanent expression of personality. Hammer (1958:600–601) believes that this expression is less influenced by the administrator than in the case of the Rorschach or TAT. He also considers it to be a more direct manifestation of personality: "The subject's Rorschach percepts must, first, be translated into, and second, be communicated in, verbal language. In drawings, on the other hand, the subject expresses himself on a more primitive, concrete, motor level."

Against the use of drawing analysis in cross-cultural studies is the argument that a subject's drawings reflect cultural traditions, local art styles and mannerisms, a point which has been demonstrated by many studies.[1] Both Jane Belo's Balinese subjects and Cora Du Bois's Alorese were unfamiliar with pencil and paper and had not drawn before. The Balinese children's drawings, however, were vigorous

---

[1] For example, Haddon (1904), Anastasi and Foley (1938), Taylor (1944), and Belo (1955).

and complex, while the drawings of the Alorese children were weak and infantile. Perhaps the reason for this contrast is that Bali has a rich art tradition, while Alor has not. Balinese children's drawings, moreover, are patterned after the classical Balinese style, while drawings of Alorese children have little or no relation to the adult art (Du Bois 1944:566).

Wayne Dennis (1960b), who expresses some skepticism of the Machover test's validity, tells us that when Bedouins are asked to draw a person, they make very small drawings, averaging only two inches high and consisting largely of straight lines and darkened surfaces. Dennis ascribes these traits to the fact that what little art is known to the Bedouins consists largely of small geometric decorations. On the other hand, Orotchen children and young people in Siberia who had never previously handled pencil and paper before and who had no traditions of figurative art made very good drawings (Schubert 1930), and I have seen drawings by Naskapi Indian children, also previously unfamiliar with pencil and paper and lacking rich art traditions, which showed very good draftsmanship. Moreover, while both Manus and Alor lack strong art traditions, Manus and Alorese children do not draw in the same way.

The problems involved here are complex and merge with the question of whether or not one can analyze the art of a people for clues to their personality tendencies. Does the character of Bedouin art itself in some way reflect the Bedouin personality? The interpretation of art will be explored in Chapter 17. In the present chapter I will present some interpretations that have been made of Alorese and Chippewa children's drawings, to which will be added a discussion of the techniques developed by Machover, Dennis, Buck and others. I will also summarize some of my own research involving Buck's House-Tree-Person drawing test.

Alorese Children's Drawings

Alorese children were given paper and pencil and asked to draw whatever they wished. Drawings were obtained from 33 boys and 22 girls. Some differences were noted in subject matter: boys showed more interest in foreign and ceremonial objects, while girls showed a predominance of tattoo designs. (They were nearing the age when tattooing takes place.) Plants formed the largest content category for both sexes, followed by animals for boys and tools for girls. Buildings came third for both groups. Human beings were drawn with relative infrequency—7 percent of the subjects portrayed for boys and only about 1 percent of those portrayed by the girls. This provides a contrast to patterns found in the drawings of Western children. Ruth Griffiths (1935), in a study of English children's drawings, found the favorite subject of children's drawings to be the human figure; houses came next; then trees and flowers. Helga Eng (1954) similarly found the human figure to be the most commonly drawn, followed by the house.

When human figures were drawn by the Alorese children, sexual organs were often omitted, despite the Alorese children's familiarity with sex. Figures with the male organ were sometimes identified as female. An interesting phenomenon was noted: house forms and human figures often seem to be combined or merged, which was also true of human figures and trees, with hands and feet resembling branches and roots. In view of some assumptions associated with the House-Tree-Person Test, these identifications are noteworthy. The Alorese children made no attempt to portray groups and showed practically no sense of composition or design. There were only four cases in which two objects were brought into some relationship—all drawn by boys. Du Bois noted no improvement in drawing over a month's time.

Dr. Schmidl-Waehner's blind analysis of this material is as follows:

> They have a feeling of aloneness as evinced by the lack of strong pressure in the lines and by the neatness of the line itself. . . . They look like children who have good abilities but are apart from each other. There are good units but there is never unity. . . . Their relationships are poverty-stricken, as evinced by the fact that each figure is lost among others. . . . The absence of free curves suggests an inability to bring themselves affectively into contact with others (Du Bois 1944:584–85).

A lack of creativeness is indicated by the smallness of the forms and the absence of unity. There are few free-flowing curves and little variation in pressure.

As was noted in an earlier chapter, these findings closely agree with blind analyses based on other data—Rorschachs and life histories, which were independently interpreted by different specialists. Schmidl-Waehner made the prediction that these subjects would lack movement responses in the Rorschach Test—which was borne out.

A problematic question concerns the omission of sexual organs. Du Bois (1944:586) remarks that, in the light of the children's knowledge of anatomy, this omission should indicate either strong castration fears or their opposite—a lack of concern about sex. The latter alternative was considered more likely. This is a point on which Géza Roheim (1950:264) strongly disagreed; in fact, he claimed that fear of castration was *the* outstanding factor in the make-up of the Alorese. We need not become involved in this controversy. Either way, it seems that Schmidl-Waehner's pioneer blind analysis was a very successful one.

Chippewa Children's Drawings

Aside from Schmidl-Waehner's Alorese interpretation, the best study that I know of in the blind analysis of a collection of drawings is by Michal S. Lowenfels. The drawings in question were 267 spontaneous drawings made by 78 Chippewa children (44 boys, 34 girls) collected by Ruy Coelho at Lac du Flambeau in 1946 as part of A. I. Hallowell's group study. (The age range was from below 6 to 16 years of age.) Lowenfels assayed a group characterization based on a blind analysis of these drawings.

> The writer did not have access to either the Rorschach or TAT data until she had completed her analysis of the drawings and had written the group interpretations, nor did she study the recent work of Dr. Hallowell and others on the psychological characteristics of the Ojibwa. The writer made no systematic study of Ojibwa ethnology (Lowenfels 1950:31).

The drawings were scored according to a system combining the criteria of formal analysis devised by Elkisch and Schmidl-Waehner, with more weighting given to the latter's system. Drawings of human figures were analyzed according to Machover's method, by and large, "such as profile as an indicator of evasiveness in personal relationships, and the significance of arms and arm placement for indication of the quality of contact with the environment" (Lowenfels 1950:43).

Statistical methods of interpretation were not used. "It was felt that the total pattern of characteristics a child manifested were more important than the presence or absence of a single trait. The crucial question in group personality derivation is the way in which certain traits tend to cluster together" (Lowenfels 1950:45). The children were, however, rated for 64 personality traits, such as rigidity, constriction, and so forth.

Some of the author's conclusions are as follows:

> Approximately two-thirds (63%) of the children approach the world in an essentially constricted, rigid fashion. In general this group tends to be overcontrolled and to manifest strong compulsive tendencies. Within this framework of inflexibility and a need to control the situation at all times, we find that 30% are in addition markedly introversive, passive and withdrawn.
>
> The other major grouping represents the remaining third (37%) of the children and differs more in degree than in quality. This group, while also manifesting constriction and overcontrol, tends to show less compulsivity and less of inflexible static approach (Lowenfels 1950:47–48).

In general, there is evidence of an avoidance of emotional involvement with others; evasive, stereotyped, and superficial relationships prevail. Lowenfels illustrates this by the treatment of human figures. Of the 47 percent of children who drew some human form, 37 percent drew only heads; 68 percent drew figures in profile—an indication of evasiveness, according to Machover.[2] If two human figures were drawn on the same page, they tended to be drawn back to back or front to back. Only one child drew a group of interacting human figures. There is a lack of emotional drive, a sense of defeat and resignation, combined with a good deal of anxiety and depression.

"Twenty-five percent of the total group used no color and an additional ten percent used only one or two colors. The children using more color tended to use either a pale or a dark color scale. The children who used less than three colors, or used a pale or dark color scale, usually coupled this with the violent and aggressive use of red" (Lowenfels 1950:50). There was little evidence of spontaneity, except for aggressive outbursts. "In child after child there was expression of affect hunger, of frustrated passive-dependency needs coupled with a fear of affective involvement" (p. 52). Lowenfels hypothesizes that this must stem from parental rejection, since parents probably have the same kind of personality as the children—aloof and insecure.

This assessment agrees strikingly with interpretations based on other data concerning the Chippewa—life histories, Rorschachs, and TATs, as has been noted in previous chapters.

Lowenfels (p. 56) goes on to note some differences between boys and girls. The latter show more rigidity, constriction, and stereotypy, but also more emotional control than the boys. They manifest a preoccupation with glamor and sex. However, they portray the male figure as "weak, ineffectual, and smaller than the female." Many of the girls show tendencies toward sexual delinquency, which may stem from the need to satisfy affect hunger.

Boys are more withdrawn, introversive, and passive. There is more repression but also less emotional control, with outbursts of aggression manifest. The girls behave in a more conventional and socially approved manner than the boys. The author presents a series of individual cases, accompanied by photostats of some drawings and the associated scoring charts. These analyses seem unstrained and convincing, at least to me.

We have, then, two cases of blind analysis of drawings—Alor and Chippewa. In both, considerable agreement appeared in relation to interpretations based on projective tests, life history material, and observational data. In both cases the children were free to draw whatever they liked—not required to draw a person, house, or tree, for instance. Both analyses were based primarily on formal criteria—largely those suggested by Schmidl-Waehner. The success of these

---

[2] The drawing of heads rather than full figures is paralleled by the emphasis on human detail responses in the Lac du Flambeau Rorschachs.

two experiments suggests that drawing analysis can be profitably pursued cross-culturally. But I think that future studies in this field should not depend on formal criteria alone, but should draw on the symbolism of content. This can best be done, I believe, by using Buck's House-Tree-Person (H-T-P) Test. Within the latter, Machover's Draw-a-Person (DAP) Test can be incorporated. The DAP Test has been applied cross-culturally, although with some negative results (Honigmann and Carrera 1957). Let me describe the administration of the Machover and Buck tests and discuss some of the assumptions associated with them.

THE DRAW-A-PERSON (DAP) TEST

In the Machover test the subject is given a medium-soft pencil with an eraser on it and a blank sheet of 8½ × 11 inch paper. He is asked to draw a person. These purposefully vague instructions leave the sex of the person drawn to the subject's choice. Once the first drawing is completed, the subject is given a second blank sheet and asked to draw a female, if he has drawn a man first, or a male, if he has drawn a woman. The words *female* and *male* are used instead of *woman* or *man* because the subject may prefer to draw a boy or girl instead of an adult (Machover 1949:29).

After the second drawing, the subject may be interrogated about the figures he or she has drawn and asked to describe them or to make up a story about them. However, this part of the test is optional.

Machover assumes that the drawings made by a person are projections, to some extent, of his or her own *body image*. This important, if somewhat vague, concept must be examined briefly.

The Body Image, Ideal Type, and Group Values

Everyone has some sort of conception of what one's body is like. This "image" is built up from different sources; not only from what we can see and feel of the body, but also from cultural traditions about the body and from how other people regard us and treat us. One's body image may be at variance with the physical facts. A man who is paralyzed may deny it. An attractive woman may feel ugly. A physiologically normal man may experience a confusion of sexual identification and feel somehow feminine, and a woman may have obsessive, unfounded notions that she gives off an awful odor. A man's concept of himself as potent or impotent may be shaped by the attitudes of his sexual partner. Thus, a person's body image has social and cultural sources, as well as physiological ones. The body image is plastic and undergoes changes with growth and in response to illness, traumatic experiences, and mental disorder.

Clothes may become part of the body image and may supplement felt deficiencies. This suggests a possible symbolic explanation for a woman's concern with hats and handbags, or a man's with ties. Seeing clothes as extensions of the body image lends added interest to cross-cultural studies of dress, tattooing, and bodily decoration, the use of masks in primitive rituals and practices of transvestism in cultures like the Iatmul (see Schilder 1950 and Fisher and Cleveland 1958).

Wayne Dennis (1966), who has made a large collection of children's drawings from different parts of the world, states that most boys, when asked to draw a man—a whole man, not just the head and shoulders—draw men who are young or middle aged, not old men; and they draw men in good health, not deformed or crippled men. Only 5 drawings in Dennis's cross-cultural collection of 2,550 drawings had mouth corners turned down. No crippled man was drawn, and only three fat men. Negative, cartoonlike figures are seldom drawn by children under 14 years of age. Dennis's assumption is that children get their values from adults and that what the children draw expresses *group* values.

An alternative to both the body image hypothesis and Dennis's value hypothesis is that children draw what they are familiar with. However, Dennis points to some data which are inconsistent with this view. In Sudan, traditional clothes—long, unbelted cotton gowns—are worn by the majority, but 85 percent of the urban children drew people in Western clothing. In San Cristobal, Chiapas, Mexico, where dominant Ladinos and the more submissive lower class Chamula Indians live in proximity (like the Mixtecans of Juxtlahuaca, Mexico, and Gillin's Ladinos and Indians of San Carlos, Guatemala), no Indians were drawn in 400 Ladinos' drawings, while the Chamula Indian boys, though wearing Indian dress, drew 70 percent Ladinos and only 30 percent Indians.

These findings suggest that ideal types and values are expressed in these drawings more than body image or what is familiar to the drawer. In the case of children's drawings, at least, it seems that children tend to draw what they admire, envy, or would like to be.

Aspects of DAP Interpretation

There are many approaches to the interpretation of DAP drawings, such as consideration of the size and placement of the drawn figures, a comparison of the male and female figures with respect to size and treatment. Formal characteristics may be interpreted in the manner of Elkisch (1945), Schmidl-Waehner (1942), and others who pay attention to such features as line pressure, size and placement of the drawn figure, rigidity of forms, and so forth.

Machover and Levy cite examples of possible diagnostic indicators.

They note that an emphasis on the mouth may reflect an "oral" dependent tendency. If the nose is made unduly large, this may represent compensatory efforts on the part of a man who has feelings of impotence. Enlargements or distortions of the ear may express sensitivity to social criticism or paranoid tendencies. A subject's treatment of the neck is significant because it represents a link between the head (rational control) and the body (impulse life). (A similar "link" is the waist.) Omission of the neck may indicate immaturity or regression, while a very long, extended neck may be an indication of a schizoid or schizophrenic personality. The manner of portraying arms and hands may reflect the nature of the subject's ego development, social adaptation, and mastery of the environment, and from their treatment one may get clues to the sense of confidence, efficiency, ambition, or aggression of the subject. Emphasis on rounded hips in a male subject is said to be a possible indication of homosexuality. Sexually disturbed subjects sometimes refuse to complete the drawing below the waistline or sketch it in only vaguely. Omission of feet may be an expression of insecurity.

Some Adult Chippewa Drawings

In the summer of 1944, I collected Draw-a-Person drawings from Tom Badger and his wife, Julia. After my return to New York, I asked Dr. Werner Wolff of Bard College if he would assay a blind interpretation of these drawings, and he consented.

It may be of interest here to supplement Lowenfels's analysis of children's drawings with Dr. Wolff's interpretation of drawings made by two adults: (1) Tom Badger, a conservative old-timer, priest of the Medicine Dance religion, in his 70s, and (2) Julia Badger, his wife, whose fantasies were discussed in Chapter 14.[3] The drawings appear in Figures 4, 5, and 6. It may be noted that Julia drew a woman and a man together on one page at the top left-hand corner. Tom first drew a man, then was asked to draw a woman on a separate sheet of paper.

Dr. Wolff pointed out the continuous interruption in Tom Badger's line and said:

> He stutters in his drawing. There is also an absence of pressure. The man's head is very large compared with the rest of the body, and there is a strong emphasis on the mouth. Although the man is naked, he has no sex organs.
>
> In Tom's drawing of the woman there is an emphasis on the breasts. She is dressed; he covers her sex organs. Both figures have very weak arms and legs.

---

[3] Julia's autobiography appears in the appendix to Barnouw, *Acculturation and Personality among the Wisconsin Chippewa* (1950); Tom's autobiography may be found in Barnouw, "Reminiscences of a Chippewa Mide Priest" (1954).

FIGURE 4
Tom Badger's Drawing of a Man

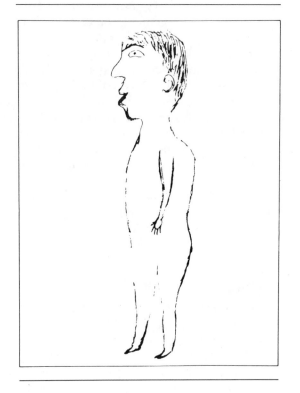

The emphasis on the head would indicate a stress on matters of the intellect over things of the body. This is supported by the weak arms and legs. He is probably a passive person, always dreaming, thinking, and not acting.

The woman is given more importance than the man through more detail, more realistic observation, more perseverance, more strokes. The woman is bigger in both horizontal and vertical size; she has attributes, such as clothing.

His strokes indicate strong inhibition, which is supported by the sexual frustration implied in his omission of the man's sexual organs.

The entire picture is very primitive. If we used a Freudian interpretation in explaining his emphasis on the mouth, we might say that frustration in the sexual sphere has resulted in a transfer to the oral region. All of the interest is centered in the upper half of the body, not below.[4]

From my personal impressions of Tom Badger, I would not have described him as being so passive and ineffectual. Tom struck me as

---

[4] Dictated to me by Dr. Werner Wolff.

FIGURE 5
Tom Badger's Drawing of a Woman

being rather practical and quite competent in manual crafts. When I knew him, he was still making serviceable birchbark canoes. He had some ability in carpentry. However, he may well have been an emotionally dependent person, for similar impressions along these lines appear in some analytic remarks made by Dr. Pauline Vorhaus about Tom Badger's Rorschach record at a Rorschach Workshop at Crafts, New York, in 1946:

> Human relationships are smooth enough. There is no underlying hostility (*Fc, FC, M*). But there is some confusion about sex. His form level is good, except for the sexual responses. He has a great deal of sensitivity and tact and gives the impression of being a conformer (*P%*). His *M*'s have a passive, holding-on quality, indicating his dependency.

Here are Dr. Wolff's comments on Julia Badger's drawing:

> She is younger. On the whole, however, she is in an even more childish level than her husband, although she has much more artistic ability and a greater "life of the soul" than he. He might have a greater

FIGURE 6
Julia Badger's Drawing of a Woman and Man
(Drawn in the Upper Left-Hand Corner of a Page)

intellectual life. She sees more details, ornaments, more individualized expression. Tom's approach is schematic. Hers is individual.

She has a high feeling for proportion, distributions in space. For instance, the distance from the head line on the woman to the breast line is equal to the distance from the breast line to the line of the feet. Her drawing is very symmetrical. The feet are right in the center of the woman's skirt. The two figures are mirroring and complementary. Notice the two bands which go to the left and the right. The woman's left foot is big, her right foot small. The man's left foot is small, his right foot big.

She shows more inner shape, patterning, and order than he; but this may be either positive or negative. Many neurotics and psychotics have a high degree of order in their drawings. They may be striving for order, because they really have none.

She shapes the woman more than the man. He has no real face, no neck, no hands. The thing the man holds is smaller than the one the woman holds. The man has no hair, but she has. She is conscious of her leading role and of her dominance over him. But she has the feeling of belonging to him—a motherly attitude, perhaps—although we can't tell from the drawings. She tries to emphasize that the woman and the man belong to each other. This is indicated by the feather on both of the heads.[5]

Much of this analysis seems valid and in agreement with data from other sources.[6] While some of Dr. Wolff's deductions are hard to assess, there is nothing in these interpretive comments which is in contradiction to the known facts about Tom and Julia Badger. With the knowledge of hindsight. I feel that some aspects of Julia's drawings might have given a cue to her rather schizoid nature. The placement of the figures high on the page would be interpreted by John N. Buck as a tendency to involvement in fantasy. It is of interest in this connection to note that in Kotkov and Goodman's (1953) study of obese women's drawings, the female drawing was found to be more often in the top left-hand third of the page than in the case of the ideal weight control group.

The stunted, flipperlike limbs suggest Mrs. Badger's passivity. The narrowness of the woman's neck is a bit exaggerated, and the conventional turned-up smile has a stereotyped, childish character. Dr. Wolff did not label Julia "schizoid," but he did point out that she is a dreamy person.

THE HOUSE-TREE-PERSON TEST

Buck's House-Tree-Person (H-T-P) Test (1948–49) can incorporate, and add to, Machover's DAP Test, particularly if a chromatic series of drawings is added to the pencil drawings. A four-page form sheet, with pages smaller ($7 \times 8\frac{1}{2}$ inches) than those used in the Machover test is given to the subject. One surface is exposed at a time, at first with the long axis of the page placed horizontally before him. (Later, for the tree and person drawings, this axis is vertical.) The subject is asked to draw as good a house (and later, as good a tree and person) as he can. He may erase as much as he wishes and take as much time as he wants.

While the subject is drawing, the tester makes observations on his behavior and times his performance. After the drawings are completed, the subject is given a rather lengthy interrogation incorporating 64 questions.

It is believed that a subject is apt to feel less self-conscious about drawing a house or tree than a person, and is less aware that he may

---

[5] Dictated to me by Dr. Werner Wolff.

[6] See Julia Badger's fantasies in Chapter 14.

be giving himself away. The house and tree were selected for this test because of their symbolic associations, their universal familiarity, and because they form among the earliest subject matter of children's drawings.

Interpretation of the test is based partly on stylistic features (for instance, shading is believed to indicate anxiety), placement on the page (use of the upper half of the page, for example, is held to indicate a preoccupation with fantasy), and symbolic interpretations of the content.

The latter have been particularly developed by Buck. Some of his symbolic equations seem aprioristic and subject to many qualifications. However, Buck's individual H-T-P analyses carry a good deal of conviction.

A subject's drawing of a house may involve many different things. The drawing may reflect such things as (1) his present home situation, (2) his past home situation, (3) his "dream house" of the future, (4) a symbolization of the mother, or (5) a symbolization of the self.[7]

Emphasis on chimneys—if they are detailed or lofty—is believed to indicate sexual inadequacy, with a compensatory assertion of virility, comparable to the drawing of a large nose or tie on the male person drawing. Abundant smoke may indicate anxiety.

The tree drawing is considered to be often the subject's most revealing self-portrait, since it involves less awareness of self-revelation than the person drawing. It is believed to express a "deeper" level of personality than the person drawing. According to Hammer (1958:172), it is less susceptible than the latter to change on retesting.

Some of the symbolic meanings attached to the tree and its parts in H-T-P literature are as follows: The choice of tree is considered significant—whether a depressed weeping willow, sturdy oak, or heavily laden apple tree. The trunk is said to represent ego strength. The branches represent reaching out toward the environment. The roots indicate the nature of contact with reality. Reinforcement of the trunk lines may suggest a striving to maintain one's personality intact, while very sketchy trunk lines may indicate a sense of impending personality collapse (Hammer 1958:184).

Holes in the tree may be expressive of traumatic experiences, and it has been suggested that their height from the ground may give a clue to the age of the trauma (Levine and Galanter 1953). Children frequently draw apple trees and seem to sometimes identify themselves with the apples. Mothers may also draw apple trees, but identify their children with the apples and themselves with the tree. A dead tree is considered a bad sign, with a poor prognosis. So is a "split" tree, in which the two sidelines of the trunk form no connection at top or bottom; this is considered to indicate schizophrenia. Many more fea-

---

[7] E. F. Hammer, lecture at Workshop on Projective Drawings, New York, summer 1961.

tures of the tree drawing are interpreted in symbolic fashion; these examples will have to suffice.

After the subject has completed the four drawings—house, tree, person, and person of sex opposite to the one already drawn—he or she may be given the same test once more, but this time with colored crayons. This series is believed to tap a "deeper" layer of personality than the pencil drawings. The subject's reactions to color may be studied, as in the Rorschach Test. The selection of colors may be of diagnostic significance—whether depressive browns and blacks are used, explosive reds, or inhibited cool colors. It has been suggested that the association of crayon with childhood may lead to the tapping of deeper personality levels. With crayons, erasing is not possible. This factor, together with the requirement to do the test all over again, may lead to a more emotional self-expression on the subject's part. Hammer (1958:208–35) has presented some case histories which support these assumptions rather well.

A possible drawback of the H-T-P Test for ethnological fieldworkers is the length of the inquiry following the test. In this inquiry Buck asks questions such as these: How many stories does that house have? Is that your own house? Whose house were you thinking about while you were drawing? Would you like to own that house? Why? Is that a happy, friendly, sort of house? Do you feel that way about most houses? Why? What kind of tree is that? About how old is that tree? Is that tree alive? Is any part of the tree dead? What part? Is that tree by itself or is it in a group of trees? What is the weather like in this picture? What does that tree make you think of? Is it a healthy tree? What is there about it that gives you that impression? Is it a strong tree?

For the person drawing, Buck asks for the age, sex, and identity of the person, what he is doing, thinking, and feeling. Is he well? Is he happy? How do you feel about that person? Do you feel that way about most people? Why?

Buck (1948–49:328–41) also asks what the house, tree, and person need most, and many other such questions.

I have made use of a modified form of the H-T-P technique in two cross-cultural studies, and it seems to me to be a promising technique. My two studies involved (1) comparisons of H-T-Ps of Japanese, Indian, and American college students and (2) an experiment designed to gauge the psychological effects of voluntary sterilization among married men in rural Maharashtra, India. Each of these experiments will be briefly described.

Japanese, Indian, and American H-T-Ps

The H-T-Ps were administered on a group basis to introductory psychology classes in Tokyo, Japan, and Poona, India, and to an introductory anthropology class in Milwaukee, Wisconsin. Most of the students in all three groups were freshmen, 18–19 years of age. There were 84 females and 28 males in each sample.[8] The students were asked to write their age and sex but not their names. Two person drawings were asked for in the manner described earlier. Students were allowed about 10 minutes for each drawing.

After the drawings were completed, the students were asked the following questions:

1. How old is the house? How old is the tree? How old are each of the two persons?
2. What is the best part of the house? What is the best part of the tree? What is the best part of each of the two persons?
3. What is the worst part of the house? (Same question asked for the tree and each of the two persons.)
4. What does the house (the tree, each of the two persons) need most?
5. Is the tree alive or dead?
6. Write a description of each of the two persons.

The Indian students were also asked to write a description of the house.

These questions, suggested by Emanuel F. Hammer, were designed as a substitute for Buck's postdrawing interrogation.

The instructions and questions were given in both English and Marathi in Poona, and in Japanese in Tokyo by the instructors of the class. Answers were generally written in the native language, later translated into English by interpreters.

It was my impression that in each H-T-P administration the students enjoyed taking the test, a welcome break in the academic routine.

No particular hypotheses were established beforehand. The aim was to see whether there were any characteristic differences in the drawings of these three groups of students, and, if so, whether they seemed to reflect differences in cultural traditions, personality patterns, or some combination of the two.

There turned out to be various characteristic differences in the three collections of drawings. Profiles and back views were more common among the Poona students than in the other two groups. Nine Indian girls drew a woman as seen from behind; three Tokyo girls drew rearview female figures, while none of the Milwaukee girls did so. According to Buck, profile and back views indicate a reluctance of the subject to face his environment, a desire to withdraw and hide his inner self. But the frequency of Indian female back views may be influenced by the fact that all three groups of girls empha-

---

[8] For an explanation of this sample and details on range of ages, see Victor Barnouw, "Cross-Cultural Research with the House-Tree-Person Test" (1969:420). The two studies are discussed in more detail in this publication, from which Tables 3 and 4 have been drawn.

sized the hair, and an Indian girl's hair, either rolled up at the back of the head or hanging down in a pigtail, is best seen from a rearview perspective.

Partial figures, showing only head and shoulders, were rare among the Japanese drawings but common in both the American and Indian samples. American heads tended to be larger than the Indian ones. Nine Milwaukee students drew large heads, filling up most of the page. This was not done by any Japanese or Indian students.

The groups of students differed in the age of the person drawn. Twenty of the Poona girls drew girls below the age of 12 years; only 11 Tokyo girls and 8 Milwaukee girls did so. 18 Poona students drew children playing (e.g., skipping rope); only 6 Tokyo and 5 Milwaukee students did so. The Poona students also tended to give lower ages for the tree in the tree drawing than did the Japanese or American students. 40 Indians gave an age below 16, as against 21 Japanese and 23 Americans. One gets an impression that in this sample of Indian girls there was some clinging to childhood or nostalgia for it. The Poona girls did not draw persons of their own age as often as did Tokyo and Milwaukee girls; nor did they draw as many "glamorous" pretty girl drawings, which may be related to the greater stress on romantic love in the United States and Japan. The Indian girls come from a conservative (mostly Brahman) section of Poona, where marriages are generally arranged and where dating does not usually take place.

References to religion appeared more frequently in the Indian girls' H-T-P descriptions (16), than in the Japanese (4), or American (1).

The Tokyo students tended to draw larger figures than did the Indian or American students, and they drew fewer small figures. This gave me the impression that there is a sense of self-confidence among the Japanese students; on the other hand; it may be related to the art instruction they receive, for according to Wayne Dennis (1966:71), "The Japanese child is taught that whatever the size of his paper his drawing should occupy most of the space available." However, the Japanese drew more small houses than did the other groups. 15 Tokyo students drew a house about two inches long or less, as opposed to only 1 Poona student and 3 in Milwaukee.

In writing descriptions of the house, the Indian students often wrote in a euphoric vein, not at all characteristic of the American students.

In their descriptions of the persons drawn, the Japanese often referred to the pressures of schoolwork and a drive for achievement. The Milwaukee girls often described the female person drawn as being popular, well-liked by others, fun to be with, intelligent, well-balanced, and warm-hearted, evidently a wish-image or ideal type.

While the data are not self-explanatory, we seem to have material here which can be compared cross-culturally. There clearly are group differences in these H-T-Ps. Some of the most interesting information to be derived from them comes not from the drawings themselves but from the written descriptions of the persons drawn.

The Sterilization Project

A second experiment with the H-T-P concerned the psychological effects of voluntary sterilization among married men in rural Maharashtra, India. Thousands of men have been sterilized by vasectomy in the state of Maharashtra in recent years in the effort to check population growth. Although interviews have been conducted with vasectomized men to assess their reactions to the operation, no "depth" techniques had been used to gauge whether or not there might be any harmful psychological consequences. That was the purpose of my own research, which had the cooperation of the Office of Family Planning in Poona.

In 1963, I gave the Rorschach Test and the House-Tree-Person Test to 100 men from three rural villages near Poona. 50 of these men had been sterilized; 50 had not. The subjects were selected by officials of the Office of Family Planning. I was not told which men had been sterilized and which had not. They were all married men, generally with two or three children or more; most were poor farmers with little education. Data were collected from each subject as to his age, number of children, occupation, approximate income, caste, religion, and number of years of school attendance. I had an excellent interpreter. The tests and interviews were given in the villages where the men lived.

In the modified H-T-P, our subjects were asked to draw a house, a tree, and the persons in the usual manner. The interpreter and I went over the drawings with each subject, asking for clarification of ambiguous features. We asked for the sex and ages of the persons drawn, the age of the tree, what type of tree it was, and what the persons were doing.

Two sorting experiments were undertaken with the data. The first experiment was to determine to what extent I and two of my colleagues, Emanuel F. Hammer and Blanche G. Watrous, could guess from the projective data which of the men had been sterilized. Hammer was chosen for this project because of his work with eugenically sterilized patients in the United States, to whom he gave the H-T-P Test. Hammer (1953) showed that castration anxiety appears in symbolic form in the H-T-P drawings of a group of subjects about to undergo eugenic sterilization. Their drawings were contrasted with those of a control group, and some rather consistent differences were found in the treatment of chimneys, branches, tree trunks, arms, legs, feet, and other items which may be seen, in traditional Freudian fashion, as having a phallic significance.

A correct list of the sterilized men was kept on file at the Office of

Family Planning in Poona. Our guesses as to which 50 men had been sterilized were sent in to the Office of Family Planning. Then we received the correct list.

A second experiment involved our drawing up a list of the 50 men whom we judged to be better adjusted and a list of 50 less well-adjusted men. On reception of the correct list of sterilized men, we were able to see what correlation there might be between the experience of sterilization and the degree of adjustment, as measured by our tests. Details of the procedures involved in the construction of our lists will not be given here; they are set forth in the article cited. Suffice it to say that our guesses for the list of the 50 men who had been sterilized were poorer than chance. We had 22 correct hits, while 25 would have been chance. But this does not mean that our experiment can be written off as a failure, for an interesting association was found between our list of better adjusted men and the sterilized list. This association is shown in Table 3.

TABLE 3
Association between Sterilization and Adjustment Ratings

	Sterilized Men	Unsterilized Men	Total
Better adjusted	33	17	50
Less well-adjusted	17	33	50
Total	50	50	100

Here it will be seen that 33 of the men whom we rated as better adjusted fell in the sterilized group. This figure exceeds chance expectations and is significant at the level of 1 percent.

Two interpretations of these data suggest themselves. One is that it was only the better adjusted men who were able to decide on and to go through with the sterilization operation. Perhaps it was the men with *less* castration anxiety who elected to be sterilized. This explanation has the virtue of accounting for our inability to correctly guess which men had been sterilized. We may have been looking for castration anxiety in the wrong group of men.

Table 4 shows that the unsterilized men seemed to show more body preoccupation in giving anatomical and sexual responses than did the sterilized men. Some of the unsterilized men, indeed, gave what we considered to be classic castration responses. One man, in responding to Rorschach Card I, said "Sterilization. Something is cut there." (A Whole response.) Another saw a broken penis in both Cards I and VI; the one seen in Card VI (upper central detail) was "broken from an operation." Still another man saw a "penis which may be cut in two" in the bottom central detail of Card V. We guessed that these men had been sterilized, but they actually had not.

TABLE 4
Anatomical and Sexual Responses in the
Rorschach Test

	Sterilized Men	Unsterilized Men	Total
Anatomical	18	34	52
Sexual	8	20	28
Total	26	54	80

Body preoccupation seems to be a widespread characteristic among these Maharashtrian peasants. According to Carstairs (1958:87), anxiety about loss of semen is the "commonest expression of anxiety neurosis among the Hindu communities of Rajasthan, and perhaps elsewhere as well." This kind of anxiety may therefore be common among both the sterilized and unsterilized men in our sample.

A second possible interpretation of the association between better adjustment and sterilization shown in Table 3 is that sterilization removes the fear of further pregnancies. Such men might have less fear of economic disaster, and thus have a more relaxed view of life. Both interpretations may have some validity. They are not conflicting.

If further work is done with projective tests in exploring the psychological consequences of sterilization, it is suggested that the men be tested both before and after the operation. Ideally, three tests should be made: (1) shortly before the operation, (2) shortly after the operation, and (3) after the lapse of several months.

To conclude, the H-T-P seems to me to be a useful research technique whose potentialities deserve further exploration in cross-cultural studies in culture-and-personality. It is easy to use, requires little equipment, and the drawings provide a permanent record of a subject's expression of personality. Allowances must be made for cultural factors, such as the differences in house types and trees present in different parts of the world. But rich material seems to be available in the use of the H-T-P technique, as well as in other procedures in drawing analysis, such as those used by Wayne Dennis, Trude Schmidl-Waehner, and others.

KINETIC FAMILY DRAWINGS

A promising field for further development is provided by Kinetic Family Drawings. Robert C. Burns and S. Harvard Kaufman (1970, 1972) have published two books on this technique, used with children, in which these instructions are given: "Draw a picture of everyone in your family, including you, doing something." This method often elicits revealing clues to the relations between the child and members of his or her family. A frequent way of handling the assignment is *compartmentalization*, placing each family member in a separate box or partition. Mothers are most often drawn cooking, cleaning, or ironing; fathers are reading the paper, paying bills, mowing the lawn, playing with the kids, or watching TV. According to Burns and Kaufman, light bulbs and lamps are often drawn by children with unsatisfied needs for love, while lines drawn under figures may mean attempts at stabilization. Much of the analysis by the authors is speculative, but many of their comments on the drawings carry conviction. This approach has not yet been tried cross-culturally, as far as I know.

SUGGESTIONS FOR FURTHER READING

I recommend the books by Machover, Dennis, Buck, Hammer, Alschuler and Hattwick, and Burns and Kaufman cited in this chapter and the articles by Schmidl-Waehner and Elkisch.

17

The Analysis of Folklore and Art

THREE APPROACHES TO FOLKLORE

One may distinguish three general kinds of studies which concern folklore in relation to personality. First, there are explorations by such pioneer psychoanalysts as Freud, Jung, Abraham, Rank, Reik, and Roheim, which sometimes range over the field of mythology and folklore at large. The aim of such studies has generally been to demonstrate the occurrence of Oedipal motifs and other Freudian features in the folklore of various societies and to provide evidence for the universality of Freudian symbolism, or, in Jung's case, archaic archetypes.[1]

A second, very different approach to folklore involves cross-cultural surveys, with scoring systems and statistical correlations. There are three studies which make use of the Human Relations Area Files and attempt to relate certain emphases in folklore to certain patterns in child training. McClelland and Friedman (1952) have studied Coyote stories taken from eight American Indian groups and scored them for the need for achievement evidenced in the tales. Their next step was to see how these findings correlated with child-training patterns in the different groups. A study along similar lines was undertaken by Child, Storm, and Veroff (1958), who obtained a sample of 12 tales from each of 46 cultures. The stories were scored for n-Achievement; the socialization practices of the groups in question were then analyzed in relation to achievement-oriented behavior. In another study, George O. Wright (1954) scored 12 folktales for each of 33 societies—drawn from Oceania, Asia, Africa, North and South America—for aggressive and nonaggressive acts. Again, an effort was made to relate the presence of aggressive themes in folklore to patterns of child training.

A third approach to folklore and its relation to personality is one which involves a more or less intensive analysis of the folklore of a

---

[1] For a bibliography of such literature, see Weston La Barre (1961).

particular society. Such an approach generally rests, at least implic-
itly, on two assumptions: first, that there is a basic or modal personality structure characteristic of the society in question; second, that
cultural integration tends to develop a certain consistency in folklore.
Contrasts may be made between the folklore of this group with that
of other societies, to highlight its characteristic patterns. Parallel features may be noted in other aspects of the culture, or in the Rorschach
or TAT protocols of members of the group. One example of such a
study is Virginia Heyer's analysis of the relations between men and
women in 60 Chinese stories (1953). Another is Margaret Lantis's
analysis of Nunivak Eskimo mythology (1953). In this case, however,
Lantis (p. 162) explicitly states that she is *not* trying to derive the basic
personality structure of the Nunivak Eskimos from their folklore,
although she *is* trying to find some "major central tendencies in emotion, attitude, and behavior and to give a 'personality construct.' "

In any event, the present chapter will be devoted to the third
approach, the one just mentioned. It does not seem necessary at this
point to review the exhaustive surveys of the pioneer psychoanalysts.
Nor will the second approach be dealt with here. This is largely because these cross-cultural studies seem rather inconclusive. The
Child, Storm, and Veroff study does not confirm the previous study
by McClelland and Friedman. Moreover, Child and his co-workers
confess that their analysis of *n*-Achievement in folktales has led to no
very conclusive results.

Wright (1954:528) is more confident and claims that "Enough consistency of trends has been found in the present study to suggest that
the relationships of child-training practices and the expression of aggression in folk tales are real and not accidental or spurious." Be that
as it may, the focus of this chapter will be on the third approach, the
analysis of the folklore of a particular society.

PERSONALITY CLUES IN FOLKLORE

Our primary question, then, is: Can one learn something about the
personality tendencies in a particular society from a study of its folklore? Certainly, the values and attitudes prevalent in a society are
often clearly expressed in its folklore. Kwakiutl folktales, for example,
reflect the great concern with rank and prestige described by Benedict, Boas, and others. As Boas (1935:176) has written: "There are
tales that consist of nothing else than the enumeration of crests and
privileges obtained by marriage or war, and in other tales also names,
crests and privileges occupy an inordinate amount of space."

The Ifugao of the Philippines are similarly concerned with status
and with the payment of debts—concerns which are, again, manifest
in their folklore. "The only emotional situations to be found in any
myths are those connected with the increase of the pigs, the chickens

and the rice, the collection of debts (or the reverse—escape from the clutches of creditors), the overcoming of enemies, the shunting aside of sorceries, evil spirits, and sickness" (Barton 1955:17). It would seem likely, therefore, that the analysis of a people's folklore would provide insights into their personality tendencies.

However, three objections may be raised against such analyses. First is the argument that the folklore may reflect culture-and-personality patterns of an earlier stage in the society's history and not those of the present. Old folktales, such as those of Grimm, may persist as a kind of cultural lag and may not be particularly relevant to the current scene. Conservatism of folklore appears in Zuñi folklore, as well as in our own. In Zuñi tales, as Benedict (1935:xiv) tells us, "entrance to the house is by means of a ladder to the roof and down another ladder from the hatchway, yet doors have been common in Zuñi since 1888 and are today universal except in the kivas." In the same way, archaic stone knives figure in the stories, rather than the store-bought knives known to the present-day Indians. We will come back to this problem presently.

A second objection to the psychological analysis of a society's folklore is that folktales diffuse widely from one society to another. For example, many stories, like the Magic Flight, and various trickster episodes, were told widely throughout aboriginal North America.

A third objection is that we cannot tell, from the presence of particular folklore motifs, whether these directly express a characteristic pattern in the society, or whether they represent wish fulfillment or reaction formations. Eskimo folklore, to cite an illustration, is full of tales expressing tension between husband and wife; aggressive women seem to be feared. Can we assume from this that male-female relations were less satisfactory among the Eskimo than in societies where such folklore motifs are less prominent? Love stories with happy endings, on the other hand, are a notable feature of our own culture. But does this mean that our marriages are happier than marriages in societies where such themes are not stressed? (There are, of course, stories of contrasting type in our culture.)

Our problem, then, is: Does a particular theme express actual relationships, wishful fantasies, fears, or reaction formations? And how can one determine which is the case?

In answer to the first of the objections mentioned, one might say that stories will not continue to be told if they are too much at variance with the prevailing values and attitudes of the society. David Riesman et al. (1953:120–31) have shown that present-day children's stories have assumed quite a different complexion from those of our more inner-directed forebears, and Martha Wolfenstein (1955b) has pointed out differences between a modern American version of "Jack and the Beanstalk" and the earlier English one. This point, reminiscent of Spengler's and Benedict's demonstrations of selectivity in the borrowing of cultural items, would apply to the second objection as well. A folktale may be borrowed but subtly transformed in the process. Such distortions and changes of emphasis should provide clues to the dominant attitudes and values of the group.

The Tlingit, Tsimshian and Kwakiutl of the Northwest Coast are neighboring tribes which share a host of folktales in common. Nevertheless, these bodies of folklore have different emphases, as Franz Boas (1916:874) has pointed out. For instance: "In the tales of marriages with supernatural beings or animals, the theme of the offended animal seems to belong primarily to the Tlingit, while the theme of the helpful animal is much more frequent among the Tsimshian." (Boas did not try to account for this difference; he simply pointed it out.) In the same way, Boas (1935:174) drew attention to a number of contrasts between Kwakiutl and Tsimshian mythology. The Tsimshian have tales in which a father turns down all of his daughter's suitors; daughters are most carefully guarded. There are, however, stories of girls who marry against their father's wishes. Such themes do not form the foundation of Kwakiutl plots. Moreover: "The love between husband and wife, between brothers and other members of the family is dwelt upon in Tsimshian tales and forms one of the motives used to develop the plot. This is rarely the case among the Kwakiutl."

Neighboring tribes, then, may share folktales in common, and much diffusion may take place between them. But characteristic patterns and emphases may still be found in the folklore of such groups. This point has been made for other culture areas than that of the Northwest Coast—for instance, by Haeberlin (1916) in his contrast of the Pueblo and Navaho tribes.

The third objection to analyzing folklore for clues to personality tendencies is that one cannot tell whether certain themes or motifs reflect existent patterns, or whether they express reaction formations or wish elements. The main answer to this must lie in familiarity with the culture and with the members of the society. Some further considerations may be added, however. The folklore of a society does not express all aspects of its people's life; and it is interesting to note which aspects of it form the focus of stories and which aspects are ignored. For example, one might expect the Eskimo to emphasize cold weather, snow, and ice, but weather is not an important feature of most of their stories. Instead, there is an emphasis on interpersonal relationships (Lantis 1953:15). Sheepherding, at the present time, occupies an important part of Zuñi life, but there is no mention of it in Zuñi tales (Benedict 1935:xiv). In the Northwest Coast area where the Clackamas Chinook Indians lived, there was a widespread interest in seasonal rituals, girls' puberty ceremonials, marriage negotiations and rituals. Despite the interest, however, Clackamas Chinook folklore does not touch on these matters. Their culture was also characterized by fears of sorcery and an interest in shamanistic cures, but there were few stories dealing with such concerns. Melville Jacobs explains this by saying that the society "had long since devised the daily means for airing feelings about these things," and goes on to conclude:

> The point, then, is that the literature served needs for which the society had not provided public outlets. That which the culture truly repressed was the tension about women, grandparents, some other relatives, and in-laws. Here is the area of tensions where the screen of culture served. This is why poisoning, shamanism, rituals, and girls' puberty rites are so conspicuously absent from the stories. . . . It was the suppressed tensions which found their way as if by subterranean streams, out into the light of literature and which thereupon dominated its expressive content (Jacobs 1959:130).

This is a useful hypothesis, which may help to explain the presence or absence of certain areas of life in the folklore of a group.

I have tried to answer three objections to the analysis of folklore for clues to personality tendencies in a particular society. (There may, of course, be other possible objections.) I have also stated two assumptions on which such analyses depend: (1) that the society in question is characterized by a more or less distinctive basic (or modal) personality type, and (2) that cultural integration develops some consistency in the folklore material, thus imbuing it with characteristic features which may offer contrasts with folklore patterns in other societies.

Folklore from two hunting-gathering cultures will now be discussed to illustrate this approach: (1) the Eskimo of Nunivak Island, and (2) the Chippewa. Let us start with Margaret Lantis's analysis of Nunivak Eskimo mythology.

ESKIMO FOLKLORE: NUNIVAK ISLAND

Margaret Lantis collected folklore at Nunivak Island, off the Alaskan coast, where she also administered the Rorschach Test to 32 Eskimo subjects. The Rorschachs were interpreted independently by two analysts, Eugenia Hanfmann and Alice Joseph. We will turn to their Rorschach analyses later. First a few general comments on the folktales.

Lantis says that the stories show a good orientation to reality. A strong ego-ideal is presented in them. Lantis (1953:139) deduces that Nunivakers have a clear picture of their own goals and work toward them realistically. "This is not a morbid mythology in which most of the characters die, overcome by the inherent conflict of their situation. Almost always, destructive forces are combated successfully." Nevertheless, there is a good deal of aggression and bloodshed in the folklore. Lantis presents a "Table of Physical Dangers in Nunivak Mythology," in which the most frequently mentioned dangers are cutting or stabbing (usually both), and biting or eating. There are many tales of decapitation and dismemberment of bodies. When supernaturals are involved, it is the spirits who cut and bite the protagonist, not vice versa. Lantis (1953:131, 135) points out that there are remarkably few cases of trickery and deceit, in contrast to Plains mythology. This contrast applies to Chippewa mythology as well, as will be apparent in the discussion of Chippewa folklore below.

A common theme in Eskimo folklore is that of a hero who overcomes obstacles. An unpublished Ph.D. thesis by Frank J. Essene, cited by Lantis (1953:156) stated that roughly one third of all Eskimo folklore falls under this heading. About half of these tales are about a poor orphan boy who ultimately triumphs over his enemies. He usually lives with a female relative—a grandmother or sister. Individual achievement is stressed in Eskimo stories, rather than group cooperative effort, which may, however, appear in war narratives. There are not many parent-child tales.

An important theme is that of the haughty girl, who rejects her suitors or leaves her husband and insists on living alone. A husband, on the other hand, is rarely shown as leaving his wife (Lantis 1953:116, 126). Mother and grandmother figures are always depicted as good, but wives are often shown to be arrogant or aggressive. Lantis accounts for this negative picture of the wife by reference to some features of the old Nunivak culture. Men and boys of five years and over spent almost no time in the family home, but lived in a ceremonial house. At the age of 11 to 13 years a girl was usually married to a strange man of between 20 and 30 years. Such marriages, according to Lantis, were difficult and full of tension. Not only were the girls reluctant, but the men were apt to be disappointed in marriage, due to the early loss of the mother (through removal to the ceremonial house) and due to their frustrated hopes for a cherishing maternal wife.

This explanation may apply to the Nunivak Eskimo, but it should be noted that aggressive and dangerous women are also depicted in the folklore of the Central Eskimo, who do not have the institution of the men's ceremonial house.

A motif singled out for discussion by Lantis is that of oral aggression. She notes that Eskimo frequently use their lips and teeth in moistening and working skins, chewing boots, and eating meat. Thus, "the people always have before themselves images of both men and women cutting and biting some part of the animal. The cannibal women cutting off human heads and boiling them is not hard for a Nunivaker to imagine even though he has never known a case of cannibalism" (Lantis 1953:135). Moreover, the Eskimo seem to have some sense of guilt for killing animals in order to live (p. 136).

Lantis deduces from Nunivak mythology that the "id-needs" of these people are not repressed. Sex and other bodily functions are presented naturally. There are strong restraints, however, on aggression. The Eskimo like to be with other people, but wish to maintain their individuality. Lantis finds that the most common defenses are wish-fulfillment, altering of reality, avoidance or flight, projection, reaction formation, and repression (p. 164).

Turning now to the Rorschach analysis, Drs. Hanfmann and Joseph scored each subject on a personality rating sheet. Lantis also scored them on the basis of her personal acquaintance. These ratings did not agree very well, but there was good agreement on the summaries, according to Lantis. She does, however, point to some areas of disagreement in the Rorschach generalizations made by Hanfmann and Joseph. While some of these may be of minor importance, others seem hard to reconcile. For example, Joseph says that the Rorschach records indicate a free expression of emotion and great spontaneity, while Hanfmann finds a high degree of constriction. Joseph sees more aggression and anxiety and describes the anxiety as "focused," while Hanfmann labels it "diffuse."

However, there are also areas of agreement. The level of intelligence is declared to be "high average"; energy is rated high, and socialization is good. The Nunivak Islanders are declared to be prevailingly extroverted and conforming, but not submissive. There is evidence of preoccupation with sex, but no conflict or guilt about it, and an indication of dependency, associated with oral aggression. Although some features, such as oral aggression, were noted both by Lantis in the folklore and by the Rorschach specialists in the protocols, the Rorschach analyses do not seem to throw much light on the folklore, or vice versa. The fact that some serious differences of opinion appear in the Rorschach analyses further complicates matters.

CHIPPEWA FOLKLORE

In contrast to the Eskimo, Chippewa tales do not stress achievement, and there are many stories of trickery and deception. This is illustrated in a long Chippewa origin myth which I collected from Tom Badger in the summer of 1944 (Barnouw 1977:chap. 2). This story tells of the experiences of Wenebojo, the Chippewa trickster culture hero. Many of the themes in this origin myth have their parallels in the trickster stories of other American Indian tribes, for example the flood and Earth-Diver episodes. But there are some characteristic features in the Chippewa cycle. If, for example, we compare this Chippewa origin myth with a Navaho one,[2] a number of contrasting features emerge.

---

[2] Aileen O'Bryan, *The Dîné: Origin Myths of the Navaho Indians* (1956). In order to have the lengths of the two narratives roughly comparable, my remarks about the Navaho legend will be confined to its first 34 pages.

Social Relations

The Navaho myth has much more collective action in that it describes the experiences of classes of animals and human groups, while the Chippewa myth describes the adventures of a lone individual, Wenebojo.

Wenebojo's mother and grandmother disappear from the story after the opening section, while the father (the sun) plays no role beyond that of impregnation. Wenebojo calls all of the animals "brother," but he trades on alleged kinship ties for purely selfish exploitative purposes. Wenebojo seems to be happiest when he is all alone. In this version of the Wenebojo cycle he never marries. William Jones (1917:423–39) presents a story in which the culture hero (here called Nanabushu) gets married, and the Wisconsin Chippewa tell a story, which had a wide distribution in aboriginal America, of how Wenebojo "married" his two daughters through a ruse. But in most of the Chippewa tales about him, Wenebojo either lives alone or is described as living with his grandmother. In the origin myth I collected, the grandmother and mother soon drop out of the story.

The Navaho origin myth represents a marked contrast in these respects. Women figure as prominently as men in the Navaho myth, and the relationship between them is one of the main motifs. Men and women have their differences; at one point they attempt a separation, but soon find that they can't live without each other and make up again: "First Woman came and threw her right arm around her husband. She spoke to the others and said that she could see her mistakes, but with her husband's help she would henceforth lead a good life. Then all the male and female beings came and lived with each other again" (O'Bryan 1956:8). Later, yucca is rubbed over the woman's heart and the man's heart. "This was done so they would love each other; but at the same time there arose jealousy between the man and the woman, his wife" (p. 33).

In the Chippewa cycle mother figures appear in the first and last episodes. In the first, Wenebojo and his two brothers are conceived when the sun causes a wind to blow up a girl's skirt and make her pregnant. In the last episode, the spirits give Wenebojo a set of "parents," who become the first members of the human race. Apart from these two episodes and the murder of a "grandmother" figure in another, women play no role in the myth whatever. The closest emotional bond in the Chippewa myth is that between Wenebojo and his adopted "nephew," a young wolf. Apart from this relationship, themes of close friendship and loyalty are absent.

Consider Wenebojo's relationships with his two brothers. The youngest brother is a stone, so he can't hunt with the other two and stays at home all the time. This begins to annoy Wenebojo, since their range of travel is limited. They must return to camp every day. Wenebojo tells his other brother that he would like to kill the stone. The brother remains noncommittal. The stone-brother has magically heard what Wenebojo said and asks, "Why don't you do what you were talking about? If you can do it, go ahead and start right now." Wenebojo accordingly tries to kill his brother.

Wenebojo beats the stone with a poleax but can't even scratch him. The stone says that he won't succeed that way. He instructs Wenebojo to build a fire and put the stone in it, and then, when the fire is red-hot, to throw water over it. Wenebojo does this; the stone cracks and dies.

This is the first death, the first murder. Now the two boys are free to travel wherever they wish. However, Wenebojo's brother walks more slowly than Wenebojo and easily gets tired. Wenebojo always has to wait for him to catch up. Finally he suggests to his brother that they dig a hole in the ground for the brother to stay in. After four days Wenebojo will come back and dig him up again. The brother agrees to this. Wenebojo digs the hole, the brother gets in, and Wenebojo covers him up. He sets up a stone to identify the place and goes off. More than four days go by, however. Wenebojo has forgotten all about his brother. When he finally remembers, he returns to the place, but his brother has gone by then and has made a road to the other world, over which Indians in the future will have to travel when they die.

Three times in this cycle irritation is expressed at being held back by others, and at one point an implicit regret is voiced that children take so long to mature and reach independence, whereas animals can walk shortly after birth.

Aggression and Duplicity

Very few themes of aggression are found in the Navaho origin myth, while murders abound in the Chippewa narrative, the victims including Wenebojo's two brothers, his "nephew," two kings of the underwater spirits, the "grandmother" figure previously referred to, and various animals. Wenebojo is himself killed, but he revives.

There are also masochistic themes. The stone gives Wenebojo instructions as to how to kill him. In one episode Wenebojo pulls out his own intestines; in another he roasts his behind over a fire; in a third he chops off his own calf muscles.

Themes of duplicity, which are rare in the Navaho myth and in Eskimo folklore, are common in the Chippewa cycle. To give one example: Wenebojo meets a collection of water birds and tells them that he is going to make a place where they can dance. Wenebojo makes a sturdy wigwam, with only one entrance, and covers all the holes in the structure. Then he tells the birds that he wants them to dance with their eyes closed. Anyone who opens them will have red eyes forever. While the birds dance with their eyes shut, Wenebojo goes about wringing their necks.

However, although it is never explicitly stated, there seems to be some notion of retribution in these stories, some conception that crime does not pay. At least, Wenebojo usually suffers punishment in these trickster episodes. On two occasions, after killing animals through trickery (one involving the birds just mentioned), Wenebojo is deprived of his meat, and someone else eats it all. The expression of hostile impulses seems to be attended by danger and some expectation of retribution.

In reading a collection of Chippewa folktales, like that of William Jones, one is struck by the recurrence of aggressive themes. A particularly cruel story, for example, concerns Wenebojo's revenge against his grandmother for making him fast. He comes home to find his grandmother enjoying sexual relations with his grandfather. Wenebojo then applies a burning stick to his grandfather's buttocks. The old man runs away. Wenebojo hopes to get something to eat, but his grandmother gives him nothing, and the next morning she says that he must fast for another day and go out hunting. Wenebojo goes to find his grandfather, kills him, cuts him up, and takes home some of the meat, which he asks his grandmother to cook. After they have eaten, he suggests that they go and bring home the rest of the meat. At the scene of the murder, the grandmother recognizes her husband's remains. Wenebojo makes her carry home some of the meat, and when they get home he tells her to cook it and to dance about the fire while the kettle is boiling. Then Wenebojo makes her eat some of the meat and tells her that she is eating her husband's penis (Jones 1917:465).

This story might be labeled an Oedipal legend. Elsewhere I have described two Chippewa stories of father-son conflicts which seem to be more directly Oedipal (Barnouw 1950:49–50).[3]

Oral Themes

The importance of corn to the Navaho is suggested by reference to it on the first two pages of their origin myth and elsewhere. Some vegetables are referred to, and there are some themes of hunger, and a mention of bread cake (O'Bryan 1956:6, 7, 8, 16, 18). But oral themes do not seem to be prominent, especially when comparison is made with the Chippewa origin myth. In the latter there are references to the mouth and to food or tobacco in various sections. As I mentioned, there are themes of oral frustration, in which food is cooked and ready to eat, but someone else enjoys the meal. Seemingly unpleasant food substances are referred to in some places, such as intestines

---

[3] The presence of such themes may be significant, for Stephens (1962:159) reports that for nearly all societies father-son conflict motifs in folklore are rare.

and vomited food. In two episodes feces float around Wenebojo's mouth.

Anal Themes

There are no anal motifs in the Navaho origin legend. The presence of such themes is a striking aspect of the Chippewa narrative. There are many examples.

A bird indicates to Wenebojo that he would defecate if he ate a certain type of grass. Wenebojo is skeptical but eats some of it. Soon he begins to defecate and can't stop. He jumps into a deep hole, which fills up with feces, in which Wenebojo floats, with the feces around his mouth and nose. Later, Wenebojo is frightened by an unfamiliar sound; he is breaking wind—something he'd never heard before.

Wenebojo envies a fox who makes a nice tinkling noise. He begs the fox to make him the way he is, so that he can make a noise like that. The fox is reluctant, but at last he agrees. He makes Wenebojo find a round stone for him and asks Wenebojo to bend over. The fox then cuts around Wenebojo's rectum and ties the end of his intestines to the stone. When Wenebojo moves, it sounds like bells ringing. Wenebojo likes that. After he has walked a little way, however, the sound becomes fainter. He turns and sees that his intestines now stretch into the distance behind him. When he grabs them, they break off in his hands. Wenebojo then hauls in his guts and throws them over an elm tree, saying, "My aunts will have the benefit of eating this stuff when they are hungry." (When Wenebojo speaks of his "aunts" and later of his "uncles," he is thinking of the future race of Indians.) Wenebojo does this a second time, throwing his guts over another tree and says, "This kind will taste sweet. That's what they'll eat as long as the earth lasts."

While waiting for some birds to cook, Wenebojo becomes sleepy and decides to have a nap. He asks his rear end to keep watch and to warn him if the South Wind men approach. After Wenebojo has gone to sleep, the South Wind men come around a bend. Wenebojo's rear end breaks wind to warn him. Wenebojo wakes up, but the South Wind men hide. Since Wenebojo can't see anything, he goes back to sleep. The South Wind men again approach. This time they have some red dye, with which they plug up Wenebojo's rectum, so that it can't make a sound. They eat all the birds and then leave.

When Wenebojo wakes up, he finds that all the birds have been eaten. He feels the red dye in his rectum and pushes it in as far as it will go, saying, "All right, you can have this, if you want it so badly. You can keep it."

Angered at his rear end and determined to punish it, Wenebojo builds a fire and roasts his rear end over it. Then he walks through some brush, leaving a trail of scabs and blood. This is the origin of tobacco. Wenebojo walks through different kinds of brush in this way, creating different types of tobacco, one kind of which tastes "very good and sweet." He also slides down a mountain, leaving a trail of scabs, and says, "My aunts will cook these when they are hungry," thus creating another type of food.

It is striking that tobacco, the Indians' sacred link with the supernatural world, has its origin in the bloody scabs trailing from Wenebojo's rectum. Note that in two of the episodes just cited products of the anal region are labeled "sweet"—a type of tobacco, and the intestines which Wenebojo throws over the tree.

The anus appears in association with the mouth in many Chippewa stories. One character believes that he is feeding his brother in the dark, while in reality he is pushing food into a woman's anus. In another story Wenebojo makes his grandmother swallow some of her own fecal matter (Jones 1917:447). Again, in Jones's folklore collection Painted-Turtle feeds Bear his own feces, telling him that they're blueberries; and Bald-Eagle suckles her children at her buttocks (Jones 1919:669, 455, 767). In an anecdote told at Court Oreilles, Coon tricks Wolf into eating his own feces. In a recent Chippewa story, which bears various marks of acculturation, the villain is punished by being thrown head first into a toilet at the order of the "king" (ōgima).

Some Chippewa stories stress the theme of punishment or penetration of the rectum. This is notable in the episode above where Wenebojo roasts his rear end until it bleeds. Other Chippewa folktales have similar features. In one anecdote Wenebojo kills a *windigo* (cannibal giant) by telling a weasel to run up the giant's anus. Reference has already been made to the story in which Wenebojo applies a burning stick to his grandfather's buttocks.

In a story told in northern Wisconsin, Wenebojo captures a buzzard by pretending that he is a dead caribou. All the birds flock down to eat his body. When the buzzard comes to eat the flesh around the rectum and pushes his head inside, Wenebojo tightens his sphincter muscles and clamps the bird's head so that he can't escape. This story accounts for the bad smell and the scabby neck which the buzzard has (Barnouw 1977:89).

Colors, Darkness, and Light

Colors play a prominent role in the Navaho origin myth, but not in the Chippewa myth. Black, white, blue, and yellow are mentioned on page one of the Navaho myth; blue, yellow, white, and turquoise on page two; these colors continue to be mentioned with frequency in succeeding pages. Colors are associated with different directions and with different worlds or layers. The second world, for example, is a blue world, containing blue jays, blue herons, and other blue birds, while the third world is a yellow world.

Only three colors are mentioned in the Chippewa origin myth: black, white, and red. Of these red is mentioned the most frequently. Wenebojo's brother becomes a "red-hot coal"; red bark is used for anklebands and headbands in one episode, red dye is stuffed into Wenebojo's anus, and his red scabs become tobacco.

Darkness and light are referred to in symbolic fashion. To enter the other world, one must cross a log (which is really a snake) over a river. On the right hand of the snake-log, the water is clear; on the left-hand side, the water is black. We also learn that at the topmost layer of sky (which has four layers), it is "always day," while at the lowest layer of the earth (which also has four layers), it is always night. Navaho color symbolism is much more elaborate and more frequently involved in the narrative.

Locality

Various specific landmarks in the regional environment are mentioned in the course of the Navaho origin myth. These cover a broad territory: Mount Baldy near Alamos, Colorado; Mount Taylor, New Mexico; San Francisco Mountain, Arizona; El Huerfanito Peak, New Mexico; Shiprock, and various other mountains and mesas (O'Bryan 1956:4 n, 26).

The Chippewa origin myth, in contrast, is lacking in such references except for a few allusions to the Lake Superior region. Indeed, the narrative is very expressive of a wandering nomadic way of life. "Wenebojo traveled here and there in every direction, and traveled and traveled and traveled. He didn't know which way he was going. He was just traveling." "The wolves had no place they could call home. They traveled just like Wenebojo did." This restless and rootless spirit is characteristic of the narrative.

The Character of Wenebojo

Wenebojo is clearly not the Western Promethean type of hero who struggles against evil for the good of mankind. When he creates something for the future race of human beings, it is usually done as a capricious afterthought, as in his creation of food for his future "aunts," and in the making of tobacco.

Apart from his murder of the two kings of the underwater spirits, Wenebojo possesses no long-range goals or purposes. He assumes various forms and manifestations in an apparent (but haphazard) quest for some sort of personal fulfillment or identification, asking animals whom he happens to encounter if they will make him look or sound the way they do. One is tempted to observe that Wenebojo is not "emotionally mature." At one point he engages in a sort of temper tantrum. This episode, and its outcome, are worth a brief summary.

In his travels Wenebojo suddenly remembers how the underwater spirits killed his "nephew," the wolf with whom he lived and who hunted for him. Wenebojo has killed the kings of the underwater spirits in revenge, but now the recollection makes him unhappy again. He sits down by the beach with his feet nearly in the water and cries and cries. He speaks to the earth and says, "Whoever is underneath the earth down there, I will pull them out and bring them up on top here. I can play with them and do whatever I want with them, because I own this earth where I am now." (Wenebojo created the world we live in.) Wenebojo then speaks to the sky: "Whoever is up there, those *mánidog* [spirits] up there, I will get them and pull them down. I will play with them here and do just as I please with them. I will even knock down the sky." Wenebojo sniffs from crying, and the sky makes a loud noise like the cracking of ice.

The two chief spirits of the universe are alarmed by these threats. They send a series of messengers to Wenebojo, asking him to attend a council of the spirits, but Wenebojo ignores them all. Finally, a white otter addresses Wenebojo as "cousin" and asks him to come to the meeting. This is one case in which Wenebojo responds sincerely to kinship relations, for he agrees, since they are related. At the subsequent meeting of all the spirits Wenebojo is given a set of "parents," the founders of the human race.

Other Wisconsin Chippewa Folklore

The outstanding features of the Lac du Flambeau myth are the isolation of the hero, the absence of close social bonds, and the recurrence of oral and anal themes.

Between 1941 and 1944, 60 folktales were collected from Wisconsin Chippewa informants at Lac Court Oreilles and Lac du Flambeau by Joseph B. Casagrande, Ernestine Friedl, Robert E. Ritzenthaler, and myself at a time when we were graduate students in anthropology at Columbia University (Barnouw 1977). These stories have many of the traits noted for the origin myth. Many tales are about two or three people living alone. We find the following combinations: two man-and-nephew, four man-and-grandmother, one man-and-daughters, two husband-and-wife, three brother-sister, one brother-brother. At the beginning of one story a young man asks his sister if they are the only people in the world. In another tale, a girls says to her sister, "I guess we're not really alone in the world." Such remarks are not apt to be made in the mythology of a densely populated society like Zuñi, but there are parallels in Nunivak Eskimo tales, in one of which a man says to his brother, "Are we the only people in the world? Are there others somewhere?" (Lantis 1946:270). Oral preoccupations are common in our collection of tales, including tales of oral frustration comparable to those already cited. There is also a common reverse theme. A grandmother figure cooks food for the hero in a tiny kettle with a grain of wild rice. The hero thinks that this small amount of food will never be enough to satisfy him. But it is a magic self-replenishing kettle, which endlessly produces more food, much more than he can eat.

A difficulty in assessing the psychological significance of oral themes in Chippewa tales is that the same sort of emphasis appears in North American Indian folklore, in general, both among hunting-gathering peoples and sedentary agriculturalists. Oral themes are common, for example, in Nunivak Eskimo folklore.[4] Tsimshian tales about Raven have the common theme of Raven's voracity, and so the whole series is marked by oral motifs. The folklore of the Zuñi also contains many oral themes. The most prominent expression of this is the descriptions of meals which often accompany the stories, one manifestation of the Zuñi tendency to embellish a narrative with details.[5]

The situation is different with anal themes. There does seem to be more emphasis on the anal zone in the folklore of the Chippewa and their neighbors than in that of most other North American tribes. Anal themes are also noticeable in the folklore of some Plains tribes,[6] and occur further west in Oregon among the Clackamas Chinook and their neighbors (Jacobs 1959:238). However, many collections of North American Indian folklore have very few anal references; for example in Boas's *Tsimshian Mythology* (1916) and Benedict's *Zuni Mythology* (1935), one can find only two or three such references. It does not seem to be an emphasis in Navaho folklore. Anal themes are not prominent in Nunivak Eskimo tales. There are several references to people going outdoors to defecate, but this is only incidental to some action that takes place outdoors and merely provides an explanation for the person's going outside. There are no themes of anal penetration, being engulfed in dung, or the other anal motifs found in the Chippewa material.

Hallowell (1947:554) noted the prevalence of anal humor among the Lac du Flambeau Chippewa: "We were not long on the reservation before all of us were struck by the fondness of these Indians for dirty stories embodying an anal type of humor. The men told them to

---

[4] In Lantis's collection of tales (1946), which is a little larger than our Wisconsin Chippewa collection, the following pages contain oral themes: 268, 270, 271, 273–76, 278, 279, 287, 290, 291, 294, 295, 299, 300, 304, 307.

[5] Benedict's two-volume collection of Zuñi folklore is much larger than ours. See the following pages: vol. 1—79, 81–82, 90, 119, 125, 133, 143, 146, 150–51, 162, 170, 188, 213, 220, 229, 238; vol. 2—6, 25, 33, 78, 80, 96, 103, 104, 109, 113, 150, 151, 169, 181, 193, 200, 209, 211, 213, 235.

[6] See Kroeber (1907:71); Dorsey and Kroeber (1903:60 n); Wissler and Duvall (1908:26, 38–39); Jones (1907:279–89); and Skinner (1916:351).

us with evident relish, and often repeated the same story on different occasions." Landes (1937:24) has noted anal humor among the Ontario Ojibwa. This seems to be an old and persistent pattern.

Why this anal emphasis? *A priori* one would not expect undue insistence on cleanliness in a seminomadic culture such as this. In the first year of life the Chippewa baby spent most of its time in the cradleboard surrounded by dried padded moss which absorbed its urine and feces. The moss was thrown away and replaced when necessary. Thus there would seem to be no pressure on the child to develop self-restraint. Nevertheless, one informant said that sphincter control was started while the child was still on the cradleboard. The baby generally slept between the parents at night. So there may have been rather early toilet training among the Chippewa. Moreover, there seems to have been some concern with constipation. One section of the Lac du Flambeau origin myth deals with Wenebojo's discovery of an herbal physic. It is also striking that these Indians, in aboriginal times, independently invented the enema syringe (Hallowell 1935; Heizer 1939). Syringes are still used nowadays to relieve constipation.[7]

Our Chippewa collection of tales is marked by a rarity of courtship themes. There is a much greater proportion of courtship themes in Benedict's collection of Zuñi tales. Benedict gives 30 tales of courtship in Volume I, which make up nearly 180 pages. Courtship themes also occur in 11 other tales. Thus there are 41 tales dealing with courtship in a total of 104 stories. The initiative in courtship may come from either the boy or girl; both kinds of tales are given. The emphasis on courtship themes is probably related to the fact that Zuñi is both matrilineal and matrilocal and had permissive attitudes toward sex. Courtship also forms a relatively prominent theme in Nunivak Eskimo tales, occurring in 19 out of 60 stories. Courtship is also fairly prominent in Tsimshian tales, but these are mostly about a man or woman who marries a supernatural-animal lover. Boas (1916:747, 759) gives 6 examples of the former and 10 of the latter.

As mentioned earlier, the family units referred to in the tales are often small and isolated. In keeping with this, we find both incest and Oedipal themes. There is one tale in our collection of incest between brother and sister and one between father and daughter. One story is about a girl who runs away from her sister, who threatens to "marry" her.

From a Freudian point of view, judging from the rarity of courtship themes and the abundance of oral and anal themes, there would

---

[7] One northern Wisconsin female informant said, "When the children get feverish, and I know they're constipated, I syringe them and make them sit right on the pot. They can't go out after that. I even syringed my husband like that. He only went to the toilet about once or twice a week. I often wondered how he could stand it. He never used anything except when he got sick" (Ernestine Friedl, field notes).

seem to have been a tendency to regression in the old culture, resulting from fearful attitudes toward the world in general—an attitude
implied in many of the tales. The absence of color references in the
origin myth may be a parallel to the characteristic color avoidance by
Chippewa subjects in the Rorschach Test and by Chippewa children
in the drawings analyzed by Lowenfels. It will be seen that this analysis agrees in many ways with the findings of Hallowell, Landes,
Watrous, Caudill, and others who have worked with the Chippewa.

STYLE

An aspect of folklore which will only be touched on here but which
deserves at least brief mention is the question of style. Frank J. Essene
refers to the Eskimo style of narration as being "terse and stiff"
(quoted in Lantis 1953:157). Boas has vividly described the method of
telling narratives in the Central area:

> Old traditions are always related in a highly ceremonious manner.
> The narrator takes off his outer jacket, pulls the hood over his head,
> and sits down in the rear part of the hut, turning his face to the wall,
> and then tells the story slowly and solemnly. All the stories are related
> in a very abridged form, the substance being supposed to be known.
> The form is always the same, and should the narrator happen to say
> one word otherwise than is customary, he will be corrected by his
> listeners (Boas 1888:564).

The "terse and stiff" style of Eskimo folklore may be contrasted
with the prolix style of Ifugao folklore which, as Barton tells us, is
hampered by the inclusion of "an enormous number of tiresome
details."

> If the myth relates the setting forth of a character on a journey, it has
> him pound his rice, winnow it twice, put water in a pot, sift in the rice,
> fire the pot, force the fire, boil the rice, take off the pot, set it by the fire
> to roast ("dry"), paddle the rice out onto a basket or wooden bowl, eat,
> put the utensils away, untuck his hip bag, take out betels, lime them,
> place the quid between his teeth, crunch it, turn the spittle red and
> thick and then spit it out (Barton 1955:18).

The character then packs what he must take on his journey, also
itemized, after which the journey itself is described in detail.

This recalls Huizinga's description of stylistic features in the late
Middle Ages:

> Art and letters in the fifteenth century share the general and essen-
> tial tendency of the spirit of the expiring Middle Ages: that of accentu-
> ating every detail, of developing every thought and every image to the
> end, of giving concrete form to every concept of the mind. [Huizinga
> gives the example of a series of sermons, described by Erasmus, to
> which a preacher devoted all of Lent. The sermons concerns the Prodi-

gal Son.] He described his journeys on his setting out and on his return, the bill of fare of his meals at the inns, the mills he passed, his dicing, etc. (Huizinga 1924:255).

Huizinga sees this tendency to elaboration as a symptom of decadence. It would be interesting to compare and contrast bodies of folklore from this standpoint and to see what features, if any, are shared by those which have a terse Eskimo-like style of narration and those which have an Ifugao-medieval prolixity.

STUDIES OF SINGLE TALES

The foregoing pages have been mainly concerned with analyzing the folklore of a particular society. Another kind of research deals with the analysis of single tales which may have a wide distribution. Many such studies are in the Freudian tradition mentioned at the outset of this chapter. Ignoring cultural differences, they emphasize presumably generic human traits, such as the Oedipus complex.

One example of such work is Alan Dundes' interpretation (1962) of the widespread Earth-Diver myth in which a culture hero, stranded in a watery landscape, asks a series of animals to dive down and bring up some mud from which he can fashion the earth. Several of the animals die in the attempt, but finally one of them comes up with some mud with which the culture hero makes the world on which we now live.

According to Freud, children usually develop a cloacal theory of birth, assuming that children are born from the anus, like feces. Bruno Bettelheim (1954) and some other psychiatrists have argued that males envy women's ability to give birth. Dundes puts these two notions together to provide an interpretation of the Earth-Diver myth. Mud and feces are unconsciously equated; in the myth a male "gives birth" to the earth made from feces.

Michael P. Carroll (1979) has produced a similar kind of analysis of another widespread tale, the Star-Husband myth, which he thinks expresses a daughter's longing to have sexual relations with her father. In another article, however, Carroll (1982:31) expresses skepticism of Dundes' analysis of the Earth-Diver tale, asserting, "I can find *no* elements in the story that support the second part of the Dundes interpretation, namely that the myth is concerned with birth-envy."

In northern Wisconsin I collected both an Earth-Diver myth and a Star-Husband tale from Chippewa informants. In looking at the distribution of Earth-Diver tales, I was struck by the fact that they have generally been reported from hunting-gathering societies, in contrast to another widespread type of creation story, the Emergence myth, in which human beings, in plantlike fashion, come up to the surface from a hole in the ground. In North America, Emergence myths are often found in settled horticultural tribes of the South, East, and

Mississippi region, while Earth-Diver stories are told by northerly hunting-gathering groups such as the Hare, Dogrib, Kaska, Beaver, Carrier, Chipewyan, Sarsi, Cree, and Montagnais (Barnouw 1977:57–60, including distribution maps).

In an analysis of the Rolling Head story, Carroll is concerned, as I was, to show what sort of society the tale is told in. As with the Earth-Diver motif, he found that the rolling head tale is told mainly in hunting-gathering societies. In the most common version of this story, a man, his wife, and children live alone. When the man finds out that his wife is having sexual relations with a snake, he kills them both and cuts off his wife's head. The children run away, and the woman's rolling head pursues them. The children try to delay her approach by throwing magical objects behind them. Finally the head is destroyed.

Carroll's analysis (1982), like that of Dundes, is based on Freudian symbolism. Decapitation stands for castration. The story expresses male castration anxiety, for in most versions it is a boy, or a boy along with a girl, who is pursued by the mother's head. In hunting-gathering societies, adult males are away from home much of the time, hunting game. The close mother-son relationship, combined with father-absence, accentuates the Oedipus complex and leads to greater castration anxiety. In this way Carroll accounts for the story's presence in such societies. Moreover, he argues that the Earth-Diver tale also reflects castration anxiety. These tales diffuse from one region to another, but not all audiences would be receptive to them.

Carroll's interpretation can be—and has been—criticized (see Graber 1983), but I think that it provides a good procedure for combining the analysis of a single tale with the focus on the folklore of a particular society that has been the main concern of this chapter.

It would seem that the analysis of folklore is a promising field for culture-and-personality investigations. Obviously, it must be supplemented by techniques which more directly gauge the personality characteristics of members of the society. Moreover, the culture in question should be well known; otherwise, interpretations may be wide of the mark.

THE INTERPRETATION OF ART

Can one learn something about the modal personality tendencies of a particular society from an analysis of that society's art? Some anthropologists have thought so and have attempted interpretations of art—of both style and content—from this point of view. In these efforts anthropologists have been preceded by culture historians and art historians, whose writings often verge on the field of culture-and-personality. We have just noted Huizinga's interpretation of the elaborate style of narration characteristic of the late Middle Ages in

France and the Netherlands. Huizinga found the same tendency in the painting of this period, notably in the work of Jan van Eyck, who paid the most extraordinary attention to detail. Huizinga also noted analogous features in the architecture and sculpture, in the costumes and festivals of the time and in art.

> There, too, we find the tendency to leave nothing without form, without figure, without ornament. The flamboyant style of architecture is like the postlude of an organist who cannot conclude. It decomposes all the formal elements endlessly, it interlaces all the details; there is not a line which has not its counter-line. The form develops at the expense of the idea, the ornament grows rank, hiding all the lines and all the surfaces. A *horror vacui* reigns, always a symptom of artistic decline (Huizinga 1924:227–28).

Curt Sachs (1946:93, 274) has made similar generalizations about corresponding tendencies in the arts of 14th-century Europe, including the music of that time.

A parallel may perhaps be pointed out in the arts of Bali. Here sculpture has an elaborate and flamboyant quality.

> The gates of a North Balinese temple are tall and slender, with a flaming, ascendant tendency as if trying to liberate themselves from the smothering maze of sculptured leaves and flowers, out of which peer, here and there, grotesque faces and blazing demons, their shape almost lost in the flames that emanate from their bodies (Covarrubias 1937:185).

Balinese painters of the conservative style take pains to fill all of the available space covered by a design, even to the spaces between groups of figures. As offerings to the gods, women make very intricate structures of fruit, flowers, cakes, meat, stomach tissue, and so forth which seem to present a "baroque" appearance (Covarrubias 1937:189–90, 161). Balinese music is very complex, a "delicious confusion," as it seemed at first to Colin McPhee (1946:37), who later began to discover "a feeling of form and elaborate architecture" in the music. Perhaps we can say that there is a kind of *horror vacui* in Bali, both in music and the visual arts.

Now, *horror vacui* is said to be often found in the art of schizophrenics (Kris 1951:107, 152). Perhaps in cultures having *horror vacui* tendencies in art there may be common features in the upbringing of children which tend toward a schizoid adult personality.

Herbert Barry III has made a cross-cultural survey, examining the pictorial art of 30 nonliterate societies for which Whiting and Child have data on socialization; 549 works of art were rated on 18 criteria of art style on a seven-point scale. Eleven art variables were considered to be measures of complexity of art style. Barry found a correlation between severity of socialization and complexity of design in art works.

> In the majority of cultures with complex art style . . . the typical individual learns self-reliant behavior to a high degree and is punished or frustrated for overt expression of dependence. . . . . The correlation of complex art style with severe socialization . . . apparently applies primarily to severe socialization pressures toward independent behavior rather than toward obedient behavior (Barry III 1957:382).

Among the cultures rated as having complexity of design above median, we find both the Kwakiutl and the Balinese. It seems to me, however, that Kwakiutl art does not have the same degree of *horror vacui* that one finds in Bali and in the Lowland Maya area. There is some *horror vacui* in Northwest Coast art, as manifest in slate carvings, shaman's rattles, and Chilkat blankets, but much Northwest Coast art is powerful and stately, without any fussiness.[8]

Among the societies whose art is rated as complex we also find both the Alorese and the Arapesh. In view of Barry's hypothesis, this is rather paradoxical, since the Alorese are described as being unmaternal and the Arapesh as very maternal and cherishing. Besides, the Alorese are said to have little interest in the arts (Kardiner et al. 1945:127).

Correspondences in stylistic features of the different arts of a culture or of a particular period have preoccupied many writers on the arts, such as Curt Sachs and Wylie Sypher. For Sypher there is a mannerist drama and mannerist poetry, as well as mannerist painting. His book, *Four Stages of Renaissance Style,* traces the development of the arts from 1400 to 1700, showing that analogous features appear in the literature, architecture, and painting of a particular period. "Not all kinds of styles are available at any given time, since a style is modified by the artist's own vision, and his vision, in turn, by the world he inhabits. Vision has its own history. There are 'period' styles, period techniques, period angles of approach, periods of history" (Sypher 1955:13).

The same assumptions underlie Egon Friedell's three-volume work, *A Cultural History of the Modern Age.* See, for example, Friedell's perceptive description of the rococo period, with observations about the different arts of the age: costume, furniture, porcelain, *chinoiserie,* style of conversation, and so forth (1931:vol. 2, chap. 3).

An approach similar to those just noted has been followed by the anthropologist Francis L. K. Hsu, in illustrating some contrasts between Western (particularly American) and Chinese ways of life. However, Hsu places more emphasis on content than on style. He points out that human subjects are prominent in Western paintings but relatively scarce in Chinese. When figures do appear in Chinese paintings, they are submerged in and dominated by the landscape. Moreover, these figures express no emotion; their faces are blank.

---

[8] However, Drucker (1955:170) states *horror vacui* to be a characteristic of Northwest Coast art.

Western paintings, on the other hand, are full of emotion and the depiction of human feelings. There is a great deal of suggestive sexuality, which is generally absent in Chinese formal art, although present in pornography.

Hsu believes that Western culture is "individual-centered," with an emphasis on the predilections of the individual, while Chinese culture is "situation-centered," with a stress on the individual's awareness of his proper place and behavior in relation to others. Thus, "In Western art the focus is on man or woman as an individual. In Chinese art the important thing is the individual's place in the external scheme of things. In addition, American art often reflects the inner tension of the individual; this concern is practically absent from Chinese art" (Hsu 1972a:18).

The diverse attitudes toward sex in relation to art are explained in terms of this contrast. In America sex is regulated more by internal restraints; in China it is regulated more by external barriers. There is more guilt in the Western world, but the tabooed material exerts a force which leads to its sublimated expression and enjoyment in art.

Hsu finds the same contrasting patterns evident in the literature of the two cultures. Chinese novels describe external behavior, while American novels are more concerned with what the characters think and feel. Western literature is more introspective. The union of hero and heroine is the climax of an American love story. Many obstacles may have to be surmounted to reach that point and a great deal of emotion generated in the process. Chinese novels, however, treat sex more casually.

> Sexual union usually occurs early in the narrative; it is never the climax of the story. The balance of the novel is concerned with how the hero goes about marrying the heroine properly, with the rectifying wedding ceremony tediously described to the last detail. Mutual attraction between an individual man and woman is not enough. Their personal feelings are never more important than the sanctions and assistance of the family and the society (Hsu 1972a:25).

Hsu's method, like that of Spengler, Huizinga, Friedell, and Sypher, lies in finding parallel expressions of a particular "world view" in the different arts of a society.

The same approach is also followed, although not, to my mind, with so much success, in Nikolaus Pevsner's book, *The Englishness of English Art* (1956). Pevsner finds certain "English" tendencies reflected not only in the work of some selected painters—Hogarth, Reynolds, Blake, and Constable—but also in the perpendicular style in architecture. This general method, then, is one that has been widely followed by culture historians and art historians who wish to characterize the salient characteristics of a nation, a culture, or an age.

Meyer Schapiro has pointed out some difficulties in this approach.

There are cultures which have two or more styles at the same time. Men and women may practice different arts having different traditional styles. There may be class or regional variations within a culture, and the religious art may differ from the secular. Moreover, one of the arts may serve as an important avenue of expression, while others are relatively neglected.

Schapiro points out that there was no style of painting in England that corresponded to Elizabethan poetry and drama, nor was there a true parallel in 19th-century Russian painting to the achievements of Russian literature.

> In these instances we recognize that the various arts have different roles in the culture and social life of a time and express in their content as well as style different interests and values. The dominant outlook of a time—if it can be isolated—does not affect all the arts in the same degree, nor are all the arts equally capable of expressing the same outlook (Schapiro 1953:295).

This may be granted. But most art historians have dealt with the changing styles of Western Europe, which has undergone tremendous cultural changes since the Middle Ages. We may expect to find more homogeneity in the arts of non-Western cultures which have had enough stability to achieve some cultural integration. And if there is such a thing as basic or modal personality, it should find some expression in the different arts of a society.

Very little has been done in the psychological interpretation of non-Western art, but some explorations in this field may be singled out. Douglas Fraser, for example, has contrasted Mundugumor and Tchambuli sculpture in ways that seem to accord with Mead's generalizations in *Sex and Temperament* (see Chapter 5). Fraser speaks of Mundugumor art as having "an overpowering emphasis on aggressive qualities," while of Tchambuli art he writes:

> The forms and their expression, in comparison with those of the Mundugamor [*sic*], are markedly less aggressive; they are more lucid in their internal relationships, more languid in their quality. But Tchambuli art is limited in projection and range. . . . The Tchambuli, while not exactly all sweetness and light, is graceful and sensuous. Essentially it is self-involved. The Mundugamor, on the other hand, is filled with double images, positive-negative relationships, and uneasy juxtapositions. Its formal structure is difficult to grasp; its total effect is completely disturbing (Fraser 1955:19–20).

Influence of the Arts on Thought and Behavior

In this chapter we have considered ways in which folklore and art express personality patterns, but these arts must also be seen as influencing thought and behavior. The Balinese drama of Rangda and

Barong, while perhaps expressing projections of parental figures,[9] also seems to reinforce these identifications in the minds of the audience, which includes young children. This is a field which needs more investigation. A pioneer effort in this direction is an analysis of Indonesian proletarian drama (*ludruk*) by James L. Peacock (1968). The author shows that some of the plots in these dramas glorify proletarian young men who rise in status without their parents' help. In various ways the plots encourage modernization and the judging of people in terms of what they can do instead of class origin. The dynamic nature of this drama is contrasted with the escapist ritual drama of Bali. "By encouraging people to break with parents, speak Indonesian, be egalitarian, join national groups, go to school, follow youthways, ludruk fosters the flowering of friendship as an institution" (p. 228). Peacock's adventuresome analysis of *ludruk* should encourage others to explore the influence of the arts on thought and behavior in other sociocultural contexts.

SUGGESTIONS FOR FURTHER READING

On oral literature in general, see Alan Dundes, "Oral Literature," in *Introduction to Cultural Anthropology. Essays in the Scope and Methods of the Science of Man,* ed. James A. Clifton (Boston: Houghton Mifflin, 1969), pp. 117–29; Alan Dundes, ed., *The Study of Folklore* (Englewood Cliffs, N.J.: Prentice-Hall, 1965), and Stith Thompson, *The Folktale* (New York: Dryden Press, 1951). For sociopsychological emphasis, see J. L. Fischer, "The Sociopsychological Analysis of Folktales," *Current Anthropology* 4 (1963), pp. 235–95. I have discussed recurrent themes in Central Eskimo folklore in Victor Barnouw, *An Introduction to Anthropology, vol. 2: Ethnology,* 3d ed. (Homewood, Ill: The Dorsey Press, 1978), pp. 275–78. A good source of Central Eskimo folklore is Knud Rasmussen, *Intellectual Culture of the Iglulik Eskimos,* Report of the Fifth Thule Expedition, 1921–24, vol. 7, no. 1 (Copenhagen, 1929). There are many published collections of Chippewa folklore, perhaps the best of which is William Jones's *Ojibwa Texts.* See also J. P. B. de Josselin de Jong, *Original Odžibwe Texts* (Baessler-Archiv, V) (Leipzig and Berlin, 1913), pp. 5–30, for a version of the Wenebojo cycle. Recurrent themes in Aymara folklore are presented in Weston La Barre, "The Aymara: History and Worldview," in *The Anthropologist Looks at Myth,* ed. Melville Jacobs and John Greenway (Austin, Texas: University of Texas Press, 1961), pp. 130–44. L. Bryce Boyer, a psychoanalyst who has had a long personal acquaintance with Apaches, has written about Apache childhood, personality patterns, and folklore in *Childhood and Folklore: A Psychoanalytic Study of Apache Personality* (New York: Library of Psychological Anthropology, 1979).

A classic of art history which approaches the border of culture-and-personality is Heinrich Wölfflin, *Principles of Art History. The Problem of the Devel-*

---

[9] See pages 124–26.

opment of Style in Later Art, trans., M. D. Hottinger (New York: Dover Publications; first published in 1915). See also Arnold Hauser, *The Social History of Art* (New York: Vintage Books; 4 volumes, 1957–61).

For an imaginative paper on art styles which, like that of Herbert Barry III, makes use of the cross-cultural files, see J. L. Fischer, "Art Styles as Cultural Cognitive Maps," *American Anthropologist* 63 (1961), pp. 79–93.

PART FIVE

Some Applications

18

Culture and Mental Disorders

Large-scale surveys of both urban and rural areas in North America have shown apparently high incidence rates of emotional disorder. Marvin K. Opler (1967:265), for example, claimed that 80 percent of New Yorkers suffer from some emotional disability,[1] while a large-scale investigation of a rural area in Canada classified 18 percent of the population as significantly impaired psychiatric cases and found only 19 percent of the total sample free of any symptoms (Leighton 1961:29–31). At the same time, some writers who wish to remove the stigma of sickness from those so characterized assert that there is no such thing as mental illness. Thomas Szasz (1961) has argued that the model of organic ailment is a false analogy.

In support of the "no sickness" model is the fact that many cases of mental disorder seem to have no organic impairment; they are "functional," psychogenic in origin. But not all psychiatrists or psychologists would agree to that. Bernard Rimland (1969), for one, believes that most mental disorders probably do have an organic basis, but our present limited knowledge does not allow us to identify the organic defects in many cases.

Related to these issues is the question of cultural relativity. Ruth Benedict (1934:chap. 8) pointed out that some behavior (trance, possession, visionary experience, homosexuality) which is considered abnormal in our society is held to be normal in others, while some behavior considered normal in our society is seen as abnormal in others. For example, a man with strong achievement motivation and initiative might be branded as a witch by the Zuñi. Should we adopt a statistical view of abnormality, counting those who deviate from a norm as "sick" persons? Benedict counseled against such an approach. Erich Fromm (1944) even argued that the majority of persons in a society may suffer from "culturally patterned defects" associated

---

[1] His figure is based on the Midtown Manhattan study of 1962, which revealed a serious mental health impairment rate of 23.4 percent of the population as compared with a "well" frequency of 18.5 percent and a combined "mild-moderate" representation of 58.1 percent (Srole et al. 1962).

with behavior which is culturally approved but which may be emotionally crippling. Fromm, then, would tend to have an absolute view of emotional health, transcending cultural differences, in keeping with a fulfillment model of personality. Fromm (1955:7–10) has made use of multiple criteria to gauge the relative sanity of societies: not just hospital admission rates (which might only reflect increasing care), but also rates for suicide, homicide, and alcoholism.

The sickness model of mental health has been associated with a taxonomy of disorders, such as those for organic ailments. We use terms such as manic-depression, schizophrenia, hebephrenia, catatonia, hysteria, neurosis, and many others. The putative advantage of such classifications is that a differential diagnosis should lead to a specific course of treatment. A drawback, however, is that different psychiatrists often apply different labels to the same patient. Walter Mischel (1968:194) observes that although it is possible to get reasonable agreement among raters for very broad categories of deviant behavior, such as "organic," "psychotic," or "characterlogical," less gross psychiatric classifications cannot reliably be made.

Karl Menninger (1963:32) who has campaigned for nearly 50 years against the psychiatrists' urge to classify mental disorders, argued that the best way of conceiving of mental illness and health is as a continuum with the sicker persons ranged at one end and the "weller" ones at the other. All persons, in his opinion, have mental illness of different degrees at different times.

The present chapter is based on the assumption that there are, after all, such things as mental or psychiatric disorders, which may be defined as "patterns of behavior and feeling that are out of keeping with cultural expectations and that bother the person who acts and feels them, or bother others around him, or both" (Leighton 1969:180).

Opler's figures on the high rate of emotional disability in New York City lead one to ask some questions: Is mental disorder on the increase? Is there more mental disorder in modern, complex civilizations? Are there lower rates of mental disorder in simpler, nonliterate cultures? Are some societies harder to live in or adjust to than others, and is this reflected in comparative rates of mental breakdown? Are different cultures characterized by different types of mental or emotional disturbance?

These questions, unfortunately, are not easy to answer. Some writers (Seligman 1929; Devereux 1939) have claimed that psychoses are rare or absent in primitive societies, while Paul K. Benedict and Irving Jacks (1954) tentatively conclude that the major functional psychoses occur in all human populations. Unfortunately, it is difficult to make cross-cultural comparisons.

Most studies of incidence in the Western world are based on hospital admissions rates, which cannot be used for truly primitive groups. Some studies in Africa have made use of hospital statistics, but mentally disturbed persons in Africa, unless they are particularly violent, are often kept at home with their families and never reach a hospital. Hospital facilities are often inadequate in such underdeveloped countries, and diagnoses may be unreliable. It is, therefore, difficult to get adequate figures for the incidence of different types of mental disorders.

For example, some authorities (Laubscher 1938:300; Carothers 1948:80–81; Tooth 1950:25) stated that very few cases of depression appear in Africa. Both Carothers and Tooth explain this rarity by saying that there is a relative absence of self-blame and guilt among Africans. M. J. Field, however, found depression to be the most common mental illness among women in rural Ghana. Field did not work in a hospital but attended shrines where anxious persons came for help. She interviewed such individuals and accumulated abundant case material. It is Field's belief (1960:149) that African women suffering from depression would not be apt to go to a European hospital; hence the rarity of reported cases.[2]

But when we make cross-cultural comparisons, may we impose on other cultures our own conceptions of normality and abnormality? Or should we consider as abnormal only those persons who are so regarded in the communities where they live?

It would be easy to make errors either way. Let us take a particular example. W. Lloyd Warner has described a man called Laindjura, a member of the truly primitive Murngin tribe in northeastern Arnhem Land in Australia. Laindjura is famous in the southeastern Murngin country as a killer and sorcerer. He described many of his murders to Warner. These murders could not possibly have taken place as the man describes them. Laindjura tells of tomahawking a young girl between the eyes, after which he pushed his arm up through her vagina, pulled out some of her intestines, and grasped her heart. Laindjura collected some of her heart's blood and sprinkled ants on the girl's intestines, which stood out several feet. Then he pushed the intestines back into her body and fixed up the wounds so that nothing untoward was visible. After this, the girl got up. Laindjura told her that she would live for two days and then die. She went off to gather lilies with some other women, and Laindjura heard them laughing. Two days later she died.

This is only one of several such stories told by Laindjura, each of which is full of similar ghoulish detail. Warner is certain that Laindjura believed a great part of these stories. If that is so, isn't Laindjura insane? The mere fact that the alleged murders follow traditional

---

[2] There may, of course, be regional differences involved in these contradictory findings, although Tooth worked in the same general area as Field.

cultural patterns does not make Laindjura a normal man. Yet, his fellow Murngin tribesmen do not regard him as peculiar, and Warner (1958:198) says that he was not very different from the ordinary man in the tribe, although perhaps a bit more alert. "He was a good hunter as well as an excellent wood carver, and had several wives and a number of children. There was nothing sinister, peculiar, or psychopathic about him; he was perfectly normal in all of his behavior." This seems hard to credit, in view of his stories.

Let us take another example. The Saora of Orissa in central eastern India are hill people who feel themselves to be much inferior to Hindus. They believe that after death they go to a vague sort of place where life is much the same as on earth, although the quality of the palm wine is not as good. Hindus, on the other hand, go to a more splendid afterworld, where they live in palaces and fly about in airplanes. It sometimes happens, however, that a Hindu in the other world takes a fancy to a living Saora girl and appears to her, asking her hand in marriage. Verrier Elwin (1955) collected many autobiographical accounts of such courtship, telling of exciting rides through the air with Hindu suitors on horseback or by airplane, and other dramatic episodes.

Perhaps we may shrug off these accounts as the erotic dreams and fantasies of shy young girls. (One also thinks of the imaginary playmates of lonely children.) But the important point about these fantasies is that for many Saora they persist for a lifetime. If the girl continues to refuse her suitor's hand in marriage, she falls ill. Her parents, therefore, arrange a wedding with the invisible groom. This makes the girl a shaman. Henceforth, she has contact with the other world through her husband's mediation. She may become possessed; then he and other spirits speak through her. The same applies to men who become shamans by marrying Hindu women in the other world. The shaman, whether male or female, may marry a living Saora and have children. But they also have children by their spouses in the other world. The Saora women suckle them at night. They keep track of the progress of their children in the other world as they grow older and tell stories about them.

Doesn't there seem to be something abnormal about this lifetime involvement in fantasy—a fantasy which becomes extraordinarily complicated and elaborate, as Elwin's pages testify? Yet, neither the Saora nor Elwin himself consider the shamans to be abnormal. According to Elwin (1955:57, 567) the Saora are, in general, a happy people, devoted to their children. One seldom hears crying in a Saora village. The people sing as they work. They have few repressions or inhibitions, and their attitudes toward sex are frank and simple. As for the shamans, they are "almost always very good people, by any standards. They are kind and affectionate, hard-working and unselfish . . ." (p. 568).[3] Shaman girls are described as being very self-possessed, dignified, and motivated by ideals of charity.

We are faced here with the same problem as in evaluating the behavior of the Murngin sorcerer. Both the people themselves and the ethnographer in each case judge the individuals in question to be normal.

Perhaps this is the right approach, since in each case the behavior is culturally patterned, and, in contrast to such culturally patterned disorders as *windigo, latah, imu, saka,* and *pibloktoq,* which are discussed below, they are not held to be pathological by members of the society. This view would be in keeping with Ludwig von Bertalanffy's notion (1971:109) that soundness of mentality is determined by whether or not the individual has an integrated universe consistent within a given cultural framework. The Murngin cultural framework may contain ideas which are bizarre from our point of view, but Laindjura's "integrated universe" is consistent with it; so perhaps he should not be regarded as mentally ill. Laindjura's crazy notions are culturally patterned; there are other men who have the same delusions. Since ideas of this kind are rather widespread in Australia, they must be rather old. Is it possible that there have been men in every generation with the same delusions for a thousand years or more? The delusions, in their patterned form, have to be kept alive by being experienced in each generation by men like Laindjura. This is a selective kind of cultural transmission. Only some men in each generation have such delusions, just as only some men become shamans.[4]

The Murngin and Saora cases illustrate the difficulties of assessing normality and abnormality in non-Western cultures. But in the Western world there are also ambiguous cases. Many Nazi officials who were well adjusted to the Germany of the Hitler regime might be regarded as emotionally disturbed (Kelley 1947). For reasons such as these it is hard to say whether there is more mental disorder in one nonliterate society than in another.

It seems likely that some cultures bear down more heavily on the individual than do others and cause more stress. One thinks of the Egyptian town of Silwa and of the Aymara discussed in Chapter 2. By contrast there are the Okinawans of Taira, described in Chapter 8, who give an impression of being happier people. But we have no

---

[3] In evaluating Elwin's observations, it must be said that he is an excellent ethnographer but that he has a tendency to champion and perhaps idealize the hill peoples of India.

[4] Some similarities may be noted between Laindjura's "murders" and the experiences of Arunta men in central Australia who seek to become shamans. Some such men lie down before a cave and go to sleep. It is believed that during the night a spirit comes out from the cave, "kills" the man, removes his entrails, replaces them with a new set, and then brings the man back to life. The Arunta shaman's fantasy is passive; he is the victim. Laindjura's fantasy is active; he is the aggressor who does the killing and disemboweling.

comparative figures on the incidence of mental disorders in these communities.

Perhaps a general measure of stress or anxiety could be applied to subjects in different cultures. An effort in this direction has been made by Charles P. Spielberger and his colleagues, who distinguish between Trait anxiety (A-Trait) and State anxiety (A-State). The former is a more stable disposition, while the latter is a transitory emotional state. "Persons who are high in A-Trait, for example, psychoneurotic patients, are more strongly disposed to perceive the world as dangerous or threatening than low A-Trait persons. Consequently, high A-Trait individuals are more vulnerable to stress and tend to experience A-State reactions of greater intensity and with greater frequency over time than persons who are low in A-Trait" (Spielberger and Diaz-Guerrero 1976:6). These features have been measured by Spielberger's State-Trait Anxiety Inventory, a self-report schedule which has been translated into Spanish, Portuguese, Hindi, Turkish, and French, and is now being translated into Japanese, Malay, Russian, Vietnamese, Lugandan, Swahili, Danish, German, Greek, Hebrew, Hungarian, Norwegian, Polish, and Slavic. As was noted in Chapter 12, there are problems with questionnaires and self-report schedules, but this would seem, all the same, to be one way of getting a rough measure of the incidence of stress in a selected group of cultures.

Marvin K. Opler (1967:271) believes that there is proportionately much more mental disorder in our modern civilization than in simpler primitive cultures. The implication is that as civilization advances and tensions increase, the rates of mental disorder go up. This notion would be in keeping with some of the studies cited in earlier chapters, such as Malinowski's picture of the well-adjusted Trobriand Islanders and Margaret Mead's contrast of carefree Samoan adolescence with the storm-and-stress of European and American youth.

As noted in Chapter 1, the idea is also in keeping with a conflict model of personality like Freud's. If culture is repressive, an individual should be better off in a simpler culture with fewer restrictions. In *Totem and Taboo*, Freud interpreted fear of ghosts of the recently dead among primitive peoples in terms of emotional ambivalence and projection or displacement of the survivor's hostility onto the ghost. Freud noted that such fear of the dead has practically disappeared among ourselves, and suggested that perhaps this was because primitive peoples were more ambivalent than we are. This interpretation would imply that we are less neurotic than our primitive ancestors were. But in a later work, *Civilization and Its Discontents*, Freud (1930:115) expressed a different view, claiming that primitive man was better off than we in lacking restrictions on his instincts. Thus, as civilization has increased, so has sexual repression. And with an increase in such repression, one would expect an increase in mental disorder.[5] However in the large-scale cross-cultural examination by Leighton and his associates (1963) of psychiatric disorders among the Yoruba of Nigeria on the one hand and in Stirling County in Canada on the other, the similarities in the findings for the two culture areas were more striking than the differences, despite the great differences in the two cultures. Moreover, rates of hospitalization for mental disorder in the United States have been going down, not up, largely due to the use of biochemical antipsychotic drugs.

SCHIZOPHRENIA

Schizophrenia is our nation's major mental health problem, followed closely by depression. Schizophrenics make up more than half of the resident patients in American public psychiatric hospitals, and the ailment is said to affect 1 percent of all adults (Bleuler 1979:1407). In 1972 a psychologist from the National Institute of Mental Health claimed that possibly 60 million Americans were borderline schizophrenics, while there were at least 500,000 schizophrenics in hospitals and more than 1.75 million walking the streets (*Milwaukee Journal*, April 24, 1972).

Schizophrenia is not a single disease but a complex of ailments, sometimes referred to as "the schizophrenias." Schizophrenic disorders are characterized by delusions, hallucinations, or thought confusion. The patient, for example, may believe that his thoughts are broadcast from his head so that others can hear them, and he may hear voices. There may be "flattened" or inappropriate affect, with a lack of emotional responsiveness to others. There is generally a lack of drive and of goal-directed behavior, while the patient withdraws into a preoccupation with fantasies that are often bizarre. There may also be disturbances in motor behavior, with the patient either assuming rigid postures or lapsing into waxy flexibility, or else exhibiting "apparently purposeless and stereotyped excited motor activity not influenced by external stimuli" (Spitzer et al. 1978:676). Adolescence or early adult life is often the time of onset, although it may occur in late adult life, or, less frequently, in childhood. The sex ratio is about equal in the United States. In the late 19th century, Emil Kraepelin gave this ailment the name of *dementia praecox* and described it as being marked by progressive deterioration. Manfred Bleuler (1979:1407), however, now claims that nearly one third of all schizophrenics recover for good and that the psychosis does not progress after five years, but improves. Moreover, very late improvements and recoveries may take place.

---

[5] As early as 1897 Freud wrote in a letter to a friend: "incest is anti-social; civilization consists in this progressive renunciation" (extracts from the Fliess Papers, 1950, vol. 1 (1966), p. 257).

Schizophrenia and Culture

Not only are there conflicting theories about what causes schizophrenia, but there are differences of opinion as to whether schizophrenia is a universal ailment, found in all societies, or whether it is mainly associated with the modern industrialized world. Some authors, such as Mishler and Scotch (1963), deny that schizophrenia is a "disease of civilization," for it exists in primitive societies (see also Benedict and Jacks 1954). George Devereux (1980:216), on the other hand, claims that schizophrenia is the ethnic psychosis of the modern complex, civilized world. He believes it to be absent in truly primitive societies (pp. 187, 214). Cooper and Sartorius (1977) point out that good descriptions of chronic schizophrenia are rare in European medieval literature or earlier. Institutionalization for the mentally disturbed first developed in Europe in the 19th century, which made it easier for psychiatrists to discover the common features in this ailment. At the same time, improved medicine saved the lives of many infants, which allowed a greater proportion of those vulnerable to it to survive to an age when schizophrenia becomes manifest. Cooper and Sartorius also point to the influence, in nonindustrialized societies, of large extended families which may provide help and support to patients. Industrial societies, on the other hand, tend to have small nuclear families. We will return to this subject of the cultural milieu in a section on methods of therapy.

E. Fuller Torrey agrees with the notion that schizophrenia is associated with advanced civilization. Unlike some others who hold this view, however, he does not find the cause to be in the complexities and stresses of modern life. Instead, he suggests that viruses are a probable factor in the development of schizophrenia. City life, bringing large numbers of people together, creates a new vulnerability. "Many viral diseases do not exist until a critical number of people are in contact with one another and can thus spread them. Measles, rubella, and influenza, for example, have been determined to be unknown or rare among hunter-gatherer or early agricultural societies . . ." (Torrey 1980:178). Torrey points out that "A virus-like agent has . . . been detected in the cerebrospinal fluid of approximately one-third of schizophrenic patients" (p. 177), and he cites various studies that point to a biological etiology for this ailment rather than a psychosocial one. He recommends that environmental contaminants and dietary factors should also be considered.

In his review of ancient and medieval literature concerning insanity, Torrey finds no clear reference to schizophrenia until modern times. The first clinical descriptions were made simultaneously in 1809 by Philippe Pinel in Paris and John Haslam in London. Torrey provides much documentation for what seems to have been a rapid increase of schizophrenia from that time on, especially in urban centers in Europe and the United States. He rejects reports about the presence of schizophrenia in primitive societies, claiming that "there are a number of organic diseases (such as temporal lobe epilepsy, pellagra, trypanosomiasis, and brain tumors) which mimic schizophrenia" (Torrey 1980:56).

That, of course, makes cross-cultural surveys of schizophrenia difficult to carry out. Nevertheless, Torrey does draw on such studies, for he finds that many of them show that people in developing countries have a greater incidence of schizophrenia when they have been exposed to Western life and modern technology. In a review of prevalence studies, Torrey finds that northern European countries, especially the more northern Scandinavian ones, have more schizophrenia than the southern nations. In the United States, although there are some exceptions, the states with high rates for schizophrenia are mainly in the Northeast, while the low-schizophrenia states are concentrated in the less populous southern and western sections of the nation.

Does culture influence the *content* of a patient's delusions? That would seem to be the case. For example, when a patient has fantasies of mixing 1,000 Cadillac engines into the brains of all the people in his hometown and sending them spinning at a terrific speed into the sky (Billig and Burton-Bradley 1978:85), we can see that we are dealing with a member of modern industrialized society. A common delusion in the Western world is that of being controlled or influenced by rays or electricity. The delusion of control by electric currents was first reported in Europe around the beginning of the 20th century (Draguns 1980:122). This notion will be absent among people with no knowledge of electricity, as among unacculturated African Negroes. However, among more acculturated African Negroes, this pattern does occur (Tooth 1950:52). The same contrast appears between lower class and better educated middle-class Bahian patients in Brazil, among whom the latter, but not the former, entertain notions about being influenced by electricity (Stainbrook 1952:333). Some knowledge about robots is necessary if one is to act like a robot—a delusion reported in the 20th century, after the production of Karel Čapek's play *R.U.R.*, which introduced the word and concept of robot in 1921. Culture thus influences the *content* of delusions and hallucinations.

On the other hand, the general picture of schizophrenic symptoms seems to be fairly uniform cross-culturally. This was shown by a large-scale cross-cultural survey of schizophrenia first carried out by the World Health Organization (WHO) in 1966, with follow-up studies two and five years later. Nine countries—Colombia, Czechoslovakia, Denmark, India, Nigeria, Taiwan, the United Kingdom the United States, and the USSR—were included in this survey. From a

total of 1,202 patients examined, 811 were diagnosed as schizophrenic, with similar groups of symptoms being reported in the different field centers.

> The schizophrenic groups of all Centres have high scores on lack of
> insight, predelusional signs (such as delusional mood, ideas of refer-
> ence, perplexity), flatness of affect, auditory hallucinations (except
> Washington), and experiences of control. Centre scores are also high
> on delusions, derealization, and disturbances of mood, although these
> are not uniformly as high as for the first-mentioned group of symptoms
> (World Health Organization 1973:405).

Nevertheless, there may still be variations in behavior and characteristic symptoms in different groups. It has been noted, for example,
that hospitalized schizophrenic patients are less violent and aggressive in India, Africa, and Japan than in the Western world (Wittkower
and Fried 1959:424), and William Caudill (1959:233) has observed that
reports from some non-Western countries, like Japan, indicate that
schizophrenic patients manifest less withdrawal than they do in the
United States. Catatonic rigidity, negativism, and stereotyped behavior are more often reported in India than in other countries (Wittkower and Rin 1965). Schizophrenic patients in Iraq are more expressive
and show more aggression than schizophrenic patients in the United
States (Bazzoui and Al-Issa 1966:428). An African psychiatrist reports
that delusions of grandeur are rare among Yoruba paranoiacs, and he
explains this by saying that Yoruba culture demands total allegiance
and submission to ancestral cults and deities. In such a cultural climate, delusions of persecution may develop, but not those of grandeur (Lambo 1955:251).

Within the Western world, there may also be variations in behavior
and symptomatology among schizophrenic patients from different
ethnic or national groups. Marvin K. Opler has reported differences
between Italian and Irish schizophrenic patients. He found that Irish
patients had preoccupations with sin and guilt related to sex; this was
not true of the Italians.

The Italian patients did not have the elaborate systematized delusions often found among the Irish patients; instead they were given
to hypochondriacal complaints and body preoccupation. There was
more open rejection of authority among the Italians.

> [The Italians] had more prominent problems of overflow (schizoaf-
> fective features) which took the form of elated overtalkativeness, curi-
> ous mannerisms, grinning and laughing hyperactivity, or even assault-
> iveness. . . . While Italian patients might oscillate between hyper-
> activity and underactivity, or show an inability to time their activities,
> thoughts, or emotions effectively, the Irish, with no such difficulties in
> estimating time or guarding their emotions, showed an inversely large
> proportion of rich and extensive fantasy (Opler 1959b:437–38).

Fantl and Schiro (1959) discovered similar contrasting patterns among Irish and Italian female schizophrenics. They found, for example, a higher degree of sex guilt in a small group of Irish patients and more impulsive, unruly behavior and conflicts with authority figures in a corresponding group of Italians.

Anne Parsons has compared the behavior of southern Italian schizophrenic patients with American schizophrenics. In south Italy psychotic delusions concern the family or neighborhood, while in the United States delusions often relate to large-scale institutions, such as the hospital, the Communist movement, or an advertising agency. American delusions, according to Parsons (1969), tend toward abstraction, while south Italian delusions are more concrete.

The coexistence of both common transcultural patterns and local cultural differences in psychiatric syndromes is indicated in a survey by Robert B. Edgerton (1966) of conceptions about psychosis in four East African tribes: the Sebei, the Pokot, the Kamba, and the Hehe, who were discussed earlier in Chapter 10. Over 500 persons, chosen by probability sampling techniques, excluding highly Europeanized subjects, were questioned. All males included were heads of households; the females were their wives. The interviews were held in private under standardized conditions.

A striking finding of this survey is that there was considerable agreement among the four tribes in their conceptions of psychosis, and also much agreement on the part of all four tribes with conceptions of psychosis in the Western world. There were also some differences, however. "Going naked" was often mentioned as an aspect of psychotic behavior. Murder, attempted murder, or serious assault were also cited, to a degree which would exceed Western-based expectations. On the other hand, hallucinations were seldom mentioned as aspects of psychotic behavior, although the author states that they do occur in East African mental hospitals.

Edgerton does not claim that his survey supports either the view that psychoses are essentially the same transculturally or the view that they differ according to the nature of the culture. Support for either position could be derived from the results of his survey.

Rates of Recovery from Schizophrenia

The WHO follow-up surveys in the nine countries studied, mentioned earlier, showed that there were differences in the outcome of schizophrenia between more advanced industrial nations and the less industrialized developing countries:

> On the whole, two of the centres in developing countries, Ibadan [Nigeria] and Agra [India] appeared in many of the analyses among the five best predictors of favourable course and outcome, while some

centres in the developed countries, London and Aarhus [Denmark], for example, tended equally often to be predictors of unfavourable course and outcome (World Health Organization 1979:306).

Course and outcome were rated best in Ibadan, next best in Agra, and third in Cali, Colombia (WHO: 369). Offering a possible explanation, the WHO report remarks: "In both Ibadan and Agra there is a strong emphasis on maintaining the contact between the patient and his family during the acute phase of his illness, and family members often live together with and take care of the patient during the time of the patient's hospitalization" (p. 371).

Similar findings were made in a follow-up study of 66 first-admission patients (all Sinhalese Buddhists) from rural Sri Lanka (or Ceylon) five years after their discharge from a psychiatric hospital ward. Nancy E. Waxler (1979:156), who interviewed the patients and their families, using standardized schedules (and who also examined their hospital records), claims that there were consistently good outcomes among these subjects. "While WHO reports that 8 and 2 percent of sampled schizophrenics in Denmark and the USSR, respectively, are asymptomatic at follow-up, we found 45 percent of Sri Lankan schizophrenics in that category."

After ruling out some possible alternative explanations for the favorable outcomes, Waxler found the crucial consideration to lie in sociocultural factors: the traditional family structure, native treatment systems, and common beliefs and values. Waxler, therefore, prefers a social labeling model to a medical model in relation to schizophrenia. Presumably, the Sri Lankan patients were not stuck with a pejorative label and subjected to isolation, as patients so often are in the Western world.

The supportive role of the family has been noted in reports in some other developing nations, as in Guthrie and Szanton's description of folk treatment (1976) for schizophrenia in the Philippines and J. G. Kennedy's account (1967) of Nubian Zar ceremonies. "Treatment goes on within the family structure; the patient is not put away or even sent to the hospital. . . . The family keeps him in their midst . . . They do not hold him personally responsible for his aberrant behavior" (Guthrie and Szanton 1976:161).

DEPRESSION

Depression and mania are classified as affective disorders. Manic-depression is a bipolar disorder in which the patient fluctuates between depressed and manic phases, but persons suffering from a major depression may never have a manic episode. Depression is one of the most widespread mental disturbances, although it is difficult to characterize precisely, and it has sometimes been said to be absent in some non-Western societies. The symptoms reported by patients in more than three fourths of cases include: "feelings of inadequacy and helplessness, loss of motivation, psychomotor retardation, indecisiveness, crying spells, loss of interest and enjoyment, fatigability, sleep disturbance, pessimism, dejected mood, and self-devaluation" (Glazer, Clarkin, and Hunt 1981:4). Manic episodes, on the other hand, are characterized by hyperactivity and grandiose feelings of self-confidence, accompanied by distractibility. The patient may be very talkative with flights of ideas, jumping erratically from one topic to another.

Several studies (Weissman and Klerman 1977; Seiden 1982) claim that women have a higher incidence of depression than men. Such reports are based on *treated* depressives. On that basis it is said that women outnumber men by two to one in the United States, England, and Sweden, and by three to one in Denmark (Fredén 1982:59). In rural Ghana, according to Field (1960:149), the majority of depressed patients are women. In Zambia 42 percent of all new female patients in 1974–75 were diagnosed as suffering from depression (Rwegellera and Mambwe 1977).

Various explanations have been offered for the higher incidence of female depressives, including physiological and hormonal interpretations on the one hand and sociocultural explanations on the other. The experiences of menstruation, childbirth, and menopause have been invoked, along with female lower status, household drudgery, and the greater difficulty for women than for men to express feelings of aggression. This blocked aggression, it has been argued, becomes turned against the self. Gove and Tudor (1973) believe that the woman's role in modern industrial societies is particularly vulnerable to mental illness, leading to higher rates for women than for men. Preadolescent males may experience more stress and have higher rates of illness than females, but by late adolescence females seem to undergo more stress (Gove and Herb 1974). Another explanation for higher female rates of reported cases is that it is less shameful for women to admit unhappiness and weakness than for men, and hence they are more apt to consult a psychiatrist. Nowadays manic-depression is treated by drugs, such as lithium, so that most manic-depressives need not be hospitalized for any great length of time.

While the basic disorder may be the same, depression may take on different manifestations. Fredén (1982:62) claims that depression in men may take the form of alcohol abuse. *Susto*, an ailment found in Central and South America, referring to "soul loss," has symptoms similar to those of "agitated depression" in Western psychiatry. It is characterized by sudden fright and fear of witchcraft (Marsella 1980:255; Gillin 1948). In rural Ghana depressed women often accuse themselves of being witches. "Witchcraft meets . . . the depressive's needs to steep herself in irrational self-reproach and to denounce herself as unspeakably wicked" (Field 1960:38).

There has been disagreement among psychiatrists as to whether feelings of guilt and unworthiness are found in unacculturated non-Western societies. Marsella (1980:261) states that they are often absent and that "Oftentimes, it is only when individuals in non-Western societies become more Westernized that we find similarities in the patterns of depression found in the Western world." In a review of psychiatric cases in sub-Saharan Africa, G. Allen German (1972) claims that guilt and self-depreciation are rare. In Ghana, however, they certainly seem to be present, judging from Field's data, and in a general transcultural review, K. Singer (1975:297) has expressed doubt that there are significant deviant features in non-Western societies: "Similarities considerably outweigh differences across cultures. A conglomeration of features—depressive mood, diurnal variation, fatigue, insomnia, loss of interest, weight loss, periodicity, and the biphasic nature of the illness—appears to be found consistently in all cultures."

CULTURALLY PATTERNED DISORDERS

In studying mental disorders in non-Western societies, one can either look for the traditional neuroses and psychoses of the Western world, as we have done for schizophrenia and depression, and so classify mentally disturbed individuals, or else one can approach the subject from the indigenous viewpoint. In most societies there are terms for mental disorders; one can learn what these terms are and then find to which persons they are applied. The Berndts (1951) used this approach in a study of Australian aboriginal concepts of abnormality. But the most elaborate application of this method is in a work by George Devereux.

Devereux (1961:19, 20) presents Mohave terms for different types of sickness and the traditional symptoms associated with them. He points out that the patient's knowledge of what disease he is suffering from may lead to a kind of unconscious "malingering," so that the appropriate symptoms appear in due course. That such processes are at work is suggested by the fact that the shamans who specialize in certain cures are frequently most effective in removing the symptoms.

This suggests one way in which culturally patterned disorders may come to characterize certain societies. Among disorders which appear to be culturally patterned are *windigo, latah, imu, saka,* and *pibloktoq.* These ailments appear to be sufficiently distinct, so that the native terms for them have been retained when they are discussed in the literature.

Windigo

The *windigo,* or *wiitiko,* psychosis is a form of disorder formerly found among Chippewa, Cree, and Montagnais-Naskapi Indians in

Canada, characterized by cannibalistic impulses and delusions. In these cases the affected individual, who is usually deeply depressed, may believe that he has been possessed by the spirit of a *windigo*, or cannibal giant with a heart or entrails of ice. He may also have symptoms of nausea, anorexia, and insomnia and may see the people around him turning into beavers or other edible animals (like Charlie Chaplin's famished companion in *The Gold Rush*). Indeed, the disorder has been attributed to the experience of starvation and isolation in wintertime (Landes 1938a; Cooper 1933).[6]

Charles A. Bishop believes that *windigo* beliefs developed particularly after the period of fur trade competition between the Northwest Company and the Hudson's Bay Company from the 1780s to 1821, which led to such depletion of game that after 1810 starvation became a serious danger for the Ojibwa. "Thus it was through both increasing occurrences of human cannibalism and the extension of the belief system to include this stress-induced behavior, that human Windigos and the concomitant psychosis were invented" (Bishop 1975:247).

Seymour Parker is skeptical about the emphasis on famine conditions to account for *windigo* behavior for two reasons: First, those who suffer from the psychosis are not always threatened by starvation. Second, there are peoples, such as the Eskimo, among whom starvation is a frequent danger but where no analogue of the *windigo* psychosis has developed. Hence Parker suggests a psychoanalytic interpretation, influenced by Abram Kardiner's views, in which the pattern is ultimately traced to frustrated dependency needs in childhood. The prototype of the cannibal giant is seen to be the frustrating mother. Parker accepts a statement by Landes to the effect that women rarely succumb to this ailment; it particularly affects men who have had repeated failures in hunting. Parker suggests that such men feel abandoned and worthless, not only because they have no food, but because they feel bereft of their power.

> Under these conditions, the dam (constituted by ego defenses) is shattered and the repressed cravings for the expression of dependency and aggressive needs bursts forth. The depressive conflict between the rebellious rage and the submissive fear is resolved. If this interpretation is correct, then the psychotic symptoms serve, at the same time, to allay dependency cravings (by becoming one with the object of dependency) and to aggress against this frustrating object (by killing and eating it) (Parker 1960:620).

---

[6] Vivian J. Rohrl (1970) has suggested the possibility that biological factors, particularly vitamin deficiency, contribute to *windigo* psychosis. Rohrl notes that a traditional "cure" of *windigo* symptoms was to feed the victim fatty meat, and she suggests that the Indians somehow acquired a half-conscious "knowledge" of the relationship between dietery deficiency and psychosis, as this custom implies. Jennifer Brown (1971), however, has taken issue with this suggestion, pointing out that fatty meat eating is seldom mentioned as a *windigo* cure. Moreover, in the two such cases which are cited its main purpose was not to give nourishment but to induce the vomiting up of the cannibal's "heart of ice."

In criticism of Parker, both Raymond D. Fogelson and Thomas H. Hay (discussed later) point out that most American Indians have been described as having strong "oral" dependency needs, but they do not all have the *windigo* syndrome. Hence, an explanation of the *windigo* psychosis in terms of Ojibwa modal personality would not seem to be sufficient. However, there seems to be some support for a psychoanalytic interpretation of *windigo* psychosis in William M. Bolman's account of a 37-year-old single white female patient, a secretary whose symptoms had some similarities to *windigo* cases. The patient obsessively bought and hoarded hamburgers. For the first two years of this behavior, she bought from 2 to 5 pounds of raw hamburger a day, but this steadily increased to huge quantities of about 60 pounds a day. The patient was acutely anxious. Indeed, Bolman states that "anxiety" is too mild a word, "stark terror" being more appropriate. After nearly three years of treatment, the patient began to express some ideas about herself. She had had a fantasy that she was a dangerous, murderous person, who killed people as they slept and ate them. Her mother, her dead father, and her younger sister were all associated with the hamburgers. Fear of separation or loss of these ambivalently regarded persons seems to have contributed to the obsessive hamburger hoarding. The patient did not, however, eat the hamburgers but kept the raw meat until after it became rotten. An interesting parallel with the *windigo* syndrome is that the patient said that when she was out at night looking for places where she could buy hamburgers, she was like ice inside. The cannibalistic impulse seems to have been mainly unconscious, although expressed in fantasy and enacted symbolically in her rituals with hamburgers (Bolman 1966).

Raymond D. Fogelson (1965) holds that the *windigo* "psychosis" is not a unitary phenomenon. He has tried to break down the reported *windigo* cases into five basic types, with some subtypes. Fogelson believes that these variants represent different forms of mental disorder ranging from mild and severe episodes of anxiety neurosis to full-blown psychoses.

Morton Teicher (1960) has canvassed the available literature on the *windigo* psychosis and has identified 70 cases, of which 45 were Chippewa (or, following Teicher, Ojibwa with 30 cases and Saulteaux with 15). The others were Montagnais-Naskapi (11 cases), Cree (9), Beaver (1), Tête de Boule (1) and 3 of unknown source. Most of the cases were from northeastern Canada and occurred in the 19th century. In 44 of the episodes, cannibalism actually took place; it was a real threat in the others as well. About half of the *windigo* sufferers were killed by members of the community. Of the 44 cases involving cannibalism, members of the immediate family were eaten in 36 cases. Teicher believes that this is because of the nature of the social order, with small isolated families often living alone. Forty of the 70 cases were males; 29 were females, and in one case the sex was not specified.

(The relatively high number of female *windigo* sufferers does not argue well for Parker's theory.) Teicher estimates that, at most, 25 of the 70 cases were associated with famine conditions. In these cases the term *psychosis* seems to be inappropriate, for Teicher points out that these individuals killed from hunger and sometimes had the support of others in violating the taboo on cannibalism. It was only in their later behavior that members of this group showed mental disturbances, which would suggest a different psychodynamic picture for the development of the disorder in these cases.

Teicher thinks that *windigo* cases must have been rare. The number must have been much greater than the 70 cases he records, since these depended on the presence of a white recorder. Even so, Teicher is struck by the rarity of reported cases.

Thomas H. Hay (1971:17) writes that "Since cannibalistic impulses are frequent among psychotic people in all societies, *windigo* cannibalism is not to be explained by peculiarities of the psychodynamics common to the Northern Algonkians." As mentioned earlier, Hay rejects Parker's psychoanalytic interpretation. At the same time, he gives some weight to psychodynamic considerations, such as Freud's idea that by introjecting (eating) a lost love object, a bereaved person may have the feeling that he is bringing him or her back to life. Hay cites Fenichel's suggestion that cannibalism may have the unconscious significance of preserving a relationship. In many cultures ritual cannibalism has this connotation, and there seems to be a manifestation of this notion in the strange behavior of the hamburger hoarder described earlier. Cannibalism was regarded with horror, at least on a conscious level, by the northern Algonkians, and patterns of ritual cannibalism were not available. But an opening wedge for *windigo* behavior, which Hay cites as a contributory factor, was the Algonkian emphasis on individual acceptance of unconscious promptings, as reflected in dreams.

Kiowa Apache Ghost Sickness

As Freeman, Foulks, and Freeman (1976:125) have noted, Ghost Sickness involving delusions and fantasies is remarkably prevalent among the Kiowa Apache.

> Eighty-five percent of Kiowa Apache adults report having experienced a partial syndrome restricted to cannibalistic fantasies with concomitant gastrointestinal psychophysiological reactions, occurring at the time of mourning. In 69 percent of the population, these cannibalistic features were accompanied by overt ghost fears. In 46 percent the ghost fears and cannibalistic fantasies were sufficient to cause a severe eating disturbance. Fifteen percent developed the fullblown "Ghost Sickness" reaction, including all of the previous features plus an actual attack and twisting by the ghost.

The authors attribute delayed maturation and ambivalence of emotions to Kiowa Apache youths of the past culture, continuing into the present, and they see Ghost Sickness as a form of regression at the time of mourning. "The mourner is both pulled toward the ghost, in his wish for reunion, and is terrified of the touch of death and of oral incorporative reengulfment" (Freeman, Foulks, and Freema 1976: 169). Some aspects of this syndrome are reminiscent of *windigo*. It would seem that the Kiowa Apache must experience a good deal of general stress or Trait anxiety, in Spielberger's terms.[7]

Latah, Imu, Saka, and Pibloktoq

These disorders are grouped together (although they are reported for different geographical areas), since they have a number of features in common and are generally considered to be forms of hysteria, primarily affecting women. *Latah,* found in Southeast Asia and Indonesia, involves a startle reaction; the subject is easily frightened and may cry out. She then engages in compulsive imitative behavior, repeating actions she has observed (echopraxia) or phrases she has heard (echolalia) (Van Loon 1926).

David F. Aberle has described *latah* behavior in Mongolia, which is similar except that here men seem to be often the victims.

> He may put his hand in the fire when the investigator merely gestures toward it, or undress completely when some one takes off an outer garment, or jump in the river when some one pretends to start to jump. . . . A severe latah may react imitatively in any novel or disturbing situation, such as meeting a stranger or a superordinate, even when the other person has no wish to provoke imitation. The latah may imitate natural objects or animals, in the absence of any human audience (Aberle 1961:471).

Aberle says that a man who has been frightened may shout obscene exclamations (coprolalia), especially words for male and female genitalia.

Imu is a somewhat similar condition found among the Ainu of northern Japan. It particularly affects older women, although it is sometimes found among young girls. Winiarz and Wielawski (1936) report that its incidence is frequent. In three Ainu villages of 1,000 there were 12 *imu* cases. In five of these the symptoms developed right after the woman had been bitten by a snake. Other cases were also related to snakes, either through seeing or dreaming about one. The attack may be started if someone pronounces the word for snake or any loud sharp sound. The woman affected may then curse and engage in excited aggressive behavior or else run away in panic. Echopraxia and echolalia also appear. As in Indonesia and Mongolia,

---

[7] See page 358.

the victim is aware of the incongruity of her behavior but cannot stop herself, and she continues with her compulsive mimicry until worn out. Women often claim to feel better after an attack.

Although it is not known why, there has been a dramatic decrease in the incidence of *imu* in recent years, dropping from 111 cases in 1934 to only 1 case in 1958 (Kumasaka 1964).

Not all writers agree in classing *latah* and *imu* as forms of hysteria. Tadeusz Grygier (1948:92) says that the symptoms of *imu* correspond roughly to the Western standard of catatonia and not of hysteria. Benedict and Jacks (1954:386) take the same view of *latah*, and, with some qualifications, of *pibloktoq*.

Marvin K. Opler (1967:279–80) classifies *latah, imu, pibloktoq,* and *amok* as "nuclear forms of schizophrenias" (distinguishable from chronic and paranoid types) which are open to spontaneous remission or curable by shamanism or other techniques. They could also be called forms of "hysterical psychosis," which are characterized by "a sudden and dramatic onset temporally related to a profoundly upsetting event or circumstance. Its manifestations include hallucinations, delusions, depersonalization and grossly unusual behavior" (Hollender and Hirsch 1964:1073).

Saka is described as a form of hysteria found among women of the Wataita tribe in Kenya. Grace Harris gives the following picture:

> Women beginning to have attacks of saka sometimes show evident signs of a generalized restlessness and of anxiety. However, sometimes without any obvious warning a woman begins the characteristic convulsive movements. The upper part of the body trembles but often the head and shoulders are more affected so that, while the shoulders shake rapidly, the head is moved rhythmically from side to side. As the attack continues the eyes may close and the face becomes expressionless. Some women perform certain simple acts in monotonous repetition, or they repeat strange sounds which are supposed to be foreign words (Harris 1957:1047–48).

Harris states that in some localities half the married women have occasional *saka* attacks. The precipitating cause might be the sight of a motor car, some bright cloth, or some bananas, or the sound of a train whistle or the sight or smell of a cigarette.

One form of cure for *saka* is to have the woman drink water in which a man's lower garment has been washed. A woman may also ask to suck some of her husband's blood. There is also a public form of therapy, a *saka* dance, in which the women wear bright cloth garments saved for such occasions, a red fez or a man's felt hat, bandoliers, and perhaps a man's belt around the waist. The purpose of the dance is to get the women "all danced out," so that they won't have more attacks.

Pibloktoq is a disorder found among Polar Eskimo in northern

Greenland. It may affect both sexes, but more commonly women. The subject is at first irritable or withdrawn, then engages in a burst of violent excitement. He may shout, tear off his clothes, break things, and then run out across the ice. Friends and relatives chase after him and try to keep him from harming himself. After this period of excitement, the subject sometimes has convulsive seizures and then may fall asleep. On awakening he may be perfectly normal and have no memory of the attack. In this respect there seems to be a contrast with *latah* and *imu*, also in the lack of emphasis on echolalia and echopraxia. *Pibloktoq* sometimes has a high incidence, especially in winter, and a number of persons living in a small community may be afflicted in the course of a season (Wallace 1972:370–72).

Somewhat similar disorders have been described for the Ona and Yahgan of Tierra del Fuego, but the information is scanty (Coriat 1915–16).

Some Interpretations

A number of theories have been put forth to account for the manifestations of *latah*, *imu*, *saka*, and *pibloktoq*, either separately or as a group. Some have attributed *latah*-like reactions to racial factors (since they often appear among Mongoloids) or to climatic extremes. P. M. Yap (1951) observes that both of these theories are rendered unlikely by the fact that similar disorders have been reported for Caucasoids in Maine—the "jumping Frenchmen." The similarity of *saka* in Kenya to *latah* has also been noted. Yap (1952) points out, as Van Loon has also done, that most cases of *latah* are middle-aged women. These women, moreover, tend to come from the lower social strata of their communities and to be uneducated. Yap remarks that those subject to *latah* do not have strongly integrated personalities and are passive, submissive individuals. He also claims that a low level of technological development is characteristic of all cultures where *latah*-like behavior appears.

David F. Aberle suggests that *latah* behavior is a form of defense against the fear of being overwhelmed. This defense consists partly in identifying with the aggressor—through imitation.

> They "go over to" (identify with) the stimulus, flee from it, destroy it—or stifle the unconscious material with a cry. . . . My present guess (and it is only that) is that the latah 's problem is one of disturbance and ambivalence with respect to submissive behavior, that this disturbance is based on an unconscious connection between submission and a dreaded and desired passive sexual experience akin to being attacked, and on the idea that the world stands ready to "overwhelm" the victim in this double sense (Aberle 1961:474–75).

H. B. M. Murphy (1976) believes that *latah* subjects probably have repressed sexual wishes and masochistic tendencies resulting in a failure to defend against the initiating stimulus. They are hypersuggestible and have an inflexible impulse control which accounts for their exaggerated startle reactions. He suggests that such personality tendencies are fostered by child-rearing practices that are widespread in Malaysia: "much body contact between parent and infant, a detachment of feeling from behavior, the surrender of one's body to guidance by others, repression as the main method of handling intrapsychic conflicts, and evasion or denial as the way of handling interpersonal conflict" (p. 9).

However, Murphy also points out that the incidence of *latah* changed greatly at different times during the period of European influence, which suggests the importance of sociological factors. *Latah* was uncommon before 1890 in Malaysia, but soon after that was widely observed in many cities and villages and was reported for both men and women, both upper and lower classes, and both old and young adult subjects. In the following three decades, however, the incidence dropped sharply, and the few cases reported were mainly of female servants.

Grace Harris presents an ingenious analysis of *saka*. She points out that the things which bring on attacks in susceptible women, and which may also appear in the therapeutic measures used to cure them, have some features in common. They fall into three overlapping categories: (1) things which are the concern of men, normally forbidden to women, such as cigarettes, male attire, bananas (which are planted by men), and water in which a man or his clothes have been washed; (2) purchased goods such as clothing, sugar, and cloth; (3) foreign items, such as automobiles, a fez, a train whistle, foreign words.

The second category consists of "women's things," bought mainly with money earned by the men. The third category consists of things outside of the usual experience of women, but with which the men have more contact through their wage work away from home. "Thus all the objects and acts which, in the context of saka, seem to excite strong fear and desire in women and which also appear to relieve the symptoms accompanying these emotions, have to do with the differences between men and women with respect to goods and activities" (Harris 1957:1051).

Harris explains that in this Kenya society men are the owners of land and livestock, which women cannot inherit. Women earn very little money, the trading and wage work being done mainly by men. Women are in a dependent and relatively inferior position in relation to men. Harris suggests as one possible interpretation for *saka* behavior that the symptoms reflect envy of the men and ambivalence about the female role:

> Here one would note the obviously Freudian symbolism of cigarettes, bananas, dirty water, blood, and dancing staves, as well as the

appearance of both fear and desire accompanying the convulsive movements. Giving women the objects they desire, protecting them from what they fear, and giving them an opportunity to be the center of attention might then be thought compensatory or even therapeutic (Harris 1957:1054–55).

The author's analysis is more extensive than this and cannot be dealt with in full. Harris does not refer to *latah* or *imu* in her paper, but as we shall consider presently, there may be similar relationships between men and women in other cultures where *latah*-like behavior appears.

Turning to *pibloktoq*, a psychoanalytic interpretation of this disorder was made by A. A. Brill (1913), who considered it to be a form of hysteria in which the seizures express frustration at lack of love. Zachary Gussow (1960) elaborated on this theme and interpreted the flight of the victim as an invitation to be pursued, an infantile attention-getting maneuver to gain love and reassurance.

Freeman, Foulks, and Freeman (1978) believe that arctic hysteria tends to occur in dependent individuals who suffer from separation anxiety; it may be triggered by physical separation or the death of a mother or mother-substitute.

Seymour Parker believes that hysteria is relatively common among the Eskimo. He cites a condition known as *kayak fright* and other hysterical manifestations in this area. Parker makes the suggestion that hysterical behavior tends to prevail in societies:

> (a)   Where early socialization experiences are not severe and involve minimal repression of dependency needs and sexual drives. . . .
> (b)   Where there is an emphasis on communalistic values, a relatively great amount of face-to-face cooperative patterns, and high expectations of mutual aid.
> (c)   Where the female role involves considerable disadvantages and lower self-esteem compared to the role of the male.
> (d)   Where the religious system involves beliefs in supernatural possession, and where "hysterical-like" behavior models are provided in the institutionalized religious practices (Parker 1962:81).

Parker then proceeds to show that these patterns prevail among the Eskimo. They also seem to apply to the Kenya tribe described by Harris, where the female role seems to be subject to various disadvantages. The position of Ainu women is also said to be very low; belief in possession, moreover, is related to the *imu* syndrome, for *imu* means "possessed" in the Ainu language.

A complicating factor is that Anthony F. C. Wallace has pointed to the need to consider possible biological factors in the etiology of hysteria. It appears that calcium deficiency may produce symptoms such as those of *pibloktoq*. Wallace (1972:374) provides some evidence for the existence of low calcium resources in this arctic area. He also suggests that the apparent decline in cases of hysteria in the Western world since the 19th century may have been due to changes in dress, diet, and other factors which have provided for better calcium intake in the population of Europe since 1900; and he notes that the discovery of the values of sunlight, milk, foods containing vitamin D, and the improvement of living conditions in the 20th century was accompanied by a great decrease in the frequency of rickets, tetany, and hysteria. If calcium was not sufficiently available to many 19th-century Europeans, the same state of affairs was very likely present in many areas where *latah*-like behavior has been found. Biological factors (of which, as Wallace indicates, calcium deficiency may be only one) are, therefore, possible causative agents in the development of such behavior.

Foulks and Katz (1975) made a study of 10 Eskimos with a history of attacks of arctic hysteria and also a matched group of 21 normal Eskimos. The authors failed, however, to find chronic hypocalcemia in the afflicted Eskimos or significant differences in calcium levels in the two groups, and they concluded that no single explanation such as hypocalcemia can account for the occurrence of arctic hysteria.

Incidentally, although Wallace accepts the view that cases of hysteria have declined in the Western world, some psychiatrists would disagree. Thomas Szasz (1961:76–77) claims that hysteria is still prevalent in America and Europe, mainly among lower class, relatively uneducated persons, who do not go to psychiatrists but consult physicians. The latter generally refer them to neurologists and other *medical* specialists. Hollender and Hirsch (1964:1066) also believe that there has been no decline in cases of hysterical psychosis in the past half century.

"Wild Man" Behavior in New Guinea

Two authors, Philip L. Newman and Lewis L. Langness, have written articles about what Newman has termed "wild man" behavior and what Langness has classified as "hysterical psychosis" in the highlands of New Guinea. There are both similarities and differences in these two accounts. The seizures described by the authors affect only young males, roughly between the ages of 22 and 35.

A kind of "running amok" pattern characterized by hyperactivity, running, and jigging up and down was described for the Bena Bena case reported on by Langness (1965). Some break with reality is suggested by the glazed eyes of the young man at a high point in his excitement and by the fact that he did not react to loud shouts in his ear. The young man gave panting gasps, and his skin was cold to the touch. It is believed by the Bena Bena that this behavior is brought about by malevolent ghosts of the same clan as the young man, who has evidently offended one or more of them. Langness reports that this disturbance is rarer among acculturated men, who have more mobility and may be less hemmed in by the social world, the pressures of which weigh heavily on young newly married men who are often lectured to and scolded by older men.

A somewhat similar picture is given by Newman (1964) of an episode affecting a man of the Gururumba tribe. In this case the man asked various people to give him certain objects, which he placed in a stolen net bag. These demands were accompanied by aggressive, threatening gestures and sometimes blows. Newman's "wild man" was hyperactive and sometimes seemed to be not in full control of his body. In such cases there is said to be an increase in respiratory and circulatory rates, sweating, and a drop in skin temperature. The "wild man" sometimes appears not to hear what is said to him, and there seems to be some reduction in his ability to speak.

On the evening of the third day of "wild man" behavior, the Gururumba man described by Newman ran into the forest. He reappeared briefly the next day, without his bag of stolen loot, and said that he was going off to collect pandanus nuts. The man was gone for 13 days; on his return to the community he was accepted by the villagers and resumed normal life.

Like Langness, Newman draws attention to the social stresses which affect young married men in highland New Guinea tribes. Marriages are arranged by kinsmen and village-mates, not by the parties involved, and the betrothal periods are long, so that men are often in their mid-20s before they begin to lead an active married life. The establishment of a family entails economic obligations and payment of debts, which place the young men under considerable pressure, to which may be added the problems of having a dissatisfied young wife. Wives often run away, and tensions then develop between a man and his in-laws and between the respective kin groups. Newman (1964:13) believes that the economic pressures that beset young Gururumba males are related to some aspects of the "wild man" behavior. "The accumulation and destruction of objects becomes an understandable outlet for a man beset by difficulties arising from his inability to effectively control objects."

There are still other culturally patterned disorders; for instance, the fear of sorcery which can lead, not only to sickness, but even to death (Cannon 1942). There is the condition of *amok*, found in Indonesia and elsewhere, in which a brooding depression succeeds to a dangerous explosion of violence. There is the anxiety state known as *koro*, found in Southeast Asia, in which the patient is afraid that his penis will withdraw into his abdomen and cause his death (Linton 1956:67–69; Yap 1965). There is also the condition known as *susto*, or magic fright, sometimes found in peasant communities in Latin America, and the trancelike state reported for Formosa, known as *Hsieh-ping* (Wittkower and Fried 1959:425).

There is the phenomenon of tarantism which has a recorded history of 600 years in Europe and is still to be found in some peasant communities in south Italy. Here there is a notion that a kind of madness is inflicted by the bite of a spider or tarantula, which can be alleviated by dancing until exhaustion, to the music of an orchestra. That the toxic effects of an actual spider bite are not crucial in this syndrome is shown by the fact that the dancing delirium is for many persons an annual event, occurring shortly before the festal day of St. Peter and St. Paul at Galatina in south Italy. Victims of such seizures are generally women, beginning in adolescence or early adult life, but often continuing until old age. Somehow the figure of St. Paul has become identified with the tarantula. Those who have recently been affected by tarantism and have recovered go to the chapel to give thanks to the saint.[8]

We have now reviewed a wide variety of culturally patterned disorders. The existence of such variety seems to show that most cultures have some traditional form or forms of aberrant behavior. They are maintained over the generations by folklore, memory, and gossip. People who display aberrant behavior may be typed, let us say, as being *windigo*, even though this category may include a wide range of deviant behavior. The existence of such a category and label may induce deviants to behave in ways that accord with the stereotype, especially when the deviant is in a confused suggestible state. As Thomas J. Scheff (1966:82) has put it: "In a crisis, when the deviance of an individual becomes a public issue, the traditional stereotype of insanity becomes the guiding imagery for action, both for those reacting to the deviant and, at times, for the deviant himself." This view is in keeping with George Devereux's suggestion, mentioned earlier in this chapter, that a Mohave patient's knowledge of what ailment he is suffering from may lead to a kind of unconscious "malingering" and adoption of the appropriate symptoms.

CLASS AND MENTAL DISORDERS

In an often-cited study, Faris and Dunham (1939) showed that rates for schizophrenia in Chicago were highest in the central part of the city, in the "hobohemia," rooming house area where many migrants, blacks, and foreign-born lived. Rates for schizophrenia were much lower in the better class residential sections of the city. Manic-depression showed no such clustering but seemed to have a random distribution. This indicated that schizophrenia was influenced by socioeconomic factors. Tietze, Lemkau, and Cooper (1941) reported findings along similar lines—that there was more schizophrenia in

---

[8] This is reported in "Tarantism, St. Paul and the Spider," *Times Literary Supplement*, London, England, April 27, 1967, pp. 345–47. No author's name is given.

lower-class groups and relatively more manic-depressive psychosis in higher classes.

A similar state of affairs has been claimed for Chinese communities in Taiwan, where T. Y. Lin (1953) found a high rate of schizophrenia in the lower class and more manic-depression in the upper. He even found the tendency, reported by Faris and Dunham, for schizophrenia to occur more frequently in the central zone of each area than in the peripheries. This zonal distribution of schizophrenia has now appeared in nine studies of American cities, although some other investigations have found somewhat different distributions (Dunham 1959:141–45). A high incidence of suicide has also been found in central, socially disorganized rooming house areas of some large American cities (Henry and Short 1954:135).

In 1953 a paper was published by Robert M. Frumkin (1955) which showed that there was a high incidence of mental illness among low-income, low-prestige, and low socioeconomic status groups in first-admissions cases in Ohio state mental hospitals.

Two studies of New Haven have demonstrated that the lower the socioeconomic class, the greater the proportion of mentally disturbed patients in the population. The incidence of psychoses in the lowest class (Class V) is almost three times greater than in the two highest socioeconomic groups (Classes I and II) and twice the rate for Class IV. Hollingshead and Redlich (1958) were able to rule out the hypothesis of "downward drift" which some critics have invoked to explain the Faris and Dunham findings—that is, the idea that persons drift toward the slums as they become affected by schizophrenia. Indeed, Myers and Roberts (1959:130–33) showed that a majority of schizophrenics had been *upwardly* mobile—more so than their siblings. The upward mobility of schizophrenics has also been discussed by E. Ellis (1952).

A possible contributory factor to the class differences in rates for schizophrenia is the availability of treatment in psychotherapy. Those who are better off are more apt to be accepted by psychiatrists or clinics for treatment. Moreover, cultural differences may make communication more difficult between lower-class patients and therapists (Myers and Schaffer 1954).

Still another way of looking at these matters has been provided by Braginsky, Braginsky, and Ring (1969). Lower-class patients whose life is difficult in the outer world and who are not deterred by the social stigma of institutionalization may—at least in some of the better mental hospitals—find many advantages in the "last resort" of the mental hospital and may make the quite "rational" choice of trying to prolong their time in the hospital under the diagnosis of chronic schizophrenia. If this should be so, an understandable correlation between lower-class membership and hospital diagnosis of schizophrenia could be brought about.

In reviewing epidemiological studies, H. Warren Dunham (1965:256) concludes that schizophrenia is found in every social class, and that its prevalence in lower-class groups is due to the extreme competitiveness of American life, for which the preschizophrenic personality is poorly equipped. Findings such as these in the United States have been reported from some other countries. Reference has already been made to Lin's data from Taiwan. But there is also said to be much more schizophrenia in the lower socioeconomic classes in Ireland than in the higher classes, and the same has been reported of Norway and Iceland (Torrey 1980:104, 130). As with schizophrenia, there is said to be a higher incidence of depression in lower-class groups in the United States and England (Brown and Harris 1980:125–27).

However, there are also some contradictory findings elsewhere. Jaco found that while incidence rates were highest among the unemployed in Texas, the highest standardized rates for those employed at the time of becoming psychotic were found among professionals and semiprofessionals. Jaco (1960:141, 178) points out that studies in Singapore and Norway have found high incidence rates among professional groups. For India, Torrey (1980:59–61) cites a number of studies reporting a higher incidence of schizophrenia in the better-educated higher castes, especially Brahmans, than in the lower castes; and he also cites a Chinese study which reports higher rates of schizophrenia in more educated families. Torrey doubts the adequacy of the stress theory, such as Dunham mentioned earlier. "Even in cultures undergoing rapid disintegration, only a small percentage of people become schizophrenic; so to explain this selectivity one has to add other factors such as genetic vulnerability" (p. 174). He is also skeptical of a childhood determinist approach:

> epidemiologic studies of schizophrenia have provided no support whatsoever for psychodynamic theories. Given the wide variety of child-rearing practices in different cultures, one would expect to find marked differences in schizophrenia prevalence as the mothering or fathering approached ideal schizophrenogenic standards. Nothing of the sort has been found (Torrey 1980:173).

MIGRATION AND MENTAL DISORDERS

There is evidence from various parts of the world for a connection between migration and mental disorder. Needless to say, this association is not invariable; many migrants are free of mental ailments and many stay-at-homes succumb to them. But there seems to be some connection, all the same, either because mentally disturbed persons are driven to leave home and try their chances elsewhere, or because of the stresses involved in adjusting to a new environment.

Ødegaard made a study of Norwegian-born immigrants in Minnesota and found that over a period of four decades their rate of hospital admissions for mental disorders was much higher than those for either native Americans or Norwegians in Norway. Interestingly enough, a still higher rate of mental disorder was found among emigrants to the United States who later returned to Norway. There seemed to be more schizophrenia and fewer affective psychoses among the Norwegian-born of Minnesota than in Norway (Ødegaard 1932:80–83, 103, 176).

Another interesting finding is that internal migration within Norway was not accompanied by increased mental disorder; on the contrary, migrants have lower admission rates than those who remain in their natal communities. Oslo constitutes an exception, either because the migrants represent a less favorable selection, or because they meet with more difficulties there. Ødegaard (1945) concludes that migration within Norway is not so drastic a move as emigration to the United States and does not involve so marked a break with the family, friends, home community, and traditional customs. Thus, it is less traumatic in its effects.

In a study of New York State admissions, Malzberg and Lee (1956:119–22) found that, over a three-year period, migrants greatly exceeded nonmigrants, both for schizophrenia and manic-depression, as well as for other psychoses. The rates were much higher for recent than for earlier migrants. Foreign-born patients with mental disorders have also been shown to have higher admission rates than native-born in practically all age groups from 1917 to 1933 in Massachusetts (Dayton 1940:104).

Isaac Frost found that psychoses often develop among foreign domestic servants in Britain, usually within 18 months of their arrival. Reporting on a study of 40 Austrian and German domestic servants, Frost (1938:801) notes that acute confusional and schizophrenic disturbances associated with bodily signs of toxemia usually occur, and that about 60 percent of the victims recover within about a year.

Libuse Tyhurst (1955) made a study of European displaced persons in Montreal who, like Frost's subjects, were working at domestic or unskilled labor. Among those newly arrived, the author noted a sense of well-being, for the first two months or so, with an increased psychomotor activity which served to release tension. This phase was followed by a sense of strain with a greater awareness of the social situation, difficulties encountered with the language, and unfamiliar customs. Nostalgic fantasies of a happy past provided escape from these realities. About six months after arrival various symptoms were noted: suspiciousness and paranoid tendencies, anxiety and depression, and a variety of somatic and psychosomatic complaints.

Migration has been related to mental disorder in other parts of the world besides Europe and the United States. Laubscher (1938:256) interpreted the higher rate of male over female admissions for mental disorders among South African natives in terms of the fact that the men were more migratory.

Carothers (1948:57), who found the rate of mental disorder among Kenya Africans to be very low, also found that the rates were higher among men who were not living in their native villages.

Okinawans are well known for their low rate of mental disorder, but Okinawans who have migrated to Hawaii have a very high rate of psychosis, significantly higher than that for any other major group in Hawaii, and two and a half times as high as that for the total population (Wedge 1952).

Patterns similar to those found by Tyhurst in the Montreal study have been observed among Andean highland migrants to lowland Peru. Here, however, the picture is complicated by the change in altitude, which brings about various physiological consequences. Seguin (1956) found that young migrants, aged 15 to 25, often develop what he calls a psychosomatic maladjustment syndrome, which may appear from within a week or two after arrival in Lima, to a year later. Upsetting experiences of various kinds may be the precipitating factors. Homesickness is associated with this picture, as among the immigrants in Montreal. The symptoms are varied and include cardiovascular failures, gastritis, peptic ulcer, constipation, colitis, hemorrhoids, bronchitis, pseudotuberculosis, neuritis, neuralgias, headaches and migraines.

Jacob Fried, who has discussed the problems facing migrants to Lima, sent a questionnaire to psychiatrists in a number of countries to see if similar patterns appear elsewhere in connection with migration. From the replies he received there seems to be evidence for psychosomatic disorders being associated with migration in other regions. A doctor in Taiwan, for example, writes:

> The outstanding characteristic of the clinical picture of both neurotics and psychotics among the group of migrated patients [i.e., Mainland Chinese] as compared with the group of Formosan born [is the] . . . great tendency to utilize somatic symptoms in neurotic patients of the migrated group (Fried 1959:120).

One is reminded here of De Vos's Rorschach studies of Algerians who had left their native communities and moved to the Casbah, and of Japanese living in the United States. In both groups he found more body-preoccupation content in the Rorschach responses than for comparable rural samples in Algeria and Japan. De Vos (1961:608) remarks, "These results suggest that there may be a turning in of hostility and/or an emotional withdrawal from difficult object relationships within a social context into an unhealthy self-preoccupation."

Distinctions should probably be made between different kinds of migration and migrants—voluntary migrants, overseas students, indentured workers or servants, displaced persons, refugees, and so forth. Different types of stress are no doubt associated with different sorts of migration. H. B. M. Murphy (1961) has pointed out that in Israel and Singapore immigrants are reported to have less mental hospitalization than the natives, and he suggests that the large main cities of a country, such as Oslo, Paris, and New York, may attract different types of migrants than do other communities.

Miriam L. Gaertner (1955) has made a comparison between the adjustments of European refugees and Puerto Rican immigrants to New York soon after World War II. She found that the former were much more successful in making a place for themselves. They were better equipped culturally for assimilation and for getting jobs and were financially better off than the Puerto Ricans. The latter could return home whenever they wished, but the Europeans were forced to make good in their country of adoption and made a more aggressive effort to do so. The Puerto Ricans tended to fail to learn English, which further handicapped them. The European refugees, moreover, met with a more favorable reception in the new country. The nature of the migration and the assets and resources of the migrants must, therefore, be taken into consideration.

The age of migrants should also be considered, for, as Murphy (1955:310–11) has noted, rates of hospitalization for migrants are generally highest in youth and old age. Children do not seem to be much affected by displacement, as long as they remain with their parents; persons of middle age also seem to be less affected by the stress of migration.

ACCULTURATION AND CULTURE CHANGE

Acculturation and culture change are closely related to migration, although culture change may take place without either migration or acculturation, and migration may take place without either acculturation or culture change. High rates of mental disorder have often been attributed to rapid acculturation in formerly colonial, underdeveloped countries (Murphy 1955:309).

But, again, it is necessary to qualify. Margaret Mead (1956a) has described the dramatically swift transformation of Manus culture which has taken place within a generation, but which has not, as far as one can gather from her book, been accompanied by any increase in mental disorders—unless the Cargo Cult in which many Manus participated be taken as a manifestation of such disorder. One gets the impression that, if anything, the Manus are happier now than they were in the old days.

To cite another example, Eric Berne (1959) reports that acculturation processes do not seem to have increased rates of mental disorder in the Fiji Islands. Citing census figures since 1911, Berne claims that such disorders were actually more frequent in the preindustrial, pre-war era than in the recent period. There may, then, be exceptions to the stressful nature of acculturation and culture change.

What are some of the consequences common to the experiences of migration, acculturation, and rapid culture change? One may be a kind of confusion and disorientation, sharpened by a sense of emotional isolation. Murphy (1955:321) has listed some types of situations which may provoke acute confusional states—for example, students in their first year at college, immigrants arriving off a ship, soldiers recently inducted. An abrupt change in cultural context may have effects similar to the emotional isolation of rooming house life noted by Faris and Dunham and others, as among young Africans who go to Britain to study and who often have mental breakdowns there (Field 1960:318; Prange 1959).

A study of recent conditions in western rural Ireland suggests that cultural breakdown there has led to a widespread condition of anomie. According to Nancy Scheper-Hughes:

> On a given census day in 1971, two out of every hundred males in western Ireland were in a mental hospital. Nearly all of those hospitalized men (89%) were lifelong celibates, most were between the ages of thirty-five and fifty, and more than half were diagnosed as suffering from schizophrenia. . . . per unit of population, the Republic of Ireland has about three times as many schizophrenic patients in hospitals as England. . . . in Ireland schizophrenia is most frequently the disease of male bachelors (Scheper-Hughes 1979:65, 69).

The highest rates are from the western part of Ireland, where Scheper-Hughes did fieldwork and interviewed and tested psychiatric patients in 1975.

She describes the current sociocultural setting there. Since the potato famine of 1845, there has been a steady exodus of people, shrinkage of population, and a decline of both farming and fishing. The former extended families have shrunk to increasingly isolated nuclear family households. Scheper-Hughes states that the predominant household in the community of Ballybran, where she worked, is a nonconjugal unit, with most middle-aged adults living alone or with some member of their family of origin (1979:35). Girls leave home for England or the United States. Before the Great Famine of 1845–49, Ballybran had a population of 2,772, families were large, and people married young. Now the population is only 461, and only one out of three adult males is married, with 34 being the average age of marriage for males. A deep-seated strain of asceticism and shyness about sex further inhibits marriage. Couples are seldom seen together in public. Men and women move in different worlds, with men spending their evenings in the pub with male companions. Alcoholism is widespread.

Scheper-Hughes notes that some other rural communities that have high rates of schizophrenia, such as those studied by Alexander Leighton in Canada and among the Yoruba, are also marked by social disintegration, as measured by such factors as low income, broken homes, and few recreational activities (1979:190–91). Scheper-Hughes claims that the situation in western Ireland is worse for males than for females, and worse for younger than elder sons, for the females and older sons tend to leave the community, while the younger sons are often obliged to maintain the family farm and to look after the old parents, a role that does not carry as much prestige today as it formerly did. As noted earlier, Torrey does not think that stress and social disintegration adequately account for high rates of schizophrenia. Concerning western Ireland, he cites an analysis by Dalen (1977) which notes a statistical association between schizophrenia and advanced maternal age. Since the average age of childbearing in western Ireland is higher than in most other places, a genetic or other biological factor may be involved, affecting the children of such mothers, as in the case of Down's syndrome (Torrey 1980:132–33, 184).

METHODS OF THERAPY

Related to the topic of mental disorder is that of therapeutic techniques. As Ari Kiev (1964:25) has pointed out, "As cultures produce characteristic tensions, they also provide mechanisms for the release of tensions." Anthropologists did not formerly pay much attention to such mechanisms. Some interest was, of course, taken in the performances of shamans, diviners, and priests, but usually without considering the possibility that their actions might actually have some therapeutic value. More attention is now being given to this subject, partly because of a growing skepticism about the efficacy of our own techniques for dealing with mental illness. There are different schools of psychiatry with different basic assumptions and therapeutic techniques. One would think that some practitioners or schools of thought would be closer to the basic truths about the human personality than others and would consequently have a higher incidence of cures. But it seems that the various schools and methods of treatment do not vary much in their rates of cure. "Most statistical studies show that 65–70% of neurotic patients and 35% of schizophrenic patients improve after treatment regardless of the type of treatment received" (Kiev 1964:5). Since many mentally disturbed persons make a spontaneous recovery without any treatment at all, the role of the physician in such recoveries is obscure. A combination of confession by the patient and suggestion and reassurance by the physician may often be enough to bring about a cure. These services are also performed by shamans and priests, perhaps as successfully as by psychiatrists in many cases, or even more successfully. Thus we might as well give some serious attention to how practitioners in non-Western societies go about their cures.

The book edited by Ari Kiev cited earlier addresses this subject. It includes an article by Weston La Barre on the use of confession as cathartic therapy in American Indian tribes; an article by Jane B. Murphy on the therapeutic aspects of shamanism among the St. Lawrence Island Eskimos; and other essays on "folk psychiatry" among the Yoruba, Ndembu, Temne, Shona, and Luo of Africa, the Balahis of Central India, the Cochiti, Apache, and Navaho Indians, Australian aborigines, Yemenite Mori, Turkish villagers and natives of south Texas.

Commenting on the therapeutic methods used in these various societies, Kiev (1964:461) points to the fact that they generally serve to allay fear and anxiety on the part of the patient and mobilize a sense of hope, features which are often more important for recovery than a correct diagnosis. While there may be some mumbo jumbo in a particular shamanistic performance, the mumbo jumbo plays a part in giving the patient the feeling that he is in good hands.

As another aspect of non-Western therapeutic methods, William Sargant (1957:65–80) has drawn attention to the role of abreaction in the curing practices of some nonliterate peoples. If a mentally disturbed patient is worked up to a state of excitement, followed by collapse, his symptoms may disappear on his recovery, in a manner similar to the experience of a person who has undergone electric shock therapy.

Two recent works on folk psychiatry deal with therapeutic measures in more detail than the earlier surveys: Richard Katz's description of community healing among the Kalahari Kung and John M. Janzen's analysis of healing practices in lower Zaire. In accounting for the relatively favorable prospects of recovery from schizophrenia in less industrialized societies, the suggestion was made that close contacts are maintained between patient and family members, including the extended family.[9] Pejorative labeling and isolation of the patient are thus not apt to occur, as they are in the industrially advanced Western world. In that case, the Kung of the Kalahari region of South Africa should have good prospects of mental health, since they always live in close-knit social groups. Until recently they were hunting-gathering people. The subject of Katz's book on the Kung is their weekly evening dances, in which a central cluster of women clap and sing, while male and female dancers circle around them. Some of these dancers go into a trance state and lay their hands on afflicted members of the group, a contact believed to be charged with spiritual energy.

The dancers are not shaman specialists. Katz estimates that more

---

[9] See page 364.

than half of the adult men and 10 percent of the women are healers. Traditionally, the healers do not charge a fee but regard their work as a community service. While in trance they believe themselves to be charged with "boiling energy" which they transfer to others. A healer lays one hand on a patient's chest and with the other hand "pulls out" the sickness and casts it into the darkness, while shrieking and howling. This may continue for hours.

This procedure is not only considered to heal particular ailments but is felt to benefit the group as a whole. "The patient is not always cured. In fact, establishing a more general sense of balance through-out the community takes precedence over any specific cure. . . . This balance is what allows the camp to stay together, helping maintain the reciprocating network which is so important to hunting-gathering life" (Katz 1982:297).

The farming people of lower Zaire are culturally more advanced than the Kung, but they retain a communal emphasis in healing, manifest in what Janzen calls the *therapy managing group.*

> A therapy managing group comes into being whenever an individual or set of individuals becomes ill or is confronted with overwhelming problems. Various maternal and paternal kinsmen, and occasionally their friends and associates, rally for the purpose of sifting information, lending moral support, making decisions, and arranging details of therapeutic consultation (Janzen 1978:4).

The Bokongo of Zaire believe that sickness may be brought about by stress and anxiety. Hence, part of the therapy is directed to reassur-ing the patient and having his friends and kinsmen show their sup-port and encouragement.

At the opposite extreme from the close-packed laying on of hands among the Kung are some procedures which David K. Reynolds (1980) calls "the quiet therapies" of Japan. Here the emphasis is on withdrawal rather than immersion in a group, which may be related to the fact that Japanese live in such densely crowded cities. In Morita therapy, a neurotic patient spends the first four to seven days in bed and is not allowed to meet or talk with others. Even reading, writing, and eating between meals are taboo. In the second stage of treatment (three to seven days), the patient gets out more but is still forbidden to talk with others or to engage in physical exercise. In the evenings, however, he or she writes in a diary which is read and criticized by a doctor. During the third stage (7–20 days), the patient is assigned various chores to carry out; and in the final, fourth stage the patient is allowed more leeway. The patient can now go shopping and do some reading, but only of practical and scientific works and not literary or philosophical books (Miura and Usa 1974:416–18).

In Naikan therapy the patient is required to review his life and to think about the benevolence he has received from others and to what extent he may have repaid them.

"The patient begins his Naikan recollections and reflections at 5:30 in the morning and continues them until 9:00 in the evening. He sits in a quiet place surrounded on two sides by a Japanese screen and walls on the other two so that he is cut off from distractions and is free to concentrate exclusively on his inner world. . . . For seven successive days he follows the same schedule so that at the end he has sat for more than 100 hours almost continuously except while sleeping" (Murase 1974:432).

A counselor interviews the patient at intervals to make sure that he is following the prescribed procedures. According to Murase, Naikan therapy is effective with different kinds of patients, except for psychotics. "Notable success has been achieved with delinquents, criminals, and drug addicts" (1974:434).

There are various other types of Japanese "quiet therapy" which promote rest and meditation. Although the usual treatment involves some isolation, the ultimate goal is to get the patient to assume a responsible position in his social group with a renewed sense of respect and gratitude toward authority figures, a goal which contrasts with the more individualistic aims of Western therapy.

According to Paul B. Pedersen (1977:367) there is a basic difference between Asia and the West in this respect:

Western theories, such as psychoanalysis, rational-emotive therapy, reality therapy, Gestalt therapy, Rogerian theory, and existential psychology, stress the individual achievement motivation, rationally defined evidence, the scientific method, and direct self-disclosure. Asian theories, in contrast, emphasize corporate welfare, experiential evidence, intuitive logic, religiophilosophical methods, and subtle indirection in personal relationships.

S. Pande (1968:432) refers to the Western

emphasis on work rather than relationships and love; self-direction and independence in life rather than interdependence and acceptance of guidance from others; a directional and linear attitude toward time rather than an ahistorical view of time; encapsulated individual consciousness rather than social if not cosmic consciousness; and a problem-solving, cerebral approach to life's conflicts rather than one emphasizing absorption and integration of experience.

SUGGESTIONS FOR FURTHER READING

For some reviews of the literature, see Ihsan Al-Issa, ed., *Culture and Psychopathology* (Baltimore: University Park Press, 1982); Harry C. Triandis and Juris G. Draguns, eds., *Psychopathology. Handbook of Cross-Cultural Psychology*, Vol. 6 (Boston: Allyn and Bacon, 1980); E. Fuller Torrey, *Schizophrenia and Civilization* (New York: Jason Aronson, 1980); John G. Kennedy, "Cultural Psychiatry," in *Handbook of Social and Cultural Anthropology* ed. John J. Honigmann (Chicago: Rand McNally, 1973), pp. 1119–198. For studies of mental disorders in non-Western cultures, see especially *Culture and Mental Health, Cross Cultural Studies,* ed. Marvin K. Opler (New York: Macmillan, 1959); M. J. Field, *Search for Security. An Ethno-Psychiatric Study of Rural Ghana* (Evanston, Ill.: Northwestern University Press, 1960); and George Devereux, *Mohave Ethnopsychiatry and Suicide: The Psychiatric Knowledge and the Psychic Disturbances of an Indian Tribe,* Smithsonian Institution, Bureau of American Ethnology, Bulletin 175 (Washington, D.C. 1961).

For descriptions of non-Western systems of psychotherapy, in addition to those mentioned in the text, see Arthur Kleinman, *Patients and Healers in the Context of Culture. An Exploration of the Borderland Between Anthropology, Medicine, and Psychiatry* (Berkeley: University of California Press, 1980).

Altered States
of Consciousness

The term *altered states of consciousness (ASCs)* has come to be used for
states of consciousness that are deviations from the normal waking
state, such as dreams, trances, and hypnosis. I find it hard to see why
dreaming, any more than the waking condition, should be characterized as "altered," but there is no point in quibbling about a term that
has been so widely accepted. In recent years the use of drugs such as
LSD, cocaine, and marijuana have focused public attention on this
subject. In the use of such drugs we do have a deliberate alteration of
consciousness which has consequences for patterns of culture-and-
personality. As Ruth Benedict argued, there are Dionysian cultures in
which such experiences are valued and sought, and there are Apollonian cultures, such as the Zuñi, in which they are mistrusted and
avoided.[1] There are also societies in which states of possession are
cultivated and others in which that does not occur. In this chapter we
will consider some of these cultural variations, but since dreams form
the subject of Chapter 14, they will not be included here.

DISSOCIATION AND SUGGESTIBILITY

An important aspect of ASCs is the hypersuggestability of the
subject while in a dissociated state. Arnold M. Ludwig (1969:17) comments as follows:

> With the recession of a person's critical faculties there is an attendant
> decrease in his capacity for reality testing or his ability to distinguish
> between subjective and objective reality. This, in turn, would tend to
> create the compensatory need to bolster up his failing faculties by seek-
> ing out certain props, support, or guidance in an effort to relieve some
> of the anxiety associated with the loss of control. In his attempt to
> compensate for his failing critical faculties, the person comes to rely
> more on the suggestions of the hypnotist, shaman, demagogue, inter-

---

[1] See pages 61–64.

rogator, religious healer, preacher, or doctor, all representing omnipotent authoritative figures.

This helps to explain how cultural patterning enters into ASCs. To begin with, the subject brings his or her own mental and cultural expectations into the experience, and the hypnotist or shaman further structures what is going on.

The hypnotic state provides some clues to the nature of ASCs. Looking at hypnosis from a psychoanalytic perspective, Merton M. Gill and Margaret Brenman (1959:xix–xx) see the hypnotic state as a form of regression. "Hypnosis is a particular kind of regressive process which may be initiated either by sensorimotor-ideational deprivation or by the stimulation of an archaic relationship to the hypnotist."

MEANS OF TRANCE INDUCTION

Arnold M. Ludwig (1968) lists various ways in which ASCs, including trance states, may be brought about. The first is through reduction of exteroperceptive stimulation and/or motor activity, as exemplified by experiments in sensory deprivation. Experiments of this sort have shown that isolated subjects lying for a few days in a semidarkened room may see illusions or hallucinations. In these experiments not only are visual cues reduced, sometimes by having the subjects wear goggles, but hearing may be muffled by headphones and tactile sensations reduced by the use of gloves or by wrapping arms and hands in cotton wool. Another procedure is to submerge subjects wearing head masks in a water tank. In a critical review of such experiments, Suedfeld and Borrie (1978) claim that, contrary to early reports, actual hallucinations are not common under these conditions. The subject often falls asleep and dreams. Since he cannot clearly differentiate states of sleep and waking, it is difficult to distinguish between dreams and hallucinations in his reports. For our purposes here this distinction is not crucial, for this general method has been used to induce trance states in some societies, as will be seen later. In the experimental laboratory sessions, the subjective experiences that result are not usually structured by the experimenter, but in religious cults where similar procedures are followed, a priest or shaman may assume this role.

In some societies, there are cases where sensory deprivation is voluntarily undertaken by individuals in search of supernatural guidance. In this case most of the resulting visionary experience must be the product of the seeker's mental set and autosuggestion. For example, beginning at around five years of age Chippewa or Ojibwa children were sent out to fast for a dream or vision of a guardian spirit. Ideally, one should have such a dream or vision before puberty. It was in this way that one supposedly acquired the power to become a shaman. Instruction in shamanistic procedures was said to be provided by the guardian spirit, who appeared to the faster, announcing that he had come "to take pity" on the child, a phrase which had the connotation of "to adopt" or "take care of" the child. The child might also be told that he would become a great hunter. Before leaving the boy, the guardian spirit was apt to assume a particular animal form.

Although children were sent out periodically without food, they often failed to report the hoped-for dream or vision. As puberty approached, therefore, a boy might build a platform for himself, high up in a tree, where he would lie alone without food or water for a week or more until the right sort of hallucinatory experience resulted. Some men claimed that they had fasted in this way for 10 or 15 days. In such cases there was no shaman at hand to monitor the boy's experience, but the neophyte did have certain culturally patterned expectations. Since medicine men told about their fasting revelations before embarking on a cure, and since there were other occasions for the public recital of guardian spirit visions, boys could learn the general nature of approved visionary experiences. Autosuggestion must, therefore, have been at work in maintaining this pattern.

A less isolated form of sensory deprivation is used by some Shakers of St. Vincent in the Caribbean, whose members are lower-class Protestants of mainly African descent. Those who aspire to the status of "elders" go through a ceremony known as mourning, although the elders are not necessarily old, and the mourning is not for the dead but for one's own sins. Mourning involves a period of isolation lying on pallets, blindfolded, for a week or two with a reduced diet. However, the mourners have contact with an official to whom they describe the "trips" they have taken, and he can end their period of isolation when he thinks that the time is right. Like the Chippewa fasters, the St. Vincent aspirants have some culturally patterned ideas of what to expect. Before their retreat, the official in charge draws a chalk design known as a "map" to give them his final instructions (Henney 1974).

The role of suggestion and prior knowledge in situations of sensory deprivation has been demonstrated in a laboratory experiment, in which 14 male college students were subjected to only one hour of sensory deprivation. They were informed beforehand that previous subjects had had peculiar perceptual and cognitive experiences, although their nature was not specified. It was indicated that it was quite normal under the circumstances to experience hallucinations. The students were also told that they would be administered a hallucinogenic drug, although they were actually given only a placebo. All but 2 of the 14 subjects had visual experiences, many of them complex, involving people, colors, and geometrical shapes; and all reported auditory experiences, such as the sounds of airplanes, trains, water, or wind. Jackson and Kelly (1962) concluded that the results were mainly due to a combination of suggestion and the establishment of a receptive attitude toward the experience of hallucinations. Note that in this experiment, although the influence of suggestion was shown, very little structuring of the experience occurred.

While the two cases of the Chippewa and the St. Vincent Shakers illustrate the use of sensory deprivation to bring about a trance or dissociated state, the same result may be induced by the opposite tactic of sensory bombardment. Drumming, in particular, is often used for this purpose. Laboratory research has shown that rhythmic drumming affects the central nervous system, sometimes producing hallucinations, muscle twitching, and a distortion of the sense of time (Neher 1962). In religious ceremonies in Haiti, Siberia, and elsewhere, there is a tendency to slowly increase the rhythm until a fast tempo has been reached. Possession states are often induced by the use of drums or other noisemakers, as, for example, in Ghana, West Africa:

> Drumming, singing, clapping and the rhythmic beating of gong-gongs and rattles, alone or all together, are the commonest inducers of possession. The drumming is exciting, the clanging iron is a harsh monotony from which consciousness readily recoils. More possessed people are likely to be seen at a well-orchestrated dance than on any other occasions (Field 1969:7).

In settings like these, dissociation is brought about not only by the noise and rhythmic beat but also by the physical exertion of dancing. "The violent dancing and gestures make hyperventilation a possibility and increase the production of adrenaline, as well as cause a decrease in blood glucose." (Neher 1962:157). As a result, in many societies, some dancers fall to the ground and twitch spasmodically.

To give an example of the energetic dancing that induces trance states, consider this description of a Moroccan Muslim religious leader of the Hadamsha sect: "He leaps, turns in mid air, lands on his knees, leaps again, and stabs at his chest with his fists as he lands" (Crapanzano 1973:193). His male followers alternately raise and lower their shoulders exhaling with a hissing noise, but the initial dance steps of the women, who fall into trance more readily than the men, are said to be more violent (p. 195). Some lapse into a trance condition while watching as spectators and make their way forward to join the dance. "Before falling to the ground, the female dancer appears semi-conscious—sleepy, one might say—and disoriented. Her eyes are glazed and unfocused, and she seems to be oblivious to her surroundings" (p. 197).

We have, then, two quite different strategies for reaching a state of dissociation. The first combines sensory deprivation with passive immobility, while the second combines sensory bombardment with muscular exertion. Both strategies manage to accomplish the same objective.[2] Still another approach is through the use of drugs, which will be discussed later.

TYPES OF TRANCE STATES

While contrasting methods are used in different societies to bring about trance, there are also differences in the utilization of the trance state, once achieved, and here again cultural patterning is at work. In some societies the entranced person is believed to be possessed; the subject's body is thought to be invaded by an external spirit that takes charge of the body for the time being. Possession may be involuntary and resisted, in which case rites of exorcism may be performed to drive out the unwelcome spirit. On the other hand, in societies that have spirit medium cults, the shaman or medium may welcome possession in order to gain access to spirits and information not otherwise attainable. These beliefs and practices, although widespread, are not universal. In the 1920s, Franz Boas pointed out that the possession concept is widespread in the Old World but rare in the New. Edwin M. Loeb (1929) made a distinction between shaman and seer, seeing the shaman as a medium through whom spirits speak, while the seer has visions of spirits who talk to him.[3] According to Loeb, the seer is an earlier type of religious specialist, found among American Indian tribes and among the more primitive and isolated peoples of the Old World.

More recently, Erika Bourguignon (1973:11) and her colleagues have made use of Murdock's *Ethnographic Atlas* to draw up a more quantitative picture of the distribution of possession and allied states. In their sample of 488 societies, drawn from all parts of the world, they find that "437, or 90 percent are reported to have one or more institutionalized, culturally patterned forms of altered states of consciousness." They then make a distinction between *possession trance*, in which the trance state is interpreted as due to spirit possession, and *trance*, in which this interpretation is not made, a contrast which roughly parallels Loeb's distinction between shaman and seer. With regard to possession beliefs, Bourguignon states that "such beliefs occur in 74% of our sample societies, with a maximum of 88% in the Insular Pacific and a minimum of 52% in North America" (p. 17). An association appears between possession trance and societal complexity, indicated by such institutions as social stratification and slavery. "Among 114 societies, possession trance was significantly related to the presence of slavery and to the presence of a stratification system of freeman (*sic*) of at least two social classes. Among 103 societies,

---

[2] On the effects of these two strategies, see Sargant (1969:510).

[3] Most anthropologists use the term *shaman* in a looser, more general sense than Loeb does here.

relationship of possession trance to either or both slavery and stratification was unusually strong" (p. 54).

More recently, Bourguignon (1979:254, 258) has reported that trance, the visionary form, is practiced much more by men than by women, while possession is mainly practiced by women. Trance is brought about by fasting, sensory deprivation, or drugs, while possession trance is usually induced by drumming and dancing in a crowd setting. Moreover, possession trance is a performance. "A performance is carried out in front of an audience; indeed, it requires an audience for possession trance typically is followed by amnesia, so without an audience no memory of the event is recorded" (p. 261). The experience of trance, on the other hand, such as the guardian spirit vision of the Chippewa boy, is remembered and reported by the faster himself.[4]

POSSESSION TRANCE: SOME INTERPRETATIONS

A psychological interpretation along neobehaviorist lines has been supplied by Walter and Frances Mischel in an account of the syncretic lower-class Shango cult of Trinidad in the West Indies, which stems from the religious beliefs of the Yoruba of Nigeria combined with Christianity. Here, as in several other areas where possession occurs, the possessed person is referred to as a "horse," who is ridden and controlled by the invading spirit. This conception clearly places the possessed person in a subordinate relationship to the spirit, but by identifying with the spirit, the "horse" temporarily plays a most commanding role.

> In the most extreme examples the possessed is virtually in absolute control of those around him. His slightest wish is immediately carried out; the onlookers are utterly at his disposal. . . . Oil, rum, implements such as axes, swords, food, and candles, are quickly brought in response to his signals. . . . The domestic who thirty minutes earlier was submissive to the whims of her British mistress is, under possession, transformed into a god; the unemployed laborer is master of an audience of several hundred people (Mischel and Mischel 1958:254–55).

In behaviorist terms, one can see how actions of this sort would readily find reinforcement. But the possessed person may also roll on the ground, beat himself, and tear his clothes. The Mischels suggest that the reinforcement in such cases concerns the reduction of guilt

---

[4] While possession may be more commonly practiced by women, it should be noted that shamanism is more commonly a male than female pursuit, although there are exceptions, such as the Saora shamanins described on page 356. The *tang-ki* (spirit medium) of Singapore and Taiwan is more often male than female. Elliott (1955:46) states that "Youths of under twenty are the most suitable candidates," and Jordan's account (1972:69n) of Taiwanese possession trance is "based largely on the more common male *tâng-ki*."

and anxiety. The possessed person also comes into close physical contact with others, massaging them, crawling between their legs, and so forth, which is seen as expressing sexual or hostile impulses or a need for intimacy. Many females claim to be possessed by male spirits, which allows for a reversal of sex roles.

Apart from all this acting out under socially sanctioned circumstances, there is the advantage of referring problems to the spirit powers for solution, which frees the subject from the responsibility of managing his or her own life.

In analyzing a case of possession in Sri Lanka, Gananath Obeyeskere presents a similar picture. Members of the possessed woman's family are tolerant of her behavior, since it is not she but the invading spirit who is responsible.

> Thus a pattern of behavior has been established: whenever the strains become intolerable the patient gets possessed, acts out her impulses and, after a period of illness that may last for a couple of days, reverts to her normal role. The temporary relief experienced and the secondary compensations of attention and parental solicitude for her welfare reinforce that pattern of behavior (1977:252).

I. M. Lewis offers a sociological interpretation on a more global scale. Lewis (1971:31) sees possession, to which women are mainly subject, and the institution of female possession cults which incorporate the victims of possession, as "thinly disguised protest movements directed against the dominant sex." They normally occur in male-dominated societies in which women have little freedom. Males who become possessed tend to be men of lower status in stratified societies, who use the same strategy of protest as the women. In either case the invading spirits are characterized by Lewis as being "amoral" and "peripheral," since they play no part in the central religion or in the moral code of such societies. It is on this point that Lewis has been criticized by some anthropologists, although they may acknowledge the applicability of his generalizations, at least in part. Bourguignon (1976:35), for example, considers Haitian vodou to be a "central morality" religion, in Lewis's terms, rather than a peripheral cult or a protest religion. Moreover, vodou possession is not a prelude to cult membership, as it is in many African cultures.

Lewis's own fieldwork was done among the Somali of northeast Africa. These people are Muslims in a society that is male-dominated both in its patrilineal descent and in the predominant male role in religion. Women are excluded from mosques and generally play a submissive part in life. Women fall ill when they are possessed by a jinn or spirit. In a ceremonial setting a possessed woman is questioned—or rather the invading spirit is questioned—to find out its identity. In this case the spirits are peripheral to the dominant Muslim religion, just as the women are relatively peripheral in the male social system (Lewis 1971:32). Part of the woman's protest is expressed in the amounts of money that her husband has to pay for the ceremonial treatment of her case. The invading spirit may demand fine clothes, perfume, and fancy dishes before abandoning her body.

Bourguignon (1976:35) points to a striking feature of East African possession cults:

> the transformation of the spirits in their relation to their human hosts as a result of initiation into the cult. . . . Ritual initiation leads not only to controlled, voluntary possession trance and the cure of the illness. It also transforms a harmful dangerous spirit into a helpful one, an ally. Where involuntary illness-causing possession in Europe and in India leads to exorcism, in these East African cults it leads to an accommodation with the possessing spirit.

A similar pattern occurs in Morocco, where possession may be handled either by exorcism or by establishing a "working relationship" with the invading jinn (Crapanzano 1973:158). In the latter case, when the jinn has been named, a symbiotic relationship is formed with him or her. The patient joins a cult and must do various things to appease the jinn, burning incense, wearing special colors, and dancing to particular musical phrases which can send the subject into trance (pp. 158–63). By joining the cult group, the patient is no longer isolated but acquires allies and sympathetic support and gains a new status as a member of the cult.

On the other hand, Alice Morton (1977:197–98) notes that there are some negative features in this situation as it affects members of an Ethiopian possession cult, for such members are at the mercy of cultist leaders and they may be cut off by their families, which leads them to become even more dependent on the cult group and its leaders. Various outcomes are possible in such cases. The Sri Lankan woman discussed by Obeyeskere (1977:290) was not only helped by her cult congregation but underwent a real transformation: "Earlier she had been possessed by evil, troublesome demons; now the possibility exists for her to be possessed by the goddess Pattini, the ideal female in Sinhalese culture." In a later revisit Obeyeskere found this former patient to have made a good adjustment. "Obviously her propensity for possession has been harnessed in a creative and meaningful way" (p. 292).

In Crapanzano's introduction to *Case Studies in Spirit Possession*, which includes the studies by Morton and Obeyeskere just cited, he points out that "Twelve of the fifteen cases presented involve women, and the theme of female powerlessness, as well as the manner in which possession phenomena permit both temporary and long-term increases in women's power and control, is conspicuous in most of the histories" (Crapanzano and Garrison 1977:xi–xii). This is in keeping with Lewis's generalizations, which are particularly well supported by Clive S. Kessler's account (1977) of Kelantanese Malay spirit seances. However, Lewis's scheme may not apply so well in all cases of possession. After pointing out that there are four different types of possession among the Kalabari of West Africa which have different significance for both the subjects and their audiences, Robin Horton (1969:44) remarks: "I can think of no single line of interpretation, either sociological or psychological, which could possibly do justice to the diversity of these phenomena." Similarly, there are three types of possession among the Tonga of Zambia, each supposedly brought about by a different class of spirits (Colson 1969). I think we must acknowledge the likelihood of different etiologies for different sorts of possession and even, for that matter, in the same class of possession.

Lewis Langness (1976:57), who is dissatisfied with Bourguignon's ASC classification, makes a distinction between possession and hysterical psychosis, claiming that the term *possession* "is simply inappropriate for the purposes of transcultural psychiatry." Possession, he explains, is sought and deliberately induced; it is institutionalized and "sacred," whereas hysterical psychoses are not sought and are considered "profane" and also abnormal—by both the local members of the society and by the ethnological investigator.[5]

MYSTICAL STATES

In different times and cultures some people have had ASCs that have been characterized as mystical states (James 1929), cosmic consciousness (Bucke 1923), or peak experiences (Maslow 1968). Sometimes these states have been achieved by spiritual exercises and meditation. Benson, Beary, and Carol (1974) describe the meditation technique as a "relaxation response" which involves physiological changes that are the opposite of flight or fight responses.

Mystical states may also be spontaneous and unexpected. Richard M. Bucke described his own experience of "cosmic consciousness" as a spontaneous one. He had spent an evening with two friends discussing poetry and philosophy and left at midnight, feeling peaceful but deeply influenced by their conversation.

> All at once, without warning of any kind, I found myself wrapped in a flame-colored cloud. For an instant I thought of fire, an immense conflagration . . . ; the next, I knew that the fire was within myself. Directly afterward there came upon me a sense of exultation, of immense joyousness accompanied or immediately followed by an intellectual illumination impossible to describe. . . . I did not merely come to believe, but I saw that the universe is not composed of dead matter,

---

[5] Langness uses the term *hysterical psychosis* for the "running amok" pattern in New Guinea described earlier on page 375.

but is, on the contrary, a living Presence; I became conscious in myself
of eternal life (James 1929:390).

This experience has, in common with many others collected by
Bucke (1923), the feelings of joy and strong conviction, combined
with ineffability, the impossibility of describing the event in words.
Many other accounts also refer to the experience of light, which one
commentator suggests may have a physical basis: " 'Illumination'
may be derived from an actual sensory experience occurring when in
the cognitive act of unification, a liberation of energy takes place, or
when a resolution of unconscious conflict occurs, permitting the experience of 'peace,' 'presence,' and the like. Liberated energy experienced as light may be the core sensory experience of mysticism"
(Deikman 1969:38).

On the basis of his collection of reported cases, both ancient and
contemporary, Bucke suggested that this experience usually occurs
among men between 35 and 40 years of age, but he thought that it
was an emergent form of consciousness that, although rare at
present, is destined to increase in the course of evolution. Prince and
Savage express skepticism of this hypothesis of Bucke's, pointing out
that such mystical states and some psychotic states have much in
common. They (Prince and Savage 1972:114) quote one patient's description of an early stage of psychosis: "I was suddenly confronted
by an overwhelming conviction that I had discovered the secrets of
the universe, which were rapidly made plain with incredible lucidity.
The truths discovered seemed to be known immediately and directly
with absolute certainty." Some other examples of psychotic episodes
marked by mystical convictions are given by Bowers and Freedman
(1966). Prince and Savage (1972) suggest that mystical states are instances of regression in the service of the ego,—a very different point
of view from Bucke's.

A problem is the exact cognitive significance of "cosmic consciousness," which is made more difficult by the ineffable nature of the
experience. William James (1929:415) acknowledged that mystical
states are usually authoritative for those who have had them, but
"mystics have no right to claim that we ought to accept the deliver-
ance of their peculiar experiences." Although the basic experience
may be much the same, religious mysticism has taken quite different
forms: "It has been both ascetic and antinomianly self-indulgent
within the Christian church. It is dualistic in Sankhya, and monistic in
Vedanta philosophy. I called it pantheistic; but the great Spanish
mystics are anything but pantheists" (p. 416).

One may take a pragmatic view and point to the creative lives
carried out, after their mystical illuminations, by saints such as Saint
Teresa and John of the Cross and by poets such as Edward Carpenter
and Walt Whitman. However, perhaps these people could have been

successful saints and poets without undergoing their mystical experiences, although they might not have been such effective saints and poets without them. As against these positive examples, in any case, we have the negative examples of the psychotics for whom their moments of illumination heralded a period of insanity. Bucke (1923:317 n) himself noted that almost everyone who has had such an experience wonders if he is going mad. Some saints and poets, at least, can emerge from the illumination strengthened and inspired, while more vulnerable persons may become insane.

Perhaps the mystical experience is a partially dissociated state under the influence of autosuggestion. This is one interpretation that could be given to explain the results of a double-blind controlled experiment carried out by Walter W. Pahnke (1972), in which 20 middle-class Protestant theological student volunteers listened to a solemn Good Friday religious service. Half of the students had been given psilocybin one and a half hours earlier, while the other half were given 200 mg. of nicotinic acid, which causes only a transient tingling sense of warmth. Neither the experimenter nor the students knew the specific contents of the various capsules. Although a receptive, trusting attitude toward the experiment was encouraged, there was no effort to suggest the nature of the mystical experience that might perhaps result.

Within a week of this experiment, all the students completed a long questionnaire designed to measure its effects, based on a nine-category typology by W. T. Stace of the characteristics of mystical experiences. The experimental students scored significantly higher in each of the nine categories than did the control students who had taken the nicotinic acid. "The experience of the experimental subjects was certainly more like mystical experience than that of the controls, who had the same expectation and suggestion from the preparation and setting" (Pahnke 1972:270). The main difference between the two groups was that the experimental students had taken psilocybin and were therefore in a more dissociated state than were the controls. "After an admittedly short follow-up period of only six months, life-enhancing and enriching effects similar to some of those claimed by mystics were shown by the higher scores of the experimental students when compared to the controls."

HALLUCINOGENIC DRUGS

This brings us to a consideration of the effects of hallucinogenic drugs, which include, among others, psilocybin, LSD, mescaline, peyote, and *yagé*, used by some South American tribes. The effects of such drugs are quite variable, but at the same time there are some regularities, even cross-culturally, in how people react to these different drugs.

Ronald K. Siegel and Murray E. Jarvik (1975) have provided a review of experiments in drug-induced imagery. A common early reaction in subjects who have taken a drug is to see a very bright light in the center of a visual field. Imagery tends to pulsate and move toward this center or away from it. When there is movement toward the center, a spirallike effect may be produced, which may also give the impression of a tunnel. Some subjects report that they are traveling through the inside of a tube. The original images may next be replaced by geometric forms, checkers, lattices, gratings, honeycombs, and the like, and then by more complex forms, including human beings and animals. Such imagery may first seem to overlay the lattices and tunnels, generally on their peripheries.

A similar sequence has been reported for the Tukano Indians of Colombia by Reichel-Dolmatoff (1971). The Tukano decorate their homes and pottery with geometrical motifs based on the early stages of their *yagé* imagery: curves, lattices, spirals, and the sun.

Ronald K. Siegel, who cross-examined Huichol Indians in Mexico about their peyote visions, notes: "there were numerous reports of geometric patterns, spirals, lines, tunnels, and lattices" (Siegel and Jarvik 1975:138). A center, or source of light toward which motion flows, was reported by experimental volunteer subjects in Chile who had taken *yagé* (Naranjo 1973). R. Gordon Wasson, who consumed hallucinogenic mushrooms in Oaxaca, Mexico, together with a friend under the aegis of a native curandera, writes:

> At first we saw geometric patterns, angular not circular, in richest colors, such as might adorn textiles or carpets. Then the patterns grew into architectural structures, with colonnades and architraves, patios of regal splendor, the stone-work all in brilliant colors, gold and onyx and ebony, all most harmoniously and ingeniously contrived, in richest magnificence extending beyond the reach of sight, in vistas measureless to man (Wasson 1957, 2:253).

Michael Harner (1973:158–73) noted some common themes in the visions produced by *yagé* among South American Indians, including the concept of a "trip," involving sensations of vertigo and flying, visions of snakes and jaguars, scenes of landscapes and distant cities and visions of demons or deities. Harner (p. 16) himself, after consuming a drug made from the vine *Banisteriopsis caapi* during fieldwork in the upper Amazon Basin, tried "to fly through the far reaches of the Galaxy."

Another common experience is human-animal metamorphosis. Masters and Houston (1966:76–78, 293) describe the experiences of an anthropologist who had taken LSD; he thought of himself as a tiger and saw himself as a tiger in the mirror. Some other such cases are given. After taking yagé, one man felt himself being transformed into various animal forms: frog, sea lion, and snake (Aaronson and Osmond 1970:52–55, 59–61). Harner (1973:140–45) has suggested that the alleged European cases of lycanthropy are explainable in terms of hallucinogenic drugs being used by the men who believed that they had turned into wolves.

As we saw at the end of the preceding section, there may also be a sense of religiosity or illumination. An example is given by Masters and Houston (1972:307) of a normal American subject who was handed a picture of a Japanese Buddha while under the influence of LSD. He reports: "I experienced a shattering thunderbolt of ecstasy and my body dissolved into the flow of matter or energy of which the universe is made. I was swept into the core of existence from which all things arise and into which all things converge."

Finally, there is an experience of mythic themes while under the influence of hallucinogenic drugs. Masters and Houston (1966:224 f.) state that myths are often experienced in drug states by American subjects, including hero myths, myths of creation, of incest, and parricide, myths of polarity (light and darkness, order and chaos). Myths are also experienced by Tukano neophytes in the Amazon rain forests who undergo initiation under the supervision of a shaman who helps to structure the experience for them. The purpose of taking the drug, they say, is to return to the uterus, the center of all things, where the person sees the enactment of mythical themes, which come in the later stages of the experience. "On awakening from the trance, the individual remains convinced of the truth of the religious teachings . . . . he has seen Vai-mahsë [the Master of Game Animals] and the Daughter of the Sun, he has heard her voice; he has seen the Snake-Canoe float through the rivers, and he has seen the first men spring from it." (Reichel-Dolmatoff 1971:174). Similar to this is an account of the initiation of a Cahuilla boy in California:

> Datura enabled him to glimpse the ultimate reality of the creation stories in the Cahuilla cosmology. The supernatural beings and aspects of the other world that he had been told about since childhood were now brought before his eyes for the ultimate test—his own empirical examination. He has seen them. They are real . . . (Bean and Saubel 1972:62–63).

To illustrate the relation of mythic themes to hallucinogens, let me summarize a remarkable sequence of images experienced in a drug state reported by Masters and Houston (1966:230–36). The subject (S) was a woman in her late 20s who had taken peyote. After a preliminary period S began to describe a medieval setting in which she found herself: the courtyard of an evil-looking old castle crowded with ugly-looking people who had come to watch a beheading. The executioner chopped off the head of a young woman. As it lay on the ground, S recognized it as her own face. The body ran around like a bleeding, headless chicken and finally fell at S's feet, with one of its hands grasping her ankle. She could not pull away from its grip. The executioner then came to rescue her. When S found that she could not walk, the executioner picked her up and carried her into the castle.

The executioner was a brutal-looking man whose face was covered by a black sack with eyeholes. His sensual lips were visible. It seemed to S that he somehow resembled her husband. The executioner asked if she was hungry, and she found that she was indeed. So he walked to an oaken sideboard on which threatening symbols were carved and brought back a large bowl of grapes. S was just about to eat two of these, when she realized that the grapes were two malevolent black eyes. She screamed and ran out of the castle into the forest. For a long time she ran through a dark, sinister wood until she came to a pleasant, sunny glade, where she lay down to rest. Here S fell into a drowsy state and then awoke to find a man standing over her.

The man asked if anything was wrong, and S explained that she had hurt her ankle while running through the woods. Like the executioner, this man wore a mask, but he seemed kindlier and better looking. He somewhat resembled both the executioner and her husband. The man carried S to a lovely stream, gave her some clear water to drink, and asked if she were hungry. She was indeed, so the man brought her a bowl of grapes. S was just about to eat two of them when she saw that they were two sad brown eyes. S cried out and dove into the stream, where she was carried along until she was finally washed up on a shore where a castle stood. This castle looked new and did not seem evil like the first one.

Limping on her wounded ankle, S entered the castle. She sat down on a wooden chest carved with reassuring symbols. A man entered the room, masked like the other two men but younger, warmer, and better looking than they. He asked her in a kindly way what she was doing there, and she explained that she had hurt her ankle and would like to stay in the castle for a while. The man carried her to a dining room and asked if she would like some food. She found that she was more hungry than ever; so the man brought her a bowl of grapes. She was just about to eat two of them when she saw that they were two clear blue eyes. Although S was frightened, she did not run away this time. Instead, she placed the eyes on the table and said that she had lost her appetite.

Then she asked the man to take off his mask. He said that although he did not really have a mask, she could not see his face, just as she had been unable to see the faces of the other two men. What she needed, he explained, was a new pair of eyes, which he had offered her. So S put the two eyes into her mouth and gulped them down. She then saw a handsome young man who looked like her husband. S realized that he was the same as the other two men and that there had been no beheading at all.

This was the end of the drug imagery. S immediately analyzed the story, seeing it as a representation of her relationship with her husband, whose motives she always mistrusted and misinterpreted. This hallucinogenic experience gave her a new insight into her attitudes and brought about an immediate improvement in her marriage, according to Masters and Houston.

This drug experience was a product of and commentary on the subject's life, but it is also a product of Western culture, although not of the present time. No unacculturated Australian aborigine or Chippewa or Hopi Indian could have seen this sequence of images, with its castles and medieval European trappings. The story reported by S is remarkably well organized, as if the "dream work," to use Freud's term, had all been prepared beforehand. The story exemplifies some characteristics which Axel Olrik (1965) claimed to be typical of folktales, especially the Law of Repetition, in which the same action is repeated in successive episodes. As Olrik noted, this repetition is almost always tied to the number three, at least in Europe. In a North American Indian tale, four, is the magic number.[6] In S's case, the three male figures represent three stages in a change of viewpoint in her own mind, with each stage having appropriate associated symbolism—evil, ugliness, and darkness, at first, with a shift to more positive and hopeful symbolism in the later episodes. There are many Lévi-Straussian polarities in the story: ugly–handsome, cruel–kind, sinister–pleasant, black eyes–blue eyes, darkness–light; and there are contrasting settings: forest and castles or nature and culture. This case, once again, illustrates the point that, although the drug-induced state departed widely from normal everyday consciousness, it was organized not only by the subject's personal problems and their clarification but also by the cultural background of the subject.

SUGGESTIONS FOR FURTHER READING

Tart's reader would be a good place to begin on this subject: Charles C. Tart, ed., *Altered States of Consciousness. A Book of Readings* (New York: John Wiley & Sons, 1969. See also John White, ed., *The Highest State of Consciousness* (New York: Doubleday Anchor Books, 1972) and A. Arthur Sugerman and Ralph E. Tarter, eds., *Expanding Dimensions of Consciousness* (New York: Springer, 1978).

On hallucinations, see R. K. Siegel and L. J. West, *Hallucinations. Behavior, Experience, and Theory* (New York: John Wiley & Sons, 1975).

A classic work on possession, which is still worth consulting, is T. K. Oesterreich, *Possession. Demoniacal and Other. Among Primitive Races, In Antiquity, the Middle Ages, and Modern Times*, D. Ibberson, trans. (New Hyde Park, N.Y.: University Books, 1966; first published in 1921). For a good series of field studies dealing with possession, see Vincent Crapanzano and Vivian

---

[6] In the remarkable vision of Black Elk, an Oglala Sioux seer, reported by John G. Neihardt (1961:22–47) the numbers 4, 6, and 12 are prominent.

Garrison, eds., *Case Studies in Spirit Possession* (New York: John Wiley & Sons, 1977).

On hallucinogens and visions, see Peter T. Furst, *Flesh of the Gods: The Ritual Use of Hallucinogens* (New York: Frederick A. Praeger, 1972); Michael J. Harner, *Hallucinogens and Shamanism* (London: Oxford University Press, 1973); and Peter T. Furst, *Hallucinogens and Culture* (San Francisco: Chandler & Sharp, 1976). See also Chapter 7, "Ritual. The Hallucinations of Social Solidarity," in *To Hunt in the Morning* ed. Janet Siskind (New York: Oxford University Press, 1973).

There are several interesting articles about the endorphins and related subjects in Volume 10 of *Ethos* (1982), including the following: Raymond Prince, "The Endorphins. A Review for Psychological Anthropologists," pp. 303–16; Murray Saffran, "The Amino Acid in the Brain," pp. 317–25; Wolfgang G. Jilek, "Altered States of Consciousness in North American Indian Ceremonials," pp. 326–43; Bruce Pomeranz, "Acupuncture and the Endorphins," pp. 385–93; and Raymond Prince, "Shamans and Endorphins. Hypotheses for a Synthesis," pp. 409–23.

20

Culture Change in the Western World

When the culture of a society changes and it develops new institutions, the members of the society must adapt themselves to the new conditions. Such adaptation may involve changes in personality which may, in turn, lead to further changes in culture. For example, a number of writers have discussed the changes in values and attitudes that developed in Europe as the feudal system broke down and as mercantile capitalism increased in importance.

BURCKHARDT ON THE RENAISSANCE

A pioneer in the analysis of such topics was Jacob Burckhardt, whose book, *The Civilization of the Renaissance in Italy,* was published in 1860. Burckhardt argued that there was a great growth of individualism in 14th-century Italy, in contrast to conditions in earlier medieval times. According to Burckhardt (1945:52) there were not even any prevailing fashions in men's attire in Florence in 1390. Burckhardt was struck by the number of "complete," or many-sided men, appearing in Italy at this time, culminating in such figures as Leon Battista Alberti and Leonardo da Vinci. There was a concern with personal glory and achievement. Cults surrounded the birthplaces and graves of famous men. And there was a new development of biography and autobiography (for instance, those of Cellini and Girolamo Cardano) with a keen interest in the distinctive characteristics of individuals. Burckhardt (1945:84–92, 119 f., 275 f.) also cited the lawlessness of the times, for individualism was expressed in acts of aggression and crime as well. To support these generalizations, Burckhardt drew contrasts between the earlier Middle Ages and the Renaissance, between northern Europe and Italy. The key to these developments was seen in the political situation in Italy, with its competing states and petty despots. In the courts of such men, individualistic self-expression was encouraged, at least in some spheres. In this respect Italy was in the forefront of Europe, for the stress on individualism was to become one of the emphases in Western culture.

Burckhardt's interpretation seems convincing, although J. Huizinga (1959:260; 1924:59) pointed out that "individualistic" behavior was exalted in earlier Norse sagas, that a thirst for personal glory was present in the ideals of medieval chivalry, and that there is some difficulty in locating clear boundary lines between the Middle Ages and the Renaissance.

FROMM ON WESTERN MAN

Erich Fromm (1941:chap. 3) is another writer who has dealt with these themes. Fromm has been influenced not only by Burckhardt but by the writings of Max Weber and Richard H. Tawney as well as by those of Freud and Marx. From Fromm's point of view, the new freedom of the Renaissance had ambivalent connotations for men of the time. For those with wealth and power, it provided opportunities for self-fulfillment and intellectual and aesthetic discoveries and was congenial to well-placed persons who had an exploitative orientation. But for many persons of the lower classes, the breaking up of medieval society led to a feeling of isolation. The individual no longer had a secure and recognized position in society. Commerce and competition grew rapidly in the 14th and 15th centuries, and the condition of the peasantry and small tradesmen deteriorated. The individual was now on his own, free but alone and powerless.

Fromm sees Lutheranism and Calvinism as religions which appealed to the urban middle class, the urban poor, and the peasants because they gave expression not only to the new sense of freedom but also to the feelings of anxiety and powerlessness felt by these classes. The value of effort was stressed by Calvinism, referring at first to moral effort but later being increasingly concerned with hard work in one's occupation, success in which came to be regarded as a sign of God's grace. Fromm believes that the new ethic of hard work had a compulsive quality related to the sense of anxiety and powerlessness, which the individual sought to overcome through hectic activity. Thus, man became his own slave driver. European man's voluntary application of energy to work resulted in the rapid expansion of the new economy. But men had to pay a price for their compulsive devotion to work. Being thwarted in the areas of emotional and sensual expression, the lower and middle classes developed strong feelings of resentment and hostility.

A hoarding orientation was fostered by conditions in the 18th and 19th centuries. This involved both the positive aspects of being practical, reserved, cautious, tenacious, orderly, and methodical, but also the negative aspects of being stingy, suspicious, cold, anxious, stubborn, obsessional, and possessive (Fromm 1955:91). The exploitative orientation also found channels of expression in the 18th and 19th centuries. But, according to Fromm, conditions have changed in the capitalism of the 20th century. "Instead of the exploitative and hoarding orientation we find the receptive and marketing orientation. Instead of competitiveness we find an increasing tendency toward 'teamwork'; instead of a striving for ever-increasing profit, a wish for a steady and secure income . . ." (p. 99).

Marketing orientation refers to a man's sense of himself as a marketable commodity, his conception of his own value depending on how well he can sell himself and succeed in the business world. If he succeeds, he has a good opinion of himself; if not, he feels that he is a failure. Fromm believes that this kind of personality, characteristic of our time, is marked by a sense of alienation from the self and from others (1955:120, 142).

Fromm writes as a moralist; he is a preacher but a good one. Yet, stimulating though his insights are, they suffer from the drawback that such broad scale reconstructions are hard to adequately document with supporting evidence. Besides, the material which Fromm covers is susceptible to other historical and psychological generalizations. For example, while Fromm writes that Lutheranism and Calvinism were religions of the urban middle class, the poor in the cities, and the peasants, Abram Kardiner in a chapter on "Basic Personality and History" writes that the Reformation was not a movement of the oppressed lower classes or of the peasants but of the new burgher class which was trying to establish a secular state. Calvinism would not seem to appeal to the poor, from Kardiner's viewpoint, since the idea that success is proof of virtue easily leads to contempt for the poor and the unsuccessful (Kardiner et al. 1945:438, 440). Questions of fact as well as of interpretation are involved here. Fromm's generalizations (and Kardiner's, too) need much more documentation to carry conviction. In this respect the study of a Mexican village by Erich Fromm and Michael Maccoby, to which we will return in Chapter 22, is much more satisfactory.

PSYCHOHISTORIANS ON WESTERN MAN

Psychohistory is an endeavor to apply Freudian principles to the study of history. The main contributions so far have been in the form of psychobiography—psychoanalytic treatments of the lives of individuals, such as Freud's on Leonardo da Vinci and Woodrow Wilson, Erik H. Erikson's analyses of Luther and Gandhi, and Bruce Mazlish's books about James Mill, John Stuart Mill, Richard Nixon, and Henry Kissinger.[1] But psychohistorians are also interested in group patterns

---

[1] References to these and other contributions to psychohistory are given in the Suggestions for Further Reading at the end of this chapter.

of personality and how they have been affected by changing methods of child-rearing in the course of history. A leading contributor to this field is Lloyd deMause, editor of *History of Childhood Quarterly*, *The Journal of Psychohistory*, founded in 1973, and of the book, *The History of Childhood* (1975a).

DeMause (1975b) has an optimistic view of history, since he believes that children have been treated progressively better in the course of time. He points out that infanticide was a regular practice in antiquity, and killing children was not considered murder in Rome until A.D. 374. Infants were tightly swaddled in the Middle Ages, partly in the belief that this might keep them from turning into totally evil beings. People projected their own unacceptable, repressed impulses onto their children. It is in these terms that deMause treats the European notion of the changeling. A changeling was a fretful infant who cried too much and was, therefore, suspected of being under the influence of a demon. Baptism was a form of exorcism.

DeMause (1975b:50) suggests that children may have been retarded physically as the result of poor care, a combination of swaddling, neglect, and abuse; he cites the late ages of first walking of some prominent persons in support of this suggestion. DeMause presents a catalog of horrors concerning child-rearing practices in Europe during the Middle Ages and the Renaissance. He claims that children were controlled through scaring devices—bogeyman, masks, and tales of horrible ghosts, and that they were taken to witness hangings, executions, and graveyards.

Wealthy parents turned infants over to wet nurses in medieval Europe and Renaissance times. After infancy they were cared for by other servants, so they spent little time with their parents. Fosterage was a common European practice; children were dispatched to be reared in another family, and well-to-do children were sent out to apprenticeship, monastery, or school by the age of seven. The following four stages characterized the lives of middle-class urban boys in Renaissance Italy: (1) removal from mother to wet nurse, (2) return to the family after two years' absence, (3) school education at seven, and (4) apprenticeship at a bank or shop at 10 to 12 (Ross 1975:215).

If the childhood years are important in personality formation, the modal personality of medieval and Renaissance Europe must have had some pathological features. Indeed, James Bruce Ross (1975:216), who describes child rearing in urban Italy from the 14th to early 16th centuries, asks: "How could the deprived and neglected infants of the middle classes develop into the architects of a vigorous, productive, and creative era which we call 'the Renaissance'?"

But perhaps this negative picture of child-rearing practices has been overdone. In his earlier study of European childhood, Philippe Ariès (1965) took a quite different view. He argued that childhood was a relatively happy time in the Middle Ages, when children were treated as adults, wore the same kinds of clothes, and played the same games. People had more leisure in those days and spent more time sharing entertainment and play with children. But this freedom was surrendered when boys began to go to school in large numbers in the late 16th and early 17th century, with a concomitant loss in naturalness and spontaneity.

Polar opposites in interpretation, like those of Ariès and deMause, are apt to be expressed when a new field of investigation is opening up, as in the case of the history of childhood.[2] It may be pointed out that both Ariès and deMause's books deal only with the Western world. Accounts of some non-Western societies, such as Japan, show that children have often been brought up in a very nurturant fashion in other parts of the world. Trobriand, Manus, and Hopi children until six or seven seem to have had quite happy childhoods. This consideration seems to weaken the cultural evolutionary picture presented by deMause.

Turning to a later period of history, Bruce Mazlish (1975), who counts himself a psychohistorian, has analyzed the lives of James Mill and John Stuart Mill along Freudian lines. He thinks that an Oedipus complex such as he attributes to John Stuart Mill was apt to be fostered by sociocultural patterns in 19th-century Europe. He points to pre-Freudian works dealing with father-son conflict, such as Turgenev's *Fathers and Sons* (1861) and Edmund Gosse's *Father and Son* (1907). The Industrial Revolution and concomitant demographic, political, and social changes in Europe established a new set of environmental conditions to which people had to adjust; these often precipitated conflicts between generations. Mazlish (1975:15–21, 216) discusses the hypothesis that frustrating social conditions may increase patterns of oral dependence and depression. He points out that the early 19th century was just such a period, and that depression seems to be often reflected in the literature of the time.

A still more recent time period which has received psychohistorical treatment is the one preceding the Nazi regime in Germany. Peter Loewenberg (1971) deals with the generation or cohort of young people who suffered from the hardships of World War I: the absence of their fathers, food shortages, the defeat of Germany, and the subsequent return of the fathers, who were often unable to find work in the postwar period. The cohort that grew up in Germany between 1914 and 1929 provided the followers and converts to Hitler's movement. Loewenberg argues that each cohort carries throughout life the influence of early common experiences, such as wars and revolutions, which have different effects on people at different age levels. The young people who grew up during World War I also went through the armistice blockade and later the Great Depression, which

---

[2] See the thoughtful review essay by Stone (1974).

hit Germany harder than other countries. Loewenberg gives data on the extent of hunger and malnutrition, decline of the birthrate, and increase of such diseases as influenza, pneumonia, tuberculosis, diphtheria, typhus, and dysentery, among others. There was a decline in weight and size of infants at birth. There was also a decline in breast feeding from 1915 to 1919, attributable both to war work and malnutrition. Right after the war, since children were so weak, school hours were reduced from seven to two hours daily.

Since many mothers worked in industries during World War I, and since fathers were away at the front, family life was often disrupted. While this was also true in other European countries, Loewenberg argues that conditions were more severe in Germany, which also suffered defeat. All this led to strong emotions of frustration, hatred, and violence. Loewenberg discusses the effects of maternal deprivation and father absence on growing children, including Oedipal conflicts among boys in latency. A boy's struggle against feminine identification would be heightened under such circumstances.

The Nazi movement had much to offer young Germans who went through these experiences. Loewenberg claims that there is ample evidence that this generation was more given to "acting out" than previous youth cohorts. Splitting and projection provided outlets for aggressive impulses and alleviated feelings of unworthiness. Homosexual tensions were relieved through submission to the Führer.

One source of information used by Loewenberg in this analysis is a series of autobiographical essays collected in 1934 by Theodore Abel of Columbia University in a contest offering a prize for the best life-history account by a follower of the Hitler movement. There are nearly 600 such essays.

RIESMAN ON THE CHANGING AMERICAN CHARACTER

Like Bruce Mazlish and some other psychohistorians, David Riesman is interested in the changing characterological patterns in the Western world. However, he does not emphasize child-rearing practices or early experiences in their formation. Riesman criticizes what he sees as a contemporary overemphasis on early childhood and "the tricks of the child-rearing trade," such as feeding schedules and toilet training (Riesman with Glazer and Denney 1953:55). Instead, Riesman and his co-authors, Nathan Glazer and Reuel Denney, are interested in determining the characteristic way in which a society ensures the conformity of its members. In *The Lonely Crowd* they argue that there have been different modes of ensuring conformity at different periods of history, related to the nature of the population curve. In the Western world there has been an S-shaped population curve. "The bottom horizontal line of the S represents a situation where the total population does not increase or does so very slowly, for the number of births equals roughly the number of deaths, and both are very high" (p. 21). This is a condition of "high growth potential," for a population boom could result from a drop in the death rate. When such a spurt occurs (represented by the climbing bar of the S), a society is said to be in a stage of "transitional growth." Then, when the rate of population growth slows down, at the top bar of the S, the society is in a stage of "incipient population decline."

Riesman suggested that each of these three stages is associated with a characteristic mode of ensuring conformity. Societies of high growth potential are dependent on *tradition*-direction; in societies of transitional growth, conformity is achieved through *inner*-direction, while societies of incipient population decline depend on *other*-direction.

In conservative underdeveloped countries, such as India and Egypt, and among nonliterate tribal peoples and "folk societies," one finds the first of these methods of ensuring conformity, tradition-direction. Such societies have a rather rigid etiquette regarding kinship relations, clan or caste membership, and age and sex groups. Not much effort is devoted to finding new solutions to old problems. A quasi-automatic acceptance of traditional culture is instilled in the child, who is not apt to become aware of cultural alternatives.

Inner-direction is associated with transitional growth societies which are experiencing expansion and economic development, such as occurred in Europe from the time of the Renaissance. As Burckhardt suggested, there is greater individualism and personal mobility and more accumulation of capital. It is a period of opening frontiers. More choices and alternatives confront the individual; the weight of tradition is lighter, and the circumstances favor persons who, early in life, have internalized a set of values which will enable them to cope successfully with all kinds of new challenges and situations. Instead of rigid traditions, a rather rigid personality is required. Goals such as wealth, fame, or achievement are pursued by the individual.

The hard work of several inner-directed generations finally brings about an advanced industrialized economy which now requires different virtues of its participants. There is a decline in the numbers and proportion of persons engaged in industrial production and agriculture and an increase in white-collar and service trades. What this system demands is harmonious working within an established organization. An other-directed personality is in keeping with this need, a personality which is sensitive to the moods and feelings of others and adaptable to external influences. Riesman and associates (1953:21, 38) find this type to be American rather than European, appearing especially in the upper middle class of our larger cities.[3]

---

[3] A similar analysis, although couched in different terminology, appears in *The Organization Man* by William H. Whyte, Jr., (1956). Whyte believes that the Protestant ethnic of orderliness, thrift, and hard work is being replaced in our time by a social ethic that emphasizes the virtue of belonging in a group, which is seen as the source of creativity. See also Kluckhohn (1958).

In application to the American scene, Riesman's picture of the inner-directed character of the transitional growth period is reminiscent of Frederick Jackson Turner's thesis (1920) that American national character was decisively shaped by the experience of frontier life, leading to the development of such traits as independence, resourcefulness, and self-reliance. With the closing of the frontier, there was presumably less need for these qualities.

Some articles by Leo Lowenthal and by de Charms and Moeller give support to Riesman's views. In a review of the kinds of persons who served as topics of popular magazine biographies between 1901 and 1941, Leo Lowenthal (1944) found that the more recent publications emphasized "idols of consumption," such as film stars, baseball players, and night club entertainers, rather than "idols of production," such as the business tycoons written about in earlier years. In a study of 150 years of children's readers, Richard de Charms and Gerald H. Moeller (1962) found a consistent decline in achievement imagery after the 1880s. But this is indirect evidence; it tells us what was being published and offered to the public, which might not necessarily reflect the attitudes of the readers. A more direct reflection has been provided by Fred I. Greenstein (1964) in an analysis of a "forgotten body of survey data," consisting of a number of studies giving questionnaire findings about children's expressed ideals between 1902 and 1958. In these investigations children were asked what person they would most like to resemble. Greenstein's analysis of this material showed that although identifications with business and political leaders are rare today, they were also rare at the turn of the century. Greenstein found little evidence for a change in values along the lines suggested by Riesman.

Riesman's writing, like Fromm's, is persuasive; but when examined critically in detail, it shows various weaknesses, which have been noted by such critics as David M. Potter, Carl N. Degler, Seymour M. Lipset, and David Riesman himself. The role of incipient population decline in bringing about other-direction has been questioned by David M. Potter, professor of history at Stanford University. Potter (1954:61) points out that incipient population decline is characteristic of England and France, but he doubts that typical Englishmen or Frenchmen could be said to be other-directed. Seymour M. Lipset, professor of sociology at Harvard, notes that in 1961 the United States had one of the highest rates of population growth in the Western world, which should presage a return to inner-direction, if the correlation is valid (Lipset 1961:157).

In a new preface to *The Lonely Crowd* in 1961, Riesman conceded that the use of the population cycle was probably less effective than would have been a discussion of economic development, urbanization, and the spread of education.

Carl N. Degler (1963) observes that Riesman's analysis of American character deals only with the middle class, not with the lower class, and only with city people, not rural people, while David M. Potter has pointed out that Riesman's generalizations, like those of Frederick Jackson Turner, apply mainly to men and not to women. According to Potter (1962), women have always been dependent, other-directed, and sensitive to the moods and interests of others; but at present, with growing economic opportunities, many women now seem to be becoming less other-directed.

Both Degler and Lipset agree that other-direction is an important aspect of American national character, but they do not believe that it is a recent phenomenon related to our advanced economy and incipient population decline. Instead, both Degler and Lipset trace other-direction back as far as the early 19th century, relating it to early American egalitarian democratic traditions, and citing in evidence such early commentators on American character as Alexis de Tocqueville and Harriet Martineau.

Some documentation for Riesman's views is provided by interview and life history material in *Faces in the Crowd. Individual Studies in Character and Politics* by David Riesman in collaboration with Nathan Glazer (1952). But Riesman's claims for this documentation (p. vi) are very modest: "there is, it should be clear, no proof offered here for the generalizations in that book [*The Lonely Crowd*] . . . reasonably conclusive judgments concerning large-scale historical hypotheses, especially perhaps in typological form, cannot be made on this kind of evidence alone." He also says (p. 7) that we are a long way from relating other-direction to modern urban America, or tradition-direction to any particular preliterate society. Besides, the three types overlap one another; they are not discrete. Thus, we are left with some rather blurry generalizations, the validity of which has not been demonstrated.

It is interesting to note, however, that there is some correspondence between Riesman's views about the shift from tradition-direction to inner-direction and the contrasts made by Whiting and Whiting between the simpler and more complex cultures of the Six Cultures project described in Chapter 8. The simpler cultures, you will recall, are characterized by subsistence farming with little economic specialization, while the more complex cultures have a cash economy, class or caste stratification, and a centralized political and legal system. There are more chores for children and more emphasis on obedience in the simpler cultures, more individualism and competitiveness in the more complex cultures. Robert A. LeVine's comment about folk and peasant societies is worth repeating in this context. LeVine (1970:594) suggested that the severe aggression training in such groups "may be part of a larger tendency to make children orderly, obedient, and pacific, producing an inhibitedness that manifests itself in performance on cognitive tasks." This might be a way of characterizing tradition-direction.

THE GAP BETWEEN GENERATIONS

A number of commentators on the American scene, including Margaret Mead, Geoffrey Gorer, and Urie Bronfenbrenner, have written about the break between generations and the consequently dominant role of the peer group in this country. This is an old theme. In 1933 an American mother complained about the loss of parental influence on children: "Their standards and their ideals are formed in the school atmosphere, and more by their companions than their teachers" (Rapson 1965:522).

Mead (1942) and Gorer (1948) both explain the break between generations in terms of the experience of immigration to the New World. The children of immigrants became ashamed of their parents, with their Old World ways, and tried to become more American than they—which they could learn better from their peers than from their parents. American parents expect their children to be different from them and to surpass them. More likely than not, the son will take up a profession different from his father's and move away from home. According to Gorer, the Old World immigrant father lacked the authority of the European father and was rejected by his son. This established a new pattern for father-son relations in the New World. But the mother, being associated with food, love, and care, retained an important emotional role and assumed a dominant position in the family, disciplining the children and becoming their source of moral conduct.

Bronfenbrenner on American Children

A more recent analyst of the changing American scene is Urie Bronfenbrenner, a professor of psychology at Cornell University. Bronfenbrenner (1970) has made studies of children in both the United States and the Soviet Union, and he makes comparisons between the two national groups, mostly to the advantage of the USSR. This is suggested by the fact that Part 1 of his book has the heading "The Making of the New Soviet Man," while Chapter 4 is entitled "The Unmaking of the American Child."

What is unmaking the American child? Largely, according to Bronfenbrenner, it is the decreasing contact which a child has with its parents and other adults. By default, children spend most of their time with their peers, so that our society is becoming segregated not only by race and class but also by age. Families are smaller, and a child has fewer meaningful contacts with adults than formerly. In one study, 766 sixth-grade children reported spending, during the week-end, an average of two to three hours a day with their parents, slightly more time with groups of friends, and an additional two or three hours per day with a single friend. An analysis of their data led Bronfenbrenner and his colleagues to conclude that the peer-oriented children are more influenced by lack of attention at home than by the attractiveness of the peer group.

The vacuum left by parental withdrawal is also filled by the television set. According to one study, the average viewing time for children between 6 and 17 years of age is 22 hours per week. In another study, TV viewing time was said to range from 17 hours per week at second grade to 28 hours per week at sixth grade.

Bronfenbrenner cites some studies which indicate that the waching of violent TV films leads to increased aggressiveness. At the same time, decrease in parental concern contributes to a decrease in qualities of responsibility and leadership and to lowered self-esteem.

The peer group also plays a large role in the Soviet Union but in a more constructive way, being directly influenced by adults, while the American peer group is more autonomous, having little contact with the adult world. If these current trends persist, Bronfenbrenner (1970:95–119) predicts increasing alienation among American children and adolescents, more indifference, antagonism, and violence.

The Hippie Scene

A highly visible manifestation of the generation gap today is the difference in appearance of the older and many of the younger generation, who in the 1960s and 1970s often had long hair, faded patched blue jeans, and such features as beads and Indian headbands. Not all who dressed in this style were hippies, but there was a period in the 1960s when the hippie cult was a recognized phenomenon and when hippies were proud to claim the title.

Lewis Yablonsky (1968:36), a professor of sociology at San Fernando Valley State College, California, who conducted interviews with many hippies in New York and California in 1967, estimated that there were then about 200,000 identifiable hippie dropouts in the United States, another 200,000 teeny-boppers (teen-age part-time hippies), several hundred thousand "Clark Kent" hippies who used drugs and interacted with hippies but who kept regular jobs or attended college, and millions of hippie "fellow travelers," many of whom were in the academic community.

Yablonsky gave over 700 questionnaires to hippies. According to his data, over 70 percent came from middle- and upper-class families; 77.6 percent had graduated from high school, and 50.6 percent had attended some college. There were more male (75.5 percent) than female (24.5 percent) hippies. Most hippies smoked marijuana; some took LSD, methedrine, or amphetamines. About half had been locked up at some time, either in a prison or mental hospital (1968:340–48).

Evidently this was a new way of life or subculture in the United States which rejected the dominant life-style and the traditional goals and values of middle-class America. Like militant blacks, white hippies were against the system, but the blacks seemed to want to get out of the ghetto and share the opportunities and advantages enjoyed by middle-class whites, while many hippies had left comfortable middle-class homes to live in the ghetto.

Nathan Adler (1968) labeled hippies as examples of "the antinomian type," which he claims has emerged at various times in the history of the Western world in periods of crisis and transition: the Gnostics and Manicheans from the time of the collapse of the Roman empire, the later Cathars, Albigensians, Waldensians, and Anabaptists, and the 19th century Romantic movement. In all of these cases, according to Adler, there is a stress on the immediate moment, on intuition and feeling rather than reason, on self-actualization and transcendance, and a rejection of traditional morality.

How Much of a Gap?

To what extent did this movement signalize a real generation gap? Some writers consider the generation gap to be profound. According to Margaret Mead (1970), the gap is a worldwide phenomenon, not limited to the United States. The generation born after World War II, she tells us, has spent its whole life with a knowledge of the existence of the atom bomb. Members of the older generation are now immigrants, not in space but in time, strangers in a postwar world which may be better understood by the young. Indeed, Mead (1970:68) states that none of the young "is untouched by the sense that there are no adults anywhere in the world from whom they can learn what the next steps should be." A similar view is set forth in the optimistic best seller, *The Greening of America* (1971) by Charles A. Reich. Reich, who teaches law at Yale University Law School, believes that members of the younger generation are acquiring a consciousness different from that of their parents; he calls it Consciousness III. Reich's sentimental faith in the young is expressed in this quotation: "the young people of Consciousness III see effortlessly what is phony or dishonest in politics, or what is ugly or meretricious in architecture and city planning, whereas an older person has to go through years of education to make himself equally aware" (p. 283). Reich predicts that Consciousness III will bring about a bloodless revolution which will change our country's political system as its final act.

The impressionistic views of Mead and Reich about differences in the generations are based on their reading and conversations, not on any organized interviews or questionnaires. A more balanced view, to my mind, is provided in an essay by Joseph Adelson, "What Generation Gap?" (1970). Adelson points out that it is common for writers on this subject to generalize about the young on the basis of only a segment of the younger generation, usually those in college rather than noncollege workers, and usually left-wing activists rather than more conservative students. Adelson considers some different criteria for the generation gap. One is conflict or lack of understanding between parents and children. Four studies on this topic are cited, including one by Adelson and Elizabeth Douvan of 3,000 young people aged 12 to 18. All four studies give similar findings: most interviewees report good relationships with their parents. One study estimates that about 10 percent of the students interviewed were seriously at odds with their parents.

Another criterion for the generation gap is differences of opinion about politics, with the young being assumed to be more radical. Adelson points out that in most cases (about 75 percent) children vote for the same party as their parents. Adelson also cites a *Fortune* poll of 18 to 24 year olds, in which more than 80 percent reported that they do not think that there are any great differences in values between themselves and their parents.

There is no doubt that the hippies represented a break with the dominant culture and that many young people share some hippie beliefs and values; but in general, there does not seem to be as marked a cleavage between today's generations as some writers have claimed.

SUGGESTIONS FOR FURTHER READING

A general bibliography on psychohistory is available in Lloyd deMause, ed., *Psychohistory: A Bibliographic Guide* (New York: Garland Publishing, 1975). Freud's pioneer studies are "Leonardo da Vinci and a Memory of his Childhood," *Collected Works*, Standard Edition, vol. 11, pp. 63–137; and Sigmund Freud and William C. Bullitt, *Thomas Woodrow Wilson: A Psychological Study* (Boston: Houghton Mifflin, 1967). Erik Homburger Erikson's two leading psychobiographies are *Young Man Luther. A Study in Psychoanalysis and History* (New York: W. W. Norton, 1958) and *Gandhi's Truth. On the Origins of Militant Nonviolence* (New York: W. W. Norton, 1969). Bruce Mazlish is the author of *In Search of Nixon. A Psychohistorical Inquiry* (New York: Basic Books, 1972), *James and John Stuart Mill. Father and Son in the Nineteenth Century* (New York: Basic Books, 1975), and *Kissinger. The European Mind in American Politics* (New York: Basic Books, 1976). See also Dana Ward, "Kissinger: A Psychohistory" in *The New Psychohistory*, ed. Lloyd deMause (New York: Psychohistory Press, 1975, pp. 69–130). Former President Jimmy Carter has been given a psychohistorical treatment in Lloyd deMause and Henry Ebel, eds., *Jimmy Carter and American Fantasy: Psychohistorical Explorations* (New York: Two Continents/Psychohistory Press, 1977).

21

Ethnic Minorities

In recent years social scientists from different academic disciplines have given much attention to the study of ethnic minorities. Two issues concerning such groups are addressed in this chapter. One is the relationship between national character and ethnic group. This concerns such questions as: How have particular immigrant groups adjusted to conditions in the host country? To what extent is the nature of their adjustment explainable in terms of personality tendencies that originated in the mother country? A second issue concerns the factors that strengthen or weaken a sense of ethnic identity. Some third-generation Americans, for example, have a strong sense of being Polish, Italian, or Irish, despite their long assimilation in the United States, while others lack such identifications. What psychological factors are involved in the emphasis or deemphasis of ethnic boundaries?

THE CONCEPT OF ETHNIC MINORITY: HISTORICAL BACKGROUND

Before turning to the issues just mentioned, we must define *ethnic minority* and consider the historical background for the current interest in this field. Webster's Seventh New Collegiate Dictionary defines a *minority* as "a part of a population differing from others in some characteristics and often subjected to differential treatment." Webster's definition of *ethnic* is rather ambiguous: "of or relating to races or large groups of people classified according to common traits and customs." This definition combines both racial and cultural criteria. It is true that ethnic groups are sometimes racially distinguishable, but often they are not. Louis Wirth (1945:347) defines a minority as a group of people who have been singled out by others for differential and unequal treatment and who, therefore, feel discriminated against. Because he defines *minority* in this way, Wirth paradoxically claims that a minority may actually make up a numerical majority. It seems to me, however, that minorities do not necessarily feel discriminated against in all cases, at least not to the same degree.

Membership in an ethnic group is both an ascribed and an achieved status. A child is born into a minority group, grows up in it, and learns its special ways of life. If the group is characterized by a particular language or religion, the child will learn to speak the language and acquire knowledge of the religious beliefs and practices. To that extent, ethnic minority status is ascribed. But there is also a voluntary aspect to this group membership, since learned patterns of behavior may be changed. The individual may reject the traditional religion, stop speaking the language, and try to change his or her identity. Or the individual may decide to affirm the ethnic identity; to that extent it becomes an achieved status.

The existence of an ethnic minority, which usually has one or more names as labels, depends on its acknowledgment by both members and outsiders. Sometimes the insistence on a group's separateness comes more from the outside than from within. This seems to be the case, for example, of the Eta, a discriminated-against minority group in Japan that was formerly associated with leather work and still is, to some extent. Eta are not happy to acknowledge their minority status, but they don't have much choice. There is little to distinguish them from other Japanese. They have no distinctive physical characteristics, which is why De Vos and Wagatsuma (1966) refer to them as Japan's "invisible race." Nor do they differ from other Japanese in cultural traits. Nevertheless, they are identifiable; they have a group name and have traditionally been treated much as untouchable leather workers are treated in India.

In the case of the Eta, then, insistence on their separateness comes more from outsiders than from the Eta themselves. In the case of some other ethnic minority groups, the insistence on separateness may come mainly from the group's members themselves. For example, the Matinnecock Indians of Long Island want very much to be regarded as Indians, although in most respects they do not differ much from their Long Island neighbors. They have few traditional Indian customs but are now trying to learn Indian ways, as William Hawk, a member of this group, has informed me.

Language and religion were referred to earlier as markers that identify ethnic boundaries. In some cases clothing (as among the Gypsies) is another marker. The Lubovitcher Hassidic Jews of Brooklyn can be distinguished by language, religion, and dress. They place value on learning Yiddish and have special schools in which instruction is in Yiddish. A Lubovitch man usually wears a narrow-brimmed black hat and a dark suit, and he is apt to be bearded. Some have sidelocks which are tucked behind the ears. A Lubovitch male should always have his head covered. If he is not wearing a narrow-brimmed hat, he wears a skullcap, and many wear skullcaps under their hats (Levy 1973).

For the Hassidim, religion is the main integrating factor that maintains the separateness of the group. Groups which might otherwise form a single unit may be divided along religious lines. Thus, most Serbs are Orthodox Christians, while most Croats are Roman Catholics. Religion may also unify groups that otherwise form separate categories, as in the case of the Roman Catholic Poles, Irish, and Italians.

In cases where the religious emphasis is strong, there may be a tendency toward group endogamy, as among the Lubovitch Hassidim, whose marriages are arranged by families. Even in the absence of such arrangements, marriages may take place mainly within the group if most social relationships occur within it, due to the common language and the traditional customs that serve to isolate its members to some extent. Ethnic neighborhoods can often be identified. When Italian immigrants came to New York City, those from Naples settled in the Mulberry Bend area, those from Sicily on Elizabeth Street, and those from Genoa on Baxter Street (Jones 1960). Chinatowns also exist in many larger American cities.

Some minority groups are associated with particular occupations—in some cases because when they immigrated they had to accept low-paying unskilled jobs. This was the case among the southern Italians who arrived in New York in large numbers between 1880 and 1920. Most of them had been peasants in the old country, and about 70 percent were illiterate (Lopreato 1970:32). However, many first-generation Italian immigrants, despite their lack of commercial experience, started stores, restaurants, and other enterprises to a much greater degree than did Irish immigrants (Glazer and Moynihan 1970:206). The Irish, who had come in large numbers during the 1840s, also took low-paying unskilled labor jobs but did not usually branch out into commerce. Many became policemen. The Chinese often established laundries and restaurants.

Consciousness of separate identity and minority status may lead to the formation of organizations to campaign for the rights of the group. The Jews, for example, have the American Jewish Committee, the Anti-Defamation League of B'nai B'rith, and the American Jewish Congress as three major organizations concerned with civil rights. There may also be organizations which provide social centers and organize get-togethers for members of the group. Religious centers may serve these functions. Political organizations, such as Tammany Hall for the New York Irish, may also do so.

Special foods sometimes characterize an ethnic group, either due to tradition, as with Italian spaghetti and Chinese chow mein, or else for religious reasons, as in Jewish Kosher foods.

It used to be assumed that the ethnic differences of immigrant groups would disappear within a few generations in the New World. In practice, we often find them to be tenacious. That was the point made by Glazer and Moynihan in *Beyond the Melting Pot*, which was first published in 1963. *The Melting Pot* was the title of a play by Israel Zangwill, performed on Broadway in 1908, in which one character stated: "America is God's Crucible, the great Melting Pot where all the races of Europe are melting and reforming!" (Glazer and Moynihan 1970:289). This notion of growing cultural homogeneity was in keeping with the idea that each nation has its own culture. If American culture is heterogeneous, it is because this country was populated by waves of immigrants from different parts of the world. But with the passage of time cultural integration should develop, and these differences will disappear. Such, at least, were the earlier assumptions, which have not worked out as expected.[1]

NATIONAL CHARACTER AND ETHNIC GROUP

We turn now to the first of the two issues singled out at the beginning of this chapter: the relationship between national character and the nature of a group's adjustment to conditions in the host country. A good test for the significance of national character in this connection is to see if similar personality traits are in evidence when emigrants from a particular nation settle in two or more different countries. For example, De Vos, Hauswald, and Borders (1979:252) were struck by the similarities of the TAT stories told by Chinese in Taiwan and Chinese in San Francisco, describing the two sets as "indistinguishable."

> It is remarkable how distinctively "Chinese" profiles have been obtained from the sample of Chinese who have in the one instance migrated to Taiwan three hundred years ago and, in the other instance, Chinese from the vicinity of Canton who have come to the American continent at various times over the past hundred years (pp. 253–54).

The two settings—Taiwan and San Francisco—were very different. In Taiwan the Chinese immigrants became the dominant group, while in San Francisco they made up "an encapsulated minority within American culture." The authors argue that the results suggest a "basic similarity in culture throughout Southeast China" (pp. 253–54).[2]

An even more striking example of continuity is seen in connection with the Japanese who settled in Hawaii, the United States, and Brazil, The first Japanese arrived in Hawaii in 1885. Colleen Johnson

---

[1] Since *Beyond the Melting Pot* was published, there has been an outpouring of books and articles on ethnicity, ethnic pluralism, and ethnic identity. Fredrik Barth's *Ethnic Groups and Boundaries* appeared in 1969. Then in 1971 Michael Novak's book, *The Rise of the Unmeltable Ethnics*, drew attention, with a kind of defiant pride, to America's "white ethnics," including Poles, Italians, Greeks, and Slavs, who have, to some extent, resisted assimilation. A symposium on *White Ethnics* (Ryan 1973) followed in due course. There are now several journals:. *Ethnicity, Journal of Ethnic Studies*, and *Ethnic and Racial Studies*.

[2] See page 301.

(1976) notes that third-generation Japanese in Hawaii still strongly endorse respect for elders and filial piety, but they have also accepted a self-assertive ethic of success and have moved into middle-class white-collar jobs, seeking for more education and higher income. The first Japanese came to the United States in 1891, many in secondary migration from Hawaii. E. K. Strong (1934) observed that while Japanese-American children in California scored about the same as other children on IQ tests, they got strikingly better grades, suggesting the presence of a strong drive for achievement.

We saw in Chapter 2 that Japanese in Japan manifest strong achievement motivation, even among the rural villagers of Niiike, whose TAT stories were analyzed by George De Vos. This seems to have been the case among Japanese-Americans as well. From 1947 to 1950 William Caudill and his co-workers studied some of the 20,000 Japanese-Americans who had moved from war relocation camps to the city of Chicago. Despite the existence of racist and anti-Japanese attitudes in the larger population, the Japanese-Americans soon moved into well-paying white-collar and skilled labor jobs, particularly the Nisei, or those of the second generation. Moreover, they were generally well regarded by their employers and fellow workers. The Nisei showed the same desire for higher education and training as did the Japanese in Japan and in Hawaii.

> In the skilled trades the Nisei men worked as printers, welders, electricians, mechanics, and jewelry and watch repairmen. . . . In the white collar field the Nisei men worked as clerks, draftsmen, laboratory technicians, commercial artists, and studio photographers. . . . As managers (5.5 percent) they worked in personnel departments, as laboratory heads, and as editors. As professional men (6.5 percent) they were doctors, dentists, lawyers, pharmacists, research workers, and teachers (Caudill 1952:21–22).

Most of the Nisei were relatively young men, between the ages of 20 and 30, who had not been in Chicago very long. In commenting on the stories told in the Thematic Apperception Test, Caudill (1952:51) remarked, "Like the Issei [first-generation], the Nisei value, and are strongly self-motivated toward, long-range goals which they try to achieve no matter what the obstacles."[3]

There are about 750,000 Japanese in Brazil, where the environment and the immigrants' experiences were quite different from those in the United States. The Japanese came later to Brazil than to the United States, the first arriving in 1908, with the migration peak appearing between 1926 and 1935. Most Japanese in Brazil came as agricultural laborers contracted to work on coffee plantations in Sao

---

[3] See p. 52. See also Caudill and De Vos (1956).

Paulo. They arrived in family units, as required by the government. Opportunities for education were limited. The Japanese bought land, as they did in California, and made it flourish. They pioneered in the establishment of agricultural cooperatives and built settlements and schools. Despite the existence of racial prejudice, the Japanese came to be admired by the Brazilians for their reliability and organizing ability. There is a strong demand for Nisei for jobs that require the handling of money, and they are now well established in commerce and the professions (Smith 1979). We can find a strain of consistency, then, in the picture of Japanese social character as described in Chapter 2 and the information from Hawaii, the United States, and Brazil. About 85 percent of the Japanese that came to the United States were of rural origin, but they were not former serfs, and they had what George De Vos (1972:456) calls "an internalized sense of self-respect . . . which was useful in overcoming the severe racism of American society. . . . They did not evaluate themselves according to the American attitudes directed towards them as peasants or immigrant workers, or 'yellow' Asians."

De Vos (1980a:122) has drawn some contrasts between the reactions of Mexican-Americans and Japanese-Americans in the United States. "What is very apparent in the studies we conducted among Japanese-Americans, and is apparent equally in Japan, is that the school peer group by and large socially reinforces the parental directives of socially cohesive families rather than acting to the contrary." As a result, juvenile delinquency or discipline problems at school are minimal. De Vos (1980a:121) contrasts this with the picture in many Mexican-American families:

> A good number of Mexican children seek out the peer group as a refuge from what is felt to be an unhappy family relationship. These peer groups are antagonistic to the schools. For many Mexicans there is a feeling that authorities in the United States, whether found in schools or in other social agencies, are alien "Anglos" not concerned with "Chicano" youth. These peer groups become delinquent in orientation and the individual becomes involved in delinquent activity in concert with others.

Dealing with the same topic in another publication (1980b), De Vos writes:

> Japanese on the west coast from the early thirties up to the present time manifest a rate of delinquency in police statistics that has hovered about one-eightieth that of the majority population of the state, while Mexican-American and black youths in California have rates that hover between four and six times that of the majority "white" category in California statistics.

ETHNIC IDENTITY

Let us now consider the second issue mentioned at the beginning of this chapter: the factors that strengthen or weaken a sense of ethnic identity. Despite the recent emphasis on cultural pluralism in the United States, it must be admitted that there is some truth in the melting pot idea, since there are groups that *have* become absorbed into the larger society and culture. Glazer and Moynihan claim that the Germans of New York City are a case in point, partly as a result of the anti-German feelings which developed during World War I and II, which led to a deemphasis on Germanness on the part of the Germans themselves. The authors point to the large German percentage of New York's population, perhaps one third, second only to the Irish in the late 19th century.

> But today, while German influence is to be seen in virtually every aspect of the city's life, the Germans *as a group* are vanished. No appeals are made to the German vote, there are no German politicians in the sense that there are Irish or Italian politicians, there are in fact few Germans in political life and, generally speaking, no German component in the structure of the ethnic interests of the city" (1970:311).

Some writers suggest that there is something rather phoney or artificial in the emphasis on cultural pluralism and ethnic identity. G. James Patterson (1979) states that writers on this subject often have a tendency to exaggerate the cultural differences of minority groups. Culture patterns which are in fact rather weak in the United States may be more noticeable and exotic in this setting and thus seem to be more important than they really are. Herbert J. Gans (1979) used the term *symbolic identity* for the superficial significance of such cultural persistence. Ethnic foods and picnics don't add up to a separate culture. Polish-Americans in Milwaukee are probably not very different from other Americans and often speak no Polish. However, a sense of national origin and distinctiveness is retained.

Gans (1979:3) claims that some writers who stress ethnicity "are looking primarily at poorer ethnics, who have been less touched by acculturation and assimilation than middle class ethnics." This point was also made by Warner and Srole (1945): New ethnic groups originally got unskilled labor jobs at the bottom of the social ladder. As they climb up the ladder, they lose their ethnicity. Meanwhile, a sense of symbolic identity may be easily satisfied by participation in occasional religious holidays or rites of passage which involve no deep commitment; "they do not take much time, do not upset the everyday routine, and also become an occasion for family reunions to reassemble family members who are rarely seen on a regular basis" (Gans 1979:10). Commercial firms provide easy-to-cook ethnic foods which take little time to prepare. "Old countries are particularly useful as identity symbols because they are far away and cannot make arduous demands on American ethnics. . . ."[4]

A deeper psychological analysis is made in a study by Howard F. Stein and Robert F. Hill (1977) of ethnic identity among Slovak, Polish, and Ruthenian Americans in Pennsylvania. The authors argue that the new eastern European immigrants in the United States greatly wished for assimilation in the New World and regarded their escape from Europe as a kind of liberation. To them the American slogans of "life, liberty, and the pursuit of happiness" were very appealing; "the paradox is that the New Ethnicity was created not when traditional *ethnic* culture was threatened, but when the *American Dream* was threatened, that is, when members of various 'groups' felt the dream to be unrealizable for them" (p. 43; Stein and Hill's emphasis). Stein and Hill point out that white ethnic Americans are largely lower middle class and working-class persons who feel themselves threatened by poverty and by the black power movement. "The white ethnic counter-counterculture is an attempt to reinstate caste through the guise of ethnicity, or culture—thereby putting blacks again in their 'place'—while being able to rationalize and deny that this motive has anything to do with racial exclusion" (p. 144).

The frustrations of the Poles-Italians-Greeks-Slavs (hence the acronym PIGS) were compounded when "the working-class whites were called 'pigs' and 'hardhats' by self-righteous white liberals, college students, and blacks" (1977:188). The traditional European culture now became idealized and served as a bond and symbol for the alienated white ethnic minorities, while hostility was directed toward both WASPs and blacks.

Joseph Lopreato (1970:168–69) believes that obsessive sensitivity is common in all minority groups and that self-hatred and efforts toward ego-enhancement are also common. He finds these patterns among Italian-Americans. In the presence of such emotions, it would not be surprising for some outward projection to take place, channeling hostility toward other groups. As Gus Tyler (1973:131) put it, "Our white worker is ready for battle. But he does not quite know against whom to declare war."

One advantage in finding an enemy, from the viewpoint of individual psychology, is to clarify one's self-identity by making distinc-

---

[4] It may be noted that when Gans gives examples of ethnic groups in this article, he always refers to Jews and Italians, to European-Americans; he never refers to Asian-Americans of Chinese, Japanese, or Indian origin. The experiences of Asian-Americans have probably been quite different from those of European-Americans. For example, although Germany and Italy were enemies in World War II, there was no rounding up and deporting to concentration camps of German-Americans and Italian-Americans as there was of Japanese-Americans, including those who were American citizens.

tions between "us" and "them." "Ethnic identity can be a positive affirmation containing a negative potential for becoming a hysterical or paranoid defense. . . . How one learns about oneself by contrasting oneself to other individuals and groups is important, for only in this way does one develop a strong sense of self" (De Vos and Romanucci-Ross 1982:366, 368).

It would be best, of course, if one could develop such a sense without creating scapegoats or enemies; but this analysis helps one to understand some of the factors involved in strengthening or weakening ethnic identity. The leaders of ethnic movements often seem to be people who have had identity conflicts themselves. In the process of rallying others to a common cause, the leader heightens his group's solidarity. Gananath Obeyeskere (1982:250) describes the career of one such leader in Sri Lanka or Ceylon, Anagarika Dharmapala (1864–1933), who was exposed to Christian teachings at school but to Buddhism at home. After a period of confusion over divided loyalties he swung to the side of Buddhism, which he sought to regenerate in a nation that had become mainly Protestant under British rule. It was due to Dharmapala's influence that Ceylonese stopped using European personal names and surnames and switched to giving their children Sinhalese or Buddhist names instead, while Ceylonese women exchanged their former Western-style dress for Indian *sārīs*. This process is what Obeyeskere calls a new *identity affirmation*—in this case an affirmation of Sinhalese Buddhist identity. "The psychological function of identity affirmation is to enhance a group's low self-esteem."

SUGGESTIONS FOR FURTHER READING

For a brief bibliography on American ethnic studies, see Josef J. Barton, *Brief Ethnic Bibliography. An Annotated Guide to the Ethnic Experience in the United States* (Cambridge, Mass.: Press of the Langdon Associated, 1976).

For the American scene, a good introduction to the study of ethnic groups is Nathan Glazer and Daniel P. Moynihan's *Beyond the Melting Pot. The Negroes, Puerto Ricans, Jews, Italians, and Irish of New York City*, 2d ed. (Cambridge, Mass.: MIT Press, 1970). For particular groups, see Joseph Lopreato, *Italian Americans* (New York: Random House, 1970); Abram Kardiner and Lionel Ovesey, *The Mark of Oppression. Explorations in the Personality of the American Negro* (Cleveland: World Publishing Co., 1961); and Howard F. Stein and Robert F. Hill, *The Ethnic Imperative. Examining the New White Ethnic Movement* (University Park, Pennsylvania: Pennsylvania State University Press, 1977).

Some anthologies include: *The New Ethnicity. Perspectives from Ethnology* edited by John W. Bennett (St. Paul: West Publishing Co., 1973); Nathan Glazer and Daniel P. Moynihan, eds., *Ethnicity. Theory and Experience* (Cambridge, Mass.: Harvard University Press, 1975); and George De Vos and Lola

Romanucci-Ross, eds., *Ethnic Identity. Cultural Continuities and Change* (Chicago: University of Chicago Press, 1982).

See also Anya Peterson Royce, *Ethnic Identity. Strategies of Diversity* (Bloomington: Indiana University Press, 1982). On an ethnic minority in Japan, see Changsoo Lee and George De Vos, *Koreans in Japan: Ethnic Conflict and Accommodation* (Berkeley: University of California Press, 1981).

22

Economic Development and Personality

Related to the works by Fromm and Riesman[1] is the question of the relationships between economic development and personality. Why have some nations, such as those of Western Europe, experienced a surge of economic advance within a relatively short time, while other less-developed nations have struggled along slowly, having great difficulty in raising living standards and increasing industrial production? Max Weber was a pioneer in examining this problem cross-culturally and in suggesting that it was not a question of economic factors alone. Weber noted that the great economic advance in Europe was associated with Protestant rather than Catholic countries. He concluded that the new independence and autonomy of Protestantism and its emphasis on asceticism and hard work led to a new breed of men, "men who had grown up in the hard school of life, calculating and daring at the same time, above all temperate and reliable, shrewd and completely devoted to their business, with strictly bourgeois opinions and principles" (Weber 1952:39).

This is a personality characterization, a personality associated with a particular religious movement. As we have seen, Fromm carried this analysis further by arguing that the lower and middle classes of Europe were drawn toward Protestantism because they experienced anxiety and powerlessness with the collapse of the feudal social system, while Riesman related these developments to the transitional growth phase of the population cycle.

In 1961 two books were published which made further contributions to the study of the relationship between economic development and personality. One was by a psychologist from Harvard, David C. McClelland, who concerned himself with economics; the other was by an economist from M.I.T., Everett E. Hagen, who became involved in studying personality. Both authors echoed Weber's point that development is not understandable in solely economic terms, with McClelland citing G. M. Meier and R. E. Baldwin (1957:119) to the effect that "economic development is much too serious a topic to

---

[1] See pp. 406–7, 410–13.

be left to economists." At the same time, both McClelland and Hagen criticized Weber's stress on the Protestant ethic as the source for economic advance in Europe. For McClelland, the emphasis on work connected with the Protestant ethic is only a special case of a more general phenomenon, for there has been a similar emphasis on hard work in other societies which are not Protestant, such as modern Japan and the Soviet Union. McClelland saw the key psychological factor as being the need for achievement (n-Achievement).

ACHIEVEMENT MOTIVATION

The strength of the achievement motive varies among individuals and among societies; it has been more in evidence at some time periods than in others. How can one gauge its relative strength at different times in the past? McClelland found an index of n-Achievement in children's readers. He and his colleagues collected 1,300 children's stories from 23 countries, all translated into English. The stories came from readers used in the second to fourth grades in two time periods: around 1925 and around 1950. Codes were used on proper names, so that scorers would not guess the story's country of origin. The tales were mixed up and coded for n-Achievement.

McClelland also needed an index for a country's degree of economic development. The one he selected was the amount of electricity produced in kilowatt-hours per capita. "The correlation between the n-Achievement level in the children's readers in 1925 and the growth in electrical output between 1925 and 1950, as compared with expectation, is a quite substantial .53, which is highly significant statistically" (McClelland 1963:81). A concern for achievement, as expressed in the children's stories, was thus related to a more rapid rate of economic development, as measured by increase in use of electricity. This generalization applied not only to such Western democracies as England and the United States but also to Communist countries such as Russia, Bulgaria, and Hungary (McClelland 1961:105). McClelland pointed out that the 1950 n-Achievement level was not correlated with *prior* economic growth between 1925 and 1950. Evidence for high n-Achievement *precedes* economic growth, suggesting that the achievement motive is a causative factor, not an epiphenomenon, in opposition to the assumptions of economic determinism.

A study of Spanish economic development by Juan B. Cortés (1960) is based on this same psychological determinism. Cortés predicted that a rise in the level of achievement motivation would directly precede a rise in Spanish economic growth. This was tested by scoring Spanish literary material from three time periods: 1200–1492, a period of economic growth; 1492–1610, a period of economic climax; and 1610–1730, a period of economic decline. Various indexes were used to measure economic production, such as the number of sheep (important in the woolen trade) and the amount of shipping from various key ports. Achievement motivation was judged to be highest in the early period; it had dropped by the time of economic climax.

A similar study has been made of English industrial growth from around 1400 to around 1830 (Bradburn and Berlew 1960).

What conditions favor the development of *n*-Achievement? A number of studies (Rosen 1962; Bradburn 1963) indicate that parental attitudes in childhood are important: a setting of high standards combined with the granting of autonomy to the child, so that he or she can learn to work things out independently and enjoy doing so. A favorable combination seems to be a somewhat dominating mother with high standards and a father who allows his children considerable autonomy. An authoritarian father-dominated family is less likely to foster need for achievement.

GROUP STATUS AND ECONOMIC DEVELOPMENT

In the course of his discussion of the Protestant ethic, Max Weber pointed out that national or religious minority groups, excluded from positions of political influence, often turn to economic activities as a way of gaining recognition for their abilities. Weber cited as examples the Jews, the Poles in Russia, the Huguenots in France under Louis XIV, and nonconformists and Quakers in England. A similar theme has been pursued by Everett E. Hagen (1962), who argues that leaders in the transition to economic growth are apt to come from groups which have lost some of their former status and are looked down on by the leading social group. In a traditional society the leading elite lacks the interest in innovation required for economic development. Elite members believe themselves to be essentially different from what Hagen calls "the simple folk," a category which includes peasants, artisans, craftsmen, shopkeepers, and menials. Since one general distinctive trait of the simple folk is that they work with their hands and become dirty in the process, members of the elite pride themselves on not doing such work. A "Protestant ethic" is not for them. The elite members have an authoritarian, as opposed to an innovational, character. An authoritarian individual, according to Hagen, does not see the world as forming an orderly system, capable of analysis. Hence he is a dependent, rather anxious person. The authoritarian person sees power as stemming from ascribed status, rather than from achievement. The innovational person, in contrast, conceives of the phenomena of the world as being susceptible of analysis, and he sees the world as valuing him. He is high in the needs for autonomy, achievement, and order.

In a traditional society adults discourage initiative, exploration, and innovation among children. The superior authority of the father is insisted on, especially during the "Oedipal period" in a boy's development. The son's consequently submissive attitude becomes generalized to other persons in authority. In such societies, according to Hagen, repressed feelings find an outlet in sexual conquests, occasional outbursts of aggression, and attitudes of *machismo*, or emphasis on masculinity. The pain and frustration experienced by the individual find an explanation in the hierarchy of the unseen supernatural realm which rules the world.

Because of this general picture of traditional society, says Hagen, rapid economic development is not likely to occur. But disturbing events may affect some groups in the society which have lost status and seek to regain it. Their first reaction to the shock of lowered status is apt to be *retreatism*, an increasing abandonment of traditional cultural goals and institutionalized norms of behavior. But this creates new conditions of home life which affect children in a different way than in the traditional upbringing, making possible a more innovational personality. Hagen (1962:217) suggests the following characteristic sequence: authoritarianism, withdrawal of status respect, retreatism, creativity. Hagen's generalizations are illustrated by accounts of economic development in England, Japan, Colombia, Indonesia, and Burma. His observations on Burma will be discussed later in this chapter.

ACHIEVEMENT MOTIVATION IN NIGERIA

It is useful to generalize on a broad scale, as both McClelland and Hagen have done. But it is necessary also to investigate particular areas where economic growth is occurring. In the following pages, accordingly, we will deal with some more restricted studies dealing with (a) Nigeria, (b) a Mexican village, (c) India, and (d) Japan. First, let us briefly consider Robert A. LeVine's analysis (1966) of three Nigerian ethnic groups: Hausa, Yoruba, and Ibo.[2]

LeVine's work seems to give support to the theories of both McClelland and Hagen, but perhaps particularly to the latter, since LeVine notes that the Ibo, much more than either the Hausa or Yoruba, suffered from withdrawal of status respect. The Ibo have also been the greatest innovators. The Hausa, who scored lowest on *n*-Achievement, was the group which suffered least in social disparagement under colonial rule.

The accomplishments of the Ibo were not limited to economic advancement but involved most branches of education, in which there has been a steady increase since the early 1920s. As one example, in the early 1920s there were 12 Nigerian physicians, of whom 8 were Yoruba and none Ibo. By the early 1950s, however, there were 160

---

[2] LeVine's work was discussed earlier in the chapter on dreams and visions; it will be recalled that he sought evidence for the strength of *n*-Achievement in the dream reports of Nigerian male students. The research methods used by LeVine, and his findings, are described in Chapter 14.

Nigerian physicians, of whom 76 were Yoruba and 49 Ibo, a remarkable increase from zero to more than 30 percent of the nation's physicians (LeVine 1966:74).

ECONOMIC CHANGE IN A MEXICAN VILLAGE

A careful and detailed study of the relationship between community development and social personality is Fromm and Maccoby's
study (1970) of a Mexican village in the state of Morelos. The interview methods used in this study were discussed in Chapter 12. On
the basis of an interpretative questionnaire, supported by findings
from the Rorschach and TAT, the authors concluded that most of the
villagers have a helpless, receptive orientation, particularly landowners who raise sugarcane, while a minority group of productive
exploitative entrepreneurs are able to take the initiative in capitalistic
ventures. Since these entrepreneurs are agents of change, it might
seem, at first glance, that productive-exploitative tendencies should
be encouraged. But Fromm and Maccoby warn that not all psychological traits which spur economic development are desirable from a
human standpoint. They would rather see the development of a
strong cooperative movement which would restrain the development
of class stratification and the exploitation of the peasants by entrepreneurs. Fromm and Maccoby visualize something like an Israeli kibbutz or a progressive Mexican *ejido*. But they realize that such a goal
would be difficult for peasants who are individualistic and suspicious
of one another—traits summed up in Banfield's phrase (1958), *amoral
familism*, which refers to the peasant's focus on his own particular
family to the exclusion of all other entanglements.[3] This tendency
occurs in the Mexican village. Mutual suspicion, a "hoarding orientation," and strong sense of private property militate against the development of cooperatives. Nevertheless, Fromm and Maccoby
(1970:203–25) are able to cite some successful efforts in that direction.
However, their final conclusions are not optimistic. They point out
that industrialism is destroying traditional values in Mexico, with
nothing to replace them except for longings for the good life of the
city. Movies have taken the place of fiestas, and radio has replaced
the local band. The peasant "not only is materially poor, but is made
to feel humanly backward, 'under-developed.' He dreams of the
good life for his children, yet only very few of them can ever attain it.
And if they attain it, is it the good life?" (pp. 237–38).

Most studies of economic growth and the need for achievement
have assumed that economic development is desirable. Particularly in
the work of Hagen, there is a tendency to see the creative innovators

---

[3] Banfield's *The Moral Basis of a Backward Society* (1958) is a pessimistic account of an isolated
Italian peasant community, in which the author expresses doubt of the possibility of making any
changes in the peasants' outlook and behavior.

with their high *n*-Achievement as the Good Guys and the authoritarian traditionalists as Bad Guys. From this perspective, economic development would seem to be a self-evident boon. But in Fromm and Maccoby's study, we find that assumption questioned.

ECONOMIC DEVELOPMENT IN INDIA

India seems to exemplify Hagen's description of a traditional society. The caste system, with its hierarchical structure and notions of pollution stemming from contacts with members of lower castes, confirms in the elite the notion of their own essential superiority. The dislike for practical and menial work and the reluctance to get one's hands dirty is certainly present in the higher ranks of society.

In a review of the possible reasons for the relatively slow pace of India's economic advance, N. V. Sovani, an Indian economist, found part of the explanation in two culture-and-personality studies of Indian life. One is by William Stephens Taylor, an article entitled "Basic Personality in Orthodox Hindu Culture Patterns" (1948); the other is G. Morris Carstairs's *The Twice-Born. A Study of a Community of High-Caste Hindus* (1958). Sovani (1962) concludes, after citing these works, that the slow pace of progress in India must be partly attributable to the presence of "a widely common personality pattern devoid of personal initiative, purposefulness, involvement, etc."

Let us briefly consider the works by Taylor and Carstairs to see what the source of such alleged patterns might be. Taylor points out that traditional Hindu culture limits an individual's opportunities for making significant decisions. In many parts of rural India there is a system of economic exchange of goods and services which has come to be known as the *jajmani system*. Under the usual operation of this system, a person's occupation is determined by birth—through membership in a particular caste. What is more, the individual's clientele—if he belongs to one of the service castes—is also determined by birth, since there are hereditary ties linking particular families; a barber serves the families formerly served by his father, and so on. While this system is now breaking down in many parts of India, with the growing incursion of a money economy and an increasing involvement of India's villages in the larger national economy, a person's choice of occupation is still limited, to a considerable extent, by the caste into which he was born.

Another area in which decision making is limited is marriage. Marriages are generally arranged by parents, almost always within the same caste. With regard to choice of occupation, clientele, and marriage, therefore, the individual in much of traditional village India has little to say. It is consonant with this system that the individual is brought up to be relatively passive and compliant. He is rewarded for his submission by the assurance of support from family and caste and by his recognized position in the social order.

According to Taylor (1948:123), Hindu society is thus able "to create a basic personality pattern in which personal initiative is replaced by the sense of conformity, in which responsibility is exercised without personal authority, in which security is associated with a sense of helplessness, and in which opportunities for frustration and acute anxiety are minimized."

Carstairs's work (1958:67) is limited to the study of a community of high-caste Hindus in Rajasthan and is not meant to apply to all of India. However, his picture has much in common with that of Taylor. He points out that in a joint family household a man or woman may not fondle their children in the presence of the man's parents, and that a man "so long as he remains under his own father's roof, must keep up the fiction of denying that he leads an active sexual life of his own. Not to do so is to be disrespectful." Carstairs emphasizes the stress on submission, resignation, and obedience in family life and in religion (p. 147).

These generalizations seem to apply to modern Indian intellectuals as well as to less-educated persons. Shils (1961:62–63) has written that "The center of gravity of the internal life of the family is almost always determined by the more traditional members, and especially the women of the family, who in nearly all cases are more traditional than the men in the same family."

Like Carstairs, Sudhir Kakar (1981:91), an Indian psychiatrist, describes the traditional Hindu joint family household as resulting in some distance between husband and wife. Some Hindu households observe purdah, having separate sleeping quarters for men and women, and some follow post-partum sex taboos which also serve to mark this distance. Under these circumstances, according to Kakar, a woman's erotic feelings are channeled toward her son. Children usually sleep beside the mother up to the fifth year. Kakar's patients always described the mother as being loving and supportive. At the same time, the mother's erotic attitude creates anxiety in the son, who develops a fear of women. This leads to a vicious circle: "mature women are sexually threatening to men, which contributes to 'avoidance behavior' in sexual relations, which in turn causes the women to extend a provocative sexual presence toward their sons, which eventually produces adult men who fear the sexuality of mature women" (p. 95).

One kind of defense by a male child is to identify with the mother. The worship of mother goddesses in Hindu India may be seen as a projection, along with reverence for the milk-giving cow (Carstairs 1958:162).

An analysis similar to Kakar's was made by Frieda Hauswirth (Mrs. Sarangadhar Das) (1932:109–10):

> The repressed Indian bride is hardly and rarely able to find in the utter stranger to whom she is given in physical marriage . . . her perfect . . . counterpart, or to obtain through him a normal release. . . . in consequence the Indian mother is bound to pour out upon her son an abnormal amount of love.

According to Hauswirth, Hindu men become deeply introverted in the course of their childhood upbringing.

The conclusions by Kakar and Hauswirth tend to support the impressions of Taylor and Carstairs concerning a rather dependent adult male personality lacking in individual enterprise.

India is a large, complex, and diverse country. Needless to say, there must be many exceptions to the foregoing generalizations, some of which apply particularly to higher caste urban middle-class groups. As S. C. Dube has pointed out, joint families are more commonly found in cities and small towns than in villages, where they are often rare. Joint families are considered the ideal, but they tend to break up in the South Indian villages studied by Dube. In a study of 125 families, Dube (1955:135) found that 34 percent of the sons had separated from their parents within two years of marriage and 36 percent between two and three years of marriage. Only 22 percent of the sons were still found living with their parents five years after their marriage.

Dube has discussed different patterns of behavior at three socioeconomic levels studied in the village of Shamirpet, near Hyderabad on the Deccan plateau. He states that all three levels value family solidarity, respect old age and social position, and recognize the superiority of the male. But these patterns are adhered to most successfully by the highest level. In the lowest, frequent division of property makes family solidarity hard to maintain. Women have more freedom and mobility; there is more open quarreling and more divorce and remarriage (p. 138–41).

Class, caste, and regional differences must, therefore, be considered in any attempt to delineate Indian modal personality tendencies. But it is significant that an economist such as Sovani should draw attention to personality variables in a discussion of India's economic development.

The same has been done by Kusum Nair (1962) in a book on India's village development program. Mrs. Nair cites the case of a peasant in Mysore who had an irrigation channel passing through his property but who let the water flow by without tapping it; and she quotes a government official associated with the project:

> We carry manures and improved seeds in a trailer and offer to deliver them right at the door-step to induce these cultivators to use them. We offer them loans to buy the seeds and manures. We go to the fields and offer to let in the water for them. We request them to try it out first in two acres only if they are not convinced. They could quadru-

ple their yields if they would only take our advice and at least experiment. Still they are not coming forward (p. 48).

Mrs. Nair notes that community attitudes toward work vary greatly in different regions, and she believes that such attitudes may be more decisive for raising agricultural productivity than material or technological resources. "Unless a man feels the desire to have more material wealth *sufficiently to strive for it,* he cannot be expected to have much interest in new techniques; there will be little attempt on his part to innovate."

Recognition of the importance of these culture-and-personality variables leads Mrs. Nair to recommend that they be taken into account in future development programs.

> when a development scheme is projected, the relevant social and psychological attributes of each community will need to be studied and examined in the same intensive manner as an inventory of the physical resources is made at present. On the basis of such studies means will have to be found for bringing about the necessary changes in people's attitudes and behavior and the beliefs underlying them. These means and methods will have to be within the framework and in keeping with the general policy and the principles of democratic planning (Nair 1962:195).

It is evidently difficult to assess the direction of events in India. A new perspective on India's economic development is provided by Milton Singer's investigation of beliefs and attitudes among a group of industrial leaders in Madras. Judging from Singer's report these men do not seem to fit the passive, dependent picture described by Taylor, Carstairs, and Kakar. Singer (1972:272–366) describes them as being shrewd, hardworking, and enterprising. The Madras industrialists believe that their work is in the best interests of India, in accord with their *dharma,* or religious duty, and that tremendous progress has been made in India's industrialization, in which they are proud to have played a part. Although the generalizations made by Taylor, Carstairs and Kakar may be true enough for many Hindus, Singer's work shows that hard-driving, enterprising leaders are also produced by the social system.

This calls for a kind of applied culture-and-personality. Something approaching this has been attempted in a series of projects in India designed to stimulate achievement motivation in Indian businessmen (McClelland and Winter 1969:94–95). McClelland and his associates in this undertaking judge their program to have been successful; but since it was discontinued, it cannot be called an unqualified success. An Indian writer, J. B. P. Sinha, has questioned the merit of trying to increase competitiveness in India. He cites the view of C. Wright Mills that a competitive spirit can flourish only when there is consciousness of unlimited opportunity; competitiveness becomes anti-social under conditions of scarcity. In a laboratory experiment, Sinha found that if competitiveness is increased under conditions of limited resources, the group's output is less than it would be if cooperation is stressed. Sinha thinks that efforts to increase achievement motivation in India may be dangerous under present conditions of scarcity. These cautionary qualifications are like those of Fromm and Maccoby and show the complexity of the issues involved. McClelland takes issue with some of Sinha's conclusions, pointing out that competition cannot be equated with n-Achievement, which involves "competition with a standard of excellence," trying to do better than one has done before.

ECONOMIC AND POLITICAL DEVELOPMENT IN BURMA

Two members of the Center for International Studies at Massachusetts Institute of Technology have done research on economic and political development in Burma and have written books in which they draw attention to culture-and-personality factors affecting such matters. The first writer is Everett E. Hagen, whose theories were presented earlier in this chapter; two chapters of his book are about Burma. The second author is Lucian W. Pye, who also has written about Chinese "political culture" in psychocultural terms, a topic to be discussed in Chapter 23. Both authors believe that the Burmese socialization process and the formation of personality in childhood have an important influence on the economic and political behavior of Burmese in adult life. Both Hagen and Pye refer to studies of Burmese child-rearing and personality by Lucien M. Hanks (1949), Hazel Marie Hitson (1959), and Geoffrey Gorer (1943a). Both authors draw attention to the seeming contradiction of mild, carefree, happy-go-lucky behavior among Burmese on the one hand and a high rate of violence and homicide on the other. Hagen is struck by the sluggishness of Burma's economic development, while Pye is concerned with the psychological obstacles to "nation building" in Burma.

Since the two authors draw from the same sources, they give similar pictures of the Burmese socialization process. Infancy is described as characterized by indulgence, demand feeding, and soothing of the child to keep it from crying. But in later childhood, the mother alternates between warm and cold behavior; she may be teasingly cruel to her child. Children are deliberately frightened with threats of being carried away, given to strangers, or attacked by evil spirits. Most Burmese adults are said to believe in the existence of evil spirits and to see the world as being full of dangers (Spiro 1967:73).

Burmese consider children to be thoughtless and unable to learn by themselves. In contrast to the Rajputs and Mixtecans[4], and the Chi-

---

[4] See pages 156–57, 160–61.

nese to be discussed in the next chapter, a child is not scolded or punished for aggression against neighboring children unless it gets the parents into trouble. Deference to elders and loyalty to the family are emphasized. The discipline of boys is reinforced when they go to a Buddhist monastery at about eight years of age, where they are drilled in rote learning and given severe punishments. The outcome of this childhood gamut of experiences is an outwardly disciplined, submissive person, who, at the same time, is full of fear and repressed hostility. According to Hagen (1962:170), there is self-doubt and often an escape into celibacy. One of every 30 or 35 adult men in Burma is a monk. The happy-go-lucky behavior of Burmese is interpreted by Hagen (p. 174) as a defense against repressed rage.

Pye (1962:141) considers the manifest level of Burmese politics to be characterized by friendliness and the latent level by tension. Hatred and violence may flare up without warning. Political power is highly valued by Burmese. At the same time, a power seeker is held back by the need to show deference and respect for others, a conflict which brings about feelings of paralysis and resentment (p. 146–49). Burmese politicians realize that open debate about issues is essential in a democracy, but they find it hard to prevent such debates from turning into personal aggression (p. 163). There is an individualistic stress in this society. According to Pye, the idea of improving the national economy has little meaning for Burmese. People are oriented to the present and have little sense of history or concern with planning for the future (p. 202–3).

Hagen states that Burmese politicians often express enthusiastic interest in economic development, but actual undertakings to that end are generally unsuccessful, often marked by irresponsibility and poor planning. Hagen cites several examples of failures in leadership and management. He does not think that corruption is a sufficient explanation for such failures, although corruption exists. Nor is it enough to say that the Burmese have "traditional" personalities, resistant to change. Rather, Hagen suggests that the Burmese find it difficult to focus on actual problems of economic development, not because of lack of intelligence but because of certain personality tendencies accentuated by the experience of colonial rule. British administration led to a destruction of the traditional Burmese community life. Burmese administrators had somehow to identify with the aggressor and become like him, an experience that must have been uncomfortable and conflicting but at the same time valued for the enjoyment of power.

After independence, Burmese political leaders knew that it was necessary to industrialize and build factories, and so they launched such projects but without carefully considering what they were doing. "[T]heir behavior was compulsive; the common sense of a normal traditional individual would not have permitted him to behave so irresponsibly as they have done" (Hagen 1962:467). Elsewhere Hagen (p. 461) observes: "They acted, so it seemed to observers, as though the substance of those problems had at best only a shadowy significance to them." In a way, such administrators were continuing in the tradition of British colonial officialdom, which did not have much interest in the technical details of projects. "[T]he concept of government office involved rote administrative paper work, correct attitude, and pride of position rather than effective entrepreneurship" (p. 467).

The insights and speculations of Hagen and Pye are stimulating, but it still is not clear just how Burmese socialization practices have influenced economic development and "nation building" in Burma.

ECONOMIC DEVELOPMENT IN JAPAN

In contrast to India and Burma, Japan has seen remarkably rapid economic development. John Whitney Hall (1965:538–39) has written: "A century ago Japan was a land bound by a traditional technology, meager resources, and a policy of national isolation. Today Japan ranks fifth in production among the advanced industrial nations. . . ." By 1971, only six years after this was written, Japan's economy had moved to third place after those of the United States and the Soviet Union.

A Weberian interpretation of this signal 100 years' accomplishment is suggested by Robert N. Bellah's analysis of the religion of the Tokugawa period (1600–1867) and the early development of Japan's polity and economy. The concepts of *on* and *giri* discussed in Chapter 2 were emphasized in both Buddhist and Confucian teachings. These teachings were particularly stressed in the warrior class of samurai. Tokugawa Mitsukuni (1628–1700) wrote that the samurai's only business was to maintain *giri*. "[If] there were no *samurai*, right (*giri*) would disappear from human society, the sense of shame would be lost, and wrong and injustice would prevail" (Bellah 1957:90). Duty to one's parents and one's feudal lord were emphasized, as in this quotation from the Budò Shoshinshu, dating from the 17th century:

> For he who is born brave will be loyal and filial to his lord and parents, and whenever he has any leisure, he will use it for study, neither will he be negligent in practicing the military arts. He will be strictly on his guard against indolence and will be very careful how he spends every penny. . . . And so, ever obedient to his lord and parents he preserves his life in the hope some day of doing a deed of outstanding merit, moderating his appetite for eating and drinking and avoiding overindulgence in sex (Bellah 1957:96–97).

Bellah notes that there was a clear-cut distinction between upper and lower samurai, with little mobility between them. The upper samurai received sufficient stipends to support themselves; the lower did not but had to supplement their income by spinning, handicrafts, and surreptitious trade. Bellah states that the lower samurai, more than any group, was responsible for the Restoration of 1868; the new Meiji government was largely formed from their ranks, and they became the leaders in new political and economic enterprises (Bellah 1957:45). The notions about *on* and *giri* emphasized in the samurai code of conduct may have provided part of the impetus to hard work and saving in the manner of the Protestant ethic in Europe.

Everett E. Hagen (1962:chap. 14) has applied his theoretical approach, outlined earlier in this chapter, to the case of Japan. Hagen notes that during the Tokugawa period the merchant class advanced economically but still held an inferior status. At the same time, the economic position of the *daimyo* or feudal lords was worsening, leading them to reduce their samurais' stipends. Merchants, samurai, and peasants all experienced withdrawal of status respect. According to Hagen's scheme, this should lead to retreatism, and he claims that it did, but he does not provide much evidence to support that view. Some of the developments cited under the heading "Manifestations of Retreatism" seem to be more indicative of creativity than retreatism: the development of new forms of drama, such as *kabuki*, and the new wood-block prints of scenes of everyday life. However, Hagen (1962:336–43) claims that this was a period of frivolity and dissipation. Following this "retreatism," many samurai and merchants found new meaning in Confucian and Zen Buddhist tenets and the inspiration needed for a regimen of hard work and capital accumulation.

George De Vos (1965b:578) has also applied a culture-and-personality approach to the understanding of Japanese economic development. He stresses the importance of the Japanese family, whose characteristics were discussed in Chapter 2. "This adventure in modernization was peopled by participants in government, in education, and in newly founded enterprises that were guided and organized by a quasi-religious paternalistic familism that united more than it divided into economic classes, created more harmony than dissension, more morale than alienation." De Vos contrasts this familism with the "amoral familism" of the south Italian community described by Banfield. The individual Japanese does not mistrust his fellowman, does not feel defeated by the environment, and is not pessimistic, but sustains himself with hard work, not just for individual gain but from a sense of self-realization and devotion to family and nation. The importance of the family in relation to economic development was pointed out by Bellah (1957:187), who noted that the vast majority of Tokugawa businesses were small family enterprises. "It was these small businesses with the help of electrical equipment later on, which produced the bulk of Japanese light goods, always the main export and the basis of the economy."

But even in the large industrial companies that developed later, the individual employee has a somewhat familistic attitude, which is fostered by the paternalism of such companies. "The company president, in the fantasy of many Japanese, has replaced the *daimyo* or feudal lord. Individuals are still motivated by feelings of loyalty to the organization" (De Vos 1965b:588). De Vos concludes that "Psychological factors contribute both in respect to achievement motivation and in respect to the effectiveness of the social organization in bringing about commonly accepted new goals" (p. 589).

These generalizations should be considered in connection with the discussion of Japanese national character in Chapter 2.

To conclude this chapter on economic development and personality, it seems to me that the studies of Nigeria, the Mexican village described by Fromm and Maccoby, and the studies of India, Burma, and Japan, all provide good evidence for the importance of culture-and-personality factors in economic development.

SUGGESTIONS FOR FURTHER READING

See Everett E. Hagen, *On the Theory of Social Change. How Economic Growth Begins* (Homewood, Ill.: Dorsey Press, 1962). This book, which examines economic development in England, Japan, Colombia, Indonesia, and Burma from Hagen's theoretical viewpoint, contains an extensive bibliography. See also Erich Fromm, *Escape from Freedom* (New York: Rinehart, 1941); David C. McClelland, *The Achieving Society* (Princeton, N.J.: D. Van Nostrand, 1961); David C. McClelland and David G. Winter et al., *Motivating Economic Achievement* (New York: Free Press, 1969); George A. De Vos et al., *Socialization for Achievement. Essays on the Cultural Psychology of the Japanese* (Berkeley: University of California Press, 1973); and Ronald Dore, *British Factory Japanese Factory. The Origins of National Diversity in Industrial Relations* (Berkeley: University of California Press, 1973).

On Hindu personality, beside the works cited in this chapter, see also Alan Roland, "Psychoanalytic Perspectives on Personality Development in India," *International Review of Psychoanalysis* 7 (1980), pp. 73–87. Taylor, Kakar, Carstairs, and Roland are concerned mainly with personality development in males. For female Hindu personality, see Manisha Roy, *Bengali Women* (Chicago: University of Chicago Press, 1975); and Manisha Roy, "The Oedipus Complex and the Bengali Family in India. A Study of Father-Daughter Relations in Bengal," in Thomas R. Williams, ed., *Psychological Anthropology* (The Hague: Mouton, 1975), pp. 123–34.

23

Revitalization, Revolution, and Reform

The anthropological literature contains many accounts of different kinds of movements, variously labeled nativistic, messianic, millenarian, or utopian movements. Examples include the Seneca Handsome Lake religion, the Ghost Dance of the Plains, and the cargo cults of Melanesia. Some writers have tried to make distinctions between different types of such movements; Ralph Linton (1943), for example, provided a typology of *nativistic movements*. Anthony F. C. Wallace (1956), however, has grouped them all under the single rubric of *revitalization movement*, by which he means a deliberate concerted effort by members of a society to create a more satisfying culture. Wallace would include the Russian Communist Revolution of 1917 under this heading. Presumably the Chinese Communist Revolution could be included as well.

The idea of revitalization depends on an organismic analogy; a society is compared with a living organism, as suggested by Wallace's title, *The Death and Rebirth of the Seneca* (1970b). If a society is threatened by some traumatic experience, such as defeat in war or disorganization brought about by acculturation, the old way of life is disrupted. A revitalization movement may then seek to bring about a new order of things, which may also bring about changes in social character.

The key agent in such a movement is a charismatic leader who sometimes experiences hallucinations in which a supernatural being appears and explains what has gone wrong with the society and what should be done about it. Such a visionary experience may cause personality changes in the recipient, who now becomes a prophet, seeks converts, and launches the movement. Revitalization movements, then, are seen as responses to stress and disappointment, initially on the part of a single person, and later among other disaffected persons who rally to his cause and find satisfaction of their dependency needs in so doing (Wallace 1956).

An ethnic movement like that described by Obeyeskere[1] may have the same character.

Similar analyses have been provided by David F. Aberle (1962) and Weston La Barre (1970:44), among others. Aberle uses the term *relative deprivation* for the feeling among members of a traumatized group that their current lot is not as good as it used to be or might be, or not as good as that of members of some other group.

CARGO CULTS

Thus, in the Melanesian cargo cults, the natives felt a sense of relative deprivation by seeing that the whites had all kinds of fancy equipment, such as refrigerators, electric ranges, and other goods. There was no way of knowing how these things were made. They came by ship or airplane. The advantages shared by the whites must be due to some special relationship with spirits, perhaps connected with the flagpoles and marching rituals performed by the whites. Various charismatic Melanesian leaders have appeared from time to time, announcing that a cargo will soon be coming in, destined, this time, for the natives themselves, and the ancestors will return, bringing the goods with them. These prophetic cults have sometimes involved imitative features, such as marching, drilling, and flagpole ceremonies. Sometimes the cultists have been urged to throw away their old belongings so that the new cargo will come. A cult of this kind flourished among the Manus of New Guinea and may have contributed to the rapid culture change which has occurred there. These cults do not usually last long, since the predicted ships or planes don't materialize, and disillusionment finally sets in. Nevertheless, the belief and the hope may remain in a latent state, ready to break out again, as has happened in parts of Melanesia.

An analysis of cargo cults in terms of the relative deprivation theory is given by Cochrane (1970), who states that Melanesian status concepts had two polar extremes, the "big man" and the "rubbish man." The big man was the giver of feasts and was formerly a leader in war. The rubbish man, incapable of such accomplishments, was lazy and powerless. When the European appeared, he replaced the big man and, in effect, demoted everyone to the rubbish man position, while former avenues to high status were no longer available. But the European big man did not behave as the former Melanesian big man had done. He did not eat with the Melanesians or enter into reciprocal relationships with them, which heightened their sense of degradation.

Theodore Schwartz (1976:159) considers cargo cults to be related to aspects of psychocultural adjustment in Melanesia. Such movements

---

[1] See page 426.

with very similar characteristics have often appeared in different parts of Melanesia but not in the same fashion in the adjacent island clusters of Micronesia, Polynesia, or Indonesia. "They have occurred among matrilineal and patrilineal peoples, among fishermen and gardeners, among small, isolated communities, and in larger, more complex settlements" (p. 160).

Schwartz, like Cochrane, notes that the Melanesians highly value the display of wealth and that the greater show of wealth by Europeans gave them an unbearable feeling of inferiority. The Europeans also brought peace, ending a long period of warfare in the islands. This opened up contacts between formerly warring groups as well as with Europeans. "Past hostilities and insecurity, however, left residues of tension and distrust" (1976:166). Elsewhere Schwartz (1973) has described Melanesians as having a "paranoid ethos," which he thinks may have been prevalent in primitive societies during the course of cultural evolution. This ethos was due to the uncertainties of life, short life span, social atomism, and the prevalence of warfare, among other factors. In such a setting few people can be trusted outside of family members and close relatives.

Pacification and foreign domination did not necessarily increase the level of stress, as some analysts have inferred. Schwartz thinks that in many respects the level of stress was reduced. He also believes that the role of the Melanesian cult leader has been overemphasized. Some of the behavior of cult members has been described as pathogenic, including convulsive seizures, shaking, and trembling. Schwartz (1976:185) notes that these features are associated with possession and may be assumed to validate the cult or one's position in it. "Displaying such symptoms may mark a claim to status in the cult, in the community, or as an object of therapy, depending on the situation." The heightened feeling of expectation generated by the cult is not abnormal, according to Schwartz. "This state is a kind of 'high' which, when it collapses, swings into a 'low' state. . . . Regardless of its failure to produce the cargo, the cult-state itself was so rewarding that the residual cultist became addicted to attempts to revive and relive its excitement" (p. 187).

The Melanesian paranoid ethos is a contributing factor to the appearance of cargo cults, according to Schwartz:

> The ethos is part of the cultural context in which such cult occurrences were precipitated and within which they made sense to emotionally and cognitively attuned participants. . . . Just as credulity and suspicion are conjoined aspects of a single process, the perception by an individual or group of being the object of benevolent forces or beings is the positive counterpart of the negative perception of malevolence (1976:191, 193).

Analyses like those of Cochrane and Schwartz help to explain why cargo cults have been a recurrent feature in various parts of Melanesia but not in Micronesia, Polynesia, or Indonesia, where Europeans also assumed power.

CHINESE POLITICAL CULTURE AND PERSONALITY

Two works on Chinese "political culture" seek to apply a psycho-cultural approach to the understanding of the Chinese Communist revolution. The first, a speculative essay by Lucian W. Pye (1968), need not be discussed at length, since the author does not supply much evidence to support his hypotheses. The book will serve, however, to introduce a weightier work along similar lines by Richard H. Solomon (1971), a professor of political science at the University of Michigan. Pye and Solomon make references to each other's work and seem to have influenced one another. One of the ideas which they have in common is that the traditional Chinese socialization process strongly restricts the expression of aggression, leaving the individual with a fund of repressed hostility, which political leaders such as Mao have known how to manipulate and direct in the process of attaining and maintaining political control. According to Pye, the strict Chinese restraint of aggression is related to the hierarchical nature of the Chinese family and society in general and to the stress on ritual and etiquette. Pye thinks it significant that many Chinese Communist leaders had violent confrontations with their fathers, a topic also discussed by Solomon, particularly in connection with the life history of Mao Tse-tung.

Solomon believes that the surprising developments of Mao's Cultural Revolution indicate the value of a culture-and-personality approach to an understanding of Chinese politics. Solomon has made use of traditional culture-and-personality techniques in research with Chinese refugees in Taiwan and Hong Kong. He and his associates administered a questionnaire on social attitudes and life experiences, a biographical schedule, an attitude survey, the Rorschach Test, and a modified Thematic Apperception Test. The sample of subjects interviewed was 91. Although the Rorschach Test was given, no reference to the results is made in the book; the author notes in a footnote that the Rorschach Test will be dealt with in a future publication. However, considerable use is made of the modified TAT, the nine plates of which are reproduced in the appendix of Solomon's book. More material on the TAT and questionnaire findings appear in a separate article by Solomon (1969). The TAT drawings are of excellent quality.

The culture-and-personality sections of Solomon's work, however, are open to criticism; but before finding fault, let us first see what some of his conclusions are.

Solomon believes that to understand China's "political culture," one must have an understanding of the Chinese socialization process. The attitudes toward persons in authority formed within the family later become extended to authority figures elsewhere. Since the Chinese tend to go through the same general socialization process and share the same culture, their characteristic values and attitudes toward authority should be widely shared.

The period of infancy and early childhood is described as being one of great indulgence and oral gratification, which Solomon believes sets the stage for the frequent use of oral metaphors in Chinese conversation. But a great change occurs between five and seven years of age, when the father, in particular, drops his playful indulgent manner and becomes remote, strict, and severe. This is in agreement with a study of child training made by Margery Wolf in Taiwan. According to Wolf (1970:41), Chinese fathers say that you cannot be a son's friend and at the same time correct his behavior; it is necessary to be aloof and strict if you want to encourage the behavior required of an adult.

A child's inquisitive, exploratory tendencies are discouraged; such activities as swimming and tree climbing are considered dangerous and are often punished. Of Solomon's interviewed subjects who gave information on childhood punishments, 79 percent recalled receiving frequent physical punishments, such as beatings with boards, whips, or rulers (Solomon 1971:51). Strict controls reinforce the dependency needs established in the happier days of infancy. The threat of isolation from the family is also used as a parental sanction. Ambivalent attitudes toward parents and other authority figures develop in such a setting. As one of Solomon's interviewees remarked, "When you saw him [his father] you would both fear him and want to get near him" (p. 60).

At the beginning of this strict period in childhood, children often respond by throwing temper tantrums, but adults neither comfort nor scold them for this behavior, and the children eventually give it up. Henceforth, there is an emphasis on reserve and emotional control.

One reason for the parents' switch from indulgence to strictness is that they expect their children to take care of them in old age, and they do not want the child to become too self-indulgent.

Punishment for any aggression, even in self-defense, is particularly swift. One of Solomon's informants said, "We hold things in our hearts, *in our stomachs*. . . . We hold hatred in . . . ," an "oral" statement of the repression of hostility. Another remarked, "*I swallow my anger, put it in my stomach*" (Solomon 1971:70). One of Mao's techniques in political action, according to Solomon, was to try to make peasants conscious of their repressed hostility and to direct their rage against exploitation toward the enemies of the revolution. A means to that end is the *su-k'u* or "speak bitterness meeting," at which peasants were encouraged to "vomit the bitter water" of injustices suffered from the local gentry.

Mao wanted peasants to be active and to overcome the passivity brought about by fear of authority. Dependency must be replaced by aggressive action. We find an echo of Mao's thought in the writings of another revolutionary activist, Frantz Fanon (1966:117), who viewed resort to violence as a cleansing force for the repressed masses, freeing them from despair, inaction, and the sense of inferiority. "Violence alone, violence committed by the people, violence organized and educated by its leaders, makes it possible for the masses to understand social truths and gives the key to them." We have noted before that many peasant societies are characterized by apathy, passivity, and repressed hostility. In line with Solomon's analysis, such societies should be amenable to revolutionary uprisings through Mao's techniques of promoting consciousness of repressed hostility.

Solomon's analysis on the whole is plausible and internally consistent, so it may seem almost pedantic to raise questions about it. The criticisms that follow concern not the conclusions, but the evidence on which they are based—the interviews, questionnaires, and TATs. Since the questionnaires required literacy, Solomon's 91 subjects (all males) were all literate and mostly from middle- or upper-class families. In a footnote on page 82, Solomon tells us that the literate segment of China's population between 1600 and 1900 was between 1 and 2 percent of the total. According to J. L. Buck's *Land Utilization in China* (1937), a survey of 46,601 rural families in different parts of China in the 1930s showed that 69.3 percent of the men and 98.7 percent of the women were illiterate (Lang 1946:72–73). Solomon's subjects were thus from a minority group; none of them were peasants, who formed the target of Mao's propaganda efforts, and who make up the vast majority of China's population. Solomon gives thumbnail biographies of his 91 subjects in an appendix; it is clear from these sketches that many of these men came from wealthy families.

The TAT pictures to which the subjects responded generally show well-dressed men in Western-style clothing in middle- or upper-class settings, not farmers in rural peasant environments.

Solomon frankly admits that his subjects were not peasants, but he thinks that this does not matter, since China's traditional culture is so uniform that class and rural-urban differences have no great significance. But this is a convenient assumption, not something which can be taken for granted.

Part of Solomon's analysis of Chinese socialization has to do with the parents' expectation that they will live with their children in their old age and that their children will take care of them. This expectation assumes the existence of a joint family household consisting of grandparents, their children and grandchildren—the kind of family we are apt to think of as being characteristic of China. But even before the Communist period, the joint family was not the normal type of Chinese family. Olga Lang (1946:137) presented statistics which showed that the joint family predominated only among landlords. In a broad-scale survey of Chinese farming families, Irene B. Taueber (1970:81) reported that more than 60 percent were nuclear, including only father, mother, and children.[2]

We find, then, that Solomon has made deductions about illiterate Chinese peasants' attitudes toward authority largely based on questionnaire and TAT responses given by literate, considerably urbanized middle- and upper-class refugees, of whom about one third had formerly been associated with Chiang K'ai-shek's Nationalist government (Solomon 1971:116). His conclusions thus seem to rest on a shaky foundation. The only way to get around this difficulty is to emphasize the uniformity of Chinese culture. "Our data reveal no significant variation in concern with social conflict or differences in conception of authority associated with socioeconomic class or educational level. Direct observations of peasant life by anthropologists support this [sic] data" (Solomon 1971:93).

Solomon does not at this point cite any anthropologist in particular. A leading figure in this field, however, is Francis L. K. Hsu, who has the advantages of being Chinese and an anthropologist who has done fieldwork in China; moreover, Hsu's main focus of interest is culture-and-personality. Some of Hsu's generalizations about the community which he studied in southwestern China are at variance with Solomon's picture. In various ways Hsu contrasts the lifestyles and attitudes of the rich and poor. He also makes a point which does not jibe well with Solomon's analysis: although, like Solomon, Hsu (1967:265) emphasizes the submissive attitude toward authority in the Chinese villager, he mentions as a second outstanding quality a strong drive for success and a competitive spirit. A strong drive for success would seem to be at odds with the passive dependency depicted by Solomon. While both rich and poor are described by Hsu as being competitive, their goals are said to be different. The poor compete to keep going and to stay alive, while the rich compete to outshine others in conspicuous consumption and display. To reach their objectives, the poor must be frugal, the rich extravagant (Hsu 1967:8–9, 210–12). Thus, one would assume that TAT stories and questionnaire answers given by Solomon's refugees would reflect many differences from the protocols of poor peasants in mainland China. These considerations seem to be damaging to Solomon's thesis. It is, however, a well-done work in many ways.

CHILD-REARING IN AN ISRAELI KIBBUTZ

The Israeli kibbutz movement represents a remarkable effort not only to establish a progressive, collective egalitarian society but also

---

[2] During the present period of Communist rule, the sanctity of the joint family and the importance of the age hierarchy have been under considerable attack. The traditional joint family system is even weaker today than formerly (C. K. Yang 1959:chap. 5).

to achieve a new kind of social character through collective child-rearing practices which involve rejection of the traditional nuclear family. According to Bruno Bettelheim (1969:35), this rejection was influenced by the German *Wandervogel* (migratory bird) movement, a revolt on the part of middle-class youth against their authoritarian families and the strict German education of the early 20th century. (There seems to be a parallel here to the development of hippie cults and the formation of communes in the United States in the 1960s and 1970s.) In the eastern European *shtetl* communities from which the Israeli kibbutz founders migrated, the family was a particularly exclusive unit. The mother was mainly occupied with rearing and feeding the children. In describing his mother, a man from a *shtetl* expressed the ideal: "She was a perfect Jewish woman, clean, patient, hard-working, and silent, submissive to God and to her husband, devoted to her children . . . her own well-being was unimportant. . . . I don't remember my mother sitting at the table when we ate, except for Friday night and Saturdays." (Zborowski and Herzog 1962:130)." The family meal not only bound the family together but had religious functions.

In rebelling against what seemed to them a stifling ingrown family system, the kibbutz founders removed the tasks of child-rearing and food-preparation from the mother. In some kibbutzim (not all), children sleep with their peers from infancy on in a separate children's house. There are no family meals. Husband and wife have quarters of their own and eat with other kibbutzniks in a communal dining room, while children eat separately with their peers. Freed from the demands of cooking and child-rearing, women now take part in the collective work of the kibbutz as the equals of men.

The kibbutz founders were influenced not only by the Communist teachings of Marx, but also by the doctrines of Freud. As they saw it, the ingrown family breeds mother fixation, Oedipus complex, and neurosis. These features should be obviated by collective child-rearing, leading to the formation of a healthier, sturdier, and more cooperative personality.

The first kibbutz was founded in 1909. There are now over 230 settlements with a total population of nearly 100,000, the typical kibbutz having about 500 members. The history of this collective movement has thus been quite different from those of most Utopian communal settlements, such as those of the United States, which generally lasted only a short time. The latter were aberrant islands within a larger society which regarded them with hostility or indifference, while the kibbutz in Israel is a valued, accepted institution. The kibbutz also contrasts with the collective units of the Soviet Union, in that membership is voluntary and not determined by the central government. One may leave a kibbutz if one wishes (Rabin 1965:1–9).

Let us now consider some features of the collective child-rearing system, keeping in mind that not all kibbutzim have such features as separate children's houses, for some let children sleep in their parents' quarters. The picture presented here is based mainly on Rabin's report and secondarily on those by Melford E. Spiro, Gerald Caplan, and Bruno Bettelheim, each of whom has tried to assess how the collective child-rearing system influences the personalities of those involved in it.

After a child is born, it is taken to an infant house, where there may be five or six babies in a room. Although the child does not sleep with the mother, she breast-feeds it and for the first six weeks is always available for demand feeding during the day; about five times a day after that. She also changes diapers, carries, and plays with the child. The mother returns to part-time work after six weeks and to full-time work after four months. The child is weaned by about six months.

The nurse in charge of an infant house is called a metapelet. Between six and nine months a group of about five children is assigned a permanent metapelet who stays with the group for the next four or five years, until they enter kindergarten. She accompanies them when they move to a toddler's house, where they stay for about three years. The metapelet is the main person involved in feeding, dressing, and toilet training the children. Parents continue to visit their children daily and put them to bed at night. Children may also visit their parents' quarters, where some toys may be kept for them.

Children leave kindergarten and enter elementary school at age 7, which involves moving to a new building and acquiring a new metapelet and teacher-counselor who stay with the group until they enter the Mosad, a kind of high school, at the age of 12. There is no grading system in this school. Everyone gets promoted from one grade to the next; there are no dropouts.

The solidarity of age mates in a peer group is said to be very strong. But the kibbutz authorities also want children of different ages to interact and work with one another. Hence, there is a Children's Society for grades two to six, to foster contacts between older and younger children. This takes such forms as working on a newspaper, sports, and farm work.

In the high school, young people are expected to put in about three hours of work a day for the kibbutz. This is an apprenticeship period, during which the youngsters are exposed to the various sectors of the kibbutz economy, learning shopwork, agriculture, and animal husbandry. As adolescents spend more time at these tasks, they also spend less time visiting their parents.

Equality of the sexes is the ideal. Before 1950 there was no separation of sexes in dormitories or showers, but there was much modesty and a somewhat puritanical attitude. Boys and girls of the same kibbutz tended to think of one another as brothers and sisters and rarely married a member of the same kibbutz. Although there is no formal regulation about this, a kind of incest taboo or rule of group exogamy seems to have developed (Rabin 1965:10–34; Spiro 1954:846).

The reader will remember that Chapter 1 contained a discussion of the psychological consequences of maternal deprivation and institutionalization. There does not seem to be maternal deprivation in the kibbutz, since the child continues to see the mother daily, although he or she does not sleep in the parents' quarters. There also seems to be no lack of stimulation, and there is a high ratio of caretakers to children. Nevertheless, some investigators found evidence of a relative lack of maturity among young kibbutzniks, although this is apparently counteracted and overcome at a later stage of development.

In one study, Gerald Caplan (1954) reported that there was much more thumbsucking, enuresis, temper tantrums, and lack of control over aggression among communally raised children below six years of age than among children of the same age reared in families. But signs of emotional disturbance generally disappeared by 10 or 11 years of age, and young adult kibbutzniks were seen to be remarkably nonneurotic. On the other hand, Melford E. Spiro (1954:424) did not consider kibbutz adolescents to be so well adjusted; he described them as being shy, introverted, hostile, and seldom forming close friendships. It should be remembered that life in a kibbutz may be hard and exacting. Before entering high school, children have six hours of classes; then, after an hour of rest, they have three hours of work; then homework and visits with parents and various social activities. The schedule becomes still more demanding in high school, with even less free time (Bettelheim 1969:251). Tensions during adolescence may thus stem from current situational conditions rather than being carry-overs from early childhood frustrations.

The most detailed study of the effects of early childhood experiences on personality in the kibbutz is that of A. I. Rabin (1965). Rabin divided his subjects into four groups: (1) infants (10–18 months), (2) 10-year-olds, (3) adolescents (17–18 years old), and (4) army young men (19–20 years old). The subjects came from six kibbutzim. A control group was provided by a moshav or moshavim (plural). A moshav is a cooperative, primarily agricultural settlement, much like the kibbutz but with the traditional family structure unchanged. Members of both the kibbutzim and the moshavim came from similar countries of origin, had about the same educational level, and shared the same general ideals and values. Among the psychological tests given to these groups were a Mental Development Scale and a Social Maturity Scale (for the infants); Draw-a-Person (DAP), Sentence Completion, Rorschach, and Blacky Pictures (for the 10 year olds); and Thematic Apperception Test (for the adolescents and army young men, who were also given a Sentence Completion Test).

When the two infant groups (kibbutz and moshav) were tested, the moshav children were found to be superior to those of the kibbutz both in general development and social maturity. Rabin suggests that perhaps the experience of multiple mothering is frustrating to the kibbutz child, who withdraws from interpersonal relationships, which reduces identification and retards learning.

Spiro has pointed out that kibbutz children are left alone at night and that the departure of parents and nurses at night may be a threatening experience for young children. This may be one source of anxiety. Another may be the fact that their caretakers are often changed (Spiro 1958:431–33).

In defense of their system, the kibbutzniks have argued that it protects the child from bad mothering. If there are many caretakers, it does not matter much if some of them do a poor job, since there will also be some good ones to make up for it, whereas a child with only one mother is at her mercy, if she is a bad mother.

Although Rabin's control group of moshav infants performed more successfully than the kibbutz children, the discrepancy between the two groups is apparently overcome by age 10. Rabin found that the intellectual development of the 10-year-old kibbutz children equaled or surpassed that of the control group. The kibbutz children were better in ego strength and overall maturity, although they showed more anxiety. There was more guilt manifest in the nonkibbutz children and more signs of Oedipal attachments. The kibbutz children showed more positive attitudes toward the family and less intense sibling rivalry, while the nonkibbutz children showed more indications of having long-range personal goals. Among the kibbutz children there was less clear-cut identification with a parent of the same sex and less superego development. Contrary to Spiro's impressions, however, Rabin did not find more hostility in kibbutz children than in the control group.

Apparently, judging from Caplan's and Rabin's findings, there are some negative aspects of infancy in the kibbutz child-rearing system which retard mental development and social maturity to some extent; but there are enough positive countervailing tendencies after the first year of life to overcome the initial setback. The goals of the kibbutz system seem to be furthered through their child-rearing methods, producing a personality which is in keeping with the collective social order.

Since the foregoing was written, there have been more reports about kibbutz life, the most interesting of which is Spiro's *Gender and Culture* (1979). In 1975 Spiro revisited a kibbutz which he calls Kiryat Yedidim, where he had studied child development in 1951. Those children are now adults. In 1976 Spiro interviewed 10 *sabras* (people born and raised in the kibbutz) in six other kibbutzim, making a total of 60 subjects. Meanwhile, *Women in the Kibbutz* by Lionel Tiger and Joseph Shepher (1975), which gave further statistical support to Spiro's findings, was published.

The main conclusion is that there has been a reversion to traditional family life and a preference among female sabras for "feminine" roles in contrast to the philosophy of the kibbutz founders. As noted earlier, the pioneer founders wanted to liberate women from the household tasks of cooking, cleaning, and child-rearing, so that they could take part in collective life as the equals of men. The rearing of children and serving of meals were collectivized, and women worked in the fields along with the men. But by now that has changed. In Kibbutz Artzi, the most radical of the four kibbutz federations, only 9 percent of the women work in farming (Spiro 1979:17). Tiger and Shepher's general figures (1975:90–91) show the following percentages for male workers: They make up 87 percent of farm workers, 77 percent of industrial workers, and 99 percent of construction workers, while women constitute 84 percent of service and educational workers. Sabra women see the current sexual division of labor as natural, although they were not brought up in such a system.

> the need of pioneer women to demonstrate their equality with men by successful achievement in physically demanding farm labor is no longer an issue among contemporary kibbutz women. . . . Women, they say, are most fulfilled by working with and helping other people, while men are most fulfilled when working with machinery and in tasks which give them a sense of power and domination (Spiro 1979:18–19).

Nowadays males are offered courses in manual arts, while female sabras take courses in domestic science. Management positions tend to be held by men (64 percent at Kibbutz Artzi), and women seldom head committees. The women say that they aren't interested in such work.

In keeping with these sexual distinctions, high schools now have separate showers and dormitory rooms for boys and girls. In the early days of the kibbutz, marriages were informally handled; nowadays traditional weddings are customary. Apartments are larger than they used to be, and they have private bathrooms, refrigerators, stoves, radios, stereo and TV sets (Spiro 1979:26–28).

Joseph Blasi (1978) has described the revolution brought about by the introduction of radios in Kibbutz Vatik. In the late 1930s a girl got married, and her parents gave her a radio, the first in the kibbutz. A general meeting was held, at which it was decided that the girl would have to return the radio to her parents. But a few years later another radio was introduced. As one member reported, "then we had two choices, to decide to fight this again or to buy everybody radios" (p. 32). They bought radios for everyone.

Another turning point concerned clothing. "Usually all took the clothes they needed each week, often different clothes each week, which sometimes fitted and sometimes did not" (p. 33). But then private clothes began to be accepted. "Regarding personal cars, the members narrowly favor personal cars by 48.6% to 40.1% with 11.3% undecided" (p. 133).

At Kiryat Yedidim the women now wear feminine clothing, jewelry, perfume, and cosmetics. The kibbutz has a beauty parlor (Spiro 1979:42–43). Women now bake pies in their kitchens. "The private apartment, rather than the communal dining room, has become the locus of the couple's social life" (p. 28). At present children spend almost all day Saturday in their parents' apartment, instead of a few hours as formerly, and they often have an evening meal there, too. Furthermore, more children sleep at home instead of in the children's houses. Three fourths of the kibbutzim in one federation have switched to family sleeping arrangements.

There is a trend to having larger families. "A generation ago, not one couple in Kiryat Yedidim . . . had more than two children. Today, three and four are typical, while five and even six are not unheard of" (p. 33).

Spiro found these developments surprising.

> As a cultural determinist, my aim in studying personality development in Kiryat Yedidim in 1951 was to observe the influence of culture on human nature or, more accurately, to discover how a new culture produces a new human nature. In 1975 I found (against my own intentions) that I was observing the influence of human nature on culture; alternatively, I was observing the resurgence of the old culture (in modern garb) as a function of those elements in human nature that the new culture was unable to change (p. 106).

Spiro attributes the "counterrevolutionary" changes that he has described to the existence of precultural human needs. This emphasis on "human nature" is in keeping with Spiro's belief in the universality of the Oedipus complex.[3]

RESTUDIES

We may conclude this discussion of culture, personality, and culture change by noting that anthropologists are in a good position to study culture change through the medium of restudies. Writers such as Fromm, McClelland, and Riesman have made inferences about personality patterns in past times from historical accounts. In their ethnographic work anthropologists are able to observe such processes more directly.

The anthropologist who writes an ethnographic account is also writing history; he or she preserves for later generations an account of the customs and behavior of a given society at a particular moment in time. If the anthropologist is a culture-and-personality researcher, he

---

[3] See pages 87–92.

or she also records something of what the people were like as individuals—their degree of reserve or emotionality, passivity, or aggression. From such information, we may be able to understand more clearly why members of that society responded as they did when faced with alternative courses of action.

In a restudy a community which has formerly been described is visited again, either by the same ethnographer (as in Spiro's case) or by another.

While various purposes may be served by restudies, one is the investigation of culture change, in which the first study serves as a base line. One example of such an investigation is Margaret Mead's restudy of Manus, which she first visited in 1928 and described in *Growing up in New Guinea* and other publications. 25 years later, in 1953, Mead returned to Manus and found this culture transformed to an almost unbelievable extent. In 1928 the Manus lived in pile dwellings in a lagoon; the women wore aprons of sago leaves, while the men had barkcloth G-strings. Today the Manus live on shore and wear Western-style clothing. In 1928 their religion involved a cult of the recently deceased family head in each household; diviners and mediums were consulted to learn the disposition of these and other spirits. This religion has been completely abandoned, and the Manus are now churchgoing Christians. Mead's description of a Sunday service sounds like something out of the Middle West, with the congregation in their Sunday best and the Manus children wearing ready-made clothes which are imported from Australia in cellophane packages (Mead 1956a:266).

Anthropologists have often emphasized the resistance to culture change found in various parts of the world, even in cases where potential changes would bring tangible benefits to the people. Benjamin Paul's volume, *Health, Culture, and Community* (1955), provides a number of examples of such resistance—persistent efforts to induce Peruvian villagers to boil their water have met with little success; an inexpensive medical clinic fails to attract patients in a Mexican town; and so on. Since resistance of this type is such a common experience, the Manus receptivity to change is all the more remarkable.

In *Growing Up in New Guinea*, Mead provided a possible key to understanding this receptivity. She described the Manus as having a sort of Protestant ethic; the men were traders, bent on making profits and valuing hard work, thrift, and prudence. Perhaps it is not surprising, then, that the Manus were able to identify with and to emulate the American soldiers stationed in their islands during World War II. In *New Lives for Old*, however, Mead (1956a:158, 365) offers another kind of interpretation. She believes that the old culture implanted feelings of dissatisfaction and restlessness in the Manus child, and that new ways of living were eagerly received because of this underlying discontent. Whatever the reason, the Manus seem to have had the makings of what McClelland calls an "achieving society."

Henceforth, it will be possible to check on many communities in different parts of the world at recurrent time intervals. Since the cultures studied by anthropologists are often in the throes of sweeping culture changes—or soon will be—we are now able to observe the psychological concomitants of acculturation in a variety of settings.

SUGGESTIONS FOR FURTHER READING

Anthony F. C. Wallace's views on revitalization movements are set forth in his paper "Revitalization Movements," *American Anthropologist* 58 (1956), pp. 264–81, and in *The Death and Rebirth of the Seneca* (New York: Alfred A. Knopf, 1970). See also David F. Aberle, *The Peyote Religion Among the Navaho* (Chicago: Aldine, 1966).

For Melanesian cargo cults, see the works by Cochrane and Schwartz cited in the text and also Peter Lawrence, *Road Belong Cargo. A Study of the Cargo Movement in the Southern Madang District, New Guinea* (Manchester: Manchester University Press, 1964).

Apart from the works on Communist China by Pye and Solomon cited in the text, see also William L. Parish and Martin King Whyte, *Village and Family in Contemporary China* (Chicago: University of Chicago Press, 1978).

For the Israeli kibbutz, see Melford E. Spiro, *Gender and Culture: Kibbutz Women Revisited* (Durham, N.C.: Duke University Press, 1979) and Lionel Tiger and Joseph Shepher, *Women in the Kibbutz* (New York: Harcourt Brace Jovanovich, 1975).

24

Retrospect, Prospects, Criticisms, and Justifications

Culture-and-personality research was initiated with the pioneer studies of Malinowski, Benedict, and Mead discussed in Part Two of this book. A clinical approach, influenced by psychoanalytic theory, was later introduced by the school of Linton, Kardiner, and Du Bois, which drew attention to the importance of early childhood experiences and the need for getting life history material and projective test data. There was a high level of confidence and enthusiasm in work along these lines in the 1940s.

The first serious criticism of culture-and-personality research came in reaction to the sweeping childhood determinist generalizations about national character made by Geoffrey Gorer and others during and shortly after World War II. It had been asserted that Japanese national character was derived from strict early toilet training; Russian national character was brought about by the swaddling of infants. Although this simplistic determinism was denied by some of its exponents, such as Gorer (Gorer and Rickman 1949:128–29) and Mead (1954), the impression remained that this was, in effect, what they had stated.

A critical review of childhood determinist writings, in general, was made by Harold Orlansky (1949), who questioned the adequacy of the basic Freudian assumptions underlying such work. The field of culture-and-personality was subjected to a probing analysis by Alfred R. Lindesmith and Anselm A. Strauss (1950). These authors did not limit their criticism to the childhood determinists, but included as well configurationists such as Ruth Benedict and others. Among their criticisms were that investigators in this field do not describe very clearly or in detail how their characterizations are arrived at; that oversimplification and selectivity are in evidence, with neglect of inconsistent data; and that while the results of projective tests are some-

457

times offered as confirmatory evidence, the test results are not self-explanatory but must be interpreted like other data and may, like them, be subject to bias. The critics also charged culture-and-personality researchers with a lack of attention to alternative hypotheses and cited Orlansky's criticisms of the childhood determinist school.

A general commentary on culture-and-personality research appears in the 1948 edition of A. L. Kroeber's encyclopedic work, *Anthropology*. Because of the author's commanding position in his field, Kroeber's views deserve our attention. Here are some of his observations:

> It seems possible, theoretically, for two peoples to show much the same psychological character or temperament and yet to have different cultures. The reverse seems also to hold: namely, that culture can be nearly uniform while national character differs. Western Europe, for instance, has basically much the same civilization all over, yet the temperaments of its peoples are sharply distinguishable. . . . the psychologies seem in part to vary independently of the cultures.
>
> If this is correct, then recent attempts to assign each culture a strict counterpart in a "basic personality structure" or "modal personality" type go too far (Kroeber 1948:587–88).

Thus, by the 1950s there was some disillusionment about the field of culture-and-personality, and anthropology graduate students began to be attracted to other kinds of research, such as the renewed interest in cultural evolution engendered by Julian H. Steward and Leslie A. White. There continued to be a great interest in culture-and-personality, however, as is indicated by the number of readers, texts, and articles published in the 1950s and 1960s and by the appearance of two journals, *Ethos* and *Journal of Psychological Anthropology,* later rechristened *The Journal of Psychoanalytic Anthropology.*

It seems likely that one reason why fewer anthropology graduate students have been specializing in culture-and-personality is that, as our understanding of the problems in culture-and-personality has increased, there has been a correspondingly greater reluctance to enter a field where there is so much ambiguity, where it is so difficult to demonstrate anything conclusively. A graduate student would have to think twice before committing himself to writing a doctoral dissertation on a culture-and-personality topic when there are simpler, more manageable subjects available.

One salutory result of the criticisms and skepticism about culture-and-personality research is that those who have done work in the field since the 1950s have shown greater attention to problems of methodology, sampling, and research design than did their predecessors. This may be seen, for example, in the studies by William Caudill, Robert A. LeVine, and Robert B. Edgerton. Some of the best recent work has involved rather large-scale group enterprises with many participants: the Six Cultures project, the Harvard values project at Rimrock, the Cornell-Aro project, the Culture and Ecology in East Africa project, and the Fromm-Maccoby study of social character in a Mexican town. All these projects have been characterized by careful planning and coordination. The vitality of these undertakings is sufficient to show that culture-and-personality is not dying or dead, as is sometimes alleged. However, there are some serious problems which researchers in the field will have to come to terms with in one way or another.

One of these is the selection of a workable model or conception of personality. Many of the early writers in culture-and-personality were influenced by Freudian psychoanalytic theory, although only a few, such as Weston La Barre and George Devereux, have been consistent advocates and exponents of it. Like projective testing, Freudian theory continues to be assailed by academic psychologists and seems to be losing ground in psychiatry. To keep some alternatives in mind, I presented in Chapter 1 the three models of personality distinguished by Salvatore Maddi: the conflict model, the fulfillment model, and the consistency model. Reference to these alternatives has been made from time to time in this book. There would be no reason for culture-and-personality to collapse as a field of research if one of these models should prove to be unworkable.

Related to the issue of what model of personality to accept is the question of what sort of terminology should be used by culture-and-personality researchers. The use of such terms as *id* and *superego*, of course, implies acceptance of the Freudian scheme. But there is also the question of using diagnostic clinical terms—such as paranoid, hysteria, megalomania, and whatnot—which anthropologists have often used. If you are going to characterize the personality of an individual or group, some adjectives are necessary. But, as pointed out in Chapter 18, critics such as Walter Mischel, Karl Menninger, and Thomas Szasz object to clinical classifications of individuals and the use of such terms. If the practice is of doubtful validity when applied to individuals, its application to whole groups of people should be even less justified.

If, when using clinical terms to characterize a group, an anthropologist presents a negative picture of the people he or she has studied (and more reports seem to stress negative rather than positive features), one opens oneself to the charge of stereotyping and prejudice.[1] If the anthropologist wants to avoid such criticisms (and who would not?), he or she would have to write only favorable descriptions or else decide not to publish descriptions which have negative

---

[1] See, for example, the blast of criticism by Harold Hickerson (1967) against anthropologists, including the author, who have made unflattering analyses of the Chippewa or Ojibwa. For other charges of stereotyping and prejudice, see Jessie Bernard (1949), Géza Roheim (1950:394), C. W. M. Hart (1954:260), and some of the comments to the papers by Lewellen (1981) and Bolton (1984).

features. This dilemma could lead to the end of culture-and-personality research. The world is smaller now, literacy greater, and the writings of anthropologists are beginning to find their way back to the communities which they have described. Nancy Scheper-Hughes (1979:15) was understandably uneasy, when she wrote in the introduction to her book about mental illness in rural Ireland: "In the final analysis, I am less concerned with what my anthopological colleagues and critics will think and say than I am about what my friends in Ballybran will *feel* about what is written here."

This dilemma is further compounded by the fact that culture-and-personality research has been largely an American enterprise. Hardly any work in this field has been done in Europe (Heine-Geldern 1960:61). It would thus be easy for critics to link culture-and-personality research with charges of American imperialism and prejudice. This poses a problem for anyone contemplating culture-and-personality as a field for research.

Where the use of projective tests is involved, this may also raise ethical problems. Apart from the issue of invasion of privacy, projective tests are often administered with some deceptive explanation, such as that the TAT pictures are a test of the imagination. In this connection Louise H. Kidder and Donald T. Campbell (1970:334) have referred to the "deceptive-deprecatory-exploitative attitude toward 'subjects' " on the part of some social psychologists, a potential danger in culture-and-personality research. If some people studied by an anthropologist subsequently learn that they have been given personality tests without realizing what they were, they may very well feel resentment.

This raises the question of whether such projective tests should be used and whether the information to be gained from them is worth the deception. As noted in Chapter 15, there has been a barrage of criticism of projective techniques, and there has been a decline in their use, especially the Rorschach, in culture-and-personality research in recent years. At the same time, some of the best culture-and-personality studies, such as those of Alor and Truk, have made productive use of projective tests. Cora Du Bois's use of the Rorschach, together with ethnographic and life history material and children's drawings, with the projective tests and life histories being independently analyzed blind by different specialists, seemed an excellent way to get around the problem of an ethnographer's subjective impressionism. If such supplementary devices as the Rorschach Test are not used, we will have nothing against which to check the anthropologist's fallible judgments about the personalities of the people being studied. To abandon projective testing without some substitute would take us back to the kind of early ethnographic reports by Ruth Benedict and Margaret Mead, in which everything depended on the anthropologist's observation of behavior and interviews and on the anthropologist's deductions and intuitions from such information. There are those, such as Jules Henry, who consider this method to be still the best. A person who now sets out to do research in culture-and-personality must choose between two alternatives: (1) abandon the use of projective tests or (2) make such productive use of projective tests that criticism will be ineffectual. The second would seem to be the happier outcome, but it depends on a gamble; success cannot be guaranteed.

It seems that, at the present time, there is some opposition to analyses of social character. This has a counterpart in clinical psychology's growing use of behavior modification therapy, in which particular isolated traits of an individual are changed through conditioning processes. No attempt is made to analyze the personality of the patient; that is not considered necessary. This movement away from diagnosis, classification, and analysis may also have some influence on anthropologists contemplating work in culture-and-personality.

Much of the work in culture-and-personality has been devoted to finding aspects of personality common to a particular group of people, as in the concepts of social character, basic personality structure, and national character. If more attention were given to individual personalities, the charge of stereotyping might be obviated. Some anthropologists currently seem to focus more on the individual. Both Mary Ellen Goodman (1967) and Robert B. Edgerton (1971b), for example, have emphasized the independence and autonomy of individuals at all levels of cultural development.

If culture-and-personality research is so full of difficulties and open to charges of stereotyping and bias, there would have to be some very good reasons for persisting in such research. What justification, then, can it have? On behalf of culture-and-personality research, I suggest the following three main reasons:

1. As mentioned in Chapter 1, culture-and-personality research provides an alternative way of learning about human personality which can check and supplement the findings of psychology and psychiatry. The anthropologist studies people in their natural spheres of action, neither as patients nor as the subjects of a laboratory experiment.

It is valuable to have descriptive ethnographic accounts of the everyday lives of people in such societies and to see how personality tendencies are directed in one direction or another. Without such documentation we would have a much more limited conception of the range of possibilities in human behavior.

2. Related to the foregoing point is the consideration that culture-and-personality research contributes to an understanding of the relationship between culture and mental disorders, as discussed in Chapter 18. Anthropologists have shown that some patterns of behavior which we would consider abnormal in our society, such as trance,

possession states, or transvestism, are accepted without stigma in other societies and may even be a source of prestige. This knowledge should contribute to a more relativistic and tolerant view of forms of deviant behavior to which we are often quick to assign pejorative clinical labels. Cross-cultural research should help us to learn what factors are commonly at work in such cases. Learning to think in new ways about what it means to be "mentally ill" may be facilitated by culture-and-personality research.

3.   Culture-and-personality research may contribute to an understanding of historical events, of why particular human groups responded as they did to particular challenges. We cannot make sense of history only in terms of economic and political factors, holding human nature constant.

In much historical writing one finds an economic determinism which does hold human nature constant. To give an example, here is a statement by George T. Hunt in his book, *The Wars of the Iroquois:*

> If Indians of other nations or institutions had lived in the country in which the Iroquois lived, they would have been subject to the same pressure of circumstance; the trade of other nations would have been desirable and even necessary to them; and they would, presumably, have taken about the same steps to obtain it as did the Iroquois. Had the position of the Hurons and the Ottawa been exchanged for that of the Iroquois, it is scarcely a mere conjecture that the Iroquois would then have used the Ottawa River highway and that the tribes living in New York would have blockaded it and attempted to destroy them (Hunt 1940:159).

In an earlier publication, I contrasted this passage with one by Abram Kardiner: "We can assume with complete confidence that the history of the Alorese would be different from the Comanche even if both were subjected to the same external vicissitudes, because each culture is characterized by different life goals and values" (Kardiner et al. 1945:414).

I commented as follows:

> It is evident that the imaginary experiment of substitution suggested by Hunt, of placing one society in the shoes of another, is an impossible one. No two societies having different historical traditions and patterns of culture can ever be said to be in the "same" situation, or be exposed, as Kardiner suggests, to the "same" external vicissitudes. But since the problems of group personality and history call for some sort of comparative approach, a reasonable approximation to a controlled experiment may be found in cases where two or more adjoining cultures have been affected by the same general sweep of historical events, by equivalent pressures and social dislocations (Barnouw 1950:7).

As an example, consider the adjoining Hausa, Yoruba, and Ibo tribes of Nigeria discussed earlier in Chapters 14 and 20. Although all three tribes have been affected by acculturation, the Ibo seem to have manifested the most enterprise and achievement motivation. It is clear that the three groups did not respond in the same way to the new challenges and opportunities. This suggests that human nature should not be held constant and that group differences in personality, in attitudes, values, and ethos partly determine how different peoples respond to the "same" situation.

In the Rimrock area of the Southwest, five groups live in close proximity: Spanish-Americans, Texans, Mormons, Navaho, and Zuñi. They share the same geographical environment but have different cultural traditions. People act in terms of their dominant values, beliefs, and assumptions about reality; so the members of these five groups probably respond to the "same" situations and challenges in characteristically different ways. Hence, in order to understand how a particular group of people behave in a particular historical situation, we should have knowledge of their culture, their values and attitudes. That is why I claim that culture-and-personality research may contribute to an understanding of historical events.

In Chapter 22 we saw that different societies have shown differences in achievement motivation. Social cooperation is more easily secured in some societies than in others. There is more art, more individualism and freedom of self-expression in some societies than in others. Researchers in the field of culture-and-personality try to learn what factors bring about such differences. If it is true that character is destiny, some knowledge of the social character of a group may contribute to an understanding of its history.

This book has provided a review of accomplishments in the field of culture-and-personality, the main contributions and criticisms thereof, the advantages and drawbacks of the research methods used, and the dilemmas which confront further work in this field. We cannot predict the future of such research, but at least it can be said that something of substantial value has been accomplished so far. Within about half a century a considerable body of literature has appeared in culture-and-personality, the best works of which will surely serve as permanent contributions to man's long effort to understand himself.

SUGGESTIONS FOR FURTHER READING

For some retrospective reviews of the field, see John J. Honigmann, "Psychological Anthropology: Trends, Accomplishments, and Future Tasks," in *Psychological Anthropology*, ed. Thomas R. Williams (The Hague: Mouton Publishers, 1975), pp. 601–26; Richard A. Shweder, "Rethinking Culture and Personality Theory. A Critical Examination of Two Classical Postulates," *Ethos* 17 (1979), pp. 255–78; "Rethinking Culture and Personality Theory. Part II: A Critical Examination of Two More Classical Postulates," *Ethos* 7

(1979), pp. 279–311; "Rethinking Culture and Personality Theory. Part III: From Genesis and Typology to Hermeneutics and Dynamics," *Ethos* 8 (1980), pp. 60–94.

George D. Spindler has assembled retrospective reviews of their own work by 20 psychological anthropologists in George D. Spindler, ed., *The Making of Psychological Anthropology* (Berkeley: University of California Press, 1978). The contributors are John and Beatrice Whiting, Victor Barnouw, Margaret Mead, Francis L. K. Hsu, Louise Spindler, Anthony F. C. Wallace, George De Vos, Weston La Barre, John J. Honigmann, Melford E. Spiro, George Devereux, Theodore Schwartz, Robert B. Edgerton, Erika Bourguignon, Theodore and Nancy Graves, Victor Turner, Douglass Price-Williams, and Michael Cole.

A Glossary of Psychiatric and Psychological Terms That Appear in the Text

Acting out. The expression of unconscious emotional conflicts in active behavior in which the individual is not consciously aware of the deeper motivations for his or her actions.

Ambivalence. The coexistence of conflicting emotions and attitudes, such as love and hate, toward the same person, object, or goal.

Anal stage. According to Freudian theory, a pregenital phase of human psychosexual development during the second year of life when pleasurable sensations are experienced in the anal zone.

Authoritarian personality. According to T. W. Adorno et al., a personality type that results from a strict and relatively affectionless upbringing. Hostility is repressed and projected or displaced against minority groups, while strong leaders are admired.

Basic personality. A personality configuration shared by the members of a particular society as a result of the childhood experiences which they have had in common.

Castration complex. A group of unconscious ideas centered around the fear of loss or damage to the genital organs, usually in punishment for having felt tabooed sexual desires.

Cognitive dissonance. The simultaneous coexistence of conflicting, contradictory cognitions.

Compulsive personality. *See* Obsessive-compulsive personality.

Concrete operations. In Piagetian psychology, mental operations that become possible during the latency period, when children are first able to group objects according to different attributes and to understand the principle of conservation.

Conflict model of personality. Salvatore Maddi's term for a theoretical approach that conceives of personality as being always caught between opposing forces, between which the individual must make compromises.

Conservation. In Piagetian psychology, a concrete operation involving the ability to attribute invariance to some matter undergoing transformations, such as when the same amount of liquid is poured into containers of different size and shape.

Consistency model of personality. Salvatore Maddi's term for a theoretical approach to personality that emphasizes its role in maintaining consistency in life experiences.

Core of personality. The basic inherent aspects of personality that are shared by all human beings and that do not change very much in the course of life.

Depression. An affective state or disorder marked by very depressed mood and motor retardation.

Ego. In Freudian terms, a part of the personality that is in contact with the environment.

ESP. Extrasensory perception, a general term for the hypothetical faculties of telepathy and clairvoyance. *Telepathy* is the communication of ideas from one mind to another independently of the usual sense organs. *Clairvoyance* is the awareness of an event or physical object independent of the sense organs but not through telepathy.

Field dependence. A global cognitive set in which there is some difficulty in separating figure from ground in such tests as the Embedded Figures Test.

Field independence. An analytic cognitive set in which there is little difficulty in separating figure from ground in such tests as the Embedded Figures Test.

Fulfillment model of personality. Salvatore Maddi's term for a theoretical approach that sees personality as representing a life force that seeks fulfillment or actualization.

Genital primacy. In Freudian terms, the culminating phase of human psychosexual development in which a person is able to sustain a mature relationship with a sexual partner.

Hysterical personality. A personality disorder characterized by excitability, emotional instability, and attention-seeking self-dramatization.

Id. In Freudian terms, part of the personality consisting of instinctual energy and drives that seek discharge.

Interactional school. A psychological school that emphasizes the current situational factors in a person's life and that also tends to deemphasize the influence of early childhood experiences in the formation of personality in later years.

Klinefelter's syndrome. A glandular disturbance in males resulting from the presence of an extra x-chromosome, leading to testicular atrophy and feminization of appearance.

Latency. A period of human psychosexual development from about six years to the time of puberty, when there seems to be a cessation or diminution of sexual interests, although this may be influenced by cultural conditions.

Latent content. The unconscious meaning of a dream or fantasy.

Libido. A Freudian concept of psychosexual energy that is invested in particular erogenous zones, such as oral, anal, and genital.

Longitudinal study. The study of an individual or group of persons over a period of several years, such as from infancy to adolescence.

Manic. An affective state or disturbance characterized by excitability, elation, flight of ideas, and irritability.

Manic-depressive psychosis.   An affective disorder characterized by strong alterations of mood from a manic state to a state of depression. (*See also* Depression *and* Manic.)

Manifest content.   The remembered content of a dream or fantasy, in contrast to its unconscious latent significance.

Modal personality.   Central tendencies in personality among the members of a particular society, not necessarily shared by all its members.

Obsessive-compulsive personality.   A personality disorder characterized by excessive concern with conformity or overconscientiousness, resulting in a rigid, inhibited personality.

Oral stage.   In Freudian terms, the earliest phase of human psychosexual development during the first year of life.

Paranoid personality.   A personality disorder characterized by rigidity, exaggerated suspicions of others, jealousy, envy, and excessive ideas of self-importance.

Personality.   A more or less enduring organization of forces within the individual that is associated with a complex of fairly consistent attitudes, values, and modes of perception which account, in part, for the individual's consistency of behavior.

Phallic stage.   In Freudian terms, a period of human psychosexual development between about two and a half to six years of age characterized by the development of erotic sensations in the genital areas, prior to the stage of latency.

Projection.   Personal apperceptive distortion in the interpretation of reality. The term was also used by Freud for a defensive process in which the ego ascribes its own drives and feelings to other persons or objects.

Projective test.   A test, such as the Rorschach Test or the Thematic Apperception Test, in which a subject reveals aspects of personality through the nature of his or her responses to the stimuli.

Psychosis.   A major mental disorder that may be of either organic or emotional origin, in which the individual loses the ability to meet the usual demands of life and may experience delusions or hallucinations. *See also* Schizophrenia *and* Manic-depressive psychosis.

Schizoid personality.   A personality disorder manifested by shyness, daydreaming, and avoidance of close personal relationships, often involving the repression of aggressive feelings.

Schizophrenia.   A form of mental disorder characterized by thought disturbances—sometimes including delusions and hallucinations—and also by mood changes, constriction, and lack of empathy with others.

Situational approach.   An approach to personality that emphasizes the current roles, activities, and interpersonal relationships in the life of an individual, rather than the influence of early childhood experiences.

Social character.   Erich Fromm's term for the aspects of character structure that are shared by most members of a particular society or group.

Super-ego.   Freud's term for the internalized voice of parental authority and the parents' code of ethics, equivalent to conscience.

Turner's syndrome.   A chromosomal defect in women that leads to abnormal ovarian development and sometimes mental retardation.

References Cited

Aaronson, Bernard, and Humphrey Osmond, eds.
1970 Psychedelics. The Uses and Implications of Hallucinogenic Drugs. New York: Doubleday.

Abel, Theodore
1941 The Element of Decision in the Pattern of War. American Sociological Review 6:853–59.

Abelson, Robert P., et al.
1968 Theories of Cognitive Consistency: A Sourcebook. Chicago: Rand McNally.

Aberle, David F.
1960 The Influence of Linguistics on Early Culture and Personality Theory. *In* Essays in Honor of Leslie A. White, eds. Gertrude E. Dole, and Robert Carneiro, pp. 1–29. New York: Thomas Y. Crowell.
1961 "Arctic Hysteria" and Latah in Mongolia. *In* Social Structure and Personality. A Casebook, ed. Yehudi A. Cohen, pp. 471–75. New York: Holt, Rinehart & Winston.
1962 A Note on Relative Deprivation Theory as Applied to Millenarian and Other Cult Movements. *In* Millennial Dreams in Action. Essays in Comparative Study. Comparative Studies in Society and History. Supplement 2, ed. Sylvia Thrupp, pp. 209–14. The Hague: Mouton.

Abt, Lawrence E., and Leopold Bellak
1959 Projective Psychology. New York: Grove Press.

Adams, Richard N., and Jack J. Preiss, eds.
1960 Human Organization Research, Field Relations and Techniques. Homewood, Ill.: The Dorsey Press.

Adelson, Joseph
1970 What Generation Gap? *In* The Character of Americans. A Book of Readings, rev. ed., ed., Michael McGiffert, pp. 378–88. Homewood, Ill.: The Dorsey Press.

Adler, Nathan
1968 The Antinomian Personality: The Hippie Character Type. Psychiatry 31:325–38.

Adorno, T. W., Else Frenkel-Brunswik, D. J. Levinson, and R. Nevitt Sanford
1950 The Authoritarian Personality. New York: Harper & Brothers.

Ainsworth, Mary D. Salter
1967 Infancy in Uganda: Infant Care and the Growth of Love. Baltimore: Johns Hopkins Press.

Aitken, Barbara
   1930   Temperament in Native American Religion. Journal of the Royal Anthropological Institute 60:363–87.

Al-Issa, Ihsan, ed.
   1980   Culture and Psychopathology. Baltimore, Md.: University Park Press.

Allport, Gordon W.
   1937   Personality. A Psychological Interpretation. New York: Henry Holt.

Allport, Gordon W., and Philip E. Vernon
   1933   Studies in Expressive Movement. New York: Macmillan.

Alschuler, Rose H., and La Berta Weiss Hattwick
   1947   Painting and Personality. A Study of Young Children. Chicago: University of Chicago Press.

Ammar, Hamed
   1966   Growing Up in an Egyptian Village. New York: Octagon Books.

Anastasi, Anne, and John P. Foley, Jr.
   1938   A Study of Animal Drawings by Indian Children of the North Pacific Coast. Journal of Social Psychology 9:363–74.

Angoff, Allan, and Diana Barth, eds.
   1974   Parapsychology and Anthropology. New York: Parapsychology Foundation.

Ardrey, Robert
   1961   African Genesis. A Personal Investigation into the Animal Origins and Nature of Man. New York: Atheneum.
   1966   The Territorial Imperative. A Personal Inquiry into the Animal Origins of Property and Nations. New York: Atheneum.
   1976   The Hunting Hypothesis. A Personal Conclusion Concerning the Evolutionary Nature of Man. New York: Atheneum.

Ariès, Philippe
   1965   Centuries of Childhood: A Social History of Family Life, Robert Baldick, trans. New York: Random House, Vintage Books.

Aronoff, Joel
   1967   Psychological Needs and Cultural Systems. A Case Study. Princeton, N.J.: D. Van Nostrand.

Arsenian, Jean M.
   1943   Young Children in an Insecure Situation. Journal of Abnormal and Social Psychology 38:225–49.

Ashley-Montagu, M.F.
   1937   Coming Into Being Among the Australian Aborigines. London: George Routledge & Sons.

Austen, Leo
   1934   Procreation Among the Trobriand Islanders. Oceania 5:102–13.

Austin, Lewis
   1977   Visual Symbols, Political Ideology, and Culture. Ethos 5:306–25.

Bacon, Margaret K., Irvin L. Child, and Herbert Barry, III
   1963   A Cross-Cultural Study of Correlates of Crime. Journal of Abnormal and Social Psychology 66:291–300.

Bacon, Margaret K., Herbert Barry, III, and Irvin L. Child
1965   A Cross-Cultural Study of Drinking: II. Relations to Other Features of Culture. Quarterly Journal of Studies on Alcohol. Supplement no. 3.

Badcock, C. R.
1980   The Psychoanalysis of Culture. Oxford: Basil Blackwell.

Bailey, Flora L.
1942   Navaho Motor Habits. American Anthropologist 44:210–16.

Bandura, Albert, and Richard H. Walters
1959   Adolescent Aggression. New York: Ronald Press.

Banfield, Edward C.
1958   The Moral Basis of a Backward Society. Glencoe, Ill.: Free Press.

Barker, Roger G., and Louise Shedd Barker
1961   Behavior Units for the Comparative Study of Cultures. *In* Kaplan 1961:457–76.

Barker, Roger G., and Herbert F. Wright
1951   One Boy's Day. A Specific Record of Behavior. New York: Harper & Brothers.
1955   Midwest and its Children. The Psychological Ecology of an American Town. Evanston, Ill.: Row, Peterson.

Barnouw, Victor
1946   Paranormal Phenomena and Culture. Journal of the American Society for Psychical Research 40:2–21.
1949   The Phantasy World of a Chippewa Woman. Psychiatry 12:67–76.
1950   Acculturation and Personality among the Wisconsin Chippewa. American Anthropological Society Memoir no. 72.
1954   Reminiscences of a Chippewa Mide Priest. Wisconsin Archeologist 35:83–112.
1961   Chippewa Social Atomism. American Anthropologist 63:1006–113.
1967   Comments. Current Anthropology 8:328–29. (*See* Hickerson 1967.)
1969   Cross-Cultural Research with the House-Tree-Person Test. *In* Advances in the House-Tree-Person Technique: Variations and Applications. ed. John N. Buck and Emanuel F. Hammer, pp. 417–47. Los Angeles: Western Psychological Services.
1977   Wisconsin Chippewa Myths and Tales and Their Relation to Chippewa Life. Madison: University of Wisconsin Press.
1978   An Interpretation of Wisconsin Ojibwa Culture and Personality: A Review. *In* Spindler 1978:64–86.
1983   Review of *The Tibetan Symbolic World: Psychoanalytic Explorations* by Robert A. Paul. The Journal of Psychoanalytic Anthropology 6:221–25.

Barry Herbert, III
1957   Relationships between Child Training and the Pictorial Arts. Journal of Abnormal and Social Psychology 54:380–83.

Barry Herbert, III, Irvin L. Child, and Margaret K. Bacon
1959   Relation of Child Training to Subsistence Economy. American Anthropologist 61:51–63.

Bartlett, Frederick C.
1932   Remembering. A Study in Experimental and Social Psychology. Cambridge, England: The University Press.

Barton, Roy F.
1955   The Mythology of the Ifugaos. Memoirs of the American Folklore Society, vol. 46.

Bateson, Gregory
1949   Bali: The Value System of a Steady State. *In* Social Structure: Studies Presented to A. R. Radcliffe-Brown. ed. Meyer Fortes, pp. 35–53. Oxford: Clarendon Press. (Reprinted in Bateson 1972:107–27.)
1958   Naven. 2d ed. Stanford, Cal.: Stanford University Press.
1972   Steps to an Ecology of Mind. New York: Ballantine Books.

Bateson, Gregory, and Margaret Mead
1942   Balinese Character: A Photographic Analysis. Special Publications of the New York Academy of Sciences, vol. 2, New York.

Bateson, Gregory, Don D. Jackson, Jay Haley, and John H. Weakland
1956   Toward a Theory of Schizophrenia. Behavioral Science 1:251–64. (Reprinted in Bateson 1972:201–27.)

Bazzoui, W., and I. Al-Issa
1966   Psychiatry in Iraq. British Journal of Psychiatry 112:827–32.

Beal, James B.
1977   The Formerly "Supernatural": Electrical and Psi Fields in Medical Anthropology. *In* Long 1977a:99–125.

Bean, Lowell J., and Katherine Siva Saubel
1972   Temalpakh: Cahuilla Indian Knowledge and Usage of Plants. Banning, Cal.: Malki Museum Press.

Beardsley, Richard K.
1965   Personality Psychology. *In* Twelve Doors to Japan. ed. John Whitney Hall and Richard K. Beardsley, pp. 350–82. New York: McGraw-Hill.

Beardsley, Richard K., John W. Hall, and Robert E. Ward
1959   Village Japan. Chicago: University of Chicago Press.

Beattie, John, and John Middleton, eds.
1969   Spirit Mediumship and Society in Africa. London: Routledge & Kegan Paul.

Beck, Samuel J.
1952   The Experimental Validation of the Rorschach Test. IV. Discussion and Critical Evaluation. American Journal of Orthopsychiatry 22:771–75.

Bellah, Robert N.
1957   Tokugawa Religion. The Values of Pre-Industrial Japan. Glencoe, Ill.: Free Press.

Bellak, Leopold
1959   On the Problems of the Concept of Projection. A Theory of Apperceptive Distortion. *In* Abt and Bellak 1959:7–32.

Belo, Jane
1935   The Balinese Temper. Character and Personality 4:120–46.
1955   Balinese Children's Drawings. *In* Mead and Wolfenstein 1955:52–69.
1960   Trance in Bali. New York: Columbia University Press.

Benedict, Paul K., and Irving Jacks
1954   Mental Illness in Primitive Societies. Psychiatry 17:377–89.

Benedict, Ruth
1930   Psychological Types in the Cultures of the Southwest. Proceedings of the 23rd International Congress of Americanists, pp. 570–81. New York.
1934   Patterns of Culture. Boston: Houghton Mifflin.
1935   Zuni Mythology. 2 vols. New York: Columbia University Press.

1938 Continuities and Discontinuities in Cultural Conditioning. Psychiatry 1:161–67.

1946 The Chrysanthemum and the Sword. Patterns of Japanese Culture: Boston: Houghton Mifflin.

Bennett, John W.
1946 The Interpretation of Pueblo Culture. Southwestern Journal of Anthropology 4:361–74.

Bennett, John W., and Michio Nagai
1953 Echoes: Reactions to American Anthropology: Japanese Critique of Benedict's "Chrysanthemum and the Sword," American Anthropologist 55:404–11.

Benson, Herbert, John F. Beary, and Mark P. Carol
1974 The Relaxation Response. Psychiatry 37:37–46.

Berlin, Brent, and Paul Kay
1969 Basic Color Terms: Their Universality and Evolution. Berkeley: University of California Press.

Bernard, Jessie
1945 Observations and Generalization in Cultural Anthropology. American Journal of Sociology 50:284–91.

1949 Sociological Mirror for Cultural Anthropologists. American Anthropologist 51:671–77.

Berndt, Ronald M.
1951 Kunapipi, New York: International Universities Press.

Berndt, Ronald M., and Catherine H. Berndt
1951 The Concept of Abnormality in an Australian Aboriginal Society. In Psychoanalysis and Culture. Essays in Honor of Géza Roheim. ed. George B. Wilbur, and Warner Muensterberger, pp. 75–89. New York: International Universities Press.

Berne, Eric
1959 Difficulties of Comparative Psychiatry: The Fiji Islands. American Journal of Psychiatry 116:104–9.

Berreman, Gerald D.
1966 Concomitants of Caste Organization. In De Vos and Wagatsuma 1966:308–24.

Berry, John W.
1966 Temne and Eskimo Perceptual Skills, International Journal of Psychology 1:207–29.

1976 Human Ecology and Cognitive Style. Comparative Studies in Cultural and Psychological Adaptation. New York: Sage Publications.

1981 Developmental Issues in the Comparative Study of Psychological Differentiation. In Munroe, Munroe, and Whiting 1981:475–99.

Bettelheim, Bruno
1954 Symbolic Wounds. Puberty Rites and the Envious Male. Glencoe, Ill.: Free Press.

1969 The Children of the Dream. New York: Avon Books.

Bettelheim, Bruno, with Morris Janowitz
1950 Dynamics of Prejudice. A Psychological and Sociological Study of Veterans. New York: Harper & Brothers.

Biesheuvel, S.
1958 Methodology in the Study of Attitudes of Africans. Journal of Social Psychology 47:169–84.

Billig, Otto, and B. G. Burton-Bradley
1978   The Painted Message. Cambridge, Mass.: Schenkman.

Birdwhistell, Ray
1952   Introduction to Kinesics. Washington D.C.: Department of State, Foreign Service Institute.

Bishop, Charles A.
1975   Northern Algonkian Cannibalism and Windigo Psychosis. *In* Williams 1975: 237–48.

Blasi, Joseph Raphael
1978   The Communal Future: The Kibbutz and the Utopian Dilemma. Norwood, Pa.: Norwood Editions.

Bleuler, Manfred
1979   On Schizophrenic Psychoses. American Journal of Psychiatry 136:1403–09.

Block, Jack, and Jeanne Block
1951   An Investigation of the Relationship between Intolerance of Ambiguity and Ethnocentrism. Journal of Personality 19:303–11.

Blum, Richard H.
1954   The Validity of the Machover DAP Technique. Journal of Clinical Psychology 10:120–25.

Blum, Richard, and Eva Blum
1965   Health and Healing in Rural Greece, Stanford, Cal.: Stanford University Press.

Boas, Franz
1888   The Central Eskimo, Bureau of American Ethnology Report no. 6. Washington D.C.: Smithsonian Institution.
1911   The Mind of Primitive Man. New York: Macmillan Co.
1916   Tsimshian Mythology. Bureau of American Ethnology Report no. 31. Washington D.C.: Smithsonian Institution.
1928   Anthropology and Modern Life. New York: W. W. Norton.
1935   Kwakiutl Culture as Reflected in the Mythology. Memoirs of the American Folklore Society, vol. 28.
1938a   ed., General Anthropology. New York: D.C. Heath.
1938b   An Anthropologist's Credo, The Nation, Aug. 27:201–02.
1943   Recent Anthropology. Science 98:311–14, 344–37.
1955   Primitive Art. New York: Dover Publications.
1963   Introduction to the Handbook of American Indian Languages. I. Bureau of American Ethnology Bulletin 40, part 1. Reprinted by Georgetown University Press, Washington D.C. (First published in 1911.)

Bogoras, Waldemar
1909   The Chukchee. Memoir of the American Museum of Natural History, Jesup North Polar Expedition. New York.

Bolman, William M.
1966   Hamburger Hoarding. A Case of Symbolic Cannibalism Resembling Whitico Psychosis. Journal of Nervous and Mental Diseases 142:424–28.

Bolton, Ralph, Carol Michelson, Jeffrey Wilde, and Charlene Bolton
1975   The Heights of Illusion. On the Relationship between Altitude and Perception. Ethos 3:403–24. ·

Bolton, Ralph
1984   The Hypoglycemia-Aggression Hypothesis: Debate Versus Research. Current Anthropology 25:1–53.

Bornstein, Marc H.
1973a   Color Vision and Color Naming: A Psychophysiological Hypothesis of Cultural Difference. Psychological Bulletin 80:257–85.
1973b   The Psychophysiological Component of Cultural Differences in Color Naming and Illusion Susceptibility. Behavior Science Notes 8:41–101.

Boshier, Adrian K.
1974   African Apprenticeship. *In* Angoff and Barth 1974:273–93.

Boss, Medard
1958   The Analysis of Dreams. New York: Philosophical Library.

Bourguignon, Erika
1973   Religion, Altered States of Consciousness, and Social Change. Columbus: Ohio State University Press.
1976   Possession. San Francisco: Chandler & Sharp.
1979   Psychological Anthropology. An Introduction to Human Nature and Cultural Differences. New York: Holt, Rinehart & Winston.

Bowers, Jr., Malcolm B., and David X. Freedman
1966   "Psychedelic" Experiences in Acute Psychoses. Archives of General Psychiatry 15:240–48.

Bowlby, John
1946   Forty-Four Juvenile Thieves. Their Characters and Home Life. London: Baillère, Tindall & Cox.
1969   Attachment and Loss. Vol. I. Attachment. New York: Basic Books
1973   Attachment and Loss. Vol. II. Separation, Anxiety, and Anger. New York: Basic Books.

Boyer, L. Bryce, George De Vos, Orin Borders, and Alice Tani-Borders
1978   The "Burnt Child" Reaction among the Eskimos. Journal of Psychological Anthropology 1:7–56.

Boyer, L. Bryce, Ruth M. Boyer, and George A. De Vos
1982   An Apache Woman's Account of her Recent Acquisition of the Shamanistic Status. Journal of Psychoanalytic Anthropology 5:299–331.

Bradburn, Norman M.
1963   N-Achievement and Father Dominance in Turkey. Journal of Abnormal and Social Psychology 67:464–68.

Bradburn, Norman M., and David E. Berlew
1960   Need for Achievement and English Industrial Growth. Economic Development and Cultural Change 10:8–20.

Braginsky, Benjamin M., Dorothea D. Braginsky, and Kenneth Ring
1969   Methods of Madness. The Mental Hospital as a Last Resort. New York: Holt, Rinehart & Winston.

Brewer, W. D.
1951   Patterns of Gesture among the Levantine Arabs. American Anthropologist 53:232–37.

Brill, A. A.
1913   Pibloktoq or Hysteria among Perry's Eskimos. Journal of Nervous and Mental Diseases 40:514–20.

Brislin, Richard W., Walter J. Lonner, and Robert M. Thorndike
1973   Cross-Cultural Research Methods. New York: John Wiley & Sons.

Brockman, John ed.
1977   About Bateson. New York: E. P. Dutton.

Bronfenbrenner, Urie, with the assistance of John C. Condry, Jr.
1970   Two Worlds of Childhood. U.S. and USSR. New York: Russell Sage Foundation.

Brown, George
1910   Melanesians and Polynesians, Their Life-Histories Described and Compared. London: Macmillan and Co.

Brown, George W., and Tirril Harris
1980   Social Class and Affective Disorder. In Al-Issa 1980:125–56.

Brown, Jennifer
1971   The Cure and Feeding of Windigos. A Critique. American Anthropologist 73:19–22.

Brown, Judith K.
1963   A Cross-Cultural Study of Female Initiation Rites. American Anthropologist 65:837–53.

Brown, Roger, and Eric H. Lenneberg
1954   A Study of Language and Cognition. Journal of Abnormal and Social Psychology 49:454–62.

Bruner, Jerome S., and Renato Tagiuri
1954   The Perception of People. In Lindzey 1954, vol. 2:634–54.

Buck, John N.
1948–49   The H-T-P Technique. A Qualitative and Quantitative Scoring Manual. Journal of Clinical Psychology, part 1, 4:317–96: part 2, 5:37–74.

Bucke, Richard Maurice
1923   Cosmic Consciousness. A Study in the Evolution of the Human Mind. New York: E. P. Dutton.

Buechler, Hans C., and Judith-Maria Buechler
1971   The Bolivian Aymara. New York: Holt, Rinehart & Winston.

Bunzel, Ruth
1933   Zuñi Texts. Publications of the American Ethnological Society, vol. 15.
1938   Art. In Boas 1938a:535–88.
1952   Chichicastenango. A Guatemalan Village. Publications of the American Ethnological Society, no. 22.

Burckhardt, Jacob
1945   The Civilization of the Renaissance in Italy. Oxford: Phaidon Press. (First published in 1860.)

Burling, Robbins
1964   Cognition and Componential Analysis: God's Truth or Hocus-Pocus? American Anthropologist 66:20–28.

Burns, Robert C., and S. Harvard Kaufman
1970 Kinetic Family Drawings. An Introduction to Understanding Children Through Kinetic Drawings (KFD). New York: Brunner/Mazel.
1972 Actions, Styles, and Symbols in Kinetic Family Drawings. An Interpretative Manual. New York: Brunner/Mazel.

Burton, Roger V., and John W. M. Whiting
1961 The Absent Father and Cross-Sex Identity. Merrill-Palmer Quarterly of Behavior and Development 7:85–95.

Bushnell, John, and Donna Bushnell
1975 Projective Doll Play Reconsidered: The Use of a Group Technique with Rural Mexican Children. *In* Williams 1975:163–220.

Buss, Arnold H.
1966 Psychopathology.New York: John Wiley & Sons.

Campbell, A.
1943 St. Thomas Negroes. A Study of Personality and Culture. Psychological Monographs, vol. 55.

Campbell, Angus, and Howard Schuman
1968 Racial Attitudes in Fifteen American Cities. Supplemental Studies for the National Advisory Committee on Civil Disorders. New York: Frederick A. Praeger.

Campbell, Donald T.
1961 The Mutual Methodological Relevance of Anthropology and Psychology. *In* Hsu 1961a:332–52.

Campbell, Donald T., and Robert A. LeVine
1968 Ethnocentrism and Intergroup Consistency. *In* Abelson et al. 1968:551–64.

Cannon, Walter B.
1942 "Voodoo" Death. American Anthropologist 44:169–81.

Caplan, Gerald
1954 Clinical Observations on the Emotional Life of Children in the Communal Settlements of Israel. *In* Problems of Infancy and Early Childhood, ed. Milton J. Senn, pp. 91–120. New York: Josiah Macy Jr. Foundation.

Carothers, J. C.
1948 A Study of Mental Derangement in Africans, and an Attempt to Explain its Peculiarities, More Especially in Relation to the African Attitude to Life. Psychiatry 11:47–86.

Carreón, A. Bouroncle
1964 Contribución al Estudio de los Aymaras. América Indígena (Mexico) 24:129–69.

Carroll, John B., ed.
1956 Language, Thought, and Reality. Selected Writings of Benjamin Lee Whorf. Boston: Technology Press of Massachusetts Institute of Technology.

Carroll, John B., and Joseph B. Casagrande
1958 The Function of Language Classification in Behavior. *In* Readings in Social Psychology, 3d ed. ed. Eleanor E. Maccoby, Theodore M. Newcomb, and Eugene L. Hartley, pp. 18–31. New York: Henry Holt.

Carroll, Michael P.
1979 A New Look at Freud on Myth. Reanalyzing the Star-Husband Tale. Ethos 7:189–205.

1982   The Rolling Head: Towards a Revitalized Perspective on Myth. Journal of Psychoanalytic Anthropology 5:29–56.

Carstairs, G. Morris
1958   The Twice-Born. A Study of a Community of High-Caste Hindus. Bloomington, Ind.: Indiana University Press.

Carter, William E.
1968   Secular Reinforcement in Aymara Death Ritual. American Anthropologist 70:238–63.
1977   Ritual, the Aymara, and the Role of Alcohol in Human Society. In Drugs, Rituals, and Altered States of Consciousness. ed. Brian M. Du Toit, pp. 101–10. Rotterdam: A. A. Balkema.

Caudill, William
1949   Psychological Characteristics of Acculturated Wisconsin Ojibwa Children. American Anthropologist 51:409–27.
1952   Japanese-American Personality and Acculturation. Genetic Psychology Monographs, no. 45.
1959   Observations on the Cultural Context of Japanese Psychiatry. In Opler 1959a:213–42.
1962a   Patterns of Emotion in Modern Japan. In Japanese Culture: Its Development and Characteristics. ed. Robert J. Smith and Richard K. Beardsley, pp. 115–31. Chicago: Aldine.
1962b   Anthropology and Psychoanalysis: Some Theoretical Issues. In Anthropology and Human Behavior. ed. Thomas Gladwin and William C. Sturtevant, pp. 174–213. Washington, D.C.: Anthropological Society of Washington.
1970   The Study of Japanese Personality and Behavior. In The Study of Japan in the Behavioral Sciences. ed. Edward Norbeck and Susan Parman, pp. 37–52. Houston: Rice University Press.

Caudill, William, and George De Vos
1956   Achievement, Culture and Personality: The Case of the Japanese-Americans. American Anthropologist 58:1102–126.

Caudill, William, and David W. Plath
1966   Who Sleeps by Whom? Parent-Child Involvement in Urban Japanese Families. Psychiatry 29:344–66.

Caudill, William, and Harry A. Scarr
1962   Japanese Value Orientations and Culture Change. Ethnology 1:53–91.

Caudill, William, and Helen Weinstein
1969   Maternal Care and Infant Behavior in Japan and America. Psychiatry 32:12–43.

Chagnon, Napoleon A.
1977   Yanomamö. The Fierce People. 2d ed. New York: Holt, Rinehart & Winston.

Chase, Richard
1959   Ruth Benedict: The Woman as Anthropologist. Columbia Forum 2:19–22.

Child, Irvin L., Thomas Storm, and Joseph Veroff
1958   Achievement Themes in Folk Tales Related to Socialization Practice. In Motives in Fantasy, Action, and Society. ed. John W. Atkinson, pp. 479–92. Princeton, N.J.: D. Van Nostrand.

Christie, Richard, and Marie Jahoda
1954   Studies in the Scope and Method of "The Authoritarian Personality." Continuities in Social Research. Glencoe, Ill.: Free Press.

Clarke, Ann M., and A. D. B. Clark
1976 Early Experience: Myth and Evidence. New York: Free Press.

Clifton, James A., ed.
1968 Introduction to Cultural Anthropology. Essays in the Scope and Methods of the Science of Man. Boston: Houghton Mifflin.

Clifton, James A., and David Levine
1961 Klamath Personalities. Ten Rorschach Case Studies. Printed at the University of Oregon Press for private distribution by the authors. Eugene, Ore.

Cochrane, Glynn
1970 Big Men and Cargo Cults. New York: Oxford University Press.

Codere, Helen
1950 Fighting with Property: A Study of Kwakiutl Potlatching and Warfare 1792–1930. Monographs of the American Ethnological Society, 18.
1956 The Amiable Side of Kwakiutl Life: The Potlatch and the Play Potlatch. American Anthropologist 58:344–51.

Cohen, Morris
1942 Causation and its Application to History. Journal of the History of Ideas 3:12–29.

Cohen, Yehudi A.
1961a ed.: Social Structure and Personality. A Casebook. New York: Holt, Rinehart & Winston.
1961b Food and its Vicissitudes: A Cross-Cultural Study of Sharing and Non-Sharing. *In* Cohen 1961a:312–50.
1961c Patterns of Friendship. *In* Cohen 1961a:351–82.
1964a The Transition from Childhood to Adolescence. Cross-Cultural Studies of Initiation Ceremonies, Legal Systems, and Incest Taboos. Chicago: Aldine.
1964b The Establishment of Identity in a Social Nexus: The Special Case of Initiation Rites and Their Relation to Value and Legal Systems. American Anthropologist 66:529–52.
1966 On Alternative Views of the Individual in Culture-and-Personality Studies. American Anthropologist 68:355–61.
1968 Macroethnology: Large-Scale Comparative Studies. *In* Clifton 1968:402–48.

Cole, Michael, John Gay, Joseph A. Glick, and Donald W. Sharp
1971 The Cultural Context of Learning and Thinking: An Exploration in Experimental Anthropology. New York: Basic Books.

Colson, Elizabeth
1969 Spirit Possession among the Tonga of Zambia. In Beattie and Middleton 1969:69–103.

Cook, P. H.
1942 The Application of the Rorschach Test to a Samoan Group. Rorschach Research Exchange 6:52–60.

Cooper, John, and Norman Sartorius
1977 Cultural and Temporal Variations in Schizophrenia: A Speculation on the Importance of Industrialization. British Journal of Psychiatry 130:50–55.

Cooper, John M.
1933 The Cree Witiko Psychosis. Primitive Man 6:20–24.

Coriat, Isador
1915–16 Psychoneuroses Among Primitive Tribes. Journal of Abnormal Psychology 10:201–08.

Cortés, Juan B.
  1960   The Achievement Motive in the Spanish Economy Between the 13th and 18th Centuries. Economic Development and Cultural Change 9:144–63.

Covarrubias, Miguel
  1937   Island of Bali. New York: Alfred A. Knopf.

Crapanzano, Vincent
  1973   The Hamadsha. A Study in Moroccan Ethnopsychiatry. Berkeley: University of California Press.
  1975   Saints, Jnun, and Dreams: An Essay in Moroccan Ethnopsychology. Psychiatry 38:145–59.
  1980   Tuhami. Portrait of a Moroccan. Chicago: University of Chicago Press.

Crapanzano, Vincent, and Vivian Garrison, eds.
  1977   Case Studies in Spirit Possession. New York: John Wiley & Sons.

Dalen, P.
  1977   Maternal Age and Incidence of Schizophrenia in the Republic of Ireland. British Journal of Psychiatry 131:301–305.

D'Andrade, Roy G.
  1961   Anthropological Studies of Dreams. In Hsu 1961a:325–56.

Dasen, Pierre R.
  1972   Cross-Cultural Piagetian Research: A Summary. Journal of Cross-Cultural Psychology 3:23–39.
  1977   Are Cognitive Processes Universal? A Contribution to Cross-Cultural Piagetian Psychology. In Studies in Cross-Cultural Psychology, vol. I. ed. Neil Warren, pp. 155–201. New York: Academic Press.

Davis, Allison, Burleigh B. Gardner, and Mary R. Gardner
  1941   Deep South. A Social Anthropological Study of Class and Caste. Chicago: University of Chicago Press.

Davis, Bernard D., and Patricia Flaherty, eds.
  1976   Human Diversity: Its Causes and Social Significance. Cambridge, Mass.: Ballinger.

Davis, W. A., and R. J. Havighurst
  1946   Social Class and Color Differences in Child Rearing. American Sociological Review 2:698–710.
  1947   Father of the Man. Boston: Houghton Mifflin.

Dawson, John L. M. B.
  1977   Developmental Effects of Different Levels of Protein and Environmental Stimulation on Growth, Endocrines, Brain and Spatial Activity Skills. In Poortinga 1977:95–105.

Dayton, Neil A.
  1940   New Facts on Mental Disorders. Springfield, Ill.: Charles C Thomas.

De Charms, Richard, and Gerald H. Moeller
  1962   Values Expressed in American Children's Readers: 1800–1950. Journal of Abnormal and Social Psychology 64:136–42.

Degler, Carl N.
  1963   The Sociologist as Historian: Riesman's The Lonely Crowd. American Quarterly 15:483–97.

De Gubernatis, Angelo
  1872   Zoological Mythology. New York: Macmillan.

Deikman, Arthur J.
1969   Deautomatization and the Mystic Experience. *In* Tart 1969:23–43.

DeMause, Lloyd, ed.
1975a   The History of Childhood. New York: Harper Torchbooks.
1975b   The Evolution of Childhood. *In* deMause 1975a:1–73.

Dennis, Wayne
1943   Animism and Related Tendencies in Hopi Children. Journal of Abnormal and Social Psychology 38:21–36.
1960a   Causes of Retardation Among Institutionalized Children: Iran. Journal of Genetic Psychology 90:47–59.
1960b   The Human Figure Drawings of Bedouins. Journal of Social Psychology 52:209–19.
1966   Group Values Through Children's Drawings. New York: John Wiley & Sons.
1973   Children of the Crèche. Englewood Cliffs, N.J.: Prentice-Hall.

Dennis, Wayne, and M. G. Dennis
1940   The Effect of Cradling Practices Upon the Onset of Walking in Hopi Children. Journal of Genetic Psychology 56:77–86.

Devereux, George
1939   A Sociological Theory of Schizophrenia. Psychoanalytic Review 26:315–42.
1961   Mohave Ethnopsychiatry and Suicide: the Psychiatric Knowledge and the Psychic Disturbances of an Indian Tribe. Smithsonian Institution, Bureau of American Ethnology, Bulletin 175. Washington, D.C.
1980   Basic Problems of Ethnopsychiatry. Chicago: University of Chicago Press.

De Vos, George
1955   A Quantitative Rorschach Assessment of Maladjustment and Rigidity in Acculturating Japanese-Americans. Genetic Psychology Monographs, no. 52.
1960   The Relation of Guilt toward Parents to Achievement and Arranged Marriage among the Japanese. Psychiatry 23:287–301.
1961   Symbolic Analysis in the Cross-Cultural Study of Personality. *In* Kaplan 1961:599–634.
1965a   Social Values and Personal Attitudes in Primary Human Relations in Niiike. Occasional Papers, Center for Japanese Studies, pp. 53–91. Ann Arbor, Mich.: University of Michigan.
1965b   Achievement Orientation, Social Self-Identity, and Japanese Economic Growth. Asian Survey 5:575–89.
1972   Social Stratification and Ethnic Pluralism: An Overview from the Perspective of Psychological Anthropology. Race 13:435–60.
1980a   Ethnic Adaptation and Minority Status. Journal of Cross-Cultural Psychology 11:101–24.
1980b   Delinquency and Minority Status: A Psychocultural Perspective. *In* Crime and Deviance: A Comparative Perspective. ed. Graeme R. Newman, pp. 130–80. Beverly Hills, California: Sage Publications.

De Vos, George, and Hiroshi Wagatsuma
1961   Value Attitudes Toward Role Behavior of Women in Two Japanese Villages. American Anthropologist 63:1204–30.
1966   Japan's Invisible Race. Caste in Culture and Personality. Berkeley: University of California Press.

De Vos, George, Lizabeth Hauswald, and Orin Borders
1979   Cultural Differences in Family Socialization: A Psychocultural Comparison of

Chinese and Japanese. *In* Japan: A Comparative Perspective. ed. Albert M. Craig, pp. 214–69. Princeton, N.J.: Princeton University Press.

De Vos, George, and Lola Romanucci-Ross
1982 Ethnicity: Vessel of Meaning and Emblem of Contrast. *In* Ethnic Identity. Cultural Continuities and Change. ed. George De Vos and Lola Romanucci-Ross, pp. 363–90. Chicago: University of Chicago Press.

Divale, William Tulio, and Marvin Harris
1976 Population, Warfare, and the Male Supremacist Complex. American Anthropologist 78:521–38.

Dobzhansky, Theodosius
1962 Mankind Evolving. The Evolution of the Human Species. New York: Holt, Rinehart & Winston.

Doi, L. Takeo
1962 *Amae:* A Key Concept for Understanding Japanese Personality Structure. *In* Japanese Culture. Its Development and Characteristics. ed. Robert J. Smith and Richard K. Beardsley, pp. 132–39. Chicago: Aldine.

Dollard, John
1957 Class and Caste in a Southern Town, 3d ed. New York: Doubleday Anchor Books.

Dollard, John, Neal E. Miller, Leonard W. Doob, O. H. Mowrer, R. R. Sears et al.
1939 Frustration and Aggression. New Haven: Yale University Press.

Dorsey, G. A., and A. L. Kroeber
1903 Traditions of the Arapaho. Field Columbian Museum Publications, no. 81, vol. 5.

Douglas, J. W. B., and J. M. Blomfield
1958 Children Under Five. London: George Allen and Unwin.

Draguns, Juris G.
1980 Psychological Disorders of Clinical Severity. *In* Triandis and Draguns 1980:99–174.

Driver, Harold E.
1966 Geographical-historical *versus* Psycho-Functional Explanations of Kin Avoidances. Current Anthropology 7:131–82.

Drucker, Philip
1955 Indians of the Northwest Coast. New York: McGraw-Hill.

Dube, S. C.
1955 Indian Village. Ithaca, N.Y.: Cornell University Press.

Du Bois, Cora
1944 The People of Alor. A Socio-Psychological Study of an East Indian Island. Minneapolis: University of Minnesota Press.
1960 The People of Alor. Cambridge, Mass.: Harvard University Press.

Dundes, Alan
1962 Earth-Diver: Creation of the Mythopoeic Male. American Anthropologist 64:1032–51.

Dunham, H. Warren
1959 Sociological Theory and Mental Disorder. Detroit, Mich.: Wayne State University Press.
1965 Community and Schizophrenia. An Epidemiological Analysis. Detroit, Mich.: Wayne State University Press.

Dunning, R. W.
1959 Social and Economic Change among the Northern Ojibwa. Toronto: University of Toronto Press.

Dyk, Walter
1938 Son of Old Man Hat. A Navaho Autobiography. New York: Harcourt, Brace.

Dyson-Hudson, Rada, and Eric Alden Smith
1978 Human Territoriality: An Ecological Reassessment. American Anthropologist 80:21–41.

Edgerton, Robert B.
1966 Conceptions of Psychosis in Four East African Societies. American Anthropologist 68:408–25.
1971a The Individual in Cultural Adaptation. A Study of Four East African Peoples. Berkeley: University of California Press.
1971b Anthropology, Psychiatry and Man's Nature. In Interface Between Psychiatry and Anthropology. ed. Iago Galdston, pp. 28–54. New York: Brunner/Mazel.
1980 Traditional Treatment for Mental Illness in Africa: A Review. Culture, Medicine and Psychiatry 4:167–89.

Efron, David
1941 Gesture and Environment. New York: King's Crown Press.

Eggan, Dorothy
1943 The General Problem of Hopi Adjustment. American Anthropologist 45:357–73.
1949 The Significance of Dreams for Anthropological Research. American Anthropologist 51:177–98.
1952 The Manifest Content of Dreams: A Challenge to Social Research. American Anthropologist 54:469–85.
1955 The Personal Use of Myth in Dreams. Journal of American Folklore 68:67–75.
1961 Dream Analysis. In Kaplan 1961:551–77.

Eibl-Eibesfeldt, Irenaüs
1972 Love and Hate. Geoffrey Strachan, trans. New York: Holt, Rinehart & Winston.

Ekman, Paul, and Wallace V. Friesen
1969 A Tool for the Analysis of Motion Picture Film or Video Tape. American Psychologist 24:240–43.

Elkisch, Paula
1945 Children's Drawings as a Projective Technique. Psychology Monographs 1.

Ellefson, John O.
1968 Personality and the Biological Nature of Man. In The Study of Personality. An Interdisciplinary Appraisal. ed. Edward Norbeck, Douglass Price-Williams, and William M. McCord, pp. 137–49. New York: Holt, Rinehart & Winston.

Elliot, Alan J. A.
1955 Chinese Spirit-Medium Cults in Singapore. Monographs on Social Anthropology, No. 14. London School of Economics and Political Science.

Ellis, E.
1952 Some Psychological Correlates of Upward Mobility among Unmarried Career Women. American Sociological Review 17:558–63.

Elwin, Verrier
1955 The Religion of an Indian Tribe. London: Oxford University Press.

Embree, John F.
1964   Suye Mura. A Japanese Village. Chicago: University of Chicago Press.

Endler, Norman S., and David Magnusson, eds.
1976   Interactional Psychology and Personality. New York: John Wiley & Sons.

Eng, Helga
1954   The Psychology of Children's Drawings. London: Kegan Paul.

Erikson, Erik H.
1963   Childhood and Society. New York: W. W. Norton.

Fanon, Frantz
1966   The Wretched of the Earth, trans. by Constance Farrington from the French. New York: Grove Press.

Fantl, Berta, and Joseph Schiro
1959   Cultural Variables in the Behavior Patterns and Symptom Formation of 15 Irish and 15 Italian Female Schizophrenics. International Journal of Social Psychiatry 4:245–53.

Faris, Robert E. L., and H. Warren Dunham
1939   Mental Disorders in Urban Areas. Chicago: University of Chicago Press.

Field, M.J.
1960   Search for Security. An Ethno-Psychiatric Study of Rural Ghana. Evanston, Ill: Northwestern University Press.
1969   Spirit Possession in Africa. *In* Beattie and Middleton 1969:3–13.

Field, Peter B.
1962   A New Cross-Cultural Study of Drunkenness. *In* Society, Culture, and Drinking Patterns. ed. David J. Pittman and Charles R. Snyder, pp. 48–74. New York: John Wiley & Sons.

Fischer, John L., and Ann Fischer
1966   The New Englanders of Orchard Town, U.S.A., Six Cultures Series, vol. 4. New York: John Wiley & Sons.

Fisher, Seymour, and Sidney E. Cleveland
1958   Body Image and Personality. Princeton, N.J.: D. Van Nostrand.

Fogelson, Raymond D.
1965   Psychological Theories of Windigo "Psychosis" and a Preliminary Application of a Models Approach. *In* Spiro 1965:74–99.

Ford, Clellan S.
1941   Smoke from Their Fires. New Haven, Conn.: Yale University Press.

Ford, Clellan S., and Frank A. Beach
1951   Patterns of Sexual Behavior. New York: Ace Books.

Fortune, Reo F.
1932   Sorcerers of Dobu. The Social Anthropology of the Dobu Islanders of the Western Pacific. London: Routledge & Sons.
1935   Manus Religion. Memoirs of the American Philosophical Association, Vol. 3.
1939   Arapesh Warfare. American Anthropologist 41:22–41.

Foster, George M.
1965   Peasant Society and the Image of Limited Good. American Anthropologist 67:293–315.

Foulks, Edward F., and Solomon H. Katz

1975   Biobehavioral Adaptation in the Arctic. *In* Biosocial Interrelations in Population Adaptation, pp. 183–93. The Hague: Mouton.

Fox, Robin

1973   Encounter with Anthropology. New York: Harcourt Brace Jovanovich.

1980   The Red Lamp of Incest. London: Hutchinson.

Frank, George H.

1965   The Role of the Family in the Development of Psychopathology. Psychological Bulletin 64:191–205.

Fraser, Douglas

1955   Mundugamor Sculpture: Comments on the Art of a New Guinea Tribe. Man 55:19–20.

Fredén, Lars

1982   Psychosocial Aspects of Depression. No Way Out? Chichester: John Wiley & Sons.

Freedman, Daniel G.

1974   Human Infancy: An Evolutionary Perspective. Hillsdale, N.J.: Lawrence Erlbaum Associates.

1979a   Human Sociobiology. A Holistic Approach. New York: Free Press.

1979b   Ethnic Differences in Babies. Human Nature 2:36–43.

Freeman, Daniel M. A., Edward F. Foulks, and Patricia A. Freeman

1976   Ghost Sickness and Superego Development in the Kiowa Apache Male. *In* The Psychoanalytic Study of Society, Vol. 7:123–71.

1978   Child Development and Arctic Hysteria in the North Alaskan Eskimo Male. Journal of Psychological Anthropology 1:203–10.

Freeman, Derek

1983   Margaret Mead and Samoa. The Making and Unmaking of an Anthropological Myth. Cambridge, Mass.: Harvard University Press.

Freeman, James M.

1978   Collecting the Life History of an Indian Untouchable. *In* American Studies in the Anthropology of India. ed. Sylvia Vatuk, pp. 65–94. New Delhi: Manohar.

1979   Untouchable: An Indian Life History. Stanford, Calif.: Stanford University Press.

Frenkel-Brunswik, Else

1949   Intolerance of Ambiguity as an Emotional and Perceptual Personality Variable. Journal of Personality 18:108–43.

Freud, Sigmund

1900   The Interpretation of Dreams. *In* Collected Works, Standard Edition, vols. 4–5. London: Hogarth Press, 1953.

1908   Character and Anal Erotism. *In* Collected Works, Standard Edition, vol. 9. London: Hogarth Press, 1959.

1913   Totem and Taboo. *In* Collected Works, Standard Edition, vol. 8. London: Hogarth Press, 1953.

1915–16   Introductory Lectures on Psycho-Analysis. *In* Collected Works, Standard Edition, vol. 15. London: Hogarth Press, 1961.

1916–17   Introductory Lectures on Psycho-Analysis (Part III). *In* Collected Works, Standard Edition, vol. 16. London: Hogarth Press, 1963.

1927   The Future of an Illusion. *In* Collected Works, Standard Edition, vol. 21. London: Hogarth Press, 1961.

1930   Civilization and its Discontents. *In* Collected Works, Standard Edition, vol. 21. London: Hogarth Press, 1961.

1933   The Dissection of the Psychical Personality. *In* Collected Works, Standard Edition, vol. 22:57–80. London: Hogarth Press, 1964.

1955   Moses and Monotheism. trans. Katherine Jones. New York: Viking Books (First published in 1939).

Fried, Jacob

1959   Acculturation and Mental Health among Indian Migrants in Peru. *In* Opler 1959a:119–37.

Friedan, Betty

1975   The Feminine Mystique. New York: Dell.

Friedell, Egon

1931   A Cultural History of the Modern Age. The Crisis of the European Soul from the Black Death to the World War, 3 vols., trans. by Charles Francis Atkinson from the German. New York: Alfred A. Knopf.

Friedl, Ernestine

1975   Women and Men: An Anthropologist's View. New York: Holt, Rinehart & Winston.

Friedman, F. G.

1967   The World of "La Miseria." *In* Peasant Society. A Reader. ed. Jack M. Potter, May N. Diaz, and George Foster, pp. 324–46. Boston: Little, Brown.

Fromm, Erich

1941   Escape from Freedom. New York: Rinehart.

1944   Individual and Social Origins of Neurosis. American Sociological Review 9:380–84.

1951   The Forgotten Language. An Introduction to the Understanding of Dreams, Fairy Tales, and Myths. New York: Rinehart.

1955   The Sane Society. New York: Rinehart.

1959   The Oedipus Complex and the Oedipus Myth. *In* The Family: Its Function and Destiny. ed. Ruth Nanda Anshen, pp. 420–48. New York: Harper & Brothers.

Fromm, Erich, and Michael Maccoby

1970   Social Character in a Mexican Village. A Sociopsychoanalytic Study. Englewood Cliffs, N.J.: Prentice-Hall.

Frost, Isaac

1938   Home-sickness and Immigration Psychoses. Austrian and German Domestic Servants: the Basis of Study. Journal of Mental Science, vol. 84.

Frumkin, Robert M.

1955   Occupation and Major Mental Disorders. *In* Mental Health and Mental Disorder. A Sociological Approach. ed. Arnold M. Rose, pp. 136–60. New York: W. W. Norton

Furst, Peter T.

1972   Flesh of the Gods. The Ritual Use of Hallucinogens. New York: Frederick A. Praeger.

Gaertner, Miriam

1955   A Comparison of Refugee and Non-Refugee Immigrants to New York City. *In* Murphy 1955:99–112.

Gans, Herbert J.
1979   Symbolic Ethnicity: the Future of Ethnic Groups and Cultures in America. Ethnic and Racial Studies 2:1–19.

Gay, John, and Michael Cole
1967   The New Mathematics and an Old Culture. A Study of Learning Among the Kpelle of Liberia. New York: Holt, Rinehart & Winston.

Geertz, Clifford
1965   The Impact of the Concept of Culture on the Concept of Man. *In* New Views on the Nature of Man. ed. J. R. Platt, pp. 93–118. Chicago: University of Chicago Press.
1967   Under the Mosquito Net. New York Review, September 14, 1967, pp. 12–13.

German, G. Allen
1972   Aspects of Clinical Psychiatry in Sub-Saharan Africa. British Journal of Psychiatry 121:461–79.

Gill, Merton M., and Margaret Brenman
1959   Hypnosis and Related States. Psychoanalytic Studies in Regression. New York: International Universities Press.

Gillespie, James M., and Gordon W. Allport
1955   Youth's Outlook on the Future: A Cross-National Study. New York: Doubleday.

Gillin, John
1948   Magical Fright. Psychiatry 11:387–400.

Gladwin, Thomas, and Seymour B. Sarason
1953   Truk: Man in Paradise. New York: Viking Fund Publications in Anthropology, No. 20.

Glazer, Howard I., John F. Clarkin, and Howard F. Hunt
1981   Assessment of Depression. *In* Depression. Behavioral and Directive Intervention Strategies. ed. John F. Clarkin and Howard I. Glazer, pp. 1–30. New York: Garland STPM Press.

Glazer, Nathan, and Daniel P. Moynihan
1970   Beyond the Melting Pot. The Negroes, Puerto Ricans, Jews, Italians, and Irish of New York City, 2d ed. Cambridge, Mass.: MIT Press.

Goffman, Erving
1961   Asylums. Essays on the Social Situation of Mental Patients and Other Inmates. New York: Doubleday Anchor Books.

Golden, M.
1964   Some Effects of Combining Psychological Tests on Clinical Inferences. Journal of Consulting Psychology 28:440–46.

Goldfarb, William
1945   Psychological Privation in Infancy and Subsequent Achievement. American Journal of Orthopsychiatry 51:247–55.

Goldfrank, Esther S.
1945   Socialization, Personality, and the Structure of Pueblo Society. American Anthropologist 47:516–39.

Goldschmidt, Walter, with the assistance of Gale Goldschmidt
1976   The Culture and Behavior of the Sebei. A Study in Continuity and Adaptation. Berkeley: University of California Press.

Goldschmidt, Walter, and Robert B. Edgerton
    1961 A Picture Technique for the Study of Values. American Anthropologist 63:26–47.

Goodenough, Ward
    1957 Cultural Anthropology and Linguistics. *In* Report of the 7th Annual Round Table Meeting on Linguistics and Language Study. ed. Paul L. Garvin, pp. 167–73. Monograph Series on Languages and Linguistics, no. 9. Washington D.C.: Institute of Languages and Linguistics, Georgetown University.

Goodman, Mary Ellen
    1957 Values, Attitudes, and Social Concepts of Japanese and American Children. American Anthropologist 59:979–99.
    1967 The Individual and Culture. Homewood, Ill.: The Dorsey Press.

Goody, Jack
    1977 The Domestication of the Savage Mind. Cambridge, England: Cambridge University Press.

Gordon, Hiram L.
    1953 A Comparative Study of Dreams and Responses to the Thematic Apperception Test. I. A Need-Press Analysis. Journal of Personality 22:234–53.

Gorer, Geoffrey
    1943a Burmese Personality. New York: Institute for Inter-Cultural Studies. Mimeographed.
    1943b Themes in Japanese Culture. Transactions of the New York Academy of Sciences, Series 2, V:106–24.
    1948 The American People. A Study in National Character. New York: W. W. Norton.
    1953 The Concept of National Character. *In* Personality in Nature, Society and Culture. ed. Clyde Kluckhohn, Henry A. Murray, and David M. Schneider, pp. 246–59. New York: Alfred A. Knopf.

Gorer, Geoffrey, and John Rickman
    1949 The People of Great Russia. A Psychological Study. London: Crescent Press.

Gough, Kathleen
    1961 Variation in Interpersonal Kinship Relationships. *In* Schneider and Gough 1961:577–613.

Gould, Harold A.
    1971 Jules Henry 1904–1969. American Anthropologist 73:788–97.

Gouldner, Alvin W., and Richard A. Peterson
    1962 Notes on Technology and the Moral Order. Indianapolis, Ind.: Bobbs-Merrill.

Gove, Walter R., and Terry R. Herb
    1974 Stress and Mental Illness Among the Young: A Comparison of the Sexes. Social Forces 53:256–65.

Gove, Walter R., and Jeannette F. Tudor
    1973 Adult Sex Roles and Mental Illness. American Journal of Sociology 78:812–35.

Graber, Robert Bates
    1981 A Psychocultural Theory of Male Genital Mutilation. Journal of Psychoanalytic Anthropology 4:413–34.

1983 The "Rolling Head" Revisited: Toward a Psychocultural Materialism. Journal of Psychoanalytic Anthropology 6:331–37.

Grant, Peter
1890 The Sauteux Indians: About 1804. *In* Les Bourgeois de la Compagnie du Nord-Ouest. ed. L. F. R. Masson, vol. 2, pp. 303–66. Quebec: A. Cote.

Greenfield, Patricia Marks
1966 On Culture and Conservation. *In* Studies in Cognitive Growth. ed. Jerome S. Bruner, Rose R. Olver, and Patricia M. Greenfield, pp. 225–56. New York: John Wiley & Sons.

Greenstein, Fred I.
1964 New Light on Changing American Values: A Forgotten Body of Survey Data. Social Forces 42:441–50.

Griffith, Richard M., Otoya Miyagi, and Akira Tago
1958 The Universality of Typical Dreams: Japanese vs. Americans. American Anthropologist 60:1173–79.

Griffiths, Ruth
1935 A Study of Imagination in Early Childhood. London: Kegan Paul, Trench, Trübner.

Grinnell, George Bird
1923 The Cheyenne Indians. 2 vols. New Haven, Conn.: Yale University Press.

Grygier, Tadeusz
1948 Psychiatric Observations in the Arctic. British Journal of Psychology 39:84–96.

Guest, Robert H.
1960 Categories of Events in Field Observations. *In* Adams and Preiss 1960:225–39.

Gurney, Edmund, Frederic W. H. Myers, and Frank Podmore
1886 Phantasms of the Living. London: Trübner.

Gussow, Zachary
1960 Pibloktoq (Hysteria) among the Polar Eskimo. An Ethnopsychiatric Study. *In* The Psychoanalytic Study of Society, vol. 1. ed. Warner Muensterberger and Sidney Axelrad, pp. 218–36. New York: International Universities Press.

Guthrie, George M. and David L. Szanton
1976 Folk Diagnosis and Treatment of Schizophrenia: Bargaining with the Spirits in the Philippines. *In* Culture-Bound Syndromes, Ethnopsychiatry, and Alternate Therapies. Mental Health Research in Asia and the Pacific ed. William P. Lebra, pp. 147–63. Honolulu: University Press of Hawaii.

Hadfield, J. A.
1954 Dreams and Nightmares. New York: Penguin Books.

Haeberlin, H. K.
1916 The Idea of Fertilization in the Culture of the Pueblo Indians. American Anthropological Association Memoirs, vol. 3, no. 1.

Hagen, Everett E.
1962 On the Theory of Social Change. How Economic Growth Begins. Homewood, Ill.: The Dorsey Press.

Hall, Calvin S.
1947 Diagnosing Personality by the Analysis of Dreams. Journal of Abnormal and Social Psychology 42:68–79.

1953   A Cognitive Theory of Dream Symbols. Journal of General Psychology 48: 169–86.

1959   The Meaning of Dreams. New York: Dell.

Hall, John Whitney

1965   Aspects of Japanese Economic Development. *In* Twelve Doors to Japan, ed. John Whitney Hall and Richard K. Beardsley, pp. 538–86. New York: McGraw-Hill.

Hallowell, A. Irving

1935   The Bulbed Enema Syringe in North America. American Anthropologist 37: 708–10.

1938   Fear and Anxiety as Cultural and Individual Variables in a Primitive Society. Journal of Social Psychology 9:25–47.

1941   The Rorschach Method as an Aid in the Study of Personalities in Primitive Societies. Character and Personality 9:235–45.

1942a   Acculturative Processes and Personality Changes as Indicated by the Rorschach Technique. Rorschach Research Exchange 6:42–50.

1942b   The Role of Conjuring in Saulteaux Society. Philadelphia: University of Pennsylvania Press.

1945   Popular Responses and Cultural References: An Analysis Based on Frequencies in a Group of American Indian Subjects. Rorschach Research Exchange 9:153–68.

1947   Myth, Culture, and Personality. American Anthropologist 49:544–56.

1955   Culture and Experience. Philadelphia: University of Pennsylvania Press.

1956   The Rorschach Technique in Personality and Culture Studies. *In* Klopfer, Ainsworth et al. 1956, vol. 2:458–544.

Hambly, Wilfrid D.

1931   Serpent Worship in Africa. Field Museum of Natural History. Publication no. 289. Chicago.

Hammer, Emanuel F.

1953   An Investigation of Sex Symbolism: A Study of H-T-P's of Eugenically Sterilized Subjects. Journal of Projective Techniques 17:401–13.

1958   The Clinical Application of Projective Drawings. Springfield, Ill.: Charles C Thomas.

Hanks, Lucien M.

1949   The Quest for Individual Autonomy in Burmese Personality with Particular Reference to the Arakan. Psychiatry 12:285–300.

Haring, Douglas G., ed.

1956a   Personal Character and Cultural Milieu, 3d ed. Syracuse, N.Y.: Syracuse University Press.

1956b   Japanese National Character: Cultural Anthropology, Psychoanalysis, and History. *In* Haring 1956a:424–37.

Harlow, Harry

1962   The Heterosexual Affectional System in Monkeys. American Psychologist 17: 1–9.

Harner, Michael J.

1973   Hallucinogens and Shamanism. London: Oxford University Press.

Harrington, Charles C.

1968   Sexual Differentiation in Socialization and Some Male Genital Mutilations. American Anthropologist 70:951–56.

1970   Errors in Sex-Role Behavior in Teen-Age Boys. New York: Teachers College Press.

Harris, Grace
1957 Possession "Hysteria" in a Kenya Tribe. American Anthropologist 59:1046–066.

Harris, Marvin
1964 The Nature of Cultural Things. New York: Random House.
1968 The Rise of Anthropological Theory. A History of Theories of Culture. New York: Thomas Y. Crowell.

Harrison, Richard J., and William Mantagna
1969 Man. New York: Appleton-Century-Crofts.

Hart, C. W. M.
1954 Sons of Turimpi. American Anthropologist 56:242–61.

Hartmann, Ernest L.
1973 The Functions of Sleep. New Haven, Conn.: Yale University Press.

Hasegawa, Nyozekan
1966 The Japanese Character. A Cultural Profile, trans. by John Bester. Tokyo: Kodansha International Ltd.

Hauswirth, Frieda
1932 Purdah: The Status of Indian Women. New York: Vanguard Press.

Hawley, Florence
1937 Kokopelli of the Prehistoric Southwestern Pueblo Pantheon. American Anthropologist 39:644–46.

Hay, Thomas H.
1971 The Windigo Psychosis: Psychodynamic, Cultural, and Social Factors in Aberrant Behavior. American Anthropologist 73:1–19.

Heath, Dwight B.
1966 The Aymara Indians and Bolivia's Revolution. Inter-American Economic Affairs 19:31–40.

Heine-Geldern, Robert
1960 Recent Developments in Ethnological Theory in Europe. In Men and Cultures. Selected Papers of the Fifth International Congress of Anthropological and Ethnological Sciences. ed. Anthony F. C. Wallace, pp. 49–53. Philadelphia: University of Pennsylvania Press.

Heizer, R. F.
1939 The Bulbed Enema Syringe in the New World. Primitive Man 12:85–93.

Henney, Jeannette H.
1974 Spirit Possession Belief and Trance Behavior in two Fundamentalist Groups in St. Vincent. In Trance, Healing, and Hallucination. Three Field Studies in Religious Experience by Felicitas D. Goodman, J. H. Henney, and Esther Pressel, pp. 1–111. New York: John Wiley & Sons.

Henry, Andrew F., and James F. Short, Jr.
1954 Suicide and Homicide: Some Economic, Sociological, and Psychological Aspects of Aggression. Glencoe, Ill.: Free Press.

Henry, Jules
1941 Rorschach Technique in Primitive Cultures. American Journal of Orthopsychiatry 11:230–34.
1945 Review of The People of Alor. American Journal of Orthopsychiatry 15:372–73.

Henry, Jules, and Zunia Henry
  1944   Doll Play of Pilagá Indian Children. An Experimental and Field Analysis of the
         Behavior of Pilagá Indian Children. Research Monograph no. 4. New York: Ameri-
         can Orthopsychiatric Association.

Henry, William E.
  1947   The Thematic Apperception Technique in the Study of Culture-Personality Rela-
         tions. Genetic Psychology Monographs no. 35:3–135.
  1951   The Thematic Apperception Technique in the Study of Group and Cultural
         Problems. *In* An Introduction to Projective Techniques and Other Devices for Under-
         standing the Dynamics of Human Behavior. ed. Harold H. Anderson and Gladys I.
         Anderson, pp. 230–78. Englewood Cliffs, N.Y.: Prentice-Hall.

Hewes, Gordon W.
  1955   World Distribution of Postural Habits. American Anthropologist 57:231–44.

Heyer, Virginia
  1953   Relations Between Men and Women in Chinese Stories. *In* Mead and Metraux
         1953:221–34.

Heyns, Roger W., and Ronald Lippitt
  1954   Systematic Observational Techniques. *In* Lindzey 1954:370–404.

Hickerson, Harold
  1960   The Feast of the Dead Among the Seventeenth Century Algonkians of the
         Upper Great Lakes. American Anthropologist 62:81–107.
  1962   The Southwestern Chippewa. An Ethno-Historical Study. American Anthropo-
         logical Association Memoir no. 92.
  1967   Some Implications of the Theory of Particularity or "Atomism" of Northern
         Algonkians. Current Anthropology 8:313–43.

Hickman, John M.
  1964   The Aymara of Chinchera, Peru: Persistence and Change in a Bicultural Con-
         text. Dissertation Abstracts, no. 7, xxiv. Ann Arbor, Mich.: University Microfilms.

Hinde, R. A.
  1974   Biological Bases of Human Social Behavior. New York: McGraw-Hill.

Hitson, Hazel Marie
  1959   Family Patterns and Paranoidal Personality Structure in Boston and Burma.
         Ph.D. dissertation, Radcliffe College.

Hockings, Paul
  1975   Principles of Visual Anthropology. The Hague: Mouton.

Hoebel, E. Adamson
  1949   Man in the Primitive World. New York: McGraw-Hill.
  1954   The Law of Primitive Man. Cambridge, Mass.: Harvard University Press.
  1960   The Cheyennes. Indians of the Great Plains. New York: Henry Holt.

Hoijer, Harry
  1954   The Sapir-Whorf Hypothesis. *In* Language in Culture. Proceedings of a Confer-
         ence on the Interrelations of Language and Other Aspects of Culture. ed. Harry
         Hoijer, pp. 92–105. American Anthropological Association Memoir no. 79.

Hollender, Marc H., and Steven J. Hirsch
  1964   Hysterical Psychosis. American Journal of Psychiatry 120:1066–74.

Hollingshead, August B., and Fredrick C. Redlich
1958 Social Class and Mental Illness. A Community Study. New York: John Wiley & Sons.

Holloway, Jr., Ralph L.
1968 Human Aggression: The Need for a Species-Specific Framework. *In* War: The Anthropology of Armed Conflict and Aggression. ed. Morton Fried, Marvin Harris, and Robert Murphy, pp. 29–48. Garden City, N.Y.: Natural History Press.

Holmes, Lowell D.
1958 T'au. Stability and Change in a Samoan Village. Wellington, New Zealand. Reprint of the Polynesian Society, no. 7.

Holmes, Lowell D., Gary Tallman, and Vernon Jantz
1978 Samoan Personality. Journal of Psychological Anthropology 1:453–72.

Holtzman, Wayne H.
1968 Holtzman Inkblot Technique. *In* Projective Techniques in Personality Assessment. A Modern Introduction. ed. A. I. Rabin, pp. 136–70. New York: Springer Publishing.

Holtzman, Wayne H., Joseph S. Thorpe, Jon D. Swartz, and E. Wayne Herron
1961 Inkblot Perception and Personality. Holtzman Inkblot Technique. Austin, Tex.: University of Texas Press.

Honigmann, John J.
1949 Culture and Ethos of Kaska Society. Yale University Publications in Anthropology no. 40. New Haven, Conn: Yale University Press.

Honigmann, John J., and Richard N. Carrera
1957 Cross-Cultural Use of Machover's Figure Drawing Test. American Anthropologist 59:650–54.

Hopkins, Keith
1980 Brother-Sister Marriage in Roman Egypt. Comparative Studies in Society and History 22:303–54.

Horton, Donald
1943 The Functions of Alcohol in Primitive Societies: A Cross-Cultural Study. Quarterly Journal of Studies on Alcohol 4:199–320.

Horton, Robin
1969 Types of Spirit Possession in Kalabari Religion. In Beattie and Middleton 1969:14–49.

Howey, M. Oldfield
1949 The Encircled Serpent. London: Rider.

Hsu, Francis L. K.
1954 ed.: Aspects of Culture and Personality. New York: Abelard-Schuman.
1961a ed.: Psychological Anthropology. Approaches to Culture and Personality. Homewood, Ill.: The Dorsey Press.
1961b American Core Value and National Character. *In* Hsu 1961a:209–30.
1967 Under the Ancestors' Shadow. Kinship, Personality, and Social Mobility in Village China. New York: Natural History Library.
1969 The Study of Literate Civilizations. New York: Holt, Rinehart & Winston.
1972a Americans and Chinese. New York: Doubleday/Natural History Press.

1972b   ed: Psychological Anthropology, rev. ed. Cambridge, Mass.: Schenkman Publishing.

Huizinga, J.
1924   The Waning of the Middle Ages. A Study of Forms of Life, Thought, and Art in France and the Netherlands in the XIVth and XVth Centuries. London: Edward Arnold.
1959   Men and Ideas. History, the Middle Ages, the Renaissance, trans. by James S. Holmes and Hans van Marle. New York: Meridian Books.

Hunt, George
1940   The Wars of the Iroquois. Madison: University of Wisconsin Press.

Hutt, S. J., and Corinne Hutt
1970   Direct Observation and Measurement of Behavior. Springfield, Ill.: Charles C Thomas.

Hyman, Herbert H., and Paul B. Sheatsley
1954   "The Authoritarian Personality" — A Methodological Critique. *In* Christie and Jahoda 1954:50–122.

Inkeles, Alex, and Daniel J. Levinson
1954   A National Character: The Study of Modal Personality and Sociocultural Systems. *In* Lindzey 1954, vol. 2:977–1020.

Isaacs, Harold R.
1964   India's Ex-Untouchables. New York: John Day.

Jackson, Jr., C. Wesley, and E. Lowell Kelly
1962   Influence of Suggestion and Prior Knowledge in Research on Sensory Deprivation. Science 135:211–12.

Jaco, E. Gartly
1960   The Social Epidemiology of Mental Disorders. New York: Russell Sage Foundation.

Jacobs, Melville
1959   The Content and Style of an Oral Literature. Clackamas Chinook Myths and Tales. Viking Fund Publications in Anthropology, No. 26.

Jahoda, Gustav
1966   Geometric Illusions and Environment: A Study in Ghana. British Journal of Psychology 57:193–99.

Jahoda, Gustav, and Harry McGurk
1982   The Development of Picture Perception in Children from Different Cultures. *In* Wagner and Stevenson 1982:77–104.

James, William
1929   The Varieties of Religious Experience. A Study in Human Nature. New York: Modern Library. (First published by Longmans, Green in 1902).

Janis, Irving L., George F. Mahl, Jerome Kagan, and Robert R. Holt
1969   Personality Dynamics, Development, and Assessment. New York: Harcourt Brace Jovanovich.

Janzen, John M., with the collaboration of William Arkinstall
1978   The Quest for Therapy in Lower Zaire. Berkeley: University of California Press.

Jenness, Diamond
1935 The Ojibwa Indians of Parry Island. Their Social and Religious Life. Canada Department of Mines. National Museum of Canada, Bulletin No. 78.

Jersild, Arthur T., and Frances B. Holmes
1935 Children's Fears. New York: Teacher's College Press.

Johnson, Colleen Leahy
1976 The Principle of Generation Among the Japanese in Honolulu. Ethnic Groups 1:13–35.

Johnson, H. M., and G. E. Weigand
1927–28 The Measurement of Sleep. Pennsylvania Academy of Science Proceedings, 2:43–48.

Jones, Ernest
1925 Mother-Right and the Sexual Ignorance of Savages. International Journal of Psycho-Analysis 6:109–30.
1948 Papers on Psychoanalysis. Baltimore: Williams & Wilkins.

Jones, Maldwyn Allen
1960 American Immigration. Chicago: University of Chicago Press.

Jones, William
1907 Fox Texts. Publications of the American Ethnological Society. Leyden: E. J. Brill.
1917 Ojibwa Texts, Part 1. Publications of the American Ethnological Society, vol. 7.
1919 Ojibwa Texts, Part 2. Publications of the American Ethnological Society, vol. 7.

Jordan, David K.
1972 Gods, Ghosts, and Ancestors. The Folk Religion of a Taiwanese Village. Berkeley: University of California Press.

Jordan, Winthrop D.
1968 White Over Black: American Attitudes toward the Negro, 1550–1812. Chapel Hill: University of North Carolina Press.

Kadushin A.
1970 Adopting Older Children. New York: Columbia University Press.

Kagan, Jerome, Richard B. Kearsely, and Philip R. Zelazo
1978 Infancy. Its Place in Human Development, Cambridge: Harvard University Press.

Kakar, Sudhir
1981 The Inner World. A Psychoanalytic Study of Childhood and Society in India, 2d ed. Delhi: Oxford University Press.

Kaplan, Bert
1954 A Study of Rorschach Responses in Four Cultures. Papers of the Peabody Museum of American Archaeology and Ethnology. Harvard University, Vol. 42, No. 2.
1961 ed.: Studying Personality Cross-Culturally. Evanston, Ill.: Row, Peterson.

Kaplan, Bert, and Richard Lawless
1965 Culture and Visual Imagery: A Comparison of Rorschach Responses in Eleven Societies. *In* Spiro 1965:295–311.

Kardiner, Abram
1939 The Individual and his Society. The Psychodynamics of Primitive Social Organization. New York: Columbia University Press.

Kardiner, Abram, et al.
1945   The Psychological Frontiers of Society. New York: Columbia University Press.

Kardiner, Abram, and Edward Preble
1961   They Studied Man. New York: World Publishing Co.

Katz, Richard
1982   Boiling Energy. Community Healing Among the Kalahari Kung. Cambridge, Mass.: Harvard University Press.

Keesing, Felix M.
1934   Samoa. Stanford, California: Stanford University Press.
1937   The Taupo System of Samoa. A Study of Institutional Change. Oceania 8:1–14.

Kelley, Douglas M.
1947   22 Cells in Nuremberg. New York: Chilton.

Kelly, George A.
1955   The Psychology of Personal Constructs, Vol. 1. A Theory of Personality. New York: W. W. Norton.

Kennedy, J. G.
1967   Nubian Zar Ceremonies as Psychotherapy. Human Organization 26:185–94.

Kessler, Clive S.
1977   Conflict and Sovereignty in Kelantanese Malay Spirit Seances. *In* Crapanzano and Garrison 1977:295–331.

Kidder, Louise H., and Donald T. Campbell
1970   The Indirect Testing of Social Attitudes. *In* Attitude Measurement. ed. Gene F. Summers, pp. 333–85. Chicago: Rand McNally.

Kiev, Ari
1964   The Study of Folk Psychiatry. *In* Magic, Faith, and Healing. Studies in Primitive Psychiatry Today. ed. Ari Kiev, pp. 3–35. London: Free Press of Glencoe.
1969   Transcultural Psychiatry: Research Problems and Perspectives. *In* Plog and Edgerton 1969:106–27.

King, Glenn E.
1975   Socioterritorial Units Among Carnivores and Early Hominids. Journal of Anthropological Research 31:69–87.

Kinsey, Alfred C., Wardell B. Pomeroy, and Clyde E. Martin
1948   Sexual Behavior in the Human Male. Philadelphia: W. B. Saunders.

Kitahara, Michio
1976   A Cross-Cultural Test of the Freudian Theory of Circumcision. International Journal of Psychoanalytic Psychotherapy 5:535–46.

Klatskin, Ethlyn Henry
1952   An Analysis of the Effect of the Test Situation Upon the Rorschach Record: Formal Characteristics. Journal of Projective Techniques 16:193–99.

Klopfer, Bruno, and Douglas M. Kelley
1942   The Rorschach Technique. A Manual for a Projective Method of Personality Diagnosis. Yonkers-on-Hudson: World Book.

Klopfer, Bruno, Mary D. Ainsworth, Walter G. Klopfer, and Robert R. Holt
1954, 1956   Developments in the Rorschach Test, 2 vols. Yonkers-on-Hudson: World Book.

Kluckhohn, Clyde
1938   Participation in Ceremonials in a Navaho Community: American Anthropologist 40:359–69.
1944   The Influence of Psychiatry on Anthropology in America During the Past One Hundred Years. *In* One Hundred Years of American Psychiatry. ed. J. K. Hall, G. Zilboorg, and H. A. Bunker, pp. 589–617. New York: Columbia University Press.
1945   The Personal Document in Anthropological Science. *In* The Use of Personal Documents in History, Anthropology, and Sociology. ed. Lewis Gottschalk, Clyde Kluckhohn, and Robert Angell, pp. 79–173. New York: Social Science Research Council Bulletin 53.
1958   Have There Been Discernible Shifts in American Values During the Past Generation? *In* American Style: Essays in Value and Performance. ed. Elting E. Morison, pp. 145–217. New York: Harper & Brothers.
1959   Recurrent Themes in Myths and Mythmaking. Daedalus: Journal of the American Academy of Arts and Sciences 88:268–79.

Kluckhohn, Clyde, and Janine Chappat Rosenzweig
1949   Two Navaho Children over a Five-Year Period. American Journal of Orthopsychiatry 19:266–78.

Kluckhohn, Clyde, Henry A. Murray, and David M. Schneider, eds.
1953   Personality in Nature, Society, and Culture. 2d rev. ed. New York: Alfred A. Knopf.

Kluckhohn, Florence Rockwood, and Fred L. Strodtbeck et al.
1961   Variations in Value Orientations. Evanston, Ill.: Row, Peterson.

Köbben, A. J. F.
1967   Why Exceptions? The Logic of Cross-Cultural Analysis. Current Anthropology 8:3–34.

Koluchová, Jarmila
1972   Severe Deprivation in Twins: A Case Study, Journal of Child Psychology and Psychiatry 13:107–14; *reprinted in* Clarke and Clarke 1976:45–55.
1976   A Report on the Further Development of Twins after Severe and Prolonged Deprivation. *In* Clarke and Clarke 1976:56–66.

Kotkov, Benjamin, and Morris Goodman
1953   The Draw-a-Person Tests of Obese Women. Journal of Clinical Psychology 9:362–64.

Krause, Aurel
1956   The Tlingit Indians. Results of a Trip to the Northwest Coast of America and the Bering Straits, trans. by Erna Gunther. Seattle, Wash.: American Ethnological Society.

Kretschmer, E.
1925   Physique and Character, trans. by W. J. H. Sprott. New York: Harcourt, Brace.

Kris, Ernst
1951   Psychoanalytic Explorations in Art. New York: International Universities Press.

Kroeber, A. L.
1907   Gros Ventre Myths and Tales. Anthropological Papers of the American Museum of Natural History, vol. 1, part 3.

1920   Totem and Taboo: An Ethnologic Psychoanalysis. American Anthropologist 22:48–55.

1948   Anthropology. New York: Harcourt, Brace.

Krout, M. H.

1935   Autistic Gestures. Psychological Monographs 46, no. 208.

Kumasaka, Y.

1964   A Culturally Determined Mental Reaction among the Ainu. Psychiatric Quarterly 38:733–39.

La Barre, Weston

1945   Some Observations on Character Structure in the Orient: The Japanese. Psychiatry 8:319–42.

1947   The Cultural Basis of Emotions and Gestures. Journal of Personality 16:49–68.

1948   The Aymara Indians of the Lake Titicaca Plateau, Bolivia. American Anthropological Association Memoir no. 68.

1954   The Human Animal. Chicago: University of Chicago Press.

1961   Art and Mythology. *In* Kaplan 1961:394–403.

1966   The Aymara: History and Worldview. *In* The Anthropologist Looks at Myth. ed. Melville Jacobs and John Greenway, pp. 130–44. Austin: University of Texas Press.

1970   The Ghost Dance. Origins of Religion. New York: Doubleday.

Lambo, T. Adeoye

1955   The Role of Cultural Factors in Paranoid Psychoses among the Yoruba Tribe. Journal of Mental Science 101:239–66.

Landauer, Thomas K., and John W. M. Whiting

1964   Infant Stimulation and Adult Stature of Human Males. American Anthropologist 66:1007–028.

1981   Correlates and Consequences of Stress in Infancy. *In* Munroe, Munroe, and Whiting 1981:355–75.

Landes, Ruth

1937   Ojibwa Sociology. Columbia University Contributions to Anthropology no. 29. New York: Columbia University Press.

1938a   The Abnormal among the Ojibwa. Journal of Abnormal and Social Psychology 33:14–33.

1938b   The Ojibwa Woman. Columbia University Contributions to Anthropology, vol. 31. New York: Columbia University Press.

Landy, David

1960   Methodological Problems of Free Doll Play as an Ethnographic Field Technique. *In* Men and Cultures. Selected Papers of the Fifth International Congress of Anthropological and Ethnological Sciences. ed. Anthony F. C. Wallace; pp. 161–67. Philadelphia: University of Pennsylvania Press.

Lang, Olga

1946   Chinese Family and Society. New Haven, Conn.: Yale University Press.

Langness, Lewis L.

1965   Hysterical Psychosis in the New Guinea Highlands: A Bena Bena Example. Psychiatry 28:258–77.

1976   Hysterical Psychoses and Possessions. *In* Culture-Bound Syndromes, Ethnopsychiatry, and Alternate Therapies. ed. William P. Lebra. Mental Health Research in Asia and the Pacific, Vol. IV; pp. 56–67. Honolulu: The University Press of Hawaii.

Langness, Lewis L., and Thomas Gladwin

1972   Oceania. *In* Psychological Anthropology. ed. Francis L. K. Hsu, pp. 167–200.

Lanham, Betty B.
1956 Aspects of Child Care in Japan: Preliminary Report. *In* Haring 1956a:565–83.

Lantis, Margaret
1946 The Social Culture of the Nunivak Eskimo. Transactions of the American Philosophical Society 35:153–323. Philadelphia.
1953 Nunivak Eskimo Personality as Revealed in the Mythology. Anthropological Papers of the University of Alaska 2:109–74.

Laska-Mierzejewska, Teresa
1970 Effects of Ecological and Socio-economic Factors on the Age at Menarche, Body Height and Weight of Rural Girls in Poland. Human Biology 42:284–92.

Laubscher, B. J. F.
1938 Sex, Custom, and Psychopathology: A Study of South African Pagan Natives. London: Routledge and Kegan Paul.

Lebra, Takie Sugiyama, and William P. Lebra
1974 Japanese Culture and Behavior. Selected Readings. Honolulu: University Press of Hawaii.

Lee, Richard Borshay
1979 the !Kung San. Men, Women, and Work in a Foraging Society. Cambridge: Cambridge University Press.

Lee, Richard B. and Irven DeVore, eds.
1968 Man the Hunter. Chicago: Aldine-Atherton.

Lee, S. G.
1953 Manual of a Thematic Apperception Test for African Subjects. Pietermaritzburg: University of Natal Press.
1958 Social Influences in Zulu Dreaming. Journal of Social Psychology 47:265–83.

Leighton, Alexander H.
1969 A Comparative Study of Psychiatric Disorder in Nigeria and Rural North America. *In* Plog and Edgerton 1969:179–99.
1961 The Stirling County Study: Some Notes on Concepts and Methods. *In* Comparative Epidemiology of the Mental Disorders. ed. Paul H. Hoch and Joseph Zubin, pp. 24–31. New York: Grune & Stratton.

Leighton, Alexander, et al.
1963 Psychiatric Disorder Among the Yoruba. A Report from the Cornell-Aro Mental Health Research Project in the Western Region, Nigeria. Ithaca, N.Y.: Cornell University Press.

Leighton, Dorothea, and Clyde Kluckhohn
1947 Children of the People. Cambridge, Mass.: Harvard University Press.

Lessa, William A.
1956 Oedipus-Type Tales in Oceania. Journal of American Folklore 69:63–73.

Lessa, William A., and Marvin Spiegelman
1954 Ulithian Personality as Seen Through Ethnological Materials and Thematic Test Analysis. University of California Publications in Culture and Society, vol. 2, no. 5:243–301.

Lévi-Strauss, Claude
1966 The Savage Mind. Chicago: University of Chicago Press.
1967 Structural Anthropology, trans. by Claire Jacobson and Brooke Grundfest Schoepf from the French. New York: Doubleday.

1969   The Elementary Structures of Kinship, rev. ed. Trans. J. H. Bell and J. R. von
        Sturmer. ed. Rodney Needham. Boston: Beacon Press.

Levine, M., and E. Galanter
1953   A Note on the "Tree-and-Trauma" Interpretation in the H-T-P. Journal of Con-
        sulting Psychology 17:74–75.

LeVine, Robert A.
1970   Cross-Cultural Study in Child Psychology. *In* Carmichael's Manual of Child
        Psychology, 3d. ed., vol. 2, Paul H. Mussen, ed., pp. 559–612. New York: John
        Wiley & Sons.

LeVine, Robert A., with the assistance of Eugene Strangman and Leonard
Unterberger
1966   Dreams and Deeds. Achievement Motivation in Nigeria. Chicago: University of
        Chicago Press.

LeVine, Robert A., and Barbara B. LeVine
1966   Nyansongo: A Gusii Community in Kenya. Six Cultures Series, vol. 2. New
        York: John Wiley & Sons.

LeVine, Sarah, in collaboration with Robert A. LeVine
1979   Mothers and Wives. Gusii Women of East Africa. Chicago: University of Chi-
        cago Press.

Levy, David M.
1939   Sibling Rivalry Studies in Children of Primitive Groups. American Journal of
        Orthopsychiatry 9:205–14.

Levy, Sydelle Brooks
1973   Shifting Patterns in Ethnic Identification among the Hassidim. *In* The New
        Ethnicity. Perspectives from Ethnology. ed. John W. Bennett, pp. 25–50. St. Paul:
        West Publishing Co.

Lévy-Bruhl, Lucien
1926   How Natives Think. London.

Lewellen, Ted C.
1981   Aggression and Hypoglycemia in the Andes. Another Look at the Evidence.
        Current Anthropology 22:347–61.

Lewis, Hilda
1954   Deprived Children. The Mersham Experiment: A Social and Clinical Study.
        London: Oxford University Press.

Lewis, I. M.
1971   Ecstatic Religion. An Anthropological Study of Spirit Possession and Shaman-
        ism. Baltimore, Md.: Penguin Books.

Lewis, Oscar
1951   Life in a Mexican Village. Tepoztlán Restudied. Urbana: University of Illinois
        Press.
1959   Five Families: Mexican Case Studies in the Culture of Poverty. New York: Basic
        Books.
1961   The Children of Sánchez. Autobiography of a Mexican Family. New York: Ran-
        dom House.
1968   La Vida. A Puerto Rican Family in the Culture of Poverty—San Juan and New
        York. New York: Random House.

Lewis, Oscar, Ruth M. Lewis, and Susan M. Rigdon
1977 Living the Revolution: An Oral History of Contemporary Cuba: Four Men. Four Women. Neighbors. (3 vols.) Urbana: University of Illinois Press.

Li An-Che
1937 Zūni. Some Observations and Queries. American Anthropologist 39:62–76.

Lieberman, Philip, Edmund S. Crelin, and Dennis H. Klatt
1972 Phonetic Ability and Related Anatomy of the Newborn and Adult Human Neanderthal and the Chimpanzee. American Anthropologist 74:287–307.

Lin, T. Y.
1953 A Study of the Incidence of Mental Disorders in Chinese and Other Cultures. Psychiatry 16:313–36.

Lincoln, Jackson Steward
1935 The Dream in Primitive Cultures. Baltimore: Wilkins and Wilkins.

Lindesmith, Alfred R., and Anselm A. Strauss
1950 A Critique of Culture-Personality Writings. American Sociological Review 15:587–600.

Lindzey, Gardner, ed.
1954 Handbook of Social Psychology. ed. Gardner Lindzey, and Elliot Aronson. Reading, Mass.: Addison-Wesley.
1968 Handbook of Social Psychology, 2d ed. Reading, Mass.: Addison-Wesley.

Linton, Ralph
1939 Marquesan Culture. In Kardiner 1939:137–96.
1943 Nativistic Movements. American Anthropologist 45:230–40.
1945 The Cultural Background of Personality. New York: Appleton-Century.
1956 Culture and Mental Disorders. Springfield, Ill.: Charles C Thomas.

Lipset, Seymour M.
1961 A Changing American Character? In Culture and Social Character. The Work of David Riesman Reviewed. ed. Seymour M. Lipset, pp. 136–71. New York: Free Press of Glencoe.

Loeb, Edwin M.
1929 Shaman and Seer. American Anthropologist 31:60–84.

Loewenberg, Peter
1971 The Psychohistorical Origins of the Nazi Youth Cohort. American Historical Review 76:1457–1502.

Long, Joseph K., ed.
1977a Extrasensory Ecology. Parapsychology and Anthropology. Methuen, N.J.: Scarecrow Press.
1977b Extrasensory Ecology: A Summary of Evidence. In Long 1977a:371–96.

Lopreato, Joseph
1970 Italian Americans. New York: Random House.

Lorenz, Konrad
1966 On Aggression. Translated by Marjorie Kerr Wilson. New York: Bantam Books.

Lowenfels, Michal S.
1950 Free Drawings as a Projective Test in Cross-Cultural Investigations. Unpublished master's thesis, University of Pennsylvania.

Lowenthal, Leo
  1944   Biographies in Popular Magazines. *In* Radio Research 1942–43. ed. Paul F. Lazarsfeld and Frank N. Stanton. pp. 507–48. New York: Duell, Sloan, and Pearce.

Ludwig, Arnold M.
  1968   Altered States of Consciousness. *In* Trance and Possession States. ed. Raymond Prince, pp. 69–95. Montreal: R. M. Bucke Memorial Society.
  1969   Altered States of Consciousness. *In* Tart 1969:9–22.

Lynn, D. G., and W. L. Sawrey
  1959   The Effects of Father-Absence on Norwegian Boys and Girls, Journal of Abnormal and Social Psychology 59:258–62.

Maccoby, Eleanor E., and Nathan Maccoby
  1954   The Interview: A Tool of Social Science. *In* Lindzey 1954, vol. 1:449–87.

Macfarlane, Aidan
  1977   The Psychology of Childbirth. Cambridge, Mass.: Harvard University Press.

Machover, Karen
  1949   Personality Projection in the Drawing of a Human Figure. Springfield, Ill.: Charles C Thomas.

Maddi, Salvatore R.
  1976   Personality Theories. A Comparative Analysis, 3d ed. Homewood, Ill.: The Dorsey Press.

Mahler, Margaret S., Fred Pine, and Anni Bergman
  1975   The Psychological Birth of the Human Infant. New York: Basic Books.

Malinowski, Bronislaw
  1922   Argonauts of the Western Pacific. An Account of Native Enterprise and Adventure in the Archipelagoes of Melanesian New Guinea. New York: E. P. Dutton.
  1924   Psychoanalysis and Anthropology. Psyche 4:293–32.
  1926   Crime and Custom in Savage Society. New York: Harcourt, Brace.
  1929   The Sexual Lives of Savages in Northwestern Melanesia. New York: Harcourt, Brace.
  1932   Pigs, Papuans, and Police Court Perspective. Man 32:133–38.
  1935   Coral Gardens and Their Magic, 2 vols. London: Allen and Unwin.
  1948   Magic, Science and Religion and Other Essays. Glencoe, Ill.: Free Press.
  1955   Sex and Repression in Savage Society. London: Routledge and Kegan Paul. (First published in 1927.)
  1967   A Diary in the Strict Sense of the Term. New York: Harcourt, Brace & World.

Malzberg, Benjamin, and Everett S. Lee
  1956   Migration and Mental Disease. A Study of First Admissions to Hospitals for Mental Disease 1939–1941. New York: Social Science Research Council.

Mandelbaum, David G., ed.
  1949   Selected Writings of Edward Sapir in Language, Culture, and Personality. Berkeley: University of California Press.
  1973   The Study of Life History: Gandhi. Current Anthropology 14:177–206.

Maretzki, Thomas W., and Hatsumi Maretzki
  1966   Taira. An Okinawan Village. Six Cultures Series, vol. 7. New York: John Wiley & Sons.

Marriott, McKim
  1955   Little Communities in an Indigenous Civilization. *In* Village India. Studies in the
         Little Community. ed. McKim Marriott, pp. 171–222. American Anthropological
         Association Memoir no. 83.

Marsella, Anthony J.
  1980   Depressive Experience and Disorder Across Cultures. *In* Triandis and Draguns
         1980:237–89.

Martin, M. Kay, and Barbara Voorhies
  1975   Female of the Species. New York: Columbia University Press.

Maslow, Abraham H.
  1968   Toward a Psychology of Being, 2d ed. New York: Van Nostrand Reinhold.

Masters, R. E. L., and Jean Houston
  1966   The Varieties of Psychedelic Experience. New York: Holt, Rinehart & Winston.
  1972   The Experimental Induction of Religious-Type Experiences. *In* White 1972:303–
         21.

Mazlish, Bruce
  1975   James and John Stuart Mill. Father and Son in the Nineteenth Century. New
         York: Basic Books.

McClelland, David C.
  1951   Personality. New York: William Sloane Associates.
  1961   The Achieving Society. Princeton, N.J.: D. Van Nostrand.
  1963   The Achievement Motive in Economic Growth. *In* Industrialization and Society.
         ed. Bert Hoselitz and Wilbert E. Moore, pp. 74–95. The Hague: Mouton and
         UNESCO.

McClelland, David C., and G. A. Friedman
  1952   A Cross-Cultural Study of the Relationship Between Child Training Practices
         and Achievement Motivation Appearing in Folk Tales. *In* Readings in Social Psychol-
         ogy, rev. ed., ed. Guy E. Swanson, Theodore W. Newcomb, and Eugene L. Hartley,
         pp. 243–49. New York: Henry Holt.

McClelland, David C., and David G. Winter et al.
  1969   Motivating Economic Achievement. New York: Free Press.

McDougall, Lorna
  1975   The Quest of the Argonauts. *In* Williams 1975:59–101.

McPhee, Colin
  1946   A House in Bali. New York: John Day.

Mead, Margaret
  1928   Coming of Age in Samoa. A Psychological Study of Primitive Youth for Western
         Civilization. New York: William Morrow.
  1930   Growing Up in New Guinea. New York: William Morrow.
  1932   The Changing Culture of an Indian Tribe. Columbia University Contributions to
         Anthropology, vol. 15. New York: Columbia University Press.
  1935   Sex and Temperament in Three Primitive Societies. New York: William Morrow.
  1937a The Arapesh of New Guinea. *In* Cooperation and Competition among Primi-
         tive Peoples. ed. Margaret Mead, pp. 20–50. New York: McGraw-Hill.
  1937b A Reply to a Review of Sex and Temperament in Three Primitive Societies.
         American Anthropologist 39:558–61.

1939   From the South Seas. Studies of Adolescence and Sex in Primitive Societies. New York: William Morrow.

1940   The Mountain Arapesh, 3 vols. Anthropological Papers of the American Museum of Natural History, vol. 37.

1942   And Keep Your Powder Dry. An Anthropologist Looks at America. New York: William Morrow.

1949a   Male and Female. A Study of the Sexes in a Changing World. New York: William Morrow.

1949b   Ruth Fulton Benedict: 1887–1948. American Anthropologist 51:457–68.

1949c   The Mountain Arapesh, 5. The Record of Unabelin, with Rorschach Analyses. Anthropological Papers of the American Museum of Natural History.

1954   The Swaddling Hypothesis. Its Reception. American Anthropologist 56:395–409.

1955   Children and Ritual in Bali. *In* Mead and Wolfenstein 1955:40–51.

1956a   New Lives for Old. Cultural Transformation: Manus 1928–53. New York: William Morrow.

1956b   Some Uses of Still Photography in Culture and Personality Studies. *In* Haring 1956:79–105.

1959   An Anthropologist at Work. Writings of Ruth Benedict. Boston: Houghton Mifflin.

1970   Culture and Commitment. A Study of the Generation Gap. New York: Natural History Press.

Mead, Margaret, and Rhoda Metraux, eds.
1953   The Study of Culture at a Distance. Chicago: University of Chicago Press.

Mead, Margaret, and Martha Wolfenstein, eds.
1955   Childhood in Contemporary Cultures. Chicago: University of Chicago Press.

Meier, G. M., and R. E. Baldwin
1957   Economic Development. New York: John Wiley & Sons.

Menninger, Karl, with Martin Mayman and Paul Pruyser
1963   The Vital Balance. The Life Process in Mental Health and Illness. New York: Viking Press.

Mensh, Ivan N., and Jules Henry
1953   Direct Observation and Psychological Tests in Anthropological Field Work. American Anthropologist 55:461–80.

Midgley, Mary
1978   Beast and Man. The Roots of Human Nature. Ithaca, N.Y.: Cornell University Press.

Milgram, Stanley
1974   Obedience to Authority: An Experimental View. New York: Harper & Row.

Miller, Daniel R., and Guy E. Swanson
1958   The Changing American Parent. A Study in the Detroit Area. New York: John Wiley & Sons.

Miller, Walter D.
1958   Lower Class Culture as a Generating Milieu of Gang Delinquency. *In* The Sociology of Crime and Delinquency. ed. Marvin E. Wolfgang, Leonard Savitz, and Norman Johnston, pp. 351–63. New York: John Wiley & Sons.

Nair, Kusum
    1962   Blossoms in the Dust. The Human Factor in Indian Development. New York: Frederick A. Praeger.

Naranjo, Claudio
    1973   Psychological Aspects of the Yagé Experience in an Experimental Setting. *In* Harner 1973:176–90.

Naroll, Raoul
    1961   Two Solutions to Galton's Problem. Philosophy of Science 28:15–39.
    1964   On Ethnic Unit Classification. Current Anthropology 5:283–312.
    1965   A Fifth Solution to Galton's Problem. American Anthropologist 66:863–67

Naroll, Raoul, and Roy G. D'Andrade
    1963   Two Further Solutions to Galton's Problem. American Anthropologist 65:1053–67.

Neher, Andrew
    1962   A Physiological Explanation of Unusual Behavior in Ceremonies Involving Drums. Human Biology 34:151–60.

Neihardt, John G.
    1961   Black Elk Speaks. Being the Life Story of a Holy Man of the Oglala Sioux. Lincoln, Neb.: University of Nebraska Press. (First published in 1932.)

Neilon, P.
    1948   Shirley's Babies after Fifteen Years. Journal of Genetic Psychology 73:175–86.

Nerlove, Sara Beth, and Ann Stanton Snipper
    1981   Cognitive Consequences of Cultural Opportunity. *In* Munroe, Munroe, and Whiting 1981:423–74.

Newman, Philip L.
    1964   "Wild Man" Behavior in a New Guinea Highlands Community. American Anthropologist 66:1–19.

Norbeck, Edward, and George De Vos
    1961   Japan. *In* Hsu 1961a:19–47.

Norbeck, Edward, and Margaret Norbeck
    1956   Child Training in a Japanese Village. *In* Haring 1956a:651–73.

Norbeck, Edward, Donald E. Walker, and Mimi Cohen
    1962   The Interpretation of Data: Puberty Rites. American Anthropologist 64:463–85.

Nydegger, William F., and Corinne Nydegger
    1966   Tarong: An Ilocos Barrio in the Phillipines. Six Cultures Series, vol. 6. New York: John Wiley & Sons.

Obeyeskere, Gananath
    1977   Psychosocial Exegesis of a Case of Spirit Possession in Sri Lanka. *In* Crapanzano and Garrison 1977:235–94.
    1982   Sinhalese-Buddhist Identity in Ceylon. *In* Ethnic Identity. Cultural Continuities and Change. ed. George De Vos and Lola Romanucci-Ross, pp. 231–58. Chicago: University of Chicago Press.

O'Bryan, Aileen
    1956   The Diné: Origin Myths of the Navaho Indians. Smithsonian Institution. Bureau of American Ethnology, Bulletin 163. Washington D.C.

Ødegaard, Ørnulv
    1932   Emigration and Insanity. A Study of Mental Disease among the Norwegian-born Population of Minnesota. Acta Psychiatrica et Neurologica, supp. 4. Oslo.

1945   The Distribution of Mental Diseases in Norway. A Contribution to the Ecology of Mental Disorder. Acta Psychiatrica et Neurologica 20:270–76. Oslo.

Olrik, Axel
1965   Epic Laws of Folk Narrative. *In* The Story of Folklore. ed. Alan Dundes, pp. 129–41. Englewood Cliffs, N.J.: Prentice-Hall.

Opler, Marvin K.
1959a   ed.: Culture and Mental Health. Cross-Cultural Studies. New York: Macmillan.
1959b   Cultural Differences in Mental Disorders: An Italian and Irish Contrast in the Schizophrenias—U.S.A. *In* Opler 1959a:425–42.
1967   Culture and Social Psychiatry. New York: Atherton Press.

Opler, Morris E.
1945   Themes as Dynamic Forces in Culture. American Journal of Sociology 51:198–206.
1968   The Themal Approach in Cultural Anthropology and its Application to North Indian Data. Southwestern Journal of Anthropology 24:215–27.

Orlansky, Harold
1949   Infant Care and Personality. Psychological Bulletin 46:1–48.

Osgood, Cornelius
1951   Culture, Its Empirical and Non-Empirical Character. Southwestern Journal of Anthropology 7:202–14.

OSS Assessment Staff
1948   Assessment of Men. Selection of Personnel for the Office of Strategic Services. New York: Rinehart.

Pahnke, Walter N.
1972   Drugs and Mysticism. *In* White 1972:257–77.

Pande, S.
1968   The Mystique of "Western" Psychotherapy: An Eastern Interpretation. Journal of Nervous and Mental Disease 146:425–32.

Parker, Seymour
1960   The Wiitiko Psychosis in the Context of Ojibwa Personality and Culture. American Anthropologist 62:603–23.
1962   Eskimo Psychopathology in the Context of Eskimo Personality and Culture. American Anthropologist 64:76–96.
1964   Ethnic Identity and Acculturation in Two Eskimo Villages. American Anthropologist 66:325–40.

Parsons, Anne
1959   Abstract and Concrete Images in Paranoid Delusions: A Comparison of American and South Italian Patients. *In* Belief, Magic, and Anomie, ed. Anne Parsons, pp. 204–11. New York: Free Press.

Parsons, Elsie Clews
1938   The Humpbacked Flute Player of the Southwest. American Anthropologist 40:337–78.
1939   Pueblo Indian Religion, 2 vols. Chicago: University of Chicago Press.

Pastore, Nicholas
1949   The Nature-Nurture Controversy. New York: King's Crown Press.

Patterson, G. James
1979   A Critique of "The New Ethnicity." American Anthropologist 81:103–05.

Paul, Benjamin D.
1953   Interview Techniques and Field Relationships. *In* Anthropology Today. ed. A. L. Kroeber, Pp. 430–51. Chicago: University of Chicago Press.

Paul, Robert A.
1976   Did the Primal Crime Take Place? Ethos 4:311–52.
1978   Instinctive Aggression in Man: The Semai Case. Journal of Psychological Anthropology 1:65–79.
1982   The Tibetan Symbolic World: Psychoanalytic Explorations. Chicago: University of Chicago Press.

Peacock, James L.
1968   Rites of Modernization. Symbolic and Social Aspects of Indonesian Proletarian Drama. Chicago: University of Chicago Press.

Pedersen, Paul B.
1977   Asian Personality Theory. *In* Current Personality Theories. ed. Raymond J. Corsini, pp. 367–97. Ithaca, Ill.: F. E. Peacock.

Peter, Prince of Greece and Denmark
1953   Peculiar Sleeping Postures of the Tibetans. Man 53:145.

Pevsner, Nikolaus
1956   The Englishness of English Art. New York: Frederick A. Praeger.

Phillips, Herbert P.
1965   Thai Peasant Personality. The Patterns of Interpersonal Behavior in the Village of Bang Chan. Berkeley: University of California Press.

Pilling, Arnold W.
1962   Statistics, Sorcery, and Justice. American Anthropologist 64:1057–59.

Plog, Stanley C., and Robert B. Edgerton
1969   Changing Perspectives in Mental Illness. New York: Holt, Rinehart & Winston.

Plummer, John H.
1966   Another Look at Aymara Personality. Behavior Science Notes. HRAF Quarterly Bulletin 1:55–78.

Pollack, R. H.
1963   Contour Detectability as a Function of Chronological Age. Perceptual and Motor Skills 17:411–17.

Pollack, R. H., and S. D. Silvar
1967   Magnitude of the Müller-Lyer Illusion in Children as a Function of the Pigmentation of the Fundus Oculi. Psychonomic Science 8:83–84.

Poortinga, Ype H., ed.
1977   Basic Problems in Cross-Cultural Psychology. Amsterdam: Swets and Zeitlinger.

Posinsky, S. H.
1956   Yurok Shell Money and "Pains": A Freudian Interpretation. Psychiatric Quarterly 30:598–632.

Potter, David M.
1954   People of Plenty. Economic Abundance and the American Character. Chicago: University of Chicago Press.
1962   American Women and the American Character. Stetson University Bulletin 62:1–22. De Land, Fla.

Powdermaker, Hortense
1945   Review of "The People of Alor." American Anthropologist 47:155–61.

Prange, Arthur J.
  1959   An Interpretation of Cultural Isolation and Alien's Paranoid Reaction. International Journal of Social Psychiatry 4:354–63.

Preston, Caroline E.
  1964   Psychological Testing with Northwest Coast Alaskan Eskimos. Genetic Psychology Monographs, 69:323–419.

Price-Williams, Douglass R.
  1968   Ethnopsychology 1: Comparative Psychological Processes. *In* Clifton 1968:304–15.
  1975   Explorations in Cross-Cultural Psychology. San Francisco: Chandler & Sharp.
  1981   Concrete and Formal Operations. *In* Munroe, Munroe, and Whiting 1981:403–22.

Price-Williams, Douglass R., W. Gordon, and M. Ramirez
  1969   Skill and Conservation: A Study of Pottery-Making Children. Developmental Psychology 1:769.

Prince, Morton
  1929   The Unconscious. New York: Macmillan.

Prince, Raymond, ed.
  1968   Trance and Possession States. Montreal: R. M. Bucke Memorial Society.

Prince, Raymond, and Charles Savage
  1972   Mystical States and the Concept of Regression. *In* White 1972:114–34.

Pye, Lucian W.
  1962   Politics, Personality, and Nation Buiding: Burma's Search for Identity. New Haven, Conn.: Yale University Press.
  1968   The Spirit of Chinese Politics. A Psychocultural Study of the Authority Crisis in Political Development. Cambridge, Mass.: MIT Press.

Rabin, A. I.
  1965   Growing up in the Kibbutz. New York: Springer Publishing.

Rabin, A. I., and Josefina Limuaco
  1967   A Comparison of the Connotative Meaning of Rorschach's Inkblots for American and Filipino College Students. Journal of Social Psychology 72:197–203.

Radcliffe-Brown, A. R.
  1952   The Mother's Brother in South Africa. *In* Structure and Function in Primitive Society. Essays and Addresses. ed. A. R. Radcliffe-Brown, pp. 15–31. Glencoe, Ill.: Free Press.

Randall, Betty Uchitelle
  1949   The Cinderella Theme in Northwest Coast Folklore. *In* Indians of the Urban Northwest. ed. Marian W. Smith, pp. 243–85. New York: Columbia University Press.

Rapson, Richard L.
  1965   The American Child as Seen by British Travelers, 1845–1935, American Quarterly 17:520–34.

Redfield, Robert
  1941   The Folk Culture of Yucatan. Chicago: University of Chicago Press.
  1957   The Primitive World and Its Transformations. Ithaca, N.Y.: Cornell University Press.
  1960   The Peasant View of the Good Life. *In* The Little Society and Peasant Society and Culture. ed. Robert Redfield, pp. 60–79. Chicago: University of Chicago Press.

Reich, Charles A.
1971   The Greening of America. New York: Bantam Books.

Reich, Wilhelm
1946   The Mass Psychology of Fascism, 3d ed. New York: Orgone Institute Press.
1949   Character-Analysis. trans. by Theodore P. Wolfe. 3d enlarged ed. New York: Orgone Institute Press.

Reichel-Dolmatoff, Gerardo
1971   Amazonian Cosmos. The Sexual and Religious Symbolism of the Tukano Indians. Chicago: University of Chicago Press.

Reichel-Dolmatoff, Gerardo, and Alicia Reichel-Dolmatoff
1961   The People of Aritama. The Cultural Personality of a Colombian Mestizo Village. London: Routledge and Kegan Paul.

Reik, Theodor
1958   Ritual. Psychoanalytic Studies. New York: International Universities Press.

Rentoul, Alex G.
1931   Physiological Paternity and the Trobrianders. Man 31:152–54.
1932   Papuans, Professors and Platitudes, Man 32:274–76.

Reynolds, David K.
1980   The Quiet Therapies: Japanese Pathways to Personal Growth. Honolulu: University Press of Hawaii.

Reynolds, V.
1965   Some Behavioral Comparisons Between the Chimpanzee and the Mountain Gorilla in the Wild. American Anthropologist 67:691–706.

Rhine, J. B.
1947   The Reach of the Mind. New York: William Sloan Associates.

Rieff, Philip
1959   Freud: The Mind of the Moralist. New York: Viking Press.

Riesman, David, in collaboration with Nathan Glazer
1952   Faces in the Crowd. Individual Studies in Character and Politics. New Haven, Conn.: Yale University Press.

Riesman, David, with Nathan Glazer and Reuel Denney
1953   The Lonely Crowd. A Study of the Changing American Character. Abridged. New York: Doubleday Anchor Books.

Riesman, Frank and S. M. Miller
1958   Social Class and Projective Tests. Journal of Projective Techniques 22:432–39.

Rimland, Bernard
1969   Psychogenesis versus Biogenesis: The Issues and the Evidence. In Plog and Edgerton 1969:702–35.

Rimm, David C., and John C. Masters
1974   Behavior Therapy. Techniques and Empirical Findings. New York: Academic Press.

Rink, Heinrich Johannes
1875   Tales and Traditions of the Eskimo, William Blackwood.

Ritchie, James E.
1956   Basic Personality in Rakau. Victoria University College Publications in Psychol-

ogy, no. 8. Monographs on Maori Social Life and Personality, no. 1. Department of Psychology, Victoria University College, Wellington, New Zealand.

Ritchie, Jane
1957   Childhood in Rakau. The First Five Years of Life. Victoria University Publications in Psychology, no. 10. Monographs on Maori Social Life and Personality, no. 3. Department of Psychology, Victoria University, Wellington, New Zealand.

Rivet-Carnac, J. R.
1879   The Snake Symbol in India. Journal of the Royal Asiatic Society of Bengal, vol. 48.

Robinson, Leonard Wallace
1959   What We Dream—and Why? New York Times Magazine February 15, pp. 52–60.

Roheim, Géza
1941   Play Analysis of Normanby Island Children. American Journal of Orthopsychiatry 11:524–49.
1950   Psychoanalysis and Anthropology. Culture, Personality, and the Unconscious. New York: International Universities Press.

Rohner, Ronald P.
1970   Parental Rejection, Food Deprivation, and Personality Development: Tests of Alternative Hypotheses. Ethnology 9:414–27.
1976   Sex Differences in Aggression: Phylogenetic and Enculturation Perspectives. Ethos 4:57–72.

Rohrl, Vivian J.
1970   A Nutritional Factor in Windigo Psychosis. American Anthropologist 72:97–101.

Rokeach, Milton
1943   Generalized Mental Rigidity as a Factor in Ethnocentrism. Journal of Abnormal and Social Psychology 48:259–78.
1960   The Open and Closed Mind. Investigations into the Nature of Belief Systems and Personality Systems. New York: Basic Books.

Romney, Kimball, and Romaine Romney
1966   The Mixtecans of Juxtlahuaca, Mexico. Six Cultures Series, vol. 4. New York: John Wiley & Sons.

Rorschach, Hermann
1941   Psychodiagnostics. New York: Grune & Stratton.

Rose, Ronald
1956   Living Magic: The Realities Underlying the Psychical Practices and Beliefs of Australian Aborigines. New York: Rand McNally.

Rosen, Bernard C.
1962   Socialization and Achievement Motivation in Brazil. American Sociological Review 27:612–24.

Rosenthal, David
1971   Genetics of Psychopathology. New York: McGraw-Hill.

Rosenzweig, Saul, and Edith E. Fleming
1948–49   Apperceptive Norms for the Thematic Apperception Test. II. An Empirical Investigation. Journal of Personality 17:483–503.

Ross, James Bruce
1975   The Middle-Class Child in Urban Italy, Fourteenth to Early Sixteenth Century. *In* deMause 1975a:183–228.

Rubel, Arthur J.
1977 "Limited Good" and "Social Comparison": Two Theories, One Problem. Ethos 5:224–38.

Ruesch, Jurgen, and J. F. Finesinger
1941 The Relation of the Rorschach Color Response to the Use of Color in Drawings. Psychosomatic Medicine 3:370–88.

Ruesch, Jurgen, and Weldon Kees
1956 Nonverbal Communication. Notes on the Visual Perception of Human Relations. Los Angeles: University of California Press.

Rwegellera, G. G. C., and C. C. Mambwe
1977 Diagnostic Classification of First-Ever Admissions to Chainama Hills Hospital, Lusaka, Zambia. British Journal of Psychiatry 130:273–80.

Sachs, Curt
1946 The Commonwealth of Art. Style in the Fine Arts, Music, and the Dance. New York: W. W. Norton.

Sachs, Wulf
1947 Black Anger. New York: Grove Press.

Sapir, Edward
1928 The Meaning of Religion. The American Mercury 15:72–79.

Sargant, William
1957 Battle for the Mind. New York: Doubleday.
1969 The Physiology of Faith. British Journal of Psychiatry 115:505–18.

Sarnoff, Charles
1976 Latency. New York: Jason Aronson.

Schachtel, Ernest G.
1943 On Color and Affect. Psychiatry 6:393–409.
1966 The Interpersonal Meaning of the Rorschach-Test Situation. *In* Experimental Foundations of Rorschach's Test, Ernest G. Schachtel, ed., pp. 268–328. New York: Basic Books.

Schaeffer, Joseph H.
1975 Videotape: New Technique of Observation and Analysis in Anthropology. *In* Hockings 1975:253–82.

Schaller, George B.
1963 The Mountain Gorilla. Ecology and Behavior. Chicago: University of Chicago Press.

Schaller, George B., and Gordon R. Lowther
1969 The Relevance of Carnivore Behavior to the Study of Early Hominids. Southwestern Journal of Anthropology 25:307–41.

Schapiro, Meyer
1953 Style. *In* Anthropology Today: An Encyclopedic Inventory, ed. A. L. Kroeber, pp. 287–313. Chicago: University of Chicago Press.

Scheff, Thomas J.
1966 Being Mentally Ill. A Sociological Theory. Chicago: Aldine.

Scheper-Hughes, Nancy
1979 Saints, Scholars, and Schizophrenics. Mental Illness in Rural Ireland. Berkeley: University of California Press.

Schilder, Paul
1950   The Image and Appearance of the Human Body. New York: International Universities Press.

Schmeidler, Gertrude R.
1945   Separating the Sheep from the Goats. Journal of the American Society for Psychical Research 39:47–49.

Schmeidler, Gertrude R., and R. A. McConnell
1958   ESP and Personality Patterns. New Haven, Conn.: Yale University Press.

Schmidl-Waehner, Trude
1942   Formal Criteria for the Analysis of Children's Drawings. American Journal of Orthopsychiatry 12:95–103.
1946   Interpretation of Spontaneous Drawings and Paintings. Genetic Psychology Monographs 33:3–72.

Schneider, David M., and Kathleen Gough, eds.
1961   Matrilineal Kinship. Berkeley: University of California Press.

Schneider, David M. and Lauriston Sharp
1969   The Dream Life of a Primitive People. The Dreams of the Yir Yoront of Australia. Anthropological Studies, no. 1, American Anthropological Association. Ann Arbor, Mich.: University Microfilms.

Schubert, Anna
1930   Drawings of Orotchen Children and Young People. Journal of Genetic Psychology 37:232–44.

Schwartz, Norman B.
1977   A Milpero of Peten, Guatemala. Autobiography and Cultural Analysis. University of Delaware Latin American Studies Program. Occasional Papers and Monographs, no. 2.

Schwartz, Theodore
1973   Cult and Context. The Paranoid Ethos in Melanesia. Ethos 1:153–74.
1976   The Cargo Cult: A Melanesian Type-Response to Change. *In* Response to Change. Society, Culture, and Personality. ed. George A. De Vos, pp. 157–206. New York: D. Van Nostrand.
1983   Anthropology: A Quaint Science. American Anthropologist 85:919–29.

Scott, John Paul
1975   Aggression. 2d ed. Chicago: University of Chicago Press.

Sears, Robert R., Eleanor E. Maccoby, and Harry Levin
1957   Patterns of Child Rearing. New York: Row, Peterson.

Segall, Marshall H., Donald T. Campbell, and Melville J. Herskovits
1966   The Influence of Culture on Visual Perception. Indianapolis, Ind.: Bobbs-Merrill.

Seguin, Alberto
1956   Migration and Psychosomatic Disadaptation. Psychosomatic Medicine 18:404–9.

Seiden, Anne
1982   Depression and Women. *In* Affective Disorders: Psychopathology and Treatment. ed. Eduardo R. Val, F. Moises Gaviria, and Joseph A. Flaherty, pp. 389–415. Chicago: Year Book Medical Publishers.

Seligman, C. G.
1924   Anthropology and Psychology. A Study of Some Points of Contact. Journal of the Royal Anthropological Institute of Great Britain and Ireland 54:13–46.

1929   Temperament, Conflict, and Psychosis in a Stone-Age Population. British Journal of Medical Psychology 9:187–202.

Shack, D. N.
1969   Nutritional Processes and Personality Development Among the Gurage of Ethiopia. Ethnology 8:292–300.

Sharff, Jagna Wojcicka
1975   Speaking to the Man: Residual Authority in Two Low Income Households. Paper presented at the 74th Annual Meeting of the American Anthropological Association, San Francisco, Dec. 2–6, 1975.

Sheldon, W. H.
1940   The Varieties of Human Physique. New York: Harper & Brothers.
1942   The Varieties of Temperament. New York: Harper & Brothers.

Sherwood, Edward T.
1957   On the Designing of TAT Pictures, with Special Reference to a Set for an African People Assimilating Western Culture. Journal of Social Psychology 45:161–90.

Shils, Edward A.
1954   Authoritarianism: "Right" and "Left." In Christie and Jahoda 1954:24–49.
1961   The Intellectual Between Tradition and Modernity: The Indian Situation. Comparative Studies in Society and History. Supplement 1. The Hague: Mouton.

Shirley, M. M.
1933   The First Two Years. A Study of Twenty-Five Babies. Vol. III. Personality Manifestations. Institutes of Child Welfare. Monograph Series. Minneapolis: University of Minnesota Press.

Shonle, Ruth
1925   Peyote, the Giver of Visions. American Anthropologist 27:53–75.

Shore, Bradd
1982   Sala'ilua. A Samoan Mystery. New York: Columbia University Press.

Siegel, Ronald K. and Murray E. Jarvik
1975   Drug-Induced Hallucinations in Animals and Man. In Hallucinations. Behavior, Experience, and Theory, ed. Ronald K. Siegel and L. J. West, pp. 81–161. New York: John Wiley & Sons.

Sikkema, Mildred
1947   Observations on Japanese Early Training. Psychiatry 10:423–32.

Simmons, Leo, ed.
1942   Sun Chief. The Autobiography of a Hopi Indian. New Haven, Conn.: Yale University Press.

Simonds, Paul E.
1974   The Social Primates. New York: Harper & Row.

Singer, K.
1975   Depressive Disorders from a Transcultural Perspective. Social Science and Medicine 9:289–301.

Singer, Milton
1972   Industrial Leadership, the Hindu Ethic, and the Spirit of Socialism. In When a Great Tradition Modernizes. An Anthropological Approach to Indian Civilization. ed. Milton Singer, pp. 272–366. New York: Praeger.

Sipes, Richard G.
1973   War, Sports, and Aggression: An Empirical Test of Two Rival Theories. American Anthropologist 75:64–86.

Skinner, Alanson
  1916 Plains Cree Tales. Journal of American Folklore 29:341–67.

Slater, Philip E., and Dori A. Slater
  1965 Maternal Ambivalence and Narcissism: A Cross-Cultural Study. Merrill Palmer Quarterly of Behavior and Development 11:241–59.

Smith, Marian W.
  1959 Boas' "Natural History" Approach to Field Method. In The Anthropology of Franz Boas: Essays on the Centennial of his Birth. ed. Walter Goldschmidt, pp. 46–60. American Anthropological Association Memoir No. 89.

Smith, Robert J.
  1962 The Life Cycle. In Japanese Character and Culture. A Book of Selected Readings. ed. Bernard S. Silberman, pp. 187–213. Tucson: University of Arizona Press.
  1979 The Ethnic Japanese in Brazil. The Journal of Japanese Studies 5:53–70.

Smith, Watson, and John M. Roberts
  1954 Zuñi Law, A Field of Values. Papers of the Peabody Museum, Vol. 43, No. 1. Cambridge, Mass.

Sofue, Takao
  1979 Aspects of the Personality of Japanese, Americans, Italians, and Eskimos: Comparisons Using the Sentence Completion Test. Journal of Psychological Anthropology 2:11–52.

Solomon, Richard H.
  1969 Mao's Effort to Reintegrate the Chinese Polity: Problems of Authority and Conflict in Chinese Social Processes. In Chinese Communist Politics in Action. ed. A. Doak Barnett, pp. 271–361. Seattle: University of Washington Press.
  1971 Mao's Political Revolution and the Chinese Political Culture. Berkeley: University of California Press.

Soskin, W. F.
  1959 Influence of Four Types of Data on Diagnostic Conceptualization in Psychological Testing. Journal of Abnormal and Social Psychology 58:69–78.

Southall, Aidan
  1975 Ecology and Social Change in Madagascar: Linton's Hypothesis on the Tanala and Betsileo. American Anthropologist 77:603–608.

Sovani, N. V.
  1962 Non-Economic Aspects of India's Economic Development. Administration and Economic Development in India. Duke University Commonwealth Studies Center. Durham, N.C.

Spengler, Oswald
  1939 The Decline of the West, trans. by C. F. Atkinson, 2 vols. New York: Alfred A. Knopf.

Spielberger, Charles D., and Rogelio Diaz-Guerrero, eds.
  1976 Cross-Cultural Anxiety. New York: John Wiley & Sons.

Spindler, George D.
  1955 Sociocultural and Psychological Processes in Menomini Acculturation. University of California Publications in Culture and Society, no. 5. Berkeley: University of California Press.
  1978 ed.: The Making of Psychological Anthropology. Berkeley: University of California Press.

Spindler, George, and Louise Spindler
  1965   Researching the Perception of Cultural Alternatives: The Instrumental Activities Inventory. *In* Spiro 1965:312–27.

Spindler, Louise, and George Spindler
  1961   A Modal Personality Technique in the Study of Menomini Acculturation. *In* Kaplan 1961:479–91.

Spiro, Melford E.
  1954   Is the Family Universal? American Anthropologist 56:839–46.
  1958   Children of the Kibbutz. Cambridge, Mass.: Harvard University Press.
  1959   Cultural Heritage, Personal Tensions, and Mental Illness in a South Sea Culture. *In* Opler 1959a:141–71.
  1965   ed.: Context and Meaning in Cultural Anthropology. New York: Free Press.
  1967   Burmese Supernaturalism. A Study in the Explanation and Reduction of Suffering. Englewood Cliffs, N.J.: Prentice-Hall.
  1970   Buddhism and Society. A Great Tradition and its Burmese Vicissitudes. New York: Harper & Row.
  1977   Kinship and Marriage in Burma. A Cultural and Psychodynamic Analysis. Berkeley: University of California Press.
  1978   Culture and Human Nature. *In* Spindler 1978:331–60.
  1979   Gender and Culture: Kibbutz Women Revisited. Durham, N.C.: Duke University Press.
  1982   Oedipus in the Trobriands. Chicago: Chicago University Press.

Spitz, René A.
  1945   Hospitalism. An Inquiry into the Genesis of Psychiatric Conditions in Early Childhood. *In* The Psychoanalytic Study of the Child, Vol. I, pp. 53–74. New York: International Universities Press.

Spitzer, Robert L., Nancy Andreasen, Jean Endicott, and Robert A. Woodruff, Jr.
  1978   Proposed Classification of Schizophrenia in DSM-III. *In* Wynne, Cromwell, and Matthysse 1978:670–85.

Srole, Leo, et al.
  1962   Mental Health in the Metropolis. The Midtown Manhattan Study. New York: McGraw-Hill.

Stainbrook, E.
  1952   Some Characteristics of the Psychopathology of Schizophrenic Behavior in Bahian Society. American Journal of Psychiatry 109:330–35.

Stein, Howard F., and Robert F. Hill
  1977   The Ethnic Imperative. Examining the New White Ethnic Movement. University Park: Pennsylvania State University Press.

Stephens, William N.
  1961   A Cross-Cultural Study of Menstrual Taboos. Genetic Psychology Monographs 64:385–416.
  1962   The Oedipus Complex. Cross-Cultural Evidence. Glencoe, Ill.: Free Press.

Stevenson, Harold W.
  1982   Influences of Schooling on Cognitive Development. *In* Wagner and Stevenson, 1982:208–24.

Stevenson, Ian
  1970   Telepathic Impressions: A Review and Report of Thirty-Five New Cases. Proceedings of the American Society for Psychical Research, 29. New York.

Stevenson, Matilda Coxe
1904   The Zuni Indians. Their Mythology, Esoteric Fraternities, and Ceremonies. Bureau of American Ethnology. 23rd Annual Report. Washington, D.C.: Smithsonian Institution.

Steward, Julian H.
1968   Causal Factors and Processes in the Evolution of Pre-Farming Societies. *In* Lee and DeVore 1968:321–34.

Stewart, Louis H.
1955   The Expression of Personality in Drawings and Paintings. Genetic Psychology Monographs 51:45–103.

Stocking, George W.
1968   Race, Culture, and Evolution. Essays in the History of Anthropology. New York: Free Press.
1974   ed.: The Shaping of American Anthropology 1883–1911. A Franz Boas Reader. New York: Basic Books.

Stoetzel, Jean
1955   Without the Chrysanthemum and the Sword. A Study in the Attitudes of Youth in Post-War Japan. London, Paris: William Heinemann, UNESCO.

Stone, Lawrence
1974   The Massacre of the Innocents. New York Review, Nov. 14, 1974:25–31.

Storr, Anthony
1972   Human Destructiveness. London: Sussex University Press.

Strong, E. K.
1934   The Second Generation Japanese Problem. Stanford: Stanford University Press.

Suedfeld, Peter E., and Roderick A. Borrie
1978   Altering States of Consciousness through Sensory Deprivation. *In* Expanding Dimensions of Consciousness. ed. A. Arthur Sugerman and Ralph E. Tarter, pp. 226–52. New York: Springer.

Super, Charles M.
1981a   Behavioral Development in Infancy. *In* Munroe, Munroe, and Whiting 1981:181–270
1981b   Cross-Cultural Research in Infancy. *In* Handbook of Cross-Cultural Psychology, Vol. 4. Developmental Psychology. ed. Harry C. Triandis and Alastair Herons, pp. 17–53. Boston: Allyn & Bacon.

Sweetser, Dorrian Apple
1966   Avoidance, Social Affiliation, and the Incest Taboo, Ethnology 5:304–16.

Swenson, C.
1957   Empirical Evaluations of Human Figure Drawings. Psychological Bulletin 54:431–66.

Symonds, Percival
1931   Diagnosing Personality and Conduct. New York: Century.

Sypher, Wylie
1955   Four Stages of Renaissance Style. Transformations in Arts and Literature 1400–1700. New York: Doubleday Anchor Books.

Szasz, Thomas
1961   The Myth of Mental Illness. Foundations of a Theory of Personal Conduct. New York: Harper & Row.

Tart, Charles T., ed.
1969   Altered States of Consciousness. A Book of Readings. New York: John Wiley & Sons.

Taueber, Irene B.
1970   The Families of Chinese Farmers. *In* Family and Kinship in Chinese Society. ed. Maurice Freedman, pp. 63–85. Stanford, Cal.; Stanford University Press.

Taylor, William Stephens
1944   A Note on Cultural Determination of Free Drawings. Character and Personality 13:30–36.
1948   Basic Personality in Orthodox Hindu Culture Patterns. Journal of Abnormal and Social Psychology 43:3–12.

Teicher, Morton I.
1960   Windigo Psychosis. A Study of the Relationships between Belief and Behavior among the Indians of Northeastern Canada. Proceedings of the American Ethnological Society. Seattle, Wash.

Thomas, William I., and Florian Znaniecki
1958   The Polish Peasant in Europe and America. New York: Dover Publications, 2 vols. (Originally published in 1917–18.)

Thurnwald, R.
1936   Review of Sex and Temperament in Three Primitive Societies. American Anthropologist 38:558–61.

Tietze, Christopher, Paul V. Lemke, and Marcia Cooper
1941   Schizophrenia, Manic-Depressive Psychosis, and Socio-Economic Status. American Journal of Sociology 47:167–75.

Tiger, Lionel
1969   Men in Groups. New York: Random House.

Tiger, Lionel, and Robin Fox
1971   The Imperial Animal. New York: Holt, Rinehart & Winston.

Tiger, Lionel, and Joseph Shepher
1975   Women in the Kibbutz. New York: Harcourt Brace Jovanovich.

Tinbergen, N.
1968   On War and Peace in Animals and Man. Science 160:1411–18.

Titiev, Mischa
1939   The Story of Kokopele. American Anthropologist 41:91–98.

Tooth, Geoffrey
1950   Studies in Mental Illness in the Gold Coast. Colonial Research Publications, No. 6. London: H. H. Stationery Office.

Torrey, E. Fuller
1980   Schizophrenia and Civilization. New York: Jason Aronson.

Triandis, Harry C., and Juris G. Draguns, eds.
1980   Psychopathology. Handbook of Cross-Cultural Psychology, Volume 6. Boston: Allyn & Bacon.

Triandis, Harry, and Martin Fishbein
1963   Cognitive Interaction in Person Perception. Journal of Abnormal and Social Psychology 67:446–53.

Tschopik, Harry, Jr.
1951   The Aymara of Chucuito, Peru. I. Magic. Anthropological Papers of the American Museum of Natural History, vol. 44, part 2.

Turner, Frederick Jackson
1920   The Frontier in American History. New York: Henry Holt.

Turner, George
1884   Samoa a Hundred Years Ago and Long Before. London: Macmillan and Co.

Tyhurst, Libuse
1955   Psychosomatic and Allied Disorders. *In* Murphy 1955:203–13.

Tyler, Gus
1973   White Workers: Blue Mood. *In* White Ethnics: Their Life in Working Class America. ed. Joseph Ryan, pp. 124–32. Englewood Cliffs, N.J.: Prentice-Hall.

Tylor, Edward B.
1877   Primitive Culture. Researches Into the Development of Mythology, Philosophy, Religion, Language, Art, and Customs, vol. 1. New York: Henry Holt. (First published in 1871.)
1889   On a Method of Investigating the Development of Institutions, Applied to Laws of Marriage and Descent. Journal of the Royal Anthropological Institute of Great Britain and Ireland 18:245–69.

Van de Castle, Robert L.
1974   An Investigation of Psi Abilities Among the Cuna Indians of Panama. *In* Angoff and Barth 1974:80–100.

Van de Koppel, Jan M. H.
1977   A Preliminary Report on the Central African Differentiation Project. *In* Poortinga 1977:282–88.

Van Lawick-Goodall, Jane
1971   In the Shadow of Man. Boston: Houghton Mifflin.

Van Loon, F. H. G.
1926   Amok and Lattah. Journal of Abnormal and Social Psychology 21:434–44.

Vogel, Ezra F.
1963   Japan's New Middle Class. The Salary Man and His Family in a Tokyo Suburb. Berkeley: University of California Press.

Von Bertalanffy, Ludwig
1971   System, Symbol, and the Image of Man (Man's Immediate Socio-Ecological World). *In* The Interface Between Psychiatry and Anthropology. ed. Iago Galdston. New York: Brunner/Mazel.

Voth, H. R.
1901   The Oraibi Powamu Ceremony. Field Columbian Museum Anthropological Series, vol. 8. Chicago.

Wagner, Daniel A., and Harold W. Stevenson, eds.
1982   Cultural Perspectives on Child Development. San Francisco: W. H. Freeman & Co.

Wallace, Anthony F. C.
1956   Revitalization Movements. American Anthropologist 58:264–81.
1970a   Culture and Personality, 2d ed. New York: Random House.
1970b   The Death and Rebirth of the Seneca. New York: Alfred A. Knopf.
1972   Mental Illness, Biology, and Culture. *In* Hsu 1972:255–95.

Walsh, Maurice N., and Barbara G. Scandalis
1975   Institutionalized Forms of Intergenerational Male Aggression. *In* War, Its Causes and Correlates. ed. Martin A. Nettleship, R. Dale Givens, and Anderson Nettleship, pp. 135–55. The Hague: Mouton.

Warner, W. Lloyd
 1958 A Black Civilization. A Social Study of an Australian Tribe, rev. ed. New York: Harper & Brothers.

Warner, W. Lloyd, and Leo Srole
 1945 The Social Systems of American Ethnic Groups. New Haven, Conn.: Yale University Press.

Warren, N.
 1972 African Infant Precocity. Psychological Bulletin 78:353–67.

Washburn, Sherwood L., and Virginia Avis
 1958 Evolution of Human Behavior. *In* Behavior and Evolution. ed. Ann Roe and George Gaylord Simpson, pp. 421–36. New Haven, Conn.: Yale University Press.

Wasson, Valentina P., and R. Gordon Wasson
 1957 Mushrooms, Russia, and History. 2 vols. New York: Pantheon.

Watrous, Blanche G.
 1949 A Personality Study of Ojibwa Children. Ph.D. thesis, Department of Anthropology, Northwestern University, Evanston, Illinois.

Watson, John B.
 1930 Behaviorism, rev. ed. New York: W. W. Norton.

Watson, Robert I., and Henry Clay Lindgren
 1973 Psychology of the Child. New York: John Wiley & Sons.

Waxler, Nancy E.
 1979 Is Outcome for Schizophrenia Better in Nonindustrial Societies? The Case of Sri Lanka. The Journal of Nervous and Mental Disease 167:144–58.

Weakland, John Hast
 1953 An Analysis of Seven Cantonese Films. *In* Mead and Metraux 1953:292–95.

Weber, Max
 1952 The Protestant Ethnic and the Spirit of Capitalism. Trans. by Talcott Parsons. New York: Charles Scribner's Sons. (First published in German in 1904–05.)

Wedge, B. M.
 1952 Occurrence of Psychosis among Okinawans in Hawaii. American Journal of Psychiatry 109:255–58.

Weiner, Annette B.
 1976 Women of Value, Men of Renown. New Perspectives in Trobriand Exchange. Austin: University of Texas Press.

Weisner, Thomas S.
 1976 Urban-Rural Differences in African Children's Performance on Cognitive and Memory Tasks. Ethos 4:223–50.

Weisner, Thomas S., and Ronald Gallimore
 1977 My Brother's Keeper: Child and Sibling Caretaking. Current Anthropology 18:169–90.

Weissman, Myrna M., and Gerald L. Klerman
 1977 Sex Differences in the Epidemiology of Depression. Archives of General Psychiatry 34:98–111.

Werner, Oswald
 1970 Cultural Knowledge, Language, and World View. *In* Cognition: A Multiple View. ed. Paul I. Garvin, pp. 155–75. New York: Spartan Books.

Wertham, Fredric
1966 A Sign for Cain. An Exploration of Human Violence. New York: Macmillan.

White, John ed.
1972 The Highest State of Consciousness. New York: Doubleday Anchor Books.

White, Robert W.
1952 Lives in Progress. A Study of the Natural Growth of Personality. New York: Holt, Rinehart & Winston.

Whiting, Beatrice B.
1950 Paiute Sorcery. Viking Fund Publications in Anthropology. New York.
1963 ed.: Six Cultures. Studies of Child Rearing. New York: John Wiley & Sons.
1965 Sex Identity Conflict and Physical Violence: A Comparative Study. American Anthropologist 67. Special Publication: The Ethnography of Law. ed. Laura Nader, pp. 123–40.

Whiting, Beatrice B., and John W. M. Whiting
1975 Children of Six Cultures: A Psycho-Cultural Analysis. Cambridge, Mass.: Harvard University Press.

Whiting, John W. M.
1954 The Cross-Cultural Method. In Lindzey 1954, vol. 1:523–31.
1961 Socialization Process and Personality. In Hsu 1961a:355–80.
1964 Effects of Climate on Certain Cultural Practices. In Explorations in Cultural Anthropology, Essays in Honor of George Peter Murdock. ed. Ward H. Goodenough, pp. 175–95. New York: McGraw-Hill.
1968 Methods and Problems in Cross-Cultural Research. In Lindzey and Aronson 1968, vol. 2:693–728.

Whiting, John W. M., and Irvin L. Child
1953 Child Training and Personality: A Cross-Cultural Study. New Haven, Conn.: Yale University Press.

Whiting, John W. M., Irvin L. Child, William W. Lambert et al.
1966 Field Guide for a Study of Socialization. Six Cultures Series, vol. 1. New York: John Wiley & Sons.

Whiting, John W. M., Eleanor H. Chasdi et al.
1966 The Learning of Values. In People of Rimrock. A Study of Values in Five Cultures. ed. Evon Z. Vogt and Ethel M. Albert, pp. 83–125. Cambridge, Mass.: Harvard University Press.

Whiting, John W. M., Richard Kluckhohn, and Albert Anthony
1958 The Function of Male Initiation Ceremonies at Puberty. In Readings in Social Psychology, 3d ed. ed. Eleanor E. Maccoby, Theodore M. Newcomb, and Eugene L. Hartley, pp. 359–70. New York: Henry Holt.

Whyte, William H., Jr.
1956 The Organization Man. New York: Simon & Schuster.

Williams, Elgin
1947 Anthropology for the Common Man. American Anthropologist 49:84–90.

Williams, Herbert H., and Judith R. Williams
1965 The Definition of the Roschach Test Situation. In Spiro 1965:338–54.

Williams, Roger J.
1956 Biochemical Individuality. The Basis for the Gerontrophic Concept. New York: John Wiley & Sons.

Williams, Thomas R., ed.
1975 Psychological Anthropology. The Hague: Mouton.

Williamson, Robert W.
1939 Essays in Polynesian Ethnology, ed. Ralph Piddington, Cambridge, England: Cambridge University Press.

Willner, Dorothy
1983 Definition and Violation: Incest and the Incest Taboos. Man 18:134–59.

Wilson, Edward O.
1975 Sociobiology: The New Synthesis. Cambridge Mass.: Harvard University Press.
1978 On Human Nature. Cambridge, Mass.: Harvard University Press.

Wilson, Edmund
1956 Red, Black, Blond, and Olive. London: Oxford University Press.

Winiarz, W., and J. Wielawski
1936 Imu—A Psychoneurosis Occurring Among Ainus. Psychoanalytic Review 23:181–86.

Winston, Ellen
1934 The Alleged Lack of Mental Diseases among Primitive Groups. American Anthropologist 36:234–38.

Winter, Edward H.
1959 Beyond the Mountains of the Moon, the Lives of Four Africans. Urbana: University of Illinois Press.

Wirth, Louis
1945 The Problem of Minority Groups. In The Science of Man in the World Crisis. ed. Ralph Linton, pp. 347–72. New York: Columbia University Press.

Wissler, Clark, and D. C. Duvall
1908 Mythology of the Blackfoot Indians. Anthropological Papers of the American Museum of Natural History, vol. 2, part 1.

Witherspoon, Gary
1977 Language and Art in the Navajo Universe. Ann Arbor, Mich: University of Michigan Press.

Witkin, Herman A.
1969 Social Influences in the Development of Cognitive Style. In Handbook of Socialization Theory and Research ed. David A. Goslin, pp. 687–706. Chicago: Rand McNally.
1977 Theory in Cross-Cultural Research: Its Uses and Risks. In Poortinga 1977:83–91.

Witkin, Herman A., R. B. Dyk, H. F. Faterson, D. R. Goodenough, and S. A. Karp
1962 Psychological Differentiation: Studies of Development. New York: John Wiley & Sons.

Witkin, Herman A., D. R. Goodenough, and S. A. Karp
1967 Stability of Cognitive Style from Childhood to Young Adulthood. Journal of Personality and Social Psychology 7:291–300.

Witkin, Herman A., H. B. Lewis, M. Hertz, K. Machover, P. B. Meissner, and S. Wapner
1954 Personality Through Perception. An Experimental and Clinical Study. New York: Harper & Brothers.

Witkin, Herman A., P. K. Oltman, E. Raskin, and S. A. Karp
    1971   A Manual for the Embedded Figures Test. Palo Alto, Cal.: Consulting Psychologists Press.

Wittkower, Eric, and J. Fried
    1959   A Cross-Cultural Approach to Mental Health Problems. American Journal of Psychiatry 116:423–28.

Wittkower, E. D., and H. Rin
    1965   Transcultural Psychiatry. Archives of General Psychiatry 13:387–94.

Wolf, Eric
    1955   Types of Latin American Peasantry. American Anthropologist 57:542–71.
    1957   Closed Corporate Peasant Communities in Meso-America and Central Java. Southwestern Journal of Anthropology 13:1–18.

Wolf, Margery
    1970   Child Training and the Chinese Family. In Family and Kinship in Chinese Society, ed. Maurice Freedman, pp. 37–62. Stanford, Cal.: Stanford University Press.

Wolfenstein, Martha
    1955a   French Parents Take Their Children to the Park. In Mead and Wolfenstein 1955:99–117.
    1955b   Jack and the Beanstalk: An American Version. In Mead and Wolfenstein 1955:243–45.

Wolff, Werner
    1943   The Expression of Personality. Experimental Depth Psychology. New York: Harper & Brothers.
    1952   The Dream: Mirror of Conscience. New York: Grune & Stratton.

World Health Organization
    1973   Report of the International Pilot Study of Schizophrenia. Vol. 1: Results of the Initial Evaluation Phase. Geneva.
    1979   Schizophrenia. An International Follow-up Study. Chichester: John Wiley & Sons.

Wright, George O.
    1954   Projection and Displacement: A Cross-Cultural Study of Folk-Tale Aggression. Journal of Abnormal and Social Psychology 49:523–28.

Wright, Quincy
    1965   A Study of War. 2d ed. Chicago: University of Chicago Press.

Wynne, Lyman C., Rue L. Cromwell, and Steven Matthysse
    1978   The Nature of Schizophrenia. New Approaches to Research and Treatment. New York: John Wiley & Sons.

Yablonsky, Lewis
    1968   The Hippie Trip. New York: Pegasus.

Yang, C. K.
    1959   The Chinese Family in the Communist Revolution. Boston: Technology Press.

Yap, P. M.
    1951   Mental Diseases Peculiar to Certain Cultures: A Survey of Comparative Psychiatry. Journal of Mental Science 97:313–27.
    1952   The Latah Reaction: Its Pathodynamics and Nosological Position. Journal of Mental Science 98:515–64.

1965 Suk Yeong or Koro—A Culture-Bound Depersonalization Syndrome. British Journal of Psychiatry 3:43–50.

Young, Frank W.
1962 The Function of Male Initiation Ceremonies: A Cross-Cultural Test of an Alternative Hypothesis. American Journal of Sociology 67:379–96.
1965 Initiation Ceremonies. A Cross-Cultural Study of Status Dramatization. Indianapolis, Ind.: Bobbs-Merrill.

Young, Frank W., and Albert Bacdayan
1965 Menstrual Taboos and Social Rigidity. Ethnology 4:225–41.

Young, William C., Robert W. Goy, and Charles H. Phoenix
1964 Hormones and Sexual Behavior. Science 143:212–18.

Zajonc, Robert B.
1968 Cognitive Theories in Social Psychology. *In* Lindzey and Aronson 1968:488–567.

Zborowski, Mark, and Elizabeth Herzog
1962 Life is with People. The Culture of the Shtetl. New York: Schocken Books.

Zubin, Joseph
1954 Failures of the Rorschach Technique. Journal of Projective Techniques 18:303–15.

Name Index

Subject Index

*This book has been set Quadex 202 in 10 and 9 point Palatino,
leaded 2 points. Chapter numbers and titles are 24 point Palatino
Bold. Part numbers are 24 point Palatino Bold and part titles are 36
point Palatino Bold. The size of the type page is 30 by 48½ picas.*